Tax Politics

TAX POLITICS
How They Make You Pay and What You Can Do About It

by Robert M. Brandon, Jonathan Rowe, and Thomas H. Stanton

With contributions from Louise Brown and Barry Greever

Pantheon Books   New York

Copyright © 1976 by Public Citizen, Inc.
All rights reserved under International and Pan-American Copyright Conventions. Published in the United States by Pantheon Books, a division of Random House, Inc., New York, and simultaneously in Canada by Random House of Canada Limited, Toronto.

Library of Congress Cataloging in Publication Data

Brandon, Robert, 1947-
Tax Politics.

Bibliography: pp. 272-81
Includes index.
1. Income tax—United States—Handbooks, manuals, etc. 2. Property tax—United States—Handbooks, manuals, etc. I. Rowe, Jonathan, 1946- joint author. II. Stanton, Thomas H., 1944- joint author. III. Title.
HJ4652.B7 1976   336.2'00973   75-38114
ISBN 0-394-49847-X
ISBN 0-394-73092-5 pbk.

Manufactured in the United States of America

FIRST EDITION

Since the copyright page cannot accommodate all acknowledgments, they can be found on the following page.

To our families and friends
and the many people who are working hard
to make our tax system better.

Grateful acknowledgment is made to the following for permission to reprint previously published material:

American Finance Association: Chart, "Effective Rates of Federal and State-Local Individual and Corporation Income Taxes, 1966" (Figure 4), reprinted from "Distribution of Federal and State Income Taxes by Income Class" by Joseph Pechman, *Journal of Finance*, Vol. 27, No. 2 (May 1972).

The Brookings Institution: Charts, "How Erosions in the Tax Base Undermine the Ability-to-Pay Principle" (Figure 2), "The Social Security Payroll Tax" (Figure 7), and "The Shifting Burden of Income and Payroll Taxes by Income Class (Figure 11), all adapted from *Setting National Priorities: The 1974 Budget* by Edward R. Fried, Alice M. Rivlin, Charles L. Schultze, and Nancy H. Teeters. Copyright © 1973 by the Brookings Institution, Washington, D.C.; "Effective Rates of Federal, State and Local Property Taxes, 1966" (Figure 41) adapted from *Who Bears the Tax Burden?* by Joseph H. Pechman and Benjamin A. Okner. Copyright © 1974 by the Brookings Institution, Washington, D.C.; "Assessment Level Table" (p. 186) adapted from *Financing State and Local Governments*, Table 6-10, Revised Edition by James A. Maxwell. Copyright © 1969 by the Brookings Institution, Washington, D.C.

Citizens Action Program (CAP): Chart, "Taxes Lost by Chicago Public Agencies Due To U.S. Steel Underassessment" (Figure 56); also, front page of *Citizens Action Program Newsletter*, Vol. 1, No. 4 (October 1971).

Harvard University Press: Chart, "Factors Reducing the Effective Tax Rate of Corporations, 1965 and 1972 (Figure 5), reprinted from *Pathways to Tax Reform* by Stanley S. Surrey. Copyright © 1973 by the President and Fellows of Harvard College.

Hyde Park Herald and Richard Kimmel: Cartoon by Richard Kimmel captioned "Passing the Hat" (p. 252).

McCutchan Publishing Corporation: Chart, "The Relationship Between District Wealth and School Revenues in Bexar County, Texas" (Figure 47) reprinted from *Answers To Inequity* by Joel Berke. Copyright © 1974 by McCutchan Publishing Corporation.

National Tax Association-Tax Institute of America: Chart, "The Proportions of Taxed and Untaxed Property in the United States, 1966" (Figure 42), reprinted from "The Incidence of the Property Tax Revisited" by Richard Netzer, *National Tax Journal*, Vol. XXVI, No. 4 (December, 1973).

The National Urban Coalition: Chart, "City-State Comparison of Proportion of Expenditures Used for Education, 1969–1970 (Figure 46) reprinted from *Urban Schools and School Finance Reform: Promise and Reality* (1973).

The New Yorker: Excerpt from "Energy Bazaar" by Elizabeth Drew, reprinted from *The New Yorker*, July 21, 1975. Copyright © 1975 by The New Yorker Magazine, Inc.

Philadelphia Inquirer: Three charts, "Compliance Level by Audit Class," "Frequency of IRS Audits (1971–1973)" and "Where IRS Was Most Likely to Sieze Money or Property of Delinquent Taxpayers in Fiscal Year 1972," all of which were published in the *Philadelphia Inquirer* in 1974.

San Francisco Guardian: Chart, "Why High-rises in San Francisco Cost Taxpayers More Than They Provide in Revenue" reprinted from *The Ultimate Highrise* (Bay Guardian Books, 1971).

Tandem Productions, Inc.: Lines of dialogue from the television program "All in the Family" (p. 245), written by Michael Ross and Bernie West. Copyright © 1972 by Tandem Productions, Inc. All rights reserved.

Tax Analysts and Advocates: Chart, "Effective Corporate Tax Rates by Industry on Worldwide Income" (Figure 6) reprinted from *Tax Notes*.

Wallingford Post: Column by Eleanor Corazzini entitled "Tip Toe Thru The Taxes" which appeared in the *Wallingford Post*, May, 1971.

Preface

The average taxpayer works three months out of the year for the government. That is how long it takes to pay the taxes for federal, state, and local budgets. It follows, therefore, that the average taxpayer should take a few hours a year to work with other taxpayers to make sure that these tax revenues are collected fairly from the powerful and the affluent as well as from citizens with lower incomes. In contrast to average taxpayers, corporations and multimillionaires have been spending the time (or money) on Congress, the Treasury Department, and local property tax assessors to minimize their taxes. This is done by lobbying, pressure, campaign contributions, or other inducements, some quite illicit, to write the law the way they want it, interpret it by favorable regulations, or encourage it to go unenforced against them.

What are average taxpayers, the millions of unorganized people who pay so many of the governmental and corporate bills, thinking and doing? Most people are aware of the gross inequities of the tax laws and their administration. The phrase "tax loophole" is widely understood as favored treatment for special interests. Some Treasury officials have spoken of a "taxpayers revolt." But knowing is not the same as doing. This volume is designed to let the taxpayer know and do at the same time. The authors want to answer in readable and objective detail the question concerned taxpayers ask the most: "We want to do something but how do we go about it?" *Tax Politics* demystifies taxes—from the way they are shaped to the way they are applied, from Washington to Main Street, USA. It is a clear, attractive guide for all citizens who wish to perform the possible—to make income and property taxes fair and permit the raising of enough revenue for legitimate public purposes. This means that most taxpayers would be paying less in taxes and receiving a more efficient economic and governmental system in return. The following pages focus on the problems of individual taxpayers and the problems of aggregate taxpayers as an effective way to link specific awareness to general reforms. The most instrumental specific awareness is that there is no such thing as free apathy. By not becoming involved in reform of the tax systems, millions of taxpayers are paying an average "non-participation tax" of about $800 a year, according to recent calculations by the Public Citizen Tax Reform Research Group. This is the amount average income taxpayers pay which instead should be paid by the wealthy and corporations—if only all taxpayers were paying without unjust favoritism.

The average taxpayer is not a participant in tax politics; the wealthy and special-interest taxpayers play tax politics—and are missing from the tax rolls.

The obfuscation of the tax laws and their administration is one important reason why more taxpayers do not participate in tax politics. Tax loopholes—like any government subsidy program—could be explained in dollars and sense terms: who benefits, how much do they get, how efficient is the subsidy in accomplishing its purported goals. Instead, most loopholes are carefully wrapped in complexity.

Often middle-class taxpayers are lulled by token tax breaks and therefore don't react strongly to loopholes that benefit principally the rich or the corporations. It's amazing how many times that trick is used: homeowner tax deductions, capital gains preferences, even the hallowed personal exemption. Average taxpayers get such small fractions of these multi-billion-dollar loopholes that they would be better off if every loophole were closed and the tax rates lowered instead. The same happens in property taxes, notoriously with the assessment ratio: everyone thinks he is getting a bargain through undervaluation

viii TAX POLITICS

but the wealthy *keep* their money through gross underassessment.

Local, state, and federal representatives working on behalf of special interests can disguise their votes for loopholes in gobbledygook (often written by a solititous lobbyist) which they themselves often don't comprehend. As long as the average taxpayers—who pay the bill—don't demand an accounting, everybody is happy.

Even if taxpayers do not understand the gobbledygook, they do understand clearly that the tax systems are unfair. Local industries are found to be paying little or no tax on their highly profitable property; millionaires are found to be paying little or no tax on their handsome incomes; corporations are found to be deducting overseas bribes and payoffs. Little wonder that the voters reject bond issues and the IRS fears a genuine taxpayers revolt.

The cycle of deliberate confusion and taxpayer anger is broken when average taxpayers enter tax politics. The story of *Tax Politics* is the story of Akron's Bob Loitz and the citizens of Arkansas's ACORN, who helped to pressure Congress into blocking hundreds of millions of dollars in special-interest tax subsidies; it is the story of Sue and Phil Long, who sued the IRS under the Freedom of Information Act and revealed secrets of often unfair IRS practices; it is the story of Chicago's Citizens Action Program, which forced U.S. Steel to pay millions of dollars by forcing a reassessment of the company's properties.

The dramatic successes of these people are a sign: the special interests and their favored politicians are not monarchs. A small percentage of determined average taxpayers can wage successful struggles against the inequities in our income and property tax laws.

Citizen awareness and commitment can lead promptly to superior strategies for fundamental action. One such strategy is to develop the instrument which can link taxpayers all over the country into continuous professional and grass-roots organizations. The obvious mechanism for such a link is a voluntary taxpayer checkoff system right on the income and property tax forms. Such voluntary contributions can support taxpayers' watchdog and reform groups throughout the country directly controlled by the contributing citizen taxpayer. These civic institutions, operating outside of government to work on government and powerful special interests, such as corporations receiving tax subsidies, can bring together concerned taxpayers with skilled staffs of economists, lawyers, accountants, organizers, writers, and others to make our system really one of taxation with representation. Readers who wish to mobilize support for this proposal may write to their members of Congress, and for further information, to the Public Citizen Tax Reform Research Group, P.O. Box 14198, Washington, D.C. 20044.

Ralph Nader

March 1976
Washington, D.C.

Acknowledgments

There are many people to thank, not just for their help on this book but for the support, insight, and inspiration they gave us in a sometimes very difficult job.

This book relies heavily on work done by many members of the Tax Reform Research Group past and present. Specifically, our former colleague Barry Greever contributed heavily to the materials in the investigations and citizen action chapters from his experience as a community organizer. Our colleague Louise Brown contributed the major portion of Chapter 3 from her experience as Director of the group's I.R.S. Project. In addition, the work of Al Turkus, Richard Bourdon, Don Peppard, Samantha Senger, William Pietz, and Douglas Crooks advanced the group's efforts to reform the tax laws and helped to make this book possible.

Special thanks go to Professor Stanley S. Surrey, whose work developed the important concept of tax expenditures, whose efforts taught us much about power relationships, and whose support for tax reform and for the work we do is much appreciated.

We are also indebted to Professor Charles Davenport, and to John McGregor, Pamela Pecarich, and Laurence Wohl for their generous gifts of time and insight into IRS administrative practices. Special mention should go to Philip and Susan Long, Bellevue, Washington, taxpayers who have used the Freedom of Information Act, often under most trying circumstances, to retrieve and share with us invaluable IRS statistical data.

We have learned and gathered information from many others: executive branch and congressional professional staff members whose skills and public spirit were not dampened by the special-interest advocacy of some of their superiors; members of the press whose professionalism and insights taught us about power, the tax process, and public opinion; various Washington-based groups which have dedicated their efforts for tax reform on behalf of average citizens, including the AFL-CIO and its able lobbyist Ray Denison, Taxation with Representation and its public-spirited founder Tom Field, and many others; some special members of Congress who have demonstrated that those with the courage to fight for tax justice can make a difference; and dedicated citizens such as Bob Loitz of Akron, Ohio, whose efforts are a constant reminder that people do care about tax reform.

Numerous other individuals and groups were especially important in bringing the property tax sections into being. Our former colleague Sam Simon initiated the property tax project, which was the beginning of it all. The Los Angeles County assessor's office opened its doors to us and went out of its way to show us how an assessing system works. The professional staff at the International Association of Assessing Officers has also been very helpful. Mike Halpin, a former intern at the Tax Reform Research Group, developed much of the information on farmland assessment. The persistence of Margaret Sosygian of Westmoreland County, Pennsylvania, was largely responsible for alerting us to the growing problem of private mass appraisal firms.

Resourceful local citizen groups are responsible for much of our data and our inspiration. The Citizens Action Program (CAP) in Chicago, Save Our Cumberland Mountains (SOCM) in Petros, Tennessee, Arkansas Community Organizations for Reform Now (ACORN) in Little Rock, Arkansas, and the Tax Equity for America (TEA) Party in Philadelphia are just a few examples.

For the property tax sections, we are especially indebted to a number of people who gave patiently and generously of their time, knowledge, and thoughts. Among these are: John Behrens of the Census Bureau, economist Mason Gaffney, attorney Irving Lew, and John Rackham, now with the U.S. Postal Service.

We would like to specially thank Timothy Ward of our staff who tirelessly labored over illegible manuscript drafts, typing and proofreading, and helped out in countless other ways. Thanks also to the many others who helped to type the manuscript.

At Pantheon, we would like to thank Carol Lazare, Dian Smith, and especially Susan Gyarmati, who edited a lengthy and sometimes difficult manuscript and whose dedicated efforts and critical guidance went far beyond what most writers could expect.

Finally, we would like to thank all the Public Citizens who support our work through their generous contributions and citizen activity. And a patient Ralph Nader, who leads most of all by example.

Contents

Preface vii

Acknowledgments ix

List of Figures xiii

Introduction xv

PART 1

CHAPTER 1: TAXES AND TAXPAYERS 3
What is Fair Taxation? 3
Tax History 7
The Tax System Today 13
    Federal Taxes Today 15
    State and Local Taxes Today 23
Who Bears the Tax Burden? 31

PART 2 Income Taxes

CHAPTER 2: TAX EXPENDITURES: THE HIDDEN FEDERAL BUDGET—A KEY TO REFORM 33
What is a Tax Expenditure? 34
Using the Tax Expenditure Budget
    to Approach Tax Reform 35
Major Items of the Tax Expenditure
    Budget: An Analysis 54

CHAPTER 3: CONGRESS AND POLITICS 75
The Tax-Writing Committees 78
Sources of Legislation 85
The House 87
The Senate 94
The Conference Committee 101
Taxation with Representation 103

CHAPTER 4: TAX POLICY AND ADMINISTRATION: THE TREASURY DEPARTMENT AND THE IRS 107
Political Influence on Policy 108
Implementing the Law through Regulation 110
Insulating Tax Policy from
    Political Influence 113
The Internal Revenue Service 117
    Assistance in Filing Returns 118
    Audits 119
    Appeals 127
    Collection of Delinquent Taxes 130

CHAPTER 5: CHECKING OUT ELECTED OFFICIALS 137
Information about Elected Officials
    and How to Find It 140

PART 3 Property Taxes

CHAPTER 6: WHO PAYS THE PROPERTY TAX 143
Where Property Taxes Come From 143
Who Pays the Property Tax 145
Where Property Taxes Go 147
Property Tax Exemptions 148
    An Agenda for Reform 157
Farmland and Open Space 158
    Do Assessment Breaks Work? 160
    What Do We Need to Do to Save
        Farmland and Open Space? 162
Paying for Schools 166
    School Finance Reform: The Options 168

CHAPTER 7: HOW PROPERTY TAXES WORK 170
The Property Tax Calendar 170
The Tax Process 174

xii TAX POLITICS

Assessing and the Assessor	175
What is a "Fair" Assessment	183
100 Percent Full Value	183
Fractional Assessment	183
Uniformity	187
Lack of Uniformity between Homes and Commercial and Industrial Property	192
Selective Underassessment	193
Underassessment of Land	193
Revaluations	195
The Reappraisal Program	195
The Mass Appraisal Industry	196
What Local Governments and Taxpayers Can Do	200
Appealing Assessments	201
The Appeals System	201
How to Appeal Your Assessment	204
Collecting Property Taxes	208
Escrow Accounts	208
Property Tax Delinquencies	209
Tax Sales	210

CHAPTER 8: INVESTIGATING PROPERTY TAXES	211
How to Uncover Underassessment	211
Investigating Unequal Assessments	214
How to Make an Assessment-Sales Ratio Study	214
What to Find Out about Delinquencies	217
How to Check for Nonlisting	217
Exempt Property	219
Information on Property Taxes and How to Find It	220
How to Find the Law	229
Your Right to See Public Records	233
Tips for Citizen Investigators	234

CHAPTER 9: PROPERTY TAXES AND RELATED BATTLES	236
Highways	236
Pollution	237
High-rises	238

Airports	238
Shoddy Home-Construction	239
Strip-Mining	239
New Industry	242
Nuclear Power and Property Taxes	243

PART 4

CHAPTER 10: TAKING ACTION ON TAX REFORM	245
A Word about Power	245
Allies	246
Building Your Tax-Reform Organization	247
Voting Records on Tax Issues	251
Campaign Contributions	251
Financial Interests and Conflicts of Interest	251
Tactics	252
Some Specific Actions	254
Elections and Taxes	258
Pitfalls	262

Appendix

The Tax Justice Act	264
Tax Reform Groups	268

Bibliographical Note

Income Taxes	272
Property Taxes	276
Index	283
About the Authors	299

List of Figures

Figure 1.	Federal Budget Receipts, by Source, Selected Fiscal Years, 1950-1974, Show the Jump in Payroll Taxes Compared with Other Federal Revenues	9
Figure 2.	How Erosions in the Tax Base Undermine the Ability-to-Pay Principle	14
Figure 3.	Budget Receipts by Source	16
Figure 4.	Effective Rates of Federal and State-Local Individual and Corporation Income Taxes, 1966	17
Figure 5.	Factors Reducing the Effective Tax Rate of Corporations, 1965 and 1972	18
Figure 6.	Effective Corporate Tax Rates by Industry on Worldwide Income	19
Figure 7.	The Social Security Payroll Tax	20
Figure 8.	Effective Rates of Federal Excise Taxes, 1954	21
Figure 9.	Tax Revenues by Source	22
Figure 10.	Individual Tax Burden vs. Corporate Tax Burden as Percentage of Total Receipts, 1944-1974	22
Figure 11.	The Shifting Burden of Income and Payroll Taxes by Income Classes	23
Figure 12.	State and Local Total General Revenue, by State, 1971	24
Figure 13.	State Tax Collections, by Source, Selected Years, 1902-1971	25
Figure 14.	Percentage Distribution of Local Government General Revenue, 1957 and 1971	26
Figure 15.	Dates of Adoption of Major State Taxes	29
Figure 16.	Revenues from Public Enterprises and Other Non-Tax Sources, 1971-1972	30
Figure 17.	The Narrowing of the Gap in Direct Tax Burdens Borne by Average and Upper Income Families, 1953 and 1974	32
Figure 18.	Federal Tax Expenditures for Fiscal Year 1976	36
Figure 19.	Tax Preference Benefits per Individual by Adjusted Gross Income Class, Fiscal Year 1974	42
Figure 20.	Federal Subsidies, Fiscal Year 1975	45
Figure 21.	How Tax Shelters Work	48
Figure 22.	Who Benefits from the Tax Subsidy for Pensions	73
Figure 23.	The Effect of Tax Integration on Private Pensions	73
Figure 24.	The Tax Advantage Achieved Through Incorporation	74
Figure 25.	How Tax Laws are Written	76
Figure 26.	How Tax Laws Are Implemented	114
Figure 27.	Some Suggestions for Do-It-Yourself Tax Return Preparation	120
Figure 28.	Finding a Tax Preparer	121
Figure 29.	Compliance Level by Audit Class	121
Figure 30.	Frequency of IRS Audits (1971-73)	123
Figure 31.	IRS Notification Letter	124
Figure 32.	Self-Help During the Audit	126
Figure 33.	Income Tax Appeal Procedure	128
Figure 34.	Where IRS Was Most Likely to Seize Money or Property of Delinquent Taxpayers in Fiscal Year 1972	131
Figure 35.	Responding to IRS Bills and Seizure Notices	132
Figure 36.	Where to Complain	132
Figure 37.	Collection Procedure for Collecting Delinquent Taxes	134
Figure 38.	Who Pays the Local Property Tax?	144
Figure 39.	The Estimated Burden of Residential Property Taxes for a Hypothetical Family of Four, for Various Family Income Groups, Selected Cities, 1971-1972	145

xiv TAX POLITICS

Figure 40.	Real Estate Taxes as a Percentage of Family Income, Owner-Occupied Single-Family Homes, by Income Class and by Region, 1970	146
Figure 41.	Effective Rates of Federal, State, and Local Property Taxes, 1966	146
Figure 42.	The Proportions of Taxed and Untaxed Property in the United States, 1966	150
Figure 43.	Value Reported for Totally Exempt Property, by Type of Exemption, for Selected States, 1971	152
Figure 44.	Property Tax Exemptions in the State of Washington, 1970	154
Figure 45.	States with Differential Farmland Assessment Provisions, January 1, 1973	160
Figure 46.	City-State Comparison of Proportion of Expenditures Used for Education, 1969-70	167
Figure 47.	The Relationship Between District Wealth and School Revenues in Bexar County, Texas	168
Figure 48.	Tax Calendars	171
Figure 49.	Simplified Chart of Property Tax Process	172
Figure 50.	Actual Local Residential Property Assessment Levels Compared to State Legal Standards, 1971	184
Figure 51.	Assessments on Single-Family Nonfarm Houses	188
Figure 52.	Comparison of Assessments and Taxes	190
Figure 53.	How To Get Facts on a Mass Appraisal Firm	201
Figure 54.	Suggested Contract Terms for a Mass Appraisal Contract	202
Figure 55.	Comparing Your Property with Others	206
Figure 56.	Taxes Lost by Chicago Public Agencies Due to U.S. Steel Underassessment	213
Figure 57.	Sample Worksheet To Find Assessment-Sales Ratio and Coefficient of Dispersion	215
Figure 58.	Finding the Typical Assessment Error: An Illustration	216
Figure 59.	Paved Acreage in City Center	237
Figure 60.	Estimated National Air Pollution Damage Costs with No Pollution Control, 1968 and 1977	238
Figure 61.	Why High-Rises in San Francisco Cost Taxpayers More Than They Provide in Revenue	240
Figure 62.	Metro-Act of Rochester, Inc., Press Release	250
Figure 63.	Citizens Action Program Newsletter	252
Figure 64.	The T.E.A. Party Petition	255
Figure 65.	"Tip Toe Thru the Taxes," Newspaper Column by Eleanor Corazzini	260

Appendix

Figure A.	Tax Liability under Tax Justice Act Compared to Present Tax Code	265
Figure B.	Income and Taxes	266

Introduction

Tax politics is the process by which people are separated from their hard-earned money. Taxpayers complain that taxes are too high, that taxes are unfair, and, most of all, that there is nothing they can do to change them.

Taxes are an increasing burden on most taxpayers—and they hit middle- and lower-income taxpayers the hardest. In the twenty years between 1953 and 1974, the federal, state, and local tax burden on the high-income American family (making about $52,000 in 1974) rose 45 percent while the burden on the average-income family (making about $14,000) jumped 98 percent. Corporate federal income taxes continue to fall, so that corporations pay not the 48 percent the law says they should, but little more than 30 percent. As a result, the corporate tax share of federal revenues has dropped from 30 percent in 1954 to 14 percent in 1975. At the same time, the share of tax revenue paid by individuals, including social security taxes, has jumped dramatically. In similar fashion, property taxes borne by residential taxpayers have been increasing, while the share borne by business has been declining. Our tax laws are written and administered under the influence of powerful and wealthy special-interest groups. And when they succeed in paying less taxes, the rest of us pay more.

★ ★ ★ ★ ★ ★

Our tax system is unfair. A multitude of tax preferences and loopholes allow taxpayers with similar incomes or property to pay greatly differing taxes. An $18,000-a-year wage earner will pay about 25 percent in federal taxes; a person who makes $18,000 on investments in the stock market will pay only half that rate; and someone whose $18,000 comes from investment in tax-exempt bonds won't pay a penny in federal income taxes. In 1974, Western Electric paid taxes at a 39 percent rate while Westinghouse paid 16 percent. Still other corporations, such as oil companies and banks, pay 10 percent, 5 percent, or nothing in federal income taxes. A recent study showed that owners of $30,000 homes in sixty-seven American cities were paying property taxes that differed as much as $337 from one home to another. Many corporations locate in special tax haven states or districts and pay little or no property taxes while residents in neighboring communities are paying excessive rates.

Despite the principle of taxation according to ability to pay, those with higher incomes are able to pay less than their fair share and those with lower incomes pay more. In 1973, 622 individuals reporting more than $100,000 of adjusted gross income paid no federal income taxes. Many others pay far less than they fairly should. Typical high-income tax returns examined by the House Ways and Means Committee showed one individual with $427,000 in income paying about 0.3 percent in tax in 1974. A businessman with $396,000 in profits paid only 11.9 percent. Another individual with over $2 million in income paid only $25,000 or 1.3 percent in taxes.

Tax loopholes unfairly help the well-off. In fact, 53 percent of federal tax break dollars go to the top 15 percent of all taxpayers. Those people with higher incomes get an average tax break of almost $19,000 while the other 85 percent of taxpayers save an average of less than $500. And average taxpayers fare worse in their encounters with the IRS, state tax authorities, and local assessors than do their wealthier and better represented counterparts.

The complaints of average taxpayers are justified. Where they go wrong is in assuming that our tax structure cannot be changed.

Taxation with representation is what our nation's founders fought for, and taxation with representation is what we have today. But some are better represented than others. Our unfair system is the result of competing interests fighting over who will pay less taxes. And in that fight, it is the underrepresented average taxpayer who loses.

There are reasons for the imbalance. According to the Harris poll, only 50 percent of Americans even know the name of their representative in Congress. Few know who their state and local representatives are. Still fewer know the officials and bureaucrats who run our tax system.

By contrast, special interests know these people well. They pressure them through lobbying and support them with campaign contributions. They influence them with paid speaking engagements, dinners, junkets, hunting trips, and other favors, including the promise of future lucrative jobs.

The system is ready-made for politicians and bureaucrats to con the general public. Hard-hitting speeches, newsletters, or statements in favor of tax reform are designed to make the voters happy. Angry letters to officeholders or administrators are usually answered with vague promises to improve the system. By contrast, politicians and policymakers know that the special interests are watching closely and want results—the right vote or decision in their favor.

A particular group looking for a tax break will always have a greater interest in its enactment than will the general public in its defeat. The special-interest group realizes that taxes are money—big money—and that representation pays. And a clever politician realizes that he can keep both the voters and the special interests happy by posturing as a tax reformer and voting for the dull, technical tax laws that can mean millions or even billions of dollars.

For years, presidents, Congress, and state and local legislators have been giving in to demands for special treatment from those who were well represented in the political process—represented by money, highly organized lobbies, and influence. The tax system described in this book is the end result not of a theory of fairness, but of this practice of politics. Citizens can change all that only when they make politicians represent the point of view of the great majority of taxpayers by countering the influence of those who have gained from the present system.

Working with Public Citizen's Tax Reform Research Group on Congress, the Treasury, and the IRS, and working with local citizen groups around the country, we have come to realize that tax reform at any level will not happen until many more people demand it and work for it. If American taxpayers who work three months each year just to pay their taxes devoted a tiny fraction of that time to reforming their tax system, change would come.

The complexity of the tax laws and the lack of information about our tax system are major obstacles to reform. The information aimed at ordinary taxpayers is mainly the how-to-fill-out-your-return variety or propaganda provided by those who benefit most by our present tax laws. This information, far from criticizing the loophole-ridden system, raises hopes in people's minds that they might find some loopholes for themselves or that they somehow benefit in other ways. What taxpayers need is information on who influences and writes the tax laws, how they work in theory and are administered in practice, and who *really* benefits from them. We have written this book to provide people with this information. It is not merely a book to make you angry, although taxpayers deserve to be angry. It is a book to make you active—to provide the tools for turning anger into positive results.

Knowledge and citizen action can be aimed at righting the imbalance in the politics of taxation. Every letter, every meeting with representatives and officials, every new civic strategy adds up. Armed with information, citizens can organize their neighbors and pressure their elected officials. They can ask for specific action and will settle for no less. Reform will come only when enough of us demand and receive equal representation in the process that determines our tax laws, in the process that administers our tax laws, and in the process that can change our tax laws.

Tax Politics

Chapter 1
Taxes and Taxpayers

Broad based movements for reform are one of the oldest American traditions. They are older than the Declaration of Independence, the Constitution, the two-party system, and either of the major political parties today. From the colonial riots protesting the British Sugar and Stamp Acts, the Revolution itself, to the Whiskey Rebellion, the latter-nineteenth-century Populist agitation for progressive income taxes, and all the lesser-known but no less ardent battles in the states and localities, Americans have risen up against economic injustice imposed by established powers. Today, the need for reform impresses itself regularly. In June 1974, a poll by Louis Harris reported that 79 percent of the Americans surveyed agreed that the rich get richer and the poor get poorer (versus 45 percent in 1966); 78 percent agreed that special interests get more from the government than do ordinary people; and 75 percent felt that the tax laws are written to help the rich. Taxpayers have been swamping public meetings, marching and demonstrating, besieging their elected officials with letters and petitions to make known their view that the tax laws need reform.

We read in the newspapers of multinational oil companies and other major corporations enjoying record profits but paying little or nothing in taxes. We learn of well-heeled stalwarts of the expense-account set who pay a rate of tax close to, or even less than ours. The bewildering complexity of the tax laws states the case eloquently. As we try to puzzle out our federal income tax returns, or try to follow the explanations of our local assessor, it becomes very plain that whatever is in those thousands of pages of federal tax laws and regulations, and in their state and local counterparts, it wasn't put there for us. Taxes hurt, and they are hurting ordinary taxpayers increasingly. Between 1953 and 1972, the total tax bill of the typical family of four increased 70 percent as a percent of income.

★ ★ ★ ★ ★ ★ ★

People, sometimes well-meaning, sometimes not, often divert discussions of tax reform into debates over spending. Spending is indeed a crucial issue. Most people agree there is too much of it on the wrong things, and perhaps not enough of it on the right things, though they disagree on what these "right" and "wrong" things may be. The spending ploy is a tempting one. Staggered by the bulk and complexity of the tax laws, and confused by the sophisticated arguments by which special interests defend their loopholes, spending seems a much simpler and easier target on which to vent frustrations. But it misses the mark. Whether spending is large or small, the question is *how the burden of paying for this spending will be allotted.*

what *is* fair taxation?

The principle for allocation of the tax burden that the authors choose is ability-to-pay. People and corporations should contribute to the commonwealth in the proportion that they are able. This view is neither radical nor novel. No less an apostle of free enterprise than Adam Smith argued in 1776 that "the subjects of every state ought to contribute towards the support of the government as nearly as possible in proportion to their respective abilities."

Smith pointed to a basis for the ability-to-pay principle that isn't always remembered. "The expence of government to the individuals of a great nation," he said, "is like the expence of management to the joint tenants of a great estate, who are all obliged to contribute in proportion to their respective interests in the

3

4 TAX POLITICS

estate." The more one has, Smith was saying, the bigger one's stake in the social order, and therefore the more expense of maintaining and protecting that order the taxpayer should bear.

The ability-to-pay principle is the simplest and most direct. Thinkers in all ages have espoused it and without pretending to clairvoyance, we would venture that to most people "tax justice" means taxation according to ability-to-pay.

Opponents of this principle advance others on which a tax system could be based. Some of these merit attention and are discussed below. But the objections most commonly raised are little more than apologies of the wealthy in the guise of argument. For example, they will try to debunk taxation according to ability as a "soak-the-rich" scheme, yet most tax reformers are moved not by a desire to hurt anyone, rich or otherwise, but rather by a desire to protect and do justice to those less well-off. "If anyone bears less than his fair share of the burden," wrote John Stuart Mill in his *Principles of Political Economy*, "some other person must suffer more than his share, and the alleviation to the one is not, on the average, so great a good to him as the increased pressure upon the other is an evil."

Opponents of tax reform also try to tarnish the ability-to-pay ideal by twisting it into a "penalty on success." The suggestion is that taxes might cause the poor beleaguered leaders of business and industry to lose heart, causing free enterprise and the ship of state to founder as a result. The life styles of those who make such claims, opulent even by America's habit—let alone the world's—leave one wondering where and how their success has been penalized. Sociologists tell us, moreover, what we already know, that beyond a certain level of income people strive more for power and prestige than for the last dollar. And even if taxes did clip a bit the ambition of the few at the top, the effect could be to open up more opportunities for those further down, making the whole system more competitive, open, and democratic.

An alternative to the ability-to-pay principle worthy of more respect is called the benefits principle. Under this theory, people should pay taxes only to the extent that they benefit from public expenditures. The theory is not without surface appeal. "Why should I pay school taxes when my kids are grown up and married?" some people ask; or, "Why should I pay for libraries when I buy my own books?"

In practice the benefits principle has less to recommend it. Trying to determine exactly who benefits from a given public expenditure is a task to which medieval theologians might well have turned. For example, even people with no children benefit significantly from a good local school system when the time comes to sell their home—as real estate brokers are only too well aware. Besides, if Adam Smith was correct that a person's over-all stake in the system—his or her income and wealth—is the true measure of benefit from government, then the circle comes full turn, right back to ability-to-pay.

This is not to say that the benefits principle is completely useless. It is used today when property owners are charged "special assessments" for particular items—such as sidewalks and sewers—which uniquely benefit their own property, and special taxes or service charges might well be levied upon such groups as commuters who use a city's streets and other facilities but do not help support them, and upon sports promoters whose functions require extra police protection. The benefits principle has a place, in special charges for special service, but as a touchstone for the tax system it will not stand up.

In recent years a new element has entered the tax debate, almost eclipsing all others. It is called economic policy. The federal government has seized upon the tax system as a way to manipulate economic activity, heating it up, cooling it down, encouraging investment in this industry or that. Yoking the tax system to economic planning and policy has had a number of regrettable effects:

1. It has completely sidetracked discussion of taxes from matters of fairness and justice to those of economic policy, real or fabricated.

2. It has made tax matters hopelessly complex, beyond the grasp of most taxpayers and, in fact, of most representatives in Congress. This has stripped the public of any effective voice on taxes, while enhancing the power of a handful of congressmen, senators, and executive branch officials.

3. It has made the tax system even more vulnerable to loopholes

and exemptions. Business pressure groups who would not have a prayer of justifying loopholes on equity grounds have been only too ready to cast them in terms of "boosting the economy." A perpetual run on the Treasury has emerged, with one industry after another arguing that it adds to the Gross National Product, and that it too is therefore deserving of some favor. The larger the industry, the more forcefully it can make such claims, and the tax laws that ensue confirm again the old saw that the richer you are, the richer you become.

The result of turning taxes over to the economic policymakers and those who use economic policy to justify their own tax breaks has been a multibillion-dollar under-the-table subsidy system, largely for the rich and unneedy. These subsidies are often called "tax expenditures," since they are funds the public has given up just as much as if they had been collected and spent. Those who receive these tax subsidies greatly prefer them to outright grants. Lawmakers review their above-board expenditures every year or every few years, and while the probe is not always thorough, the special benefits at least see the light of day. By contrast, once a tax loophole is enacted, it lies buried in the tax laws until some inquisitive lawmaker troubles to question it—which in most cases is never.

There are three additional grounds on which taxes—or the failure to tax—are sometimes justified. Some taxes, called "sumptuary," are supposed to discourage people from certain behavior. In the past these reflected rigid moral judgments against such things as smoking and drinking. More recently they have been proposed for social concerns more broadly defined, such as pollution and the excessive use of automobiles. Taxes on cigarettes and liquor exist in virtually every state, and considering the revenues they generate — over $4 billion in 1971 — it is worth noting that the danger of taxing social ills is that government can come to depend on the revenues and thus encourage the continuation of such activities.

A related reason some taxes are imposed is to give the government a special handle for controlling certain illegal activities, or for simply gathering data. The U.S. Supreme Court has greatly curtailed the former, but as to the latter, many states impose land transfer taxes not for the revenue but so that a record of the sales price will appear on the deed.

Lawmakers and officials in particular are keen on still another way of looking at taxes—called "elasticity." A tax is "elastic" if, as economic activity expands, revenues grow even faster. Officials like elastic taxes because the bigger revenues come in without increases in the tax rate.

By the same token, however, elastic taxes dip even faster than does the economy when economic activity slows down. During the long boom following World War II this drawback was not of great concern. It appears to be looming larger now.

In general, income taxes with truly progressive rates are the most elastic taxes, because people move into higher rate brackets as their income rises. Revenues increase more rapidly than does the personal income on which it is based. Sales taxes have low elasticities, because the more people make, the smaller the portion of it they spend on goods. Property taxes are between the two, but their elasticity has been greatly underrated because assessors do not keep assessments in line with changing property values.

The benefits principle and the economic policy justifications have genuine and disinterested adherents. But the arguments are most often raised as window dressing for a rear-guard effort to erode policy decisions made long ago and stemming from traditions that go all the way back to our colonial beginnings. Early on, our nation opted for ability-to-pay as its ideal for tax justice. The earliest colonial enactments expressed it, the state constitutions adopted it directly or indirectly, and with the Sixteenth Amendment the tradition found expression in the U.S. Constitution.

Further, when the U.S. Congress passed an income tax in keeping with the Sixteenth Amendment, it made certain the tax included progressive rates as many state income taxes had done before it. Progressive taxes are a direct attempt to embody the ability-to-pay principle. The phrase arises constantly in discussions of tax reform. We should try to understand what it means.

A tax is progressive if it is larger on those who have a lot of the thing taxed than it is on those who have a little. The more the

6 TAX POLITICS

taxpayer has, the higher the rate becomes.

The reason for progressive taxes is simple and was well stated by the political philosopher Montesquieu, writing about the tax system in ancient Athens:

It was judged that each had equal physical necessities, and that those necessities ought not to be taxed; that the useful came next, and that it ought to be taxed, but less than what was superfluous; and lastly, that the greatness of the tax on the superfluity should repress the superfluity.

In other words, as applied to income taxes, people need a certain amount to acquire their basic necessities, and this amount should not be taxed. The more they have above this amount, the less they need it, and thus the more heavily it can be taxed. It bears repeating that the intent of progressive taxes is not to afflict the rich, but rather to put the tax burden where it will cause the least suffering.

Progressivity should not just be measured in terms of income. A property tax is progressive if it taxes people with lots of property at higher rates than people with little. It is common, however, to rate the progressivity of taxes solely in terms of how the taxes affect taxpayers at different income levels. This is a major blind spot in our thinking about taxes and is a reason why wealth taxes have made so little headway in the United States.

The federal income tax illustrates a progressive rate structure. The rates on unmarried individuals (in 1974) rose from 14 percent on the first $500 of taxable income, to 15 percent on the next $500, 16 percent on the next $500, on up to 70 percent on all income over $100,000. Note that the very rich do not pay the highest rates on *all* of their income, but only on the income above set levels.

The opposite of a progressive tax is a *regressive* tax, when the less a person has of the thing taxed, the higher is the rate he pays. The social security tax is a perfect example of a regressive tax. Workers making $15,000 a year pay $825, which is 5.5 percent of their income. Meanwhile an executive pulling in $100,000 a year pays the same $825, which is less than one-tenth of 1 percent of his or her income.

A tax which is neither progressive nor regressive is called proportional. This means that everyone, rich and poor alike, is taxed at the same rate. A tax rate which goes neither up nor down, but stays the same for everyone, is called a *flat rate*.

The income tax is not the only tax that can be progressive. A sales tax could be progressive, with rates increasing according to the size of the sale. A permit fee could be progressive if the fee increased according to the size of the business applying. A property tax could be progressive, with people paying a rate that was high or low according to how much property they owned. The Australians have such a progressive property tax, and in the United States it could be the most progressive tax of all, since property ownership in this country is more concentrated among a wealthy few than is income.

Similarly, progressive rates are not the only way to make a tax progressive. A tax can also be progressive or regressive according to what it taxes. For example, a sales tax could be progressive in a rough sense if food and medicines were exempted but attorneys', real estate brokers', and other professional service fees were taxed. An income tax would be roughly progressive, even with flat rates, if workers' earnings were exempted but income from stocks, bonds, and sales of property were fully taxed.

By the same token, we should not be fooled by tax rate structures. They tell only half the story. Exemptions and loopholes are the other half. The most progressive rate structure in the world is not worth much if special provisions allow the most well-off to slip through untouched. The key is not the statutory tax rate but the rates people actually pay, taking into account all exemptions, deductions, and other special provisions. This tax rate that people actually pay is called the "effective" tax rate. As we shall see, there is a vast difference between the rates listed in the Internal Revenue Code and the effective rates that taxpayers end up paying.

Despite the long tradition of the ability-to-pay principle, the lip service we pay to it, and its supposed embodiment in the federal income tax, the tax system we have today falls far short of this ideal. Nationwide, and all taxes considered, the very wealthy pay taxes at virtually the same rate as that imposed on people far less well-off.

Three trends bring this result. First, we are replacing taxes that tend to be progressive with regressive ones; raising little from estate taxes, for example, while leaning heavily on sales and payroll taxes. Second, we are undeterring our supposedly progressive taxes with special favors and loopholes, and third, weak administration of the tax laws further erodes progressivity.

How this happened is the subject of the next section.

We will be talking about tax "loopholes," so we should say what we mean by the term. Many tax experts insist that the term "loopholes" should refer only to unintended slips in the wording of the tax laws, slips that particular taxpayers can contrive to exploit. Special favors deliberately granted they dignify with the polite label "preferences."

We consider such niceties misleading. As we use the term and as we think most taxpayers understand it, loopholes are special provisions which depart from the normal pattern and give any taxpayer or group of taxpayers benefits not enjoyed by others. Whether enacted deliberately by Congress (as most are), or unintended gaps left by sloppy wording, they are still loopholes.

tax history

federal tax history

In colonial times, taxes were levied by local governments, colonial assemblies, and the British Parliament. The revolutionary banner, "No taxation without representation," sprang from two concerns. First, the colonists sent no representatives to the British Parliament which imposed taxes on them. Not that the British levies up to that time had been heavy, nor that any colonial representatives could have stopped them. But the colonists saw danger on the horizon. Britain had rung up a staggering debt in its recent war against France, and the costs of managing the territories it had gained were mounting. Britons were bearing tax burdens that the colonists were eyeing anxiously. "It could then be from no other motive than avarice," Thomas Paine wrote of Britain's stubborn fight to keep its colonies, "or a design of establishing ... the same taxes in America as are paid in England (which, as I shall presently show, are above eleven times heavier than the taxes we now pay ...)."

The other side of the revenue coin also caused concern. The colonial assemblies had as little say over how the revenues raised here were spent as they did over the taxes themselves.

The distrust of distant central governments which grew during this period carried over to the newly formed federal government. The Continental Congress had no taxing power and had to rely on grants from the states. The failure of the Continental Congress can be blamed in part on a lack of adequate funds. An early attempt to remedy the problem by amending the Articles of Confederation to allow the Congress to impose a 5 percent import duty failed because the Rhode Island Colony objected. But in 1789, the Constitution of the new United States of America went into effect. Article I, section 8, granted the new Congress the power "to lay and collect taxes, duties, imposts and excises to pay the debts and provide for the common defense and general welfare of the United States."

Under the Constitution, duties, imposts, and excises had to be "uniform through the United States," export taxes were forbidden, and direct taxes (taxes on individuals) had to be "in proportion to the census."

From 1789 until the Civil War, the federal government relied almost exclusively on excise taxes and customs. There was a national tariff of 5 percent on all imports as well as specific duties on liquors, wine, pepper, sugar, molasses, cocoa, tea, and coffee. Small tonnage duties were imposed on American ships and higher duties on foreign-owned ships. There were also luxury taxes on a number of items including snuff, whiskey, and carriages.

The whiskey tax was enacted over many objections in 1791. Opponents argued it was a direct tax; others that it was not a luxury but a poor man's necessity. So unpopular was the tax that farmers and others in western Pennsylvania, where much whiskey was made, refused to pay it—even when the rate was reduced. Finally in 1791, President Washington dispatched federal troops to enforce the tax and end the Whiskey Rebellion.

The carriage tax was challenged in the Supreme Court where it was held, in the case *United States v. Hylton,* to be an excise tax and not a direct tax which would have to be apportioned among the states according to their populations. The *Hylton* case seemed to say that an income tax would not be a direct tax within the meaning of the Constitution. In fact, just what

8 TAX POLITICS

the framers of that document meant by a direct tax besides a pure per capita tax has never been settled.

Despite the ending of the Whiskey Rebellion and the court decision on the carriage tax, the excise taxes remained unpopular, and the Jeffersonian Democrats abolished them in 1802. They were re-enacted briefly during the War of 1812, but until the Civil War federal revenues came primarily from customs duties and from some sales of public lands. From 1799 to 1859 federal revenues remained between 1 and 2 percent of national income. During this period, the tax load on the average citizen was so light that, with the exception of the whiskey tax, tax fairness never became a real issue.

The first national graduated income and inheritance tax was passed as an emergency measure during the Civil War and was in effect from 1862 through 1871. It contained a flat $600 exemption for each taxpayer and the rates increased with the taxpayer's income up to a top rate of 10 percent. To meet the high cost of war, other taxes were enacted on liquor and tobacco, manufactured goods, gross receipts of transportation companies, advertising, licenses, and legal documents.

Ironically the excise taxes on liquor and tobacco met little resistance and became permanent sources of federal revenues. Taxes on manufactured goods and gross receipts taxes were phased out as tending to check economic development. But the graduated income tax was highly controversial and was allowed to lapse in 1872 in spite of the recommendation of a congressional commission that it be retained. At its height the tax accounted for about 20 percent of total federal revenues and reached only the wealthiest 1 percent of the population. At the war's end, this small but influential group was able to defeat the tax.

They also challenged it in court, on the constitutional grounds that it was a direct tax and should have been apportioned among the states. Eight years after it expired, the Supreme Court upheld the Civil War income tax in the case *Springer v. United States*.

From 1868 to 1913, excise taxes on liquor and tobacco—hitting, once again, the bulk of the people instead of those who could most afford to pay—accounted for about 90 percent of internal revenue collection. The low incomes of farmers in the South and Midwest and laborers in the East caused opposition to this system and created pressure to restore the income tax. The Populist party gained support among these groups and included a graduated income tax in its platform. The power the Populists showed in the elections of 1890 and 1892 forced the Democratic administration of President Grover Cleveland to look on the proposal more favorably. A promised reduction in tariffs and the panic of 1893 sharply reduced federal revenues and led to the need for a new source of revenue. People were aroused over monopolies and trusts, and over wealthy individuals who paid relatively little in taxes. Finally, the Congress passed an income tax of 2 percent on all incomes over $4,000 as an amendment to the Tariff Bill of 1894.

However, only a year later, the Supreme Court, in the famous case of *Pollock v. Farmers' Loan & Trust Company*, struck it down as a direct tax. The 5-to-4 decision was assailed as a triumph of the jurists' conservative economic views over the established legal precedents in the *Hylton* and *Springer* cases. These jurists reflected the view of influential conservatives that an income tax was very dangerous, particularly when there was a depression, a railroad, strike, and the possibility of a free silver program they considered inflationary.

Proponents of the income tax were not to be put down. In 1909, they pushed passage of a 1 percent tax on the net incomes of corporations in excess of $5,000. It was labeled an excise tax on the privilege of doing business and was upheld by the Supreme Court in the case of *Flint v. Stone Tracy Company*. At the same time, Congress passed a constitutional amendment to allow a graduated income tax. In 1913, following the required number of state ratifications, the Sixteenth Amendment was born:

The Congress shall have power to lay and collect taxes on incomes, from whatever source derived, without apportionment among the several states, and without regard to any census or enumeration.

With America's entry into World War I, the recently enacted income tax was forced to bear the heavy burden of financing that conflict. According to the Revenue Act of 1918, tax rates were 6 percent on the first

$4,000 of income, and 12 percent on the remainder, with a war surcharge ranging from 1 percent on income of $5,000 to 65 percent on income over $1 million. Exemptions were set at $1,000 per single taxpayer, $2,000 for a married taxpayer, and $200 for each dependent. The corporate tax rate was 12 percent, with a $2,000 exemption. In addition, Congress enacted an excess profits tax on corporations as well as an estate tax. Although excise taxes were also increased, the income and excess profits taxes accounted for substantially larger revenue. However, even with relatively high tax rates, income taxes during World War I were very much lighter than today. Only about 5.5 million people paid income taxes out of a population of about 106 million people. Even a $10,000-a-year family paid only $558 in income taxes.

After the war, once again Congress reduced the high income taxes. By 1939, only 4 million people (4 percent of the population fourteen years and older) paid income taxes. This time, however, the income tax remained a permanent part of federal revenues.

Inevitably, World War II again brought much higher rates. And the tax cut much deeper into the population. By 1945, 43 million individuals paid income taxes. The $10,000-a-year family paid $2,245. At the same time, the corporate tax rate rose to 40 percent and the excess profits tax to a maximum of 80 percent. As Harvard Professor Stanley Surrey points out, a high point of the World War II income tax was its successful administration. Tax withholding from wage and salary checks simplified tax returns; tax tables and the standard deduction were developed during this period. In 1945 about $35 billion came from income and excess profits taxes, with only $7.5 billion coming from excise taxes.

The predictable postwar tax reductions were cut short in 1950 with the outbreak of the Korean War, when taxes went back up again. However, income-splitting for married couples reduced the impact of the new rates. The $10,000-a-year family paid $1,744 in taxes in 1951. The corporate tax was 30 percent on income up to $25,000, and 52 percent on income above that amount, the excess profits tax was an additional 30 percent.

Taxes were cut again after the war, with a major overhaul of the laws occurring in 1954. The 1954 Internal Revenue Code repealed the excess profits tax. Corporate taxes remained at 30 percent and 52 percent. Individual rates ranged from 20 percent on the lowest taxable income to 91 percent on the highest. However, Congress undercut these seemingly high rates by introducing various tax subsidies including accelerated depreciation and a special provision for tax-free stock dividends up to a certain limit.

The Revenue Act of 1964, rooted in what has become ortho-

★ **FIGURE 1. FEDERAL BUDGET RECEIPTS, BY SOURCE, SELECTED FISCAL YEARS, 1950-1974, SHOW THE JUMP IN PAYROLL TAXES COMPARED WITH OTHER FEDERAL REVENUES** ★

Source	1950	1960	1970	1974	1976 (Estimate)
Billions of dollars					
Individual income taxes	15.7	40.7	90.4	119.0	135.0
Corporation income taxes	10.4	21.5	32.8	38.6	39.5
Social insurance taxes*	4.0	14.7	45.3	76.8	92.6
Excise taxes	7.5	11.7	15.7	16.8	16.9
All other	3.3	3.9	9.5	13.6	16.8
Total	40.9	92.5	193.7	264.9	300.8
Percentage of total					
Individual income taxes	38.4	44.0	46.7	44.9	44.9
Corporation income taxes	25.4	23.2	16.9	14.6	13.1
Social insurance taxes*	9.8	15.9	23.4	29.0	30.8
Excise taxes	18.3	12.6	8.1	6.3	5.6
All other	8.1	4.2	4.9	5.1	5.6
Total	100.0	100.0	100.0	100.0	100.0

SOURCE: Derived from The Budget of the United States Government and Special Analyses. Figures may not add to totals because of rounding.
*Includes payroll taxes for social security and unemployment insurance, employee contributions for federal retirement, and contributions for supplementary medical insurance.

10 TAX POLITICS

dox economic doctrine, tried to bring the country out of a recession by cutting individual taxes. The new rates ranged from 16 percent to 77 percent for the calendar year 1964, and the following year they dropped again to the present levels—between 14 and 70 percent. By 1968 the economy was humming, and in that year a temporary tax surcharge was added to help pay for the Vietnam War. President Johnson was trying to finance the war and reduce the budget deficit at the same time without jeopardizing his Great Society programs. After some disagreement with a Congress that wanted to cut expenditures, a compromise was reached. The budget was cut slightly while a 7.5 percent surcharge was enacted for 1968, rising to 10 percent in 1969.

The so-called Tax Reform Act of 1969 reduced the surtax to 2.5 percent in 1970 and repealed it for subsequent years. That act also put a maximum tax ceiling of 50 percent on earned income (wages and salaries) while instituting a minimum tax on certain tax preference items. Finally, the 1971 Revenue Act raised the personal exemptions from $625 to the present $750 and cut corporate taxes.

Payroll taxes began much later than income taxes. The Social Security Act of 1935 established a limited social security plan, accompanied by modest payroll taxes of 1 percent of the first $3,000 in wages to pay for it. By 1939, payroll taxes were bringing the federal government some $740 million, less than either the individual or corporate income taxes but already over twice the revenues from federal estate and gift taxes. By 1950, payroll taxes reached 3 percent for employers and employees, amounting to $4 billion, less than 10 percent of government revenues. (Individual and corporate taxes amounted to 38 percent and 25 percent, respectively.)

state and local tax history

In the early colonies, state and local expenses were met largely through voluntary contributions and through revenues from the public lands and enterprises. The religious origins of many of the colonies cast a churchly hue over public functions and made contributions to them akin to giving at church. Thus in 1644 in New Haven, Connecticut, each resident "whose heart is willing" was asked to give a peck of wheat to support "poor scholars at Harvard College."

Such contributions were requested with ever-increasing regularity, and their "voluntary" nature became largely a nicety of theory. In 1680, Maryland imposed "equal assessments" on inhabitants of a county who refused to contribute to a local charity. Around the time of the Revolution, people in Maryland who would not pay a share were cited as "enemies of America" in resolutions published in the *Maryland Gazette*, and were reported to local committees of observation.

Still, the spirit of voluntary assistance to the common cause remained strong during this period. Ben Franklin left a fund of £1,000 to the city of Philadelphia to be loaned to young married couples in amounts up to £60. Stephen Girard, another wealthy Philadelphian, left his large estate to the city to help "diminish taxation."

Publicly run enterprises were another way the early colonists diminished the need for taxes. Philadelphia, for example, raised considerable revenue by renting wharves, market stalls, and other city-owned property. By 1710 the city did not even have the power under its charter to levy taxes. In the nineteenth century, gas works, water works, and like facilities were often publicly owned. The state of New York operated a salt works. Massachusetts reclaimed over one hundred acres of marsh land in Boston's Back Bay and sold it for a $4 million profit (although critics charged the property could have been leased for up to $2 million per year). Savannah, Georgia, had a plan that was even more ambitious. The city was extended only when and where the city itself had acquired the proposed new section. After making certain improvements the city would auction the lots at a profit.

Fines were a third way the colonies kept their taxes low. With taboos covering so many forms of behavior, the opportunities for such revenues were ample, as Mary Stebbins of Springfield, Massachusetts, discovered when, in 1667, she was fined ten shillings for wearing silks contrary to law.

When contributions, public enterprise, and fines could no longer carry the load, the colonies began to levy a wide assortment of license and permit fees, excise and poll taxes. But the bulwarks of their tax systems defied the rigid classifications of "income" taxes, "property" taxes, and "sales" taxes that we have today. The early colonists appear to have been much more concerned with *taxpaying ability*. Legal historian Arthur Lynn points to the English Poor Tax as a major model in the minds of the early settlers on this continent. The Poor Tax eventually evolved toward a fixed-rate levy, but for a long time tax officials tried to take each taxpayer's total financial circumstances into account. This attitude was epitomized by the "faculty" tax, a combination of income and property tax designed to reach the individual's taxpaying ability, whether it resided in revenue-producing land, a business, or a profession.

Thus assessors in New Plymouth Colony were instructed in 1643 to assess all inhabitants "according to their estates or faculties, that is, according to goods, lands, improved faculties, and psonal abillities" (sic). This mandate to reach all sources of taxpaying ability persisted up to 1777, when the instruction to tap non-real-estate sources of property and wealth was made even more explicit.

Vermont, by 1796, had, in addition to its regular property tax, an optional levy on lawyers, traders, and owners of mills, in proportion to their profits. Included in the Massachusetts tax were shops, mills, industrial works, tonnage of vessels, government securities, stock in banks, and plate. Connecticut taxed the profits of any and all gainful professions, trades, and occupations, with exemptions for public officeholders, farmers, and common labor for hire.

The taxes were often progressive even among members of the same profession. Connecticut attorneys paid a tax on their practices, the "least practitioners" at £50 and others "in proportion to their practice."

In New England in the 1700s property taxes constituted about two-thirds of direct taxes, and poll taxes only about one-third.

The pattern was quite different in the South, however, due mainly to the concentrated landownership there and the political power arising from it. The southern plantation owners stoutly resisted property taxes, promoting instead poll taxes, license fees and permits and duties on imports. Virginia, for example, levied property taxes briefly, in 1645-48, and then not again until the French and Indian War in 1755. In 1763 less than one-third of Virginia's revenues came from the land and over two-thirds from polls. Maryland did not have a tax on real estate until 1756. This tax was extended to all property in 1777, but was used little in the late eighteenth and early nineteenth centuries.

Standards used for valuing property were different as well. The "market value" standard common today was not then so widely used, in part because real estate did not change hands as frequently. Often land was assessed instead at a set amount per acre, depending roughly on how productive it could be. It was also common to classify land according to its nature and use. In Ohio, for example, there were three classes, and observers deplored the trend by which more and more land gravitated to the lowest taxed category.

To ameliorate this trend, state after state adopted laws and constitutional amendments requiring that all property be assessed and taxed uniformly. Historian Lynn points to Ohio as typical. In 1825 the state abandoned the system of classifying land and began to assess real estate according to its market value—what a "willing buyer" would pay a "willing seller." In 1846, the period of broadening the tax base was capped by the so-called Kelly Act, under which all property not specifically exempt was to be taxed according to market value.

To protect the "uniformity" clause, nineteenth-century Ohio lawmakers embedded it into the state constitution three years later. "The legislature," wrote Jens Peter Jensen, the late dean of property tax scholars, "had become disturbed in Ohio as well as in other states. It was charged with favoring certain corporations in selecting the list of taxables. It was deemed necessary to free 'man, as such, his business, occupation, and profession, from legislative caprice.'" Thus the new section of the Ohio constitution asserted that "Laws shall be passed, taxing by a uniform rule, all monies, credits, investments in bonds, joint stock companies, or otherwise, and also all real and personal property according to its true value in money."

In a like spirit, New Jersey Governor Daniel Haines exclaimed to the state legislature in his 1851 message that the tax "burden, whether great or small, shall be borne as equally as possible by all; and no proposition of political economy can be more obvious or just, than that everyone should contribute toward the support of the government in proportion to the amount of his property protected by it. The passage of a law equalizing taxation seems to be imperatively demanded by the people, and I respectfully but earnestly commend it to your early consideration, and prompt and efficient action."

After this message the New Jersey legislature enacted the state's first general property tax, subjecting all property, real, personal, and intangible, to taxation "upon an equal ratio according to actual value."

At this time property taxes provided the bulk of revenue for state as well as for local governments (New Jersey was an exception), so that the states took some role in the administration of the tax. Assessing, however, remained a local matter and the thousands of local assessors, many part-time and untrained, often lacked the ability, inclination, or both to make the ideal of uniform taxation of all property a fact in practice. Uniform assessment of real estate was rare, and much property, especially personal property and intangibles, never even got onto the tax rolls.

Viewing this failure, many observers took the stance—one still accepted widely and uncritically—that the ideal of uniform taxation, and not the paltry efforts taken to achieve it, was at fault. Thus E. R. A. Seligman's early twentieth-century denunciation of the property tax:

Practically, the general property tax as actually administered is beyond all doubt one of the worst taxes known in the civilised world. Because of its attempt to tax intangible things it sins against the cardinal rules of uniformity, of equality and of universality of taxation. It puts a premium on dishonesty and debauches the public conscience; it reduces deception to a system and makes a science of knavery; it presses hardest on those least able to pay; it imposes double taxation on one man and grants entire immunity to the next. In short the general property tax is so flagrantly inequitable that its retention can be explained only through ignorance or inertia. It is the cause of such crying injustice that its alteration or its abolition must become the battle cry of every statesman and reformer.

Two other developments around this time practically killed any hope that the states would provide adequate property tax administration. One was the way school financing evolved. "Our early schools," Lynn writes, "were essentially private and . . . prior to 1825, even public schools often derived much of their revenue from non-tax sources." Some states enacted laws *permitting* localities to impose school property taxes, but the states remained under pressure to put school finance on a dependable basis. At the same time, powerful conservatives were objecting to mandatory public schooling and the accompanying taxes as an intrusion of government upon individual rights—and incidentally, upon their pocketbooks. To squirm out of this bind, the state lawmakers went ahead with compulsory schools, but put the burden of running and paying for them onto the local governments. The main revenue source the localities had for meeting this burden was the property tax, and even today schools consume more property tax revenues than does any other public function. Having passed the buck to the localities, the states—which alone had the constitutional power to improve faltering property tax administration—could conveniently look the other way.

A related development was the rise of new sources of state revenue, such as motor fuel and vehicle taxes and, later, sales and income taxes. Scholars began to advance a theory of "separation of revenue sources." This theory held that states and localities should impose completely different taxes instead of sharing revenue from the same taxes. Accordingly the states would withdraw from the property tax and leave it more or less completely to local governments. In large measure this has happened. In 1902 the states still raised a full 51 percent of their revenue from property taxes, but by 1937 this figure had declined by half, to 26.8 percent. Ten years later only 8.7 percent of state revenues came from property taxes, and the decline has continued to just a little over 2 percent today.

Ironically, one promised result of this "separation of revenue sources" was to be better property tax administration. But the opposite has occurred. No longer relying on property taxes for revenue, state lawmakers were not greatly concerned. To this day they answer property tax complaints from constituents with a cold "I'm sorry, that's a local matter." Local officials and politicians for their part welcomed state neglect and often turned the property tax into an adjunct of their patronage machines.

Though study commissions recommended reforms and scholars like Professor Seligman harangued long into the night, the political impetus for improved property tax administration just did not arise. The alternative to reform was to throw in the towel and cease even trying to tax those forms of property that presented the most difficulty.

Assessing according to market value, in place of standards based on the yield of the property, had already made it difficult to include occupations and professions in the property tax and helped pave the way to the strict cleavage we now have between "income" taxes and "property" taxes. Now a further claim was advanced that special exemptions for business were necessary to promote industry, employment, and "growth." These arguments suited neatly, and gave respectability to, the desires of the wealthy and the special interests that otherwise could lay little claim to relief.

As a result, there has been during our century a steady erosion of the property tax base, shifting the burden more and more to residential real estate. Most states have undone the work of the colonists and the mid-nineteenth-century tax reformers and have eliminated stocks and other "intangible" property partially or entirely from the tax base.

Though the actual number of states that in theory levy taxes on at least some kinds of intangibles increased from fifteen in 1962 to twenty-seven in 1969, only a few—Ohio, Florida, and Connecticut among them—levy taxes on intangibles with some success.

A parallel erosion has taken place regarding personal property. When assessed and taxed, property falling into this category can make up a substantial part of the property tax base—about 20 to 25 percent. Some twenty-six states exempt household personal property, not without good reason. But at least five states—Delaware, Hawaii, Idaho, New York, and Pennsylvania—exempt business personal property entirely, while at least nine more are in the process of phasing out part or all of their property taxes on business inventories and/or equipment and machinery. Most of the other states have at least partial exemptions for business property of some kinds.

The outright exemption of business property and the intangible property of the wealthy, moreover, is just a more obvious form of property tax erosion. Subtler forms, such as underassessment, back-door exemptions gained through leasing government property, and low-tax zones and industrial "tax havens," have evolved in tandem. In just ten years, from 1957 to 1967, the portion of property taxes falling initially on business dropped from 45.1 percent of the total to 39.5 percent.

The over-all result of this century-long process of tax-base erosion is that the burden of property taxes is falling increasingly on real estate and individual taxpayers. "Assessed value data from the 1957, 1962, and 1967 Censuses of Governments," says the Advisory Commission on Intergovernmental Relations (ACIR), "indicate a steady growth in the proportion that is attributed to residential assessments, and a steady drop in industrial and commercial assessments."

"The property tax," the ACIR concludes, "is increasingly a tax on housing."

the tax system today

Our present tax system is the product of a continuing move away from the ideals of progressive taxation. It is important to understand that there are three basic ways in which the ability-to-pay principle has been undermined.

First, more reliance on taxes which tend to be regressive and proportional rather than on those which tend to be progressive makes the whole tax system less fair. For example, a state may have a progressive income tax and a general sales tax which includes food and medicine and is highly regressive. The over-all tax burden may be proportional, rich and poor paying about the same percentage of their income in taxes. If the same state is facing financial difficulties and must raise added revenues, the two most apparent choices would be to raise the income tax rates or to add a penny to the sales tax. By relying more heavily on the

14 TAX POLITICS

income tax, the state's burden would fall more heavily on those most able to afford it—taxes would become more progressive. Raising the sales tax would increase the tax burden on low income groups, making the state's over-all tax burden more regressive and further eroding the ability-to-pay principle.

Unfortunately, most states have chosen this latter course. The 1974 New Jersey State Legislature, for example, rejected a proposed progressive income tax to reduce the burden of the property tax and to help equalize school financing. The people of New Jersey and their representatives apparently resisted the new income tax even though the vast majority of taxpayers (low and moderate income people) would have had a lighter over-all tax burden.

In similar fashion, the federal government has been placing greater and greater reliance on the highly regressive payroll tax to fund social security benefits instead of financing these through the income tax.

The second major source of erosion of the ability-to-pay principle is the eating away of the tax base itself through exemptions and deductions. A state, for example, might have adopted long ago a comprehensive property tax on a person's total wealth—real, personal, and intangible property. This same state later might have exempted personal and intangible property such as stocks and bonds. As a result, the tax originally designed to tax total wealth would now fall more lightly on wealthy individuals and be less progressive.

The erosion of the tax base, and therefore of progressivity, in the federal income tax structure is striking. As set forth at the beginning of the Internal Revenue Code, the legal tax rates on individuals range from 14 percent on the first $500 of income, up to 70 percent on income over $100,000. These rates originally were designed to apply to "all income from whatever source derived." But the Congress, in the following hundreds of pages has exempted an ever-growing number of items from the definition of taxable income. They have excluded one-half of all capital gains income (gains from selling property), 22 percent of income from oil wells, all the income from interest on state and local bonds, and certain pension and retirement benefits. They have allowed deductions for mortgage interest and property tax payments, accelerated depreciation, oil drilling, cattle breeding, and child care. And finally, they have granted special tax rates for income splitting and heads of households. All of these erode the income tax base and do so much more for those with high incomes than for those less well-off. As a result, the federal income tax is much less progressive than the statutory rates seem to indicate (Figure 2).

Careless administration is the third and probably least noted source of tax injustice. Local governments lose billions of property tax dollars each year through faulty assessing and collection practices. State governments miss perhaps one-half of the taxes

★ FIGURE 2. HOW EROSIONS IN THE TAX BASE UNDERMINE THE ABILITY-TO-PAY PRINCIPLE

Income class* (thousands of dollars)	effective rate (%)
0-3	0.8
3-5	4.6
5-10	8.6
10-15	10.9
15-20	12.8
20-25	14.5
25-50	17.3
50-100	23.8
100-500	24.6
500-1,000	27.2
1,000 and over	29.8
All classes†	13.1

SOURCE: Edward R. Fried, Alice M. Rivlin, Charles L. Schultze, Nancy H. Teeters, *Setting National Priorities: The 1974 Budget* (Washington D.C.: The Brookings Institution, 1973).

*Income is equal to adjusted gross income as defined in the Internal Revenue Code, modified to include the full amount of capital gains plus items receiving preferential treatment.

†Includes negative income class not shown separately.

corporations are supposed to pay, because audits are so weak. Even the federal government fails to collect significant revenues, especially from businesses and recipients of stock dividends. It is the largest taxpayers with the most complicated tax situations who benefit from this weak administration. The typical wage earner's taxes are withheld from the weekly paycheck, and that's the end of it.

One form of erosion can encourage another. If, for instance, exemptions or loopholes in the estate tax system substantially erode the tax base and thereby cut down revenues, the government may make up the lost revenues by increasing the excise (sales) tax on gasoline.

Taxes and Taxpayers 15

★ **FIGURE 2. HOW EROSIONS IN THE TAX BASE UNDERMINE THE ABILITY-TO-PAY PRINCIPLE** * (Continued) ★

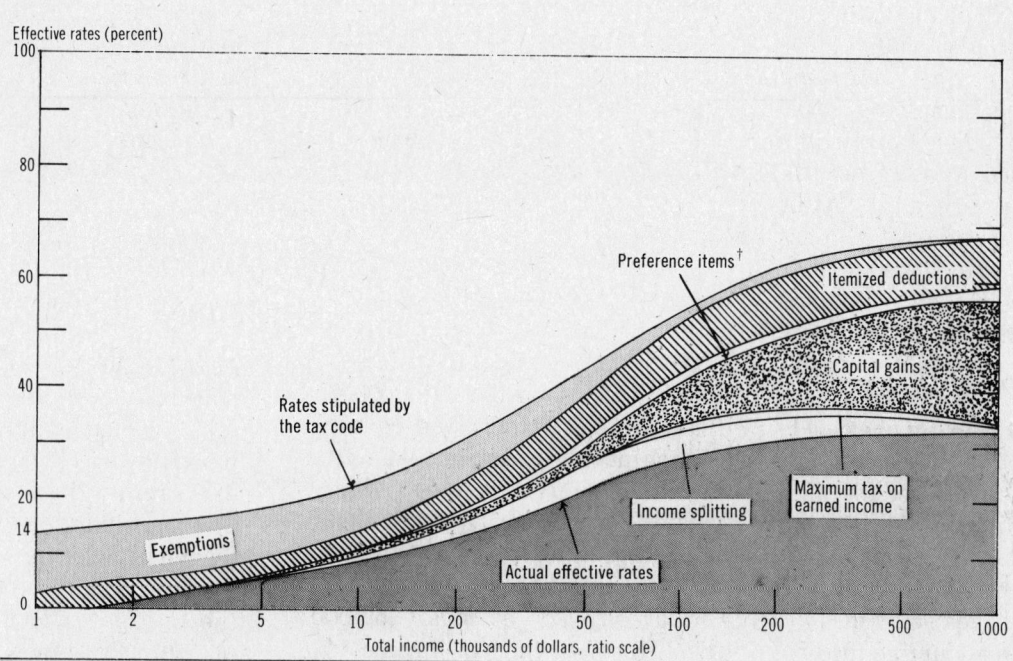

*Rates, exemptions, and other provisions of the Tax Reform Act of 1969 scheduled to apply to calendar year 1973 incomes.
†Includes accelerated depreciation, depletion, and stock options.

SOURCE: Joseph Pechman, Federal Tax Policy (Washington, D.C.: The Brookings Institution, 1971).

Another example is the corporate income tax. This tax has been so decimated by special tax breaks or subsidies since World War II that its contribution to the federal revenues dropped from 34 percent in 1944 to a paltry 14 percent in 1974. This loss of revenues had to be made up somewhere, and a quick look at federal tax receipts shows where. During the same thirty years the regressive payroll tax was rising from 3.9 percent of federal revenues in 1944 to nearly 30 percent in 1974. As the corporate tax base continues to erode, payroll taxes will continue to climb.

federal taxes today

The federal tax burden is by far the largest for most taxpayers. About two-thirds of all taxes are collected by the federal government, amounting to some $300 billion in fiscal 1976. These revenues are collected through a variety of taxes, on individual incomes, corporate incomes, payrolls (for social security and unemployment), estates and gifts, excise or sales taxes on liquor, tobacco, gasoline, and other items, and duties on imports. (Figure 3).

individual income taxes

The individual income tax is the most important source of federal tax revenues, contributing about 45 percent of total receipts. Reliance on the income tax has increased rapidly since the beginning of World War II. In 1939, the tax yielded about $1 billion, but by 1974 it was bringing in $118 billion. Lawmakers leaned on the income tax to this extent because of its supposed fairness—the close relationship between people's incomes and their taxpaying ability. Unfortunately, as the reliance on the income tax in-

16 TAX POLITICS

creased, its progressive nature was undermined.

The late Louis Eisenstein, a prosperous yet candid corporate tax lawyer, developed a wry perspective on our tax system. "Our taxes represent a continuing struggle among competing interests for the privilege of paying the least," he said. And, of course, some taxpayers are much better equipped than others to pass their burdens onto someone else.

Economists Joseph Pechman and Benjamin Okner calculate that if all of the special tax breaks were eliminated, we could cut the income tax rates by an average of 43 percent. Wealthy individuals who now effectively reduce their tax bills by more than 43 percent would then actually pay more, while the majority would pay less.

Though averages show how tax preferences have cut into the progressivity of the income tax, they do not show the great reduction in the tax burden that some individuals enjoy. In 1972, income tax breaks allowed an estimated 37,000 American families with incomes over $20,000 to get away without paying any federal income taxes. Moreover, 402 of those non-taxpayers actually made over $100,000 a year. Among them was multimillionaire Stewart Mott, heir to a large General Motors fortune who told CBS-TV: "I paid about zero tax to the federal government" in 1972 on income of roughly $1 million.

Besides those who pay no taxes, many wealthy taxpayers manage to pay very little. Ed Riley, who paid only $300 federal income taxes on the $293,000 he made in 1971, tours the country telling people—for a fee—how to use tax preferences to do it themselves. That year, with or without Ed Riley's advice, almost 100,000 Americans reduced their taxes by an average of at least $62,000 each through federal income tax preferences. Their federal income taxes were an average of only $1,700 (about 2.5 percent) each.

the corporate income tax

In most years prior to World War II, the corporate income tax was the major source of federal revenues. In 1944, corporate income tax revenues made up 34 percent of the federal receipts; since then they have steadily declined until they now account for only 14 percent of federal revenues, far behind individual income and payroll taxes. However, they are still an important source of revenues, amounting to $39 billion dollars in 1974.

Should income taxes apply to corporations at all, or should they bypass corporations and focus on the shareholder? Business interests are not the only ones raising this question. Earnest tax reformers argue that in some ways the corporate income tax opens the floodgates to tax avoidance, providing the foundation for numerous corporate tax subsidies.

Supporters of the corporate income tax say that if corporations were not taxed, wealthy shareholders could avoid taxes by keeping the business from distributing the profits as dividends. Instead, the profits would stay in the corporation, pushing up the value of its stock. The shareholders would get their piece of these profits when they sold the stock, enjoying in the process the special capital gains rates that are one-half the ordinary rates.

Opponents reply that such avoidance could easily be curbed by limiting the amounts corporations could accumulate, or by attributing retained earnings to the shareholder. They also observe

---

★ **FIGURE 3. BUDGET RECEIPTS BY SOURCE** (In Billions of Dollars) ★

This figure shows the various sources of federal tax revenues (in billions of dollars) and their contribution to over-all federal budget receipts (in percentages).

	1974		1975		1976 (estimated)	
Individual income taxes	119.0	(45%)	122.4	(44%)	130.8	(44%)
Corporation income taxes	38.6	(15%)	40.6	(14%)	40.1	(13%)
Social insurance taxes and contributions	76.8	(29%)	86.4	(31%)	92.6	(31%)
Excise taxes	16.8	(6%)	16.6	(6%)	16.9	(6%)
Other receipts	13.7	(5%)	14.0	(5%)	17.2	(6%)
	264.9	(100)	281.0	(100)	297.5	(100)

SOURCE. *Report of the House Budget Committee, FY 1976 Budget.*

that many advantages would ensue from dumping the corporate tax and taxing the shareholders directly on corporate profits. This would wipe out at a stroke the plethora of loopholes that not only permit the corporations (and thus their shareholders) to escape taxes but also distort economic activity as the corporations plot intricate strategies to qualify for the loopholes.

Is the corporate tax progressive? It can be argued that any tax on corporations can be progressive to the extent that the tax is borne by the corporation, since the holders of corporate stock are in upper income brackets. In competitive industries, the tax is more often absorbed by the company than passed on to customers in the form of higher prices. In less competitive industries, taxes can more readily be passed on to customers through higher prices. Reducing taxes in the latter instance would only mean that all taxpayers would incur a greater tax burden in order to subsidize the purchasers of the products of those industries. Because of the different assumptions as to who bears the burden of the corporate tax, there is no clear answer as to how progressive the present tax is.

Some economists argue that the tax is borne by the corporation and therefore by its shareholders. Others argue that the tax is passed forward to the consumers in the form of higher prices. Still others believe the tax is passed back to the workers in the form of lower wages. A large number hold that the tax is borne by all three groups, but primarily by the shareholders. Economist Joseph Pechman has concluded under this view that federal and state corporate income taxes are, in fact, more progressive than federal and state income taxes on individuals.

Given this high degree of progressivity, it is regrettable that the corporate income tax is bearing a diminishing share of the federal tax burden.

The idea of eliminating the corporate income tax and taxing shareholders directly for corporate profits is referred to as "integration" of the corporate and the individual income tax. This concept will be discussed in coming years as part of the tax-reform debate. As with many areas of taxation, integration can be good or bad depending on how it is accomplished. Unfortunately, most proposals that have been advanced tend simply to cut taxes for stockholders. They go only part way in integrating the two systems.

Ideally, corporate tax integration could be a progressive step that would tax stockholders at their high tax brackets while eliminating current corporate subsidies such as capital gains tax rates and accelerated depreciation. However, one version of integration proposed by Treasury Secretary Simon in 1975 is really just a reduction in the taxes stockholders pay on dividends. It does not end capital gains treatment or the other subsidies. Since 50 percent of corporation stock-

★ **FIGURE 4. EFFECTIVE RATES OF FEDERAL AND STATE-LOCAL INDIVIDUAL AND CORPORATION INCOME TAXES, 1966*** (In Percentages) ★

Adjusted Family Income Class (thousands)	Individual Income Taxes	Corporation Income Taxes	Total
$0-5	2.7	2.3	5.0
5-10	6.2	1.6	7.8
10-15	8.2	1.5	9.7
15-20	9.4	2.2	11.6
20-25	10.0	3.4	13.4
25-50	11.5	5.7	17.2
50-100	16.7	9.8	26.5
100-500	16.4	19.4	35.8
500-1,000	14.7	27.0	41.7
1,000 and over	12.7	29.4	42.1
Total	9.0	4.0	13.0

SOURCE: Joseph Pechman, "Distribution of Federal and State Income Taxes by Income Class," *Journal of Finance*, Vol. 27, No. 2 (May 1972). Footnotes omitted.
*This reflects the burden of the corporate income tax on shareholders and others by family income class.

18 TAX POLITICS

holders are in the richest 1 percent of the country's population, lowering their taxes would be a highly regressive step that would give even more federal tax money to the rich. Even though integration is capable of making things better, the Simon version would only make them worse.

Profits are paid out to stockholders in two ways. About 40 percent of profits is usually paid out directly in the form of dividends. Dividends are included in a stockholder's regular income and are taxed at whatever tax rate he or she is ordinarily subject to.

The other 60 percent of a corporation's after-tax profits is paid to stockholders in an indirect way. The corporation holds these profits for expansion and investment. This makes the company richer, and the richer the company, the more valuable its stock becomes; therefore stockholders can readily regain these profits by selling their stock. The income they get in this way is treated as a capital gain and is taxed at only half the rate of dividends or wages.

Under full integration, all profits would be taxed at the stockholder level. The 60 percent of profits that is currently kept to generate capital gains would be taxed at progressive rates rather than at the special capital gains rates. Under Simon's partial integration plan, the capital gains loophole is kept, the only change being that one tax rather than two is imposed on dividends.

Of course, progressive full integration would require the elimination of capital gains rates and other preferences that reduce the actual tax rates shareholders currently pay. Without that, tax reformers should not support the idea of tax integration. It could simply lower taxes further on corporation stockholders at a time when the tax burden of corporations and their owners has already been reduced to unacceptable levels.

While tax preferences lower corporate tax rates, they do not provide uniform relief. Some corporations may pay a 40 percent tax on their profits while others pay 15 percent, 5 percent, or nothing. In 1974, for instance, G.M. paid taxes at a rate of 39 percent, while Westinghouse paid at a rate of only 16 percent. Typically, the tax laws favor one industry over another, producing wide variations in industry by industry effective tax rates. (Figure 6)

A study by Representative Charles Vanik (D-Ohio) of 143 of the nation's largest corporations showed an effective 1973 tax rate of only 27.1 percent, down from 29.6 percent in 1971. (The statutory corporate tax rate is 48 percent.) Vanik found ten corporations with combined profits of $976 million paying no federal income tax at all. These included companies such as Con Ed of New

★ **FIGURE 5. FACTORS REDUCING THE EFFECTIVE TAX RATE OF CORPORATIONS, 1965 AND 1972 (In Percentages)** ★

	1965		1972	
Statutory rate		48.0		48.0
Less surtax exemption	2.5		2.2	
investment credit	2.4		3.0	
excess depreciation on machinery and equipment				
ADR class life system			1.4	
Reduction due to general tax expenditures	4.9		6.6	
General effective rate		43.1		41.4
Less exclusion of state and local bond interest	.9		1.8	
excess percentage depletion	2.2		1.8	
capital gains rate	.8		.6	
excess exploration and development costs	.4		.4	
excess bad dept reserves	.6		.4	
excess depreciation on buildings	.5		.4	
Western Hemisphere Trade Corporation rate	.2		.2	
DISC			.1	
Reduction due to specialized tax expenditures	5.6		5.7	
Overall effective rate, including specially benefited industries		37.5		35.7

SOURCE: Stanley S. Surrey, *Pathways to Tax Reform* (Cambridge, Mass.: Harvard University Press, 1973).

York, Chemical New York Corporation, and Bankers Trust. In fact, seven companies actually received credits to reduce past or future tax bills. Another twenty corporations with 1973 profits of $5.3 billion paid between 1 percent and 10 percent in taxes. McDonnell-Douglas, for instance, the giant aircraft corporation, paid only 3.2 percent on $200 million. (The company paid no federal income tax in 1971 and 1972 on yearly incomes over $100 million.) The list goes on: Chrysler Corporation, 7.5 percent; National Cash Register, 9 percent; Uniroyal, 6.5 percent, etc. ITT, one of the nation's largest corporations, paid only 10.1 percent on $470 million profit; in 1972 ITT had paid only 1 percent on profits of $376 million.

The nation's oil companies have been unusually adept at corporate tax avoidance even while they pull in record profits. For the nineteen largest oil companies, those profits surpassed an incredible $18.5 billion in 1973. Yet according to *U.S. Oil Week*, their 1973 U.S. income tax bill averaged only 6.5 percent: Exxon paid 5.4 percent, Texaco only 1.6 percent, Mobil 2.2 percent, Gulf 1.1 percent, and Standard of California 4.1 percent.

Commercial banks also get high marks as students of applied tax avoidance. Through the use of a large array of tax breaks, commercial banks have been able to lower their effective tax rate, according to the Federal Deposit Insurance Corporation, from 38.3 percent in 1961 to less than 15 percent in 1973. Chase Manhattan, the nation's third largest bank, paid 2.5 percent in federal income taxes. First National City kicked in 14.1 percent of its $300 million profits to the U.S. Treasury, while Western Bancorp, Chemical New York, Bankers Trust, and Continental Illinois Bank paid no U.S. taxes at all on combined incomes of $330 million.

These corporations were not the great exception. Among all 143 companies, profits rose in 1973 nearly $7 billion, or 25.8 percent, while tax payments rose only $740 million, or 10 percent.

In presenting his report to Congress, Vanik said, "In 1974 during economic hard times, corporations are crying for tax relief. This study is a reminder that many giant corporations already pay little or nothing in federal income taxes and that across-the-board industry tax breaks will only add to the list of profitable corporate tax freeloaders."

social security payroll tax

The fastest growing and most regressive of federal taxes is the payroll tax. It is second only to the individual income tax as a revenue source, bringing in nearly $77 billion, or 29 percent of the entire federal budget in 1974. This share is up from only 4

★ **FIGURE 6. EFFECTIVE CORPORATE TAX RATES BY INDUSTRY ON WORLDWIDE INCOME** ★

The worldwide rate on worldwide income usually shows the real income tax burden for most industries. Their U.S. rate appears lower because foreign income taxes are credited against U.S. taxes. For the extractive industries, the U.S. rate represents their real income tax burden since their payments to foreign governments, though credited as income taxes, are actually royalty payments.

Industry	# of Co.'s	Worldwide Rate on Worldwide Income	Share to Foreign Government [# of Co.'s]	U.S. Rate on Worldwide Income
Beverages	6	39.9	(16.7) [3]	31.5
Chemical	12	36.2	(11.8) [12]	24.4
Commercial banks	12	16.1	(9.9) [12]	8.4
Conglomerates	10	29.3	(5.4) [9]	24.5
Drug companies	12	36.7	(14.5) [12]	22.4
Electronics	11	41.2	(9.1) [9]	33.7
Food processors	10	41.5	(14.6) [9]	28.3
Metals and Mining	10	25.5	(8.2) [10]	17.7
Oil	10	37.0	(25.4) [10]	11.5
Paper	8	34.5	(11.2) [5]	27.5
Retailers	11	33.5	(14.9) [3]	29.4
Steel	13	39.9	(11.7) [1]	34.2
Timber	10	40.9	(4.9) [5]	34.5
Trucks and Equipment	10	39.1	(10.4) [7]	31.7

SOURCE: Compiled by Tax Analysts and Advocates from SEC filings.

20 TAX POLITICS

percent in 1944, 10 percent in 1954, and 20 percent in 1964, and it will rise even higher as scheduled increases in the tax take effect in future years.

Payroll taxes for social security were originally designed for a system in which workers would set aside funds for their retirement, receiving future benefits based on their past earnings. Retired people today, however, receive social security benefits far greater than were their "contributions" to the system. Benefits include, in addition, social security payments, retirement income credits, supplemental security; Medicare and Medicaid are included as well. Since social security is no longer an insurance-type system at all, but actually just another federal expenditure, payroll taxes should be viewed as simply another source of federal revenues contributing to the support of a number of federal programs. Relying on it to the extent that we have, under the guise of an "insurance system," has greatly eroded the ability-to-pay principle.

The present social security payroll tax is a flat 5.85 percent on the first $14,100 a worker earns, matched by another 5.85 percent from the employer. Although in theory only half the tax is deducted from the worker's paycheck and the other half is paid directly by the employer, economists generally agree that the whole 11.7 percent tax, in fact, comes out of wages or is reflected in lower fringe benefits. If there were no payroll tax, wages would rise by approximately the amount now paid by the employer.

This payroll tax appears to be a proportional or flat-rate tax. Why, then, is the payroll tax regressive? The reason is that while the payroll tax shows a striking lack of particular loopholes—all wages are taxed—it does have one very large loophole. All income above $14,100 is completely exempt from the tax. That, combined with the flat rate, makes the payroll tax very regressive—low income families and individuals pay a much higher proportion of their income in payroll taxes than do higher income families (figure 7).

The present 5.85 percent rates will continue to rise automatically to 7.2 percent by the year 2000. The ever increasing yearly cost of social security benefits for retired persons will be paid more and more by present workers. Thus, the growing financial burden of the social security tax falls on the taxpayer, but not on all taxpayers. Instead, the wage earner alone will make up for the erosion in the social security trust fund every year at a painfully regressive rate. On the other hand, if the increased costs of social security and related benefits were paid out of general revenues raised through the corporate and individual income taxes, the cost of supporting retirees would be shared by all taxpayers and through progressive taxes.

estate and gift taxes

Estate and gift taxes have a great deal of merit on social, moral, and economic grounds. Early supporters of federal death taxation came from all income classes. Theodore Roosevelt and Andrew Carnegie, for example, saw death and gift taxes as properly limiting the transfer of excessive accumulations of wealth. Carnegie wrote that "the parent who leaves his son enormous wealth generally deadens the talents and energies of the son, and tempts him to lead a less useful and less worthy life than he otherwise would." Others have advocated the estate tax as a levy on those who escape their share of income tax during their lifetimes.

Finally, both estate and gift taxes most closely embrace the ability-to-pay principle. Bequests and gifts, like income from work or investments, represent a source of ability-to-pay. Unlike these other income sources, however, the recipients of bequests and gifts did nothing to earn them; they are windfalls.

FIGURE 7.
THE SOCIAL SECURITY PAYROLL TAX

Income (Thousands of Dollars)	Effective Rate (Percent)
0–3	4.6
3–5	4.8
5–10	7.4
10–15	8.7
15–20	7.8
20–25	6.7
25–50	5.3
50–100	2.4
100–500	0.6
500–1,000	0.1
1,000 and over	*
All classes	6.3

SOURCE: Adapted from Edward R. Fried, Alice M. Rivlin, Charles L. Schultze, Nancy H. Teeters, *Setting National Priorities: The 1974 Budget* (Washington, D.C.: The Brookings Institution, 1973).

Despite the compelling fairness of these taxes, they remain our most neglected source of federal revenues. Today's estate tax, enacted in 1916, and gift tax, enacted in 1932, have yielded only small amounts. By 1939, they accounted for only 7 percent of federal revenues, and even this small amount fell to 4.5 percent by 1941 and to 2 percent or less in the post-World War II period. In 1974, federal estate and gift taxes brought in about $5 billion, just under 2 percent of federal tax revenues.

The estate tax is imposed on property or money left at death. A rate schedule sets taxes that range from 3 percent on small estates to 77 percent on estates over $10 million. There are several exemptions: a $60,000 exemption for the estate itself, one-half the estate if left to a surviving spouse, and a 100 percent deduction for anything left to charity. The gift tax rates are three-fourths of those for estate taxes, reaching a top rate of 57.75 percent on gifts over $10,000 a year. The gift tax also has a number of exemptions and deductions including a lifetime $30,000 exemption, yearly $3,000 exemptions for each gift recipient, and deductions for charitable contributions and gifts to spouses.

All these exemptions and deductions account for a tremendous erosion in these otherwise progressive taxes. One main defect in the present estate and gift tax is that it allows wealthy individuals to give away part of their estate before they die and avoid a healthy portion of the tax. Not only do such maneuvers take advantage of the lower gift tax rates, the taxpayer gets to use the lower end of the rate schedule twice. It is as though a runner set a world's record for the mile by running a half-mile, resting up for a few days, and then running a half-mile again.

Two months before his death, industrial magnate Irénée duPont made a "gift" of about one-fifth of his $176 million estate, avoiding about $16 million in estate taxes in the process.

As with other taxes, such cases are not the exception. In 1970, forty-seven millionaire estates paid no estate tax whatsoever. In fact, people died leaving more than $50 billion that year, yet the federal estate tax collected amounted to a meager $3 billion, or 6 percent from 100,000 taxable estates—less than 5 percent of the total estates in that year.

The Treasury Department's 1969 estate tax figures show that millionaire estates paid federal estate taxes amounting to 21 percent of the net estates and 25 percent when state, foreign, and other death taxes were included. The vast accumulations in the $10 million and above category paid even less, averaging only 17 percent despite a statutory rate of 77 percent applicable to those estates.

excise and other taxes

The excise tax (the federal government's name for a sales tax) is declining as a source of federal revenues. Many excises were eliminated with the Excise Tax Reduction Act of 1965 and others were scheduled to be phased out.

Before the 1965 Act excises brought in about 12.5 percent of our tax revenues. Today, the excise tax share is about 6.5 percent, $17 billion in 1974. The 10 percent tax on automobile sales is gone and the 10 percent telephone tax is down to 6 percent, scheduled to end in 1982. The remaining federal excise taxes include: highway user taxes on gasoline; alcohol and tobacco taxes; a tax on truck parts and accessories; taxes on fishing equipment and firearms; aircraft user taxes, and regulatory taxes on phosphorus matches and gambling.

A tax whose burden falls primarily on consumers can be progressive or regressive, depending on what is taxed. For example, a tax on beer and cigarettes is highly regressive, while excise taxes on furs and jewelry would be progressive. On balance, the postwar excise tax system has been regressive (figure 8).

★ **FIGURE 8. EFFECTIVE RATES OF FEDERAL EXCISE TAXES, 1954** ★

Income Class (Dollars)	Federal Excise Taxes (Percentages)
0– 1,000 1,000– 2,000	5.0
2,000– 3,000	4.5
3,000– 4,000	4.1
4,000– 5,000	3.9
5,000– 6,000 6,000– 7,500	3.6
7,500–10,000	3.3
10,000–15,000 15,000 and over	1.9
All classes	3.4

SOURCE: Adapted from Richard A. Musgrove, "The Incidence of the Tax Structure and Its Effects on Consumption," Joint Committee on the Economic Report, 84th Cong., 1st Sess. (1955). Footnotes omitted.

22 TAX POLITICS

Given this regressivity, moves to reduce the reliance on excise taxes should be met with general approval by advocates of the ability-to-pay principle. While some regressive taxes have been eliminated, those on alcohol, tobacco, and gasoline remain.

Customs duties are another source of federal revenues, accounting for a little more than 1 percent. These duties are levied on imported items primarily to protect domestic industries and not to produce federal revenues. For this reason, this book will not discuss import duties further.

★ ★ ★ ★ ★ ★

Our quick look at the federal tax structure shows several major trends. First, the fast rise in revenues from the regressive payroll tax closely matches the decrease in revenues collected from the corporate income tax. In 1954, the payroll tax (which is borne fully by the wage earner) supplied 10 percent of the revenue receipts, while corporations kicked in 30 percent. By 1974, these figures were almost reversed with the payroll tax bringing 29 percent of Uncle Sam's revenues, while corporations provided only 14 percent. Figure 9 illustrates this trend.

When we look at the individual tax burden by adding income and payroll tax and compare it to the corporate tax burden we get figure 10.

While supplying an increasing share of total federal revenues, the tax burden on individuals has itself become more regressive. Those less able to pay have been hit the hardest to make up for taxes the corporations and the wealthy are not paying. It is true that income taxes were cut in 1969 and 1971, so that in 1974 revenues were reduced by approximately $16 billion. But payroll taxes were raised at the same time by about $19 billion. Taking the combination of income and payroll taxes, the trend toward tax reductions for higher income families but higher taxes on middle and lower income families can be seen in figure 11. It compares four-person families with one wage earner making $5,000, $10,000, and $25,000 in the years 1963, 1968, and 1973.

The individual income tax, itself, has become less progressive as a result of the many tax preferences that cast their greatest benefits on those with the greatest wealth. These trends, as well as a general failure to use the estate tax, have brought on the erosion of progressivity in the over-all federal tax system.

★ **FIGURE 9. TAX REVENUES BY SOURCE** ★

Fiscal Year	Total %	Individual Income	Corp Income	Social Security*	Excise	Other†
1944	100	44.6	33.6	3.9	9.7	8.2
1949	100	43.8	27.0	5.8	17.7	5.7
1954	100	42.4	30.3	10.3	14.3	2.7
1959	100	46.4	21.8	14.8	13.3	3.7
1964	100	43.2	20.9	19.5	12.2	4.2
1969	100	46.5	19.5	21.3	8.1	4.6
1974	100	44.8	14.6	29.1	6.3	5.2

* Includes payroll taxes, federal employee contributions for retirement, and contributions for supplementary medical insurance.
† Includes estate and gift taxes, customs duties and deposits of earnings by Federal Reserve banks.

★ **FIGURE 10. INDIVIDUAL TAX BURDEN VS. CORPORATE TAX BURDEN AS PERCENTAGE OF TOTAL RECEIPTS, 1944–1974** ★

Fiscal Year	Total	Individual Income	Corp Income	All Other*
1944	100	48.5	33.6	17.9
1949	100	49.6	27.0	23.4
1954	100	52.7	30.3	17.0
1959	100	61.2	21.8	17.0
1964	100	62.7	20.9	16.4
1969	100	67.8	19.5	12.7
1974	100	73.9	14.6	11.5

* Includes excise, estate and gift and miscellaneous taxes.

state and local taxes today

Taxes on property raise the largest share of state and local revenues—about one-quarter—followed closely by sales taxes, and then by federal aid, miscellaneous and "other," income taxes on individuals, and only last by income taxes on corporations (figure 12).

These figures are an average for all states and do not show the enormous variations from state to state and from locality to locality within states. Alabama, for example, gets over one-fourth of its state and local budget from the U.S. Treasury. Wisconsin, by contrast, gets less than half of Alabama's share of federal monies. Meanwhile, Wisconsin gets about 18 percent of its revenues from income taxes, to Alabama's 6 percent, while Alabama gets 30 percent of its revenues from consumer taxes, to Wisconsin's 19 percent. In New Hampshire—a state without an income or general sales tax—property taxes in 1971 still provided 59.1 percent of total state and local taxes, down barely 1 percent from 1942. In Montana, property taxes in 1971 were 55.6 percent of state and local taxes, while in New Jersey they were 54.7 percent. On the other hand, Louisiana leaned on local property taxes for only 19 percent of its state and local revenues, Delaware, 17.6 percent, and Alabama only 14.8 percent, down more than 50 percent from 1942.

There are three main reasons for these differences. One is the relative role of local governments in the state's revenue system. A second is the greater or lesser use of other taxes: Delaware, for example, relies heavily on its state income tax, and Louisiana receives substantial revenues from oil. A third reason is the differing extent of public activity and hence spending. Local governments do less in the rural South than they do in the urbanized Northeast.

Over the last thirty years the trend in state and local taxation has been away from taxes on businesses and toward taxes on individuals and consumers. The property tax share of revenues has fallen by 30 percent, and its burden on business is lighter than in the past. Today's general sales taxes comprise a share twice as large as three decades ago. Between 1948 and 1972, property taxes increased by an average of 8.4 percent per year, while local individual income taxes increased by 17.9 percent per year, state individual income taxes increased by 14.7 percent per year, and sales taxes jumped by 10.4 percent and 10.9 percent per year on the local and state levels, respectively. States and localities get over 200 percent more of their

---

FIGURE 11. THE SHIFTING BURDEN OF INCOME AND PAYROLL TAXES BY INCOME CLASSES

Earnings and Tax Items	1963	1968*	1973
$5,000 earnings			
Income tax	$420	$308	98
Payroll tax†	348	440	585
Total tax	768	748	683
Effective income tax rate	8.4	6.2	2.0
Effective payroll tax rate†	7.0	8.8	11.7
Total effective tax rate	15.4	15.0	13.7
$10,000 earnings			
Income tax	$1,372	$1,198	$905
Payroll tax†	348	686	1,170
Total tax	1,720	1,884	2,075
Effective income tax rate	13.7	12.0	9.0
Effective payroll tax rate†	3.5	6.9	11.7
Total effective tax rate	17.2	18.8	20.8
$25,000 earnings			
Income tax	$4,889	$4,362	$3,890
Payroll tax†	348	686	1,264
Total tax	5,237	5,048	5,154
Effective income tax rate	19.6	17.4	15.6
Effective payroll tax rate†	1.4	2.7	5.0
Total effective tax rate	20.9	20.2	20.6

SOURCE: Edward R. Fried, Alice M. Rivlin, Charles L. Schultze, Nancy H. Teeters, *Setting National Priorities: The 1974 Budget* (Washington, D.C.: The Brookings Institution, 1973).
*Includes income tax surcharge.
†Includes both employer and employee taxes.

24 TAX POLITICS

★ FIGURE 12. STATE AND LOCAL TOTAL GENERAL REVENUE, BY STATE, 1971 (Total Amount and Percentage Distribution by Major Source) ★

State	Total General Revenue (In millions)	Federal Aid	Tax Revenue Total	Property	Individual Income	Corporation Income	General Sales	Selective Sales	Other	Charges & Miscellaneous Gen. Revenue
UNITED STATES	$144,927.5	18.0	65.5	26.1	8.2	2.4	12.3	10.6	5.9	16.4
Alabama	1,943.3	27.6	49.4	7.3	4.9	1.7	14.9	15.5	5.2	23.0
Alaska	488.9	32.5	29.9	6.8	8.6	1.2	1.9	4.7	6.7	37.5
Arizona	1,318.2	17.7	64.9	25.0	5.6	2.1	18.2	10.2	3.7	17.4
Arkansas	947.9	25.8	55.2	14.1	4.7	2.8	12.7	14.8	6.2	19.0
California	18,535.1	19.3	65.8	32.3	6.9	2.9	12.2	7.6	3.9	14.9
Colorado	1,668.5	19.9	61.2	25.6	8.6	1.7	12.8	8.1	4.3	18.9
Connecticut	2,228.8	14.5	73.7	37.8	0.5	5.7	11.9	12.9	5.0	11.7
Delaware	439.6	13.4	63.3	11.1	19.1	2.8	—	10.4	20.0	23.2
Dist. of Columbia	873.7	41.3	49.7	15.4	12.7	2.3	8.9	7.5	3.0	9.0
Florida	4,069.5	14.1	64.8	21.9	—	—	17.6	16.9	8.4	21.0
Georgia	2,717.1	21.7	57.0	18.4	6.8	3.0	13.3	12.2	3.4	21.2
Hawaii	761.5	20.4	63.6	11.5	15.3	1.7	23.4	8.5	3.2	15.9
Idaho	475.0	21.2	61.5	21.6	11.9	2.7	9.6	9.3	6.5	17.3
Illinois	8,076.3	16.4	71.2	27.7	9.6	1.9	15.2	11.2	5.6	12.4
Indiana	3,140.8	13.2	67.5	34.2	7.0	0.3	12.9	9.6	3.5	19.3
Iowa	1,921.0	14.2	66.9	33.3	6.0	1.5	11.1	8.8	6.3	18.9
Kansas	1,463.1	17.1	64.3	32.4	5.6	1.7	10.8	9.5	4.2	18.6
Kentucky	1,917.2	27.6	54.1	12.0	9.9	2.1	15.1	11.1	3.9	18.2
Louisiana	2,401.2	20.4	58.2	11.0	3.4	2.1	15.4	11.3	14.9	21.4
Maine	619.7	21.7	66.5	30.1	3.9	1.4	14.9	11.3	5.1	11.7
Maryland	2,955.2	15.4	68.8	22.5	20.4	2.4	8.9	10.1	4.5	15.8
Massachusetts	4,340.3	16.8	72.8	38.0	13.1	4.7	4.4	9.0	3.6	10.3
Michigan	6,612.7	15.4	66.9	27.5	9.1	2.5	13.3	8.6	5.9	17.7
Minnesota	2,993.4	16.2	64.5	27.3	12.4	2.7	7.2	10.1	4.9	19.2
Mississippi	1,320.4	26.5	53.1	12.9	3.5	1.5	18.7	11.6	4.9	20.4
Missouri	2,660.8	19.4	64.4	26.2	8.4	1.0	12.7	10.2	5.8	16.2
Montana	526.3	28.1	56.9	31.6	8.1	1.8	—	9.6	5.8	15.0
Nebraska	1,027.6	15.4	63.5	32.5	5.3	0.9	9.3	10.1	5.5	21.0
Nevada	474.3	16.4	61.9	20.3	—	—	15.0	19.4	7.3	21.6
New Hampshire	429.7	17.8	66.5	39.4	—	—	—	16.0	11.2	15.6
New Jersey	5,067.3	15.0	71.8	39.3	0.4	2.2	10.3	13.3	6.3	13.2
New Mexico	791.1	27.7	50.9	11.4	4.5	1.3	15.3	10.0	8.4	21.3
New York	17,532.2	13.9	72.2	27.1	17.0	3.3	11.7	8.6	4.5	13.8
North Carolina	2,749.6	20.6	62.9	15.8	11.0	4.2	10.9	15.5	5.6	16.4
North Dakota	483.9	24.0	54.2	24.3	3.5	1.6	11.2	7.8	5.7	21.8
Ohio	6,006.3	14.4	65.3	30.9	4.8	—	11.5	11.8	6.3	20.3
Oklahoma	1,571.3	24.4	53.6	16.2	4.1	1.6	8.7	13.0	10.1	21.9
Oregon	1,573.9	24.6	57.1	27.9	14.4	1.6	—	6.9	6.3	18.3
Pennsylvania	7,542.6	17.2	70.0	20.6	7.6	5.7	13.4	11.9	10.7	12.8
Rhode Island	646.7	19.6	69.2	26.8	5.8	4.3	12.9	13.8	5.6	11.2
South Carolina	1,288.8	21.2	60.6	13.5	8.4	3.4	16.6	14.8	4.1	18.1
South Dakota	483.9	21.3	60.3	33.3	—	0.2	11.4	10.2	5.3	18.4
Tennessee	2,130.8	24.8	56.5	15.9	0.6	2.8	16.2	12.8	8.2	18.6
Texas	6,438.9	19.2	61.0	24.4	—	—	11.9	13.4	11.3	19.8
Utah	752.6	26.4	56.6	20.4	8.2	1.5	14.9	7.8	3.8	17.0
Vermont	366.5	25.5	61.9	23.1	11.7	1.6	5.3	14.2	5.9	12.5
Virginia	2,725.6	19.1	64.4	18.9	11.5	2.4	11.2	13.8	6.6	16.5
Washington	2,709.2	17.4	62.0	21.5	—	—	23.3	12.3	4.9	20.6
West Virginia	1,072.9	31.8	54.5	12.1	5.5	0.5	17.9	13.2	5.4	13.6
Wisconsin	3,319.6	11.9	72.1	31.2	15.3	2.7	10.2	8.4	4.3	15.9
Wyoming	326.6	26.3	50.3	23.8	—	—	10.5	8.5	7.6	23.4

SOURCE: Advisory Commission on Intergovernmental Relations.

revenue from income taxes on individuals, while the contribution of corporate income taxes has actually declined.

Looking at state taxes alone, not including localities, it is sales taxes that dominate. General sales taxes amounted to 30 percent of state tax collections in 1971, and when selective sales taxes on cigarettes, liquor, and the like are included, over one-half of state tax revenues comes from consumer taxes. At 20 percent, individual income taxes are a far second, while corporate income taxes provide merely 6 percent, and estate and gift taxes, 2.1 percent. In 1949 individual and corporate income taxes were making roughly equal contributions. Twenty-five years later, individuals are paying about three times the share of corporations (figure 13).

Looking at local governments, taxes on property have been declining in importance, but still provide the largest single source of local revenues—about 40 percent—and almost 85 percent of local tax revenues. Grants from the state and federal governments provide another large share, with sales, income, and other taxes bringing very small amounts, although in specific cities these other taxes can bulk large (figure 14).

property taxes

Taxes on property have been declining in the total state and local revenue picture, down from 53.2 percent in 1942 to 40 percent in 1971. They have been increasing less rapidly than other state and local taxes, moreover. Yet property taxes are still the mainstays of most local revenue systems, and they continue to bear much of the important burden of paying for schools. They provoke outrage among local taxpayers far in excess of their actual fiscal importance. Property taxes have declined in fairness more than any other of our revenue sources, and the potential for reform is probably the greatest. Later chapters will treat these matters in more detail.

state and local income taxes

During the early 1800s, some states began to enact income taxes of various sorts and during the Civil War income taxes were common, especially in the South, where a lid had been kept on property taxes. Many observers, however, had written off the income tax as impossible to administer. Then in 1911 Wisconsin proved these doubters wrong. It

★ FIGURE 13 STATE TAX COLLECTIONS, BY SOURCE, SELECTED YEARS, 1902–1971 ★

Year	Total Excluding Employment Taxes	Individual Income Taxes	Corporation Income Taxes	Death and Gift Taxes	General Sales Taxes	Motor Fuel Taxes	Alcoholic Beverage Taxes	Tobacco Taxes	Amusement Taxes	Public Utility Taxes	Property Taxes	Motor Vehicle and Operators' Licenses	All Other
					Percentage Distribution								
1902	100.0	—	—	4.5	—	—	—	—	—	—	5.26	—	42.9
1913	100.0	—	—	8.6	—	—	.6	—	—	—	46.5	1.7	42.5
1922	100.0	4.5	6.1	7.0	—	1.4	—	—	—	—	36.7	16.1	28.3
1927	100.0	4.4	5.7	6.6	—	16.1	—	—	—	—	23.0	18.7	25.5
1932	100.0	3.9	4.2	7.8	.4	27.9	—	1.0	—	—	17.3	17.7	19.7
1942	100.0	6.4	6.9	2.8	16.2	24.1	6.6	3.3	.7	2.6	6.8	11.0	12.6
1952	100.0	9.3	8.5	2.1	22.6	19.0	4.5	4.5	1.6	2.3	3.7	9.4	12.5
1962	100.0	13.3	6.4	2.5	24.9	17.8	3.6	5.2	1.5	2.0	3.1	8.1	11.6
1967	100.0	15.4	7.0	2.5	27.9	15.2	3.3	5.1	1.4	1.9	2.7	7.2	10.5
1971	100.0	19.7	6.6	2.1	30.0	12.9	3.0	4.9	1.2	2.0	2.2	6.2	9.1

SOURCE: Advisory Commission on Intergovernmental Relations.

26 TAX POLITICS

enacted a progressive income tax with two novel features: the tax was administered by a central state agency instead of through local officials, and the tax was collected at the point of payment, i.e., from the paycheck. (Wisconsin's progressive rates ranged from a low of 1 percent to 6 percent for all income over $12,000.)

These breakthroughs opened the way to state income taxes as we know them. Other states were quick to follow suit. By 1919, nine states and Hawaii had income taxes, with five more joining them during the next decade. Then the depression put new demands on state governments while pinching their revenues from property and other taxes. By 1937, twenty-nine states plus Hawaii had turned to income taxes for a boost.

Tax scholar L.L. Ecker-Racz has pointed out that agricultural states were the first to embrace income taxes as a way to shift the tax burden from farmers to business and professional interests. Older industrial states—such as Connecticut, Illinois, New Jersey, Ohio, and Pennsylvania—resisted. To this date, neither Connecticut nor New Jersey has a broad-based individual income tax.

After 1937, it was twenty-five years before another state adopted an income tax, since prosperity, combined with consumer taxes, met most revenue needs. Then during the sixties, with revenue deficits once again on the rise, eleven more states entered the fold, leaving only ten without broad-based income taxes (figure 15).

In general the states have enacted corporate income taxes at the same time they imposed income taxes on individuals. A few, however, such as New Hampshire, Florida, and New Jersey, have corporate income taxes but no general tax on individuals. Paralleling what has happened to federal taxes, state corporate income taxes have been declining as a source of state revenues, while income taxes on individuals have greatly increased.

More and more state legislatures have been empowering local governments to levy their own income taxes. At this writing, close to 4,000 local units in ten states were employing such taxes. In 1972 over eight cities in Ohio, including the state capital of Columbus, derived 70 percent or more of their tax revenue from income taxes. Elsewhere, Louis-

★ FIGURE 14. PERCENTAGE DISTRIBUTION OF LOCAL GOVERNMENT GENERAL REVENUE, 1957 AND 1971 ★

	\multicolumn{12}{c}{Level of Government and Year —}
	Total local		Counties		Municipalities		Townships		Special Districts		School Districts	
Revenue Source	1971	1957	1971	1957	1971	1957	1971	1957	1971	1957	1971	1957
Federal and state grants	37.5	29.6	41.8	38.0	31.7	18.9	22.3	24.8	26.4	14.1	46.1	42.1
Property tax	39.9	48.7	37.4	46.5	32.8	46.3	62.8	63.6	19.7	29.1	45.7	50.1
Income tax	1.9	0.8	0.8	–	4.6	1.9	0.8	0.3	–	–	0.4	0.1
General sales tax	2.5	2.6	2.9	0.9	5.4	6.5	–	–	0.8	–	0.2	–
˙rent charges:	10.7	10.0	11.3	9.3	11.7	10.3	4.8	3.9	41.6	49.9	5.6	5.9
Education	2.7	2.6	1.1	0.8	0.7	0.8	1.3	1.4	–	–	5.6	5.9
Hospitals	2.8	1.8	5.8		2.3	1.8	0.7	0.4	15.2	8.3	–	–
Sewerage	1.1	0.9	0.3	0.2	2.6	1.9	1.1	0.8	3.2	2.1	–	–
Housing and urban renewal	0.7	1.1	–	–	0.8	1.0	–	0.1	8.6	18.6	–	–
Other	3.4	3.6	4.2	4.7	5.2	4.7	1.6	1.2	14.6	21.0	–	–
All other gen'l rev.	7.5	8.3	5.7	5.2	13.7	16.1	9.3	7.4	11.4	6.9	2.0	1.8
Total	100.0	100.0	100.0	100.0	100.0	100.0	100.0	100.0	100.0	100.0	100.0	100.0

Advisory Commission on Intergovernmental Relations. Footnotes omitted.

ville, Kentucky, was getting 55 percent of its taxes, Detroit 35 percent, Kansas City 37 percent, and Philadelphia 62 percent from income taxes.

Most of the state income taxes claim to be progressive, with higher rates applying to higher levels of income. In fact, the progressivity of these taxes tends to be modest in the extreme. Idaho, for example, taxes the first $1,000 at 2 percent, with rates gradually increasing to 7.5 percent of all income over $5,000. Thus the person making $5,000 and the one making $500,000 pay the same rate. A few states come closer to the progressivity ideal. In Delaware, the rates rise from 1.5 percent on the first $1,000 to 18 percent on all income over $100,000. Minnesota and New York are two states with fairly progressive rates.

A number of states have flat rate systems under which all taxpayers, rich and poor, pay the same rate. These states are Illinois, Indiana, Massachusetts, Michigan, and Pennsylvania. And a few states impose taxes on just certain forms of income. New Hampshire and Tennessee, for example, tax only dividends and interest, while Connecticut taxes only income from capital gains.

State corporate income taxes are even less progressive than state individual income taxes. Flat rates are common, as are special deductions and exclusions. A growing trend has been for the states to pattern their income tax rules (but not rates) on the federal income tax. This is said to bring convenience to taxpayers, and the federal government has even encouraged the trend by offering to collect the income taxes for any state whose tax laws match closely the federal tax. Though it sounds attractive, the practice obviously tends to shift decisions on what is taxed to the U.S. Congress and away from the state legislatures.

state and local sales taxes

"That which I greatly feared has come upon me" was Job's lament. State taxpayers might say "Amen!" Sales taxes were the British levies that the American colonists greatly feared. "There is scarce an article of life [in England] you can eat, drink, wear, or enjoy, that is not there loaded with a tax," wrote Thomas Paine. "(W)ere they to effect a conquest of America, it is then only that the distresses of America would begin . . . What they want is clear, solid revenue, and the modes they would take to procure it, would operate on all alike." Today, sales taxes have become the bulwarks of the state tax systems.

There are two basic kinds of sales taxes: *general* sales taxes, covering a broad range of items, and *selective* sales taxes, aimed at particular items such as gasoline, cigarettes, or beer.

1. general sales tax: General sales taxes have been amassing an ever larger share of state and local tax collections. In 1932 less than one-half of 1 percent of state tax collections came from this source; thirty years later one-quarter of their taxes did. By 1971 the figure was closer to one-third.

In 1932 Mississippi became the first state to enact a general sales tax, and its rise thereafter was meteoric. Over the next six years one-half of the states had enacted the taxes, and by 1944 they had become the most important single state revenue source. The lead has widened since. By 1971 forty-six states had broad-based general sales taxes and over half of the states received more than one-third of their tax revenues from this source.

In the 1930s and 40s the state legislatures began to give local governments the power to levy certain "permissive" taxes to supplement their property taxes, and sales taxes were among these. New York was the first city to enact a sales tax, in 1934; New Orleans followed in 1941, and by 1973 they were in use in half of the states. Large cities such as New Orleans and Los Angeles get a quarter or more of their revenue from this levy.

Most states that have a sales tax enact a *use* tax along with it. This levy taxes the use of goods purchased out-of-state that would otherwise escape the sales tax.

General sales taxes have prodigious loopholes. All states except Hawaii and Louisiana exempt wholesale transactions. By 1971 thirteen states had completely exempted business machinery from the tax. Transfers of stocks, bonds and real estate are widely exempt, as are common services, such as storage, dry cleaning, and repairs. Since the more money people have, the more they tend to spend on services, including these in the sales tax would give it a unique boost toward fairness. Normally exempt are the services of lawyers, stockbrokers, architects, real estate brokers, and advertising

28 TAX POLITICS

agencies. While such expenditures go completely tax-free, almost two-thirds of the sales tax states apply their tax to food, while a number of others include medicines as well.

Not surprisingly sales taxes tend to be highly regressive, since people of modest means must spend a much larger share of their income on taxed necessities than those better-off.

2. special sales taxes: In addition to general sales taxes, most states have special taxes on certain items—gasoline, alcohol, tobacco, amusements, and public utilities are examples. The states enacted gas taxes in the early twentieth century, along with motor vehicle registration taxes. Until 1942 gas taxes were the most important source of state tax revenues. Since then their role has declined steadily. The importance of alcoholic beverage taxes and amusement taxes has also declined, while taxes on public utilities and tobacco have borne a fairly constant share. Together these special sales taxes comprised about one-quarter of state tax collections in 1971. Meanwhile, general sales taxes and income taxes on individuals were picking up the slack.

It is not by accident that state lawmakers have been placing ever larger shares of the tax burden on consumers. Sales taxes yield bountiful revenues at what appear to most people to be low rates. The revenue is stable since people maintain a certain level of taxable expenditures even if their income dips. The tax is easy to administer; unknown to consumers, many states allow merchants who collect the tax to keep a certain percentage of their collections as compensation.

Most important, sales taxes do not hit the consumer with one lump sum. State lawmakers learned long ago that people resist taxes less when the real cost is hidden. In fact, the broad trend in state and local taxes has been toward these semihidden taxes. Income taxes on individuals, the other fast-growing state and local revenue source, are commonly withheld from the regular paycheck, so that their impact is similarly masked. And millions of home-buyers pay their property taxes in monthly installments to their bank, along with their mortgage payment, so that the tax seems to be just another part of the mortgage.

state taxes on estates, inheritances, and gifts

Of all things to tax, estates, inheritances, and gifts seem the most apt. They arise from accumulated wealth, which the rest of the tax system leaves largely untouched. Moreover, concentrations of wealth are growing at alarming rates, and taxes on them affect only potential taxpayers most able to pay.

Yet state governments act as if these revenue sources did not exist. In 1971 they raised only 2.1 percent of their tax revenue from them. Tax expert L.L. Ecker-Racz has estimated that the total tax rate applied to estates, inheritances, and gifts comes to about 5 percent a year, federal taxes included. This is less than the sales taxes many living people have to pay when purchasing necessities.

Some states began levying so-called death taxes over a century ago, but by 1891 only nine states imposed them—and at low rates. Then public outrage grew at the enormous wealth being amassed by the "Robber Barons." "I believe in a graduated income tax on big fortunes," wrote Theodore Roosevelt in 1910 in his book *The New Nationalism*, "and in another tax which is far more easily collected and far more effective—a graduated inheritance tax on big fortunes, properly safeguarded against evasion and increasing rapidly in amount with the size of the estate." With this outrage and state revenue needs as impetus, forty-two states were raising over 8 percent of their revenue from this source by 1916.

The movement was threatened, however, when Florida, Nevada, and a few other states set out to become retirement tax havens for the rich. In 1924 Florida enacted a constitutional amendment barring income and inheritance taxes, and Nevada followed suit a year later. Meanwhile, the federal government was tapping estate and gift taxes, which the states took as an intrusion on their revenue domain. The matter was settled, after a fashion, when Congress agreed to allow a credit on federal estate taxes for any state taxes paid. This protected the state death tax revenues. It also undercut somewhat the state efforts to become tax havens. Much of the death tax savings once available to people in such states would now just go to the federal government instead.

Now, over four decades later, the states are barely touching the potential death and gift tax rev-

Taxes and Taxpayers 29

enues. Only two states, Connecticut and New Hampshire, get as much as 5 percent of their revenues from death and gift taxes, and most get considerably less. The provisions in the states vary widely. Over half the states tax inheritances—the amounts going to each heir—while others tax estates—the total amount the deceased person leaves. Oregon and Rhode Island tax both, while one state, Nevada, still taxes neither. Sixteen states also enacted gift taxes to stop people

★ FIGURE 15. DATES OF ADOPTION OF MAJOR STATE TAXES ★

Individual Income*

Before 1911	1911-20	1921-30	1931-40	1941-60	Since 1961
Hawaii, 1901; total, 1.	Wisconsin, 1911; Mississippi, 1912; Oklahoma, 1915; Massachusetts, 1916; Virginia, 1916; Delaware, 1917; Missouri, 1917; New York, 1919; North Dakota, 1919; total, 9.	North Carolina, 1921; South Carolina, 1922; New Hampshire, 1923; Arkansas, 1929; Georgia, 1929; Oregon, 1930; total, 6.	Idaho, 1931; Tennessee, 1931; Utah, 1931; Vermont, 1931; Alabama, 1933; Arizona, 1933; Kansas, 1933; Minnesota, 1933; Montana, 1933; New Mexico, 1933; Iowa, 1934; Louisiana, 1934; California, 1935; Kentucky, 1936; Colorado, 1937; Maryland, 1937; total, 16.	Alaska, 1949; total, 1.	New Jersey, 1961; West Virginia, 1961; Indiana, 1963; Michigan, 1967; Nebraska, 1967; Connecticut, 1969; Illinois, 1969; Maine, 1969; Ohio, 1971; Pennsylvania, 1971; Rhode Island, 1971; total, 11. Broad-based tax, 40. Grand total, 44.

*States without an individual income tax: Florida; Nevada; South Dakota; Texas; Washington; Wyoming. States with limited tax: Conn. (capital gains); N.H. (interest + dividends, and commuter tax); N.J. (commuter tax); Tenn. (interest and dividends).

Corporation Income*

Before 1911	1911-20	1921-30	1931-40	1941-60	Since 1961
Hawaii, 1901; total, 1.	Wisconsin, 1911; Connecticut, 1915; Virginia, 1915; Missouri, 1917; Montana, 1917; New York, 1917; Massachusetts, 1919; North Dakota, 1919; total, 8.	Mississippi, 1921; North Carolina, 1921; South Carolina, 1922; Tennessee, 1923; Arkansas, 1929; California, 1929; Georgia, 1929; Oregon, 1929; total, 8.	Idaho, 1931; Oklahoma, 1931; Utah, 1931; Vermont, 1931; Alabama, 1933; Arizona, 1933; Kansas, 1933; Minnesota, 1933; New Mexico, 1933; Iowa, 1934; Louisiana, 1934; Pennsylvania, 1935; Kentucky, 1936; Colorado, 1937; Maryland, 1937; total, 15.	Rhode Island, 1947; Alaska, 1949; Delaware, 1957; New Jersey, 1958; total, 4.	Indiana, 1963; Michigan, 1967; Nevada, 1967; West Virginia, 1967; Illinois, 1969; Maine, 1969; New Hampshire, 1970; Florida, 1971; Ohio, 1971; total, 9. Grand total, 45.

*States without a corporation income tax: Nevada; South Dakota (exclusive of the tax applicable to financial institutions only); Texas; Washington; Wyoming

SOURCE: Advisory Commission on Intergovernmental Relations.

30 TAX POLITICS

from avoiding estate and inheritance levies by giving away their wealth in their last years.

other taxes

On charts of state and local finances there is usually a column titled "miscellaneous and other." In a few cases the revenues are substantial — 25 percent for Louisiana, for example, most of which derives from severance (production) taxes on the state's large oil output. Alaska and Texas are two other states with large oil revenues.

In most cases the sum is modest — around 6 percent or less of state and local revenues. States and localities seem to have taxed just about everything at one time or another — in Virginia there was once a window tax, in Maryland a tax on bachelors over twenty-five years old (100 percent to be added for "papists"), and in New York there was once a special tax on wigs. Today these miscellaneous revenues come largely from licenses, permits, and similar levies.

public enterprises

At last count, over 15 percent of total state and local revenues came from public enterprises. The percentage is even larger when federal grants are not included in total revenue. Yet this large revenue source is largely ignored in discussions of state and local finance.

There has not always been such silence. Earlier in the century the writings of people like Carl D. Thompson of the Public Ownership League laid out in detail the remarkable array of public enterprises in the country. Far from a matter of just electrical utilities and subway systems, the record includes such endeavors as printing plants in Boston and Pasadena, slaughtering houses in Nashville, Los Angeles, and Dubuque, municipal markets in Baltimore, New York, and Philadelphia, and a municipal milk pasteurization plant in Tarboro, North Carolina, to name just a very few. As mentioned earlier, the public ownership tradition goes all the way back to the colonies, when such cities as Philadelphia raised considerable revenues from them. In 1887, almost half the receipt items in the Baltimore city budget were from public enterprises, ranging from rents of market stalls and wharves, to dividends from stock in the Baltimore and Ohio Railroad.

Textbooks on public finance discuss public enterprises only in the most cautious theoretical

★ **FIGURE 16. REVENUES FROM PUBLIC ENTERPRISES AND OTHER NON-TAX SOURCES, 1971–1972** ★

	All governments	Federal Government	State and local governments Total	State	Local
National Defense and International Relations	835	835	—	—	—
Postal Services	7,601	7,601	—	—	—
School Lunch Sales	1,419	—	1,419	—	1,419
Institutions of Higher Education	4,861	—	4,861	4,435	426
Other (Education)	766	40	726	86	640
Hospitals	4,296	33	4,263	1,181	3,081
Sewerage	1,240	—	1,240	—	1,240
Sanitation other than Sewerage	398	—	398	—	398
Local Parks and Recreation	360	—	360	—	360
Natural Resources	2,941	2,586	355	256	99
Housing and Urban Renewal	1,217	527	690	18	672
Air Transportation	657	15	642	63	580
Water Transport and Terminals	522	198	324	90	234
Parking Facilities	200	—	200	—	200
Other (Charges and Miscellaneous General Revenues)	3,893	646	3,247	1,692	1,556
Special Assessments	712	—	712	20	692
Sale of Property	823	506	317	66	252
Interest Earnings	4,675	1,463	3,212	1,536	1,676
Other (Miscellaneous General Revenue)	7,273	3,939	3,334	1,338	1,996
Utility Revenue	7,787	—	7,787	—	7,787
Liquor Stores Revenue	2,188	—	2,188	1,904	284
Insurance Trust Revenue	64,654	51,256	13,398	11,773	1,625
Total Revenues	381,849	223,378	189,724	112,309	113,162
	119,316	69,645	49,670	24,457	25,215
Total Non-tax Revenues	31.2%	31.2%	26.2%	21.8%	22.3%

SOURCE: Adapted from Advisory Commission on Intergovernmental Relations.

terms. But they continue to exist, from water, gas, electrical utilities, and telephone systems to toll bridges, ferries, terminals, and markets. Revenues from hospitals, transportation facilities, public housing projects, and the like are also important. Virtually the entire state of Nebraska is served by a publicly owned power company, as are large cities such as Los Angeles and Jacksonville, Florida. The state of Alaska derives substantial amounts of its revenue from oil leases.

The general pattern in this country has been to give away public resources for little or nothing to private industries — the great railroad land grants and low-priced monopoly franchises come to mind. Public property is regularly leased to private companies, which not only operate it for their own profit, but often are exempt from local property taxes. However, as states and localities continue their search for revenue, and the so-called public utilities keep asking for rate increases, the buying out of utility monopolies to operate them as public enterprises is more frequently raised as an option.

who bears the tax burden?

What does it all mean? The most recent and comprehensive study, *Who Bears the Tax Burden?* by Joseph Pechman and Benjamin Okner of the Brookings Institution in Washington, D.C., testing various assumptions about who bears certain taxes, found that irrespective of income, most Americans pay roughly the same rate of tax. The evidence further suggests that historically the over-all tax system—federal, state, and local—is becoming less and less fair. A study by the Advisory Commission on Intergovernmental Relations showed that between 1953 and 1974, the tax burdens on average income families increased much more rapidly than the tax burdens on higher income families. In those twenty years, the tax burden on high-income families increased by 52 percent. But the tax burden on average families increased by 98 percent (figure 17).

Most striking is the parallel erosion of the income tax and property tax and the way in which specific reductions in each tend to benefit similar special interests. Thus, today we find:

fast "write-offs" for industrial machinery under the income tax, and exemptions for machinery and often for entire industrial plants under the property tax;

income tax provisions allowing corporations and wealthy individuals to duck taxes through "tax-loss farming," and "farm-land assessment laws" enabling these same interests to avoid their share of property taxes;

"capital gains" provisions allowing investors profiting from stock and bond deals to pay only one-half the income tax rate paid by working people, and property tax exemptions for stocks, bonds, and other forms of so-called intangible property;

"depletion allowances" that shrink income taxes on profits from oil and other resources, and the notorious underassessment of these resources for property tax purposes;

Taxes and Taxpayers 31

Accelerated depreciation for business real estate, and assessment techniques which result in lower assessments on business property than assessments placed on homes;

"capital gains" treatment for income from land speculation, and the underassessment of vacant land, cutting costs and increasing profits for the same speculators.

Nor do these arm-in-arm tax breaks stop with income and property taxes. For example, investors not only benefit from property tax exemptions and capital gains income tax rates. Stock and bond sales commonly are exempt from sales taxes as well. Similarly, industrial equipment often is exempt from sales taxes, in addition to the other tax breaks its owners receive. A thorough inventory of the entire tax system would show still further benefits converging from many directions upon business and the wealthy. This is not surprising when we examine who most influences the nation's tax laws.

Legislators have increasingly favored regressive over progressive taxes. They have undercut progressivity with numerous exemptions, deductions, and special preferences. And administrators have opted for convenience over fairness in formulating and applying tax laws. We can see that in all areas of taxation reforms are needed to overcome these three trends which undermine fairness and underlie the rising protest against unfair taxes. How and why this has happened and what can be done about it is the subject of this book.

32 TAX POLITICS

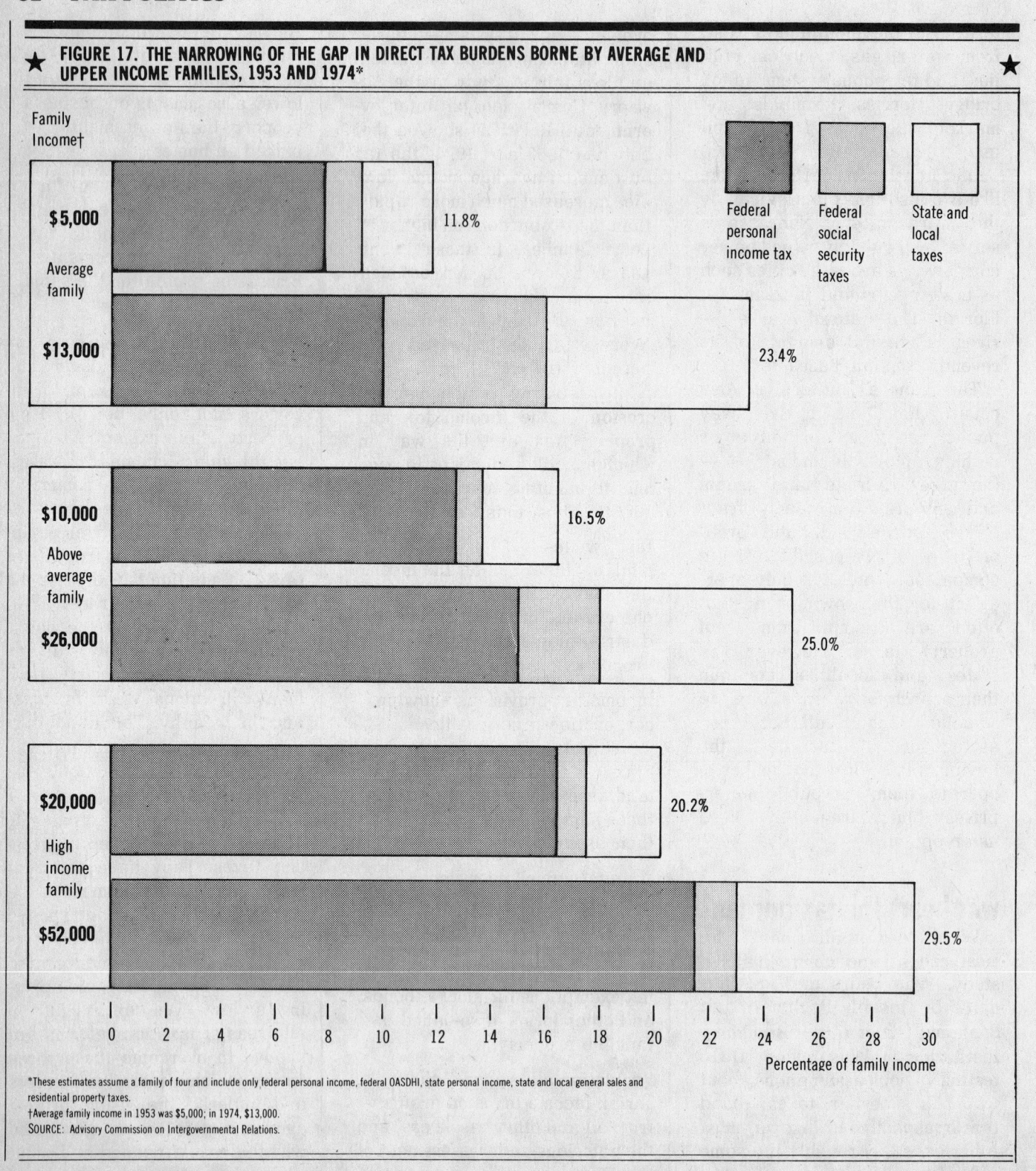

FIGURE 17. THE NARROWING OF THE GAP IN DIRECT TAX BURDENS BORNE BY AVERAGE AND UPPER INCOME FAMILIES, 1953 AND 1974*

Family Income†

Legend:
- Federal personal income tax (dark)
- Federal social security taxes (light gray)
- State and local taxes (white)

Family Income	Total Tax Burden
$5,000 (Average family)	11.8%
$13,000	23.4%
$10,000 (Above average family)	16.5%
$26,000	25.0%
$20,000 (High income family)	20.2%
$52,000	29.5%

Percentage of family income (0 to 30)

*These estimates assume a family of four and include only federal personal income, federal OASDHI, state personal income, state and local general sales and residential property taxes.
†Average family income in 1953 was $5,000; in 1974, $13,000.
SOURCE: Advisory Commission on Intergovernmental Relations.

2 Income Taxes

Chapter 2
Tax Expenditures: The Hidden Federal Budget - A Key to Reform

"I want to point out, however, that the grant of ... tax credits has precisely the same effect on the budget as an outright expenditure. The only difference is they appear as a negative receipt rather than as an expenditure. That is why I refer to... tax credits as back-door spending..."

Ways and Means Chairman
Wilbur D. Mills in a 1967
speech delivered on the House
floor entitled "Back-Door
Spending"

★ ★ ★ ★ ★ ★ ★

This chapter will take a closer look at tax preferences or loopholes. We will investigate what they are, how they work, who benefits from them—and at what cost, and why we need to reform them. Reform will come only when the majority of American taxpayers ask basic questions.

Who really benefits from tax preferences? American taxpayers are being conned into supporting tax breaks that provide very little relief for average citizens and vastly greater relief for the wealthy. Fifty-three percent of all tax break dollars go to the top 15 percent of the taxpayers. The other 85 percent of taxpayers save an average of only $437 from all individual income tax breaks while the top 15 percent save a whopping $18,977 a year. **Why should you support small tax breaks for yourself when others benefit much more from them?** By removing this unfair system of selective tax relief altogether, everyone's tax rate could be reduced substantially. Why not lower everyone's taxes, not just those of select businesses or groups powerful enough to have the tax laws written for their benefit? Many special tax preferences have been written into the law not because of good policy reasons but because of powerful special-interest lobbying. Lawmakers should respond to facts and fairness, not to pressure. **Why shouldn't special interests** prove why they should receive special relief?

Are "tax incentives" worth it? Do their benefits outweigh their costs? Presently, tax preferences cost the U.S. Treasury about $100 billion annually! Are they worth all that potential revenue that goes uncollected? Do they accomplish what they are supposed to do? Are they worth their cost to the basic fairness of our tax system?

Do tax incentives really encourage desired economic and social decisions or do they distort those decisions improperly? Don't tax incentives often represent windfalls to certain taxpayers by paying them to do what they would do anyway? **Aren't there more efficient and more equitable ways to encourage certain desired activity?**

Keeping these questions in mind will give you a framework for looking at tax proposals as they come up in the news. They are the hard questions politicians and special interests like to avoid.

what is a tax expenditure?

The concept that is central to tax reform is the concept of tax expenditures. Tax preferences or loopholes cost money. The 1971 decision to enact a 7 percent investment tax credit, for instance, meant that in order to encourage more spending on plant and equipment purchases by business, the Treasury Department would forego the collection of about $3.8 billion in taxes. A decision was made, in other words, to spend $3.8 billion of what would have been tax revenues on businesses that used the money to buy new equipment. The 7 percent credit meant that business would spend $93 on a new $100 purchase and the Treasury Department would spend the other $7. It is this spending of potential tax revenues by enacting a tax preference or loophole that we refer to as a tax expenditure.

Whether you call these income tax provisions loopholes, preferences, subsidies, incentives or expenditures, the concept is the same. Tax expenditures represent conscious decisions to reduce the taxes of particular groups of taxpayers from what they would have to pay under the normal tax structure. For this reason, tax expenditures can and should be equated with direct governmental expenditures. They both represent government spending on particular programs. The only difference is that with direct expenditures, taxes are collected in full and a certain amount is then paid back to the taxpayer, while with tax expenditures the amount to be paid back is simply never collected.

Let's look at a simple example. Suppose the president or the Congress feels that in spite of the high cost of energy, people need an additional incentive to insulate their homes and to save energy. Representative A may propose a direct subsidy payment to homeowners equal to 25 percent of the first $400 of insulation costs—a maximum of $100. Representative B proposes to make the first $400 of insulation costs a tax deduction.

This year the Smith family spent $400 to insulate their old house. Under the direct payment plan, Mr. Smith, an average income worker, pays $2,260 in taxes and receives $100 from the government as an insulation subsidy. Under the tax expenditure plan, Mr. Smith, who deducts the $400 in insulation costs, saves $100 on his taxes and pays only $2,160.

The U.S. Treasury has "spent" $100 and Mr. Smith has received a $100 savings in his insulation costs—in one case through a direct payment, in the other through his taxes. In either case the total cost to the Treasury is estimated to be $100 million. Depending on which plan is adopted, we will either have a $100 million direct expenditure program for subsidizing insulation or a $100 million tax expenditure program for subsidizing insulation.

Tax reformers often refer to tax expenditures as tax loopholes or tax breaks. It is important to note that tax loopholes are not inadvertent defects in our tax system which enable certain taxpayers to slip through, paying little or no tax. Nor are they attempts to fairly distribute the tax load. For the most part they are specifically enacted programs aimed at encouraging certain economic or social behavior. There is the mortgage interest deduction to encourage home purchases; charitable deductions to encourage charitable giving; capital gains exclusions, accelerated depreciation and investment tax credits to encourage investment; oil depletion allowances and intangible drilling deductions to encourage oil exploration; and many others. As the reader will see, tax expenditures are usually unfair, often unneeded, and almost always inefficient in achieving their stated purpose.

One final point. When the Congress spends federal monies outside the direct budget through various tax expenditures, the amount of resources available to the government for other projects is reduced. The resulting choice is to cut funds for existing programs or to raise everyone's taxes to make up the difference. In other words, if one group of taxpayers pays less tax because of a particular tax preference, the rest of the taxpayers will have to pay more.

As we have seen in the introduction, tax expenditures have resulted in the erosion of our progressive income tax system. The object of this chapter will be to determine whether the economic and social "incentives" created by tax expenditures are worth their costs in absolute terms and in terms of their effect on the fairness of the income tax system. The key to this tax expenditure analysis for tax reform is that it provides a mechanism for examining the hidden tax expenditures with an eye toward eliminating both the inequity and the inefficient subsidies that these expenditures now produce. To do this, we will turn to the list of these expenditures—the tax expenditure budget.

the tax expenditure budget— the hidden budget

When President Ford submitted his fiscal year 1976 budget he came down hard against large government spending. "I am proposing no new spending initiatives in this budget other than those for energy," Mr. Ford said in his budget message. (Actually, defense spending was up $9 billion.) Not only was Ford trying to prevent programs from growing faster than their normal rate, but he also proposed cuts of $17 billion in existing programs, including a 5 percent ceiling on increases in federal salaries and retirement and social security benefits which are pegged to cost of living increases.

"It has become a popular notion to consider some government expenditures as uncontrollable; that is, they would go on and on whether we like it or not," Ford said at a February 1, 1975, briefing. "I categorically reject that view. They are controllable, if the Congress on the one hand and the president on the other do something about them."

Mr. Ford obviously failed to study the rest of his own budget documents. For there, among hundreds of pages of material, was a list of billions of dollars of government expenditures and the largest source of uncontrollable spending—the tax expenditure budget. Thanks to an amendment to the Congressional Budget Act of 1974, the fiscal 1976 budget took a comprehensive look at the cost of tax preferences—listing them item by item—and found that taxpayers (and non-taxpayers) would benefit from those expenditures to the tune of $91.8 billion in FY 1976. The president would not have to look far to find areas where he could cut the size of this hidden budget. Any number of tax preferences could be ended, not only making our tax system more equitable but reducing the federal deficit by raising new revenues. Certainly any effort at budget cutting is misdirected if it fails to take a careful look at our present tax expenditure budget—tax subsidies that, when added together, exceed one-quarter of the present direct budget.

The concept of compiling a list of tax expenditures into a tax expenditure budget recognizes that our tax system really consists of two parts. The first part is made up of the simple structure necessary to raise taxes from corporate and individual incomes. The second part is made up of a system of tax expenditures that grant government financial assistance through special tax provisions rather than through direct government programs. The tax expenditure budget is simply an enumeration of the present "tax subsidies" in our income tax system.

Figure 18, on the next page, shows the latest tax expenditure budget.

using the tax expenditure budget to approach tax reform

Tax reformers have varying ideas about specific reforms but most can agree on two basic goals. The first is equity. We want to raise taxes within our traditional notions of fairness and one's ability to pay. This can be done through structural reforms such as simplification, less reliance on regressive taxes, removing poverty-level wage earners from the tax rolls, and the elimination of unfair tax loopholes or preferences. Second is efficiency. That means evaluating tax expenditures, as we do direct expenditures, to determine whether they are efficient and effective in achieving their stated purposes. Considering tax preferences within the context of a tax expenditure budget—an approach pioneered by former Assistant Treasury Secretary Stanley S. Surrey—enables us to evaluate existing or proposed tax preferences from the standpoint of what they cost, whom they benefit, how well they work, and whether they are worth it.

Ideally, the approach to tax reform would be to eliminate all present tax expenditures and to return to a simple, progressive revenue-raising tax system. This idea of expenditure reform is consistent with the closer scrutiny to which direct government spending has been subjected in recent years. Many reformers have al-

36 TAX POLITICS

★ FIGURE 18. FEDERAL TAX EXPENDITURE ESTIMATES FOR FISCAL YEAR 1976 (In Millions of Dollars) *

Description	Corporations 1974	Corporations 1975	Corporations 1976	Individuals 1974	Individuals 1975	Individuals 1976
National defense:						
Exclusion of benefits and allowances to Armed Forces personnel				650	650	650
Exclusion of military disability pensions				65	75	85
International affairs:						
Exclusion of gross-up on dividends of LDC corporations	55	55	55			
Exclusion of certain income earned abroad by U.S. citizens				90	95	100
Deferral of income of domestic international sales corporations (DISC)	870	1,070	1,320			
Special rate for Western Hemisphere trade corporations	50	50	50			
Deferral of income of controlled foreign corporations	620	620	620			
Agriculture:						
Expensing of certain capital outlays	170	145	155	580	480	495
Capital gain treatment of certain income	30	20	25	520	280	340
Natural resources environment and energy:						
Expensing of exploration and development costs	750	950	1,235	80	100	130
Excess of percentage over cost depletion	1,815	2,200	2,610	305	370	445
Capital gain treatment of royalties on coal and iron ore	5	15	20			
Timber: capital gain treatment of certain income	130	145	155	55	60	60
Pollution control: 5-year amortization	35	30	20			
Commerce and transportation:						
$25,000 corporate surtax exemption	3,270	3,590	3,570			
Deferral of tax on shipping companies	35	35	40			
Railroad rolling stock: 5-year amortization	70	60	55			
Bad debt reserve of financial institutions in excess of actual	1,000	1,030	980			
Deductibility of nonbusiness State gasoline taxes				865	850	850
Community and regional development: Housing rehabilitation:						
5-year amortization	35	45	35	50	70	60
Education, manpower, and social services:						
Child care facilities: 5-year amortization	5	5	5			
Exclusion of scholarships and fellowships				195	210	190
Parental personal exemption for student age 19 and over				655	670	690
Deductibility of contributions to educational institutions	155	160	155	355	405	435
Deductibility of child and dependent care expenses				230	240	250
Credit for employing public assistance recipients under work incentive program	5	5	5			
Health:						
Exclusion of employer contributions to medical insurance premiums and medical care				2,940	3,340	3,745
Deductibility of medical expenses				1,225	2,375	2,630
Income security:						
Exclusion of social security benefits:						
Disability insurance benefits				235	260	280
OASI benefits for aged				2,530	2,655	2,940
Benefits for dependents and survivors				410	435	480
Exclusion of railroad retirement system benefits				160	170	180
Exclusion of sick pay				255	275	295
Exclusion of unemployment insurance benefits				1,050	2,370	3,830
Exclusion of workmen's compensation benefits				520	570	620
Exclusion of public assistance benefits				75	85	90
Net exclusion of pension contributions and earnings:						
Employer plans				4,790	5,200	5,740
Plans for self-employed and others				230	410	710

Tax Expenditures: The Hidden Federal Budget—A Key to Reform

| | Corporations ||| Individuals |||
Description	1974	1975	1976	1974	1975	1976
Exclusion of other employee benefits:						
Premiums on group term life insurance				680	740	805
Premiums on accident and accidental death insurance				40	45	50
Privately financed supplementary unemployment benefits				5	5	5
Meals and lodging				175	180	190
Exclusion of capital gains on house sales if over 65				10	10	10
Excess of percentage standard deduction over minimum standard deduction				1,260	1,370	1,420
Additional exemption for the blind				15	15	15
Additional exemption for over 65				1,150	1,200	1,250
Retirement income credit				100	75	70
Veterans' benefits and services:						
Exclusion of veterans' disability compensation				485	525	550
Exclusion of veterans' pensions				25	30	35
Exclusion of GI bill benefits				290	255	250
General government: Credits and deductions for political contributions				10	25	50
Revenue sharing and general fiscal assistance:						
Exclusion of interest on State and local dept	2,805	3,155	3,505	1,060	1,160	1,260
Exclusion of income earned in U.S. possessions	350	350	350	5	5	5
Deductibility of nonbusiness State and local taxes (other than on owner-occupied homes and gasoline)				6,955	8,820	9,950
Business investment:						
Depreciation on rental housing in excess of straight line	105	115	120	375	405	420
Depreciation on buildings (other than rental housing) in excess of straight line	285	280	275	220	220	215
Expensing of research and development expenditures	605	630	660			
Capital gain: corporate (other than farming and timber)	745	595	755			
Investment credit	3,690	4,160	4,420	880	905	950
Asset depreciation range	1,260	1,410	1,590			
Personal investment:						
Dividend exclusion				320	340	360
Capital gain: individual (other than farming and timber)				6,150	3,280	4,165
Exclusion of capital gains at death				5,000	4,420	4,550
Exclusion of interest on life insurance savings				1,420	1,620	1,820
Deferral of capital gain on homes sales				255	285	315
Deductibility of mortgage interest on owner-occupied homes				4,870	5,590	6,500
Deductibility of property taxes on owner-occupied homes				4,060	4,660	5,270
Deductibility of casualty losses				255	275	300
Other tax expenditures:						
Exemption of credit unions	105	115				
Deductibility of charitable contributions (other than education)	290	295	285	3,820	4,485	4,840
Deductibility of interest on consumer credit				2,435	2,885	3,460
Maximum tax on earned income				330	350	385

*All estimates are based on the provisions in the Internal Revenue Code as of Jan. 1, 1975

Totals:

Fiscal year	Total	Corporations	Individuals
1974	81,115	19,345	61,770
1975	88,215	21,335	66,880
1976	98,980	23,195	75,785

38 TAX POLITICS

ready begun this process, as have some members of Congress.

In the 93rd Congress, Senator Mark Hatfield introduced a tax scheme he refers to as simpliform. It would essentially repeal all individual income tax preferences, translate the savings into lower rates, and reduce tax returns to four simple lines: gross income, a deduction for legitimate expenses used to make that income, the resulting taxable income, and a final tax owed. Wilbur Mills, while pursuing the 1972 presidential nomination, proposed systematically repealing fifty-four major tax preferences, thereby forcing Congress to re-evaluate major tax expenditures to determine if they should be re-enacted. This proposal, however, was never seriously pursued.

More recently Senator Floyd Haskell, a member of the Senate Finance Committee and a tax lawyer of thirty years' experience, introduced a tax-reform bill that eliminates a majority of present tax expenditures he considers unfair or unnecessary, urges the replacement of other tax expenditures with direct expenditure programs, and reforms still others to make them more equitable. Tax reformers have been urging the congressional tax-writing committees for some time to view tax loopholes as expenditure items in need of budgetary reform.

When the legislators finally face this fact, congressional committees can begin to view tax loopholes as a way of spending federal monies. Members of the House Ways and Means Committee and the Senate Finance Committee should be evaluating their tax actions as if they were an appropriations committee or a budget director. For each proposed or existing tax preference, they should ask the same questions that any budget director would ask:

How well does the program work? Is it efficient? What are its costs and benefits.

What are its objectives? Are those objectives being reached? Could they be achieved more economically?

Who are the intended beneficiaries of the program? Are they actually being assisted by the program? Are there any unintended beneficiaries? Are people receiving too much or too little of the benefits?

The answers to these questions call for three basic steps toward tax reform. A large number of present tax preferences should be repealed outright because they are unneeded, accomplish no worthwhile purpose, and are simply a misuse of federal tax revenues. The oil industry's depletion allowance, for instance, would fall into this category.

Other tax expenditures may provide financial assistance for worthwhile social or economic activity but would be more efficient and equitable if replaced with a direct expenditure program. Of these, many could be readily transferred to more efficient existing federal programs. For example, the same financial assistance given to states and localities through tax-exempt bonds could be given through a direct revenue-sharing program of interest subsidies at a yearly savings of $700 million to the government.

Some tax expenditure items that provide desirable financial assistance would be more efficiently and fairly operated outside the tax system but do not readily fit into existing direct programs. Here, a new direct program should be designed before the tax expenditure is repealed. The present incentive for charitable giving, the charitable deduction, is a good example of this type of tax preference. It is obvious that wealthy individuals benefit unfairly from the charitable deduction and that some direct program of matching grants would be more desirable.

Finally, there may be a small number of tax expenditure programs that can operate more efficiently and effectively than direct programs. In these few cases, it is the job of the tax reformer to make sure that the tax preference, if it remains in the tax system, is as fair as possible.

why tax expenditures are less desirable than direct expenditures

tax expenditures are inequitable

An example used by Professor Surrey is instructive: Imagine a packed hearing room of housing appropriations subcommittee. A new secretary of housing and urban development has come before it to present a program to assist in the purchase of owner-occupied homes. The HUD secretary proposes the following:

—For a married couple with more than $200,000 in income, HUD would $70 of every $100 in mortgage interest costs, leaving the couple to pay the other $30.

—For a married couple with an income of $15,000, HUD would pay the band $22 of every $100 in mortgage interest, leaving the couple to pay $78.

—For a married couple earning about $4,000 and too poor to pay any income tax, HUD would pay nothing to the bank, leaving the couple to pay the entire interest costs.

Obviously no HUD secretary or member of Congress would ever advocate or vote for such an unfair direct housing program. But that is exactly the effect of the present tax expenditure program for assistance to owner-occupied homes under the mortgage interest deduction. The same upside-down effect also occurs in the deductions for property taxes and numerous other tax deductions for exemptions. The reason that tax deductions, exemptions, and exclusions favor the wealthy over middle and low income individuals is really quite simple.

Let's return to our example of the mortgage interest deduction. If you are an average family making about $15,000 a year, your tax bracket will probably have a 22 percent rate. For each $100 of income you earn at that level, you would pay $22 in taxes. It follows, then, that for each $100 in mortgage interest you deduct from your income, you will save $22 in taxes. (That's $100 deducted X 22 percent taxes you would owe on that amount of money.)

Now take the wealthy family with an income of $200,000. Their tax bracket has a 70 percent rate. Does this rich family also save $22 on their $100 deduction? No. They save much more—for each $100 of mortgage interest they can deduct, they save $70. (That's $100 deducted X 70 percent taxes they would otherwise owe on that amount of money.) It's a strange government subsidy that gives the rich man $70 for each $100 he spends on his home mortgage but gives the average taxpayer only $22.

So even if you and your neighbor have identical houses and identical mortgages, your neighbor may effectively get much more help buying it because he or she has more income. Of course, rich families can afford more expensive houses and larger mortgages. They might even have a vacation home at the beach. Since there are no limits on the amount of mortgage interest deducted, the tax break from this preference can be huge. There are also those families that cannot afford houses at all who receive no benefit from this "housing subsidy," even though it may be costing them as much each year to rent an apartment or house.

There are other examples which highlight the unfairness of using tax deductions as a subsidy program. For instance, the $4 billion tax expenditure to promote charitable giving—the charitable deduction. Take our same taxpayers. For each $100 the rich person donates, $70 is actually given by the government in the form of reduced taxes. Only $30 actually comes out of his pocket.

A Note on Income Figures

Adjusted gross income [AGI] is the basis for almost all Treasury Department statistics relating to an individual's income. Hence it is also the basis for most of the charts and tables in this book that refer to information *by income class.*

Adjusted gross income understates many people's real income. AGI relates to income which does not include a number of items exempt from income such as municipal bond interest, the untaxed half of capital gains, oil and mineral income not taxed because of depletion allowances, and several other items of non-taxed income. The result of all this is that tables listing individuals with AGI of, say, $10,000 may actually include a number of individuals with very high incomes. The tax benefits that go to these "lower" income brackets, then, are actually overstated since much of the benefit is conferred on wealthy people who use the tax preferences to lower their adjusted gross income.

40 TAX POLITICS

When the average family gives $100, they take $78 out of their own pocket. Only $22 is picked up by the Treasury in the form of reduced taxes. And the generous giver who takes the standard deduction (58 percent of all taxpayers in 1972) gets no government subsidy at all. The effect is that the rich not only get a greater tax break, but the government subsidizes their favorite charities to a much greater extent than the charities of average taxpayers.

If these tax deductions are going to remain in the tax code, they need to be made fairer. The way to benefit all taxpayers fairly without regard to their income tax bracket is to replace tax deductions and exemptions with tax credits.

In 1972, for example, living individuals gave about $16 billion to charity. That year, the federal income tax deduction for charitable contributions cost the government $3.4 billion in tax subsidies. An income tax credit of 24 percent of the dollars a taxpayer gives to charity would benefit each taxpayer, irrespective of income, $24 per $100 donation. In other words, a tax credit benefits each taxpayer equally according to the amount he gives.*

In spite of the obvious upside-down benefits of tax deductions, wealthy recipients of these tax breaks and their political allies continue to defend them with reference to struggling widows, hard-working small businessmen, and average wage earners. The Treasury Department's own statistics, published annually by the Ways and Means Committee, perpetuate the myth of the middle class loophole. According to the 1974 Treasury statistics, a great deal—a total of $900 million of the $4.9 billion mortgage interest tax expenditure—went to middle class taxpayers (earning $10,000 to $15,000 per year.) A much smaller amount — only $95 million — went to the wealthy ($100,000 per year or more). In that year, however, there were 16 million taxpayers in the first category, so the average saving was $55.54. On the other hand, there were only 160,000 taxpayers reported in the $100,000 bracket, so they saved an average of $593.75—more than ten times as much as the average taxpayers. In fact, if this tax expenditure were completely repealed and the savings passed on in lower taxes, every taxpayer could save about $70 each year.

The inequity is even greater in the charitable deduction. The average income taxpayer (including all those who received no benefit because they took the standard deduction) benefited an average of $28 from the deduction. Taxpayers with incomes of $100,000 and more benefitted an average of $6,200 each.

There are many other tax preferences which subsidize activity almost exclusively within the province of the rich or of large corporations. The capital gains exclusion, for example, works just like a deduction by excluding one-half of the income from capital gains but is only available to those well off enough to own stocks and bonds and real estate investments. The latest survey of stock ownership shows that the top 1 percent of taxpayers own 51 percent of the nation's stocks and bonds. Here the distribution of the benefits is even more lopsides. The capital gains exemption disregards one-hals of the income from investments and is our single largest tax expenditure, costing the Treasury $6.1 billion in 1974. The average family saved less than $20 in taxes with this tax expenditure, but the wealthy tax payer saved an average of nearly $20,000.

Thus, tax expenditures are inequitable for a number of reasons. In the form of deductions, exemptions, or exclusions, they benefit high bracket taxpayers more than low or middle bracket taxpayers. Many of the favored activities, such as investment, are activities in which wealthier people predominate and therefore are the only real beneficiaries. Even in those areas where middle income people do receive tax preferences, they receive less than do wealthier people because they usually have smaller deductions. And, finally, since many tax expenditures are in the form of itemized deductions (medical expenses, mortgage interest and property tax and charitable deductions), taxpayers who do not itemize get no benefit from these tax preferences at all.

Figure 19 is a chart of all major tax expenditure budget items

---

*Assuming no change in the amount of charity, the cost of the 24 percent tax credit would be about the same as the present tax deduction (24 percent x $16 billion in gifts = $3.8 billion, close to the 1972 $3.4 billion cost).

which shows the average savings of each by income class.

tax expenditures are usually less efficient than direct expenditures

We have seen that subsidies are unfairly distributed among taxpayers. But can these unfair expenditures be excused because of their benefits to the economy or the country? It turns out that tax subsidies frequently waste money without efficiently promoting the economic or social purposes with which they are associated.

There are several reasons why tax subsidies tend to be less efficient than direct subsidies of the same cost. But there is one major reason why those that are wasteful continue as a permanent part of our tax subsidy system.

1. **The congressional procedures for enacting tax subsidies are much less rigorous than those followed in appropriating direct subsidies.**

Tax subsidies, once written into the tax laws, remain there indefinitely unless and until the tax-writing committees happen to take another look. By contrast, direct subsidies are annually subjected to the authorization and appropriation process. Each year the proponents of direct subsidy programs come before the Congress to argue the case for their particular program. The burden of proof is on them to show evidence that the program is working and that it's worth the money.

Moreover, in the executive branch, the Office of Management and Budget subjects direct subsidies to further hard analysis, many times recommending retention of effective programs and elimination of wasteful programs. This is not the case with tax subsidies and only adds to a loose process that cannot help but produce much less efficient programs.

In 1969, for the first time, there was an attempt to force the re-evaluation of several new and controversial tax expenditure programs. Proponents of a new tax subsidy in the form of fast write-offs (rapid amortization) for buying railroad cars, mine safety equipment, and pollution control equipment agreed to have the tax expenditure end after five years. The idea was to give the Congress, the Treasury, and the industry an opportunity during that time to study whether these tax breaks encourage enough new purchases of this equipment to be worth the more than $100 million annually they would cost the government. It would also give Congress a chance to determine whether it wanted to subsidize these investments at all.

This approach failed. The Treasury Department made no study of these expensive government subsidies. The tax-writing committees of Congress made no study as to their usefulness. And the industries involved offered no proof that the expenditures were worthwhile. But they really didn't have to. Businesses receiving the tax breaks simply sent their lobbyists up to Capitol Hill urging the renewal of these still untested subsidies. They seemed to be saying, "Trust us, we need this incentive. It would be unfair to take it away after you gave it to us. We've counted on it to continue." At the very end of the legislative session in 1974, the Congress cheerfully agreed. The Senate Finance Committee quietly tacked onto a minor tariff bill a one year's extension of these fast write-off tax provisions. Subsequent extensions will undoubtedly be granted.

Even when the Congress does look at tax expenditures, they consider them in a very sloppy manner. The congressional tax-writing committees almost never require any kind of cost-benefit studies of tax subsidies. Instead, special interests present rhetoric and closed-door justifications for programs depriving the government of billions of dollars in revenue.

A similar example is provided by the investment tax credit or, as it was called when re-enacted in 1971, the "job development credit." Treasury Secretary John Connally told Congress the job development credit would create jobs, increase productivity, and (by increasing productivity) enhance American competition in world markets. What Connally omitted was to explain *how many* jobs would be created, and *how much* productivity would be increased. And Congress, in its haste to cut corporate taxes (almost all of the credit benefits corporations rather than individual taxpayers), neglected to ask.

The job development credit allows a business a 7 percent tax credit on purchases of machinery and equipment. If General Motors buys a new $1,000 pneumatic riveter for one of its assembly

42 TAX POLITICS

FIGURE 19. TAX PREFERENCE BENEFITS PER INDIVIDUAL BY ADJUSTED GROSS INCOME CLASS, FISCAL YEAR 1974 (In Dollars)

Adjusted gross income class	(1) Exclusion of benefits and allowances to Armed Forces personnel	(2) Exclusion of military disability pensions	(3) Exclusion of certain income earned abroad by U.S. citizens	(4) Expensing of certain agriculture capital outlays	(5) Capital gains treatment of certain agriculture income	(6) Expensing of exploration and development costs	(7) Excess of percentage over cost depletion	(8) Capital gains treatment of certain timber income	(9) Deduction of nonbusiness State gasoline taxes
0 to $3,000	2.46	0.25	3.70	2.46	2.46	...	0.25	...	0.25
$3,000 to $5,000	17.81	1.72	1.72	4.62	3.96	0.13	.66	0.26	.66
$5,000 to $7,000	19.34	1.93	.85	7.25	6.65	.12	.48	.24	2.66
$7,000 to $10,000	10.94	1.14	.79	7.88	7.00	.18	.96	.26	7.09
$10,000 to $15,000	6.90	.69	.44	7.21	6.58	.63	1.19	.25	12.41
$15,000 to $20,000	5.58	.61	.71	7.10	6.09	.81	2.13	.30	21.81
$20,000 to $50,000	5.55	.56	2.66	13.88	12.77	2.11	8.44	1.11	34.09
$50,000 to $100,000	6.11	...	9.16	61.07	53.44	19.85	94.66	13.74	42.75
$100,000 and over	6.25	...	12.5	218.75	187.50	162.50	662.50	137.50	50.00

Adjusted gross income class	(10) Housing rehabilitation 5-yr amortization	(11) Exclusion of scholarships and fellowships	(12) Parental personal exemptions for student age 19 and over	(13) Deduction of contributions to educational institutions	(14) Deduction of child and dependent care expenses	(15) Exclusion of employer contributions to medical premiums and medical care	(16) Deduction of medical expenses	(17) Exclusion of social security disability insurance benefits	(18) Exclusion of social security OASI benefits for aged	(19) Exclusion of social security benefits for dependents and survivors
0 to $3,000	.49	1.48	...	...	...	6.41	0.99	10.85	115.85	19.72
$3,000 to $5,000	...	5.15	1.06	...	.13	9.63	5.01	5.67	60.69	9.90
$5,000 to $7,000	...	5.80	4.60	0.12	.85	15.83	13.54	4.23	45.93	7.25
$7,000 to $10,000	...	3.59	8.75	.18	2.71	24.94	23.10	3.85	41.13	6.56
$10,000 to $15,000	.13	1.94	13.29	.19	5.33	41.50	30.15	1.94	20.69	3.45
$15,000 to $20,000	.20	1.93	13.09	2.03	9.33	66.46	38.15	1.32	14.20	2.03
$20,000 to $50,000	.67	1.22	8.22	7.11	1.55	91.83	70.84	2.22	23.87	3.89
$50,000 to $100,000	21.37	...	111.45	99.24	...	294.66	221.37	6.11	68.70	7.63
$100,000 and over	150.00	...	131.25	1,250.00	...	550.00	443.75	6.25	125.00	31.25

Adjusted gross income class	(20) Exclusion of railroad retirement system benefits	(21) Exclusion of sick pay	(22) Exclusion of unemployment insurance benefits	(23) Exclusion of workmen's compensation benefits	(24) Exclusion of public assistance benefits	(25) Net exclusion of pension contributions and earnings — Employer plans	(26) Plans for self-employed and others	(27) Exclusion of premiums on group term life insurance	(28) Exclusion of premiums on accident and accidental death insurance	(29) Exclusion of privately financed supplementary unemployment benefits	(30) Exclusion of employer furnished meals and lodging	(31) Exclusion of capital gain on house sales if age 65 or over
0 to $3,000	7.39	2.46	12.32	6.16	7.39	3.70	...	1.23	...	...	0.25	0.25
$3,000 to $5,000	3.83	2.11	10.56	5.28	3.30	6.60	...	1.98	0.13	...	.53	...
$5,000 to $7,000	2.90	2.05	12.09	6.04	1.81	13.30	0.12	3.63	.24	0.12	.97	...
$7,000 to $10,000	2.63	2.10	14.00	7.00	.44	25.38	.18	5.69	.35	.09	1.49	.09
$10,000 to $15,000	1.32	4.14	15.67	7.52	...	49.52	.38	9.72	.56	.13	2.44	.06
$15,000 to $20,000	.91	6.09	15.22	7.61	...	100.45	1.12	15.73	.91	.10	3.96	.10
$20,000 to $50,000	1.44	6.33	22.21	11.10	...	193.20	11.88	21.10	1.22	...	5.55	.22
$50,000 to $100,000	4.58	6.11	76.34	38.17	...	832.06	132.82	68.70	4.58	...	18.32	3.05
$100,000 and over	6.25	6.25	62.50	31.25	...	1,625.00	100.00	125.00	6.25	...	31.25	12.50

FIGURE 19. TAX PREFERENCE BENEFITS PER INDIVIDUAL BY ADJUSTED GROSS INCOME CLASS, FISCAL YEAR 1974 (Continued)

Adjusted gross income class	(32) Excess of percentage standard deduction over minimum standard deduction	(33) Additional exemption for the blind	(34) Additional exemption for age 65 or over	(35) Retirement income credit	(36) Exclusion of veterans disability compensation	(37) Exclusion of veterans pensions	(38) Exclusion of GI bill benefits	(39) Credits and deduction for political contributions	(40) Exclusion of interest on State and local debt	(41) Exclusion on income earned in U.S. possessions	(42) Deduction of non-business State and local taxes (other than on owner-occupied homes and gasoline)
0 to $3,000	......	......	1.73	0.25	15.04	4.19	8.38	......	......	......	0.25
$3,000 to $5,000	0.13	0.13	12.53	2.37	5.15	1.06	16.36	......	......	......	1.72
$5,000 to $7,000	1.57	.36	22.36	2.66	5.32	......	7.25	0.12	......	......	6.65
$7,000 to $10,000	5.60	.26	23.45	1.75	5.86	......	3.06	.09	0.09	......	20.91
$10,000 to $15,000	40.43	.19	12.29	1.19	6.39	......	1.00	.13	.25	0.06	41.44
$15,000 to $20,000	35.71	.20	10.75	.91	7.31	......	1.01	.20	2.23	.20	103.08
$20,000 to $50,000	19.76	.22	23.43	1.11	9.66	......	1.00	.33	10.88	.22	329.56
$50,000 to $100,000	9.16	1.53	85.50	1.53	15.27	......	3.05	1.53	593.89	......	1,622.90
$100,000 and over	6.25	......	162.50	......	18.75	......	......	......	3,412.5	......	5,868.75

Adjusted gross income class	(43) Depreciation on rental housing in excess of straight line	(44) Depreciation on buildings (other than rental housing) in excess of straight line	(45) Investment credit	(46) Dividend exclusion	(47) Capital gain (other than farming and timber)	(48) Exclusion of interest on life insurance savings	(49) Deferral of capital gain on home sales	(50) Deduction of mortgage interest on owner-occupied homes	(51) Deduction of property taxes on owner-occupied home
0 to $3,000	0.49	0.49	0.25	0.74	18.73	2.46	.25	......	0.25
$3,000 to $5,000	.79	.40	1.58	1.06	4.49	7.92	.92	1.72	3.17
$5,000 to $7,000	1.21	.73	3.87	1.33	9.79	10.88	1.09	6.29	7.98
$7,000 to $10,000	1.84	1.14	6.21	2.28	13.83	10.50	1.66	23.10	19.34
$10,000 to $15,000	2.63	1.57	9.34	2.63	19.06	12.54	2.63	55.54	36.55
$15,000 to $20,000	3.86	2.23	13.70	4.67	28.61	17.25	4.77	114.96	78.23
$20,000 to $50,000	14.21	8.33	33.31	14.88	126.25	46.64	10.88	230.74	196.98
$50,000 to $100,000	122.14	71.76	164.89	56.49	1,479.39	297.71	32.06	531.30	621.37
$100,000 and over	300.00	168.75	450.00	81.25	19,4321.25	968.75	68.75	593.75	1,331.25

Adjusted gross income class	(52) Deduction of casualty losses	(53) Deduction of charitable contributions (other than for education)	(54) Deduction of interest on consumer credit	(55) Untaxed capital gains at death [1]	(56) Deferral of income of controlled foreign corporations	(57) Asset depreciation range	Total average benefit for all preferences
0 to $3,000	......	0.74	......	4.44	......	......	267.44
$3,000 to $5,000	0.40	2.37	.92	1.06	......	......	229.32
$5,000 to $7,000	.48	8.10	3.14	2.18	......	.60	284.90
$7,000 to $10,000	1.58	16.63	11.64	3.15	......	.79	385.28
$10,000 to $15,000	3.39	27.90	27.77	4.39	.06	.63	556.36
$15,000 to $20,000	4.26	55.60	57.53	6.49	.20	1.01	901.08
$20,000 to $50,000	8.22	138.91	115.37	21.54	.78	4.00	1,933.60
$50,000 to $100,000	51.91	772.52	265.65	170.99	10.69	38.17	9,337.40
$100,000 and over	162.50	4,950.00	287.50	1,125.00	81.25	62.50	45,662.50

44 TAX POLITICS

lines or, for that matter, a $1,000 air conditioner for the office of its president, it is permitted to credit 7 percent of the cost—$70 in this case—against taxes. GM simply pays $70 less in taxes that year. The theory is that the $70 works as a reduction in cost; the credit is supposed to be an incentive for new purchases because the cost is lowered. In effect, it's subsidy equivalent to GM sending the government the $1,000 receipt and getting a $70 government rebate check by return mail.

The price tag on this simple tax subsidy is $4.5 billion annually. (The new 10 percent credit has raised this cost by at least $3 billion.) Instead of providing this corporate tax benefit, the government could cut individual taxes for every taxpayer in the country by almost $100 a year, stimulating consumer demand and creating new jobs.

The only complicated question about this simple, if expensive, tax device is: why attempt "'job development" by subsidizing the purchase price of new machinery? New machinery uses less labor than old; how many jobs can the government expect to create with a tax credit for machinery?

Former top Treasury tax economist Gerard Brannon was unable to discuss this crucial question while Congress passed the 1971 Revenue Act. Then, in 1972, he presented a technical paper showing the credit would create roughly 250,000 jobs annually. At $4.5 billion, the credit costs roughly $18,000 per new job. Concluded Brannon: "An important argument in the paper is that these incentives (the job development credit and accelerated depreciation] do not really relate to the level of employment. You can have full employment with or without high investment. . . . Full employment depends on the total fiscal program and the momentary policy, plus our ability to control inflation . . . ."

Besides predicting job development, Treasury Secretary Connally also foresaw the credit leading to important gains in industrial productivity. He was disputed by prominent economists, including Nobel prizewinner Paul Samuelson. In 1973, President Nixon's economic consultant, Pierre Rinfret, documented for Congress the weakness of Connally's prediction. Over 75 percent of major corporations replying to Rinfret's survey reported they would make "no change" in their investment programs because of the credit. This is a clue to the inefficiency of many tax incentives. Even though businesses didn't buy extra machinery because of the credit, they got the full 7 percent benefit on machinery they planned to buy anyway. A credit limited to extra purchases of machinery would have been much less expensive. Many businesses recognized that the more efficient credit would give them less money; it is no surprise that they lobbied for the less efficient, more generous subsidy.

The average taxpayer who foots the bill for such tax subsidies wasn't the only one who forgot to pay attention to the 1971 Revenue Act. The House of Representatives, which has constitutional responsibility for initiating all tax laws, spent a total of one hour and thirty-nine minutes debating the expensive bill. And its sponsor, Chairman Mills of Ways and Means, managed to bring the bill for a vote during lunch, so that only about thirty representatives were present! One hour and thirty-nine minutes of debate on a $7.8 billion annual corporate tax subsidy works out to roughly $80 million spent per minute of deliberation.

2. **Many tax incentives waste money by paying taxpayers for doing what they would do anyway**. We say this in the "job development credit," above. Another part of the 1971 Revenue Act, the DISC export subsidy, provides another good example of this wastefulness. As originally designed, DISC (the *Domestic International Sales Corporation* plan) essentially exempted businesses from paying federal income tax on one-half of their export profits.

Treasury Secretary Connally touted DISC as a means of increasing exports by $1.5 billion annually. But Connally didn't make clear to Congress what that meant. In 1971, American exports totaled roughly $40 billion. DISC, by increasing exports $1.5 billion, would mean a gain of a mere 4 percent over trade without DISC. But to get the extra 4 percent, DISC inefficiently wasted money on the other 96 percent of exports which are already there without the tax subsidy! The administration proposed essentially to exempt all export profits from income tax, not just extra exports. Much more efficient would have been a direct subsidy program which paid for *new* exports. As it

Tax Expenditures: The Hidden Federal Budget—A Key to Reform

is, we have a DISC program which costs $2 in lost tax revenue for every $1 of new exports! Fortunately, Congress hesitated to buy the whole idea, and only granted the subsidy for one-half of export profits. But the annual cost remains high: $1.3 billion in FY 1976, still a juicy corporate tax cut.

Why would Congress design a tax "incentive" which pays corporations mostly for activities they already carry out? One reason is equivocal data from the special interests hoping to benefit. The Union Carbide Corporation and Hewlett-Packard Corporation both submitted data to show how DISC would help them promote exports. In fact, economic analysis of the data revealed that both of the giant corporations would benefit most from DISC if they pocketed the tax windfall without increasing exports a single penny! By the time Senator Gaylord Nelson exposed the contradictions, it was too late for reform senators to mount an effective action to stop this expensive corporate tax give-away.

3. **Many tax incentives waste money because of fundamental flaws in design.** The tax exemption for state and local bonds is a classic example. The expensive tax subsidy benefited states and localities by some $1.9 billion in 1972, but at a $2.6 billion annual cost to the federal government. The "slippage" of $700 million amounts to 27 percent! The beneficiaries of the $700 million are banks and wealthy investors. Many alternatives are available. Direct revenue-sharing is one. Another is a direct federal subsidy for state and local bonds. By eliminating the wealthy middle people, the states and localities can receive more cash benefit, at the same cost to the federal government.

Other poorly designed tax subsidies include tax-exempt foundations, oil and mineral depletion allowances (which have cost us billions without forestalling the energy "crisis" we reportedly face), and the tax subsidy for pollution control facilities.

4. **Many tax incentives waste money by helping the rich rather than the economy.** Assuming for the moment that it is important to subsidize homeowing in America, a direct subsidy program would subsidize people who need just a bit more boney to buy a home; or it might concentrate on speciific regions, with special benefits for inner city homeowners or homeowners in the less populated regions of America, or whatever. The subsidy would be directed to accomplishing a specific national goal.

The home-mortgage interest tax deduction is a $3.5 billion annual tax subsidy which is *completely unrelated* to effective promotion of homeownership as a national goal. Any many, including the then Ways and Means Chairman Wilbur Mills, ask "Who can really say whether we might not have more and better housing in the United States if there were more of a market for rentals," rather than the expensive home-owner subsidy?

5. **Tax subsidies have often been wasteful because there has been no effort to coordinate tax expenditure programs with direct expenditure programs in the same area.** Tax expenditures are by far the largest single source of government subsidies, yet how can we formulate or evaluate our housing programs if we focus on the $3 billion in assistance administered by HUD and ignore almost $9 billion in tax expenditures for housing? Not surprisingly, this lack of coordination has resulted

★ **FIGURE 20. FEDERAL SUBSIDIES, FISCAL YEAR 1975 (In Millions of Dollars)** ★

Function	Direct Subsidies	Tax Subsidies	Loans	Benefits in Kind	Total
Agriculture:	$ 642	$ 1,100	$ 710	$ 17	$ 2,469
Food				5,863	5,863
Medical care	638	5,800	26	10,178	16,642
Manpower	3,334	700	0	68	4,102
Education	4,955	1,040	59	400	6,454
International trade	0	1,545	882	13	2,440
Housing	1,706	8,965	1,143	0	11,814
Natural resources	121	4,125	0	124	4,370
Transportation	574	50	0	1,724	2,348
Commerce & economic development	316	16,800	43	1,853	19,012
Other	0	13,050	54		13,104
	$12,286	$53,175	$2,917	$20,240	$88,618

SOURCE: Joint Economic Committee, Staff Study, "Federal Subsidy Programs," 1974.

in subsidy programs that often work at cross purposes or are at least inconsistent with stated national policy objectives.

Tax expenditures also account for billions of dollars in accelerated depreciation and preferential capital gains treatment which encourages many landlords to take tax losses out of their investments, let their properties deteriorate, and then sell them in five or six years to a new owner to start the process all over again. While many housing experts recognized that present tax preferences speed the deterioration of many rental units, the government has other direct programs and even a $100-million rapid tax write-off to encourage housing rehabilitation.

Of course tax expenditures for substantive programs are approved by congressional committees with no real expertise in the areas involved. Direct housing programs are developed and authorized by House and Senate subcommittees on housing that do nothing but study housing problems and solutions. Aid to education is approved by education committees that regularly look into the area. Energy programs are developed by energy subcommittees, and so on. There has often been criticism of congressional committees for not developing sufficient expertise to adequately handle the nation's problem. By and large this criticism has some basis. But the legislative committees involved do have expert staff and even the most uninvolved committee member has to develop some familiarity with the subject area. Indeed, a number of representatives are acknowledged experts in the areas of their committee jurisdiction.

But in the House Ways and Means Committee, where all tax legislation originates, there is little opportunity to develop expertise in many areas the committee has subsidized through our present tax expenditure program.

6. **Many tax expenditures are completely unneeded and are simply the product of successful lobbying effort on behalf of a particular special-interest group or the product of a tax expenditure phenomenon we call "me-too-ism."** Examples of the first are found throughout the tax code. They range from tailor-made provisions for unnamed but well-known individuals and corporations such as Louis B. Mayer, the DuPont family, and American Motors to powerful special interests like banking, oil, railroads, coal, and timber.

Often "me-too-ism" follows successful lobbying efforts by others. A good example of this would be the percentage depletion allowance. As with the apple Eve gave to Adam, the oil industry, with the help of oil baron and, then, Treasury Secretary Andrew Mellon polished up the 27.5 percent depletion allowance for oil and gas and presented it to the Congress in 1926. Since the Congress took a bite of that apple fifty years ago hundreds of industries have argued that they too should receive a depletion allowance, until today 114 different "minerals," including clay, gravel, sand, and even clam shells, are entitled to a depletion allowance. In 1974, the me-too process reached its logical extreme when the recycling industry asked for a depletion allowance for its junk—scrap metal, aluminum can throwaways, wastepaper, etc.—in order to be able to compete with virgin materials that presently received the depletion tax subsidy. They wanted a tax break in order to encourage recycling of the materials that other tax breaks encourage to be used up.

Ways and Means Committee member Sam Gibbons (D-Fla.), wondering about the logic of this "me-too" request, suggested that if we wanted to encourage recycling rather than the use of virgin material his committee should repeal all the existing depletion allowances instead of granting a new one. Obviously, Mr. Gibbons had not digested the rules of tax subsidy me-too-ism. Fortunately, for the industry, most of his committee did, and voted for a special tax break for the recycling industry.

7. **Tax subsidies can encourage the misallocation of resources and distort the normal market mechanism.** Obviously, this is what tax incentives and direct incentives are designed to do, but often many of the distorting effects of the system go unnoticed. The investment tax credit, for instance, makes it more profitable for a business to spend money on a new machine than to spend the same amount on teaching workers a new skill, even if both investments would increase the company's production by an identical amount.

Similarly, tax incentives for installing pollution control equip-

Tax Expenditures: The Hidden Federal Budget—A Key to Reform

ment make it more economical to install such devices than to spend an identical amount on controlling pollution by, for instance, purchasing low-sulfur fuel or developing a cleaner manufacturing process.

The depletion allowance is a good example of a tax subsidy that misallocates resources. It discourages the production of cheaper and more abundant sources of energy. First of all, depletion benefits for minerals are based on the value of those minerals in the ground and not in their final processed form. Therefore, a $7 barrel of crude oil gets the full benefits of the depletion allowance while a $7 barrel of oil made from coal will only receive depletion benefits on the value of the original coal. Since coal costs less than oil, the bulk of the $7 cost of liquefication lies in processing expenses. These do not qualify for depletion.

At present, a company that produces a $7 barrel of crude oil gets a tax bonus of about $1.30. A company producing the same $7 barrel from coal liquefaction would receive a bonus from the taxpayers of only ten cents. Of course, someone who develops solar energy at an equivalent price or designs a more efficient gas engine would receive no tax incentives at all.

When a tax subsidy is actually necessary to encourage a certain type of activity, it means that that activity cannot be economically pursued in the normal market. To put it another way, tax incentives are needed only where the undertaking is uneconomical and where it becomes profitable solely because of the tax subsidy. There may be some instances where, because of our national policy, we want to spend money to subsidize activity that would otherwise not be pursued. For example, we may want to give a subsidy, direct or indirect, to encourage the commercial development of electric cars that would otherwise not be built because they are too expensive and non-competitive.

But most tax subsidies are wasteful because they misallocate resources. Our present tax laws encourage the construction of new housing units and make them profitable from a tax point of view even if there is not a great market for that type of housing in a given area. Without all the tax subsidies a builder would only build an apartment house if people in the area needed apartments. If they needed houses, he would build houses because the demand would ensure that he could sell them. Thanks to tax incentives, in many areas in the country, money that should be spent on fixing up existing housing is instead spent on building suburban apartments or houses that may remain vacant.

In many instances these tax incentives become packaged as tax shelters for doctors, lawyers, executives, actors, and others far removed from the particular industry involved. These are the unintended beneficiaries of tax subsidies and account for a great deal of waste and inefficiency. They invest billions of dollars a year, often in questionable enterprises, simply to shelter their high income from taxes.

Tax shelters usually operate in three ways. The high income investor uses accelerated deductions generated from an investment to offset other income that would otherwise be taxed at high tax rates in the year earned. Using the rapid write-offs postpones payment of the tax to a later year when the investment is sold. This is the deferral aspect of a tax shelter. Deferral of taxes is similar to the government making a loan of the tax deferred without asking for interest or collateral. It is obviously of great benefit to the taxpayer.

The investor often will borrow money to invest in a tax shelter. (Interest on the loan is deductible.) Both his actual investment and this larger borrowed sum qualify for the deductions, often enabling the taxpayer to get deductions far in excess of his actual investment. That enables him to shelter even more of his ordinary income. This is known as the leverage aspect of the tax shelter.

In many tax shelter investments an investor isn't even liable for the borrowed money. This "non-recourse" financing occurs when a loan is made to the partnership backed up by the parnership's assets and not by the personal liability of the individual investor. But even though he has no personal stake in "his portion" of the loan, the investor can deduct his entire portion of the artificial losses.

Finally, when the taxpayer sells his investment and receives the ordinary income he originally sheltered, it is often taxed as a capital gain and only at one-half

48 TAX POLITICS

the rate that the original income would have been taxed.

A doctor, for example, may earn $50,000 a year from professional fees on which he would have to pay a 50 percent tax. But the doctor takes $1,000, borrows $9,000 more from his bank, and invests the full $10,000 in a cattle-feeding tax shelter syndicate. The syndicate takes his $10,000 and buys cattle feed at the end of the year even though it will not be delivered until the following spring. Ordinarily such expenses could only be deducted against related income from selling the cattle. But the Congress has permitted "farmers" to deduct immediately or "expense" those costs in the year they are made. The wealthy city investor becomes the beneficiary of this farm tax subsidy. This tax preference allows the doctor to deduct a $10,000 "loss" from his income that would otherwise be taxed at 50 percent—a tax savings of $5,000. With cattle feeding this could go on for five years sheltering, and therefore deferring taxes on, $5,000 a year, or $25,000 in tax savings. Typically, at the end of five years, the syndicate will sell the doctor's share of the cattle for, say, $50,000—the amount of the original investment. It looks like the doctor breaks even. But actually he is a big winner. He has been able to offset $50,000 ($10,000 a year for five years) of professional fees, otherwise taxable at 50 percent by the "tax loss" from the cattle feeding investment and, on the sale of the investment, has, in effect, included the $50,000 of fees in income that, because of our tax

★ **FIGURE 21. HOW TAX SHELTERS WORK**

As part of their work on closing tax shelter opportunities, the Ways and Means Committee, in 1975, reviewed a number of tax shelter syndicates and the tax returns of those who invested in them. Here are two of 37 individual tax returns the Committee made public (after deleting all identifying taxpayer data). They indicate how tax shelter operations generate huge artificial losses and how those losses are

CASE NO. 1
Partnership Return

Type of business: Real estate.
Date of startup: December 28.

Capital contributed by partners	225,000
Liabilities of partnership	0
Income	0
Expenses	215,000
Interest	197,000
Depreciation	0
Real estate taxes	0
Management and syndication fees	0
Net loss	215,000
Net loss as a percent of capital contribution	95.6%

Individual Income Tax Return

Occupation: Executive.

Wages and salaries	427,000
Dividends and interest	4,000
Capital gains (100%)	0
Partnership profit and loss	−410,000
Real estate (3 shelters)	−385,000
Farm	−25,000
Other income	16,000
Economic income	448,000
Adjusted gross income	37,000
Itemized deductions	27,000
Taxable income	7,000
Income tax	1,200
Minimum tax	0
Tax credits	0
Total tax after credits	1,200
Tax as a percent of economic income	0.3%

Analysis

The real estate partnership commenced operations on December 28 and lost $215,000. Expenses consisted of $151,000 of interest on a construction loan (presumably prepaid interest), $25,000 of commitment fees, $21,000 of guaranteed financing fees, and $18,000 for advertising and startup rental costs. For each $1.00 invested in this partnership, the partners were able to deduct 95 cents in the first taxable year, which was only 3 days in length.

This individual had wages of $427,000. Almost all of his income was sheltered by investments in real estate and farm partnerships.

Tax Expenditures: The Hidden Federal Budget—A Key to Reform

used by high income individuals to shelter their other income. (An analysis of all these tax returns appears in "Tax Shelter Investments: Analysis of 37 Individual Income Tax Returns," a pamphlet available from the Ways and Means Committee, U.S. House of Representatives, Washington, D.C. 20515.)

CASE NO. 13

Small Business Corporation Return

Type of business: Cattle.	
Date of startup: December 21.	
Capital contributed	150,000
Liabilities	431,000
Income	0
Expenses	225,000
Interest	16,000
Depreciation	0
Management and syndication fees	0
Feed	209,000
Net loss	225,000
Net loss as a percent of capital contribution	150.0%

Individual Income Tax Return

Occupation: Businessman.	
Wages and salaries	7,000
Dividends and interest	1,000
Capital gains (100%)	−1,000
Small Business Corporation and partnership profit and loss:	
Cattle feeding	−225,000
Business income	388,000
Other income	0
Economic income	396,000
Adjusted gross income	170,000
Itemized deductions	32,000
Taxable income	135,000
Income tax	47,000
Minimum tax	0
Tax credits	0
Total tax after credits	47,000
Tax as a percent of economic income	11.9%

Analysis

This cattle-feeding operation is a small business corporation. It was in business for only nine days but incurred $16,000 in interest and $209,000 in feed expenses. Its assets consist entirely of $75,000 in cash and $281,000 in cattle. The business is highly leveraged, with $150,000 in capital contributed by the shareholders and $431,000 in liabilities.

The owner of the corporation had $388,000 in income from his business and about $8,000 of other income. He deducted the entire $225,000 loss from the small business corporation.

laws, is considered a capital gain on the sale of an asset and taxed at only half the rate—or 25 percent. Not only has he deferred the taxes on his fees but he has cut those taxes in half. And he did it with someone else's money to boot.

The very nature of a tax shelter is wasteful. First of all, many tax shelters, billions of dollars worth annually, are "packaged" by promoters who get commissions and fees for their services—sometimes approaching 50 percent of the investment. Some of the investment dollars, even if these activities were economically sound, are siphoned off by middlemen who receive a good deal of the tax expenditure money themselves.

Secondly, because of the tax benefits of shelters, the investments don't have to be economically sound to be profitable to the high bracket taxpayer. Because of tax deferral and capital gains rates, the investment can lose money, while still providing significant economic benefits to wealthy taxpayers. The Treasury Department's Individual Statistics of Income for 1972 show that American millionaires are still the world's worst farmers even though they continue to get rich through the magic of the tax code.

In that year, 49 millionaires made $4,298,000 from farm operations—but 125 managed to lose—generally for tax purposes—$16,444,000 on farm operations. In other words, these otherwise very successful business people "lost" an average of $131,552 each in farming. A House Report on the 1969 Tax Reform Act noted that the tax laws "have allowed some high income taxpayers who carry on limited farming activities as a sideline to obtain a tax loss (but not an economic loss) which is deducted from their high-bracket non-farm income." In the strange world of tax shelters, according to representative Charles Vanik of Ohio, "going broke" for the tax-loss farmer really means making hay.

Tax-loss farming has other bad effects. The price of farmland has been artificially bid up by tax-loss farm investors. Critics have argued that the overproduction of beef which plagued the industry into a crisis during 1974 was due in part to cattle-feeding ventures set up as tax shelters for wealthy investors. And these unfair tax rules create an unfair competition for the real farmer and introduce price instability into the marketplace.

It is estimated that tax shelter operations cost the Treasury over $2 billion a year. Aside from their obvious effect on tax avoidance, tax shelters often channel money into marginally productive or nonproductive enterprises at the expense of other more productive investments. They channel money into areas where there may not be large consumer demand, or areas that are less socially desirable. In other words, they replace consumer demand as the allocation of investment. One witness during the 1973 Ways and Means Committee tax reform hearings described the tax shelter for raising rosebushes: "It is difficult to believe the United States is in the throes of a rosebush crisis." But the fact is that many investors put their money into rosebushes with the sole objective of generating "tax losses" and thereby sheltering their high incomes.

the savings interest exemption—evaluating a new tax expenditure

How does our knowledge of how tax expenditures work apply to a new tax proposal—one that almost became law in 1974? At the urging of thousands of savings and loan associations across the country dozens of members of Congress sponsored legislation to totally exempt from taxes up to $500 in interest ($1,000 for a married couple) received from deposits in a savings account. The bill, appealingly called the Small Savers Act of 1974, made two basic pitches to representatives. First, it was promoted, according to its chief Ways and Means sponsor, Donald Brotzman, as a break for the "little guy"—the average person with a small savings account. Second, according to its proponents, it would attract greater savings money into the savings and loan associations which could, in turn, increase the amount of mortgage money available to bolster the sagging housing market.

At first, the proposal attracted a great deal of support and was approved overwhelmingly by the House Ways and Means Committee. But let's ask the important budget questions that the members of Congress should have asked and answered before supporting this new tax expenditure. Who are the intended beneficiaries of the program? Will they actually be benefited? Are there unintended beneficiaries? Will people receive too much or too little of the benefits? What is the cost of the program? Do the benefits justify the costs? Can the objectives be achieved more efficiently and economically through another program?

First, let's look at the intended beneficiaries—the small saver. This sounds appealing at first blush. Small savers would like to get the same break on their savings as those wealthy individuals who can save by investing in stocks with special capital-gains treatment or tax-free bonds. The real answer, however, is to end those other special preferences. In any case, it's not much of a break for the small saver. As Ways and Means Committee member Sam Gibbons (D-Fla.) explains, "the bill would give $700 to Nelson and Happy Rockefeller and $11.97 to Edith and Archie Bunker [of TV fame]."

That's because the Rockefellers have savings of at least $19,050. At the current 5.25 percent interest rate on passbook savings, they would earn interest of $1,000—all of which is exempt. Since they're in the 70 percent tax bracket, they would otherwise have had to pay taxes of $700 on this interest. But statistics show that the average American couple has savings of only $1,200 and thus earn interest of only $63 per year. If they are in the 19 percent tax bracket, excluding this interest from taxation saves them

Tax Expenditures: The Hidden Federal Budget—A Key to Reform

only $11.97. Moreover, wealthy families with savings of more than $19,050 could place some of their savings account in the names of each of their children. For example, if they have three children, the family could receive annual interest of $2,500 tax-free.

The Treasury Department estimates that federal tax revenues would drop by $2 billion every year and half of this amount would go to the wealthiest 10 percent of the population. Those two-thirds of American families who have savings of less than $2,000 would receive few benefits. Of course, the poorest 38 percent of the population, who are simply unable to save at all, would receive nothing. This contrasts sharply with other proposals now before Congress—such as raising the low income allowance and the standard deduction—which would tend to grant more tax relief where it is needed.

So, in spite of its name, the bill benefits rich people in particular, and banks in general, which would receive the increased savings. But will it still effectively accomplish the worthwhile goal of stimulating the housing market by increasing mortgage money?

Practically speaking, most people cannot afford to save too much more money even though they'll get a tax benefit, because the cost of living is rising so rapidly. The tax exemption would also automatically apply to all savings already on deposit and this would be of little use in stimulating additional mortgage money. In addition, most new deposits would result from wealthy persons switching money out of one pocket—stocks and bonds—and into another—savings.

Once such a switch has occurred, it cannot occur again. Therefore, virtually all of the flow of funds into homebuilding would occur immediately—in future years there would be little or no benefit.

The bill was initially promoted by savings and loan associations, which frequently channel 80 percent of their deposits into home loans. Then commercial banks, which typically channel a much smaller fraction (about 10 percent) of their deposits into home loans, reluctantly decided they needed the same break to stay competitive. This is the same "me-too" process that produced a depletion allowance not only for oil but also for oyster shells and clams.

Based on historical relationships between rates of return on competing investments, economists estimate that the amount of money switched into savings institutions would total $10 billion. Such institutions would typically use one-third of their deposits, or $3.5 billion, for mortgage loans. Thus, obtaining a one-time switch of $3.5 billion out of other investments into mortgages will continue to cost the Treasury $2 billion each year that no taxes are paid on savings account interest. After, say, ten years the Treasury will have forfeited $20 billion just to have channeled $3.5 billion into housing. It would be a lot less expensive to simply give away $3.5 billion to the banks.

Obviously, this tax expenditure is very costly and almost embarrassingly inefficient. No budget director who wanted to keep his job would propose such a direct subsidy program. But is there an economical way of providing for more mortgages and stimulating house construction through a direct subsidy?

The tax expenditure program with its new $3.5 billion increase in mortgages was estimated to cause as many as 300,000 new houses to be built. At the same time, Senator William Proxmire (D-Wisc.), then Senate housing subcommittee chairman, advocated a direct subsidy to lenders to allow them to lower their mortgage interest rates. This direct subsidy would cost $300 million and was estimated to add 500,000 new houses. In other words, the direct subsidy plan would stimulate more new housing at only one-sixth the cost of the proposed tax expenditure. Obviously, members of Congress should have asked these questions, found the answers, and rejected this expensive and wasteful subsidy.

After a great deal of lobbying from public interest groups, the Treasury Department and some members of Congress, representatives began to realize that the tax expenditure was a very bad idea. Ironically, however, many who privately conceded that the bill's surface appeal is grossly misleading nonetheless insisted they dare not go on record as voting against it. Aside from lobbying pressure by savings institutions and builders these representatives feared that misinformed constituents would mis-

52 TAX POLITICS

interpret a "no" vote as a vote against homebuilding and small savers.

This cynicism as to the public's ability to understand complex tax legislation and congressional lawmaking procedures is all too commonplace. For too long, many representatives have assumed a public posture as tax reformers while quietly relying on public misunderstanding and convenient procedural roadblocks to avoid offending vested interests by actually eliminating tax loopholes. The public should learn to look behind public pronouncements and demand real results from those spending their tax revenues.

why tax expenditures are good—reasons from the other side

We have seen why tax incentives are a poor substitute for direct expenditures. But there are those—primarily the recipients of tax subsidies—who argue that there are other advantages to the use of tax expenditures as a means of subsidizing certain activities. Let's take a look at some of the asserted advantages of subsidization through the tax system.

Direct subsidies require large government bureaucracy and control. Tax subsidies are simpler and involve less government supervision.

There are really two arguments being made here. One is that tax incentives can be more efficient because of the lack of red tape and detailed control. The other is that direct incentives are often wasteful because of the large administrative costs of a government bureaucracy. Neither argument really stands up to closer scrutiny.

Professor Surrey discusses the fallacy of this first argument with regard to the work incentive (WIN) tax credit for manpower training and employment. The WIN program was described on the Senate floor by Senator Charles Percy:

Employers who participate in the program will receive a tax credit of 75 percent of wages paid to the employee for the first four months of employment, 50 percent for the next four months, and 25 percent for the balance of the individual's first year of employment. This is an uncomplicated program with the minimum of red tape. Any employer who hires a certified employee is eligible for the tax credit—it is as simple as that.

But Professor Surrey points out that, whether the subsidy is direct or indirect, this is nothing more than saying: "Let's have a manpower program under which the government pays an employer who hires a certified employee an amount calculated as a percentage of the employee's wage." He goes on to add:

Direct expenditure programs can also be structured to pay out government money with few administrative controls. Thus, if an employer can obtain government funds (i.e., a reduction in tax through the tax credit) for his employment activities by filling out a schedule or a tax return, a direct manpower program could be devised instead under which he would receive the same monetary assistance by filling out the exact same schedule on a piece of paper that had "Department of Labor" at the top in place of "Internal Revenue Service."

The point is that it is the substantive design of the program that determines its simplicity. If direct programs in the past have been overstructured with too much red tape, the answer is to create more efficiently designed expenditure programs. We cannot cure a badly designed expenditure by simply substituting the check-writing process of direct grants with tax deductions or credits.

The second argument, that direct programs have large administrative costs, ignores the fact that many tax subsidies require a huge government bureaucracy for administration. That huge bureaucracy is called the IRS. In the five years FY 1968 through 1972, IRS estimates it spent 2.3 million man-hours—at a cost of about $18.2 million—auditing and otherwise administering the depletion allowance for oils and minerals. To administer the tax subsidy for foundations and other tax-exempt organizations, IRS estimates it spent 8.9 million man-hours, at a cost of $60.3 million in the same five-year-period. And the capital gains subsidy costs IRS roughly 21 million man-hours *annually* to administer. Obviously, administrative costs occur in both direct programs and tax programs.

IRS administration raises an important question. The IRS is supposed to be expert at tax collection. Can we also demand that IRS know enough engineering and geology to administer oil and mineral depletion, enough social science to determine a "charity" for tax purposes, and enough business science to analyze transactions for capital gains? Indeed, with the many different deductions open to taxpayers, one auditing agent may have to decide on many of these at once.

At least when HUD administers a housing subsidy, or the Office of Education a school subsidy, we know the civil servants are trained in housing or education. An IRS agent may know tax law, but we can't expect he will know all of the subsidies, too.

Tax incentives promote pluralism—decision-making by individual taxpayers rather than by government.

Businessmen often complain about government intervention. They talk of the merits of the free enterprise system allowing individual choice in business planning as well as in solving social problems. Of course, what they are really arguing for, when promoting tax incentives, is massive governmental assistance without governmental interference. Such a governmental assistance program can be designed with minimum interference or central decision-making whether it is a tax subsidy or a direct subsidy. In some areas this is a desirable goal and in others there may be a need to have more accountability of government funds. But in either case the design of the program and not whether it is direct or indirect will determine the role of private decision-making.

Presently, for instance, states and localities can use the funds they borrow through tax-exempt bonds in any manner the local government chooses. The same would be true of a direct expenditure program subsidizing part of the interest they pay to the bondholders. In both cases, the local government's decision to issue the bonds would automatically trigger the federal assistance. There would be no direct federal involvement in the decision.

Similarly, a direct expenditure program of matching grants for individual gifts to charities would also promote private decision-making. A direct program could preserve the asserted virtue of the charitable deduction tax expenditure whereby the taxpayer chooses the charity and determines how much to give rather than government deciding which charities to support and not support. And, in fact, many of our tax incentives actually undermine this goal of pluralism. The present charitable deduction gives no government assistance to the charities of those taxpayers who take the standard deduction and gives inordinately high assistance to the charities of the very wealthy. This has the effect of placing decisions as to which charities the governmental assistance will go in the hands of a very small number of people. According to the American Council on Education, for example, only 1 percent of all donors gave 75 percent of the gifts to higher education in 1967-68. Pluralism could be better promoted by giving some governmental assistance to everyone's charities through matching grants and not just to the charities of a wealthy few through charitable deductions.

This, then, is the case against tax subsidies. Compared to direct government subsidies, they are hidden from public view and the democratic processes which might discover and eliminate inefficiencies. Tax subsidy programs escape cost-benefit analysis. They tend to benefit the rich instead of those who could make efficient use of a cash incentive. They tend to pay people for considerable activity that is profitable in the first place. Or they create tax shelters diverting investment into "tax-loss" situations of questionable need. Many suffer from fundamentally poor design. And all must be policed and administered by the huge IRS bureaucracy. The real problem with tax subsidies is the way Congress creates and perpetuates them: the two tax committees have not squarely faced their responsibilities for massive intervention in the American economy and society with tax subsidies amounting to some $91 billion annually.

And average taxpayers have to get the message about tax loopholes. They may think they benefit from them but they don't. They may tolerate them as necessary incentives but often there are more efficient and less expensive ways to give incentives.

Ferdinand Lundberg, author of *The Rich and the Super-Rich*, is outraged at the support of rich people's loopholes by average taxpayers. "The government encourages everyone to feel he is getting away with something by advising all to be sure to take all the deductions—exemptions they are entitled to on the labyrinthian tax form. And they are many. After correctly filling out this form the average taxpayer has the delicious feeling that he has once again outwitted a grasping bureaucracy," says Lundberg. But it is only a "con game."

"It is much like participating in a crooked card game in which, one is assured, everyone is cheating. So why not take what comes one's way? But where an ordinary player is allowed to 'get away' with $200, favored players somehow get away with $200,000, $2 million, or even $20 million. The small players pay for this in the end." The average taxpayer pays for tax breaks in reduced government services, increased taxes or huge federal deficits.

Major Items of the Tax Expenditure Budget: An Analysis

Deductibility of State and Local Taxes .... $9.950 Billion

The deduction for state and local taxes will cost the Treasury almost $10 billion in FY 1976. As a tax expenditure item, it probably presents a needed expenditure to the states. By softening the actual bite of state and local taxes, the deduction allows states and localities to increase their taxes at the expense of the federal treasury. It is really a type of revenue-sharing giving these governments about $10 billion a year in increased revenues.

Unlike revenue-sharing, however, the benefits of the deduction are unfair, increasing only as the taxpayer's income bracket increases. At the same time the deduction includes general sales taxes and, therefore, further compounds the already regressive aspects of those taxes. Low and moderate income families are asked to pay a greater percentage of their incomes in sales taxes and receive little or no relief from the deduction for those taxes.

Probably the least justifiable deduction is that for the state gasoline tax. This tax is really a charge for the use of public roads. The proceeds of the tax are used for the benefit of those who pay it. But deductibility places part of the costs of the tax on the general taxpayer who may not drive. And the deduction is unfair. On a state gasoline tax of 8 cents, a 70 percent bracket taxpayer actually pays out-of-pocket about 2.5 cents a gallon, while the average 25 percent wage earner pays 6 cents out-of-pocket as a contribution to public highways. The gasoline tax deduction should be repealed, restoring equity, and saving the government about $865 million.

A general revenue-sharing program was enacted in 1972. It would seem to make sense to "spend" the $10 billion that presently goes uncollected on additional revenue-sharing that would bring assistance directly to the states and localities rather than to high bracket taxpayers. Eliminating the present inequitable tax deductions and replacing them with a revenue-sharing program would be the most rational way to provide this assistance to state and local governments. At a very minimum, the deduction for these taxes should be replaced with a tax credit that would relieve all taxpayers' state and local tax burdens equally.

Deductibility of Home Mortgage Interest .... $6.500 Billion

Deductibility of Property Taxes .... $5.270 Billion

Homeowners are favored by two major tax expenditures which we have already discussed, the deduction for home mortgage interest and the deduction for homeowner property taxes. These tax provisions allow you to skip all federal income taxes on income you use to pay your home mortgage interest and property taxes on your home, thereby reducing your costs of homeownership. These deductions are justified on two major grounds: (1) they help promote homeownership, supposed to be a major value in American life, and (2) they provide middle class taxpayers with some tax benefits, just as wealthier taxpayers may benefit from provisions such as capital gains or tax-free bonds. In addition, the property tax deduction like other state tax deductions is justified as a means of federal relief for the state and local governments, which depend on the property tax for revenue. It is argued that the income tax deduction allows state and local governments to increase their property tax rates correspondingly. The widespread use of these homeowner tax deductions is reflected in their considerable cost: all taxpayers together save some $6.5 billion annually in income taxes through use of the home mortgage interest deduction; taxpayers save a total of $5.3 billion annually in income taxes from the homeowner property tax deductions. In 1972, some twenty-two million Americans claimed the property tax deduction and eighteen million claimed the home mortgage interest deduction.

Of course, the homeowner deductions do not benefit two groups of Americans: (1) the 58 percent of the taxpayers who do not take itemized deductions, but take the standard deduction even if they own homes; and (2) the 40 percent of Americans who rent rather than own their own homes. Moreover, as we have seen, the home mortgage interest deduction and homeowner property tax deduction benefit high income taxpayers much more than average or lower income taxpayers. In fact, in 1974 the average taxpayer saved an average of $92.09 from these deductions, while the $100,000 and above income group benefited by an average of $1.925—twenty times as much. If these deductions were eliminated completely, everyone's taxes could be cut by about $150.

Any reform of tax expenditures for housing must take place within the context of an over-all look at our present housing policies as promoted through both tax subsidies and direct subsidies. This promises to be a lengthy but necessary task to ensure some rationality to our nation's housing programs. Obviously, homeownership could be more efficiently subsidized through a system of direct interest subsidies pinpointed for particular groups and particular types of housing.

The benefit of the homeowner property tax deduction, since it so heavily favors high income homeowners, does not provide nearly the broad property tax relief to a community that could be provided by a more evenly distributed tax subsidy, a direct grant such as revenue-sharing, or some other federal subsidy method. But in the interim, several modifications should be made of the existing tax expenditures for homeownership.

They should be limited to relief for primary residences, ending the benefits they bestow for owning second homes. There should also be a limit on the amount of a mortgage and value of the property that the tax system will subsidize. Finally, the deductions should give way to a credit that gives all taxpayers the same benefits for each dollar of interest and taxes spent. One reform proposal whose cost would be equal to the present deductions is to allow a tax credit of 25 percent of the costs of homeownership but no tax benefit would be available for property taxes on the portion of the assessed valuation of a home in excess of $70,000. Interest paid with respect to the portion of any mortgage in excess of $50,000 on a primary residence would yield no tax benefit either.

Deductibility of Gifts to Charity (including Education) .... $5.430 Billion

Another major tax expenditure is the income tax deduction for charitable contributions. This subsidy allows you to skip all federal income taxes, up to certain limits, on all of your income that you contribute to charity. What this means is that every dollar you contribute to charity contains a percentage of federal subsidy in the form of income taxes the government has declined to collect. For example, a cash gift to his college by an individual in the 70 percent bracket is equivalent to a government expenditure of $70 and a net cost to the taxpayer of $30. But if a 25 percent bracket taxpayer gives $100 to the same college the government picks up on $25 of the gift. Those who do not itemize deductions or pay no federal income taxes get no help at all from the government on their $100 gift.

Professor Paul McDaniel of Boston College Law School points out that the absurdity of this kind of tax expenditure becomes clear if we view it in direct expenditure terms. A direct grant system that mirrored the present tax deduction would provide grants by the federal government of $7 for each $3 contributed to charity by $200,000-a-year families. For families earning $50,000 the government would give $5 for each $5 contributed by the family. For $16,000-a-year families, the government would give $2.50 for each $7.50 contributed. The effect of this upside-down subsidy is that the more money people have to give, the less a gift will cost them. The less money they have, the more the gift will cost.

The inequity of the charitable deduction is compounded when wealthy individuals donate property that has increased in value. Not only is the full value of the property deducted from present income but the income represented from the gain is never taxed. Suppose a wealthy 70 percent taxpayer makes a gift of a share of stock worth $100 for which he paid one dollar ten years ago. The government grants the taxpayer a $70 tax reduction for the gift plus a tax reduction of $34.65 by forgiving the 35 percent capital gains tax on the $99 gain. In other words, the government is paying $104.65 to encourage a gift of $100. Obviously, this is not a very efficient way of encouraging charitable gifts. It also points out the unfairness in a tax deduction that bestows a much greater benefit on a gift consisting of appreciated property than on cash of an identical value.

In spite of its unfairness and irrationality, the charitable deduction tax expenditure remains in its present form because of powerful and vocal support from charities, religious groups, and colleges and universities. These groups justify the deduction as an incentive for taxpayers to donate to private religious, educational, and philanthropic organizations. Recently however, several tax experts have taken issue with the claim that the $5.4 billion cost of this subsidy is worth the benefits of increased charitable giving. One major economic study indicates that the federal tax benefit had virtually no effect on over 99 percent of taxpayers with incomes below $100,000 who made charitable donations. The remaining very small fraction of taxpayers provided only 10 percent of all donations. (This is reasonable, considering that the taxpayers above $100,000 had much more to contribute.) Of course, the 58 percent of taxpayers who took the standard deduction in 1972 made their sizable charitable contributions without receiving any tax benefits at all. The actual benefits to middle income taxpayers ($10,000-$15,000) averaged only $29.15 in 1974, while the wealthy taxpayer (over $100,000) gained an average of $6,200 from the tax expenditure.

As discussed earlier, proponents of the charitable contribution argue it is an important alternative to government decision-making as to which charities or educational institutions should be supported. Ironically, however, the result of the present system is to subsidize especially those charities favored by the rich and to grant the greatest government support to educational institutions with wealthy alumni and large endowments. Perhaps the proponents of the present system should borrow a page from the recently enacted campaign finance laws and encourage more smaller gifts in an effort to increase the pluralism in American life and decrease the influence of the wealthy few who already have too much to say about how the country and its institutions are run. A system of federal matching grants or, at a minimum, a tax credit system would

Tax Expenditures: The Hidden Federal Budget—A Key to Reform

provide some incentive to all donors (government grants or credits of 25 to 50 cents on the dollar would cost no more than the present tax deduction).

Of course, some present "generous" givers would no longer find it as advantageous to give to charities in order to avoid taxes under a reformed system. The universities have complained that many of their very large donors would give much less. If this is true, we could take some of the money we would get by collecting more taxes from these wealthy people and consider increasing direct federal aid to education.

A direct program could be designed with a minimum amount of government involvement if desired. After all, should not all educational institutions receive federal assistance and not just those lucky enough to have wealthy graduates. The present system allows for the inordinate influence of a few wealthy donors in the educational affairs of these institutions and perpetuates the idea that the rich get richer.

Deductibility of Interest on Consumer Credit .... $3.460 Billion

The present tax laws allows taxpayers to deduct interest they pay on consumer loans—automobile loans, carrying charges on bank credit cards or gasoline credit cards, and similar interest charges. This tax expenditure amounts to a $3.5 billion grant of governmental assistance for buying "on time." Leaving aside the wisdom of encouraging individuals to buy on credit, the assistance is really misdirected. As with the other deductions we have studied, the deduction of interest on consumer credit benefits those who are better off and able to purchase more expensive items. For example, in 1974 the middle income taxpayer (between $10,000 and $15,000) gained an average tax savings of $27.77 from the deduction, while taxpayers in the $100,000 and over bracket saved $287.50 on the average. There is, of course, no benefit to low and middle income purchasers, who use the standard deduction or pay no tax, even though they are most burdened by installment purchases and high interest charges.

Obviously, interest on loans secured to produce income (business loans) should be deductible as a cost of making that income. But this legitimate business deduction should not be used as an excuse for allowing all interest to be deducted. Those who want to keep this expensive tax expenditure argue it would be too complicated to separate out loans made for business purposes (i.e., purchasing shares of stock) and those made to simply buy, for instance, a diswasher or a car. To get around this problem, interest up to the amount of someone's investment income could be deductible. This will ensure that the taxpayer's income is not overstated since the interest on a loan used in investment is part of the cost of producing that income. At the same time, this will result in excluding approximately 75 percent of the interest currently deducted.

Since the government does not grant assistance to people who buy automobiles, furniture, washing machines, or other consumer goods, it is difficult to rationalize giving assistance through the tax code to people who decide to buy those very same items on credit and pay interest. Not only is the deduction unfair, it is unneeded and wasteful. This very expensive tax expenditure should be ended.

Deductibility of Medical Expenses .... $2.630 Billion

Deductions for medical expenses are allowed because these types of expenses are often unpredictable and involuntary and can use up a large part of a person's income. It is felt that people in these circumstances should pay lower taxes than those in the same income group because their income has been reduced unavoidably and they, therefore, have less ability to pay taxes. But

58 TAX POLITICS

the present deduction provides the greatest help for those who least need it and no help for those who need it the most.

Few would disagree that help is needed to provide adequate health care for all Americans. Using the tax system, however, for subsidizing medical expenses and part of the cost of medical insurance (up to $150) does not provide the kind of comprehensive and fair help we need. It's hard to justify the government paying a greater percentage of a well-to-do family's doctor's bills while paying less to a middle income family. But in 1974, those well-to-do families (making more than $100,000) received an average tax break of $443.75 from these deductions, and $10,000 to $15,000-a-year families saved an average of only $30.15. The $2.6 billion involved would be much better spent on a program of comprehensive health insurance and health care for everyone.

If we are to continue giving aid through the tax system, it should be limited to truly extraordinary expenses. The present 3 percent floor, below which you get no deductions, is not a sufficient measure of extraordinary expenses and should be raised to its original 5 percent level. And the assistance above that amount should come in the form of a tax credit that gives equal assistance to everyone who has a large medical expense.

The Asset Depreciation Range (ADR) System . . . . $1.590 Billion

The fourth major tax subsidy in the form of a deduction is called "accelerated depreciation." While the homeowner and charitable deductions were for personal use, this accelerated depreciation deduction applies to business equipment.

Depreciation is simply the loss in value of property as the property gets older. For example, if you buy a new typewriter for $500, and you expect it to have an operating lifetime of five years, the average yearly depreciation is $100 per year in loss of value. If you buy the typewriter for business purposes you can deduct (or "write off," as it is also called) $100 depreciation each year as a cost of doing business. At the end of five years, just as the typewriter is ready for the junk-heap, you have written off the entire cost from your taxes. This method, of $100 a year, is so-called straight-line depreciation. The tax laws, however, offer a special kind of depreciation deduction known as "accelerated depreciation." This means, for example, that you can take a $125 deduction for the typewriter over four years, instead of $100 over five years. You are getting an extra $25 deduction in each of the first four years; in other words, you are postponing taxes on $25 each year. The result: an interest-free loan to you in the form of your tax savings over the first four years.

This may sound like a small point, but the asset depreciation range (ADR), an accelerated depreciation provision for business equipment and machinery, will amount to a tax savings of $2.9 billion annually for individual and corporate businesses over the decade: ADR allows a business or individual to "write-off" business equipment and machinery at an arbitrary 20 percent faster than they are actually wearing out or being replaced. At the same time, ADR eliminates the reserve ratio test—a Treasury device that was designed to calculate the actual replacement policies of particular businesses to ensure they were depreciating their plant and equipment properly.

Advocates of accelerated depreciation for machinery and equipment point to the incentives for business investments provided by the subsidy. On the average, one economist has calculated, ADR reduces the cost of a piece of business equipment by roughly 4 percent annually. This, combined with other tax subsidies, it is said, provides a powerful inducement for business to modernize through purchase of new equipment. Given the huge cost of this tax subsidy the question arises as to whether or not ADR is an efficient means of stimulating business investment.

There is little evidence that the ADR system has much effect on capital investment and it is a poor device to stimulate a slack economy. Most businesses make decisions on equipment purchases on what will increase profits and meet existing or anticipated levels of demand. If an industry is operating at full capacity, it will attempt to increase profits by increasing capacity through the purchase of new equipment. If it

Tax Expenditures: The Hidden Federal Budget—A Key to Reform 59

is not operating at full capacity, the purchase of new equipment would be unwise and fail to create new jobs or higher profits. In fact, when ADR was first proposed, about 25 percent of the nation's plant capacity was already unused.

The fact that businesses rely on factors other than ADR to make their investment decisions is exemplified in the small percentage of corporations who find this tax incentive useful in their economic planning. In a Capital Sentiment Survey conducted by Dr. Pierre Rinfret, 90.6 percent of those corporations surveyed indicated that the ADR incentive would not cause them to increase their capital spending for 1972. This means that in that year at least 90 percent of ADR's cost would be in expenditures to subsidize machinery and equipment purchases that would be made anyway. This accelerated depreciation simply acts as a tax cut for selected business enterprises. While some of the incentive money might go into increased investment, much of it will simply go into the pockets of investors as increased profits.

ADR is also promoted as a spur toward increased employment. But besides increasing profits, the major economic effect of a subsidy like ADR actually will be to increase the use of labor-saving machinery by business. Since depreciation provides tax savings for companies using new equipment but not for companies employing additional manpower, businesses will tend to become relatively more automated, thereby reducing the proportion of people employed.

Finally, ADR in effect discriminates against other important types of investment. ADR, like the investment tax credit, is a subsidy for capital-intensive industries—those that rely most heavily on machinery. It gives those industries a comparative advantage over less capital-intensive industries. The result is not necessarily that we will be increasing total production but, rather, that we will be producing more of those products that receive the tax subsidy and less of the less capital-intensive goods such as food. And, of course, the more basic question is whether we want to be stimulating spending on machinery as opposed to investment in human capital (training), in education, in health, or in research.

Our present tax system creates a distortion in existing markets and in the competition between different types of needed investments. Given the appropriateness of investment decisions being based on normal market assumptions the tax monies spent on purchasing plant equipment and machinery would be better spent on a general tax reduction to stimulate consumer demand. And if there is to be an incentive to increase investment spending, some form of direct subsidy or tax credit is a far more effective device. The ADR system should be repealed.

Accelerated Depreciation for Real Estate .... $1.020 Billion

Accelerated depreciation is also available for investments in real estate. Presently, rental housing can be depreciated up to twice as fast as straight-line depreciation. This tax expenditure will be worth $540 million to investors in FY 1976. Since some reforms were enacted in 1969, commercial and industrial buildings have a reduced accelerated depreciation of from 125 to 150 percent of straight-line. This more limited tax expenditure will still be worth $490 million to investors of nonresidential buildings in FY 1976. In addition, the 1969 Tax Reform Act expanded the "recapture" of accelerated depreciation of nonresidential buildings. Recapture forces the investor to pay taxes at the time the building is sold on the income that was initially deferred. But obviously recapture is not a complete remedy for excessive depreciation, since the taxpayer still has the benefit of deferring the taxes owed in earlier years to the later year of sale—another interest-free loan from the Treasury. Of course, if the taxpayer doesn't sell the building but rather gives it away or bequeaths it to his children, the excess depreciation will never be recaptured. The real estate investor also has the advantage, discussed earlier, of receiving depreciation for the entire property even though the bulk of the invested funds are borrowed or leveraged. In fact, the tax courts have ruled that with as little as 3 percent down and ninety-nine years to pay off the rest, a

60 TAX POLITICS

wealthy investor could claim depreciation deductions for 100 percent of the building cost as if every penny had come from him personally.

The chief result of accelerated depreciation and leveraging investments is to produce tax write-offs far in excess of actual economic loss of value providing a shelter for other income. Moreover, many studies have even shown that straight-line depreciation may be an overly generous tax subsidy in the real estate field. Obviously, the value of a well-situated, well-maintained rental property will decline very little, if at all, for the first fifteen years, Accordingly, even straight-line depreciation provides an all-important tax deferral for high bracket investors.

Aside from its effect on tax equity, accelerated depreciation produces a number of undesirable effects for housing development. Ostensibly designed to encourage risk-taking, our present tax system gives positive incentives to a developer to undertake the least risky development. This is because tax subsidies presently extend to luxury apartments, shopping centers, office buildings, and commercial buildings that are constructed for rent. Rents here, as opposed to low and moderate income housing, can be more flexible (higher), promising greater profits for the developer and investor. Depreciation and related deductions also tend to be greater. Accelerated depreciation provides tax shelters and quick return on investment. There is no real incentive to maintain a property in good condition. The incentive is to simply maximize the tax benefits in the first several years and then sell off to a new investor or syndicate that can begin the fast write-offs all over again. This game of musical landlords with its accompanying deterioration makes little sense for taxpayers supposedly subsidizing a national housing policy.

Incentives might be needed for priority housing areas such as the rehabilitation of urban and rural housing and the building of low and moderate income rental units. But these incentives should be made directly through the budget process. The present tax expenditures not only provide a major source of tax escape for wealthy individuals and corporations but provide subsidies to real estate developments that don't need help in attracting capital and only drain resources from higher priority areas.

Many legitimate developers will concede privately that these real estate tax expenditures are really inefficient. And one even stated it publicly before the Ways and Means Committee during a 1973 hearing. George H. Deffett, the president of a large and successful real estate development firm, candidly told the committee that:

> The present real estate tax shelter incentives perpetuate a totally unfair form of taxation . . . they are perversions of the progressive tax system . . . tax shelter gimmicks promote waste and inefficiency and do not add measurably to the stock of low and moderate income housing, an explicit social goal of Congress when it passed the Tax Reform Act of 1969 . . . I am convinced that these tax loopholes indirectly aid fragmentation and irrationality in our industry . . : and ultimately deny consumers superior housing products at lowest possible costs.

Percentage DepletionAllowances . . . . **$1.8 Billion**

Expensing of Intangible Drilling, Exploration and Development Costs . . . . **$800 Million**

Total . . . . **$2.6 Billion**

The final deduction type subsidies we shall examine are two tax expenditures supposedly designed to encourage the production of natural resources. These are the percentage depletion allowance for oil, gas, and minerals, and the expensing of exploration and development costs.

Depletion is similar to depreciation; it is a means of evaluating the way a natural resource is used up over time. When something depletes, it wears out. Originally, that's what the depletion allowance was all about: wearing out. Each year an oil company pumped a well, it wore out, or exhausted part of it. So the tax laws allowed the company to subtract from its income a suitable amount to cover the loss. These original tax provisions were called cost depletion. They were based on the cost of what the oil company actually lost. They were similar to depreciation provisions, which let a business subtract each year an amount to cover the wearing-out of its buildings and equipment.

There were problems with cost depletion, however. It is easy to determine how much a machine is worth and to spread that cost out over the machine's life. But it was difficult for the IRS to determine how much oil was left in a company's well so that it would know how much to let the company deplete each year. So in the 1920s, the present system of percentage depletion was introduced. Oil-connected congressmen argued that allowing the oil companies to subtract a set percentage of their income would be easier for the IRS to administer and might therefore prevent some of the excesses under the old law. Percentage depletion did not stop with oil and gas wells. Today, over one hundred minerals enjoy the advantage of the allowance.

Congress has taken the various minerals and assigned them different percentage depletion benefits for tax purposes: oil, uranium, sulfur, and forty other minerals mined in the United States are fixed at 22 percent; American-mined gold, copper, silver, iron, and some oil shale are fixed at 15 percent. Lower rates are established for virtually all other materials, except "soil, sod, dirt, turf, water, or mosses" or "minerals from sea water, the air, or similar inexhaustible sources." When you mine $1 million of uranium ore, for example, you are allowed 22 percent or $220,000 of tax-free income for your efforts (subject to certain total limitations unimportant here). Had you mined $1 million of coal ore you would be eligible for 10 percent depletion, or $100,000 of tax-free income. Unlike depreciation, which is limited to your total purchase price (the example of your typewriter, p. 58), depletion deductions allow an investor to receive tax-free income many times greater than the purchase price. You may take a percentage depletion deduction on any and all income from your mine or well. Oil companies, for instance, recover the value of their oil not once, but an average of sixteen times over.

Why do we have this generous depletion subsidy? Depletion advocates justify the deduction on several grounds: (1) oil and mining ventures are risky, including dry holes and unproductive mines. This great risk deserves a compensating government subsidy; (2) the depletion allowance is needed to insure a flow of investment capital into the domestic oil and mining industries to protect the nation against sudden foreign shortages; (3) the subsidy is needed to provide the oil and mining companies with capital necessary for needed exploration for and development of oil reserves.

In 1975, in response to the record profits of the oil industry and record prices for oil, Congress repealed the oil and gas depletion allowance for about 200 oil companies but left it intact for over 9,800 smaller "independents." This partial reform ended about $2 billion of this $3 billion subsidy. But the exemption of the so-called independent oil companies from the repeal of depletion defied the very reason for ending the controversial depletion allowance. The "small" independents (some gross up to $12 million a year) were reaping the biggest windfall profits from the rapid oil price rises.

In spite of the recent attacks on depletion because of the oil, gas, and coal industry's windfall profits, depletion has always been an unfair, costly, and inefficient tax expenditure. As with any subsidy, the depletion deduction results in inefficient and poor allocation of investment resources. One economist, Professor Arnold C. Harberger, once calculated that the several tax benefits for oil and mineral interests, especially including depletion, meant that at that time it was profitable for a company to spend $2.12 to mine $1 of sulfur, $2.13 to mine $1 of iron, $1.96 to mine $1 of copper, $2.27 to mine $1 of lead or zinc, $2.30 to mine $1 of coal, and $1.95 to drill $1 of oil! One of the obvious bad effects of this kind of economic equation is that it becomes much more profitable to use up the nation's virgin natural resources than to invest in recycling minerals or looking for alternative energy sources.

Our overly generous treatment of the oil industry has proved to be a highly inefficient method of encouraging increased domestic production. A study made for the Treasury Department in 1968 concluded that the depletion allowance was costing taxpayers $1.4 billion annually, but increasing oil reserves by only $150 million. More recently, a 1973 Library of

62 TAX POLITICS

Congress study concluded that, rather than stimulating exploration and development, oil tax incentives such as the depletion allowance encourage producers to overdrill in already discovered oil fields. Indeed, since only 10 percent of exploratory wells strike oil, depletion benefits only one-tenth of the exploratory drilling. Thus, oil companies prefer to spend money drilling in existing oil fields and thereby be certain to receive the depletion tax subsidy.

Former energy chief William Simon recognized this in a 1973 letter to the Senate Interior Committee, stating that: "In the short run, changes in percentage depletion should have little effect on the rate of expenditure of discovery efforts . . . in the long run, a change in depletion should have no effect, per se, on the rate of production."

Moreover, many of the benefits from percentage depletion go to nonproductive interests. A landowner receiving royalty income receives the benefits of percentage depletion even though he takes no financial risks to expand production of domestic reserves. In fact, 42 percent of depletion benefits are paid either to nonoperating interests in domestic production or for foreign production.

The "expensing" or immediate writing-off of exploration and development costs is the second major tax expenditure for oil, gas, and mineral production. The bulk of this $800 million subsidy goes to expensing of intangible drilling costs for oil and gas wells.

What the intangible drilling deduction does is allow oilmen to take an immediate deduction for labor and supply costs incurred in drilling successful wells, even though virtually all other businesses are required to spread their costs over the life of their capital investment.

Under normal tax rules, the entire cost of drilling a well would be considered part of the capital investment and depreciated over a period of years. For example, if a company built a $100,000 factory to last ten years, it would deduct $10,000 a year for depreciation. (Actually, the tax laws let businesses depreciate buildings somewhat faster.) Intangible expenses like labor are considered part of the factory's total cost. But the oil companies get a special break. If an oil company drills a ten-year well for $100,000, it can deduct the $70,000 to $90,000 for intangibles immediately and then spread the rest out over the ten years.

The larger deduction in the first year means the oil company receives all of the tax benefit at once. In effect, that year's taxes are deferred to a later year. The tax dollars they owe now can be paid later with no penalty—again, it's like an interest-free loan from the American taxpayers. Free interest may not seem like much, but on a large scale it adds up. This one provision is responsible for many independent oil companies paying no tax at all. In fact, a random survey of twenty-five independent oil companies showed that, in 1974, while their average rate of return on investment was a very profitable 26 percent—almost double all other manufacturing—most paid no taxes. And sixteen companies had additional tax deductions available to shelter income in future years. For example, Houston Oil and Minerals reported profits of $16 million in 1974 and a spectacular return on equity of around 50 percent, yet it reported a tax "loss" of $34 million.

Unfortunately, all this lost revenue is not the incentive for exploration the recipients of this tax break claim it is. Oil interests assert that they need the immediate write-off for intangible drilling costs to offset the risks in trying to find new oil. The fact is that this tax subsidy provides little incentive to explore. The oil producers receive a full write-off for the nine out of ten wells that prove dry holes. By itself, that provision could encourage exploration. But the expensing of intangibles gives the oil companies almost the same tax break—about 75 percent as much—for wells that do produce.

If producers get almost the same tax benefits for punching new holes in old oil fields as for exploring in new ones, it is clear what they will do. They will drill in the oil fields. That way the company gets the deductions, plus the depletion allowance, plus the profits. As with depletion, producers get a tax subsidy whether they undertake the risks of exploration or not. So why take the risks?

The write-off the oil companies get for the intangible capital costs of drilling more wells in the same place negates any incentive they get from being able to write off expenses of exploratory wells that turn up dry. Yet, this latter provision is the one that actually encourages exploratory drilling. If we kept it and got rid of the ex-

Tax Expenditures: The Hidden Federal Budget—A Key to Reform

pensing of intangibles, we might get some actual exploration in return for our tax dollars.

Tax "incentives" for the oil industry just haven't worked. In fact, they have encouraged exactly what the American public does not need: oil drilling and production abroad instead of at home; wasteful drilling in existing oil fields instead of exploration; monopoly control of the oil industry instead of competition; and a lack of energy sources to compete with oil. The tax incentives have helped no one except the oil industry. That is why we should get rid of them. All of them.

The obvious incentive for mining and oil and gas drilling is price. In the case of oil, gas, coal, and others, higher prices have more than made up for any loss of tax subsidies. These subsidies are inefficient and have only served to make our precious resources "cheaper" than they really are, encouraging their overuse while discouraging recycling and alternative materials or energy. It's time the taxpayer stop subsidizing the waste of our natural resources.

CAPITAL GAINS

Exclusion of One-Half of Capital Gains Income	$4.165 Billion
Non-Taxation of Capital Gains Transferred by Gift or Bequest	$4.550 Billion
Total	$8.715 Billion

The single largest tax expenditure in the income tax laws is the preferential treatment of capital gains. Capital gains are simply the gains from the sale (at a profit) of securities, real estate, or other investments. The tax laws provide that profits from such a sale, if the property was held longer than half a year (long-term capital gains), will be taxed at *one-half* the usual tax rate for wage and salary incomes.

Corporations pay a maximum of 30 percent on long-term capital gains instead of the normal rate of 48 percent on other income. Moreover, the law provides a maximum tax of 25 percent for individuals on the first $50,000 of capital gains providing additional help to taxpayers who are above the 50 percent tax bracket (those in the 70 percent bracket would otherwise pay at a 35 percent rate). Finally, capital gains on property held by the investor and transferred by gift or at his death escape income taxes altogether.

The capital gains preference is the greatest single source of tax reduction for the very wealthiest taxpayers. And only one in ten taxpayers is prosperous enough to benefit from capital gains. In fact, in 1974 those making over $100,000 a year—the top one-tenth of 1 percent of all taxpayers—received over 50 percent of the benefits from the capital gains preference. Those making over $20,000—the top 15 percent of all taxpayers—received over 85 percent of the capital gains benefits. In the same year, the average benefits to middle income taxpayers ($10,000-15,000 a year) amounted to only $19.06, while the benefits increased a thousandfold for those earning over $100,000 to an extraordinary $19,431.25. (In 1972, a more prosperous year, the average saving here reached $39,000.) Of course, if this very expensive preference were eliminated altogether, everyone's taxes could be cut by more than $100.

Why do we tax investment income so much less than salary or wage income? There are three major justifications presented for this policy.

1. When investment property is held longer than a year, it is unfair to tax all of the profits at high progressive income tax rates. (For example, take a wealthy taxpayer who bought $50,000 of oil company stock in 1970, and sold it for $150,000 in 1974. His profit: $100,000. In fairness, that income should not be taxed at ordinary income rates which go up to 70 percent. The problem is that the $100,000 total income is bunched into a single year and would be taxed at 53 percent—see your tax tables. The unfairness comes because the profit of $100,000, over four years, really works out to $25,000 a year—income which would be taxed at much lower rates [about 35 percent alto-

gether, computed from the tax tables].)

Advocates of the tax subsidy concede that the low one-half tax rate very much overcompensates for this so-called bunching problem. But they point to two other justifications.

2. Investments bought and sold over a period of years include inflation as a large part of the profits. Take a rental apartment bought in 1970 and sold in 1974. Inflation over those four years has probably exceeded 20 percent. If the apartment cost $100,000 and sold for $130,000 in 1974, the investor would have to pay tax on $30,000 of profits, even though two-thirds of this amount is really inflation. The lower capital gains tax rate helps compensate for this unfairness.

3. Advocates of the capital gains tax subsidy feel that it is important to promote investment in the economy. Why should wealthy people invest money rather than consume it, if investments are strictly taxed? Moreover, the lure of lightly taxed business investment is needed to entice investors into risky ventures which otherwise couldn't be carried out. They also feel that without the current capital gains preference, investment in capital would be overtaxed. A corporation pays a 48 percent tax on its income and if distributed to shareholders as dividends, the income is taxed again to the recipient at ordinary rates. They argue that this condition is partially corrected when the company retains its earnings. This may increase the value of the company's stock and allow the shareholder to reap the increase by selling the stock and paying tax at lower capital gains rates. To tax such sales as ordinary income, they insist, would close off even this marginally effective way to ease the burden of double taxation on capital.

Finally, advocates of special treatment for capital gains argue that subjecting such gains to tax tends to induce investors who hold appreciated assets to refrain from selling them. This "lock-in" effect, they argue, impairs the free flow of investment capital, tying up much-needed capital for long periods of time.

Although the question of capital gains raises complex economic issues, opponents of the subsidy can easily point out the fallacies of the alleged justifications that are offered.

1. First, opponents of the subsidy agree that it would be unfair to tax profits from investments in property held many years, as if they were made in a single year. However, they point out the present income tax provision for income-averaging compensates for this unfairness by allowing a taxpayer to spread unusually large profits over a period of several years. Moreover, even the most staunch opponents of the capital gains subsidy are willing to extend the present income-averaging benefits to completely compensate for the "bunching" problem. Some have advocated taxing the increased value yearly as a means of avoiding this problem.

2. Inflation is a poor excuse for the lower capital gains rate. Everyone suffers from inflation, not just wealthy investors. In fact, the investor is often quite lucky, compared with the many Americans on fixed incomes, that his profits do increase with inflation. But look at the wage or salary earner whose income goes up with inflation. A $10,000 salary in 1970 was worth over $12,000 in 1974. Progressive income taxes taxed the $12,000 income at a higher precentage than the $10,000 income. The result, even though the increase in salary income was only due to inflation, is that the tax rate has gone up. If the tax laws are going to be generous to investors with inflationary profits, they should be equally generous to wage and salary earners. That means a tax cut for everyone, and not just the wealthy beneficiaries of the capital gains subsidy.

Also, investors who hold onto assets for a number of years have the benefit of deferring taxes on the yearly gain in value of their investment. As we have seen, this deferral can be very beneficial for long-held assets, often more than making up for any loss due to inflation. Take, for example, a piece of property that has gained in value in 1966 (it may have had similar gains in later years) and is sold in 1975. Suppose the tax on that 1966 gain would have been $100. Instead, the taxpayer puts the $100 in the bank and pays the $100 in tax in 1975. The cost of paying the $100 in 1966 is $100. But in ten years, his $100 has grown to $220 (assuming an 8 percent interest rate), leaving him with $120 to offset the tax—he has actually come out $20 ahead of the game. A twenty-year deferral is of much greater benefit with the $100 in the bank swelling to $470, putting the taxpayer $270 ahead. Obviously, if there is to be any adjustment for inflation of capital gains there should be an adjustment for the deferral benefit as well—sort of an "interest" charge for the taxes deferred on yearly gains in value.

The deferral benefit reaches the heights of tax avoidance for capital assets that are given away during one's life or at death. Here the deferred taxes are never collected. For example, if someone bought ten shares of stock for $100 in 1965 and sold them for $1,100 in 1975, he would be liable for tax on one-half of the $1,000 capital gain. But if the same person had died in 1975 and left that $1,100 worth of stock to his child, he would pay no income tax on the gain. If the child sold the stock one year later, for $1,200, he would be liable for a tax only on the $100 gain that occurred since he inherited the stock. The original $1,000 gain would go untaxed forever.

Capital gains transferred at death account for some 40 to 50 percent of all estates—$10-15 billion a year that goes completely untaxed. Many opponents of the capital gains preference argue that much of the unfairness of the subsidy could be removed simply by eliminating this tax holiday feature, itself worth $4.5 billion in fiscal year 1976.

3. Finally, the economic argument. A number of economists begin by noting the difference between a direct contribution to economic growth, for example, purchase of a machine, compared with capital gains resulting from activity in the stock market or the real estate market, when one nonproducer sells at a profit to another nonproducer. These sales, about 95 percent of all capital gains, provide no increased investment but simply replace one investor's dollars for another's. If the $8 billion capital gains subsidy were removed and replaced with a $8 billion tax rate cut for all taxpayers, this would promote consumer demand since more people would have more money to spend and result in economic investment according to supply and demand.

Opponents concede that people may differ on whether to tax income or tax consumption (thereby encouraging savings and investments) or, indeed, to tax both. But if we are going to base our tax on income, then all income including capital gains (whether realized through sale or not) should be taxed; if we are going to tax consumption (all income which is spent), then all income which is saved—not just capital gains—should be excluded. There is no reason in either case to give preferential treatment just to capital gains.

As for the need to induce wealthy people to spend, rather than consume their wealth—their consumption will also stimulate business to satisfy the demand. In fact, of course, the wealthy will still invest a great amount of money, even if they are taxed at the same rates as everybody else. That is the nature of our capitalist system.

As for the need to use low capital gains taxes to lure money into more risky ventures, there are several counter-arguments. First, why subsidize an investment which isn't profitable by itself according to the laws of free competition? Second, if capital gains treatment does encourage some risk-taking, it is not at all certain that it does so at a sufficient level to justify its enormous revenue cost. Moreover, if risk-taking is to be a major aim of tax policy it could be promoted more effectively and fairly by allowing generous write-offs against ordinary income for losses incurred.

The argument that capital gains is an offset against "double taxation" should also be met with considerable skepticism. To the extent that corporate tax is passed through to the customers it does not represent a tax on the shareholders. Furthermore, only about 30 percent of all capital gains consist of return on corporate stock. The double tax argument does not apply to all other capital assets. Preferential capital gains treatment is not the way to deal with the "double taxation" problem. If there is a concern here, the answer would be to "integrate" the corporate and personal income tax systems, taxing only the shareholders on the earnings of their corporation whether or not those earnings were paid out as dividends.

Finally, the problem of "locking-in" investments is very real but, in fact, it is the present system of capital gains taxation that is its primary cause. In this instance, the supposed solution is really the problem. Obviously, "lock-in" is caused, rather than alleviated, by the capital gains preference which gives a reward to those who hold an asset for over six months. Also corporations often don't distribute dividends which would be taxed at ordinary rates (thereby allowing the stockholder to convert the income into capital gains later on when the stock is sold, its value enhanced by the retained earnings). Another important reason for not selling appreciated assets is the opportunity to defer taxes on the yearly gain, thereby enjoying an interest-free loan from the government.

Obviously, the greatest impetus to "lock-in" gain results from the failure to tax capital appreciation at death. Rather than selling an investment that has appreciated in value, paying an income tax, and reinvesting the proceeds elsewhere, the owner of an investment that has appreciated in value will simply hold onto it until he can give it to his heirs and avoid the tax altogether.

In summary, although opponents of the capital gains subsidy agree that the economic aspects are complicated, they do not see that the advocates have made a case worth $8 billion annually in tax benefits for the wealthiest one-tenth of taxpayers. There is little question that at the very minimum the tax-free transfer of capital gains at death or by gift should be ended immediately with appropriate exemptions for intrafamily transfers (small family farms, businesses, and residences). This very expensive expenditure creates no incentive for investment and, in fact, inhibits the flow of new investments.

Any thorough tax reform effort should then include taxing capital gains at the same rates as all other income with a liberal system of income-averaging or an election to pay the tax on yearly gains in value of unsold assets (unrealized gain). The treatment of capital gains as ordinary income would also call for liberal deductions for losses. The repeal of this very unfair and expensive tax incentive could also permit some lowering of the top income tax rates or the integration of the corporate and individual income tax. The over-all effect of these reforms would be to increase the over-all progressivity of the present income tax system and end a great deal of inefficiency and waste of this $8 billion tax expenditure and the tax shelters it helps create. If we need special incentives for risk-bearing, saving, and investment, we should provide them in a direct, open, and uniform manner and not as we currently do through the tax system.

Exclusion of Income - Security Transfer Payments .... $8.715 Billion

Transfer payments are money payments made by the government to certain groups from which no service is required. Examples of payments which should be included in someone's income but are exempt under current law are social security and railroad retirement, public assistance (welfare payments), workmen's compensation, unemployment insurance, and veterans disability compensation. At first glance these do not seem the kinds of income that we want to tax even though they represent real increases in economic well-being. But as with most tax expenditures there are more efficient and equitable ways of providing more income assistance than by exempting the present income security payments.

Most transfer payments are excluded because their recipients would not be subject to tax even if they were included in income, i.e., most of the people who receive the payments are poor. In many instances, these additions to their incomes would make no difference for tax purposes; but this is not the issue. The problem is that people who get these transfer payments pay less tax than other people with the same income who don't get the payments.

For example, can we really say that a couple aged sixty-five with an annual social security income of $6,000 needs more help than a younger couple with two children with the identical income. And what about another couple aged sixty-five who receives only $3,000 from social security but has additional outside income of $20,000. Is there a good reason in this case to also exempt their $3,000 which would otherwise be taxed at more than 30 percent.

Excluding social security and railroad payments from AGI (adjusted gross income) discriminates against other types of retirement income. Congress tried to correct this somewhat in 1954 by enacting a credit for retirement income, but the 15 percent retirement income credit in effect, excluding a portion of other income, is an unsatisfactory solution to the problem. Horizontal tax equity between taxpayers with equal incomes is better achieved by taxing all income equally rather than by excluding some that is taxed, in a rough attempt to make things equal.

One difficulty which arises in including social security benefits in adjusted gross income is that a part of these benefits has already been subject to tax and is a return to the recipient of money he has contributed to the social security fund. The problem lies in determining the percentage of the benefits which is prior contribution. Recent data show, however, that only about 10 percent of social security benefits are prior contributions.

In addition to exemptions for transfer payments, our tax system has other tax expenditures for income security purposes which could be more fairly distributed through direct expenditure programs. The additional $750 personal exemption for those over sixty-five is the largest such expenditure costing more than $1 billion a year. But does it really make sense? The tax benefit goes to all who reach the sixty-fifth birthday—rich and poor alike—but provides no benefit for nearly one-quarter of the elderly too poor to pay tax. For those in the lowest tax bracket it provides a saving of only $105 (14 percent of $750). And for those in the highest bracket it provides $525 of assistance. In fact, in 1974, elderly people with incomes between $10,000 and $15,000 saved an average of $12.29 from this tax expenditure while the wealthy ($100,000 and more) received an average benefit of $162.50. Because many recipients of transfer payments are not taxpayers, reform in this area is considered less important than in others. But if these payments were taxed, the increased revenue could be used to raise the low income allowance or to provide more direct aid to those who need it. The system would then make allowance for ability to pay and the fact that the benefits of the current tax preferences have no relation to the need of the recipient. This is a more rational approach to equity and tax relief for low income taxpayers, whatever their source of income.

Corporate Surtax Exemption .... $5.03 Billion

The corporate tax rate is actually made up of two rates. Up to 1975 those rates were 22 percent on all corporate income plus a 26 percent surtax on all income above $25,000. The effect was that corporations would pay a 48 percent tax on all income over $25,000 with the lower 22 percent rate applying to the first $25,000. This exemption from the higher 48 percent surtax rate was recently expanded so that, beginning in 1975, the first $25,000 of corporate income would be taxed at 20 percent, the next $25,000 at 22 percent (an average of 21 percent on the first $50,000), and everything over $50,000 at the regular 48 percent rate.

This tax expenditure in the form of an exemption from the higher corporate tax rate is projected to cost $5 billion in FY 1976. It is defended as an aid to small business but it really is a very expensive aid to wealthy corporate owners. To understand this it is important to make a distinction between small corporations and the people who own them.

Suppose the owner of a small clothing manufacturing operation makes a profit of $100,000 a year on his unincorporated small business. Suppose further that he lives on $50,000 before taxes and leaves the other $50,000 in the business. As an individual proprietor he would pay taxes of about $33,000 (assuming a family of four with taxable income, after itemized deductions, of $80,000). His after-tax earnings would be $67,000.

But if the same businessman incorporated his business he could save a considerable amount of tax. If he ran the business, he could pay himself a salary of $50,000 and leave the rest in the business. This would be basically the same as before when he lived on $50,000 before tax and left the remainder of his profit in the business. Before incorporating, this second $50,000 marked for reinvestment in the business would be taxed at an individual tax rate of about 50 percent. But by incorporating, the second $50,000 left in the business will be taxed at the favorable corporate rate averaging 21 percent (about the same rate as a working family of four with $12,000 total income would pay).

The result, then, of a graduation in the corporate income tax is that it enables the owner-operator of a small business to split his income and apply it to the bottom part of both the individual and corporate income tax brackets. The savings for the well-off businessman in our example is considerable. By taking advantage of the corporate surtax exemption he will pay only $18,000 on his $100,000 profit—a tax savings of $15,000.

Of course, if the business in question is even more profitable or if the owner has other outside income, the tax on the unincorporated business could be as high as 70 percent. But by incorporating, the owner can shelter up to $50,000 at a very low 21 percent rate of tax—a very major tax benefit to persons in high tax brackets. It is interesting to note that the shareholders of small corporations are distinctly more affluent than stockholders of large publicly held corporations. For example, according to Treasury statistics on so-called Subchapter S corporations, which they consider reflective of all small corporations, 60 percent of the corporate income goes to people with incomes in excess of $50,000.

In fact, it is the Subchapter S corporation that provides a reasonable and equitable alternative to the surtax exemption. Under Subchapter S, small business owners can elect to be taxed as a partnership with all of the income taxed to the shareholders as if they earned it directly. These corporate owners would be taxed like all other wage earners. If they made a lot of money, they would pay higher taxes; if they made a small profit, their tax rates would be lower. Unfortunately, the present surtax exemption ignores the fact that the size of the corporation is unrelated to the size of its owners' incomes. This very expensive tax expenditure should be repealed. If additional incentives are needed for small business, they should be provided through the existing direct programs of the Small Business Administration and similar programs.

Investment Tax Credit . . . . $8.760 Billion

Congress enacted the investment credit in 1962, suspended it for fifteen months in 1966, repealed it in 1969, reenacted it at 7 percent in 1971, and increased it to 10 percent for 1975 and 1976. Since 1975, the credit has provided a dollar-for-dollar offset against taxes equal to 10 percent of the cost of plant machinery and equipment purchased by a business. The 10 percent credit will produce a cut in corporate income taxes by more than 15 percent in fiscal year 1976.

As discussed in detail earlier, the investment tax credit is an inefficient way to stimulate new investment and create new jobs; it distorts the free market mechanism and, as such, leads to an inefficient allocation of resources. The misallocation of resources is obvious by the credit's operation. It is not a credit for all investment but applies only to investment in machinery by business. It does not apply to investment in new plants or to investment by government, local and federal. It does not apply to investment in housing or durable consumer goods. More importantly, it does not apply to productive investments in manpower training or research and development. Finally, the credit bypasses small businesses not requiring large capital investment and, since it offsets taxes, the credit gives no benefit to new businesses with no profit, or businesses that are operating at a loss.

The investment credit is also very wasteful. If a $100 piece of equipment will bring a $110 return in increased production, then we should expect business to invest in that equipment without a subsidy. On the other hand, why should the U.S. Treasury subsidize the purchase of new equipment costing $100 if it will produce only $95 worth of goods? If investment in new equipment cannot be economically justified, then it does not make sense for the government to provide an additional $10 in subsidy to encourage its purchase.

This is particularly true of a subsidy promoted under the guise of creating new jobs. The $8.7 billion loss in revenue is not made up in new jobs and certainly a general tax cut would be a more equitable way of stimulating the economy. In fact, purchases of most new equipment tend to displace jobs. Moreover, if there is no credit and if an industry is operating at full capacity, it will attempt to increase profits by increasing capacity through the purchase of new equipment. If an industry is not operating at full capacity, the purchase of new equipment encouraged by a credit

Tax Expenditures: The Hidden Federal Budget—A Key to Reform

develops no new jobs anyway. If there is a need to develop new jobs, we can more efficiently accomplish that goal through a general tax cut through expenditure programs in a variety of public and private sectors.

This has certainly been the case historically where the credit and other investment incentives have had little impact on unemployment. In July 1962, depreciation was liberalized, followed by the enactment of the investment credit in October. For the eighteen months between July 1962 and December 1963 unemployment actually rose from 5.4 percent to 5.5 percent although it had declined from 6.6 percent to 5.4 percent in the eighteen months prior to July 1962. Only after personal income taxes were cut in February 1964 to stimulate consumer spending did the jobless rate drop below 5 percent to 4.4 percent by July of 1965.

There just has not been a strong case made to prove that the credit sufficiently increases equipment investment to justify its enormous cost. Numerous surveys have, in fact, shown that as a practical matter plant investment decisions are determined by customer demand with little weight given to the credit. And, of course, a great deal of the credit goes to reward investment which would occur in any case. Thus while a company may increase investment outlays by only 5 percent over what was planned without the credit, they will receive a tax credit benefit on the full 100 percent of their investment.

The investment credit is less objectionable than other tax expenditures since it is easier to spot and does not distort general accepted definitions of income. But given its inequities, inefficiency, distorting effect on the economy, and marginal usefulness as a fiscal stimulant, the investment credit should be repealed and replaced with more neutral tax cuts or direct spending programs in the public sector. If the credit is retained, it should be restructured to either help all investment equally or to provide aid to specifically targetted areas of the economy that need help. It should also reward only investment that, without the credit, would not take place.

Exclusion of Interest on State and Local Bonds . . . . $4.765 Billion

State and local governments raise capital outside their tax base by selling bonds. In 1913, Congress recognized these governments' need for help in raising debt capital and decided to provide it by means of an indirect subsidy—making income invested in these bonds exempt from federal taxes.

Since investors don't have to pay tax on the interest from tax-exempt bonds, a state or local government can sell them to investors at lower interest rates. Paying lower rates saves these governments money, but at the same time costs the federal Treasury lost tax revenues. In 1972, the last year figures were available, the states saved $1.9 billion at a cost to the federal Treasury of $2.6 billion. In FY 1976, the cost to the Treasury will increase to $4.8 billion.

Two things stand out from the 1913 action. First, it subsidizes state and local governments to the extent borrowers will accept lower rates of interest in order to receive that income tax-free. Second, it has created another loophole that is of much greater benefit to the wealthy than other taxpayers. For example, assume a taxable bond is offered, under present conditions, which would have to grant interest at 9 percent. Under similar market conditions, a taxpayer in the 70 percent tax bracket would pay tax on the 9 percent, leaving 2.7 percent after tax income. Therefore, that taxpayer would be better off accepting any rate of tax-exempt interest higher than 2.7 percent. But his counterpart in the 40 percent bracket comes out ahead only on a tax-exempt yields exceeding 5.4 percent. As with all tax subsidies, the wealthy taxpayer is better off than the less wealthy taxpayer. And as bond interest increases, the advantage of the wealthy taxpayer over the less wealthy also increases.

And this tax expenditure benefits the wealthy more than any other. People in the high income brackets are responsible for most of the investment in tax-free municipal bonds. People making over $50,000 a year (the top one percent of taxpayers) own two-thirds of the municipal bonds held by individuals and receive 88 percent of the tax savings from the exemption. In 1974, the average saving from this tax preference for families with incomes between $10,000 and $15,000 was only 25 cents; $15,000 to $20,000 families saved $2.23; those with income between $50,000 and $100,000 saved $593.89, and those earning more than $100,000 a year reduced their taxes by $3,412.50.

About three-quarters of the tax-exempt bonds are held by large corporations, primarily commercial banks, seeking income that is sheltered from the normal 48 percent corporate tax rate. In 1971, banks held $75 billion worth of municipal bonds—or nearly half of all tax-free securities. The expenditure has become very profitable for commercial banks, and the major reason why they can reduce their U.S. tax rate from 48 percent to an effective tax rate of around 15 percent. Tax-exempt interest income alone, according to records filed with the Securities and Exchange Commission, actually reduced the 48 percent rate of ten of the nation's largest banks by an average of 20.6 percentage points in 1974—a tax reduction of almost 43 percent.

Not only is this tax expenditure unfair, it is also very inefficient. The 1970 bond market is a good example of the inefficiency of this system; only a little more than half the federal assistance went to the intended beneficiaries—the governments. The balance amounted to a charge by investors upon the federal government—in the form of tax-exempt income—for using this indirect financing technique.

Wealthy investors and commercial banks were able to turn from taxable bonds, paying an average interest rate of 9.11 percent, to exempts paying 6.75 percent. By purchasing tax-exempt bonds, the 70 percent bracket investor saved $6.38 (9.11 x 70) in taxes in exchange for a sacrifice of $2.73 of interest and thereby obtained a net benefit of $4.02. However, the government issuing the bond saved only $2.36—the difference between $9.11 and $6.75. Thus, the federal government paid investors $4.02 so a state or local government could save $2.36—an inefficiency of 41 percent.

This inefficiency is further compounded by the fact that the financial sources who currently benefit from the exemption, wealthy individuals and commercial banks, should be making higher-risk equity investments and loans to business. In fact, when business and federal government's financial needs require it, the banks cut back first on purchases of state and local bond issues. The organizations which should be buying these safe issues—such as private pensions, trusts, state and local retirement funds, and educational and charitable institutions—are tax-exempt themselves and hence cannot benefit from the attraction of tax-exempt interest.

It is generally accepted that state and local governments should continue to receive federal assistance in their efforts to raise capital from bond issues. The most widely advocated method of providing this financial assistance is the removal of the current tax exemption for state and local bond issues and the substitution of a direct federal subsidy for some portion of the interest yield on the taxable bonds. This would enable these jurisdictions to issue taxable bonds at a competitive interest rate, cover part of their costs with federal dollars, and eliminate the inefficiency and inequity of the present loophole.

In its 1969 tax reform bill, the House Ways and Means Committee proposed that those state and local governments electing to issue taxable bonds would receive a federal subsidy on some portion of each interest payment. The percentage was understood to be 40 percent at the time the bill passed the House. No strings were attached to the payment, leaving the governments free to plan projects without federal interference. The plan was killed in the Senate after a successful lobbying effort on the part of state and local governments and many commercial banks. Their objections were many but centered mainly around uncertainty over how the bond market would readjust, political considerations, and a lack of understanding of how the system would work.

Since that time a series of events have changed these attitudes, focusing recent attention not so much upon whether the idea should be implemented but whether the system should eliminate tax-exempt bonds altogether or partially and at what percentage the federal subsidy should be set. With interest rates on tax-exempt bonds approaching 70 percent of those on taxable bonds, states and localities, saving only 30 percent, are realizing they would gain more from a direct 40 percent subsidy.

Some critics of the present system also argue that the subsidy should not be tied to bond issues

Tax Expenditures: The Hidden Federal Budget—A Key to Reform

at all and that equivalent funds should simply be given to states in the form of additional revenue-sharing monies. They contend that a bond subsidy, either direct or through tax-exempts, forces governments to invest only in capital improvements and other types of construction—like new schools, jails, and city halls—when many would prefer to invest in such programs as job training and hiring more adult-education teachers.

Aside from giving these governments additional assistance, the direct subsidy proposal would establish a system that is more efficient and more equitable. Any loss to the Treasury under the bond subsidy program would go directly to the states and local governments, and not be wasted in tax windfalls to high-bracket taxpayers and banks, as is the case under today's tax-exempt bond subsidy. In short, a dollar spent by the federal government will mean a dollar saved by the states and localities.

Exclusion of Pension Contributions and Earnings . . . . $6.45 Billion

Our tax laws provide a major tax expenditure ostensibly to promote private pension and profit-sharing plans. Under a "qualified" plan, the salary that an employer would otherwise pay to an employee is paid instead into a pension or profit-sharing plan on behalf of that employee. (To qualify, a plan must be non-discriminatory, i.e., treat all employees alike.) The employer still gets a deduction as if he had paid his employee directly. He is, therefore, satisfied. The money paid for the employee's benefit, however, is excluded from his income and therefore is tax-free at the time of payment. Once deposited in the plan the entire employer contribution, unreduced by taxes, can be invested on behalf of the employee. Thereafter, the income from the investment and reinvestment is received by the plan free from tax to be reinvested again. So only only the original contribution but all the income from that contribution is sheltered from tax until the employee retires.

When the employee retires, his pension income is treated much more gently than if it had been taxes originally. If he takes the money out all at once there are special tax-rate and averaging provisions to reduce the tax bite. If he withdraws his share of the fund in periodic payments, he pays tax, but only as he receives the money. If he should die before he receives his full share, the remainder can be paid directly to his family, thus avoiding any estate tax. Finally, if the pension plan had invested its money in stock of the employer's company the Internal Revenue Code excludes from tax any appreciation in the stock when it is distributed to the employee after retirement.

The difference between a profit-sharing plan and a pension plan is often very minor. Traditionally, profit-sharing plans set up a fixed formula to give the employee a share in the employer's profits. However, the tax laws do not require that qualified plans assure the employees a fixed share of the profits. It is only necessary that the contributions for the plan be paid out of current or accumulated earnings.

Sometimes a profit-sharing plan is set up in place of a pension plan or in conjunction with one to let an employer reduce his contribution in a bad year and to permit unrelated withdrawals by employees. In fact, there is no requirement that profit-sharing plans are related to retirement at all. They may simply be another device for sheltering investments from tax. Some profit-sharing plans will allow an individual who may be quite well off and have ample retirement benefits to invest in this tax shelter.

A good example of this is the "cash or deferred profit-sharing plan." Here the employer will pay his employee a bonus and give him the option of taking the bonus in cash or putting part or all of it in a profit-sharing plan. In effect, the employee can chose to invest in a tax shelter, deducting the entire amount that he puts in the plan from his income for the year and allowing his investment to grow tax-free until he wants to receive payments.

Self-employed people receive a similar tax advantage for pension funds. They can set aside 15 percent of their annual earnings up to $7,500 in a Keogh plan (after its congressional sponsor). As with other pension plans, these earnings are not taxed until they are withdrawn in later years. Since the 1973 Pension Act, a similar arrangement exists for employees who are not covered by a pension plan. These individuals can set aside $1,500 a year, tax-free, toward retirement in individual retirement accounts (IRAs).

All this inducement for retirement security is a very expensive proposition. The tax expenditure budget for fiscal year 1976 indicates a cost of $6.5 billion for the special tax benefits granted qualified plans and plans for the self-employed. While these tax incentives were created to help those who could otherwise not gain retirement security, they are unduly weighted in favor of high-paid individuals. the result is that those who least need retirement income help receive the most government tax subsidy. In 1974, for example, the average benefit from this tax expenditure for those making $10,000-$15,000 was $49.90, while those making over $100,000 received an average tax benefit of $1,725.

In addition, while the cost in lost revenues of the private pension system has been growing quickly, less than half of the non-agricultural work force is covered by the ststem. And many who are "protected" by pension plans will get either no benefits at all or relatively small benefits because they change employers. Thus, well over half the work force gets little or no benefit from the private pension system, yet they are still required to help make up the hugh revenue loss through higher taxes.

There are several reasons why the present tax expenditure has worked so unfairly and inefficiently. As stated, the major tax advantage for pension plans is the right to deduct employer contributions currently while taxation to the employee is deferred until actual distribution, usually after retirement. Deferral of taxation until after retirement can have the advantage of allowing a high-paid employee to pay tax on this pension contribution when he is in a lower retirement tax bracket rather than paying tax on the money while he is in a high tax bracket. For example, a married executive making $100,000 a year pays tax at a 50 percent rate on everything above $50,000. In effect he is paying $25,000 in tax on his second $50,000 in earnings. But if that same executive drew $50,000 and had the other $50,000 put into a pension plan, his retirement income of $50,000 a year would be taxed at an average rate of only 28 percent. Here the tax on the second $50,000 is only $14,000—a tax savings of $11,000. In effect, the employee is splitting his salary in half by using the pension plan. He has split his income over two lower tax brackets.

But even if the retiree's tax bracket is the same as when he was working (because of outside income), there is another significant advantage to pension plans. Assume employee Smith is in the 25 percent tax bracket. Ordinarily if he receives $10,000 from his employer he would pay taxes of $2,500. On the other hand, if the $10,000 was contributed to a qualified pension plan, the plan gets to keep the full $10,000 and the Treasury is out $2,500 in tax until the plan distributes the money to Smith some years later (assuming he remains in the same 25 percent bracket upon retirement). In essence, the deferral of tax amounts to an interest-free loan from the Treasury. And the amount of the loan depends on the tax bracket of the taxpayer—the higher the bracket the greater the loan.

Moreover, it is not "discriminatory" to provide a larger pension for higher paid employees than for the lower paid as long as the ratio of pension to salary is the same. A plan could set up a pension equal to one-half of all employees' top salaries. This would obviously provide higher pensions to the higher paid workers. Under such a plan, a 25 percent tax bracket worker earning $20,000 a year would be entitled to a $10,000 annual pension. The annual contribution for such an employee would be about $2,000, resulting in a tax deferral—or interest-free loan—of $500. On the other hand, a 50 percent tax bracket executive making $60,000 a year would receive a $30,000-a-year pension. The $6,000 annual contribution for his pension will result in deferred taxes of $3,000, or six times as much as the average worker.

The 1973 Pension Act placed a limit for the first time on corporate contributions to pension plans. Presently, contributions sufficient to fund pensions up to $75,000 a year are tax-free. Upt to that limit, corporations may contribute as much as they want to employee plans as long as they

Tax Expenditures: The Hidden Federal Budget—A Key to Reform 73

treat all employees alike. That is, if they contribute to a pension equal to 75 percent of an executive's salary, they must do the same for assembly-line workers.

In theory, the cost of having to give all employees proportional pensions prevents corporate executives from setting up unduly high pensions for themselves. But executives can sidestep this requirement to some extent through "integration." The concept of "integration" has kept numbers of lower income employees from receiving any pension benefits at all. The rationale is that the social security system provides a basic level of retirement security. Congress has therefore permitted private pension and profit-sharing plans to operate as a supplemental retirement security system confined to wages above the $14,000 social security base. It is possible, therefore, for qualified plans to entirely exclude workers earning less than a fixed amount a year—say, $14,000. Figure 23 illustrates the effect of integration on the private pensions of low and middle income wage earners.

Limits have also been placed on the pension plans of self-employed people, like doctors and lawyers. Unlike large corporations they hire few employees. And most of those don't stay on their jobs long enough to qualify for pensions. Therefore, the requirement of treating all employees alike wouldn't work to limit the size of pensions for the self-employed. That is why the law has placed contribution limits of 15 percent of an employee's salary up to $7,500 for noncorporate pension plans.

That is also why doctors and lawyers have lobbied through professional incorporation statutes in all fifty states. The tax benefit from corporate pension plans is the sole reason why these professionals have been incorporating their practices in increasing numbers. Figure 24 indicates the advantages of becoming a professional corporation.

★ **FIGURE 22. WHO BENEFITS FROM THE TAX SUBSIDY FOR PENSIONS (In Constant Dollars)** ★

The following chart illustrates the tax benefits from pension plans available to two employees with different income levels:

If the employer contributes 15% of salary

	Executive		Employee	
	With tax benefits	Without tax benefits	With tax benefits	Without tax benefits
Starting taxable salary	$ 30,000	$ 34,500	$10,000	$11,500
Ending taxable salary	100,000	115,000	18,000	20,700
After-tax pension	25,990	12,312	8,005	5,765
"Tax subsidy"	53%		28%	

Assumptions: Participation age 35 to age 65; 6% interest; 2½% inflation; joint returns; executive has outside income equal to deductions.

SOURCE: United States Treasury.

★ **FIGURE 23. THE EFFECT OF TAX INTEGRATION ON PRIVATE PENSIONS** ★

(Private pension and profit-sharing plans may be confined to wages above the social security base)

If the employer contributes 10% of salary

Employee	Salary	Less Social Security Base	Private Pension Base	Employer Contributions	% of Salary
A	$ 10,000	$14,100	$ 0	$ 0	0%
B	16,000	14,100	1,900	190	0.1
C	20,000	14,100	5,900	590	3.0
D	100,000	14,100	85,900	8,590	8.6

74 TAX POLITICS

FIGURE 24. THE TAX ADVANTAGE ACHIEVED THROUGH INCORPORATION

	Annual Contribution Beginning at Age 40 in 1974	Annual Pension Payable in 1974 Dollars Beginning at Age 65 in 1999
Individual retirement account	$ 1,500	$ 3,236
Self-employed	7,500	16,180
Corporate	34,765	75,000

Assumes 6% interest and 3% inflation.

SOURCE: United States Treasury.

The private pension plan system is top-heavy in favor of higher paid individuals. It has not fulfilled the purpose of the tax benefit, which is to provide for an increase in retirement security for workers who would otherwise not be expected to provide it for themselves. If we are to spend such huge sums of money, it makes sense to redesign the system of retirement security. We should either increase basic social security protections or readjust the present tax benefits of the private pension system to distribute them more equitably.

Chapter 3
Congress and Tax Politics

Our federal tax system is unfair to lower and middle income taxpayers because a large majority of Americans, who in theory have the democratic power to create a favorable tax structure, have been seriously underrepresented in the politics of taxation. From Washington, it is easy to see why. The larger and more privileged taxpayers, with money to spend on effective representation, have organized themselves into influential special-interest groups. Their advocates know the tax laws, and most important, the tax political process. By contrast, the average taxpayers remain relatively unorganized and unaware of the political process they must use to free themselves from unfair taxes. Although academicians and public-interest groups stand ready to assist citizens with knowledge of the tax system, they lack the political impact of an electorate aroused to effective action based on the knowledge of the political process and how to use it.

In short, the key to changing unfair taxes is to learn the tax policy process. How are the laws made? How are they enforced? Who are the key decision-makers at each step? What are points of access to influence the system at each step? Who are our potential allies in the fight for tax reform? Who are the adversaries, and how do they operate? What are our strengths and weaknesses? Only when we learn the answers to such tactical questions will we be ready to act effectively.

★ ★ ★ ★ ★ ★ ★

As a general rule, federal government tax policy is formally determined in three places: the Congress, the Treasury Department, and the Internal Revenue Service. The Congress, as the legislative branch of government, enacts all federal tax laws. The Treasury Department, as part of the executive branch, reflects the policy of the president of the United States. It has two major policy functions: the Treasury recommends laws to Congress, and it enacts tax regulations to carry out those laws which Congress passes. Finally, the ubiquitous Internal Revenue Service collects taxes by administering the laws and Treasury regulations as they apply to each particular taxpayer.

The entire process, from congressional policy to taxpayer's wallet, is a marvel of democratic government. As the late Justice Robert Jackson observed: "That a people so numerous, scattered and individualistic annually assesses itself with a tax liability so often in highly burdensome amounts is a reassuring sign of the vitality and stability of our system of self-government. It will be a sad day for the revenues if the goodwill of the people toward their taxing system is frittered away." In order to retain the goodwill of the American people, what is now needed is that democracy go one step further: that the average and lower income taxpayers, comprising the bulk of American voters and taxpayers, act to make the tax laws and the tax system fair to them—to eliminate loopholes in the tax laws and regulations, and to eliminate abuses in tax collection by the IRS. In later chapters we shall look more closely at the tax process in the Treasury Department and the IRS. We have already seen who benefits from the present tax system. Here, we shall look at Congress to see how the expensive game of tax politics is played, who the players are, and how the average taxpayer can affect the outcome.

76 TAX POLITICS

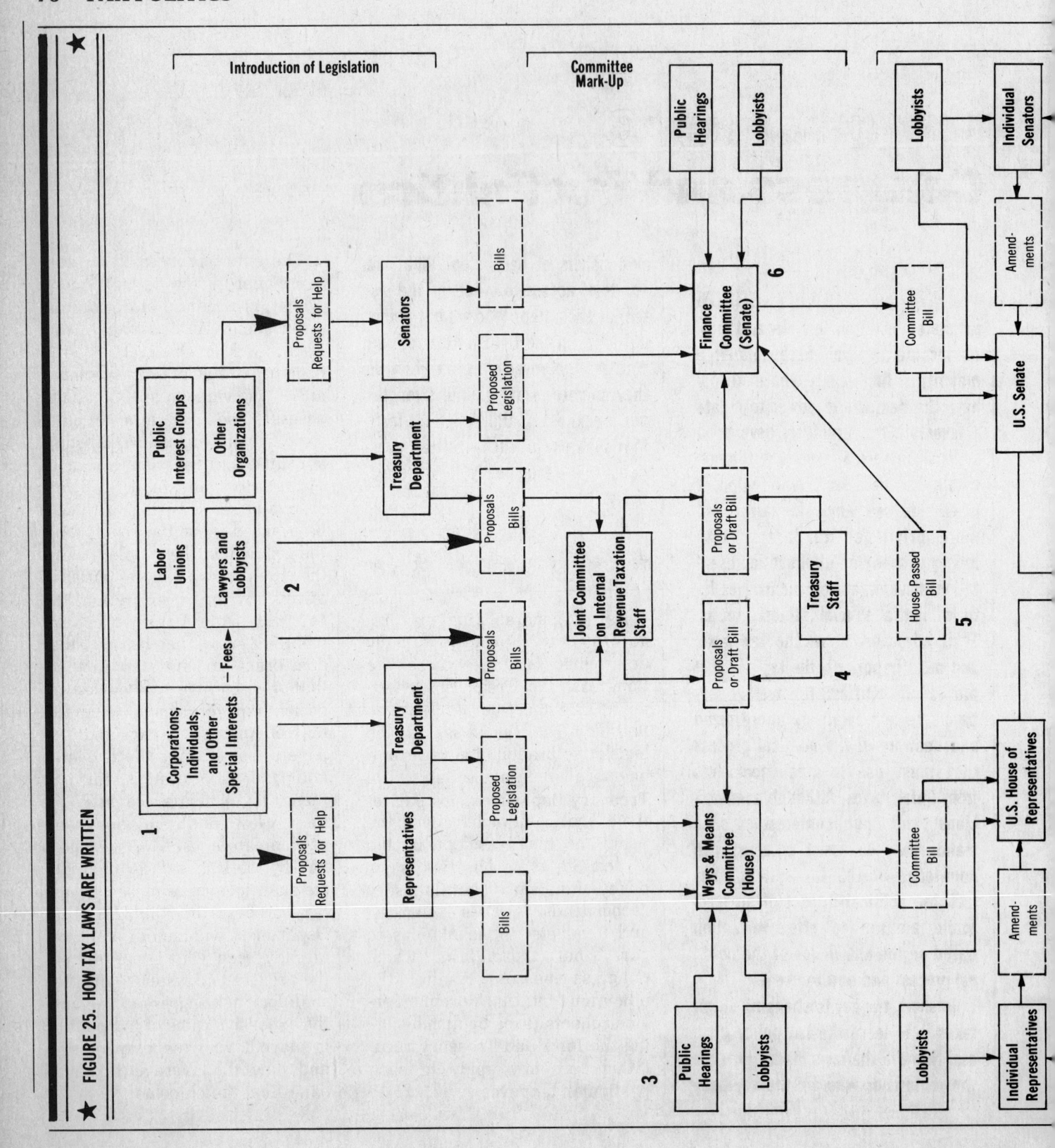

FIGURE 25. HOW TAX LAWS ARE WRITTEN

Congress and Tax Politics 77

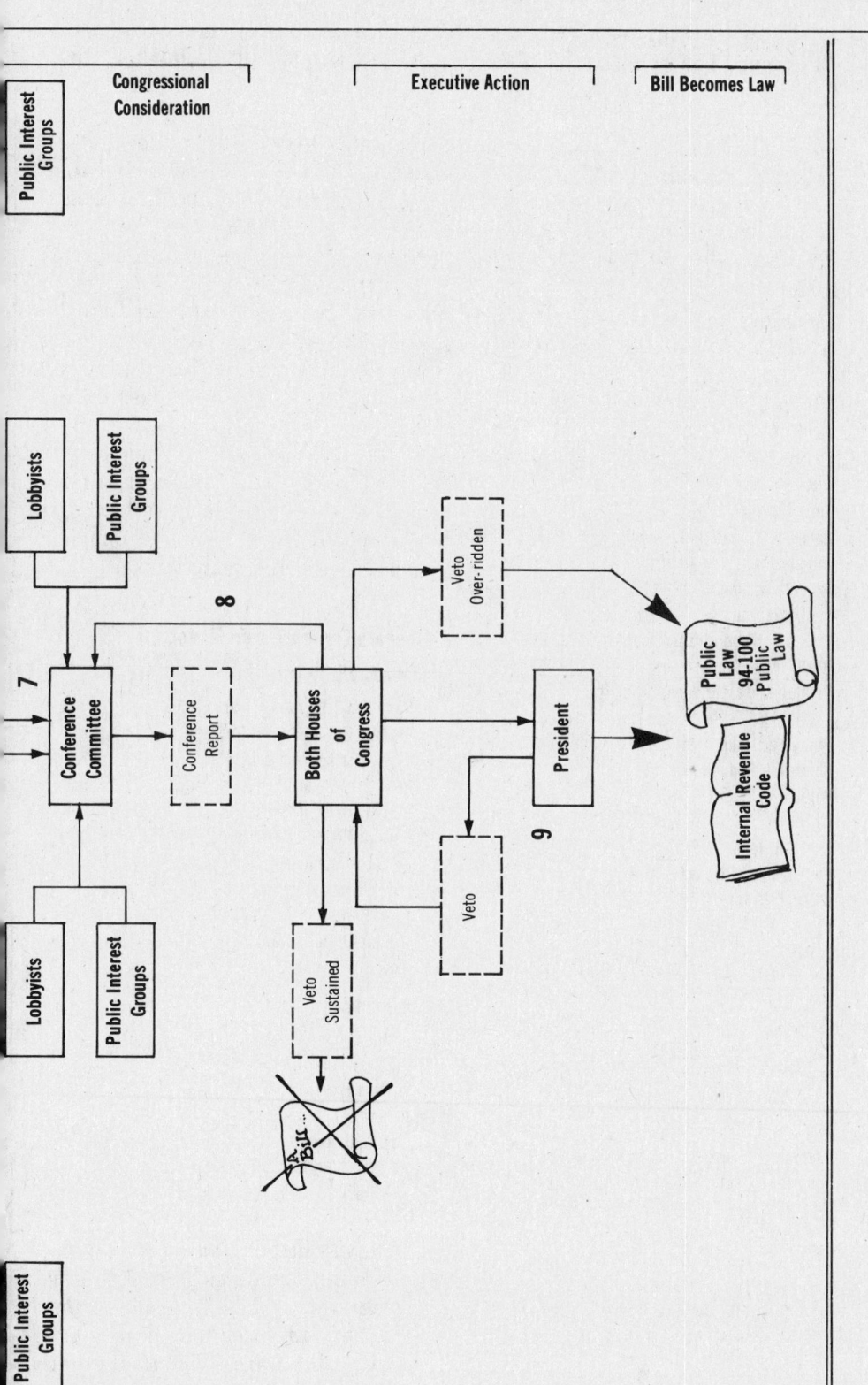

[Flowchart showing Congressional Consideration, Executive Action, and Bill Becomes Law stages, with Public Interest Groups and Lobbyists feeding into Conference Committee (7) → Conference Report (8) → Both Houses of Congress → President (9), with branches for Veto Sustained, Veto, Veto Over-ridden, leading to Public Law 94-100 / Internal Revenue Code.]

Proposed Legislation

1. Special interests and public interest groups make their proposals to sympathetic members of Congress, a sympathetic administration (Treasury), members of the committees, or committee staff. Campaign contributions help special interests get a sympathetic hearing on their proposals.
2. Special interests advance proposed tax changes themselves or by hiring lawyers and lobbyists.
3. Public hearings are useful input to committee members but direct lobbying activity during bill mark-ups has a much greater effect on committee decisions.
4. At committee mark-up sessions the staff presents alternative proposals for each subject area or a draft bill with a single set of proposals. The Treasury Department offers its opinions on these proposals and possibly the administration's alternative.
5. Under the Constitution, all revenue (tax) measures must originate in the House.
6. The Finance Committee will work from the House bill, but will often report out a substitute bill incorporating Finance Committee approved changes.
7. The House Senate Conference Committee meets to iron out differences between the House-passed and Senate-passed bills. Lobbyists work to retain favored provisions and knock out others they oppose. Only provisions where the two houses disagree can be changed.
8. Both houses either accept the Conference Committee Report or insist on their own version and send the legislation back to conference.
9. The president can sign the bill into law, or veto it. Two-thirds of both houses can override the veto; if they sustain the presidential veto the legislation is not enacted.

78 TAX POLITICS

the tax-writing committees

In order to deal with the myriad legislative tasks which must be done each year, each house of Congress has organized itself into committees according to the different areas of congressional responsibility—such as defense, banking, agriculture, and appropriations, to name a few. Since no single member of Congress can master all of these areas, the job is assigned to permanent committees which cover each area. The House and Senate, as interdependent parts of the legislative branch, have each evolved their own traditions over the years, including the development of somewhat different committee structures. For taxes, the Senate has assigned the jurisdiction to the Senate Finance Committee, while the House has assigned jurisdiction to the House Ways and Means Committee. Under congressional rules, the number of Democrats and Republicans on each committee is based on the parties' over-all ratio in each house of Congress.

In the 93rd Congress, ending in 1974, ten Democrats and seven Republicans sat on the Senate Finance Committee. One Democratic seat was added in the 94th Congress to reflect an increased Democratic Senate majority. The Finance Committee has been chaired since January 1966 by conservative Democrat Russell B. Long of Louisiana.

Through the 93rd Congress, fifteen Democrats and ten Republicans sat on the House Ways and Means Committee chaired since 1957 by Wilbur D. Mills of Arkansas. The Ways and Means Committee, however, underwent some dramatic changes in the 94th Congress. Its once powerful chairman, Wilbur Mills, facing

★

House Committee on Ways and Means, 1975

Democrats

Al Ullman, *Oregon*, Chairman
Wilbur D. Mills, *Arkansas*
James A. Burke, *Massachusetts*
Dan Rostenkowski, *Illinois*
Phil M. Landrum, *Georgia*
Charles A. Vanik, *Ohio*
Omar Burleson, *Texas*
James C. Corman, *California*
William J. Green, *Pennsylvania*
Sam M. Gibbons, *Florida*
Joe D. Waggonner, Jr., *Louisiana*
Joseph E. Karth, *Minnesota*
Otis G. Pike, *New York*
Richard F. Vander Veen, *Michigan*
J. J. Pickle, *Texas*
Henry Helstoski, *New Jersey*
Charles B. Rangel, *New York*
William R. Cotter, *Connecticut*
Fortney H. (Pete) Stark, *California*
James R. Jones, *Oklahoma*
Andy Jacobs, Jr., *Indiana*
Abner J. Mikva, *Illinois*
Martha Keys, *Kansas*
Joseph L. Fisher, *Virginia*
Harold E. Ford, *Tennessee*

Republicans

Herman T. Schneebeli, *Pennsylvania*
Barber B. Conable, Jr., *New York*
John J. Duncan, *Tennessee*
Donald D. Clancy, *Ohio*
Bill Archer, *Texas*
Guy Vanderjagt, *Michigan*
William A. Steiger, *Wisconsin*
Philip M. Crane, *Illinois*
Bill Frenzel, *Minnesota*
James G. Martin, *North Carolina*
L. A. (Skip) Bafalis, *Florida*
William M. Ketchum, *California*

★

almost certain ouster, resigned his chairmanship following the now-famous Tidal Basin incident and revelations of a serious drinking problem. The committee's second ranking Democrat, Al Ullman of Oregon, acting chairman during much of the 93rd Congress, succeeded Mills as chairman in the 94th Congress. House reformers also expanded the size of the committee, making the once conservative and senior committee younger and less conservative. The committee was increased to thirty-seven members with twenty-five Democrats and twelve Republicans, reflecting the more than two-to-one Democratic majority in the house.

★

Senate Committee on Finance, 1975

Democrats

Russell B. Long, *Louisiana*, Chairman
Herman E. Talmadge, *Georgia*
Vance Hartke, *Indiana*
Abraham Ribicoff, *Connecticut*
Harry F. Byrd, Jr., *Virginia*
Gaylord Nelson, *Wisconsin*
Walter F. Mondale, *Minnesota*
Mike Gravel, *Alaska*
Lloyd Bentsen, *Texas*
William D. Hathaway, *Maine*
Floyd K. Haskell, *Colorado*

Republicans

Carl T. Curtis, *Nebraska*
Paul J. Fannin, *Arizona*
Clifford P. Hansen, *Wyoming*
Robert Dole, *Kansas*
Bob Packwood, *Oregon*
William V. Roth, Jr., *Delaware*
Bill Brock, *Tennessee*

★

The composition of the tax-writing committees more than any other factor has determined the shape and direction of our tax laws. There are, of course, other influences on the tax legislative process which we will discuss. Any change in our unfair tax laws, though, must begin by changing the people who make those laws or changing their attitudes and actions.

who sits on the committees

Traditionally, members of the two committees have been more senior, more conservative, and less reform-minded than the rest of the Congress. Once legislators are assigned to committees, they remain until they are defeated in an election or voluntarily resign to take a preferred committee assignment.

Until recently, very few members of the Ways and Means Committee and the Finance Committee were defeated for re-election. Most had come from safe, well-established districts and, as we shall see, received significant campaign help from the special interests that benefit from favorable tax laws. Even fewer members would give up assignments to these prestigious and powerful committees.

As members of Congress become more senior and more secure in their jobs, they often become less responsive to their constituents and more responsive to the special interests and lobbyists with whom they have worked for years and who have contributed to their campaigns. Members once oriented toward tax reform tend to adapt to special-interest patterns and the status quo that characterizes the present system. Two years after he became Ways and Means chairman, Wilbur Mills wrote in *Life* magazine that "our tax system has become a house of horrors which needs rebuilding from the ground up." In the fifteen years that followed, he did very little to change those laws, often supporting new tax breaks for favored taxpayers. Some observers have also commented on the tendency of the present chairman, Al Ullman, to lose much of his enthusiasm for tax reform over the years.

Members of Congress inclined toward tax reform have become demoralized after years of unsuccessful effort and have reduced their efforts to improve the system. Consistent unsuccessful challenges to committee secrecy or special-interest activity can only incur the displeasure of the committee chairman and fellow members. As a result, some members have accepted the more immediate legislative rewards of going along with the system rather than challenging the special-interest tax practices of their respective committee chairmen.

In the Finance Committee and, until recently, in the Ways and Means Committee, few members would fight openly for reform. Without reformers making issues of secrecy, special tax giveaways, a chairman's heavy-handed approach, and other actions not in the public interest, the tax-writing committees remained insulated from public exposure and public criticism and, therefore, from reforms. As we shall see, members who do choose to buck the status quo may not be considered part of the club but can help reform the system and, as a consequence, our tax laws.

what influences the committees

Members of the tax committees, responsible for more than $100 billion in tax expenditures to various interest groups, are themselves among the largest congressional recipients of special-interest campaign contributions. In the 1972 elections, twenty-three members of the Ways and Means Committee and three members of the Finance Committee up for re-election listed more than $575,000 in campaign contributions which were reported after the election—too late for voters to have known about them before casting their ballots. A survey by the *Washington Post* disclosed that most of the $575,000, both in post-October 26th contributions and larger sums given earlier, came from special interests concerned with taxes, health insurance, pension benefits, and other legislation within the jurisdiction of the two committees. Many of the contributions were actually received after the election itself by candidates who had just won a two-year extension of the legislative activities so important to their contributors.

The major contributors are not difficult to predict. In any given election year those interests who benefit most from the tax laws lead the list. They include financial interests such as banks, savings and loans, investment houses and the securities industry, all of which benefit from preferential capital gains treatment, investment tax incentives, and a number of bank tax subsidies. Oil and mineral interests usually follow, with their stake in

80 TAX POLITICS

preserving depletion allowances, intangible drilling deductions, and foreign tax credits. Large manufacturing interests are big contributors, seeking to preserve and extend fast write-offs and investment credits for equipment and tax subsidies for exports. Real estate groups contribute heavily with an interest in accelerated depreciation, tax shelters, and tax deductions for homebuying. Medical interests, such as doctors, dentists, hospitals, and nursing homes—all with a great stake in how health insurance and Medicare legislation is written, are major contributors. Doctors, lawyers, and business executives have additional incentives to contribute considering the vast amounts of tax benefits in tax shelters and pension plans for high-paid individuals. The list goes on—insurance, railroads, drug companies, multinational companies, corporate farmers, and more.

Special-interest influence is not limited to campaign support. Many special interests and lobbyists develop strong professional and personal relationships with members of Congress. Some lobbyists have developed close friendships with key members of the tax committees. Well-known Washington tax lobbyist James "Dick" Riddell was friendly with Wilbur Mills for years. He not only lent Mill's 1972 presidential campaign $17,000, he also actually left Washington to help in the New Hampshire presidential primary. In return, Riddell could get a friendly ear for his clients' particular tax problems. He and other friendly lobbyists had better access to committee information and materials. Riddell has continued his friendship with the present chairman, Al Ullman. He can still be seen using the "members only" phone in the private anteroom off the Ways and Means main committee room.

Other lobbyists may be less brash than Dick Riddell, but they still know how to play the lobbying game. They develop congenial relationships with members and their staffs, taking them to lunch or providing an additional sweetness in the form of imported Scotch, scarce tickets to a Redskins' game, or an occasional junket. Former Senator Paul Douglas explained the process well:

The enticer does not generally pay money directly to the public representative. He tries instead, by a series of favors, to put the public official under such a feeling of personal obligation that the latter gradually loses his sense of mission to the public and comes to feel that his first loyalties are to his private benefactors and patrons.... Throughout this whole process the official will claim—and may, indeed, believe—that there is no causal connection between the favors he has received and the decision which he makes. He will assert that the favors were given or received on the basis of pure friendship.

A more subtle form of influence and, in fact, payment for laboring on behalf of a corporation or lobbying group is the potential for a high-paying job when the member retires from Congress. Subsequent employment by lobbying organizations was described in *Who Runs Congress?* as the "Congress-lobby complex." John W. Byrnes, the ranking Republican on Ways and Means until he retired in 1972, represents several interests including U.S. Steel, minerals, insurance and breweries. Charles Chamberlain, another Republican who retired in 1974, has clients interested in tax legislation in the House and Senate, among them cab owners seeking an exemption from a Ways and Means gas tax. Former Florida Senator and Finance Committee member George Smathers represents horse breeders, railroads, and scrap dealers. Former members of Congress move freely about their ex-colleagues. Moreover, they have the privilege, accorded no other lobbyists, of visiting members on the House and Senate floor.

One Washington lobbyist has carried such influence one step further. Thomas Boggs, son of the late House Majority leader Hale Boggs, used his father's position very effectively. According to the *Washington Post*, the American Medical Association had hired the younger Boggs's law firm to head off a proposed provision of the 1969 Tax Reform Act which would have cost the association millions of dollars in taxes on *AMA Journal* advertising revenues. Boggs, whose father Ways and Means Committee, was hired, according to internal AMA memos, because he was able to obtain "copies of all documents, confidential and otherwise . . . [while the bill] was being drafted" in the House and when it came before the Senate Finance Committee. He was also able to obtain "assurances that amended language submitted [by AMA friends] in the Senate would survive the ultimate House-Senate Conference." Just to be sure, the AMA also contributed $5,000 to

Hale Boggs's campaign, $2,500 of which was delivered in December 1969 while the conference committee was meeting. Tom Boggs is still considered close to the Ways and Means Committee and represents numerous special interests on tax legislative matters.

Finally, members of the tax-writing committees end up supporting much bad tax legislation because the tax code is the only instrument they have at their disposal. This problem was highlighted most effectively during the Ways and Means Committee's consideration of an Energy Conservation Bill in 1975. There were many sound non-tax conservation proposals being advanced in Congress, but the committee only had jurisdiction over tax write-offs. Part of the debate over the tax credit for home insulation illustrates the relative wisdom (or unwisdom) of adding still more tax preferences to our already cumbersome tax laws.

MR. ULLMAN: We've got to be sure that the items purchased by the taxpayer actually are useful insulaters. The [committee] staff should tighten up the technical language so that this loophole won't be so big. (Laughter greeted the use of the term "loophole" and prompted an explanation from the chairman.) Well, this is a loophole but it benefits everyone and that, nobody can deny.

MR. BAFALIS (R-Fla.): Might it not be better for the government to help people arrange long-term home improvement loans at very low rates of interest? Many people are too poor to spend $1,000 on insulation even if they do get a $300 tax break.

MR. JACOBS (D-Ind.): Do you realize how much energy savings on dentist drills we could have if we paid someone to come in and brush every citizen's teeth every morning? Why do Americans need a tax code bribe from the government every time we want them to do something sensible which they ought to do anyway on their own? I'm going to ask the staff (of the Joint Committee on Internal Revenue Taxation) to do a psychological study which profiles the average American. I want the staff to report to me on just where and why our wonderful traditional and fundamental American spirit of free enterprise has degenerated.

MR. BURKE (D-Mass.): This reminds me of my seed proposal. [Mr. Burke has been touting a bill to give each American a free packet of vegetable seeds.] Our forefathers were very self-reliant and independent. They grew their own food in their gardens. Our forefathers gave away seeds till they were coming out of their ears.

MR. JACOBS: The seeds of our destruction lie along this route. May the record show that we are drinking only water this morning.

MR. PIKE (D-N.Y.): How can we be sure people aren't sabotaging our conservation efforts by deducting electric toothbrushes as a medical expense? What I mean is the problem which Mr. Ullman has properly mentioned is simply one we always have to live with—the taxpayer must be able to somehow prove he spent the money legitimately.

MR. STEIGER (R-Wis.): If we give a tax break for installing insulation why don't we also give one for awnings or exterior siding or perhaps curtains? In many cases these will make better sense, but these people won't get any government help.

MR. ULLMAN: The point is we have to draw a line somewhere to distinguish between decoration and insulation.

MR. VANDER JAGT (R-Mich.): It seems that this committee may be rapidly proceeding to adopt an extremely costly measure, without knowing how much bang per buck we're getting. How are we going to know how much of an energy saving we're getting for each dollar this credit is costing the government. We need to know what result we're going to get to know if this is a good investment.

(The committee staff noted that several economists have used mathematical computer models to predict how much energy will be saved, although there are differences of opinion as to precisely how big a tax credit is needed to entice homeowners to act. The committee had earlier invited these economists to give expert testimony, but—perhaps through oversight—no behavioral psychologists were invited.)

Next the committee discussed a similar credit for installing solar energy collectors in homes. The following question, which is fundamental to the subject of tax expenditures, was raised.

MR. FRENZEL (R-Minn.): Do we even know how many people today can possibly afford a solar unit? Will Mrs. Horace Dodge buy it? Will she be the only one to qualify for it? [The much-celebrated Mrs. Dodge reportedly pays no federal taxes on income, from tax-exempt bond interest, of $1 million each year.]

MR. KARTH (D-Minn.): We should not blindly approve these additional write-offs for coal-hauling railroads and utilities. I'm concerned about using new tax preferences—I won't call them loopholes—to attack the energy problem. Loss guarantees or low-interest loan guarantees would be better, provided they are proven to be necessary. Our experience shows that once these tax preferences get enacted they never get repealed. In future years it becomes a hidden appropriation. The appropriations committee never sees the cost. The other way—the direct expenditure way—it's out in the open. [And, incidentally, out of the jurisdiction of the Ways and Means Committee.]

MR. ULLMAN: The tax route is better than giving them government financing. We have a long history of doing it this way. This is the most dynamic way.

MR. KARTH: I question the wisdom of it.

82 TAX POLITICS

While the committee refused to adopt tough conservation taxes, it did eventually adopt the insulation and solar heating credit and railroad write-offs. It also approved special tax benefits for businesses that recycle paper, iron, and steel; for equipment used to convert coal into liquid or gas; and for the installation by businesses of insulation and solar energy equipment. One tax reformer on the committee, Sam Gibbons of Florida, commented that the final bill was an "ounce of conservation and a gallon of loopholes."

The process was well described by Elizabeth Drew, writing on the Energy Conservation Bill for *The New Yorker* magazine:

> All this was done by the process of mutual accommodation by which the committee has operated over the years: a member who has a particular interest in one sort of tax break offers it in the form of an amendment, and the others, like poker players lending chips, go along. As the committee broke for lunch, someone who had been observing the committee said, "Now you know why the tax code is the way it is." To be sure, some of the purposes for which the "incentives" were approved might be laudable, and some of the provisions might even result in the conservation of energy. But there are questions about the suitability of the tax code as a vehicle for trying to achieve such purposes. Tax breaks tend to perpetuate both themselves and other tax breaks. They *are* harder to stop than a federal "program." Tax incentives usually benefit those who are better off. But the Ways and Means Committee adopted a number of tax credits for energy conservation, for two reasons: the tax code was the only mechanism under its jurisdiction; habit.

power relationships in the house

The traditional committee power structure is responsible for much of the special-interest oriented legislation that has emerged from the Ways and Means Committee and the Finance Committee: although average taxpayers may be better represented in Congress as a whole, they are woefully underrepresented where it counts. Moreover, the two tax committees have always wielded enough power to resist all but the most determined efforts by nonmembers to change tax legislation. The sources of that power are embedded in the structure and traditions of the Congress. Happily, some of those traditions and structures have begun to fall before a reform movement that is slowly advancing in both the House and the Senate.

When a member of Congress introduces a bill, it is sent to the proper committee. According to the Constitution, all tax bills must begin in the House. And when a representative introduces a tax bill it is referred to the Ways and Means Committee. The committee has immense power, including legislative jurisdiction over taxes, trade, social security, Medicare and Medicaid, unemployment compensation, health insurance, and welfare. Moreover, before the 94th Congress, Ways and Means Democrats served as a "committee on committees," controlling Democratic committee assignments in the House. Since such assignments are critical to a representative's career, House Democrats have been especially responsive to the committee's Democratic majority and, of course, its chairman.

Recognition of and concern over this nonlegislative source of committee influence resulted in a move at the beginning of the 94th Congress to transfer the Ways and Means Committee's committee assignment function to the Democratic Steering and Policy Committee—a nonlegislative party policy committee considered more representative of House Democrats as a whole. Predictably, committee Democrats, fighting to maintain this source of power, reminded many of the fellow legislators of past "assignment favors" in hopes of defeating the move. But the seventy-five Democratic freshmen representatives could not be so persuaded and provided the margin of victory in a 146-122 vote to strip the Ways and Means Committee of its long-held power over committee assignments.

With its growth in power, the Ways and Means Committee had developed a corresponding vanity. "The Ways and Means Committee knows that it does not operate in a vacuum," second-ranking Republican Barber Conable (N.Y.) has said of the committee's role in Congress, adding, "rather, it floats in a sea of peasants."

And the Ways and Means Committee does still retain a great deal of power and prestige within the Congress. It is a very important legislative committee holding "life and death" power over many areas of legislation important to other members of Congress who, of necessity, must rely on the Ways and Means

Committee to act on their favorite legislation. If the committee doesn't like a tax bill, the bill will die. There will be no explanation or excuse: the committee will simply not approve the bill and, most often, will not even consider it. Representatives who do not cooperate with the Ways and Means Committee will not get cooperation from the committee on their bills. In the 93rd Congress 3,370 bills (many duplicates) were referred to the Ways and Means Committee. Of these, only forty-five were reported (approved) for consideration by the full House, and many of these had been changed substantially.

The committee also holds power over the complex areas of its jurisdiction because few members of Congress outside the committee are knowledgeable in these areas. Representatives are generalists, few have the time or the interest to become informed on taxes, and most defer to the committee on these matters. This has been a major weakness in the tax legislative process. In the past, it has resulted in a small group of legislators having an iron grip on tax policy and undermining the fairness of the tax system.

The power of the Ways and Means Committee traditionally has been the power of one man, its chairman. Wilbur D. Mills was chairman from 1957 through 1974. Mills decided when to call committee meetings, when to allow public hearings, and which bills and which subjects the committee would consider. Without his approval, no representatives were appointed to fill vacancies on Ways and Means.

Ways and Means had long been the smallest legislative committee in the House, despite having the greatest legislative responsibility. It also had not delegated any of that responsibility to subcommittees. Mills had abolished subcommittees shortly after becoming chairman in 1957, and had since exercised total authority over all substantive issues and proposed legislation, and what he could not do through his prerogatives as chairman, he did through his legendary knowledge of the tax laws.

Besides Mills, Ways and Means had fourteen Democrats and ten Republicans. Theoretically, a majority of the committee could overrule the chairman, but Mills had picked his committee well. Most members were docile as long as he gave them prestige, electoral support, and the chance to introduce their own special legislation.

Most committee members had joined the committee not because of its legislative activity but because of its power and prestige. Mills was a master in letting them retain that prestige while they let him do the real legislating. His control over the committee began to slip, however, in the 93rd Congress. During the committee's consideration of the 1974 energy tax bill, tax reformers, led by junior committee member William J. Green (D-Pa.), made a concerted effort to completely eliminate the oil depletion allowance in defiance of the chairman's wishes. The mere fact of a challenge to Chairman Mills indicated that he was losing some of his power. Now with thirty-seven members and six subcommittees, the power and authority of the new committee chairman, Al Ullman (D-Ore.), will be more diffuse.

Expansion of the committee coupled with election-year retirements and defeats has significantly changed the committee's ideological makeup as well. Two of the more conservative and less intellectual committee Republicans, Harold Collier (Ill.) and Charles Chamberlain (Mich.), have retired, and two other Republicans, Joel Broyhill (Va.) and Donald Brotzman (Colo.), were defeated. On the Democratic side, liberal Martha Griffiths (Mich.) retired and Hugh Carey (N.Y.) left to run successfully for the governorship of New York.

Many of the twelve new Democrats on the committee are decidedly more pro-tax reform than incumbent committee members. And several of the new Republicans are vast improvements over the members they have replaced. While the enlargement of the tax-writing committee makes it more reform-minded, there likely will not be an absolute majority in favor of major tax-reform legislation. The new committee should, however, develop substantial minorities who will be able to press tax-reform issues in the committee and on the House floor. Tax reform in the House will succeed or fail in the next several years to the degree that these committee members can coalesce centrist committee members or a majority of House members around specific tax reforms.

84 TAX POLITICS

Of course, the committee's chairman, Al Ullman, will be the key to how the committee will operate in the future. He is generally considered as conservative as Mills on many tax-reform issues but has handled the committee in a more open and democratic way. It is not clear which way he will move on tax-reform legislation in the future. But given the recent upheavals against unresponsive committee chairmen, his views will probalby reflect those of the majority of Democrats on the committee more often than not.

power relationships in the senate

In the Senate, tax bills are referred to the Senate Finance Committee. There, with senators serving on several different committees, power relationships differ from those in the House. Historically, the Senate tax-writing committee has not had the powerful influence over the Senate that its counterpart has had over the House. But its power and influence have been considerable, and the impact of Russell B. Long (D-La.), its chairman, is well known.

Like the Ways and Means Committee, the Finance Committee has jurisdiction over many important areas of legislation—taxes, trade, social security, welfare, health insurance, revenue-sharing, and others. Very few senators will take on the Finance Committee and its chairman, knowing they have great control over so many areas of important legislation. On the contrary, most senators fall prey to the mutual back-scratching that characterizes much of Congress's activities.

Russell Long's skill at playing the game of legislative give-and-take is legendary. He's willing to approve, for instance, a minor Medicare amendment that means little to him but a great deal to several northern liberals. In return, those senators usually defer to Long's wishes on major issues such as oil taxation. As one senator observed about Long: "It's remarkable how little he gives up in return for what he gets."

Nowhere does Long play this game better than in his own committee. As a result, very few committee members march out of step with the chairman. For years, committee "tax reformers" would sit by quietly as the committee at Long's insistence passed many new tax breaks. Any opposition that did surface would protest only meekly against what was being done. On most occassions, there was no attempt to force roll-call votes to put senators on record in favor of sometimes blatantly special-interest legistlation.

Usually, committee liberals remained team players, accepting their quietly contested defeats in stride and refusing to take their opposition to the Senate floor where they might win. On the few occasions when floor fights were mounted, non-committee members led the opposition, with committee members reluctantly agreeing to join the fight. During consideration of the 1975 Tax Cut Act, committee liberals Abraham Ribicoff (D-Conn.), Gaylord Nelson (D-Wis.), and Walter Mondale (D-Minn.) concurred with Long initially in voting not to include a House-passed repeal of the oil depletion allowance. Committee newcomers Floyd Haskell (D-Colo.) and William Hathaway (D-Me.) argued alone to follow the House's lead. It was only after a major effort to include depletion in the bill was announced by noncommittee members including moderate conservative Ernest F. Hollings (D-S.C.) that the committee liberals agreed to vote to end the Long-inspired filibuster on behalf of the oil interests. They were embarrassed into taking a reform position by a conservative Southerner who apparently had a clearer sense of the importance of fighting against the depletion allowance.

Long has carried committee loyalty to a further extreme. Sometimes he gets other committee members to carry the ball for his own special-interest legislation in order to legitimatize his efforts. During consideration of a 1975 energy conservation bill Long saw an opportunity to push for a new tax incentive for the oil industry—a drilling credit for oil wells. He stated quite candidly one day that if he offered such a proposal, it would be viewed as another tax break for the oil industry but if a non-oil stater offered the same proposal it would be viewed as an energy-production incentive. The following day, Senator Ribicoff of Connecticut spoke in favor of the idea of an oil-drilling credit as an incentive to produce more oil. That kind of loyalty does not go unrewarded. Senators Ribicoff,

Nelson, and Mondale all have good working relationships with Long. And they have all had success in getting Long's cooperation on welfare and other measures. There has been a great cost involved in terms of tax legislation which the senators apparently decided was worth paying. They have consistently told tax reformers that they agree with them and will vote with them, but that they cannot take an aggressive role in fighting for certain reforms to which Long is opposed. Hopefully, new additions on the committee and more public exposure will transform these senators into active rather than passive tax reformers.

One thing is clear—the power of the tax-writing committees and their chairmen to thwart tax reform cannot be curbed from outside the committee. It must start within. Ways and Means Committee members have begun that effort and have had a few notable successes to date. Senators Haskell and Hathaway seem to recognize the importance of initiating tax reforms from within and may be able to forge their likeminded colleagues on the committee into a viable bloc that will counter the power and influence of the special-interest representatives on the committee.

sources of legislation

We have seen who the actors are in the legislative process. But where does tax legislation really come from? Who formulates over-all tax policy? Who proposes new tax laws or changes in our existing laws?

the treasury department

As we will see in Chapter 3, primary responsibility for initiating tax legislation resides in the Treasury Department. It is the president, then, who usually will advocate major changes in the tax law as he does in other areas of the law. In the past, the Treasury Department's advocacy of tax reforms or new tax policy has varied greatly, depending on the administration in power.

The Kennedy and Johnson Treasury Departments were particularly active in the tax policy area under Assistant Treasury Secretary Stanley S. Surrey. Their work culminated in an extensive study of the tax system and suggested reforms. These tax studies were released as President Johnson left office and provided the background and basis for much of the 1969 Tax Reform Act. Many issues raised in the studies but not acted upon in 1969 are still cited by tax reformers as needed reforms.

In contrast, the Nixon and Ford Treasury has done little in the area of tax reform. In the words of the former assistant treasury secretary for tax policy for these Republican administrations: "Neither former President Nixon nor President Ford felt that tax reform is a burning issue that needs to be on the front burner just for its own sake."

During the 1972 presidential campaign President Nixon had publicly promised major tax reform initiatives by the end of the year. But it was not until April 1973, after the Ways and Means Committee had completed extensive tax-reform hearings and were about to draft tax-reform legislation, that Treasury Secretary Schultz presented the administration's ideas on tax reform. Most experts agreed that those proposals were not very comprehensive and showed signs of being hastily prepared in response to the Ways and Means actions.

In 1975, Secretary Simon came before the Ways and Means Committee reiterating the earlier Nixon proposals, with two important changes. The one major reform item—a subsidy to replace tax-exempt municipal bonds—was dropped and significant new tax cuts for corporations and their shareholders were proposed to increase investment. Simon was criticized by many tax experts for proposing these new tax cuts because they were not based on any hard evidence on the need for new investment incentives and because they were not very well thought-out. In fact, one of his proposals, tax breaks on savings accounts, had been vehemently opposed by the Treasury Department only nine months earlier as an ineffective savings incentive that benefited only the well-off.

The lack of an affirmative Treasury tax policy was underscored in 1975 during the search for a new assistant secretary for tax policy to replace the retiring Frederic Hickman. A number of people who were offered the job turned it down. The top tax-policy job was hard to fill because there was no real commitment to a tax policy by the administration.

Not only had the Nixon and Ford Administrations shown little interest in formulating positive policy but their Treasury was, to a large extent, a second-class citizen in over-all administration decisions. During the Kennedy and Johnson years, the Treasury Department had strong veto powers over policy decisions affecting taxes. If the Commerce Department, for example, wanted to push for a new export tax subsidy, it had to be approved by the Treasury Department. This was not the case under Nixon and Ford.

In fact, Treasury's objection to or advocacy of a new program was often overruled by other agencies or cabinet officers. This was the case when the Treasury came out strongly against an expensive and inefficient tax credit for recycling scrap and paper. After the Environmental Protection Agency gave the proposal a something-is-better-than-nothing endorsement, the administration, through congressional Republicans, supported the proposal. It was also the case when the Council of Economic Advisors' chief, Alan Greenspan, disapproved Treasury's support for a direct subsidy to replace tax-exempt state and local bonds. Needless to say, the morale of the professional economists and attorneys who work on tax policy can only be hurt by such decisions.

The importance of the Treasury Department in proposing new legislation and reforms stems from its unique position in the executive branch. This agency has a great number of professional staff—both economists and tax attorneys—who have the time and resources to study the effects of the tax laws and to propose changes. They also have access to an extensive computer system with data on tax returns that is essential in analyzing the present laws and projecting the effects of any changes. Through the Internal Revenue Service, they also have direct feedback as to what areas need tightening up, changing, or simplifying to ensure better compliance and enforcement.

The Treasury Department's access to other federal agencies helps it determine how the tax laws affect other substantive areas, such as housing, banking, or farming. Finally, it has the resources of the executive branch and the president to present changes to the public and push for their acceptance by Congress. For these reasons, major reforms in our tax laws will rarely take place without the support of the Treasury Department.

outside interest groups

Much tax legislation originates from outside interest groups as well. Most often, these interest groups will hire tax attorneys to work on legislation to relieve a particular situation that the taxpayer feels is too burdensome. It's the tax lawyer's job to find a legislative solution, develop a convincing case or rationale for the change, and convince a member of Congress or, more likely, a member of the tax-writing committee, its chairman, or its staff, to support the proposal.

Examples abound as to how this method has been used to help particular taxpayers or narrow special interests gain tax favors. There is the $2 million loophole for movie magnate Louis B. Mayer, separate tax breaks for the estate of the DuPont Family, the estate of stockbroker Charles Merrill, the estate of a G.E. president's wife, Mary Hill Swope, a $3 million tax break for Uniroyal, a $14 million tax break for Lockheed, along with $6.5 million for its competitor McDonnell-Douglas, and a $13 million tax break for Mobil. In fact, the 1969 Tax Reform Act contained over a hundred such special provisions, as was pointed out on the Senate floor by Senator Edward Kennedy to the embarrassment of Finance Committee Chairman Long.

Other tax provisions with broader application are also the result of special-interest pressure. The $2,000 tax credit for home-buyers was drafted and lobbied for by the home-building industry which convinced members of both tax-writing committees to offer it as an amendment to the 1975 Tax Reduction Act. The home-builders saw it as a means of promoting sagging new-home sales by using a popular political argument that home-buyers need tax relief from the high costs of homes and mortgages.

tax professionals

Still other provisions are proposed by professional groups involved with tax laws. The American Bar Association sometimes develops tax proposals. Often these proposals are helpful because they come from professionals most intimately involved in tax planning in specific areas, such as estate and gift taxes. Sometimes, however, the interests of the attorneys in maintaining tax laws advantageous to their clients, and therefore their practices, get in the way of substantial reform proposals.

congress

Finally, some legislative initiatives come from the Congress itself, although most tax legislation introduced in the Congress is the result of a specific lobbying effort. The primary source of tax legislative initiatives within Congress is the staff of the Joint Committee on Internal Revenue Taxation, headed by Dr. Lawrence Woodworth. This staff serves both the Ways and Means and the Finance Committee, providing all the staff work for tax legislation. When the chairman of the Ways and Means Committee indicates an interest in having his committee consider tax legislation—either in a specific area or reform legislation generally—the Joint Committee staff will put together a series of recommendations (usually carrying the approval of the chairman) or a draft bill. Often these draft proposals will contain possible alternatives in the same area.

The staff, consisting of attorneys and economists, has considerable expertise but usually develops its tax proposals after consultation with the Treasury Department, outside-interest groups, academic experts, and the inevitable input of numerous Washington lobbyists. The role of the staff in formulating tax policy seems to bear an inverse relationship to the role of the Treasury Department. In recent years, the staff's prominence in tax legislation has grown as the influence and initiative of the Treasury Department has waned.

In addition to the committee staff and the chairman to whom it is responsible, other members of the tax-writing committees and other members of Congress propose tax legislation. Much of this legislation, as with all tax legislation, reflects the concerns of a particular group or industry who brought their problem to the attention of the sponsor. But a number of representatives have begun to develop their own tax-reform proposals, reflecting a general interest in changing the tax laws. Comprehensive tax-reform bills have been sponsored by Ways and Means member James Corman (D-Cal.). House Banking Committee Chairman Henry Reuss (D-Wis.), and Finance member Floyd Haskell (D-Colo.). In addition, the seventy-five new Democratic members of the 94th Congress have set up a tax-reform task force to develop ideas for tax legislation.

reform groups

Tax-reform groups have also developed their own legislative proposals which have been introduced in the Congress. The Tax Justice Act of 1975 (see Appendix) was sponsored by over thirty representatives in the 94th Congress. Other proposals have been proposed by tax reformers and introduced by members of the House and the Senate.

the house

hearings

When the Ways and Means Committee decides to act on a major bill, it almost always calls for public hearings. Hearings provide an ideal opportunity to hear the ideas of interested taxpayers on changes in the law and to learn the details of complicated legislative proposals. Those who may be helped or hurt by changes in the tax law come before the committee to support or oppose legislation or to suggest modifications.

The Ways and Means hearings, however, have always been held more for the benefit of those testifying than for those listening. Nearly thirty years ago, *Business Week* magazine commented that "this year's tax hearings have been staged for the witnesses. The idea is to let everyone say his piece before the Committee starts work on a bill. Then no one can argue later that his viewpoint was not considered." *Business Week* added that senior members of the committee felt "the act of giving public testimony has a soothing psychological effect on constituents," noting that for this reason committee members would decline to argue with witnesses, but would rather thank them for their contribution and proceed to write a quite different bill.

That was 1947. The last twenty-eight years have seen little change in committee style. In fact, well before the 1973 hearings on promised tax reform, Chairman Mills told the *New York Times* of his plan to use the hearings "to make a showing" to the American people that our tax laws really aren't so bad after all.

There is another important function of committee hearings. It gives Washington lobbyists an opportunity to earn their fees. The hearings may mean little to the legislative process but an appearance before the Ways and Means Committee by a lobbyist or corporate vice president (including a picture of them shaking hands with the chairman) means a lot to those who pay their salaries.

Sometimes the committee will invite panels of tax experts to discuss the tax laws. At these sessions many committee members tend to hear only what they want to hear though some of the newer members seem anxious to learn more about the subjects discussed and follow the testimony closely. In general, however, the committee's interest in expert testimony is only slightly above its interest in general public testimony.

Attendance in both instances is usually poor. In 1973, the committee invited fifty-five expert witnesses to analyze eleven major areas of tax reform. Yet only ten of the twenty-five committee members managed to attend at least half of the expert sessions—sessions designed to discuss the complicated issues in the tax bill.

Hearings which consist of special interests arguing their case are even more poorly attended. But some witnesses, labor unions, the Chamber of Commerce, or the National Association of Manufacturers are usually scheduled in the morning and draw larger attendance. Not surprisingly, other large campaign contributors such as the AMA, the oil industry, real estate groups, and banks also prompt good attendance from the beneficiaries of their support. Most questions asked of such witnesses are set up in advance with a friendly member of the committee.

The whole hearing process tends to lull the committee members, the staff, the press, and the public to sleep. It is not surprising that in 1975 the committee agreed to split attendance time so that a third of the committee would try to be there for a third of the day. At one public hearing in 1973, Congressman Burke volunteered to witnesses from the Public Citizen Tax Reform Research Group why twenty-three of the twenty-five members were missing. The committee had arranged beforehand that one member from each party would attend, leaving the rest free to go home to their districts.

But on occasion a witness may have some effect. George Deffett, a major real estate developer from the Midwest, appeared before the committee on "prime time" one morning in 1973. A fair number of committee members sympathetic to the real estate industry were there to hear more reasons why the industry needed all the tax breaks it was getting. But Mr. Deffett attacked the industry "incentives" as wasteful, unneeded, and counterproductive to proper real estate development and business management. Needless to say, his testimony had more effect than similar testimony from a number of academicians several weeks earlier. Unfortunately, most of the old friends of the industry found their long association with other industry representatives, and the campaign contributions that flow with that association, more persuasive.

mark-up or bill-drafting sessions

When the public hearings are over, the committee goes into "mark-up" sessions where it begins to consider the issues and hammers out a detailed tax bill. Drafting a tax bill involves much horse-trading and compromise. It is during these sessions that outside lobbying pressure is most crucial and, for that reason, reaches its peak.

Before 1973, all Ways and Means bill-drafting sessions were held in secret. Lobbyists had to rely on allies on the committee to find out what was going on, what issues needed to be pushed, and who needed to be worked on. Secret sessions were a fairly effective way of controlling legislation while protecting members who sided with special interests. Not only was their work generally kept out of the public view, but also votes on specific proposals were not released. Members could claim they voted in the public interest while approving special legislation. Their excuse usually was that they voted for the final bill because it represented a compromise—more good than bad.

Reforms in the 93rd Congress required that all mark-up sessions be held in public unless closed by a public vote of a majority of committee members. Representatives, in a post-Watergate atmosphere, found it difficult to go on record for government secrecy, and eventually the Ways and Means Committee began to draft legislation in the open.

Thanks to other structural reforms, any member may now demand that votes taken during mark-up sessions be recorded and made publicly available. Members of the committee can still protect each other, however, by not demanding roll-call votes on special-interest legislation or other controversial measures. During a 1974 mark-up, for instance, the committee decision to increase living-expense allowances for members of Congress was unrecorded, as was a controversial cut in the excise tax on beer. In the 94th Congress, committee members began insisting on more recorded votes on controversial proposals. In a number of cases—such as a highly publicized proposed tax bail-out for Chrysler, Pan Am, and Lockheed—putting members publicly on record on special-interest legislation has been responsible for disapproval of a number of such measures. Still, there is a tendency not to demand a recorded vote on some issues that might embarrass fellow legislators.

the chairman's role

Initial input during the mark-up session comes from the committee chairman and the Joint Committee staff. The chairman will have the staff draw up a draft bill or he will himself introduce the administration's draft bill. Other committee members will offer changes to the basic draft but the chairman obviously has the upper hand in this situation since the burden to come up with technically sound alternatives and to convince a majority of the committee of their approach falls to the members proposing the changes.

Another approach to drafting tax bills has been tried recently in response to members' complaints about the undemocratic nature of being presented with a bill reflecting only the chairman's view. The staff will write up pamphlets describing specific problem areas of taxation and provide several alternative reforms to deal with the problem. One position, usually the one favored by the chairman, will be recommended. Alternative proposals may represent the views of the professional staff, lobbying groups or members supporting those interests, individual members or a group of members, or the administration.

Knowledge and information are crucial to the drafting of complicated tax legislation. Mills's power over the Ways and Means Committee, and therefore over its legislation, was due in large part to his superior knowledge of the tax laws. His dominance also stemmed from his free and almost exclusive access to staff experts and the information they possessed.

Tax committee staff members observe privately that many Ways and Means members did not do their homework and were unfamiliar with issues on which they voted. The relatively few members who had good personal staffs could not use them to best advantage, since staffs were kept from attending closed mark-up sessions. In the past, members were often absent from mark-up, simply giving their proxy to Chairman Mills to cast as he saw fit.

the member's role

Lack of members' expertise has always plagued the Ways and Means Committee. But Mills's absolute control of information further undermined tax-reform efforts. In 1974, for example, the committee staff informed a junior member that he could not obtain staff documents explaining the DISC export tax subsidy prepared for the committee three years earlier. The excuse was that the representative had not been on the committee at that time. When a more senior member who had been on the committee made the same request a few days later, he was informed that distribution of such material was "against committee policy."

The caliber of the committee's mark-up sessions has improved somewhat since 1974. With the ascension of Al Ullman to the chairmanship, Mills's iron-clad grip on the committee staff has been broken. While the committee still remains responsive to the chairman, its members have had more access to the professional staff. Open mark-up sessions have provided an opportunity for personal staffs to observe committee actions and provide information and ex-

90 TAX POLITICS

pertise. While the personal staffs do not command the immense resources available to the Treasury or the Joint Tax Committee staff, they can make a great difference in the ability of a representative to do a good job.

Also, with public sessions, tax-reform groups have had an opportunity to provide expertise for tax reformers on the committee.

The caliber of the committee itself improved significantly in the 94th Congress with the addition of twelve Democrats and six Republicans. Many of these new members are better prepared and more informed when tax issues are discussed in the committee. This, combined with the increased expertise and activity of older members, has changed mark-up sessions perceptibly. As one veteran reporter put it during the writing of the 1975 Energy Bill, "It's amazing. Some of these members are actually asking intelligent questions and debating some of these issues." Another observer added, as if to bring it all into perspective: "They've been down so low that 'down' looks like 'up' to you. Things are getting better, but there's a long way to go."

the staff's role

The influence of the committee staff is usually considered good by tax reformers. The Joint Tax Committee staff is highly competent and reasonably free from outside pressure. If there is any criticism of the staff, it stems from their natural subservience to the boss—the committee chairmen—and their tendency not to offend senior members. To the extent that reforms have been enacted in the past, Dr. Woodworth and his staff can take a great deal of credit. Unfortunately, major tax reforms were not generally on the agenda of Mills, Long, and other senior members. After years of quietly fighting losing battles, the Joint Tax Committee staff did become prone to weak compromises. With the recent changes in the Ways and Means Committee, the Joint Tax Committee staff's reform advocacy is on the ascent again.

lobbyists

Lobbyists, as we have seen, have a pervasive influence over the entire tax-writing process. Some, like the Public Citizen's Tax Reform Research Group, represent a broad public-interest in tax reform. Others, particularly union lobbyists, represent a broad constituency of average taxpayers which is largely pro-tax reform but may have some particular parochial interests to advance as well. But most lobbyists work for a particular company, a particular industry such as oil, banking, or home building, a wealthy taxpayer, an association of large manufacturers like the National Association of Manufacturers, small business, multinational corporations or professional associations such as lawyers or doctors. All these interests have a common goal in tax legislation. They want to pay fewer taxes either by preserving a special tax advantage or by creating a new one. In the mark-up sessions, some lobbyists move beyond persuading members to their point of view. They become involved in writing legislation. Shrewd lobbyists understand that they may not always be able to prevent legislation from being drafted, but that they can help draft it.

During the drafting of a 1974 bill aimed at taxing away huge oil company profits, the oil industry lobbyists were among the most active people in the committee room. They worked through one of their strongest allies on the committee, Texas Republican Bill Archer, an articulate defender of the oil industry, who offered amendments drafted by oil lobbyists. As things changed during the bill-writing session, Archer moved to the back of the committee room to consult regularly with representatives of the American Petroleum Institute, the Independent Petroleum Producers of America, the Independent Gas Producers, and others. They handed him new amendments, discussed new tactics and, when required to, called downtown to get more information for Archer to present to the committee.

In the summer of 1975, while the Ways and Means Committee was struggling over what type of automobile efficiency tax it would adopt to force the auto industry to build more efficient cars, representatives of the Ford Motor Company handed Louisiana Joe Waggonner a weak alternative tax. In the confusion of finding a tough compromise tax, the Waggonner-Ford proposal was adopted. The automobile lobbyists had done their work well.

Congress and Tax Politics 91

These lobbyists will often enlist allies to promote their cause. The giant automobile companies received grass-roots lobbying help from the automobile dealers. Representatives may not be very responsive to a GM lobbyist but all of them have GM retail dealers in their districts. In 1974, savings and loans institutions, pushing for a new tax break that would increase deposits, wrote to their passbook savers urging them to communicate their support of the measure to their representative. The Minnesota S&Ls even paid for a television ad that ran at half-time of a Minnesota Vikings game.

Many lobbyists don't wait for the actual mark-up sessions to do their work. They often prepare a simple amendment to help them out and line up a sympathetic sponsor ahead of time. The last days of a 1974 tax reform bill mark-up saw numerous special-interest amendments proposed and adopted by the committee. There were tax breaks for beer brewers, cigar manufacturers, railroads, the movie industry, insurance companies operating in Canada, investment bankers, bank holding companies, real estate investment trusts, savings and loan associations, and many others.

Mark-ups in 1975 produced more special amendments. During consideration of the tax-cut bill, Representative Richard VanderVeen of Michigan proposed a tax break for Chrysler Corporation, Representative Charles Rangel of New York proposed a tax break for Consolidated Edison of New York, Representative Henry Helstoski of New Jersey proposed a tax break for home-buyers that was pushed by the home-building industry, Representative Joe Waggonner proposed a tax break for purchasers of used oil-drilling rigs and fleets of used cars, and Representative Omar Burleson of Texas proposed a tax break for building oil refineries and nuclear reactors.

Some of the sponsors of these special-interest amendments are convinced they're doing the right thing. Representative Vander Veen was told that the Chrysler Corporation was on the brink of disaster and needed help—in this case about $250 million in tax savings—or it might face disaster. Certainly, the congressman couldn't be responsible for the demise of a major Michigan business and employer. But, as he later discovered, Chrysler hadn't been completely honest in painting their financial picture to him. He also had not thought about other less costly ways of helping the automobile corporation or the effect of his proposal on the Treasury or on our tax laws. As Representative Pete Stark (D-Calif.) observed, in arguing against the provision, "This committee should not be in the business of bailing out mismanaged corporations." Certainly not with a quarter-of-a-billion-dollar grant from the U.S. Treasury.

the treasury department

Another important source of information to committee members during a bill mark-up is the Treasury Department. Traditionally, the Treasury staff would sit at the same table as the Joint Committee staff and freely participate in legislative discussions. In recent years, Treasury's influence during the mark-ups has been waning. They are still usually asked their opinion on the matter under discussion, but most of the input comes from Dr. Woodworth. Since 1969, the Treasury has stood silently by as many special-interest tax provisions have been approved. The department was actually the advocate for perhaps the most anti-tax-reform legislation in recent times. They had proposed and strongly supported the Revenue Act of 1971 with over $8 billion in tax cuts for corporations, including two proposals that most tax experts strongly disagreed with—the ADR accelerated depreciation and the DISC export tax subsidy.

On other occasions, the Treasury has fought against new tax loopholes. Assistant Secretary Fred Hickman strongly opposed an exemption from the oil depletion repeal for wealthy independent oil producers. He also argued against huge tax subsidies to Lockheed, Pan Am, Chrysler, and other failing corporations. And, as mentioned earlier, the Treasury opposed a new tax credit for recyclers of scrap metal and paper. The Republican Treasury's philosophy on new tax breaks is consistent with most conservatives. They defend the revenue base (no new raids on the Treasury) but will not advocate any reforms of existing tax preferences. Hickman told one Washington reporter as he was

92 TAX POLITICS

leaving his Treasury post, "I thought the tax system was basically fair before I took this job and I think it is basically fair today."

consideration by the full house

Once a tax bill is reported by the Ways and Means Committee it is ready to be considered by the entire House of Representatives. The House has devised elaborate procedures that are supposed to promote efficient House deliberation of the hundreds of different bills considered each year.

the rules committee

The main procedural structure is the fifteen-member House Rules Committee which meets in a small room on the floor above the House chamber. Each committee chairman must bring his bill before the Rules Committee. The Committee assigns priority to bills and grants a rule allotting the number of hours of general debate on the bill and specifying what floor amendments will be permitted.

Because of its purely procedural function, few citizens realize that the Rules Committee is often used in a highly political manner. But it can be used to block the wishes of a particular committee to have the House consider its legislation. This is what happened at the end of 1974 when the Rules Committee killed a Ways and Means tax-reform bill which had included a phased-out end to the oil depletion allowance. Mills reported the bill out at the very end of the session in an effort to head off mounting criticism of his committee. (He had refused to take a similar bill to the floor five months earlier for fear that liberal reformers would attach an amendment that would repeal the oil subsidy immediately.) A curious coalition on the Rules Committee killed the bill on a 9-4 vote. House Speaker Carl Albert, who has great influence over the committee he appoints, and oil state representatives had helped delay the earlier oil depletion bill and wanted to stop this one as well. Some liberals on the committee decided to go along. They argued that Mills was simply trying to save his own neck and that even if the House considered the bill, there would be no time for the Senate to act before the Congress adjourned. They also claimed that passage of the bill would dampen the enthusiasm for a comprehensive tax-reform measure in the more liberal 94th Congress. Others argued, however, that if the bill was not passed this year, the billion dollars it would add to the industry's 1974 taxes would be lost forever. The oil-staters with well-intentioned help allowed the oil companies to slip into the new year with their huge windfall profits intact. The official announcement from the Rules Committee was that, as a matter of procedure, the House could only consider priority bills before adjournment. In this case, procedure was worth a great many dollars of substance.

The Rules Committee has also been used to protect other committees and the House from having to vote on highly controversial measures. Throughout 1974, many members of Congress introduced legislation to give a tax break on interest from savings accounts. As discussed in Chapter 2, liberals and conservatives alike sponsored these bills to give the small saver a break.

Representative Donald Brotzman, the bill's chief sponsor in the Ways and Means Committee, had hoped that the apparent appeal of his "Small Savers Act" might boost his re-election campaign. The Ways and Means members decided to oblige Brotzman by reporting the bill out just before the election recess under a procedure bypassing the Rules Committee—suspension of the rules—requiring a two-thirds vote for passage. In the clublike atmosphere of the committee, one Democrat surprisingly stated he would vote for the bill because Republican Brotzman was in a close race. The Colorado representative lost the election despite what some reporters termed "the Re-elect Don Brotzman Bill."

After the elections, committee members had second thoughts about the bill. Al Ullman expressed grave reservations about the bill's merits and the advisability of suspending the rules. Treasury and several influential committee Republicans were opposed. But Mills had apparently promised a group of Arkansas savings and loans that he would get the bill out to the House floor. Some conjectured that he did it under suspension, hoping it would fail to get a two-thirds vote.

After the election and Mills's resignation as committee chairman, the committee reconvened and voted to follow customary procedures and send the bill to the Rules Committee for consideration. Most members said quietly they hoped the bill would become bogged down in Rules Committee debate and die a quiet death. Many conceded privately that the bill's surface appeal was grossly misleading but that they were afraid to vote against a popular-sounding bill. A week before the 93rd Congress adjourned, the House Rules Committee took everyone off the hook and voted not to consider the savings interest bill.

the no-amendment rule

The Rules Committee has traditionally been quite helpful to the Ways and Means Committee. For years it granted Ways and Means a special rule on tax bills: no floor amendments allowed. This is known as a "closed rule."

What do closed rules mean? They mean that the 398 representatives not on Ways and Means have two choices on a tax bill: they can vote it up or down. In 1973, the House Democrats slightly modified the closed rule procedure through a modification of caucus rules. Under the new rule, if any chairman announces he will ask the rules committee for a closed rule, fifty Democrats can call for a special Democratic caucus to vote on making any particular amendment in order on the House floor. In effect, the caucus would instruct its Rules Committee majority to vote for a rule allowing the amendments. Floor amendments to tax bills are now possible, but exceedingly difficult. For example, the threat of House tax reformers led by Representative William J. Green (D-Pa.) to amend the 1974 Ways and Means' tax bill eliminating the oil depletion allowance resulted in Chairman Mills's withholding the entire bill from House consideration.

In 1975, Green and other Ways and Means Democrats went to the caucus and got approval to attach their oil depletion repealer to the popular Tax Reduction Act. Mills's defiance of the caucus action a year earlier had angered many House members and helped bring about reforms to curb his and his committee's powers. This time the Rules Committee and Chairman Ullman followed the caucus directive to allow the House to vote on the depletion allowance. The overwhelming House vote to repeal oil depletion (248-163) demonstrated the desirability of floor amendments. For years this expensive oil industry tax break was invulnerable to attack on the House floor. With a recorded vote on the issue, however, most House members opted to end the unpopular oil subsidy.

Mills had argued for years that "the House of Representatives could make a shambles of the code of the nation's tax policy if an open rule were allowed." He argued that Ways and Means legislation is too complex and vulnerable to perforation to permit normal amending procedures on the floor. "That's a lot of crap," former Ways and Means member Thomas Curtis responded. "The way to hold power is to say to the House that this is too difficult to explain."

changing the rules

Under increasing pressure from newer members, Ways and Means asked for an open rule for the Energy Conservation Bill of 1975. The committee members felt that other House members were entitled to propose alternatives to some of the bill's controversial conservation measures. Under the rule that was granted all germane amendments (relating to subject areas in the bill) which were published in advance would be in order on the House floor. The publication requirement was to give House members a chance to study the amendments they would be voting on. Lobbyists, members, and reformers saw a golden opportunity to either propose new tax expenditures in the name of conservation, or to strike out tax incentives already in the bill. When the smoke cleared, some 160 amendments were published in the *Congressional Record*. Many of these were duplications, many related to true energy conservation measures, but the majority were new tax loopholes for everything from electric cars to strip-mining equipment.

Some of the these amendments passed while others were defeated as Ways and Means members argued against the House passing new tax loopholes. They had some trouble convincing their colleagues, though, since the committee's own bill had numerous tax breaks for special interests. Why should the Ways and Means members be the only ones who can give away money to favored taxpayers? Many well-meaning members didn't understand the concept of

94 TAX POLITICS

tax expenditures and since the energy bill before them had to do with taxes, they, like the committee, had to think of ways to use the tax system to affect energy policy. Ways and Means tax reformer Sam Gibbons warned his colleagues of the mistake they were making as debate began on the "tax incentive" section of the bill.

"I hope that the members will be extremely quiet now, because if they will be they can hear the sound of the tiny reindeer hooves as they approach this Merry Christmas season in June that we are about to see now, because we have at last come to the part of the bill that should spread peace on Earth and goodwill to all men. We are about to open the Christmas presents. This is the loophole section. There will be a lot of fine speeches made about how we need to encourage this and how we need to encourage that through the tax system.

"I feel very terrible in trying to shoot Santa Claus down, but let me remind the members that for every gift there has to be a giver. We do not know who the recipients are because they will be buried in the tax returns down there at the IRS. But do you know who the giver is going to be? It is going to be you, and me, and all the other taxpayers out there.

"What are they going to be giving? We will be giving to the fellow who has a lousy house, who got it cheap, and because he bought a lousy house we will be giving him money to insulate it. We are not going to do this for the fellow who bought a good house, but only to the fellow who bought a lousy house and who is going to insulate it.

"That is one of the things we will be giving away."

"Then we will be giving away a solar hot water heater to everybody. I have got a solar hot water heater, so perhaps I had ought to be magnanimous and make sure everybody get a hot water solar heater but, you know, I do not like to give my money away. But. again, this will be Christmas time of the year in June, so we will be asked to give help for electric cars and other things, and they are all going to sound so attractive. But remember, these are appropriation-type expenditures, just like an appropriation that is authorized and goes all through the appropriations process, but there is a difference in that these will keep going on once we put them in the code. We will never see them again, because they will just keep going on and on and on, and there is no end to it. They can start off as a small thing, and pretty soon they grow and grow and grow...."

The experience of the open rule on the energy bill was not all bad. It did allow an amendment by Bill Green, already a tax-reform hero for his successful fight against the depletion allowance, to knock out a tax credit for recyclers of scrap metal and paper which, by 1980, would have channeled $1 billion in federal revenues into the pockets of scrap processors without increasing their level of recycling.

There needs to be some way, however, to reconcile the advantages of full participation in the tax-writing process and the disadvantages of opening up the tax code to new loopholes. One answer is to educate members on the impropriety of using the tax system to accomplish social and economic goals. Another is greater public exposure of how members vote on special-interest tax breaks. Finally, there needs to be a responsible open-rule procedure.

the senate

When the House is finished with a tax bill, it goes to the Senate. There it falls into the tender hands of the Finance Committee and its chairman, Senator Russell Long (D-La.) The seventeen members of Senate Finance are not representative of the country as a whole. Instead, they come mostly from rural areas. The states of Georgia, Nebraska, Arizona, Wyoming, Arkansas, Kansas, Alaska, Delaware, Tennessee, Colorado, and Maine were represented on the Finance Committee in 1975, but not states like California, New York, Illinois, Pennsylvania, or Ohio.

Finance Committee senators frequently espouse big business or special-interest causes. Chairman Long, a vigorous supporter of oil tax subsidies, has reportedly made over a million dollars from his personal oil investments. The ranking Republican in the 93rd Congress, Wallace Bennett (R-Utah), was a former president of the National Association of manufacturers. Democratic senators like Hartke (Ind.) and Ribicoff (Conn.) miss many Finance Committee meetings. The ranking committee tax reformer is Gaylord Nelson (D-Wis.), who was joined in 1973 by Walter Mondale (D-Minn.), a senator with a good tax-reform voting record. But as we have mentioned, none have chosen to fight aggressively for tax reform within the committee. Nelson, in fact, was responsible for increasing the corporate surtax exemption during the 1975 Tax Cut Bill—a major step backward in tax reform.

One bright spot on the committee has been Senator Floyd Haskell of Colorado, a tax lawyer with thirty years experience. He has been joined at times by Democratic newcomer William Hathaway of Maine.

The Republicans have not put their best senators on the committee. Said one labor official, "Griffin is the first Republican to get on that committee in the memory of man who hasn't been an absolute troglodyte." Senator Robert Griffin (R-Mich.) later resigned from the committee to take a seat on the more prestigious Foreign Relations Committee. Senators Robert Dole, Robert Packwood, and William Roth are Republican members who joined the committee in 1973. Senator William Brock was put on the committee in 1974. These new additions have improved the Republican side somewhat, but there has been very little tax-reform activity from there.

hearings

Finance Committee Chairman Russell Long usually has his staff invite a selected list of witnesses and then makes a general announcement to the public of upcoming hearings. The deadline to request to testify, in fact the hearing itself, may be just a few days hence, leaving little time to prepare. The hearings announcement also advises that only five minutes are allotted for oral testimony and suggests that the potential witness might want to avoid the effort and submit a statement to be included in the written record. Requests by the public to appear at finance hearings are, needless to say, few.

Long sets up hearings when it is to his advantage. In 1974, a group of senators announced their intention to tack a series of tax-reform measures to a bill to increase the debt-ceiling limit. (This bill is usually viewed as veto-proof because it must be passed before the government can borrow more money.) Senate reformers had threatened to add reforms to earlier debt-ceiling bills, but in 1974 they included an attack on Chairman Long's most cherished tax loophole—the oil depletion allowance. Long decided to hold hearings on the tax-reform proposals.

Playing a game of legislative semantics, he labeled the sessions "Hearings on Tax Increase Proposals." Long's specially invited guests included the American Council on Capital Gains, the American Petroleum Institute, the Independent Petroleum Association, the National Association of Manufacturers, the National Association of Realtors, the Chamber of Commerce, the American Mining Congress, and a host of other business interests, all predicting devastating economic effects if the Senate were to repeal oil depletion, ADR and DISC, and strengthen the minimum tax on tax preference income. Treasury Secretary Simon testified against any of these reforms. Of the forty or fifty witnesses only two— Senator Edward Kennedy and economist Gerard Brannon— argued in favor of any of the reforms.

Long made good use of his hearings. They were held on June 5th through June 11th. Ordinarily hearings take several months to be printed, but miraculously, Senator Long had the two-volume set on the senators' desks at the beginning of the tax-reform debate only ten days later and took to the floor holding the volumes in his hand. He was able to say that his committee had just held hearings on the tax proposals and that the great weight of the testimony was that such "tax increase" proposals would be disastrous for the economy. The Senate tax reformers were unable to get the votes necessary to pass their complete reform package and later were unable to break a filibuster on the depletion repeal.

Earlier in the year, many members of Congress were calling for an excess profits tax on the oil industry whose income had soared as oil prices tripled. The fact is that an excess profits tax is a poor way to tax oil companies which receive $4 or $5 billion a year in tax subsidies. The proper approach would be to first repeal those tax breaks. But the excess profits tax idea was gaining momentum. Long could not risk the Senate passing such a tax as a result of public outrage against the industry. He set up a one-day hearing inviting four former IRS commissioners and a tax-reform-minded former Treasury official. All witnesses pointed out the technical difficulties of administering an excess profits tax. When a few witnesses raised the subject of ending some of the present oil tax subsidies, committee members changed the subject or moved on to the next witness. Public debate over the desirability of an excess oil profits tax was effectively shut off and Long had gained a temporary victory.

the hearings charade

Senate Finance Committee hearings could be important because they give interested parties an opportunity to testify on the specific House-passed language in the bill. Unfortunately, special-interest lobbyists have enjoyed a much better hearing by the committee than public interest witnesses.

A hearing on the national debt limit and proposed presidential spending ceiling illustrates the point. The administration bill posed a question of crucial importance to the nation: should the president be allowed complete discretion to cut $6 billion in federal programs without congressional guidance?

At noon on Wednesday, Oct. 11, 1972, the committee announced public hearings by posting a notice in the committee's office. Two administration witnesses and one U.S. senator were invited to testify. The hearings were to take place that very afternoon at 2 P.M.—two hours after the first public announcement. Much to the committee's surprise, a public witness—an author of this book—actually showed up. He had studied the issues and prepared careful testimony and asked to be heard. Committee functionaries suggested that he submit his testimony in writing. Since it is well known that the Finance Committee frequently votes on issues before the hearing record is printed, he insisted on being heard before the committee voted.

The officials turned to the book of unwritten Finance Committee rules—Catch-22. Had the witness submitted a written request to be heard? (This seemed a good move—there had been only two hours of public notice, not much time to write the committee for permission.) Happily, the witness showed he had indeed written the proper letter. The officials were visibly unenthusiastic.

Finally, Chairman Long himself was called to decide the issue. How long would the witness take, he asked. Only ten minutes. Chairman Long said he was happy to hear the witness. So, more by grace of the chairman than by virtue of the U.S. Constitution, the Finance Committee heard a member of the public on an important issue. Of course the committee asked him no questions.

Other Finance Committee hearings follow this pattern. In the debate on the Revenue Act of 1971, most witnesses represented special interests. The House version of the bill cut corporate taxes by almost 20 percent; these witnesses came to support that bill or to ask for even more. A few public-interest witnesses came on behalf of the taxpaying public to argue against the corporate tax cut and proposed instead that the money should be used to lower individual taxes. Prominent economists testified that the result would be better for the economy than the huge corporate tax break.

Finance Committee senators had been cordial to the corporate witnesses but much of the committee met the public-interest witnesses with undisguised hostility as the following exchange demonstrates:

SENATOR LONG: Thank you very much.

SENATOR FANNIN: I think it is worthless to ask some questions on such biased testimony. How do you think that our tax rates, tariffs, and incentives compare with other industrial countries of the world, our competitors?

The witness started to answer. He was interrupted.

SENATOR FANNIN: Let me ask you this. What is your background and experience in business and government?

The witness explained that he had studied the issue and was a tax attorney. Again he was interrupted.

SENATOR FANNIN: Still, you are criticizing people with long experience in government affairs and I accept your testimony on that basis. Mr. Chairman, I have no further questions.

The witness insisted on his right to answer the question, now that it had been asked.

SENATOR BENNETT: I object. I think this witness has had his time and he has indicated his bias and I think we should go on to the next witness.

SENATOR FANNIN: I think we have had enough . . . I withdraw the question.

SENATOR NELSON: I think he ought to be able to answer the question.

SENATOR FANNIN: We only have a certain length of time for these hearings and receiving testimony of witnesses that are qualified to speak on the subject.

SENATOR NELSON: He sounds as qualified to me as most of the rest I heard here.

Congress and Tax Politics

SENATOR BENNETT: May I make the point that he misstated the question deceptively. Was your question on tax incentives?

SENATOR FANNIN: Absolutely. My question was how do you think our tax rates, tariffs, and incentives compare with other industrial countries of the world?

The witness, encouraged by a question from Senator Nelson, attempted to complete his answer.

SENATOR BENNETT: Is this going to be a lecture that will take us into this afternoon?

The witness indicated that the senator had first alleged his bias; at least he should be allowed to present the facts.

SENATOR BENNETT: In how much depth? . . . It is ten minutes to twelve. How long are we going to have to sit here and listen to you?

The witness had little choice but to finally submit his answer for the written record, knowing full well that it would be printed only after the Finance Committee had voted on the bill.

mark-up sessions

The Senate Finance Committee mark-up sessions are even more bizarre than the process that has led up to them. Until 1975 all Senate Finance bill-drafting was closed to the public. Secrecy has led to serious abuses of the democratic process. It has not been unusual for the chairman to call the committee into secret "mark-up" without notifying some senators he knew would oppose him on the issues; Senators Mondale and Nelson have been excluded from such sessions in the past. Moreover, the informal procedures in secret session made it difficult for reform senators to know what was happening. Here, too, personal staff were not permitted to attend.

There were no transcripts kept of committee proceedings. Committee votes went unrecorded and were decided by head nodding or a show of hands. Senator Long has been a staunch opponent of opening mark-up sessions to the public on grounds that the committee would then have to make decisions "at breakfast" rather than at open committee meetings.

The opening of the Finance Committee bill-writing sessions in 1975 following new reforms in the Senate have made little difference in the caliber of the mark-ups. The following exchanges during the committee's consideration of the 1975 Energy Conservation Bill are illustrative:

MR. HANSEN (R-Wy.): I've been wondering—has anyone been keeping any minutes or any record of what we're saying or doing?

MR. LONG: Larry Woodworth (of the Joint Committee staff) is jotting down what we agree to.

MR. PACKWOOD (R-Ore.): I think we shouldn't proceed any further without establishing what are all the proposals under consideration so we can view them in proper perspective to each other and be properly prepared to discuss them when they come up.

MR. NELSON (D-Wis.): I understand that in my absence we passed the tax breaks for railroads, but omitted railroad over-water ferries—such as the one in Wisconsin.

MR. LONG: (possibly facetiously) Well, Gaylord, I'll be happy to give you that one without need of further discussion, but I'll expect you in exchange to vote for this next tax credit we're about to discuss.

MR. GRAVEL (D-Alaska): I'd like to explain my proposal to place a tax on energy consumption throughout our economy—"a B.T.U. tax."

MR. LONG: I'm not sure we should spend a lot of time on this. I would remind the senator that no one ever advanced his political career by having his name associated with a tax that happens to get passed.

MR. LONG: I want to read to this committee the following statement from today's *Wall Street Journal:*

"The Senate Finance Committee is lining up some major tax breaks for energy-related industries. . . .

"As the committee was making these decisions, the room was packed with lobbyists representing industries such as oil, utilities, railroads and recyclers of scrap from steel and paper. Frequently, senators or their staff aides would consult openly with these lobbyists during the deliberations."

The article is even critical of the senator from Connecticut. (The article noted that Senator Ribicoff was sponsoring the credit for drilling exploratory oil wells and that Senator Long had stated it is better politically to have oil company tax breaks proposed by lawmakers from non-oil producing states.)

Now, of course, all this openness business was not my idea in the first place. The Senate majority simply said we had to have meetings open to the public. I don't enjoy seeing this committee held up to scorn. These special tax matters are sensitive so in the future I'm going to recommend that we exclude the public, except the press, from tax-writing sessions.

MR. BROCK (R-Tenn.): I don't want to drive these meetings behind closed doors. There'd be an aura of conspiracy to that. Closing the meetings would be counterproductive. Actually there are lobbyists on both sides of an issue—for example, Common Cause people are here.

MR. DOLE (R-Kan.): People have a right to see what we've done. Someone is laughing in the back row. I assume that's someone we've just shot down.

98 TAX POLITICS

MR. MONDALE (D-Minn.): We may be overreacting. Maybe we should get a list of *Wall Street Journal* subscribers broken down by state so we can see what special interests they represent.

MR. LONG: Well, I just don't think Mr. Albert Hunt's article was up to his usual high standards.

(A vote to close the sessions drew only four votes in favor. Senator Long had seemed to assume that only lobbyists for vested interests would bother to attend tax-writing sessions, but later reportedly said he had no objection to Common Cause's presence because they are "against giving anything to anybody.")

The committee's consideration of a tax credit for homeowners who replace inefficient furnaces produced the following exchanges:

MR. MONDALE: We should also give a credit for installing home thermostats.

MR. BROCK: Can't we leave anything to the market mechanism?

MR. WOODWORTH: The furnace credit would present great administrative problems; even if the FEA could certify the efficiency of a new unit the efficiency improvement would depend on what kind of unit it replaces.

MR. LONG: Well, you'll never solve it if you don't try.

MR. BROCK: The problem is financing. What the homeowner really needs is financing and the fuel saving will pay off the loan and pay for itself. We don't need a tax credit. We should use our housing rehabilitation programs and do it there.

MR. GRAVEL: You could just assume the old unit was inefficient without having to go down into each taxpayer's basement.

MR. BROCK: You distort the market mechanism.

MR. GRAVEL: So what? We've been distorting the market mechanism all day yesterday with all the other tax credits.

MR. BROCK: You aren't going to help the average homeowner. If he doesn't have $1,500 to buy a new furnace he won't buy one regardless of what tax credit you give him.

MR. DOLE: What if someone is too poor to pay taxes?

MR. LONG: Let's make this a refundable tax credit. (Refundability means that persons who pay no taxes and cannot use the tax savings will get a payment of money from the government.) Refundability makes it clear this is a tax expenditure. Fritz Mondale put in the *Congressional Record* the other day how much tax expenditures cost. But so what? Let's call it what it is, as I said the other day. (On a previous day Senator Long had noted, "Professor Surrey and, I suppose, Ralph Nader have said these tax breaks are really tax expenditures, but that label doesn't bother me. I've never been confused about it. I've always known that what we were doing was giving government money away.") I'd like to have at least one tax expenditure in there I can brag about and say here's one I like.

Of course I understand tax write-offs can't solve all our energy problems. For example, just when we think we're making progress then here comes some young lawyer driving up to the courthouse on his motorcycle and he's found one little old lady as a client and she's taking the day off from her washing to come to the court to enjoin some new construction. We've got to find some other means to stop this little old lady in tennis shoes and this lawyer trying to make a name for himself from blocking progress.

Of course when it comes to helping homeowners, if I were on the Banking Committee, I'd favor a loan guarantee for them because that would be in my jurisdiction, but since I'm on the Finance Committee I favor the use of tax credits.

MR. DOLE: We've given away an awful lot of revenue here with tax credits and even refundable tax credits—are we going to raise any revenue to cover it? Will we have a gas tax?

Senator Floyd Haskell (D-Col.) has become the committee's most effective opponent of tax rip-offs—a fact duly noted by the chairman during a debate over tax credits for railroads.

MR. LONG: Floyd Haskell has never yet voted for an investment credit. I keep thinking someday he'll decide since everyone else in the world is getting one he'll vote for one for some special group in Colorado, but he hasn't yet.

MR. HASKELL: This discussion demonstrates the problem. Yesterday we gave a tax credit to slurry pipelines but they compete strongly with railroads so today we have to give another credit to railroads.

The same point emerged in a discussion of the credit for recycling:

MR. LONG: If you took away the depletion allowance for virgin materials you'd cause the greatest depression this country of ours has ever seen. So we should give a corresponding tax break to recyclers.

MR. HASKELL: What we're saying is one good loophole deserves another.

MR. CURTIS (R-Neb.): I accept the fact that in this bill we've got to use the tax law for social objectives. I don't like it. I think we should let the record stand in this open hearing that this committee or the Ways and Means Committee has, throughout the life of the Republic, created unfair tax provisions.

The committee reached its zenith of efficiency in passing an amendment sponsored by Senator Bentsen (D-Tex.) to provide up to $2.5 billion per year in loan guarantees for energy projects. Senator Bentsen read a brief speech and the bill passed after five or ten minutes of discussion. Within sixty seconds the noticeably elated senator distributed a detailed press release to all present. Senator Long observed, "That was quick. These $2 billion amendments we can do in a hurry.

Its those goshdarned amendments involving only tens of millions that give us all the trouble."

Openness has not shaken Long's control over the mark-up sessions. As noted earlier, tax reformers don't like to challenge the chairman. There are still few recorded votes and confusion remains the order of the day during the bill-writing sessions.

Dr. Woodworth and his Joint Committee staff provide background material for the members and of course copies of the House bill, but it is Long's loyal Finance Committee staff that controls the flow of information. Senators receive materials without time to study them. They routinely pass them on to their staffs. But many personal staff people complain that their bosses pay little attention to their advice once they enter the never-never land of a Finance Committee mark-up.

One day during the consideration of a $28 billion tax-cut bill, several members complained that they had no idea what provisions they were voting on, how much they cost, and what they accomplished. An impatient Long responded, "If every man insists on knowing what he's voting for before he votes, we're not going to get a bill reported before Monday." That statement says a lot about Senate Finance Committee mark-ups. But Albert Hunt, a veteran tax committee reporter for the *Wall Street Journal*, summed up the tax-cut bill-writing process best:

The resourceful Senator Long clearly dominated the Finance Committee deliberations. It was the first time in recent history that the committee had written a major bill in a public session. Senator Long directed the debate on almost every important issue. He was sometimes tough, frequently talkative, and always tenacious. At one point he told another member, "You vote for my amendment and I'll vote for yours." When the Louisiana Democrat thought he had the necessary support, he would force a quick vote even after only seconds of debate; when he didn't, he would talk and maneuver until he picked up the needed backing. As a result, the committee chairman got his way on almost every matter.

Whatever type of tax bill emerges from the House, the odds are very strong that it will become worse, from a tax reform point of view, in the Senate Finance Committee. The 1975 Tax Cut Bill, for instance, came over to the Finance Committee with a repeal of the depletion allowance and a reasonably fair package of individual business and individual tax cuts totaling about $20 billion. When it left the Finance Committee, the depletion repealer was gone, while about $10 billion in new tax write-offs were added. The committee had responded to nearly every major individual or business group that had sought tax relief.

Notably two tax bonanzas that were rejected by Ways and Means—a $2 billion building tax credit and $1 billion bail-out for Chrysler, Pan Am and Lockheed—were approved by the Senate committee. This is the usual pattern—the more outrageous loopholes are attended to in the Finance Committee. After losing their fight in the House for the corporate bail-out, one of the lobbyists consoled a less experienced colleague, "Don't worry, the Finance Committee will take care of us."

senate floor

At the end of mark-up sessions, the bill is reported out to the full Senate. On the Senate floor there is no closed rule and all amendments, germane and published in advance or not, are in order. The wide-open nature of Senate deliberation is a mixed blessing. On one hand, Senate reformers have an opportunity to undo what the Finance Committee has done or add new reforms to the tax bill. On the other hand, many senators will seize the opportunity to propose new tax breaks for favored constituents. But through it all Russell Long is very much in control. After he successfully fended off 150 attempted amendments to a 1964 tax bill, Senator William Proxmire said of Long's performance: "If a man murdered a crippled, enfeebled orphan at high noon on the public square in plain view of a thousand people, I am convinced after today's performance that if the senator from Louisiana represented the guilty murderer, the jury would not only find the murderer innocent, they would award the defendant a million dollars on the ground that the victim had provoked him."

Special-interest legislation is brought up attached to minor House-passed tariff bills (to get around the constitutional requirement that revenue measures must originate in the House). Long has successfully avoided Senate scrutiny of Finance Committee bills but even when they have been challenged, he has usually come out on top.

Larger tax bills are subjected to more serious debate. But here, too, Long is usually a winner.

The 1969 Tax Reform Act contained numerous special-interest provisions approved by the Finance Committee. During the floor debate Senator Edward Kennedy raised the issue of burying special interest legislation in major tax-reform bills. "It is not a secret that special provisions find a way into the various tax bills passed by the Congress, and signed by the President," he said on the Senate floor. "But it usually is a secret which groups or individuals benefit from them. And this aura of secrecy generates an impression that the provisions are hidden because their sponsors have something to hide." Kennedy then introduced into the *Congressional Record* a list of fifteen special-interest provisions. These included a special tax break on stock options for executives of the Litton Industries conglomerate, special exceptions for five influential foundations, and exemptions from the repeal of the investment credit for four corporations. Kennedy even had a price tag for the last four. Mobile Oil Corporation would save $12 million; Uniroyal, Inc., $3 million; Lockheed Aircraft Corporation, $14 million; and McDonnell-Douglas Corporation, $6.5 million.

Senator Long frankly admitted that the 1969 so-called Tax-Reform bill included between 100 and 200 such special provisions. But he didn't like Kennedy's approach. "As chairman of the committee, all I want to know is, one, what are the merits, and two, how much is involved?" he said. "We do not make a point of identifying the taxpayer in general legislation. Where anyone is so affected, he could claim the same benefits if he had the same problem."

In other words, all taxpayers—rich and poor alike—are invited to use these loopholes. There is only one small catch: the taxpayer's income must be from stock options like Litton's, special foundation business, or activities qualifying for an investment credit on aircraft, oil, or rubber production.

Satisfied with his work, Senator Long left the floor. While many newspapers carried the debate across the country, the Senate passed the Tax-Reform Act with the special provisions intact.

floor amendments

Debates on major tax bills sometimes develop into utter chaos. Such confusion usually works to the advantage of the committee bill. When the Tax Reduction Act of 1975 reached the Senate floor, members had over 200 amendments they wanted to offer. Some popular amendments to cut taxes were adopted, but most amendments fell prey to the general confusion in the Senate chamber and the desire of senators to leave on their Easter vacations.

Long was usually cheered by the adoption of further floor amendments because, as in committee sessions, more amendments meant more chips to play at the House-Senate Conference sessions. One major amendment, however, did not make Long very happy—repeal of the oil depletion allowance—an action taken earlier by the House but nullified by Long's committee. Over this issue, the debate was long, intense, and informative. In the end, Long got pretty much what he wanted.

Long, who has candidly referred to himself as "the darling of the oil industry," had been faced with a serious dilemma when the House added to the popular tax-cut bill an amendment to completely repeal the oil depletion allowance. With the support of Finance Committee liberals, he did succeed in stripping the depletion section from the tax bill with a vague promise to consider the issue separately.

Long said that the depletion question would slow down the vitally important tax bill. He also argued that there would be no time to consider the entire bill before the Senate's two-week Easter recess. The slowdown, of course, would have been due to an oil state filibuster. The fact was that Long feared a filibuster over oil might be broken if it was holding up the important and popular tax-cut bill. That was, of course, the House tax reformers' strategy in attaching the oil depletion repealer to the bill in the first place. But when a majority of the Finance Committee, fearing they would have to cancel spring vacation plans, supported Long, the real fight began.

A coalition of senators outside the committee announced their attempt to add depletion repeal to the tax-cut bill. Senators Ernest "Fritz" Hollings, Edward Kennedy, and Warren Magnuson (D-Wash.) prepared a bill to repeal depletion altogether, with a limited four-year phase-out for "independent" oil companies. The concession to the independents made to soften opposition from many senators who had such oil producers in their states. The phase-out also recognized that it made no sense to exempt permanently multimillion-dollar independent producers whose profits were even higher than the major oil companies.

Long and his allies began putting pressure on the Hollings coalition, accusing them of jeopardizing an immediate tax cut. But Hollings, an effective and energetic legislator, made it clear to Long that he was not dealing with a "wishy-washy" liberal. (In fact, the tall, gray-haired South Carolinian with a thick southern drawl amused many Capitol Hill veterans because he was able to force tax reformers to stand up to Long for fear of being outdone by a moderate conservative Southerner.) The pressure began to be applied the other way. The House Democratic caucus leader and Ways and Means Chairman Ullman both announced that the House would not accept any attempt to delete depletion repeal from the bill, raising the possibility of delay if the Senate didn't act. Senator Hollings announced he was willing to give up a scheduled Senate trip to Moscow in order to resolve the issue. Les Whitten, a journalist with Jack Anderson's column, began to call senators' offices asking where they were planning to go on vacation and why they couldn't cancel their trips to vote on the depletion allowance. Finally, several days before debate on the bill was set, the *Washington Post* ran an editorial accompanied by a cartoon picturing a senator pushing the depletion repeal bill in the wastebasket, grabbing his hat, and following a Playboy-type bunny labeled "Easter Recess" out the door.

The issue was drawn clearly in the *Post* editorial: "The Senate Democrats will meet this morning. Those senators who care most about their vacations will favor a fast tax cut and a long delay on oil depletion. Other senators will seize this opportunity for major progress in tax reform and will vote to stay at their desks until the job is finished."

Later in the day a smiling Senator Hollings emerged from that meeting. The Democrats had agreed to suspend the Easter recess until the bill was concluded and the reformers had agreed to limit themselves to two attempts at ending the anticipated filibuster.

The strategy for Long and his fellow oil staters now shifted to limiting depletion repeal to the major oil companies, thus protecting the thousands of wealthy independent oil producers who have political clout in the Senate. They promoted an exemption from the depletion for companies that produced less than 3,000 barrels per day.

As the tax-cut bill was brought to the Senate floor, a substitute amendment to the Hollings-Kennedy-Magnuson repeal was offered by Texas Senator Lloyd Bentsen. Senator Bentsen's amendment contained a permanent 3,000-barrel-a-day exemption for oil, an additional one for natural gas, and an exemption for oil royalty recipients. Another permanent exemption proposal came from a surprising source. Liberal Democratic Senator Alan Cranston of California, a large oil-producing state, offered his own version of a 3,000-barrel exemption, which apparently had the quiet approval of Russell Long. Through a parliamentary move, later ruled out of order, Cranston tried to keep the Hollings amendment from even being voted on. The Cranston proposal contained several improvements over the Bentsen plan. Apparently, it was hoped by Long and others that this would be the acceptable compromise significantly undercutting Hollings' strength.

The strategy worked. Cranston's effort picked up other liberal oil state senators—such as Gary Hart (D-Colo.), Lee Metcalf (D-Mont.), and Philip Hart (D-Mich.) The Hollings amendment was tabled by a 51 to 46 vote.

In a final flurry of activity, Senator Hollings offered a 1,000-barrel-a-day exemption. A compromise exemption of 2,000 barrels a day was finally passed by one vote. The entire oil depletion repeal (protecting all but 71 of the 10,000 U.S. oil companies) sailed through the Senate on a vote of 82 to 12.

the conference committee

Once the Senate passes a bill it goes to conference with the House. The Conference Committee is a procedural device used to iron out differences between House and Senate versions of the bill. Usually, the conference is

102 TAX POLITICS

comprised of each committee chairman and several senior members. Decisions are made by a majority of the members of each body. In order for there to be an agreement, a majority of both the House and the Senate conferees voting separately must approve it.

The Conference Committee has been secret government at its worst, though recent congressional reforms make open conferences more likely. No transcript has been taken for later record and conferees were unaccountable to the public. Senate conferees have been known to give up Senate floor amendments. During consideration of the 1971 Revenue Act a liberal Republican senator won a small tax-reform amendment in a Senate floor fight. An angry Senator Bennett stormed over and promised to do everything he could to kill the amendment in conference. The surprised sponsor protested that Senate conferees were supposed to defend Senate amendments, not kill them. But Bennett was adamant. (As it happened, Bennett's ulcer flared up and he couldn't attend the conference committee meetings. The amendment survived, although in a somewhat weakened form.)

The infidelity of Long and his fellow conferees is well known in the Senate. This has sometimes led to a devious game. Some Senators concerned about their public image will fight for a popular tax amendment. After much speechmaking they will prevail. Of course, they'll be sure to get good publicity at home. What they don't tell the public is that they know the popular measure will die in conference.

Congressman John Byrnes (R-Wis.) was ranking Republican on the Ways and Means Committee, and a frequent conferee, until his retirement in 1972. Byrnes told Ralph Nader's Congress Project that there is prior understanding among conferees that many of the Senate amendments will be killed. That way, he says, "Everybody is happy. The tax code hasn't been raped. And the senators can go home and blame the House for not passing their amendments."

For Wilbur Mills, conference committees could be a lot of fun. He took time out from the conference on the 1971 Revenue Act to jibe:

> We conferees are engaged in the unusual task of detrimming and taking down a Christmas tree before Christmas. As is always the case, it is a somber and sad chore and not nearly as much fun as was the ceremonial decoration of the tree in the Senate last month. As of seven o'clock last night we had removed and carefully packed away for the next season of goodwill about $12 billion of the assorted ornaments and tinsel hung by jolly elves on the Seante floor.

Of course, Mills didn't take away a $7.8 billion annual gift to corporations contained in the bill.

For years, when House and Senate tax conferees met, Mills had overshadowed his Senate counterpart. But in 1975, Mills was gone and Russell Long, the veteran, was up against Al Ullman, the new Ways and Means chairman. The conference on the 1975 Tax Reduction Act was the first that pitted Long and Ullman head to head. Long needed to prove he could not be run over. The outcome would probably determine the course of such conferences for years to come. Long was determined to use all those Senate amendments in his horse-trading with the House. He was willing to give up on many of the $10 billion in additional Senate amendments. If Ullman wanted those expensive amendments dropped, he would have to pay the price.

The conferees are usually the most senior members of each committee. But Long, under pressure from the Senate leadership, added pro-depletion repeal Senators Haskell and Hathaway to the Conference Committee. The catch was that Long still controlled a majority of the Senate votes. Long would caucus with his fellow senators early in the morning and at critical points throughout the conference. He effectively silenced Haskell and Hathaway by putting issues to a vote. A vote by a majority of the Senate conferees would bind the others to stick with that position. Long went to conference with a majority of Senate votes in his pocket. Now he could deal with the House from a position of strength.

On the first day, the Conference Committee voted to close the session to the public. Ullman had raised the stakes by appearing on national TV the day before, declaring that many Senate amendments were irresponsible and that he could not accept a permanent exemption to the depletion repeal. In the seclusion of a small room in the Capitol Building, the House began to offer compromises. The Senate stonewalled. Long seemed to be saying that Ullman could get on TV, but that the senator from Louisiana would get what he wants.

On the second day, Long began to compromise but wouldn't budge on the issue of the depletion allowance. As the conference advanced, several major items including oil remained stalemated. The House offered one more compromise on oil, agreeing to a smaller permanent exemption. Long said he would "check with his people" overnight. The next day, after checking with oil interests, Long turned down the House compromise. Finally, faced with the economic necessity of getting a bill out immediately and the already delayed Easter recess, Ullman and the House conferees were pressured to accept Long's terms. A tired but honest Charles Vanik (D-Ohio) remarked later, "He would have kept us there till next Christmas. We couldn't risk this tax bill over an issue [the independent exemption] that the public doesn't really understand anyway. They want their tax rebates."

Ullman had pared down the cost of the tax cut by almost $8 billion, but Long had saved all the amendments that were important to him. In the final analysis both chairmen could claim they had won. And that's exactly the way Russell Long wanted it. "Senator, isn't this a typical Russell Long compromise?" one reporter asked of the depletion repeal. "You got 99 percent of what you wanted." Long just smiled.

After conference both houses of Congress voted on the final version of the bill. Technically, either house could reject the compromise, but, as a practical matter, this never happens on complex tax bills. A vote against a final bill would negate weeks or months of work, and few members of Congress would go that far. The bill as shaped by the conferees and passed by the House and Senate then goes to the president to be signed into law.

taxation with representation

This, then, is the process which has given us the complex and unfair set of laws we call the Internal Revenue Code. The men and women who write our tax laws are elected and sent to Congress to be public servants. Unfortunately, the structure we have described facilitates the serving of private interests in the tax process to the detriment of the general public. If we are to accomplish any meaningful tax reforms, we must first right the imbalance between the influence of the average taxpayer and the influence of special groups seeking to preserve or enlarge their privileges under the tax laws.

public interest vs special interest

It's like baking a large apple pie for your twelve children. One child who loves pie more than the rest has the resourcefulness to leave the others playing outside and come into the kitchen. He begins helping out: handing you ingredients, making suggestions, and all along mentioning that he is so hungry he wants an extra big piece when it's ready. Then our pie lover disappears briefly and comes back with a present for you he made in school. He continues to help, saying how much he needs an extra piece because he's so hungry. You answer, "Parents are supposed to be fair to all their children. I've got to divide the pie up equally." The child gets angry and throws a tantrum. He threatens to run away. He pleads with you again. He mentions all the help he's given you (and the present). Finally, the pie is finished. The pesty kid is still hanging around the kitchen and the others are outside. You say to yourself, "Why not? They'll never know." You cut up the pie, making each of eleven pieces slightly smaller. That leaves one huge piece for the greedy child and more peace of mind for you. Your relations with all the kids remain good even though you favored one over the others.

Now, if you're a member of Congress, the pie is tax money, the child in the kitchen is a special interest, and the rest of the kids are all your average constituents. For each special tax provision being proposed or already in our tax laws, there is a specific interest group with a very large stake in its passage or preservation. These interests will spend substantial sums of money to hire lobbyists, attorneys, and economists to make their case. They will come to Washington,

104 TAX POLITICS

they will utilize media campaigns, and they will spend huge amounts in political campaigns—legally and illegally.

But how great a stake does the general public have in, for example, a $200 million tax break for one industry. Unfair? Sure, it's a rip-off. But even if people could be convinced it was coming out of their pockets directly through higher taxes we're only talking about $1 a person. Of course, tax breaks cost more than that because there are a lot of them and they've been enacted over the years. Public opposition has been diffuse, while support by interest groups has been direct and very intense.

The oil industry, a prime example, has easy access to senators, representatives, top-level Treasury and other agency officials, and the White House. To wield its political influence, oil is organized into three major political action groups. The American Petroleum Institute (API) is the largest, with a 1971 budget $17 million. The API is headed by Frank Ikard, a former Ways and Means congressman from Texas. The API consists of 265 corporate members and 7,000 individual members. It speaks especially for the large integrated oil companies that dominate its management committees and set its policies.

The smaller oil companies make their voices heard through the Independent Petroleum Association of America (IPAA), funded at $1.6 million in 1971. The Independent Natural Gas Association, representing the pipeline companies, is headed by former Texas congressman Walter Rogers and is budgeted at $800,000. Together, then, these three oil groups spend a total of over $19 million annually—an equivalent of the $42,500 salaries of all 435 of our representatives in Congress.

The three formal organizations and their budgets do not include the amount the oil industry spends on campaigns. In 1972, some 413 individuals directly involved in the oil industry contributed over $5.7 million is known campaign funds to President Nixon's reelection efforts. Most such contributions are hard to identify since they come from individuals involved with the organizations and not the organizations themselves. (See Chapter 5 on investigations.) The past IPAA president, Harold McClure, has been quoted as saying he contributed $90.000 to political campaigns in 1968 alone; officers and directors of the American Petroleum Institute alone gave over $450,000 (to candidates of both parties!) in the 1968 elections. In 1974 oil interests gave over $350.000 to the campaigns of eight Senate Finance Committee members. Of course, once a candidate accepts, he doesn't care to broadcast the fact. These contributions and the promise of future campaign contributions establish for the oil industry and other special-interest contributors close behind-the scenes relationships with members of Congress and the executive branch. Tax reform can never be achieved as long as the monied interests who benefit from our unfair tax laws have this influence over Congress. There will be no reform of our tax laws until our campaign laws eliminate campaign contributions as a source of undue influence. If the general public were to pay for campaigns, then the general public would be better represented in the tax-writing process. Similarly, the public must see to it that brakes are put on tax-deductible corporate advertising and lobbying.

Again, the oil industry provides a good example. During the 1969 tax deliberations in Congress, the industry sought to bolster public support for the oil depletion allowance. A new front group, "The Petroleum Industry Information Committee," was set up in New York City to pay for nationwide newspaper advertisements. In 1972, the American Petroleum Institute alone spent $4 million on television and magazine advertising campaigns. In 1973 the API spent another $1.8 billion. In addition, other oil industry groups and individual oil corporations have invested heavily in public relations.

The public relations campaigns are sound investments from a business point of view. Special interests prosper amidst public confusion. Thus the "Tax Foundation," which bills itself nonprofit, nonpartisan, and "interested solely in the goal of more efficient and economical government," according to an AP news story sought to rebut the proposition that "some big corporations do not pay taxes and profits are high." Its answer was brief and to the point: "Political observers have noted that almost

40 percent of all corporations pay no income tax. The fact is that in a typical year almost 40 percent of all corporations operate at a loss, with no income left to be taxed away." The rebuttal was also beside the point. The question was whether corporations pay their fair share on taxes. We have already seen that there are many large corporations which pay little or no federal income tax on their substantial profits.

The special interests spend generously on campaign contributions for Congress and the presidency, on skilled Washington-based lobbying organizations, and on public propaganda including advertisements in the media. In return, they receive valuable tax preferences. To add insult to injury all these lobbying expenses with the exception of direct campaign contributions are tax-deductible just like an ordinary business expense. Not only are American taxpayers paying for all the special tax breaks in the law, they are also helping to pay for the process that puts them there.

With all this power, money, and influence flowing from one side, representatives and senators often accede to the wishes of special interests. Most legislators are not corrupt. They simply support these packaged positions because they don't sound unreasonable. And, of course, they know that if they don't support these groups the groups won't support them. Or they'll finance someone who will run against them. So why not go along? Other constituents usually won't even know or care. If representatives do fight against tax loopholes in a public spirit, they usually have more to lose than gain. Voters won't send them back just because they voted *against* special-interest legislation—after all that's what they're *supposed* to do. But the special interests will work hard to defeat them.

a matter of public record

The legislative process has been helpful to representatives who wanted to hide their anti-tax reform positions. The system of nonrecorded votes and inadequate disclosure of contributions generally have insulated all members of Congress. Even now, the manipulation of news about individual legislators allows representatives to deceive or misinform their constituents. Senators and representatives have full-time staffs that write press releases, arrange canned interviews, and highlight some votes while ignoring others. Sometimes there have been outright deceptions. During his 1974 re-election bid, Ways and Means Republican Donald Brotzman defended his receipt of large sums of money from special interests—including oil—with a public statement that it was incorrect to say the special interests had bought his vote. "I voted to phase out the oil depletion allowance," he commented, adding sarcastically that "maybe they (the oil companies) want the oil depletion allowance phased out." Brotzman termed his vote on the depletion allowance "a matter of public record."

What Brotzman did not publicize was the record of his committee votes leading up to the depletion phase-out. A newspaper reporter in Brotzman's district wondered about his statement and decided to check it out himself. He discovered that on seventeen different occasions in the Ways and Means Committee, Brotzman voted for amendments to weaken the depletion repeal bill and a related windfall profits tax measure. In another instance, the reporter discovered, Brotzman had introduced a bill to create a new loophole for multinational oil companies that would be retroactive for four years. The story ran in the weekly Boulder, Colorado, paper and was picked up by Brotzman's opponent, who used it as a campaign issue. Thanks to a little research by a curious reporter, the public got the full story of Brotzman's "support" for tax reform. This exposure was one reason he lost his bid for re-election. More of this kind of monitoring is necessary to force members of Congress to be accountable for their actions.

To meet the need for systematic monitoring of congressional and Treasury tax activities in Washington, several organizations are beginning effective operation from the capital city. These include Taxation with Representation, Tax Analysts and Advocates, Common Cause, and Public Citizen's Tax Reform Research Group. (See the Appendix for a complete list of tax reform groups.) For the first time in recent years, public-interest professionals are working full time to inform citizens and citizen groups about issues in tax politics.

Meanwhile, taxpayers in communities across the country are organizing to make use of such information and bring it to the voters in each congressional district. While the Washington groups monitor the behind-the-scenes activities of senators and representatives, local taxpayer groups are working to prevent voters from being misled by the political rhetoric and complicated language that the special interests may use to disguise the real issues. Until now, the special interests have generally enjoyed tax politics their way. That's changing. When it does, we'll have a fair tax system and long-lost taxation with real representation.

Chapter 4
Tax Policy and Administration: The Treasury Department and the IRS

The Treasury Department has a great deal of influence over our tax laws. It not only formulates and initiates tax policy which helps to create and mold tax legislation, but, along with its Internal Revenue Service (IRS), the Treasury interprets the tax laws and applies them to more than 123 million taxpayers each year. These functions of policy input and administration deserve a closer look.

★ ★ ★ ★ ★ ★

The Treasury Department has several important tax policy functions. First, the secretary of the Treasury and his subordinates provide national leadership on issues of taxation. Depending on the nature of the secretary and the administration, this guidance can inspire reform or stifle it. Second, the Treasury Department and its substantial legal and economic tax staffs provide information and guidance to the congressional tax committees and to members of Congress generally. Again, the Treasury can either support or oppose tax reform. Third, the Treasury Department, with the advice of the IRS, promulgates tax regulations to fill the gaps or otherwise interpret or supplement congressional tax laws. In this quasi-legislative function, the Treasury has considerable latitude to tighten or relax restrictions on tax preferences.

The department is headed by the secretary of the Treasury, who is appointed by the president and confirmed by the Senate. The secretary is a member of the president's cabinet, serves at his pleasure, and therefore represents the particular politics of the administration in the White House. There is a deputy secretary directly under the secretary and a number of assistant secretaries below the deputy.

Tax policy is supervised by the assistant secretary for tax policy, who is also selected by the secretary. The assistant secretary, along with a deputy, sits in on congressional bill drafting sessions and indicates administration positions on various tax matters before the House Ways and Means Committee. On major tax questions the assistant secretary will confer with the president.

As a practical matter an assistant secretary either presents the administration's position or finds another job. But there is some latitude in the office in terms of policy. Stanley Surrey, the assistant secretary for tax policy during the Kennedy and Johnson administrations, had a reputation for using his position to advance tax reform positions to the administration. He, of course, could be and was occasionally overruled. During the Nixon administration, Assistant Secretary Frederic Hickman was able to assert his own positions in congressional mark-ups less often.

Treasury tax policy comes from below as well as from the top. The assistant secretary is in charge of the three professional tax policy branches of the Treasury Department. They are the Office of Tax Analysis, staffed by professional economists, the Office of the Tax Legislative Counsel, staffed by professional tax lawyers, and the Office of International Tax Counsel, staffed by experts in the international tax field.

Directly below the secretary of the Treasury and the deputy secretary is the Internal Revenue Service, headed by a commissioner appointed by the president and confirmed by the Senate. The Internal Revenue Service is also involved in tax policy through its chief counsel's Legislation and Regulations Division and the Interpretive Division, which draft and propose regulations. It also makes its views known on pro-

108 TAX POLITICS

posed legislation or suggested policy changes through the deputy secretary. But as we will see below, the IRS's major responsibility is to administer and enforce the tax laws.

political influence on policy

The Treasury Department doesn't perform its various tax policy functions in a vacuum. It is subjected to much the same kinds of pressure from outside interests as is the Congress. As we shall see, Treasury decisions are influenced by specific taxpayers, their lawyers and lobbyists, members of Congress on behalf of favored constituents, the tax section of the American Bar Association, trade associations, and academicians.

In the end, Treasury tax policy is a product of professional input from below, political input from above, and various special-interest, professional, and public-interest pressures from outside. All these are amalgamated and expressed through administration recommendations to Congress, interpretations of the tax laws through regulations, and administration of the law through the IRS.

From a tax-reform perspective, it is important that Treasury's participation in the tax legislative process represent the broad public interest as much as possible. Special interests are well represented in Congress. In order to have genuine democratic debate, it is important that the Treasury not merely mirror these same special interests. Instead, the Treasury should represent the broad interest in closing rather than opening loopholes, and in lowering tax rates for all taxpayers rather than conferring tax benefits on the influential few.

Some of the Treasury Department's work is inherently political. The secretary of the Treasury—the highest Treasury Department official and a member of the president's cabinet—almost automatically becomes an administration spokesperson on issues of domestic and international economic policy, including tax policy. Every year the secretary and ranking subordinates speak out on issues such as inflation, recession, energy policy, interest rates, tax cuts, and balancing the federal budget.

The American public hears frequently from the Treasury Department on tax issues. Usually the message comes in the form of news coverage of a presentation by the secretary, undersecretary, or possibly even the assistant secretary for tax policy to a congressional committee or private group. The use of a public presentation to provide national leadership is well illustrated in the January 17, 1969, congressional testimony of outgoing Treasury Secretary Joseph Barr. The Treasury Department during the Johnson administration had done a great deal of policy work on needed tax reforms. As the administration was about to change hands, the department released its *Treasury Tax Reform Studies*. Treasury Secretary Barr made a pitch for tax reform almost as a parting shot. He made the startling disclosure that, in 1968, 155 wealthy Americans with incomes of over $200,000 paid no federal income taxes whatsoever. He left the Congress and new administration with the following warning:

>...Mr. Chairman, I think the greatest unfinished agenda item is...tax reform...I will hazard a guess that there is going to be a taxpayer revolt over the income taxes in this country unless we move in this area.
>
>Now, the revolt is not going to come from the poor. They do not pay very much in taxes. The revolt is going to come from the middle-class, it is going to come from those people with incomes from $7,000 to $20,000 who pay every nickel of taxes at the going rate. They do not have the loopholes and the gimmicks to resort to, Mr. Chairman. ...
>
>This is a voluntary system. It will not work unless people want it. ...if we're going to maintain this magnificent tax system..., it must be a fair system.

Barr himself was surprised by the popular reaction. Middle-class taxpayers were already aroused by the high tax bills due April 15 because of the Vietnam War tax surcharge; no provision for increased withholding had been made to cover the extra amount. Following Barr's speech, Treasury and Congress were deluged by demands for tax reform. The final result was the 1969 "Tax Reform Act," a modest but good first step toward tax fairness. Good Treasury Department leadership can make a big difference in the struggle for tax reform.

Of course, as with any official statements, Treasury statements deserve careful scrutiny. In July 1972, Treasury Undersecretary Edwin Cohen, the Nixon administration's top tax policy official until his departure to a corporate law firm in early 1973, testified before the congressional Joint Economic Committee. He lightly dismissed statistics that showed 112 people with "adjusted gross incomes" (AGI) over $200,000 paying no federal income taxes in 1971. Cohen argued that "if we look at the data as a whole it is clear that persons with high adjusted incomes are paying heavy federal income taxes...." Congressman Henry Reuss, chairing the committee at the time, stopped Cohen: "Well, that sounds reassuring to someone who doesn't know what 'adjusted gross income' is.... But is it not a fact that 'adjusted gross income' is one of those lovely Treasury terms which deliberately excludes the very loophole income we are talking about—capital gain, oil depletion, tax-exempt bonds, interest on life insurance, savings, and so on?... So that these people did make millions, taken together, on which they paid no tax whatever, and this [adjusted gross income] figure merely relates to that portion of their income which wasn't loophole income. Isn't that so?" Cohen quickly backed off. "Mr. Chairman," he conceded, "I could not agree more that the use of 'adjusted gross income' as a measurement here has great defects." However, the undersecretary's concession had little impact on the publicity accompanying the Treasury Department press release of Undersecretary Cohen's statement.

Although professional and political considerations both may influence many areas of Treasury Department activity, the combination is most pronounced in tax policy. On one hand, the tax proposals of the administration in power quite clearly depend on politics: the constituencies that put a party into the White House will have an easier time persuading the administration to lower taxes for them than will anyone else. On the other hand, tax policy should be based on sound principles of taxation. Politics should properly play a role in tax policy when it involves the broad philosophy of economics and taxation. For example, the Democrats usually advocate a tax policy that stimulates the economy through tax relief to low and middle income taxpayers who will spend most of their tax cut on new products, while Republicans usually advocate a "trickle-down" theory of tax cuts for business and higher income taxpayers who will save and invest the most. The problem for tax reform arises when too much politics and too little professionalism go into the formulation of tax policy.

Unfortunately, Treasury tax policy sometimes does not reflect the best judgment of the lawyers and economists who work on it. It often becomes involved in the politics of a particular administration. On February 4, 1974, for example, Treasury Secretary George P. Shultz, after consultations with President Nixon, presented a proposal to eliminate the windfall profits that the oil companies were making as a result of the rapid increase in the price of crude oil. Nowhere in his statement did Shultz propose the repeal of any of the oil industry's generous tax preferences—the oil depletion allowance, the deduction for "intangible" drilling costs, or the foreign tax credit—which lowered the taxes of the oil companies by as much as $6 billion in 1974.

At hearings before the House Ways and Means Committee many public witnesses argued that the proper way to end windfall profits would be to end the tax breaks that led to those profits in the first place. Privately, many Treasury economists and lawyers agreed. They were under orders, however, to come up with a complicated windfall profits tax in order to preserve the oil depletion allowance—a position which President Nixon had pledged to maintain at an April 1972 Texas barbecue attended by 200 oilmen. Apparently that pledge helped to bring in over $5 million in 1972 presidential campaign funds and would not be abandoned.

Without strong administration backing of reform, the depletion allowance would remain in 1974. In fact, following an October press conference when President Ford mistakenly made an on-the-spot endorsement of a Ways and Means Committee bill which included a five-year phase-out of the depletion allowance, Treasury Secretary William Simon reiterated the administration's opposition to ending the controversial subsidy, proving his friendship with the oil industry. On the following day, the president "clarified" his position as being in line with that of Mr. Simon.

Most of the experts in the Treasury Department privately supported depletion repeal. But with the Treasury opposing such a move, its chances were reduced. Despite its often political positions, the department maintains a good deal of influence over the tax writing process.

110 TAX POLITICS

Oil is not an isolated example. Administration studies from the Treasury Department and the Office of Management and Budget on the $1.5 billion Domestic International Sales Corporation (DISC) export tax subsidy concluded that the program had little or no effect on increasing U.S. exports. In 1975, there were very few professionals in or out of Treasury that would support DISC as sound tax policy. Even those who generally supported lowering taxes on business felt it made more sense to repeal DISC and give those benefits in a more neutral manner to business generally. But DISC had gained a very important constituency: the thousands of corporations, big and small, which were the beneficiaries of this generous program. The result was that the Ford administration refused to advocate its repeal.

As mentioned in the preceding chapter, the subordination of good policy to good politics has only served to discredit the Treasury Department's traditionally strong policy role. When George Shultz was Treasury secretary in 1973 and 1974, he came down strongly against tax shelters as wasteful and inequitable. A year later under a more pro-oil secretary, William Simon, the administration did a complete about-face, opposing the end of syndicated tax shelters in the oil industry. Some members of Congress wondered aloud why good tax policy in 1974 was bad tax policy just one year later. One House Ways and Means member was heard to say, "How do they [the Treasury] expect us to take them seriously?"

implementing the law through regulations

Tax regulations fall into two broad categories: interpretative and legislative. Where Congress explicitly states what the law should be, the secretary of the Treasury is authorized to further clarify and interpret it. The resulting interpretations and clarification guidelines could be challenged if they contradict the intent or fall outside the scope of the underlying law. In regard to certain sections of the law, Congress has delegated to the Treasury Department specific authority to write detailed rules. These "legislative" regulations have the full force of law unless they clearly exceed the Treasury's congressionally delegated authority.

Both interpretative and legislative regulations can involve issues of great importance, especially financial considerations, to specific taxpayers. Lobbying and political pressure are therefore a major part of the regulations process. Regulations are subject to influence from specific taxpayers, often an industry group that will be affected by them; from the Treasury professionals who work on them; from the congressional people responsible for tax legislation; and from public and congressional reaction.

Tax regulations are thought up in many places. The IRS itself, the president or other executive departments, Congress, business interests or other taxpayers, may informally suggest the need for new or amended regulations. Regulations can also be formally requested by anyone through a petition to the IRS commissioner.

The regulations process must follow the procedures prescribed under the "Administrative Procedures Act." A proposed regulation actually begins when the assistant Treasury secretary for tax policy orders the IRS Regulations Division to draft a regulation. The IRS then sends the drafted proposed regulation back to the assistant Treasury secretary's office. Once approved there, it is published in the weekly *Federal Register* as a "Notice of Proposed Regulation." The public then has thirty days in which to file written comments or request a public hearing on the proposed regulation. After thirty days, or after a hearing, if one has been granted, the Treasury can publish the regulation as a temporary or a final regulation or it can amend it and publish another notice of proposed regulation.

In fiscal year 1973, the Treasury Department issued seventy-seven final regulations, eight temporary regulations, and fifty-two notices of proposed regulations relating to tax matters. Of the total, thirty-six of the final regulations and ten notices of proposed regulations related to the 1969 Tax Reform Act—an indication of the time it takes to resolve many tax questions because of the complexity and politics involved.

interpreting the law

Sometimes regulations can be largely ministerial, involving noncontroversial issues. But most tax regulations are of utmost importance to the taxpayers who will be affected, often involving millions of dollars in potential tax revenues. For this reason, industries will barrage the Treasury with lobbyists, lawyers, accountants, corporate executives, and sometimes letters from influential congressional people advocating the drafting of regulations in the manner most favorable to them.

One example is the case of the mineral depletion regulations issued by the Treasury Department on March 13, 1972, after many years of controversy. This case highlights another unfortunate function of tax regulations: they can be used where the intent of Congress is unclear to confer generous tax subsidies on special interests. The depletion regulations conferred an initial estimated $500 million tax benefit on the mining industry, and about $50 million annually thereafter.

The public debate over the depletion tax subsidy usually centers on oil. Often ignored is the expansion of the depletion subsidy to benefit many other interests, especially including hard minerals and gas. What remains of the oil depletion deduction is now 22 percent of gross income, but the tax laws also allow 22 percent depletion to forty other American mine minerals ranging from aluminum and asbestos through clay, mica, and quartz to talc, uranium and zinc. Fifteen percent depletion is allowed for minerals like gold, silver, and copper, and lesser depletion for other minerals and even gravel, peat, sand, and stone!

Although Congress is primarily responsible for the expensive depletion subsidy, the Treasury is also involved. Congress, having prescribed the percentage amount of depletion, leaves to the Treasury the task of defining what is the "gross income" from the mine or oil well to which depletion applies. The oil and mineral interests, of course, want the most generous possible definition of "gross income" so that their depletion deductions will be larger. And having gotten the depletion subsidy from Congress, the special interests turn to the Treasury Department for similarly generous treatment. In the case of the mining industry, the question was what was gross income from mining. Congress had set the depletion allowance for the copper industry at 15 percent of "the gross income from mines." Of course, if a large copper company mines, refines, and molds copper into industry-grade ingots, it is hard to determine the gross income from the copper mines. The Treasury has that responsibility, through the regulations process and the IRS administration of the regulations. It can develop regulations which are either cautious or openhanded in extending tax loopholes. For example, let us suppose that copper ore is worth $10 million; roughly refined copper is worth $15 million; refined and molded copper is worth $20 million. A tough Treasury regulation would give depletion on $10 million or a $1.5 million deduction. A generous Treasury regulation would give depletion on $20 million or a $3 million deduction.

The issue came to a head in the late 1960s, when the mining companies discovered that Treasury officials were attempting to restrict the subsidy through regulations narrowly defining the "gross income" subject to the depletion benefit. The oil and mining interests turned to their strong allies in the Senate. On December 5, 1967, Chairman Russell Long of the Finance Committee wrote Treasury Secretary Henry Fowler: "Recently I was contacted by representatives of a number of American cement companies with regard to proposed income tax regulations.... I have concluded that the industry's objections are in large part well-founded.... I urge you as strongly as I know how to remedy your proposed regulations with regard to the shortcomings." Less than two weeks later, on December 15, high-ranking Finance Committee Republican Wallace Bennett wrote to Fowler: "I have been contacted by an American copper company which is very much concerned [with the proposed Treasury regulations]. I am writing to express my support for the company's position."

In 1968, the special interests intensified their pressure on the Treasury through the Finance Committee. In secret meetings in July and October, committee senators roughly interrogated Treasury officials. Faced with this pressure, and Long's threats that he would pass a law forcing the Treasury to grant more generous depletion benefits, the officials finally caved in. The final depletion regulations the Treasury promised Long "should make the cement industry happy." "There was an implied threat here that if the Finance Committee did not like the regulations, they would ruin every Treasury bill that came before them," one Treasury official anonymously told the *Washington Post*.

112 TAX POLITICS

In November 1968, Richard Nixon won the presidency. Much of the Treasury resistance to Senate and industry pressure had come from Thomas F. Field, the Treasury Department depletion expert. Field's determined stand persuaded outgoing IRS Commissioner Sheldon Cohen that he should not approve the pro-industry regulations until his own staff had reviewed the issues. Outgoing IRS chief counsel, Mitchell Rogovin, similarly refused to sign the necessary documents. Despite a last-minute flurry of angry letters from Senator Long, the regulations remained incomplete when the new administration and Treasury Department officials took over in 1969.

With the post-election change of personnel, the oil and mining interests found a much warmer welcome at the department. Thomas Field resigned and was replaced by Burke Willsey, an attorney from Miller & Chevalier, the law firm representing the American Mining Congress. The new Treasury tax legislative counsel was John Chapoton, twin brother of cement industry tax attorney O. Don Chapoton. Randolph Thrower of the Sutherland. Asbill & Brennan tax law firm (one of whose attorneys represented clay producers seeking depletion benefits under the Treasury regulations) replaced IRS Commissioner Sheldon Cohen. The depletion regulations went into the new administration's bureaucratic pipeline, along with dozens of regulations based on the new 1969 Tax Reform Act. Finally, in early 1972, the department issued final regulations satisfactory to the mining industry and Finance Committee chairman Russell Long. Eager to atone for the earlier resistance, the Treasury applied many provisions retroactively—mining industry taxpayers could benefit from the new regulations back to December 31, 1955—sixteen years earlier! The industry was duly appeased.

legislating the law

At times an administration has attempted to use interpretative regulations to improperly "legislate" new tax laws. The 1971 ADR (accelerated depreciation regulations) are an example of such an attempt to cut corporate taxes by literally billions of dollars a year. ADR was announed January 11, 1971, in simultaneous press conferences at the San Clemente "Western White House" and the Treasury Department in Washington. ADR's cost to the government: $3.9 billion annually in a business tax cut. The benefits: "The changes in tax administration announced today," said Treasury Secretary David M. Kennedy, "will be good for our national economy, all of our citizens, and every American business."

Much to its surprise, the Treasury quickly ran into problems with the multibillion-dollar regulations. In trying to act fast, it had forgotten the democratic principle of public participation. President Nixon and Treasury Secretary Kennedy had announced ADR as if the regulations were an accomplished fact. Citizens were expected to accept Treasury statements at face value and acquiesce quietly in the massive corporate tax cut. To correct the Treasury misconception, two attorneys from Ralph Nader's Public Interest Research Group (PIRG) promptly filed suit in federal court to block the regulations until the Treasury considered public views as prescribed by the Administrative Procedures Act. The Treasury, caught off guard, rushed to the press to explain that there would, indeed, be public hearings. Treasury officials had simply omitted mention of that fact. The PIRG attorneys withdrew their court motion after the assistant Treasury secretary for tax policy, Edwin S. Cohen, and the commissioner of Internal Revenue, Ralph Thrower, filed sworn promises that the hearings would be held. But the Treasury had pledged only to hear the public, not to listen. Assistant Secretary Edwin Cohen stressed this point to the press the day the motion was withdrawn. "We don't anticipate changing our mind," he proclaimed. "As a very practical matter, a businessman can rely on this going into effect, in its broad outline." In short, Assistant Secretary Cohen—who had served large business clients for thirty years as a Wall Street attorney—was assuring his constituents that the public would remain powerless to change the $4 billion dollar tax subsidy, regardless of the evidence presented at the promised hearings.

Mr. Cohen remained true to his word. The hearing was conducted with strong partisan flavor. Witnesses critical of ADR were intensively and even roughly cross-examined. Those speaking for ADR—almost always on behalf of clients benefiting from the generous tax cut—were complimented on their expertise and fine statements. For public interest witnesses questions and answers were more a test of verbal agility than expertise. When Professor Martin David, the University of Wisconsin economist, spoke, it took forty-five minutes before a Treasury inquisitor managed to trip him up. When he finally stumbled, one onlooker sighed, "Well, they finally got him!" The interchange had been a verbal fox hunt, with one of the thirteen Treasury and IRS officials sure to catch him eventually, and willing to take as much time as necessary to do so. As Senator Birch Bayh put it, the hearing was truly a "charade."

But there was a stronger attack on the regulations as a usurpation of Congress's power to legislate. University of Pennsylvania Law School Dean Bernard Wolfman, appearing at the hearings for Common Cause, presented a long legal memorandum to support his contention that ADR "represents an unwarranted and unprecedented arrogation of power on the part of an administrative agency." Only Congress had the constitutional power to grant the multibillion-dollar tax cut. Members of Congress from both parties voiced concern about the Treasury action. Forty-five Democrats, led by Ways and Means Congressman Sam Gibbons (D-Fla.), wrote to the IRS urging cancellation of the proposed regulations. "Only the Congress, as elected representatives of the American people, is able, through a comprehensive legislative process, to properly evaluate [such] tax legislation," they argued. Senator Sam Ervin (D-N.C.) announced an investigation by his Subcommittee on Separation of Powers as a possible prelude to hearings on Treasury encroachment on congressional taxing powers.

Senator Edmund Muskie (D-Me.) made a dramatic contribution to the public debate by revealing that Treasury official John Nolan—as acting assistant secretary for tax policy—had warned President Nixon that the proposed changes would indeed be an unlawful taking of congressional power. In particular, Nolan pointed out that Congress, in the Internal Revenue Code, required that machinery be depreciated at a "reasonable" rate. A system like ADR would allow depreciation tax deductions at a much faster rate—which could well be ruled "unreasonable" and therefore unlawfully in excess of the Treasury's authority to prescribe. Exactly a month after Nolan sent the White House his legal memorandum, President Nixon and the Treasury Department announced the new ADR system of fast depreciation deductions.

In the months after the ADR hearings, the Treasury remained under bombardment with unfavorable comment from Congress and the press. On June 22, 1971—over half a year behind the original timetable—it issued the final ADR regulations. Mr. Cohen had remained true to his word and to the special-interest constituents. Two weeks later, a coalition including Ralph Nader, Common Cause, the United Auto Workers, and Congressman Henry Reuss (D-Wis.), took the Treasury to court to invalidate the regulations. Fearful that the courts would overturn their generous tax subsidy, the special-interests turned to their supporters in Congress. In the Revenue Act of 1971, Congress changed the depreciation law to grant corporations a smaller version of ADR, costing $2.9 billion instead of the original $3.9 billion. But the congressional battle was close. A Senate floor fight led by Birch Bayh (D-Ind.) came within two votes of killing ADR outright.

insulating tax policy from political influence

A great deal of political influence pervades the legislative and tax policy process. The Treasury Department interpretation of tax legislation has often been overly influenced by such pressure. At times this influence has spilled over into the actual process of applying and enforcing the laws and regulations on specific taxpayers. Some of this came to light most recently in the revelations of "friends" and "enemies" lists within the IRS. This is not a new phenomenon.

From 1951 to 1953 a subcommittee of the House Ways and Means Committee investigated problems of corruption and political influence in the Treasury Department and its Bureau of Internal Revenue (as the IRS was then known). After extensive hearings, the subcommittee issued its report in 1953, concluding: "It is indisputedly clear that intervention in tax cases by Treasury officials for political reasons not only produced improper decisions in tax cases, but also had an adverse affect on the entire Internal Revenue System."

The subcommittee cited six sample cases of favoritism in tax administration, involving some $10 million lost in federal revenues. The cases included sus-

114 TAX POLITICS

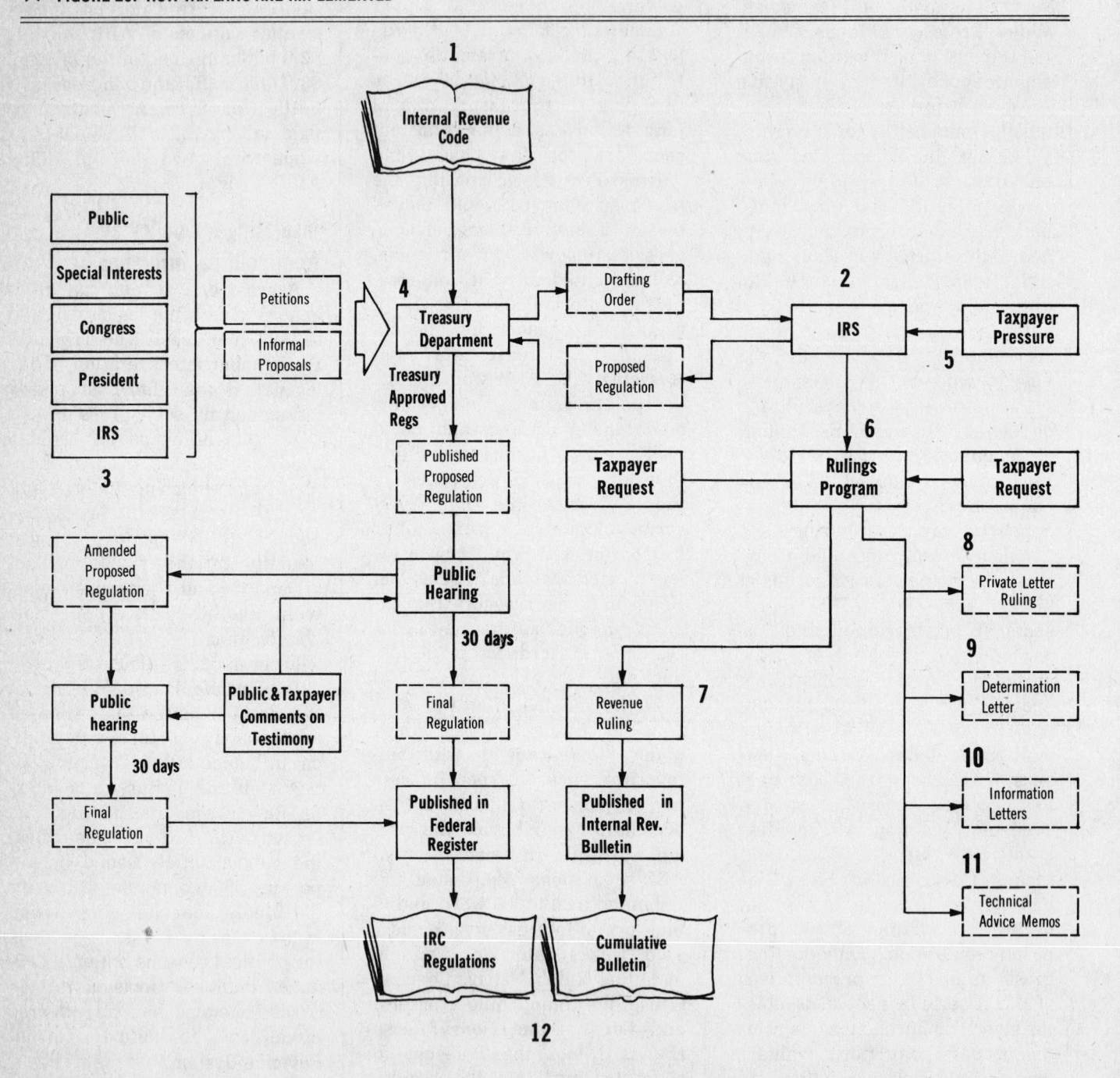

★ FIGURE 26. HOW TAX LAWS ARE IMPLEMENTED ★

1. Internal Revenue Code
2. IRS
3. Public / Special Interests / Congress / President / IRS — Petitions / Informal Proposals
4. Treasury Department — Treasury Approved Regs — Drafting Order / Proposed Regulation — Published Proposed Regulation
5. Taxpayer Pressure
6. Rulings Program — Taxpayer Request / Taxpayer Request
7. Public Hearing (30 days) — Amended Proposed Regulation — Public hearing (30 days) — Public & Taxpayer Comments on Testimony — Final Regulation — Revenue Ruling — Published in Federal Register — Published in Internal Rev. Bulletin
8. Private Letter Ruling
9. Determination Letter
10. Information Letters
11. Technical Advice Memos
12. IRC Regulations / Cumulative Bulletin

FIGURE 26. HOW TAX LAWS ARE IMPLEMENTED (Continued)

1. Our complex income tax laws are further interpreted and clarified by the Treasury Department and, under it, the IRS.
2. Under the Internal Revenue Code, the IRS is authorized, with the approval of the Treasury secretary, to prescribe all needful rules and regulations for the enforcement of the internal revenue laws.
3. Tax Regulations are thought up in a lot of places. The IRS itself, the president, or other executive departments, Congress, business interests or other taxpayers may informally suggest the need for new or amended regulations. Regulations can also be formally requested through a petition to the IRS commissioner.
4. Proposed regulations start when the assistant treasury secretary for tax policy orders the IRS Regulations Division to draft a regulation.
5. Interested taxpayers often hire attorneys to work with, or on, IRS to make regulations most favorable to them
6. In addition to official "regulations," the IRS issues "rulings" on particular fact situations made in response to requests by taxpayers. These are issued without the formality of Treasury's approval.
7. A "revenue ruling" is an interpretation issued by the IRS national office and published in its Cumulative Bulletin. It usually involves tax situations of general applicability to a number of taxpayers.
8. "Private" or "letter rulings" are issued by the IRS Technical Branch to a taxpayer. These rulings interpret and apply the tax laws to a specific set of facts. They usually involve prospective tax situations and until recently were kept confidential.
9. Before filing a tax return covering a completed transaction, a taxpayer may sometimes get a "determination letter." These are similar to private letter rulings but are issued by district directors where the law is well settled by regulation revenue ruling or court decision.
10. Information letters are issued by either the district or national office and merely point out to the taxpayer a well-settled interpretation of tax law without regard to a specific set of facts.
11. Technical advice memoranda are issued by the IRS national office to give requesting district offices guidance as to the proper interpretation of the tax laws to a specific set of facts.
12. The series of Cumulative Bulletins containing tax rulings and the published regulations comprise all the official administrative interpretations of the internal revenue laws.

TAX POLITICS

pension of tax enforcement operations, the lifting of a tax seizure designed to protect the assets of a delinquent taxpayer seeking to keep them out of government hands, and three improper tax rulings, allowing taxpayers favored treatment. "Dubious rulings were issued by the Bureau after direct expressions of interest by the then Secretary of the Treasury" and after lobbying by counsel for the taxpayer, according to the investigating subcommittee. In one case, concerning the Monsanto Chemical Company, the Bureau of Internal Revenue took a position against the taxpayer, and reversed itself within forty minutes after the company obtained the assistance of the secretary of the Treasury.

Many proposed reforming Treasury Department administration by completely separating the Bureau of Internal Revenue from the Treasury, but the department resisted strongly. It argued that the administration of the tax laws with respect to individual taxpayers should not be separated from the Treasury's tax policy responsibilities.

The subcommittee sought to draw a clear distinction between the "functions and essential political consciousness of the Treasury and the Bureau. The former is an instrument for the development and effectuation of the fiscal policies of the governing political administration. The latter should provide a quasi-judicial enforcement of revenue laws, free from any kind of political influence."

In the resulting reorganization of the IRS, the patronage system, headed by sixty-four politically appointed "collectors of internal revenue," was abolished. All positions within the agency, except for that of commissioner and chief counsel, were placed under the civil service system. Responsibility for the day-to-day operations of the tax agency was lodged with fifty-eight district directors, who replaced the sixty-four collectors. They are supervised by seven regional commissioners. The IRS national office was left with policy-making authority. These reforms did not, however, fully insulate the IRS from political pressure because the agency is a natural target for those seeking favorable interpretations of the tax law.

IRS's role in tax law implementation

While the IRS's main role is to administer and enforce the law, it also contributes to the creation of tax policy in a number of ways: regulations are normally first drafted in the IRS chief counsel's office and the IRS issues private letter rulings, revenue rulings, technical advice, determination letters, and other statements which are its interpretations of the tax law.

These statements express what the IRS thinks the law means, and to that degree they set tax policy at the level where it really counts—the taxpayer's pocketbook. As a result, taxpayers bring pressure to bear through their congressmen, through the White House, or contacts within the IRS to get interpretations favorable to them.

For example, a taxpayer concerned about a proposed IRS regulation regarding employers' withholding and social security tax payments sent his complaint to a highly placed government acquaintance—Rose Mary Woods, personal secretary to President Nixon. The petitioner was a friend, it turned out, of President Nixon. Within a week after the letter was written, Presidential Assistant John D. Ehrlichman passed it along to IRS Commissioner Randolph Thrower, pointing out the friendship with Nixon and asking for a personal reply.

tax rulings—special help for influential taxpayers

In contrast to regulations, which are written as general guides to tax law interpretation, IRS rulings are tailored to specific fact situations in what are generally considered to be complex financial transactions. A taxpayer who wishes to know how the IRS might treat a specific financial arrangement he plans to make can ask the IRS to rule prospectively on the issue. If the IRS decides to make such a ruling, it is generally binding, although the agency may later reverse itself and revoke the ruling if it finds that it was in error. These interpretations of the law, called "private letter rulings," apply only to the specific taxpayer and are secret. If they become known, they still cannot be used as precedent by others. The IRS makes some 15,000 such rulings every year, and it makes another 15,000 rulings which simply involve changes in accounting methods. Many tax experts have protested that private letter rulings are "secret law," and some courts have agreed. As a result, these rulings may not remain secret much longer. The IRS has taken steps to make them public under certain conditions, and Congress

Tax Policy and Administration: Treasury and the IRS

may soon legislate public access to them.

Since private letter rulings may amount to millions of dollars in tax savings to wealthy individuals and corporations, people who hope to benefit from them press hard for favorable action from the IRS. In 1972, Robert H. Finch, former secretary of Health, Education and Welfare, and then a counselor to President Nixon, wrote directly to IRS Commissioner Johnnie Walters on behalf of a taxpayer who had asked for a private ruling. Walters, ducking the political hot potato, threw it to his Treasury Department superiors. He wrote to Finch advising him that "because of the broad policy questions involved, we referred the matter to the Office of the Assistant Secretary for Tax Policy, where it is now under consideration." Ordinarily the IRS makes rulings unilaterally, without consulting the Treasury Department in advance. In acknowledging Walter's action, Finch asked Walters to keep him advised, and added a little more pressure, saying, "In view of the merits of the case, I hope action can be taken promptly."

Not all of the rulings which the IRS issues are private. Of the 15,000 interpretative rulings, around 600 are stripped of all identification and issued as "revenue rulings," which can be used as precedent by others with similar fact situations. Revenue rulings may also arise from significant court decisions and from requests by taxpayers for "technical advice."

Technical advice is another expression of IRS tax law interpretation and, like private letter rulings, applies to a specific set of facts. However, unlike the letter rulings, technical advice applies to the tax treatment which the taxpayer has already taken, and usually arises when the individual or corporation is being audited. IRS district offices may request technical advice from the national office on any technical or procedural question which develops during consideration of the tax liability. The national office responses to these requests, which are made by IRS personnel or by the taxpayer, frequently result in the publication of revenue rulings aimed at promoting uniformity in the treatment of tax issues.

The IRS has still other ways of letting people know its views on the tax laws. A district director may issue a "determination letter" in response to a written request by an individual or an organization. This relates mainly to qualifications of pension plans and to the qualification of certain organizations for exemption from federal income tax. The determination letter applies principles and precedents previously announced by the national office to a particular set of facts and is issued only where a determination can be made on the basis of clearly established rules as set forth in the law, regulations, rulings, and so on.

An "information letter" is a statement issued either by the national office or by a district director that merely calls attention to a well-established interpretation or principle of tax law without applying it to a specific set of facts.

While all of these procedures cost the IRS considerable time and money, they are services mainly for businesses, corporations, and the wealthy. Most of the nation's 84 million individual taxpayers do not even know about them. Their contacts with the IRS start when they get their forms in the mail, and may not end until they have received an IRS audit or met up with one of the agency's collection officials.

Let us now turn to the Internal Revenue Service and how it deals with average taxpayers. We shall see that IRS procedures have been developed by and for tax practitioners, and their affluent clients. As a result the system does not work well for moderate and low income taxpayers who cannot afford such representation in their dealings with the agency. Not only do wealthy taxpayers benefit from the complex tax law, but they may ovtain binding rulings—guaranteed tax advice—from the agency. However, the IRS refuses to be bound by the advice its employees give rank and file taxpayers who visit IRS local offices for help. Unrepresented taxpayers who do not know their rights and do not understand the law cannot protect themselves in IRS audits and appeals. Represented taxpayers can.

the internal revenue service

America could not run for a day without the revenue supplied to it by the nation's taxpayers. For that reason, Congress has given the Internal Revenue

Service more power over the lives and property of Americans than any other agency of the federal government. The American tax system depends on voluntary self-assessment, where taxpayers tell the government how much income they have and figure their own tax. The Internal Revenue Service collects the revenue and polices the self-assessment system to ensure that taxpayers obey the law. It handles some 123 million returns, 84 million of them filed by individuals. Every year many of these individuals find, unhappily, that filing a return does not end their involvement with the IRS.

In 1974, for example, the IRS audited 2.2 million taxpayers (equaling the combined populations of Philadelphia and Miami). It billed 8 million (equal to the entire population of New York City) who allegedly owed the government more than they had paid. Not all of them understood or agreed with actions taken by the IRS, and most could not afford professional representatives to help them. This chapter will explain how the IRS administers the tax law, and how people who have disputes with the agency can help themselves.

Among the extraordinary powers that Congress has granted the Treasury Department is the authority to (1) examine a taxpayer's books of account and financial records without a court order; (2) examine any of the taxpayer's records in the hands of a third party, like an employer or bank, without a court order; (3) garnish wages and seize and sell property without a court order.

Hand in hand with these powers, the Congress has established an "appallingly complicated tax law." This means that taxpayers who cannot retain professionals to represent them in disputes with the IRS face a potentially precarious situation. Since even skilled attorneys complain that they cannot always understand the complex law, it is not hard to see why ordinary taxpayers may come off second best in a confrontation with the IRS. And, although the agency tells its employees to be reasonable and fair, sometimes they are not. For example, in 1971 a Santa Cruz, California, accountant, Richard L. Goodell, owed the IRS back taxes. When it became clear that Goodell could not pay, the agency not only seized his car, golf clubs, and the watch off his wrist, but published a humiliating cartoon in a local paper announcing the public auction of his property. The cartoon depicted Goodell wearing only a necktie and a barrel. Although the IRS reportedly apologized later, Goodell is still seeking relief from the loss to his business and health which, he says, the incident caused.

assistance in filing returns

Until the early 1970s, the IRS devoted relatively few resources to educating or helping individuals meet their tax obligations. One reason was because relatively few people were required to pay federal income taxes before World War II. In 1940, out of a total population of 132 million, there were only 8 million individual taxpayers and they paid 18 percent of the total tax collected. But just three years later, millions of new taxpayers who needed help began to enter the system. By 1943, the number of individual taxpayers had jumped to 37 million. In 1973, the total population had not even doubled (it stood at 220 million), yet individual taxpayers increased to 79 million, and their taxes amounted to 53 percent of the total collected. In 1975, there were 84 million individual taxpayers.

The growth in the number of taxpayers put new pressures on the IRS and contributed to a burgeoning of commercial tax-return preparer firms across the country. In 1971, the IRS estimated that half of all taxpayers spent $600 million to have someone else prepare their returns.

But the influx of new taxpayers, combined with increasingly complex tax laws, caused problems for the IRS and for tax practitioners. The agency discovered the alarming fact that both outside tax preparers and its own employees had made an extraordinary number of errors on returns prepared in 1972. For example, the error rate hovered between 74 and 79 percent for returns with adjusted gross income from $10,000 to under $50,000. Although the IRS kept its study a secret, the press discovered the poor quality of tax return preparation on its own.

In 1972, *Washington Star* reporter John Fialka took the same tax problem to seven different commercial firms, including two H&R Block offices, a Sears and Roebuck store, and Beneficial Finance, among others. He got seven different answers to his tax problem. And when he checked in with the IRS, he got still another response. Tom Herman, a *Wall Street Journal* reporter, did a similar survey of five commercial preparers in 1971 with similar results.

The IRS is not responsible for the activities of tax preparers unless fraud is involved. However, it does have a responsibility to explain the law to taxpayers who ask for help. Many people do not know that the agency often gives incorrect advice, and they do not know that it refuses to back up its employees' advice. If the IRS audits a return and finds an error, the taxpayer is responsible, even though an agency employee made the mistake.

Faced with a growing number of complaints in the early 1970s, the IRS began to strengthen its assistance to taxpayers. It operates under persistent constraints, however, which tend to limit the amount and quality of help taxpayers can expect. The first is the complexity of the tax law. The second is the size and continuing increase of the taxpayer population. The third is the short filing season during which the IRS is hard-pressed to assist the large numbers of people who turn to it for help. The fourth is the low budget for taxpayer services. This budget is a fraction of the amount spent on IRS's audit and collection activities. For fiscal year 1976, the agency asked Congress for $122 million for taxpayer assistance, out of a total budget of $1.6 billion. In contrast, it requested $838 million to fund its compliance activities, including audits, and $651 million for accounts and collections. Yet the IRS estimated that 40 million people contacted the agency offices in 1975 asking for tax advice, help on refunds and incorrect bills, and other types of assistance. The budget request would provide only $1.50 in services for each of the 83 million individual returns filed in 1974, or $3.00 each for the 40 million people who contact the agency.

About 2,300 of the IRS's 80,000 employees work full time in taxpayer services. Called Taxpayer Service Representatives (TSRs), they needed only a high school diploma or equivalent experience until 1974. Now they must have two years' experience in addition to a high school degree. Also, the agency has added a new position, the Taxpayer Service Specialist (TSS). To qualify, applicants must pass a federal examination for professionals.

During the filing season, these employees are joined by 1,000 to 1,500 temporary employees who need not be high school graduates. At peak periods they are assisted by more knowledgeable IRS auditors and revenue agents. However, because the filing season is short (three-and-a-half months at most), the law complex, and the number of taxpayers seeking help overwhelming, not only the IRS, but tax practitioners and taxpayers themselves continue to make costly mistakes on returns. Taxpayers faced with the choice of preparing their own returns (figure 27), or having someone else do it for them (figure 28), know that in either case, they may end up in trouble with the IRS.

audits

Beginning in 1964, the IRS attempted to measure the number of errors individuals make on their returns through its Taxpayer Compliance Measurement Program (TCMP). Under the program, the IRS selects a random sample of returns and subjects them to intensive audit. Then it projects the results of the sample to cover all of the returns filed during the year. The TCMP figures were one of the IRS's best-kept secrets until Phil and Sue Long, taxpayers from Bellevue, Washington, obtained access to them in 1975 under the freedom-of-information act. One set of figures deals with 1969 tax year returns filed in 1970. According to the IRS, the data suggest that 36.2 million individual taxpayers (48.8 percent of all individuals who filed) made mistakes resulting in tax changes of $1.00 or more on their 1969 returns. Of this number 30.3 million made mistakes in their own favor. In contrast, 5.9 million (8 percent of all individual filers) overpaid their taxes. The IRS calculated that the errors added up to $6.4 billion in lost revenue. However, IRS tax examiners discovered $900 million of that amount during audits, leaving a theoretical estimated loss to the Treasury of $5.5 billion—theoretical, because the

120 TAX POLITICS

★ **FIGURE 27. SOME SUGGESTIONS FOR DO-IT-YOURSELF TAX RETURN PREPARATION** ★

Taxpayers make mistakes on their returns because they follow the advice of neighbors or friends, instead of authoritative sources, and because they do not know how to document the tax treatment they have taken. There are some ways to help solve these problems.

---

1. Examine newsstand type tax guides at a local library. Study the content and style of each guide to see if it answers questions thoroughly and is easy to read. Avoid guides that do not have an index. Without one, there is no quick way to find the answer to a question.

2. Compare the treatment each guide gives on a particular subject, like moving expense deductions. See if the guide explains the IRS view of the law as well as court decisions which differ from the IRS view. Remember that the IRS does not always follow court precedent, and that, regardless of what the court says, it may challenge anyone who uses a court decision in figuring his own taxes.

3. After choosing the guide that seems most understandable and complete, buy the latest edition at a newsstand.

4. Use it along with the IRS's Publication 17, "Your Federal Income Tax." It explains the IRS view of the tax law and is available at all IRS offices. However, even the information in this guide is not beyond dispute. That means that you can follow the guide, be challenged by the IRS, go to court, and lose.

5. Use the IRS toll-free telephone service for answers to specific questions, but remember that IRS employees make mistakes. The IRS will not back up its employees' advice and may challenge the return even if the IRS prepared it. Therefore, always ask the employee to cite the authority in law or IRS regulation for any statement which seems contradictory or questionable. Expect a delay but don't hang up the telephone. You may have a hard time getting back on the line.

6. Visit an IRS office for more assistance on the return. If you are not able to prepare your own return, the IRS may do it for you. But remember that the IRS makes mistakes and will not back up its employees' advice. Ask the employee to cite the authority for statements if they seem contradictory or questionable.

7. Read IRS Publication #552, "Recordkeeping Requirements and a Guide to Tax Publications." It explains the kind of documentation needed to back up claims made on the tax return, and is available at all IRS offices.

8. Remember, taxpayers are personally responsible for their returns, regardless of who prepares the return or who gives tax advice.

---

figures do not show how much of the $900 million figure was lowered in appeals and how much of the amount the IRS could not collect.

The TCMP estimates also suggested that both the number and dollar amounts of errors had risen since a similar survey of 1965 individual returns. According to an IRS official, more recent data do not indicate that the trend has stopped or been reversed.

By analyzing the errors which taxpayers make, the TCMP study also measures "voluntary compliance"—defined by IRS as the degree to which taxpayers actually report and pay the tax that IRS believes they really owe. The survey data are broken down into audit classes, which categorize taxpayers according to adjusted gross income and types of returns filed. According to the study, those who file the simple 1040A return have the highest compliance level—96.3 percent. In contrast, individual businessmen reporting under $10,000 in adjusted gross income have the lowest level of compliance—68.7 percent (figure 29).

Tax Policy and Administration: Treasury and the IRS

★ FIGURE 28. FINDING A TAX PREPARER ★

On April 4, 1972, the IRS issued an official news release announcing widespread evidence of fraudulent practices by a "significant number of tax preparers," and a major expansion of its own free service to taxpayers. For those who are unable to prepare their own returns, here are some suggestions for selecting a returns preparer.

1. Avoid tax preparers who:
   - Suggest the taxpayer lie about the information on the return.
   - Suggest the taxpayer sign the return before it is completely filled out.
   - Fail to provide the taxpayer with a copy of the return.
   - Refuse to sign the return as the preparer.
   - Require the taxpayer to sign over the refund to the preparer.
   - Offer to pay an "instant" tax refund.
   - Are not in business on a year-around basis.

2. Select a tax preparer who:
   - Will explain what services will be performed and how much they will cost.
   - Is a certified public accountant, a tax attorney, a public accountant who is a member of a professional society (like the National Society of Public Accountants) or an agent enrolled to practice before the IRS.
   - Will provide a signed copy of the return.

3. Remember:
   - No one can guarantee that the IRS will not challenge the tax treatment taken on the return in an audit.
   - Only attorneys, certified public accountants and enrolled agents can represent you before the IRS.

★ FIGURE 29. COMPLIANCE LEVEL BY AUDIT CLASS ★

Audit Class	Voluntary Compliance Level 1965	1969
1040A type	95.8%	96.3%
Low nonbusiness (under $10,000 adjusted gross income)	92.4	89.6
Medium nonbusiness ($10,000 to under $50,000)	96.6	96.1
High nonbusiness (over $50,000)	95.8	94.1
Low business (under $10,000)	78.0	68.7
Medium business ($10,000 to under $30,000)	90.7	87.8
High business (over $30,000)	93.3	91.2
Total	93.8%	92.7%

SOURCE: IRS Co. 6230 (7-73) TC P Phase III, Cycle 3. Summary Results Individual Returns Tax Year 1969, page 9.

Although the TCMP data for 1969 returns suggested that almost half of all individual taxpayers made mistakes resulting in a tax change, the IRS was able to audit only 1.8 percent of individual returns filed that year. In fact, the agency's audit capability is weak, although the number of people affected is significant.

The IRS uses computers to select the majority of returns it audits. When returns are filed, they go first to IRS service centers where they are checked for mathematical errors and "unallowable" items, like improperly computed medical deductions. Next, the computers score the returns under complex secret formulas. These formulas measure the "normal" characteristics of returns reflecting similar tax brackets and similar circumstances. Returns which vary from the norm are singled out for review. Audit employees in the ten IRS service centers scan them to determine if there are any ready explanations for the variations. If not, the returns are sent to district and local offices where they are reviewed again and some are distributed to tax auditors and revenue agents for examination.

Not all returns, however, are selected by the computers. Agents examine some because they may involve pockets of noncompliance, like returns of individuals who might conceal cash income or returns prepared by tax practitioners suspected of fraud. Altogether, the IRS has twenty-four different reasons for selecting returns for examination and it has audit programs that are national, regional or local in scope.

122 TAX POLITICS

The audits are conducted in two ways. One is the office audit, where the taxpayer brings his books and records into the IRS office or answers the agency's questions by mail. Most individual returns are examined this way. The other is the field audit, a more intensive review of complex corporate or individual returns conducted at the taxpayer's home or place of business. The office reviews are done by tax auditors, college-educated men and women with some accounting background, who enter government service at the G.S.-5 level (starting salary in 1974 of $8,500) and may rise to G.S.-9 ($12,841). Higher paid and better trained revenue agents conduct the field audits. They may rise to G.S. grades 11 ($15,487), 12 ($18,463) or 13 ($21,816).

In 1974, the IRS audited a total of 2.2 million returns, 2.4 percent of all returns filed. Of those audited 1,767,000 were indivdual returns. The agency has always kept secret the percentages of individuals and corporations it audits in each income class, on the grounds that public knowledge of such data would allegedly provide a "road map to tax evasion." However, in 1973, the Public Citizen Tax Reform Research Group obtained and made public an official IRS document, "The Audit Story," which contained the information the IRS had concealed. Among other things, it showed that the IRS concentrates its audit efforts on individuals and corporations who report high incomes. For example, in fiscal year 1972, the agency audited 12.1 percent of all individual non-business returns which reported adjusted gross income (AGI) of over $50,000. On the other hand, it audited only 2.4 percent of itemized returns in the under $10,000 AGI bracket. In fiscal year 1972, the IRS audited 79.5 percent of corporations with assets from $10 to under $50 million but 2.1 percent of corporations reporting assets of under $50,000.

This audit approach seems to make sense in view of the greater tax revenues collected from audits of high-income taxpayers. In those years, additional taxes assessed on individual returns of under $10,000 averaged $86 per man hour, while $293 per man hour was assessed on returns reporting over $50,000. Similarly, corporate audits yielded $92 per man hour for corporations reporting under $50,000 in assets and $403 per man hour for those reporting $10—50 million in assets. Also, other IRS data show that the changes of audit vary widely from state to state (figure 30).

The IRS notifies taxpayers about the audit in a letter which sets the date and time of the examination (figure 31). The letter explains that taxpayers may appeal the examiner's recommendations and points out that an IRS pamphlet, "Audit of Returns, Appeal Rights, and Claims for Refund" (Pub. 556), is available without charge at all IRS local offices. The audit letter and the pamphlet are designed to help people understand the procedure, yet they have not eliminated taxpayer complaints.

For example, some people report that IRS examiners have threatened to seize their assets immediately if they refused to agree with the results of an audit. Others have complained that the agency lost their files or shuffled their cases from one agent to another (with each new agent raising new issues), and that the process is fraught with general confusion and lengthy delays.

One woman had another complaint. She has been audited for five consecutive years, although her incomer never reached $4,000 and the IRS tax examiners never found anything wrong with her return. A Seventh Day Adventist, she believed in paying 10 percent of her income to the church. The IRS questioned her donations. Although she had receipts from the church, she had to take time off from her job, lose her pay for the day, and appear year after year at the IRS office in Des Moines, Iowa, for the investigation, she said. She reported that the annual audit stopped only when she moved out of the state.

The IRS does not like to waste its limited resources auditing returns that are correct to begin with, and it has tried to eliminate such occurrences. However, taxpayers may still find they are subject to repeated audits, even through the IRS does not find any errors on their returns. Some taxpayers have succeeded in stopping such audits by contacting the chief of the audit division in the IRS district office, explaining any unusual entries on the return. Others attach a letter to

Tax Policy and Administration: Treasury and the IRS

FIGURE 30. FREQUENCY OF IRS AUDITS (1971–1973)

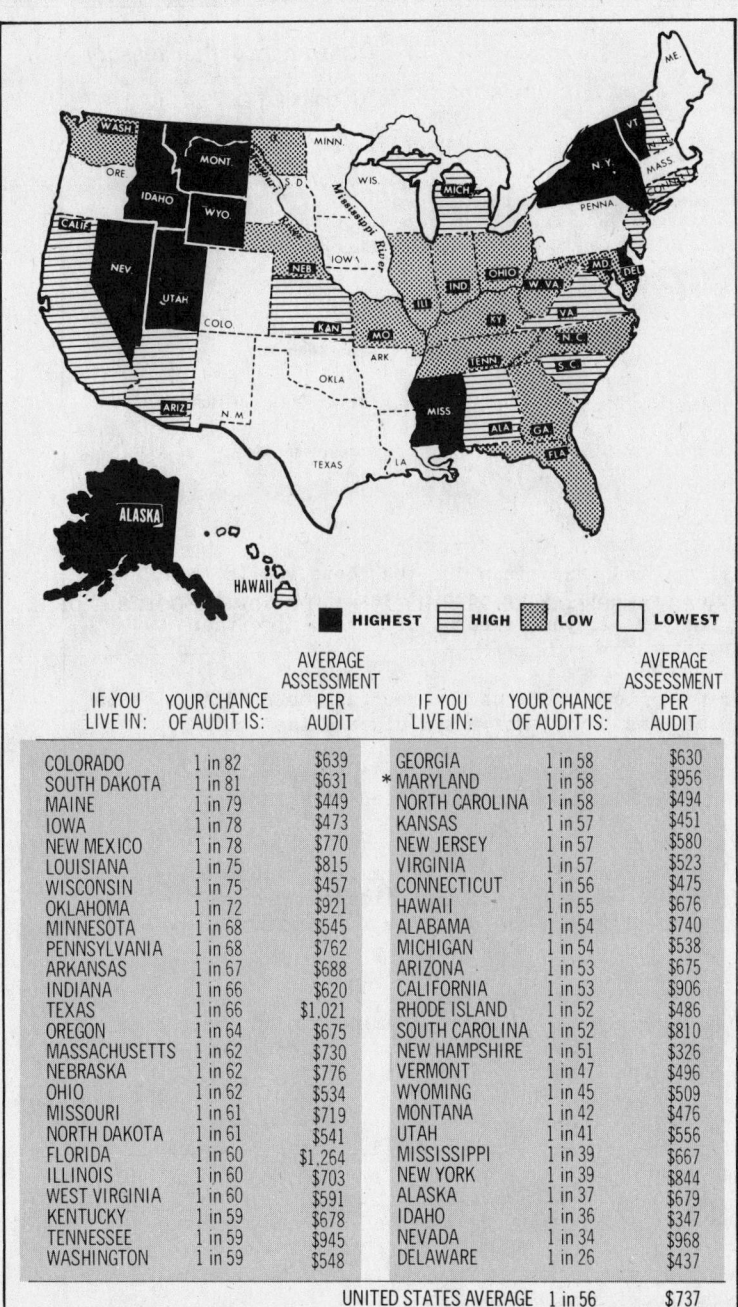

■ HIGHEST ≡ HIGH ▓ LOW □ LOWEST

IF YOU LIVE IN:	YOUR CHANCE OF AUDIT IS:	AVERAGE ASSESSMENT PER AUDIT	IF YOU LIVE IN:	YOUR CHANCE OF AUDIT IS:	AVERAGE ASSESSMENT PER AUDIT
COLORADO	1 in 82	$639	GEORGIA	1 in 58	$630
SOUTH DAKOTA	1 in 81	$631	*MARYLAND	1 in 58	$956
MAINE	1 in 79	$449	NORTH CAROLINA	1 in 58	$494
IOWA	1 in 78	$473	KANSAS	1 in 57	$451
NEW MEXICO	1 in 78	$770	NEW JERSEY	1 in 57	$580
LOUISIANA	1 in 75	$815	VIRGINIA	1 in 57	$523
WISCONSIN	1 in 75	$457	CONNECTICUT	1 in 56	$475
OKLAHOMA	1 in 72	$921	HAWAII	1 in 55	$676
MINNESOTA	1 in 68	$545	ALABAMA	1 in 54	$740
PENNSYLVANIA	1 in 68	$762	MICHIGAN	1 in 54	$538
ARKANSAS	1 in 67	$688	ARIZONA	1 in 53	$675
INDIANA	1 in 66	$620	CALIFORNIA	1 in 53	$906
TEXAS	1 in 66	$1,021	RHODE ISLAND	1 in 52	$486
OREGON	1 in 64	$675	SOUTH CAROLINA	1 in 52	$810
MASSACHUSETTS	1 in 62	$730	NEW HAMPSHIRE	1 in 51	$326
NEBRASKA	1 in 62	$776	VERMONT	1 in 47	$496
OHIO	1 in 62	$534	WYOMING	1 in 45	$509
MISSOURI	1 in 61	$719	MONTANA	1 in 42	$476
NORTH DAKOTA	1 in 61	$541	UTAH	1 in 41	$556
FLORIDA	1 in 60	$1,264	MISSISSIPPI	1 in 39	$667
ILLINOIS	1 in 60	$703	NEW YORK	1 in 39	$844
WEST VIRGINIA	1 in 60	$591	ALASKA	1 in 37	$679
KENTUCKY	1 in 59	$678	IDAHO	1 in 36	$347
TENNESSEE	1 in 59	$945	NEVADA	1 in 34	$968
WASHINGTON	1 in 59	$548	DELAWARE	1 in 26	$437
			UNITED STATES AVERAGE	1 in 56	$737

* Includes the District of Columbia

The above map and table provide a state-by-state breakdown of the average chance for audit, and the average amount of additional taxes assessed following an audit, over the last three fiscal year. For example, while persons living in Delaware had the greatest chance of being audited, 1 in 26, persons living in Florida, whose chance of audit was 1 in 60, were hit with the highest average assessment, $1,264.

Source: Internal Revenue Service

each year's return, explaining the entries which triggered the original audit. Given a satisfactory explanation, the service center examiner sometimes decides not to send the return to the district for audit. Still, it is important to remember that the IRS has a legal right to audit a taxpayer's return within three years of filing. The law requires the Treasury Department to ensure the accuracy of tax returns, and, because the taxpayer is supposed to know the facts, the burden of proof is on him. If the agent is not satisfied with the taxpayer's documentation, he has a right to require the taxpayer to produce all of his relevant books and financial records, and he can examine other documents pertaining to the taxpayer which are in the hands of third parties, like employers, banks, and other financial institutions.

However, taxpayers have rights, too. Former IRS Commissioner Mortimer Caplin listed some of them in the Spring 1972 *Tax Counselor's Quarterly*:

1. The taxpayer may have an audit in the IRS office or in his home, even though the IRS initiates an audit by correspondence.

2. The taxpayer may request a change of the time and date that the IRS sets for the examination in favor of one that is convenient to him as well as to the IRS.

3. The taxpayer may have a lawyer, certified public accountant, or an agent enrolled to practice before the IRS represent him at the audit, and need not attend himself.

4. The taxpayer may not be subjected to "unnecessary" exa-

SOURCE: *Philadelphia Inquirer*, April 18, 1974, p. 8-A.

124 TAX POLITICS

★ FIGURE 31. IRS NOTIFICATION LETTER ★

Internal Revenue Service   **Department of the Treasury**

Tax Year(s):

Date: Day and Date of Appointment:

Time:

Information Copy Only

Place of Appointment:

Room Number:

This letter supersedes L-14 (Rev. 1-73)   Contact Telephone Number:
Present stock should be destryed.

Appointment Clerk:

Dear Taxpayer:

    We are examining your Federal income tax return for the above year(s) and find we need additional information to verify your correct tax. We have, therefore, scheduled the above appointment for you. If you filed a joint return, either husband or wife may keep the appointment.

    We would appreciate your bringing to our office the records you used as a basis for the items checked at the end of this letter so we can discuss them with you.

    The enclosed Information Guides will help you decide what records to bring. It will save you time if you keep together the records related to each item. Please bring this letter also.

    Taxpayers are required by law to substantiate all information reported on their returns when requested. If you do not keep this appointment and do not arrange another, we will have to proceed on the basis of the information we have.

    About the examination and your appeal rights--

    We realize some taxpayers may be concerned about an examination of their tax returns. We hope we can relieve any concern you may have by briefly explaining why we examine, what our procedures are, and what your appeal rights are if you do not agree with the results.

    We examine returns to verify income, exemptions, and deductions. This does not always result in more tax due, nor does the selection of your return for examination imply dishonesty or suspicion of criminal liability. In many cases, the taxpayer's return is accepted as filed or he gets a refund. We are required to collect only the correct tax--no more and no less. But if taxpayers do not substantiate items when requested, we have to act on available information that may be incomplete. That is why your cooperation is so important.

    We will go over your return and records and then explain any proposals to change your tax liability. We want you to understand fully any recommended increase

★ **FIGURE 31. IRS NOTIFICATION LETTER (Continued)**

or decrease in your tax, so please don't hesitate to ask questions about anything not clear to you.

If changes are recommended and you agree with the proposals, we will ask you to sign an agreement form. By signing, you will indicate your agreement to the amount shown on the form as additional tax you owe or as a refund due you and simplify closing your case.

Most people agree with our proposals, and we believe this is because they find our examiners to be fair. But you don't have to agree. If you choose, we can easily arrange for you to have your case given further consideration. You need only tell the examiner you want to discuss the issue informally with a supervisor, and a conference will be arranged immediately. If this discussion does not result in agreement, you may take your case to a conferee for still further consideration.

In addition to these District office appeal rights, you may request the Service's Appellate Division, which is separate from the District office, to consider your case. We will be glad to explain this procedure and also how to appeal outside the Service to the courts.

We will also be happy to furnish you a copy of our Publication 556, Audit of Returns, Appeal Rights and Claims for Refund, which explains in detail our procedures covering examinations of tax returns and appeal rights. You can get a copy of this publication by writing us for it or by asking for it when you come to our office.

Your appointment is the next step. We will consider the appointment confirmed if we do not hear from you at least seven days before the scheduled date. We will make our examination as pleasant and brief as possible and will welcome any questions you raise.

Please contact us if you have any questions. Thank you for your cooperation.

Sincerely yours,

Enclosures:
Information Guides

District Director

Please bring the records to support the following items reported on your tax return:

☐ Alimony Payments	☐ Contributions	☐ Moving Expenses
☐ Automobile Expenses	☐ Education Expenses	☐ Rental Income and Expenses
☐ Bad Debts	☐ Employee Business Expenses	☐ Sale or Exchange of Residence
☐ Capital Gains and Losses	☐ Exemptions	☐ Sick Pay Exclusion
☐ Casualty Losses	☐ Interest Expenses	☐ Taxes
☐ Child and Dependent Care Expenses	☐ Medical and Dental Expenses	☐ Uniforms, Equipment, and Tools
☐ _____	☐ _____	☐ _____
☐ _____		

mination, and only one inspection of his accounts can be made for any one taxable year, unless he requests it or gets an official notice in writing that an additional examination is necessary.

The taxpayer has other rights as well. If the audit is to be held in a geographical area inconvenient to him, the taxpayer can ask for a change of location. If he cannot get along with the examiner assigned to his case, he can ask to deal with someone else—however, the IRS can refuse a request. The taxpayer has a right to confidentiality, and the IRS may not make information about his return public unless liens or lawsuits are involved. Finally, the taxpayer has the right to appeal any additional tax recommendations through the IRS and through the courts.

But these rights do not protect an individual if he does not know about them. And commonly, most taxpayers do not know their rights. In addition, although the IRS sets high standards for its tax examiners, former Commissioner Caplin confirmed that some agents may become overzealous, adopt a "policeman-on-the-beat" attitude, and "find daily satisfaction in raising every conceivable issue."

Skilled representatives can help assure that the IRS observes their clients' rights. But a person who cannot afford such help is at a disadvantage during the examination, because he may not know the law, what proof the agent will accept, or whether his case is strong or weak. And, regardless of how strong the taxpayer's case is, an agent may decide against him and let the taxpayer take the consequences. As a result, he unknowingly may pay an unwarranted assessment. Tax attorney Edward O. Hunter has recommended some ways in which unrepresented taxpayers can help themselves (figure 32). Even so, taxpayers who make sincere attempts to ensure that their facts are correct, that the law is applied correctly, and that they have solid proof of their claims may still be assessed an additional tax liability. In this case, the taxpayer's only defense is to appeal.

★ FIGURE 32. SELF-HELP DURING THE AUDIT ★

1. Taxpayers ignore IRS letters or messages which call for a response at their own risk. If the taxpayer fails to respond to an audit notice, the IRS has the legal power to make an assessment. If the taxpayer fails to pay, the IRS can garnish wages or seize and sell property to settle a tax debt.
2. The audit letter indicates which items on the return are being questioned. It also specifies a date by which the taxpayer must respond. If the date is inconvenient, the taxpayer may contact the IRS to make other reasonable arrangements. It is important to organize canceled checks, receipts, and other materials before attending the audit, and to be prepared to explain all items on the return, even though only selected items have been questioned.
3. IRS tax examiners are instructed to be polite, fair, and helpful in explaining any adjustments which they may make on the return. If they are not, IRS supervisors should be notified. The taxpayer can ask to deal with another tax examiner.
4. Anything a taxpayer says can be used against him.
5. Tax examiners who visit the taxpayer's home or place of business must carry a "pocket commission" and a "field contact card" which contain information needed to contact him or her later.
6. Noting the name, office address, and telephone number of the tax examiner and the supervisor, along with the time, date, and outcome of each encounter, helps if complaints develop later.
7. Do not rely on verbal agreements made with the tax examiner about how much the tax will be. All recommendations must be put in writing on official IRS documents and signed by a person in authority.
8. When the audit ends, taxpayers have thirty days to decide whether to agree with the audit recommendation or to appeal. They do not have to decide on the spot.
9. If taxpayers disagree with the recommendation, they have the right to appeal.
10. Taxpayers have a right to an explanation of the reasons for any action proposed or taken by the IRS.

appeals

Taxpayers may appeal after the agent has completed the audit and made his determination. Two times out of three, the agent will recommend a tax increase. In FY 1974, 67 percent of returns audited resulted in increased tax liabilities; 5 percent had refunds, and the rest resulted in no change.

If he decides on a tax increase, the examiner will present the taxpayer with a recommendation, called a "preliminary notice of deficiency." It is also referred to as a "30-day letter" because it gives the taxpayer thirty days in which to decide whether to agree or to appeal. The letter includes an explanation of the reasons for the recommendation, a Form 870 for the taxpayer to sign if he agrees to pay, and a form explaining appeal rights. Taxpayers who do not agree to pay and who do not respond to the thirty-day letter, will then receive a "statutory notice of deficiency," called the "ninety-day letter." It gives the taxpayer ninety days to appeal in court. If the taxpayer does not appeal, the IRS proceeds to assess the tax.

If the taxpayer accepts the agent's decision, he agrees by signing the Form 870. This automatically stops any further accumulation of the 7 percent annual interest which accrues from the date the tax became due. However, by signing, the taxpayer gives up his right to appeal in the tax court—the only court where he can dispute the additional tax without paying it first. Once the form is signed, the account is turned over to the IRS service center which issues a bill for the agreed tax deficiency plus any penalties and interest. At this point, the IRS generally closes the case, although it may reopen it and recommend additional assessments if new facts come to the agency's attention. On the other hand, the taxpayer can pay and sue later for a refund in the U.S. District Court or a U.S. Court of Claims.

There are several appeal routes, depending on whether the taxpayer wants to appeal without paying the assessment, or prefers to pay and sue for a refund (figure 33). He may challenge the agent's recommendation through the IRS's administrative appeals conferences without paying first. The same is true if he uses the tax court, and this forum also has another advantage—a small-case division where people can plead their own cases without a lawyer, for a simple $10 filing fee if the dispute involves $1,500 or less.

If he wishes to appeal through the two other courts available to him—the U.S. District Court and the Court of Claims—the taxpayer must pay the bill first and then sue for a refund. Except for the small-case division of the tax court, where all decisions are final, taxpayers may appeal adverse findings in lower courts, through higher courts and up to the U.S. Supreme Court.

The most important rule for people who wish to appeal without paying first is not to sign an IRS Form 870 agreeing to pay, and not to pay before receiving and responding to the ninety-day notice. Second, it is important to remember that, for every day that payment of the assessment is delayed, simple interest accrues at the rate of 7 percent per year, and this interest must be paid if the taxpayer loses his case. Taxpayers need to decide whether they can afford to pay the interest charges before setting out on the appeals route, since there may be lengthy delays before the case is finally settled.

The IRS's administrative review bodies are the district conference, available in all fifty-eight IRS district offices, and the appellate conference, available in thirty-eight offices. Most cases go to the district conference first, and then, if agreement is not reached, on to the appellate level. However, taxpayers can take their disputes directly to the appellate conference to begin with, if they wish to do so. The thirty-day letter explains how taxpayers can ask for a conference.

IRS figures show that it pays to appeal. In fiscal year 1972, in the appellate conference, the IRS settled disputes involving less than $1,000 for an average of 67 cents on the dollar. In larger tax cases, where $1 million or more was in dispute, settlements were considerably more favorable, 34 cents on the dollar. Settlements at the district conference were also favorable. In fiscal year 1972, settlements in Atlanta and Boston averaged 33 cents on the dollar; 34 cents in Denver, Colorado, and Portland, Oregon, but 74 cents in Baltimore, Maryland.

The district conference is an informal meeting between the taxpayer and/or his repre-

128 TAX POLITICS

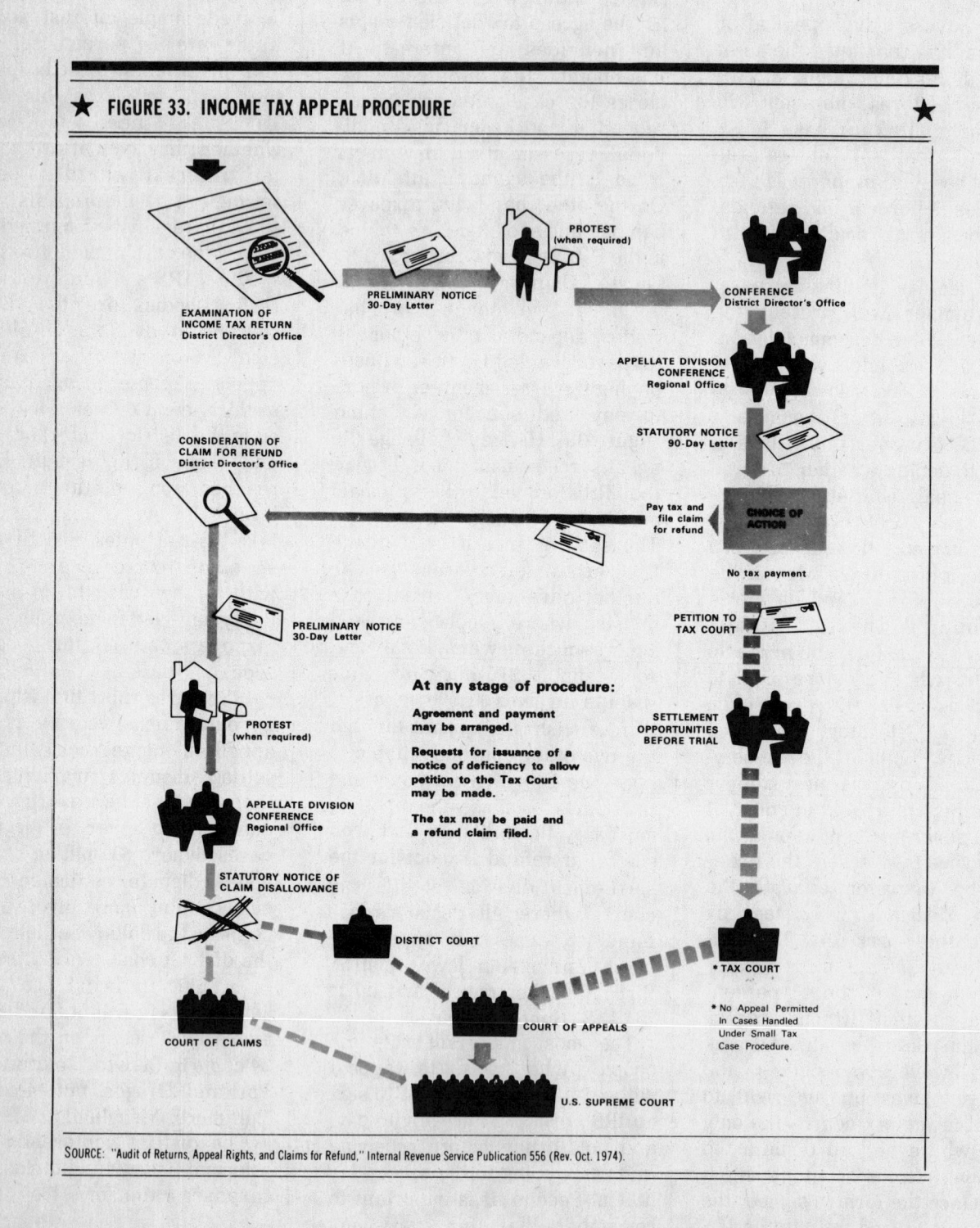

FIGURE 33. INCOME TAX APPEAL PROCEDURE

EXAMINATION OF INCOME TAX RETURN
District Director's Office

PRELIMINARY NOTICE
30-Day Letter

PROTEST (when required)

CONFERENCE
District Director's Office

APPELLATE DIVISION CONFERENCE
Regional Office

STATUTORY NOTICE
90-Day Letter

CHOICE OF ACTION

Pay tax and file claim for refund

No tax payment

CONSIDERATION OF CLAIM FOR REFUND
District Director's Office

PRELIMINARY NOTICE
30-Day Letter

PETITION TO TAX COURT

At any stage of procedure:

Agreement and payment may be arranged.

Requests for issuance of a notice of deficiency to allow petition to the Tax Court may be made.

The tax may be paid and a refund claim filed.

SETTLEMENT OPPORTUNITIES BEFORE TRIAL

PROTEST (when required)

APPELLATE DIVISION CONFERENCE
Regional Office

STATUTORY NOTICE OF CLAIM DISALLOWANCE

DISTRICT COURT

* TAX COURT

* No Appeal Permitted In Cases Handled Under Small Tax Case Procedure.

COURT OF CLAIMS

COURT OF APPEALS

U.S. SUPREME COURT

SOURCE: "Audit of Returns, Appeal Rights, and Claims for Refund," Internal Revenue Service Publication 556 (Rev. Oct. 1974).

sentative and the IRS conferee, typically a revenue agent who has been promoted to the position. If the amount in dispute is $2,500 or less, the taxpayer does not have to present his protest in writing but can simply tell the conferee his side of the story. If the conferee thinks the IRS might lose in a court fight, he can make a settlement accordingly. In cases over $2,500, this authority rests with the appellate conferee.

At either of these conferences, the taxpayer's representative (if he has one) must be a certified public accountant, an attorney, or an agent enrolled to practice before the IRS. Commercial tax preparers cannot represent the taxpayer, although they can accompany him and help explain how the return was prepared. Taxpayers can, of course, represent themselves. However, this is a risky business. Most taxpayers do not know the law or how to argue their cases in the conference. Donald C. Alexander, a tax attorney who became commissioner of the Internal Revenue Service in 1973, once pointed out how difficult the task is, even for professional tax practitioners.

In 1963 *New York University Institute of Federal Taxation* article, Alexander explained the need to ascertain the complete facts of the case and to do a thorough job of legal research—something which few taxpayers could do on their own. He emphasized how important it is to plan the strategy of the conference and to know something about the conferee. Alexander actually urged that the taxpayer stay out of the confernce altogether, at least initially: "Some taxpayers in the heat of argument cannot avoid the mistake of attacking the intelligence, motives, and even the ancestry of the revenue agent. The informal conference can thus degenerate into a shouting contest which kindles tempers but serves little other purpose." Although revenue agents no longer attend these conferences, the conferee himself is still a handy target for an aggravated taxpayer.

Also, Alexander intimated, taxpayers may talk too much and weaken their cases. For instance, the threat of a lawsuit might enhance chances of a good settlement, for the agency does not like to go to court if it does not have to. Therefore, even if the taxpayer does not intend to litigate, it is wiser not to admit it to the conferee. However, naive and talkative taxpayers can let the cat out of the bag and ruin their chances for a favorable decision. "It is bad enough," Alexander wrote of taxpayers, "to find that unrequested and irrelevant information is volunteered, but worse are the unforgettable words, 'I certainly hope we can work this out, because I could never take it to court.'"

If the district conference is not a suitable forum for the average unrepresented taxpayer, the appellate conference is less so. Appellate conferees are among the IRS's most able experts. They handle the most complex disputes that come before the agency and are skilled at developing new issues undetected by the district conferee. That leaves the alternative of the tax court for those who do not wish to pay before they appeal.

The tax court has a small-case division especially designed for those who cannot afford professional help and is generally the best forum to use if the tax dispute involves $1,500 or less. Taxpayers can ask the small case division to hear the dispute even though they also take their cases through the IRS appeals procedures. However, they can also bypass the IRS conferences and go directly to tax court. To do this, the taxpayer can ask for a "Statutory Notice of Deficiency" as soon as he receives the thirty-day letter, which is issued when the audit is concluded. The Statutory Notice of Deficiency gives the recipient ninety days in which to ask the court to hear the case.

Issuance of the ninety-day notice means that any further dickering with the tax examiner is over. The taxpayer may not petition the court for a hearing until he receives this notice, and then must act promptly, for the ninety days start on the date the notice is issued, not the date the taxpayer receives it. If the taxpayer does not ask for an appeal during this period, the IRS will bill him for the total amount assessed.

To petition the court, the taxpayer simply writes to the U.S. Tax Court, Washington, D.C. 20217, and asks for the forms to petition the small case division. The tax court clerk will send a

130 TAX POLITICS

packet containing instructions and a simple four-question petition, in which the taxpayer explains his grievance. He must fill out the petition and return it, along with a $10 filing fee, within ninety days after the date on the IRS notice of deficiency.

The court clerk lists the cases by city, and the six small case division tax court commissioners decide where and when they will hear them. The commissioners visit a total of 110 cities across the nation (although not all of them every year) in an attempt to bring the court as close as possible to the taxpayer's home town.

Before a case actually comes to trial, government attorneys usually contact the taxpayer in order to reach a settlement out of court. And, in fact, most cases are settled this way. While the small-case division heard 391 cases in fiscal year 1974, more than four times that number, 1,856, were disposed of by agreement. Another 335 cases were dismissed, mainly because taxpayers did not show up in court.

Most taxpayers do better by settling with the IRS, even at this late stage, than they do later on in court. The mere threat of litigation gives the IRS an incentive to reach an agreement which satisfies the taxpayer. In calendar year 1973, 1,831 cases were closed this way. Only 286 people paid what the IRS had said they owed. Of the others, 1,045 paid less than the IRS originally asked, and 499 paid nothing at all. One person paid more than the original deficiency.

In dollar terms, the IRS claimed $921,636.40 in extra taxes due, but settled for less than half—$427,299.75.

On the other hand, when cases actually get to court, the IRS is more likely to win, simply because it does not like to spend money on costly litigation when it might lose. For example, small tax court cases for the first six months of 1972, analyzed by columnist E. Edward Stephens, showed that taxpayers won their cases only 9.3 percent of the time. The IRS won 67.5 percent of the cases and 23.2 percent were split between the two.

collection of delinquent taxes

If taxpayers lose their appeals and still fail to pay, the IRS collection branch takes over. This division gets the overdue bills after the service center has tried but failed to collect them. Besides bills resulting from audit, the service center sends the collection division bills generated when it discovers errors on tax returns.

The district office collection divisions consist of an office branch, staffed by taxpayer service representatives and officer interviewers, and a field branch, staffed by revenue officers. The office branch first tries to collect the bills by writing or telephoning the taxpayer; if this fails, the bills are turned over to IRS revenue officers who seek out taxpayers and try to persuade them to pay. If persuasion fails, they can use forcible collection methods. In 1974, the IRS closed 2.6 million delinquent accounts by persuasion or force and collected more than $2.5 billion in delinquent taxes.

Tax authority Marvin J. Garbis described the power of IRS revenue officers in a 1971 *New York University Institute of Federal Taxation* article. He wrote, "In our nation, there is probably no other public servant who has the legal power (subject to virtually no external review) given the revenue officer over the property, reputation, and often health of a taxpayer who is behind in his tax payments."

There are approximately 7,000 IRS revenue officers. They can garnish wages, take bank accounts, and seize and sell nearly all of a delinquent taxpayer's property without a court order. (The IRS can also retain a taxpayer's refund to settle an unpaid bill. This procedure is called an "offset.")

In fiscal year 1972, IRS collectors made 937,744 seizures of wages and property—seven seizures each minute of every working day (not counting offsets). Although the IRS billed 8 million taxpayers for back taxes in calendar year 1974, the IRS's use of forcible collection dropped by nearly half, to 604,717 in fiscal year 1974. An IRS official acknowledged that the agency has recently become more cautious in its use of forcible collection.

The agency does not keep statistics on the incomes of those

Tax Policy and Administration: Treasury and the IRS

subject to forcible collection, but it does have figures which show how the IRS's use of seizure varies in different parts of the country (figure 34).

Forcible collection activities are the source of many taxpayer complaints. Some people say that they did not know they owed back taxes until the agency seized their wages. According to a former revenue officer, this may happen because the service center sends the bill to a wrong address. When the taxpayer does not respond, the service center turns the bill over to a revenue officer who locates the taxpayer and proceeds with the levy (i.e., seizure). Lewis Lederer, an IRS revenue officer for six years, wrote in a letter to the *Washington Post* that he had often levied the wages of people who did not know they owed a back tax, because the notices had gone to the wrong address. Lederer also pointed out how serious the effects of a levy could be: "Many employers will fire a man rather than get involved with the complications of tax levies."

The IRS sometimes seizes wages or property even though there is no tax due. One reason this happens is because agency employees make mistakes in posting payments to computerized accounts. As a result, the computers issue erroneous bills. If the taxpayer does not respond to such bills (because he does not receive them, or because he knows they are wrong), the account becomes "delinquent." Then the service center turns it over to an IRS collector.

Even if taxpayers protest such bills, they may not succeed in stopping the billing process. Taxpayer service representatives in local IRS offices have the authority to stop the computer notices and initiate efforts to locate the missing payments, if the accounts are not already in the hands of collection officers. However, some taxpayers say that the TSRs ignore their protests and that the corrections are not made. If the taxpayer cannot get the error corrected, his "delinquent" account is usually turned over to a revenue officer.

★ **FIGURE 34. WHERE IRS WAS MOST LIKELY TO SEIZE MONEY OR PROPERTY OF DELINQUENT TAXPAYERS IN FISCAL YEAR 1972** ★

The table shows the frequency with which the Internal Revenue Service (IRS) seizes property or money from delinquent taxpayers in different states. The percentage is calculated on th basis of the number of delinquent accounts closed and the combined total of levies and seizures. The figures are approximate since the number of delinquent accounts, as calculated by IRS, may include more than one account for a single taxpayer. Similarly, there may be more than one levy or seizure against a single taxpayer.

STATE	% OF DELINQUENT ACCOUNTS IN WHICH TAXPAYERS MONEY OR PROPERTY WERE SEIZED BY IRS	STATE	% OF DELINQUENT ACCOUNTS IN WHICH TAXPAYERS MONEY OR PROPERTY WERE SEIZED BY IRS
MARYLAND	55%	MISSISSIPPI	30%
SOUTHCAROLINA	48%	WASHINGTON	30%
ALASKA	47%	MINNESOTA	29%
CONNECTICUT	46%	NEW MEXICO	29%
NORTH CAROLINA	46%	ILLINOIS	28%
IDAHO	45%	RHODE ISLAND	27%
NEW YORK	44%	KENTUCKY	26%
DELAWARE	43%	OKLAHOMA	26%
OHIO	43%	SOUTH DAKOTA	26%
ARIZONA	42%	WISCONSIN	26%
VIRGINIA	42%	NEBRASKA	25%
GEORGIA	40%	TEXAS	25%
NEVADA	40%	COLORADO	24%
CALIFORNIA	37%	MISSOURI	24%
TENNESSEE	37%	VERMONT	22%
PENNSYLVANIA	36%	HAWAII	21%
ALABAMA	35%	MAINE	21%
MONTANA	35%	ARKANSAS	20%
OREGON	34%	LOUISIANA	20%
FLORIDA	33%	IOWA	19%
MICHIGAN	32%	NEW HAMPSHIRE	19%
INDIANA	31%	NORTH DAKOTA	19%
MASSACHUSETTS	31%	KANSAS	15%
NEW JERSEY	31%	WYOMING	15%
UTAH	31%		
WEST VIRGINIA	31%	OUTSIDE UNITED STATES	7%

SOURCE: *Philadelphia Inquirer*, April 20, 1974.

132 TAX POLITICS

Once the account is in the hands of a revenue officer, the taxpayer may have a difficult time convincing the collector he does not owe more taxes. For example, the *Las Vegas Sun* reported that the IRS lost the records of a Nevada businessman who paid his taxes in cash. Even though the man had a certified IRS receipt for his cash payment, the collector refused to honor it. The revenue officer said a canceled check was the only proof of payment he would accept, and then seized the man's bank account to settle the already-paid bill. In cases like this, it may help to complain to higher authorities (figure 35 and 36).

★ **FIGURE 35. RESPONDING TO IRS BILLS AND SEIZURE NOTICES** ★

1. Most IRS bills are computer-generated and tell where and how to respond. However, if the matter is urgent, and the notice does not have the information needed, call the local IRS office and ask for advice. Note the name of the employee, and ask what steps will be taken to solve the problem. Ask the employee to keep you informed. Make a note of the conversation.
2. If the bill is wrong, write to the office listed on the bill, and enclose Xerox copies of checks or other documents which support your claims. Keep your originals and copies of all IRS notices and any correspondence with the agency.
3. If the IRS continues to issue an incorrect bill, take steps outlined in Figure 00, Where to Complain.
4. If the IRS sends a "Final Notice of Seizure" although no taxes are due, call the IRS office and ask for the chief of collections or the senior revenue officer. Make an appointment to talk over the problem.
5. Take all canceled checks, bills, receipts, or other documents which support your claims to the meeting.
6. If an adjustment is not made, go immediately to the office of the district director and make a complaint.
7. If you discover that you do owe more taxes, try to arrange with the chief of collections or the senior revenue officer for installment payments, or, in hardship cases, to have the debt declared uncollectible.

★ **FIGURE 36. WHERE TO COMPLAIN*** ★

Type of Complaint	Contact or Write to
Threats, harassment, extortion	Assistant Regional Commissioner, Inspection. Call local IRS office for address.
Audit problems	Chief, Audit Division, IRS District Office. Call local IRS office for address.
Collection problems	Chief, Collections Division, IRS District Office. Call local IRS office for address.
Wrong tax advice, computer billing errors	Chief, Taxpayer Services Division (IRS District Office). Call local IRS office for address.

*In case of emergency, go directly to the office of the district director and make the complaint. And send copies of all correspondence to:
1. IRS District Director, your district
2. Commissioner, Internal Revenue Service, Washington, D.C. 20224
3. Your congressman
4. Honorable Charles Vanik, Chairman, House Ways and Means Subcommittee, U.S. House of Representatives, Washington, D.C. 20515

Some revenue officers urge taxpayers to pay the IRS bill and file for a refund, even if the taxpayer says he does not owe the money. One tax practitioner explained that collectors follow this practice because they are under pressure from management to close cases. Such alleged pressure has come under congressional scrutiny and is frowned upon by top IRS officials. Nevertheless, it is a fact of life, according to Vincent Connery, president of the National Treasury Employees Union. His view is supported by former IRS Deputy Commissioner William Smith, who said at Senate hearings in 1973, "You can fight it all the time, you can deal with it where you find it, but it continues to occur. I suppose it always will."

At the same hearings, Connery gave the Senate Treasury Appropriations Subcommittee a form which he said illustrated the pressures put on collectors by supervisors. The form was one which revenue officers working in the San Francisco district office were required to fill out if they wanted a promotion. It listed "points" collectors had to accumulate before qualifying for promotion. They gained points by seizing personal property, closing down businesses, and levying on taxpayers' pensions, among other things. The point system opened up possibilities that officers would take forcible collection actions, not on the merits of a case, but to win promotion. The system has been abolished.

In 1974, Connery also told the same Senate subcommittee that the IRS rewards revenue officers for making seizures but disciplines them for letting taxpayers maintain their businesses in order to repay their debts. He presented the senators with a memo written by an IRS collection group manager. It said that the group's overall position was the worst in the field branch, and that collectors could have made twenty-two seizures although "we have just three seizures...in progress." "It would appear," continued the memo, "that we are unduly concerned with a benevolent image. I would rather that we establish an image of enforcement." Another memo was placed in the hearing record by the subcommittee chairman, Senator Joseph Montoya (D-N.M.). It reprimanded IRS collectors for lack of prompt, firm action, and accused them of "undue sympathy for taxpayers."

It is a fact that a taxpayer who finds a sympathetic revenue officer may be able to save his business or prevent the seizure and sale of his property. IRS collectors have broad discretion in the way they use their powers, and can choose to seize or, conversely, to help ease the taxpayer's burden in hardship cases (figure 37). An IRS pamphlet, "The Collection Process" (Pub. 586), explains this help and something about taxpayer's rights. It is available free at all IRS offices.

IRS revenue officers can help the taxpayer by allowing him to pay his debt in installments, or by indefinitely postponing collection in hardship cases. However these arrangements are not available as a matter of right, and the taxpayer must ask about them. If the taxpayer wishes to repay his debt in installments, he will first have to give the revenue officer a complete financial statement, and agree to pay interest at the rate of 7 percent per year until the debt is paid. The officer has the right to decide whether or not he will approve an installment plan. Even if the taxpayer succeeds in arranging to pay by installments, the IRS can cancel the agreement without notice and demand immediate payment in full. Since installment arrangements do not close collection cases, revenue officers approve them sparingly. For example, out of two million delinquent accounts collected in FY 1972, there were only 48,000 installment plans.

Under certain circumstances, the IRS may declare an account "uncollectible," which means that collection is suspended indefinitely. The revenue officer may take this step if he decides that the amount due does not justify the cost involved in collecting it, or that the likelihood of collection is remote. He takes into consideration whether the balance owed is small, the taxpayer has no assets, the taxpayer cannot be located, or the collection would cause undue hardship. In FY 1972, 362,000 accounts were declared uncollectible.

Finally, if the tax liability is found to be excessive, assessed after the statute of limitations has expired, or assessed illegally or erroneously, the IRS can abate (cancel or reduce) the tax due.

Taxpayers have certain rights which revenue officers must observe. For example, a taxpayer can offer to pay less than the total amount of his debt, if he can show that there is either doubt about the liability or about the collectibility of the tax. However, the IRS is not obliged to accept the taxpayer's offer. (In FY 1972, only 1,170 such offers were approved.) To make the "offer in compromise," the taxpayer must fill out a special form available at the IRS office and submit it to the agency along with a substantial portion of the sum he wishes to pay. This usually postpones the collection process until the IRS decides whether to accept or reject the offer.

134 · TAX POLITICS

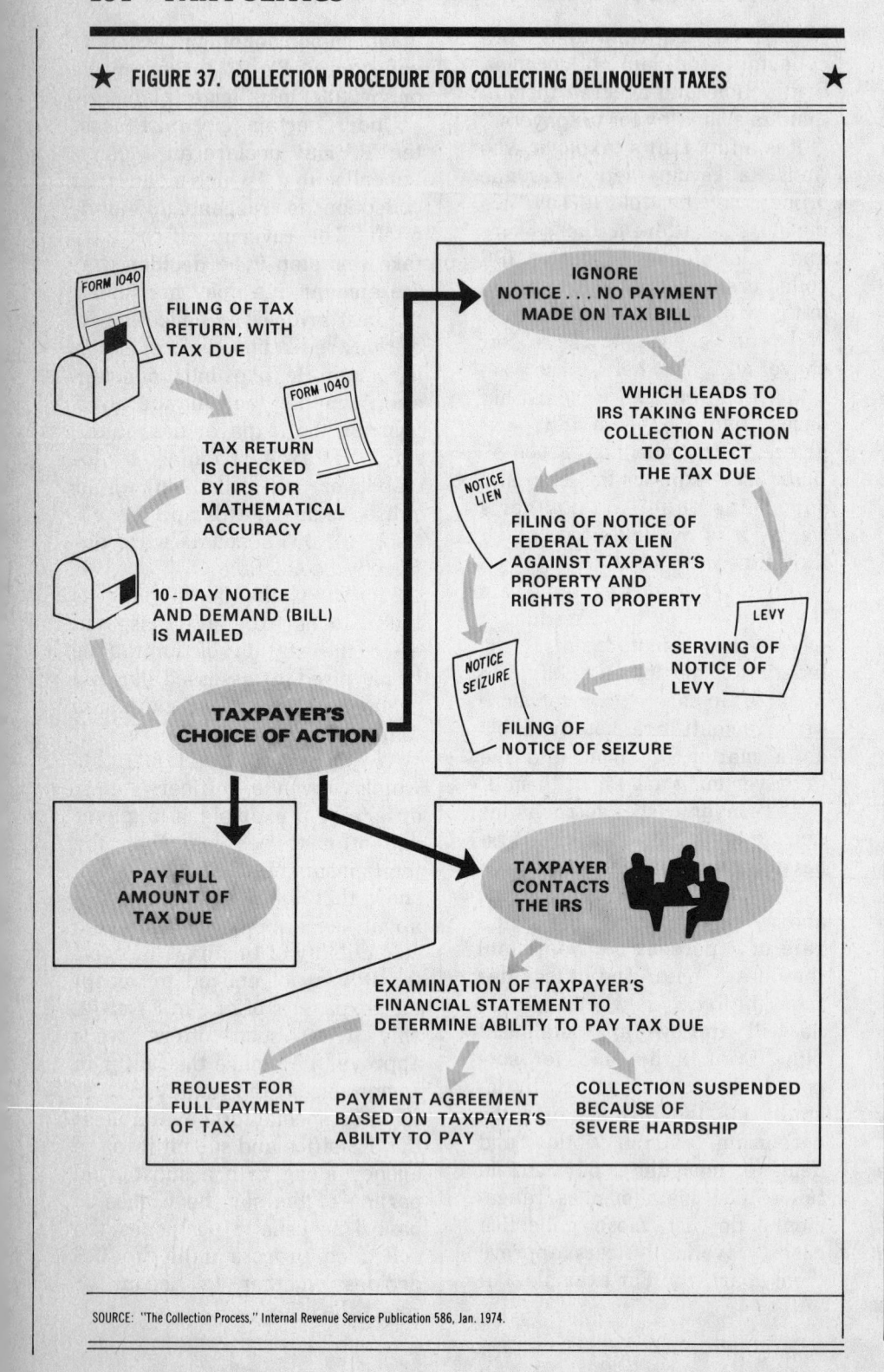

★ FIGURE 37. COLLECTION PROCEDURE FOR COLLECTING DELINQUENT TAXES ★

- FILING OF TAX RETURN, WITH TAX DUE
- TAX RETURN IS CHECKED BY IRS FOR MATHEMATICAL ACCURACY
- 10-DAY NOTICE AND DEMAND (BILL) IS MAILED
- TAXPAYER'S CHOICE OF ACTION
  - PAY FULL AMOUNT OF TAX DUE
  - IGNORE NOTICE... NO PAYMENT MADE ON TAX BILL
    - WHICH LEADS TO IRS TAKING ENFORCED COLLECTION ACTION TO COLLECT THE TAX DUE
    - FILING OF NOTICE OF FEDERAL TAX LIEN AGAINST TAXPAYER'S PROPERTY AND RIGHTS TO PROPERTY
    - SERVING OF NOTICE OF LEVY
    - FILING OF NOTICE OF SEIZURE
  - TAXPAYER CONTACTS THE IRS
    - EXAMINATION OF TAXPAYER'S FINANCIAL STATEMENT TO DETERMINE ABILITY TO PAY TAX DUE
      - REQUEST FOR FULL PAYMENT OF TAX
      - PAYMENT AGREEMENT BASED ON TAXPAYER'S ABILITY TO PAY
      - COLLECTION SUSPENDED BECAUSE OF SEVERE HARDSHIP

SOURCE: "The Collection Process," Internal Revenue Service Publication 586, Jan. 1974.

The IRS must observe the taxpayer's right to retain property which is protected under the law. This includes school books and wearing apparel (although the IRS may seize luxury items like furs); fuel, provisions, and personal effects up to a total value of $500; books and tools of trade, business, or profession up to a value of $250; unemployment benefits, undelivered mail, certain annuity and pension payments, workmen's compensation; income which a court has ordered must be paid for child support; and special Treasury fund deposits made by certain members of the armed forces and the public health service.

If an IRS collection officer tries to enter the taxpayer's home, the taxpayer has a right to refuse access. However, if refused access, the IRS officer can simply seize the taxpayer's home to settle the debt. It is illegal to use force or the threat of force (meaning threats of bodily harm) to interfere with an IRS employee acting in an official capacity and such action may result in imprisonment or fine.

As soon as possible after the IRS seizes property, it must give the taxpayer a written list of what it has taken, the value of the property seized as well as an estimate of the value of the property which remains with the taxpayer, and notice of how much more tax, if any, he still owes. The taxpayer has a right to go to court and ask the judge to stop the seizure if it can be shown that the government has absolutely no claim, that the seizure would do irreparable damage, and that no other legal remedy is available to him. Also, under some circumstances taxpayers can be relieved of paying overdue taxes by declaring bankruptcy.

After the IRS has seized property, it may sell it, but it must first give the taxpayer ten days' notice of the sale. The taxpayer can redeem his property by paying the tax, plus penalties, interest, and any costs incurred by the IRS in the seizure. If the taxpayer can prove that he has been wrongfully levied, he can get a court injunction and stop the sale.

When a tax account becomes delinquent, a lien automatically attaches to all of the taxpayer's property (except exempt property), thus protecting the government's interests. If the IRS wishes to do so, it may make this a matter of public record by filing a notice of lien in the state where the taxpayer's property is located. Filing of the notice of lien alerts creditors to the fact that the lien exists, and may adversely affect a taxpayer's financial interests. The lien is released when the tax due (including interest and any additions to the tax) has been paid or adjusted.

Generally, the IRS may not seize property without giving the taxpayer ten days' notice. However, under certain circumstances, this rule does not apply. For example, if the agency believes that the taxpayer is about to flee the country or hide his assets without paying his taxes, it may decide how much is due and demand immediate payment of the sum without notice. If the taxpayer does not pay, the IRS can seize all of his assets, except for those exempt under the law. However, it must issue a Statutory Notice of Deficiency within sixty days, giving the taxpayer a chance to appeal his case in tax court. This procedure is called a "jeopardy assessment." It is similar to another procedure, "termination of tax year," where the IRS can not only seize but sell the taxpayer's property without giving him a chance to go to tax court. In FY 1973, the IRS used these two procedures against 3,006 taxpayers.

The procedures have long been criticized by tax practitioners, the courts, and the American Bar Association, and on January 13, 1976, the U.S. Supreme Court backed up the critics by ruling that the IRS must provide taxpayers with access to tax court in termination of tax year cases.

But jeopardy and termination assessments are not the only weapons against taxpayers that have come under fire. Many of the IRS practices and procedures described in this chapter have been the subject of congressional inquiries as well as probes by other government entities. In 1975, the Administrative Conference of the United States, an independent federal agency, completed a study of how some IRS policies affect taxpayers. Among other things, the lengthy report showed that taxpayers without skilled representation fare worse in IRS audits and appeals than those who do have professional help. Further, there are few guidelines or controls over the vast powers of IRS collectors, and wide differences in the way they treat taxpayers. As a result, some collection officials go easy on likable taxpayers, while treating offensive or abrasive tax delinquents harshly. In other cases, they have used the tax law as punishment without trial against people accused of criminal violations, whose guilt has never been determined in court. The Administrative Conference report shows that much must be done to achieve equitable tax administration and to secure taypayer rights. Clearly, Congress must amend unfair laws and the IRS must improve its administration practices.

The General Accounting Office, Congress's watchdog agency, has studied IRS taxpayer services and its audit and collection practices. Also, the IRS itself has undertaken studies of its administrative processes. The studies and reviews show that, to achieve equitable tax administration and to secure taxpayer rights, Congress must amend the tax laws, and the IRS must improve its administrative practices.

IRS Commissioner Donald C. Alexander, speaking to the tax section of the New York State Bar in 1975, underlined the importance of both equitable tax laws and equitable tax administration. He emphasized that the IRS does not have sufficient resources to administer and enforce the tax laws unless the public assists by believing in and complying with the tax system.

In 1953, Supreme Court Justice Robert Jackson observed, in U.S. v. *Kahriger*," . . . that a people so

136 TAX POLITICS

numerous, scattered and individualistic annually assesses itself with a tax liability often in burdensome amounts is a reassuring sign of the stability and vitality of our system of self-government." But he also warned that, "It will be a sad day if the goodwill of the people toward their taxing system is frittered away . . ." Today, Justice Jackson might put it more strongly. He might observe that there has been an erosion of equity toward taxpayers, and an erosion in the effectiveness of the voluntary self-assessment system. He might warn the Congress and the IRS that the nation faces a grave and irreversible crisis if the goodwill of the people toward their taxing system continues to be frittered away.

Chapter 5
Checking Out Elected Officials

"Them that pays the fiddler calls the tune." This old Appalachian saying especially applies to candidates and their contributors around election time. So citizen action must begin with the question, "How much do I really know about my elected officials?" Do you know the people and groups who control the purse strings of your representative's campaign? Do you know the bills your representative has introduced in Congress and who benefits? Your investigation of these questions can tell you who your representative (and other elected officials) really represents.

In 1973, the Tax Reform Research Group studied the public records of Representative Herman Schneebeli (R-Pa.), a ranking member of the House Ways and Means Committee, to test possible investigating techniques. Schneebeli came from the 17th Congressional District of Pennsylvania, a district encompassing part of Harrisburg and surrounding smaller towns. As ranking Republican on the House committee responsible for all tax laws, Schneebeli was in an excellent position either to help tax reform or to help special interests receive further tax breaks.

★ ★ ★ ★ ★ ★ ★

For a beginning we looked at Ralph Nader's Congress Project *Profile: Herman Schneebeli*, the *Almanac of American Politics*, and *Congressional Quarterly* and its State profiles.

We discovered that in Schneebeli's home district average family income in 1970 was $8,933, below the national and state averages. 61 percent of those employed are blue collar workers and 39 percent white collar. If Schneebeli were representing the interests of his voters, he would be a strong tax-reform advocate.

We then turned to the informative weekly publication, *Congressional Quarterly*, for information about tax bills Schneebeli has actually sponsored. It turns out that in 1971-72 Schneebeli had not supported HR1040, a widely co-sponsored comprehensive tax reform bill to eliminate loopholes and lower income tax rates on average taxpayers.

Instead, we discovered that Schneebeli had sponsored a few bills, like a tuition tax credit for private schools, that would help average taxpayers, but many more bills for special interests. Two among Schneebeli's bills in 1971-72, were to benefit foundations. Under the 1969 Tax Reform Act, charitable foundations were required, in return for their tax-free privileges, to contribute a small percentage of their wealth to charity each year. Otherwise, wealthy families could use the foundation device exclusively as a way of hoarding their money, tax-free. Schneebeli's bills would reduce and postpone the 1969 requirement, and allow foundations to accumulate their tax-sheltered fortunes without significantly helping charitable causes.

Three national newspapers, the *Washington Post*, *New York Times*, and *Wall Street Journal*, are invaluable sources of information about such special interest bills. In this case, the *New York Times* broke the story. Schneebeli introduced his first bill, HR11197, to benefit the Pew Memorial Trust, a Philadelphia foundation established by the Pew family (the Sun Oil Company was their family business), and the Kellogg (cereal) family foundation. Later calculations showed that the Pew foundation

138   TAX POLITICS

would save some $40 million, and the Kellogg Foundation almost as much. The second Schneebeli foundation bill, H.R. 15448, was a milder form of the first, intended as an alternative when the Pew-Kellogg foundation bill, H.R. 11197, got into trouble.

The Office of Records and Registration at the U.S. House of Representatives maintains campaign contribution records on representatives. Under the old federal law these records were kept only for two years. Since July 1971 contributions must be kept on file for five years. The only way to get pre-1972 records is if they were required to be kept on file under state law. Requirements will vary from state to state and can be checked with the secretary of state in each state capital.

These records told an interesting story: in 1970 the Pew family contributed $7,000 to Schneebeli's congressional campaign. Voters in Schneebeli's district might be interested to know that the Pews and their foundation are located at Philadelphia and not in the district at all.

In the last two Congresses, Schneebeli introduced several bills for the steel industry. A check of Schneebeli's campaign contributions showed that in 1972 steel interests contributed $5,250 directly to Schneebeli. In addition, the Mellon bank interests of Pittsburgh—a city at the opposite end of Pennsylvania from Schneebeli's district—gave his campaign $5,000. A report of the House Banking and Currency Committee indicates that the bank, Mellon National Bank and Trust, is involved in steel companies with billions of dollars of assets, both through stock control and through interlocking directorates.

Another steel industry contribution was $400 from Edwin Hodge, Jr., listed in *Poor's Registry of Executives and Directors* as President of Pittsburgh Forgings Company of Pittsburgh, Pa.—another out-of-district special interest.

Finally, Schneebeli received a contribution from a Mr. Charles W. Davis. Schneebeli's official campaign records listed him only as an attorney located at 1 First National Plaza, Chicago, Illinois. We checked the *Martindale-Hubbell Law Directory*, where we found Davis listed as a partner of the Chicago firm of Hopkins, Sutter, Owen, Mulroy & Davis. *Martindale-Hubbell* also indicated the firm has a Washington, D.C. office and that Davis had an extensive background in tax legislation. In fact, for several years he had worked for the Ways and Means Committee.

This seemed to add up to tax lobbying activities by Mr. Davis. To find out, we consulted the list of registered lobbyists which appears quarterly in the *Congressional Record*. Sure enough, Davis was registered as a lobbyist for various special interests, including the Inland Steel Corporation. He wasn't contributing to Schneebeli's campaign out of altruism.

Our study of Schneebeli's campaign contributors revealed Schneebeli's public reports to be evasive and probably irregular in many cases. This is not unusual. Many representatives violate the election laws, sometimes in an effort to avoid full disclosure of their financial backing. For instance, a General Accounting Office report disclosed the following violations in the reporting by Congressman Wilbur D. Mills in his unsuccessful 1972 Presidential campaign:

1. The Committee failed to report the occupation and principal place of business for many individuals who contributed in excess of $100, as required by section 304(b)(2) of the Act.

2. The Committee failed to maintain a detailed account of each individual who contributed in excess of $10, but less than $100 as required by section 302(c)(2).

3. The Committee reported receipts as of the date of deposit rather than the date of receipt.

A large proportion of Schneebeli's contributions came from outside of his home district. Moreover, many of the contributors were disguised by being funnelled through groups such as the National Republican Congressional Committee and the Business-Industry Political Action Committee (BIPAC) of the U.S. Chamber of Commerce. This technique allows a contributor to secretly earmark funds to a specific candidate while appearing to donate money to a general group. Such disguising of contributions has become much less popular with voters since the Watergate scandals. The practice is especially bad when thousands of dollars come from outside the candidate's home district. Publicizing this information would make a good starting point for citizen action.

Investigation on this model of

Checking Out Elected Officials

the special interest ties to Congressman Wilbur D. Mills (D-Ark.) in his abortive 1972 Presidential race, led to these discoveries:

Mills was required by law to file campaign contribution disclosure reports in 17 states. A long-distance telephone survey revealed that he filed none of the required documents.

There was a significant correlation between campaign contributions to Mills and the legislation he has introduced or supported. For example, 23.5 percent of Mills's itemized contributions came from three dairy cooperatives; Mills cosponsored legislation raising federal price supports for milk—a bill to increase the price of milk and dairy products.

Our release of the report on Mills generated news articles in the *New York Times*, *Wall Street Journal*, *Washington Post*, *Christian Science Monitor*, and other newspapers including, of course, those in Mills's home district in Arkansas. Moreover, the report provoked editorials in the *New York Times*, *Wall Street Journal*, and *Christian Science Monitor*, as well as independent articles based on further work by investigative journalists.

The Tax Reform Research Group followed the Mills report with a report on the special interest ties to Rep. Joel T. Broyhill (R-Va.). The Broyhill report revealed the following:

Broyhill, who introduced or supported substantial legislation favoring real estate and investment interests, had a personal net worth of $3.8 million, including about $2.5 million in real estate investments.

In 1972, Broyhill received 65 percent of the itemized contributions for his congressional campaign from out-of-state interests; in 1974, 80 percent of his itemized contributions came from out-of-state.

Broyhill's campaign records included numerous irregularities. For example, one contributor, the Political Awareness Fund, claimed no special interest or private affiliation; in fact, the contribution was made by an employee of the Union Oil Company of California, the Fund's address was that of Union Oil, and the Secretary of Union Oil was a trustee of the Fund.

An examination of his legislative proposals showed a pattern of pro-real estate and banking tax bills.

About one-third of his 1972 contributions were received after the election, despite the fact that his campaign fund was not in debt. Such contributions are significant for several reasons. Being late, they cannot be known to the voters at election time. Late contributions are typically given by special interests to the winning candidates to ensure that their money goes to someone in a position to help them.

Broyhill, a 22-year veteran, was proud of his reputation for helping individual constituents with his position and influence. His staff was very efficient at handling citizen complaints and requests. What became clearer as the study of his legislation and financial deals progressed, was that the constituents were really getting crumbs in comparison to the loaves his wealthy friends got.

Using county records and deed registers, containing corporation and bank charters, land titles and leases, a pattern emerged showing a circle of business friends and relatives with whom Broyhill had personal financial connections. This same group benefited heavily from his position as a congressman. They controlled fully 65 percent of the federal government's General Services Administration (GSA) office building leases in Broyhill's district. Broyhill admitted soliciting the government's business for his friends and he was quite successful. In fact, fully 83 percent of GSA leasing in Northern Virginia was in Broyhill's district, despite the cheaper space that was available in counties nearby, and despite the fact that the area does not meet GSA's own published policy requirements for local housing.

Another, more direct, instance of congressional favors involved a piece of property near the Capitol Building complex in Washington. Broyhill sponsored a bill to have the House of Representative purchase the land for possible future development as a congressional building. The bill was traced by researchers through the legislative index in the *Congressional Record*. The appropriations subcommittee chairman who held hearings on the bill, Rep. Andrews, reported against the purchase. The land wasn't needed and wasn't close enough to the Capitol to be of much use anyway. The House voted it down.

Examination of the title to the property in the registry of deeds showed that the land belonged to some of that same circle of Broyhill's friends. They had purchased it in 1962 for $420,000 and then leased it to GSA for office space for two years at $65,000 per year until the old building was condemned and torn down. Plans to build a very profitable high-rise apartment building were rejected by the Architect of the Capitol as inconsistent with the Capitol Hill area of primarily

TAX POLITICS

old, restored brick townhouses. Rather than build townhouses on the land, Broyhill's friends sought to sell it to the government, and eventually they did.

The *Congressional Record* index for the following year showed that the bill, which had been rejected the year before, was quietly attached to a large appropriations bill and passed without comment or debate. The final sales price was $1.4 million—a profit of 330 percent. Rep. Andrews had, in the initial report on the bill, openly characterized the purchase a charity to bail Broyhill's friends out of a bad business deal and suggested that they pass the hat elsewhere. Apparently, they didn't have to.

A report was published, detailing all of these financial connections and favors and campaign reporting irregularities. The report received substantial news coverage and prompted independent investigations, one of which was published in the *Washingtonian* magazine. Joel T. Broyhill, an incumbent of 22 years and odds-on favorite to win re-election, was defeated in 1974. There were probably many factors which contributed to his defeat, but the widespread publicity about his business deals and his steadfast refusal to discuss them with his constituents played a considerable part.

information about elected officials and how to find it

who finances their campaigns?

Under most state laws, contributions to all candidates of $25 or more, given directly or through a political committee, must be reported locally: Go to your local bureau of elections or voter registration bureau and ask to see the files for the last election or previous elections.

Under federal law, contributions to congressional candidates of $100 or more must be reported. For senators write to the Office of Public Records, ST-2, U.S. Capitol, Washington, D.C. 20510. For representatives write to the Office of Records and Registration, U.S. House of Representatives, Longworth Building, Washington, D.C. 20515.

There will be photocopying charges by the House and the Senate offices—approximately $10.00 per candidate. If it is more convenient, copies of these House and Senate records are also on file with the secretary of state in your state capital. Moreover, state disclosure laws—for example that of California—may be much tougher than the federal law.

what interests do these contributors represent?

While the federal law requires the contributor's name, business address, and occupation, the records discussed above will often give only names and home addresses. If the information is incomplete, the following sources will help you trace the corporate connections involved:

The *City Directory* found in most medium or large cities will usually tell you what the contributor does for a living. Your public library will have one.

Poor's Registry of Executives & Directors will tell you if the contributor is "big business" and will list all corporate involvements. The second section of this reference book will tell you most of the board of director positions held by the contributor.

Lawyers should be checked out in *Martindale & Hubbell's Law Directory*, available in law libraries and most reference libraries. Here you can often find corporate clients of the law firm or individual lawyer, estimated economic worth, rating as to legal ability, and a biographical sketch. The Law Directory will also list any Washington offices a law firm may have.

Newspaper clipping files in the library of your local newspaper will often give more information on the contributor. Ask for any clippings the newspaper has about the contributor.

when the contributor is a lobbyist

The *Congressional Record* lists registered lobbyists four times a year and tells for whom they lobby. Your library will have it in its reference department. Look in the index to find the list of lobbyists. (However, be aware that not all lobbyists actually register as they should.) Check the list for names of contributors—especially any with a Washington, D.C. area address—or any out-of-town attorneys. It is a good idea not to limit your check to the year in which the contribution was made. Check to see if the individual was a lobbyist in the past or became one after he made the contribution in question.

The Washington Influence Directory, mentioned in the Bibliographical Note, also lists lobbyists and their clients.

what interests elected officials vote for

Tax bills that your elected officials have introduced, voted for, or made speeches about can be found in *Tax Notes*, published weekly by Tax Analysts and Advocates, in the *Congressional Quarterly*, in the *Congressional Record Index*, and by writing directly to their office—ask whom their bills benefit and compare with contributors' interests. A word of caution: often bills can be written to look like they help many interests, but closer scrutiny reveals the bill is really meant to benefit a narrow special interest or even an individual taxpayer.

Obviously, a representative's voting record is central to any investigation of tax-reform positions. For years, however, the tax-writing process had insulated members of Congress from taking public stands on tax-reform issues. As discussed in Chapter 3, traditionally no specific tax reforms came to a vote on the House floor and very few clear-cut issues were voted on in the Senate. Votes of the tax-writing committees also were not publicly disclosed. This has changed and, presently, recorded votes during committee mark-up sessions are made public. Also, in the last several years, more tax-reform amendments have been voted on separately, on the House and Senate floors. All recorded floor votes are listed in the *Congressional Record* and the *Congressional Quarterly*. Descriptions and records of tax-reform votes are now being compiled by various tax-reform groups. For voting information write to Public Citizen's *People & Taxes*, P.O. Box 14198, Ben Franklin Station, Washington, D.C. 20044, and Taxation with Representation, 2369 N. Taylor St., Arlington, Va. 22207.

needing help to understand the bills

Since most bills are written by lawyers for lawyers, most of them will be hard for the layperson to understand. You might enlist the help of a lawyer, or a friend knowledgeable in the area, to analyze the bills. On bills involving taxes, you can also write to Tax Analysts and Advocates, 732 17th St., N.W., Washington, D.C. 20006, giving the number of the bill, sponsor and date it was introduced. They will explain the bill and who benefits. Or write to the Public Citizen Tax Reform Research Group.

Sometimes professional economists and tax law experts are available to help out. Contact Taxation with Representation or the Public Interest Economics Center, 1714 Massachusetts Ave., N.W., Washington, D.C. 20036, to see if experts are available in your area.

do officials have local broadcasting interests?

Go to your local TV and radio stations. Ask to see the public ownership files. Look for the names of elected officials. Since most people don't know about the existence of these files, the station personnel will be surprised when you ask for the files. Mention to them you want the files required under Federal Regulations, Title 47, part 1.526.

do they have real estate involvements?

See Chapter 8, Investigating Property Taxes.

in what corporations are they involved?

The U.S. House of Representatives Committee on Standards of Official Conduct, Room 2360, Rayburn Bldg., lists all income of more than $1,000. Corporate involvement (stocks, bonds, etc.) will often show up on the Statement of Certain Financial Interests and Associations. Unfortunately, even the limited disclosure that is required is sometimes ignored by representatives. Therefore, these records should not be considered conclusive.

The counterpart in the U.S. Senate is the Office of Public Records, ST-2, Capitol Bldg., Washington, D.C. 20510. All speaking fees of $300 or more per year are listed here. Also see the *City Directory*, *Poor's Registry*, and newspaper clipping files mentioned earlier.

are they involved in tax-exempt foundations?

Look in the index of the *Foundation Directory*. Then turn to the appropriate pages listed after the official's name to find the foundation, its location, and its major activities.

142 TAX POLITICS

general information

Congressional Profiles written by Ralph Nader's *Congress Project* gives information on each senator and representative who ran for the 93rd Congress. These can be purchased at bookstores or from Grossman Publishers, Box 19281, Washington, D.C. 20036. Be sure to list the officials you want to study. They cost $1 each.

The *Almanac of American Politics* gives information on the district, key votes, and a biographical sketch. The Almanac can be found in your library or purchased from Gambit, Inc., 53 Beacon St., Boston, Mass. 02108.

Who's Who in American Politics gives more extensive biographical information on elected officials in state and local governments. It can be found in most libraries.

Two weekly publications can be very helpful in providing information on members of Congress (including voting records), on specific committees, and on legislation and lobbying activity on certain bills. They are *Congressional Quarterly* and *National Journal Reports* and are available in most libraries.

It's important to find out what opinions others have about your elected representatives. Local newspaper editors and reporters can often give you an invaluable perspective on local officials and members of Congress. Sometimes a Washington correspondent for the local media may also be a good source of information on your representation.

Remember, in evaluating this information, you must consider the source. While most journalists tend to be objective, relationships and friendships over the years can make some biased in their views. Others find it convenient to protect or be supportive of powerful officials. Sift through the information carefully, keeping in mind that media people and officials often can represent similar powerful groups.

Tax legislation is obviously not the only measure of special-interest representation. Other areas of legislation should also be examined to determine the types of interests your representatives support. Various Washington-based public-interest, consumer, environmental, and union groups (some with local chapters) compile legislative records which will be helpful in analyzing the types of legislation elected officials have sponsored or voted for.

how can I find out if my elected officials have ever been arrested or sued... or if they've ever had anyone else sued or arrested?

Go to the Clerk's Office of the various courts in your county or the city courthouse (they will be listed on the "directory" as you enter the building). Look in both the criminal and civil indexes for the name of your elected officials (last name first). Since there is usually a separate index for each year, you will want to go through indexes for the past several years. These will list all civil and criminal cases your representative was involved in. You can ask the Clerk for the actual file of any case in question.

investigating manuals

The Common Cause Manual on Money and Politics, published by Common Cause, 2030 M St., N.W., Washington, D.C. 20036.

Tactical Investigation for People's Struggles by Barry Greever. Order from Citizen Action Group, P.O. Box 19404, Washington, D.C. 20036. Cost $1.50.

The reader can expect to run into a few problems, trying to put this outline to use. But persistence will solve most of these.

3 Property Taxes

Chapter 6
Who Pays the Property Tax

where property taxes come from

It is called a "property tax," but "selective property tax" would be a more accurate description. Decades of chipping away at the tax have resulted in a system in which most property isn't taxed at all. Residential taxpayers are bearing an ever-increasing share of the total property tax load. Nationwide, in 1972, residences—homes and apartments—provided about 47.3 percent of the revenues, farms about 8 percent, and commercial and industrial property about 42.2 percent.

★ ★ ★ ★ ★ ★ ★

These proportions vary, sometimes drastically, community-by-community and state-by-state. New Jersey, for example, is a highly industrial state, yet commercial and industrial property bore a smaller share of New Jersey's property taxes than it did nationwide. As a result, homeowners paid proportionally more. One reason is that New Jersey exempts all business personal property except that of telephone companies and utilities.

Locally the differences can be even greater. At the one extreme are bedroom suburbs such as Hillsdale, New Jersey, where residences comprise over 91 percent of the tax base. Not far away is Teterboro, an "industrial tax haven" with few residences, where industrial property makes up 98 percent of the tax base and the tax rate is less than one-tenth that of other New Jersey localities.

There are also towns and cities which have one or more industries that bear most of the taxes. The Reynolds and Alcoa aluminum plants on the St. Lawrence River in Massena, N.Y., provide the bulk of the town's base. In little Rowe, Massachusetts (1972 population 303), two power plants—one of them Yankee Atomic, New England's first nuclear plant—pay over 90 percent of the town's taxes and provide an ample public treasury in a depressed region.

Businesses too pay uneven taxes. How much a business will pay depends on how capital-intensive it is—how much it relies on physical equipment and assets to make its product or render its service; whether it is located in a high-tax city—as banks, hotels, and insurance companies often are—or in a lower-taxed rural area, as is the case with coal mines, oil wells and timber stands; and how state tax laws and exemptions affect the business. Utilities often bear a heavier property tax burden than other businesses. They are capital-intensive, they are often assessed by state agencies that are more competent than local assessors. On the other hand, being monopolies, they pass all their taxes on to their customers.

Like the utilities, people or businesses who pay a tax bill do not always bear the tax in the long run. They may be able to shift it to someone else. A business can pass a tax forward to its customers in higher prices, or backward to its workers and suppliers in lower wages and prices of supplies. A landlord can shift a tax forward to renters, or backwards to the person who built or sold him the building, or provides services to it. Even homeowners can pass part of their property taxes back to the builder or seller by paying less for the property. (This is known as *capitalizing* the tax into the sales price.)

land

There is wide agreement that property taxes on land fall mainly, if not entirely, upon the owner. The reason, economists say, is that the supply of land is

144 TAX POLITICS

fixed (except for land-fills and the like.) Owners cannot close down their land and move it elsewhere, the way industries close down their plants when taxes cause them displeasure.

commercial and industrial property

The orthodox view that businesses pass along their property taxes to their customers is being scaled down. Professor Dick Netzer, dean of The New York University Graduate School of Public Administration, surmises that the amount of tax actually shifted to consumers is "perhaps half or less." The amount varies from case to case, depending on such factors as the local tax rate and competition from localities where tax rates are lower.

residential property

The current view is that *homeowners* bear the bulk of their residential property taxes. The picture is less clear for *rental housing*. Landlords can pass a good part of their taxes forward to their tenants, especially when housing is in short supply, as it is in many U.S. cities. Another part they can shift back to builders and sellers. Recent studies suggest that landlords may bear a larger portion than was once thought but how much more is not clear.

In 1972, about 20.2 percent of the typical family's income went to taxes; only about 3.4 percent was property taxes, compared to 3.9 percent for social security

★ **FIGURE 38. WHO PAYS THE LOCAL PROPERTY TAX?** ★

Estimated Local Property Tax Collections By Source, 1972[1]

Source	Amount (millions)	Percentage distribution
Nonbusiness		
Nonfarm residential realty[2]	$19,023	47.3
Farm realty[3]	817	2.0
Vacant lots	320	0.8
Total nonbusiness realty	$20,160	50.1
Nonfarm personalty[4]	657	1.6
Farm personalty	113	0.3
Total nonbusiness personalty	770	1.9
Total nonbusiness	$20,930	52.1
Business		
Farm realty[5]	1,860	4.6
Vacant lots	480	1.2
Other realty[6]	9,170	22.8
Total business realty	$11,510	28.6
Farm personalty[7]	454	1.1
Other personalty[8]	4,287	10.7
Total business personalty	4,741	11.8
Public utilities	3,019	7.5
Total business	19,270	47.9
Total	$40,200[9]	100.0

[1] ACIR staff estimates based on estimated 1972 collections distributed on basis of 1967 Census data, latest available statistics.

[2] Includes both single-family dwelling units and apartments. An estimated $14 billion or 36 percent of all local property taxes was derived from single-family homes; about $5 billion or 12 percent of property tax revenue came from multi-family units.

[3] Estimated collections from the taxation of the "residential" element of the farm.

[4] The collections produced through the taxation of furniture and other household effects.

[5] Estimated collections from the taxation of land and improvements actually used in the production of agricultural products—this is exclusive of the land and buildings used in a residential capacity by the farmer.

[6] Commercial and industrial real estate other than public utilities.

[7] The estimated collections from the taxation of livestock, tractors, etc.

[8] Estimated collections from the taxation of merchants and manufacturers' inventory, tools and machinery, etc.

[9] This is the estimated grand total for *local* property tax receipts. In addition, there is an estimated $1.3 billion in State property taxes. The data needed for a similar distribution of State receipts is not available. However, it is estimated that approximately $450 million of the State receipts are derived from general property taxes and could probably be distributed among the various sources of revenue in the same proportion as local receipts. The remaining $850 million in State receipts consists mainly of State special property taxes on business personal property, but includes a substantial amount from special property taxes on motor vehicles, most of which is collected by the State of California.

SOURCE: Advisory Commission on Intergovernmental Relations.

taxes and 9.7 percent for federal income taxes. Further, in the twenty-year period only federal income taxes grew less than property taxes as a percent of family income.

Just as important, in any of the over 65,000 different local property tax jurisdictions, particular taxpayers can be greatly overburdened by taxes which, on the average, are quite moderate.

Even average property tax burdens vary widely from state to state. At one extreme, the typical New Jersey homeowner in 1969 paid $626 in property taxes, while his Louisiana counterpart paid only $79. The average-income Boston homeowner paid 8.9 percent of his income in property taxes in 1971, while the figure was 2 percent in Atlanta, and only 1.4 percent in Houston.

Even more striking are the huge differences one finds in tax rates in communities within the same local area. Thus the owner of a $20,000 home in the village of Wayne in DuPage County, Ill., just west of Chicago, paid $1,005.40 in property taxes in 1973, while the owner of the same kind of home in nearby Hinsdale paid $1,565.00—about 64 percent more. In Los Angeles County, taxpayers in one plush Beverly Hills taxing district paid less than one-half the tax rate borne by taxpayers in Walnut City.

Frequently there are great differences between what inner city residents and neighboring suburbanites have to pay. The property tax rate in the Baltimore, Md., suburbs in a recent year was only 53 percent that of the central city, and for cities such as Cincinnati, Newark, and Rochester the gaps were of similar scale. This pattern does not always hold, however. In the suburbs of San Francisco, New York, Washington, D.C., and St. Louis, tax rates are higher than in the central city.

All such disparities are perfectly legal, being part and parcel of the fragmented state of the local property tax.

who pays the property tax

How these burdens are spread out among taxpayers of differing incomes is not a totally settled question. The conventional view is that property taxes are regressive, casting greater burdens on low-income people. The leading advocate of this claim is the Advisory Commission on Intergovernmental Relations (ACIR), which regularly produces tables such as figure 40 to expound its view.

The table purports to show the proportion of family income devoted to property taxes for homeowners at different income levels

★ **FIGURE 39. THE ESTIMATED BURDEN OF RESIDENTIAL PROPERTY TAXES FOR A HYPOTHETICAL FAMILY OF FOUR, FOR VARIOUS FAMILY INCOME GROUPS, SELECTED CITIES, 1971–1972** ★

Estimated residential property tax as a percentage of family income

Family Income	U.S. Average	City Average	Minn.	Boston	New York	Chicago	Atlanta (Fulton Co)	Houston	Denver	Los Angeles	Seattle
$ 7,500	3.6	6.6	7.6	13.0	7.8	6.9	2.7	1.8	5.2	8.3	6.1
$12,000	3.4	4.6	5.4	8.9	5.4	4.8	2.0	1.4	3.8	5.8	4.3
$25,000	2.9	2.7	3.0	5.1	3.0	2.7	1.3	0.9	2.2	3.4	2.5
$50,000	2.5	2.1	2.3	3.9	2.2	2.1	1.0	0.8	1.6	2.8	1.8

SOURCE: Advisory Commission on Intergovernmental Relations.

FIGURE 40. REAL ESTATE TAXES AS A PERCENTAGE OF FAMILY INCOME, OWNER-OCCUPIED SINGLE-FAMILY HOMES, BY INCOME CLASS AND BY REGION, 1970

Family Income	United States Total	Northeast Region	North-central Region	South Region	West Region
Less than $2,000	16.6	30.8	18.0	8.2	22.9
$ 2,000– 2,999	9.7	15.7	9.8	5.2	12.5
3,000– 3,999	7.7	13.1	7.7	4.3	8.7
4,000– 4,999	6.4	9.8	6.7	3.4	8.0
5,000– 5,999	5.5	9.3	5.7	2.9	6.5
6,000– 6,999	4.7	7.1	4.9	2.5	5.9
7,000– 9,999	4.2	6.2	4.2	2.2	5.0
10,000–14,999	3.7	5.3	3.6	2.0	4.0
15,000–24,999	3.3	4.6	3.1	2.0	3.4
25,000 or more	2.9	3.9	2.7	1.7	2.9

SOURCE: U.S. Bureau of the Census, *Residential Finance Survey, 1970* (conducted in 1971). Special tabulations prepared for the Advisory Commission on Intergovernmental Relations.

and in different parts of the country. It seems to indicate that without exception, the lower the family income, the greater the share of it that goes to property taxes.

Critics of this view point out that the ACIR measures residential property taxes against the homeowner's income for a particular year only. Economists widely agree, however, that housing decisions are based on the income a family expects over the long haul—its "permanent income"—not on the income of a particular year. Adjusting for this "permanent income" concept, and making other statistical refinements, Henry Aaron of the Brookings Institution found that even if one accepted the ACIR's basic premises, residential property taxes were not regressive. Instead they were proportional, affecting people at different income levels roughly the same way. In addition, it is argued that the ACIR leaves out entirely the property taxes on commercial and industrial property, which is owned largely by the rich.

The ACIR seems to assume that the property tax, like excise taxes, is passed along to consumers in the prices they pay for goods and services. Others take the view that property tax is a tax on the owners of capital. Since property ownership is even more concentrated among the wealthy than is income, this would make the property tax decidedly progressive.

This position was explored by Joseph Pechman and Benjamin Okner of the Brookings Institution in their book *Who Bears the Tax Burden?* Assuming that property taxes are indeed borne by the owners of capital, they found that the burden by income class looked like this:

FIGURE 41. EFFECTIVE RATES OF FEDERAL, STATE, AND LOCAL PROPERTY TAXES, 1966

Income classes in thousands of dollars; tax rates in percent

Adjusted Family Income	Property Tax
0–3	2.5
3–5	2.7
5–10	2.0
10–15	1.7
15–20	2.0
20–25	2.6
25–30	3.7
30–50	4.5
50–100	6.2
100–500	8.2
500–1,000	9.6
1,000 and over	10.1
All classes	3.0

SOURCE: Adapted from Joseph A. Pechman and Benjamin A. Oliver, *Who Bears the Tax Burden?* (Washington, D.C.: The Bookings Institution, 1974).

Given these assumptions, a tax on property now seems a key part of a progressive tax system.

Even the new analysis is flawed, however. It still relates tax burdens solely to the taxpayer's income, reflecting the income bias that has beset tax policymakers. Economist Mason Gaffney and others argue that property tax burdens should be measured against the taxpayer's wealth, or net worth; first, because wealth represents ability to pay sometimes better than income does, and secondly, because to use the income standard is to criticize the property tax for not being what it is not—an income tax.

The permanent income approach goes somewhat in the direction of net worth. It is not clear exactly how the property tax burden would look if the taxpayer's net worth were the yardstick. Quite possibly the apparent regressivity at the lowest income levels would be eliminated, since many in these categories are older people with reduced current incomes but substantial net worths. The property tax might appear yet more progressive at other income levels too.

where property taxes go

Property taxes pay for local government. That means streets, sewers, garbage collections, police and fire departments, libraries, parks, and schools. How our property tax dollars are divided up among these different functions depends on such factors as:

the needs of our localities for different services, such as police protection, snow removal, traffic lights, building inspectors, aid for the poor.

the amount of state and federal assistance for different functions; e.g. revenue sharing, state aid for schools.

the other revenue sources that state lawmakers made available to the local government; e.g. sales and income taxes, parking fines, revenues of publicly-owned power and water companies.

It should be noted, however, that just as taxes can be shifted to someone else, benefits from revenue expenditures do not benefit only the people or services for which they are made. Thus it is commonly assumed that the benefits from schools go to families in proportion to the number of children they have. Yet schools function as much to keep kids off the streets as to educate them, and the parents and children are hardly the only ones who benefit from this involuntary confinement.

Similarly, realtors and developers benefit directly from school expenditures. Anyone who has gone house-hunting in the suburbs knows that the quality of the local schools is a centerpiece in the broker's sales pitch. Architects, contractors, and bond attorneys have a major stake in the politics of suburban school districts and many other projects besides new schools. Another special-interest group that benefits from government expenditures for new facilities are the holders of the public debt. In 1969-70, local governments spent almost $2.8 billion dollars to pay the interest on local debt. Nationwide, this came to 3.5 percent of local expenses. But the percentage is much higher in specific cases. New Jersey cities spent 8.26 percent of their revenues on interest in 1970. In fast-growing Bucks County, Pennsylvania, the debt service for one school district in the early 1970s reached 18 percent of its budget.

In 1972, commercial banks held over 50 percent of all state and local debt, households—mainly the very wealthy—about 30 percent, and insurance companies about 14 percent. The main reason why such investors purchase this debt is that the interest is exempt from federal income taxes.

could we abolish property taxes?

Property taxes raise over $40 billion annually at this writing and the amount is steadily rising. Not including property taxes, the states collected $60.6 billion dollars in taxes in 1972. Thus to do away with property taxes, the states would have to increase their taxes—mainly income and sales taxes—by at least two-thirds. The U.S. Advisory Commission on Intergovernmental Relations has computed that if the states were to shift merely 30 percent of local property taxes to state income and sales taxes, these levies would increase over 40 percent nationwide. The increase in some states would be much more: 56 percent in California, 71 percent in Texas, 70 percent in Nebraska, 107 percent in New Jersey, and 92 percent in Connecticut.

It would even take a 30 percent increase in federal income taxes to fill in for local property taxes, not to mention the massive political problems involved in finding a formula for distributing that much money to states and localities.

All in all, it does not seem likely that taxes on property will be eliminated or even greatly

148 TAX POLITICS

reduced in the foreseeable future. To pose the issue this way is really to confuse it, in any event. The basic issue is *fair* taxes, through many measures or devices.

property tax exemptions

The property tax loophole system is much larger than most people suspect.

At last count, at least one-third of all the real estate in the country was exempt from property taxes. The taxes lost came to $310 for each American family. Put another way, over one-quarter of the typical American's property tax bill went to pay for the property that was legally or illegally exempt. These estimates for real estate are decidedly low. Many assessors keep virtually no records on exemptions. Thus nobody really knows how much property is exempt.

Exempt real estate, moreover, is just the beginning. Property consists of a great deal more than just land and buildings. Dick Netzer has estimated that in 1966 the tangible property in the nation—both real estate and personal property such as business equipment and inventories—was worth about $2,554 billion. Yet only $1,503 billion was on the property tax rolls. In other words, over 41 percent of the tangible property was not taxed.

Only about 45 percent of the property in the United States is tangible at most. The rest is *intangible*—paper property such as stocks, bonds, and patents.

Intangible property has been growing in value much more rapidly than tangible property, increasing from about 40 percent of all national assets in 1900 to about 55 percent or more today. The value of privately held corporate stocks alone has been increasing about twice as rapidly as real estate. Professor Donald Hagman of the University of California (Los Angeles) Law School has estimated that of the approximately $7 trillion worth of property—tangible and intangible—in the country in 1968, only about $1.4 trillion was taxed. "Stated another way," Professor Hagman writes in a study published by the Institute of Government and Public Affairs at UCLA, "taxes on property now taxed are on the average about five times what they would be if all property were uniformly burdened." He concludes that "The $5.6 trillion loophole is getting bigger. Legally and illegally, the property tax base is being shrunk. And the faster it shrinks, the faster it will shrink, for one property owner's exemption translates into the non-exempt property owner's increased tax, which leads him, too, to seek relief. Gone—in fact if not always in law—is the principle of the sweeping constitutional and statutory provisions of the nineteenth century that all property was to be assessed at a uniform and full value. While in 1900 the assessed value of property was some 24 percent of national assets, by 1929 it was only some 17 percent, and now it would be generous to conclude that assessed values represent 7 percent of national assets."

public property

The largest single share of exempt real estate is public property, belonging to federal, state, and local governments. The landmark U.S. Supreme Court case of *McCulloch* v. *Maryland* (1819) held that the United States Constitution bars state and local governments from taxing the property of the federal government. Most states, in turn, bar their localities from taxing state-owned property. Sometimes, however, the federal and state governments make payments voluntarily *in lieu* (instead of) taxes to local taxing units.

★ ★ ★ ★ ★ ★ ★

The exemptions for private property fall into a number of basic classes. There are relief exemptions for homeowners (*homestead* exemptions), and the elderly and disabled. There are charity or *welfare* exemptions for a virtually endless list of nonprofit institutions and groups which are said to render a public service: schools, libraries, churches, hospitals, cemeteries, orphanages, social clubs and fraternal orders.

A third class of exemption consists of rewards, bonuses, and special-interest favors that are available, regardless of need, to a widening group of beneficiaries, from veterans in certain states to racehorse owners in others. A fourth type of exemption is due to the difficulties, supposed or real, of getting the property onto the assessment rolls. The frequent exemptions for intangible property and household goods are said to be for this reason. A final class are so-called incentive exemptions to encourage one form of activity or another. Into this class fall the exemptions for new industrial plants and equipment, and the laws providing special low assessments for farmland and open space.

Some exemptions are complete exemptions. The owner pays no property taxes whatsoever. Others are partial. A certain portion of the assessed value may be exempt, or the property may be exempt from some property taxes, e.g. school or sewer taxes. The homestead exemptions are a common form of partial exemption. Many of these were adopted during the depression, especially in the South, to prevent people from being taxed out of their homes.

One could do worse than to study our property tax exemptions in order to find out who has power in our society. Michigan, for example, sports the notorious "Chrysler Exemption," so named, assessor's say, because it was enacted in response to that automaker's threats to leave the state. The exemption applies to tools, dies, and equipment supposedly used only for a single model year; the carmakers argued that this property depreciates so rapidly that taxing it is not fair. Yet they actually keep and use the equipment to make replacement parts for five years or more. In California, one of former Governor Ronald Reagan's early acts in office was to sign a bill into law providing that movie films should be assessed as though worth no more than the raw celluloid on which they were printed.

intangible property

The leading beneficiaries of property tax exemptions are the owners of "intangible" property. According to the Institutional Investor Study Report of the Securities and Exchange Commission, in 1968 intangible property came to about $3.971 trillion—about four-sevenths of all assets. At a tax rate of 2 percent, typical for property taxes, that means almost $80 billion in revenue—about twice what property taxes currently yield. Of course, not all intangibles are fit for taxation, nor at rates applied to other property. It is helpful, nevertheless, to see the size of the exemption.

The owners of this intangible property are not the poor and the needy. In 1971 around 90 percent of American families making $10,000 a year or less owned *no* stocks or bonds, while of the families making over $25,000 a year 60 percent did own such property. To take corporate stock alone—about one-fourth the nation's wealth—the wealthiest 1 percent of the population owned over 70 percent and people owning $60,000 worth of property or more held a full 88 percent. Professor Lester B. Snyder of the University of Connecticut Law School has estimated that a property tax on intangible property would reach only about 15 percent of the population—by and large the wealthiest 15 percent.

Who Pays the Property Tax 149

personal property— business and residential

Personal property, unlike real estate, can usually be picked up and moved around fairly readily. It comprises business equipment and machinery, inventories, automobiles and trucks, boats, and household goods. Increasingly, the states have been exempting personal property. To a degree, the trend is understandable, for household goods are difficult to assess and do not yield profits for their owners. Not so for business property, however. Yet at least thirteen states totally exempt business personal property and/or inventories, and most other states either tax these at special reduced rates, are phasing down the tax, or have total exemptions for certain kinds of this business *personalty*.

The revenue loss is substantial. Dick Netzer has estimated that, in 1966, the total value of business and farm tangible personal property was about $431.3 billion, and that over half of this, $228.5 billion, was not on the tax rolls. This translates into lost revenue of $16.3 billion, roughly two-thirds of what property taxes raised that year. The beneficiaries of this exemption tend to be the larger businesses and industries since they are more capital-intensive, thus use more equipment and machinery per unit of output than do smaller enterprises.

Meanwhile, taxes lost through exemptions for household personal property came to over $2 billion. Since the wealthy tend to own proportionally more

150 TAX POLITICS

property than do the less well-off, putting household property over a certain value back onto the tax rolls could provide both added revenues and fairness.

exempt real estate

As previously noted, the great bulk of exempt real estate belongs to the public, and is held by federal, state, and local governments. Drs. Martin A. Larson and C. Stanley Lowell, in their book, *The Churches: Their Riches, Revenues, and Immunities*, put the government total value in 1968 at about $455 billion worth, about 75 percent of all exempt real estate. This total is misleading, however, since a large amount of so-called public property actually is leased to private businesses, with the government acting in effect as a tax-exempt front. This point is discussed more fully below.

Of the remaining 30 percent of

★ **FIGURE 42. THE PROPORTIONS OF TAXED AND UNTAXED PROPERTY IN THE UNITED STATES, 1966** ★

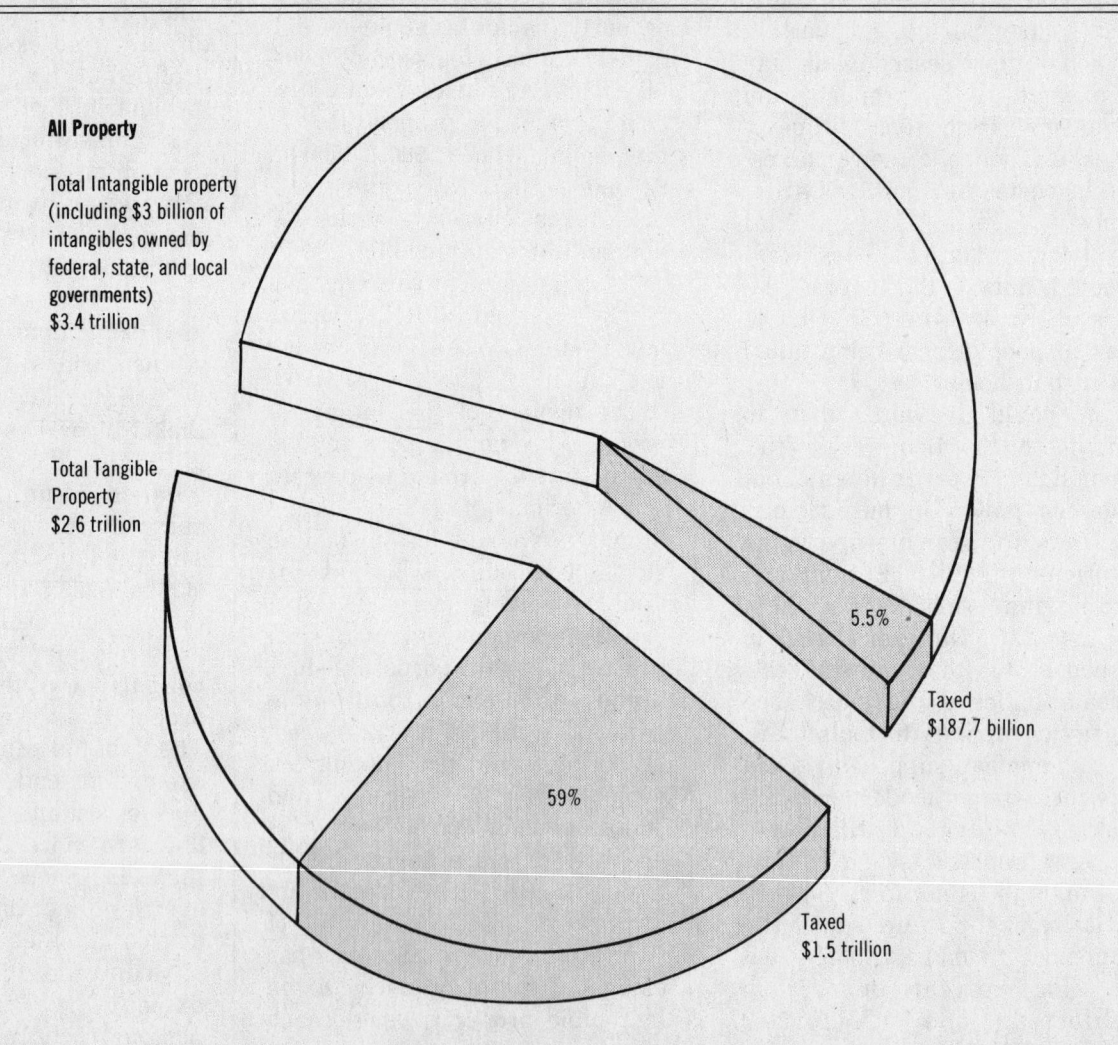

All Property

Total Intangible property (including $3 billion of intangibles owned by federal, state, and local governments) $3.4 trillion

Total Tangible Property $2.6 trillion

5.5%

Taxed $187.7 billion

59%

Taxed $1.5 trillion

SOURCE: Intangibles were estimated from Census of Governments, 1967; Institutional Investors Study Report of the Securities and Exchange Commission, 1971; Flow-of-Funds Accounts, Board of Governors of The Federal Reserve System, September 1974. Tangibles were calculated by Dick Netzer.

exempt real estate, Larson and Lowell estimated that about 18 percent—over $100 billion worth—belongs to "religious" organizations. The Roman Catholic Church had an estimated $54 billion, Protestants $41 billion, and Jews about $8 billion. This left about $68 billion in exempt property—12 percent of the total—belonging to individuals and nonreligious organizations—schools, hospitals and businesses.

These estimates are somewhat different from those of a U.S. Census Bureau survey in 1971. The census data covered just seventeen states, the only ones with information anywhere near adequate though still far from satisfactory. In these seventeen states there was about $87.6 billion in exempt real estate, including 10.4 percent religious, 12.1 percent educational, 3 percent charitable, 59 percent govern-

★ **FIGURE 42. THE PROPORTIONS OF TAXED AND UNTAXED PROPERTY IN THE UNITED STATES, 1966 (Continued)** ★

Tangible Property

Total value in billions of dollars

- Non-farm residential structures $542.3 billion — 88%
- Business and farm structures $266.7 billion — 94%
- Business and farm equipment and machinery $431.3 billion — 47%
- Household property $201.3 billion — 28%
- Land not owned by governments or tax-exempt organizations $513.5 billion — 100%
- All categories of property owned by governments or tax-exempt organizations $604.7 billion — Not Taxed

Legend: Percentage of property that is taxed

NOTE: Figures refer to total value, not to assessed valuation.
SOURCE: Adapted from Dick Netzer, "The Incidence of the Property Tax Revisited," National Tax Journal, December 1973.

mental, and 16 percent other (figure 43).

The real problem for local taxpayers, aside from there being too many exemptions, is that the exempt property is spread out so unequally among different local jurisdictions. In Boston, a center of colleges and universities, close to one-half of the property is exempt from taxes; and in Newark, New Jersey, beset by large amounts of government property, exemptions are also close to that figure. These cities have two of the highest tax rates in the country. Similarly, there are thirty-seven Appalachian counties in which the U.S. Forest Service owns over 20 percent of the land, and in fourteen of these it owns as much as 40 percent. Yet, in a city like White Plains, New York, only about 21 percent of the property is exempt. The exempt properties, moreover, provide benefits to people far removed from the locality. Boston's universities and Newark's Port Authority serve students, travelers and shippers all over the country. Appalachia's national forests provide timber for national and multinational timber companies, and recreation for people throughout the East. Yet the tax burden that should be borne by these properties falls mainly or entirely upon the local taxpayers, and upon them alone.

Adding up these three exemptions—intangible property, personal property, and exempt real estate—the total revenue loss comes conservatively to over $110 billion, which approaches three times what property taxes have been raising in recent years.

★ FIGURE 43. VALUE REPORTED FOR TOTALLY EXEMPT PROPERTY, BY TYPE OF EXEMPTION, FOR SELECTED STATES, 1971 ★

(Millions of dollars)

State	Total, All Types	Religious	Educational	Charitable	Governmental	Other or Unallocable
Total, 17 states (including D.C.)	87,648	9,089	10,618	2,698	51,296	13,944
Arizona	715	–	86	–	176	453
California	1,480	461	368	651	–	–
District of Columbia	4,480	186	156	28	3,828	282
Florida	10,198	2,710	–	–	7,327	160
Hawaii	2,551	358	–	–	2,128	64
Indiana	4,295	–	–	–	–	4,295
Kansas	402	–	–	–	–	402
Louisiana	5,653	851	–	–	–	4,802
Massachusetts	6,196	404	1,116	585	4,055	35
Minnesota	965	114	302	21	308	220
Nevada	833	15	51	–	762	5
New Jersey	8,377	1,213	–	490	5,838	836
New York	25,017	1,509	5,907	159	15,801	1,642
Ohio	4,708	732	1,523	456	1,849	146
Oregon	9,315	289	748	203	7,692	384
Rhode Island	1,344	106	297	14	730	197
South Dakota	1,119	141	64	91	802	21

NOTE: Detail may not add to totals, because of rounding.
SOURCE: Advisory Commission on Intergovernmental Relations. (Footnotes omitted.)

nonassessment and underassessment

There is a vast substratum of exemptions which is so built into the faulty structure and administration of property taxes that few people notice it at all. Nonassessment and underassessment are hidden exemptions worth billions of dollars of property that assessors have failed to put onto the tax rolls.

Industrial plants, even entire residential subdivisions, have been left off the assessment rolls, either by oversight or design. The problem is especially acute in the assessment of natural resources. These frequently are located in remote rural areas, where the assessors, housed in a small room in a country courthouse, equipped with an adding machine and a desk, and assisted by a clerk-typist, are no match for the job of assessing or even finding the resources. One result is that these localities must turn to the state and federal governments for assistance, while literally sitting atop vast wealth which should be yielding substantial revenues.

Underassessment of high-valued properties probably provides an even larger exemption than does nonassessment. Taxpayers have shrunk from the apparent difficulty of questioning assessments on such properties. When they have investigated, they have uncovered a problem as chronic as it is costly.

The most consistent type of property tax underassessment has been the underassessment of land. A 1968 study for the National Commission on Urban Problems found that land, properly assessed, would constitute about 40 percent of the property tax base. Due to underassessment it makes up only 30 percent.

Using census data for 1962, a survey in *Nation's Cities* magazine estimated the yearly revenue loss from underassessment at between $6 billion and $7 billion. Assessing has improved somewhat since then, but property values and tax rates have climbed, which means a larger tax loss for a given degree of underassessment. In addition, the census data were least adequate for large commercial and industrial properties since they were based on sales, and these high-value properties rarely change hands. They were also weighted toward urban areas, so that they did not reflect fully the underassessment of large rural acreages and mineral holdings. Indeed, separately assessed mineral rights, where underlying minerals are owned separately from the land surface, were omitted entirely; as were, of course, all cases of nonassessment. Thus $7 billion is an extremely conservative estimate of revenue losses due to nonassessment and underassessment. The actual total easily could be twice that.

Balkanization

This word, derived from the small, warring states that once dwelt on Europe's Balkan Peninsula, describes how property taxes today are levied by small, fragmented local jurisdictions—almost 66,000 at last count.

Balkanization provides a substantial exemption to wealthy property owners in low-tax jurisdictions. The dollar benefits, though difficult to estimate, easily reach into the billions of dollars per year.

leased government property

Many people do not know that the Pentagon, just for example, is in the business of building factories and then leasing them out to its contractors. In 1958, when a lawsuit over the matter reached the U.S. Supreme Court, the federal government owned $19.3 billion worth of property which it leased to private contractors, $11 billion of which belonged to the Defense Department and $8.3 to the Atomic Energy Commission. By 1973, the Defense Department alone was still reporting over $10 billion worth of property leased to private contractors. The federal government further owns one-third of the nation's land, and thus significant amounts of coal, oil, mineral reserves, timber stands and grazing lands. It leases these resources to private companies under terms which are not known for their harshness.

A case in point is the U.S. Forest Service. A study by Si Kahn, "The Forest Service in Appalachia," made for the John Hay Whitney Foundation showed that the Forest Service holds almost 5.5 million acres—close to 8,500 square miles—in Appalachia alone. A good deal of

154 TAX POLITICS

FIGURE 44. PROPERTY TAX EXEMPTIONS IN THE STATE OF WASHINGTON (1970)

Proportions of Exempt Property by Major Categories

Estimated value of exempt amounts to 48.6 percent of the estimated value of all property in the state of Washington. The following chart illustrates the proportions attributed to the major exempt categories:

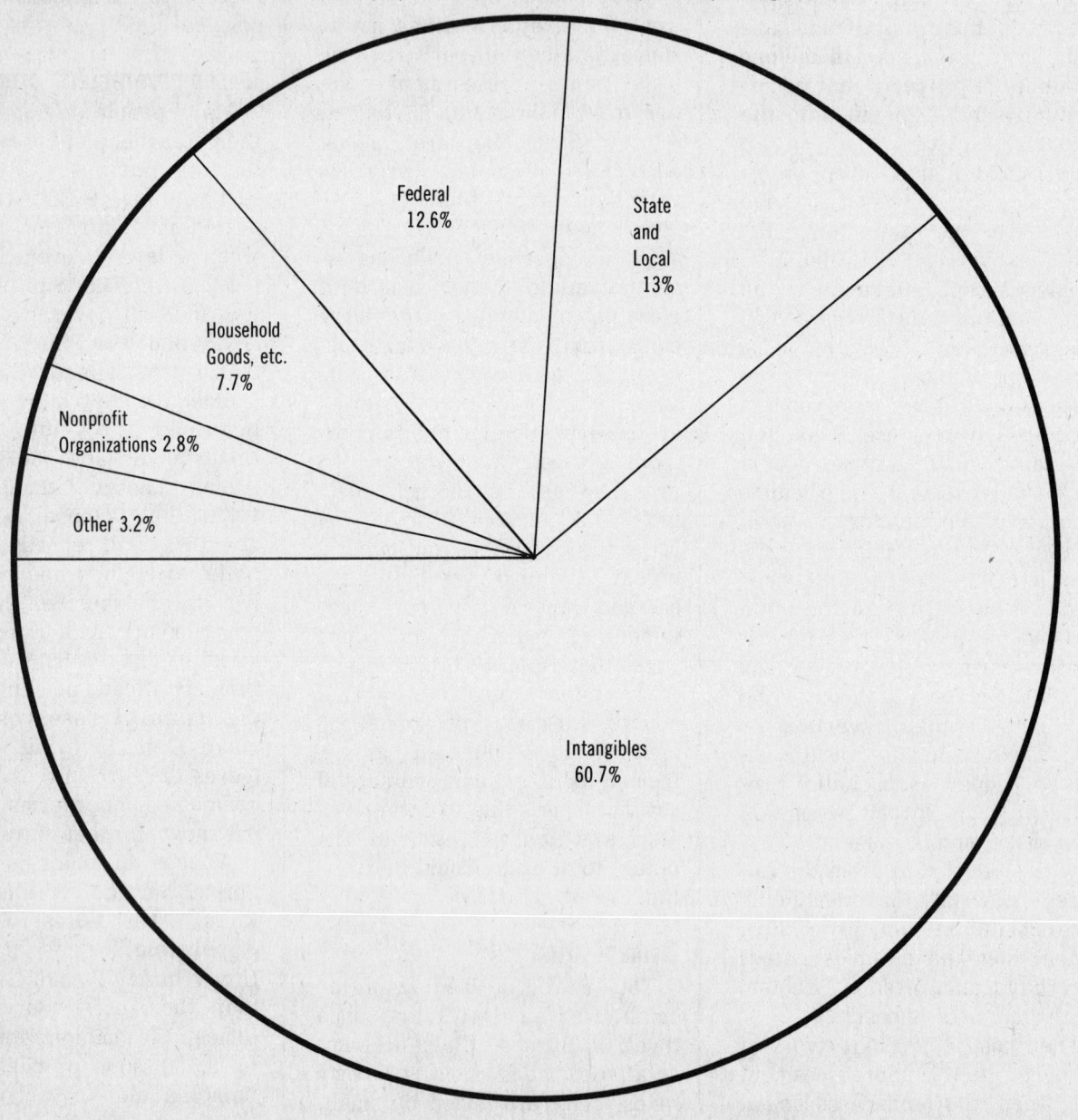

- Federal 12.6%
- State and Local 13%
- Household Goods, etc. 7.7%
- Nonprofit Organizations 2.8%
- Other 3.2%
- Intangibles 60.7%

SOURCE: State of Washington Department of Revenue (Footnotes omitted).

Estimated Value of Exempt Property in Washington State Exemption	Year Exemption Granted	Estimated Value (Millions)
I. Public Property		
Federal	1853	$ 4,288.9
State	1889	521.4
County	1889	267.3
Cities and towns	1889	749.1
Public hospital districts	1945	259.3
Port districts	1911	312.2
Public utility districts	1931	791.1
Public schools		
Colleges and universities	1889	547.8
Kindergarten through grade 12	1889	971.3
Fire districts	1933	28.6
Foreign consulates	1967	Negligible
Airport owned by municipal corporations in adjoining state	1941	Negligible
Interstate bridges	1949	None
Total – Public Property		$ 8,737.0
II. Private Property		
Cemeteries	1854	$ 19.8
Churches	1854	340.5
Nonsectarian and youth	1915/1933	55.0
Veterans	1929	6.3
Relief (Red Cross)	1945	0.5
Club libraries	1854	Negligible
Orphanages	1891	4.2
Homes for fallen women	1891	1.3
Retirement and nursing homes	1891	89.9
Hospitals	1886	220.0
Private schools		
Kindergarten through grade 12	1925	83.8
Colleges and universities	1925	119.7
Humane societies	1915	Negligible
Sheltered workshops	1970	7.9
Nonprofit associations providing education and recreation for the public	1967	Negligible
Total – Private Property		$ 948.9

Exemption	Year Exemption Granted	Estimated Value (Millions)
III. Personal Property		
Intangibles	1931	$20,673.0
Household goods/personal effects	1871/1885	2,589.4
$300 head of household	1900	35.2
Ships and vessels		
Under construction	1959	165.0
Interstate or foreign commerce	1931	31.9
Others (pleasure boats)	1931	159.5
Inventory		
Freeport–goods in transit	1961	177.6
Plywood, particle board	1967	Negligible
Ores–metals	1961	65.0
Metals in cathode or bar form	1949	Negligible
Certain agricultural crops		
Original producer	1890	188.3
Processor	1939	177.7
Soil/water conservation districts	1963	0.4
Art, scientific and historical collections	1915	0.1
Total – Personal Property		$24,263.1
IV. Miscellaneous		
Retired persons' $50 credit	1967	$ 53.6
Current land use–open space	1970	None
Air space over public stadium facilities	1967	None
Public right-of-way easements	1947	Negligible
Water distribution cooperatives	1965	Negligible
Steam-generated electricity plant	1957	80.0
Total – Miscellaneous		$ 133.6

(In Billions)
Exempt Property $34.1
Taxable Property $36.0
Total $70.1

this land is leased to large private timber companies which pay a "stumpage fee" for the timber they cut. Local governments get 25 percent of these fees *in lieu* of property taxes, but this share has proven small and unreliable compared to what property taxes would have raised. Kahn estimated that local governments in Appalachia lose about $10 million per year in property taxes because the Forest Service owns so much of their land, and that the stumpage fees make up for less than 10 percent.

Some states have made an effort to subject leased government property to property taxes. They do it by assessing the *leasehold* or *possessing* interest which the lease confers on the private company, since this interest is property just as much as is a deed of title. In California alone, county assessors put onto the tax rolls annually over $100 million worth of leasehold interests in everything from oil fields to ski resorts. Other states have backed away from such action, claiming fear of driving out industry. Former New York Governor Nelson Rockefeller persistently vetoed leasehold-interest tax bills on this ground. Whether the argument is valid for defense plants is dubious; the notion of "driving away" natural resources and their extraction strains belief.

State and local governments also hold property which they lease to private companies. They have developed a special vehicle, the so-called industrial development bond (IDB). The state or locality sells the bond, and uses the proceeds to build an industrial plant, tailormade to a particular company's specifications. The company then leases the plant, and since it technically belongs to the state or locality, it remains tax-exempt. (In some cases the company makes *in lieu* payments, however.)

The industrial development bond began in Mississippi in 1936, and for about thirty years the method was used on a modest scale primarily by southern states to lure industry away from the North. During the 1960s, the use of IDB's mushroomed, largely because corporations, faced with high interest rates, were looking for cheaper cash while competition between states to attract industry was escalating.

As state and local governments found themselves paying ever higher interest rates to borrow for schools, libraries, hospitals, and other genuinely public ventures, even the investment industry was expressing concern at the havoc the bonds were causing in interest rates and in credit markets generally.

The U.S. Congress, in 1968, limited the kinds of bonds that would enjoy a federal income tax exemption. But the Congress left so many loopholes that bond lawyers predicted the market would be more brisk than ever. One of the loopholes was for pollution control facilities, and by 1974, the pollution control loophole among others had caused the outstanding industrial development bonds to exceed an estimated $4-7 billion, several times the level that had caused congressional concern to begin with. Bethlehem Steel alone used about $100 million worth in just two years—investing in government-owned and hence tax-exempt facilities—and it saved between $40 million and $50 million in interest compared to what it would have paid on the regular corporate bond market.

Even when leased government property is supposed to be on the tax rolls, however, it does not always get there. Seattle, Washington, taxpayers learned this lesson several years ago. In March 1971, the *Seattle Times* disclosed that the city was losing millions of dollars because the assessor was being less than thorough. Firms like Lockheed shipbuilding were leasing giant cranes from the Port of Washington, multimillion-dollar floating drydocks from the navy, and other public property; the leases were supposed to be subject to property taxes, but the assessor just hadn't gotten around to it.

Finally, there are the public authorities which wed tax-exempt public bonding powers to grandiose entrepreneurial endeavors with practically no accountability to the public. One finds at the New York Port Authority's Kennedy Airport and at the Massachusetts Port Authority's Logan Airport—to name just two—hotels, restaurants, shops, banks, even industries leasing the tax-exempt property. Redevelopment authorities are notorious for buying up land over the owner's protests and razing it, in behalf of private developers, real estate and business interests.

Churches and universities are often among the wealthiest residents in a community, far more amply endowed than most of the taxpayers who must underwrite their tax exemption. Churches and universities also have pure investment property, such as apartment buildings, office buildings, and even factories, which in some states is tax-exempt even though used for clearly profitmaking purposes in competition with privately owned structures. The towering Chrysler Building in New York, which generates over $7 million per year in rent but which pays no taxes because it belongs to the Cooper Union for the Advancement of Science and Art, is only one prominent example.

an agenda for reform

Much as freeways beget more traffic, property tax exemptions give rise to more exemptions. It is not hard to see why. Once a favor is granted, other groups come rushing forward demanding equal treatment. The result can be seen in California's farmland assessment law. Originally an effort to preserve farmland and open space, it has been extended to oil fields, riding academies, archery ranges, aircraft landing strips, radio and television transmitter sites, one-half-acre single-family homesites, quarries, golf courses, salt ponds, and swamps. The best thing to do about exemptions would be to eliminate them, and to put outright grants and subsidies in their place. The funds would be appropriated in the normal legislative process, so that lawmakers and the public could know how much was spent and who was benefiting. The grants would last for just one or a few years, so there would be a regular review. Substantial savings, equity, and accountability could result. The appropriation process itself, as practiced in state and federal legislatures, is certainly no model of good government. But it offers more hope of accountability than does the current system of perpetual tax exemptions.

This approach is not without difficulty. Would taxpayers agree to replace the exemption system with outright grants? It is customary to predict dire consequences to the politician who would venture upon these waters. Reform will not come easily, and it may be necessary to resort to compromise measures along the way. Here are some steps that would help make exemptions more tolerable and would help eliminate abuses.

make exemptions a budget item

At present, legislatures enact exemptions and forget about them. They do not worry about where the revenues to pay for them will come from, nor whether the exemption is really doing what it is supposed to do. Excusing certain taxes is just as much an expenditure of the public revenue as is any other appropriation. Hence, the amount the legislature has spent on tax exemptions should be computed each year and appear in the budget. This will make both lawmakers and the public aware of these outlays. The state of California and the U.S. Treasury Department have both adopted this *tax expenditure budget* concept.

base exemptions on need

Blanket exemptions for entire classes of institutions or persons are a massive waste of public revenues. An institution is not needy because it is a church, a university, a country club, or a veterans organization. Individuals are not needy because they are homeowners, farmers or elderly. Institutions and people are needy if and when they are needy. And tax relief should be granted on this basis alone.

When exemption benefits go to all property owners of a given class, regardless of need, needy people are often bypassed. Small and struggling religious bodies, schools, and similar organizations often must rent quarters because they cannot afford to buy. They may get no relief at all when exemptions benefit only people who own property. This is also true for people who rent their homes, even though between 15 and 25 percent of their rents go to pay property taxes, and even though renters tend to be less well-off then homeowners. Small businesses normally get no relief from exemptions, but they may need relief much more than wealthy homeowners who enjoy homestead exemptions.

One method for targeting relief where it is most needed is called the "circuit breaker." Variations of the circuit breaker had been enacted in twenty-two states by 1974. Whenever a taxpayer's property tax burden becomes excessive, typically defined as a certain percentage of their income, the state steps in and picks up the overburden. Some states do so through a credit to the state income tax, the taxpayer receiving a rebate if their circuit-breaker relief due is greater than their state income tax. Other states send the circuit-breaker relief check right to the taxpayer. Some states limit circuit-breaker relief to elderly homeowners. Other states include renters and/or overburdened property taxpayers generally.

One weakness of the circuit breakers has been the test used to determine when the tax burden is excessive. Income is just one portion of taxpaying ability. There are many wealthy people who manage to show little or no income. Surely they should not be rewarded with property tax relief for their skill in avoiding income taxes. At the very least, income for circuit-breaker purposes should include any and all gains, regardless of federal income tax loopholes. Better still, the test would take account of net worth as well.

The circuit-breaker concept has never been applied to institutions—churches, universities, etc. But there is no reason why it could not be. A suitable test of need could be devised. At the very least, there should be a ceiling on the exemption benefits which such institutions enjoy.

payments in lieu of taxes

As an alternative to or in combination with a limited exemption, institutions would pay a service charge to compensate the locality for public services used—such as street and fire protection. Some institutions make such payments voluntarily—Harvard University and MIT in Cambridge, Massachusetts, and the Christian Science Church in Boston, are notable examples. Most institutions have resisted such moves, however, so legislation will be necessary.

Private businesses which lease public property should be required to pay the equivalent of state and local property taxes as a condition of their lease. Federal and state officials could adopt this policy on their own, but legislation is needed to make sure it is applied uniformly and across the board. The U.S. Congress could enact a law requiring all leases of federal property to pay the equivalent of state and local property taxes as a condition of their lease.

eliminate tax havens

Owners of vast natural resource property, power plants and large industrial plants frequently pay little or no property tax because the property is located in remote rural areas or in specially created tax-havens. These de facto exemptions can be eliminated by imposing a minimum statewide rate on all high-value commercial, industrial and natural resources.

farmland and open space

Over the last twenty-five years the number of farms in the United States has declined from 5.4 million to 2.9 million. The *Wall Street Journal* reported in 1971 that urban sprawl is wiping out 1.5 million acres of farmland a year. If cropland continued to be lost at the 1964-69 rate, there would be none left in one hundred years.

The losses have been even more striking in particular states and regions. California has been losing an estimated 375 acres to development daily. That is the equivalent of 600 generous-sized homes or ten giant discount stores every day. New Jersey, though still calling itself "America's Garden State," has lost about 44 percent of its farmland since 1950, and the federal government predicts that in fifty years only 8 percent of the state will be in farms. Around Washington, D.C., the development since 1960 of Maryland and Virginia farms, forests, and open lands, has exceeded an area twice the size of the District itself. Massachusetts has lost one-half of its farmland in the last twenty-five years.

High agricultural prices and interest rates have combined to slow this trend temporarily. But in the long run, no curbing of our destruction of food-producing land is in sight.

Farm property taxes almost doubled as a percentage of farm income between 1950 and 1968, and the United States Department of Agriculture reports that today the average farmer pays 7.7 percent of his personal income in property taxes, while the average homeowner pays 4.4 percent. In suburban areas, where land values are higher, the farmer's taxes are much higher than the national average. Farmland values have gone up over 9 percent per year during the last seven years, and the increase between 1973 and 1974 was more than 15 percent. Farmers, and others with large landholdings but small cash incomes, often find themselves hard-pressed to pay their taxes, and sell their land.

The connection between rising property taxes and the loss of farmland seems to be so clear that efforts to preserve farmland and open space have centered on property tax breaks for their owners. The reasoning is that farm operations cannot support property taxes which are levied on normal "fair market value" assessments. The solution appeared simple: change the standard for assessments. Permit assessments based on the value of the land for *farm use* only, as though developers and speculators were not interested in it. Thus the name "use-value" assessment. This is what the special farmland tax laws have done.

In some states land other than farmland can qualify for the breaks: forest land, "horticultural" land, marsh land, flood plains, quarries, and land of scenic beauty.

To lower taxes, three main types of assessment breaks have been enacted.

current-use, use-value or preferential assessment

In some states any land that meets normally broad standards can receive a special use-value assessment regardless of where it is and who owns it. The land may have to be a minimum size (five acres in Delaware), produce a minimum amount of crops ($500 worth in New Jersey), and/or have been in farm use for a minimum number of years. Owners who later sell the land for development or develop it themselves incur no penalty and are not responsible for paying back any of the taxes they avoided. This is key: under simple use-value assessment there is no deterrent to development. It is a free gift to the landowner.

deferred taxation or use-value assessment with rollback

In other states the taxes are not completely forgiven. Instead they are *deferred*. Landowners get the use-value assessment as long as they keep their land undeveloped. But when they sell their land for development, or change its use, either they or the buyer have to pay back part of the property taxes they avoided through the low assessment. This rollback pays back the community for the taxes it excused in vain; and deters the owner from developing the land.

In practice, however, the rollback is usually too weak to do either. In New Jersey, a landowner who takes a farmland assessment break and then sells his land or develops it has to pay a maximum of only two years' avoided taxes, plus regular property taxes for the current year. Similarly, in Minnesota the maximum rollback for agricultural land is three years. In some states the rollback includes interest; in others, not. Connecticut takes a slightly different approach. Instead of a rollback, Connecticut imposes a transfer tax at the time of sale. The tax is 10 percent for land held only one year. But it phases out gradually so that there is no tax at all when land held over ten years is sold.

restrictive agreement

In some states a landowner seeking a special use-value assessment must sign an agreement promising not to develop the land for a period of years— ten in California, Hawaii, and Washington, eight in New York State. In some cases, such as Pennsylvania, California, and Hawaii, land must be designated for farm or open-space use on a local land-use plan in order to qualify. Penalties are normally severe for landowners who break the contract. Also, landowners who choose not to renew their contract may be subject to rollback taxes. In Hawaii the owner of benefited land who changes its use must pay back all the taxes avoided even if the contract has expired.

As mentioned, commonly there are requirements concerning acreage, agricultural production, income, and/or inclusion in a local plan for use-value assess-

160 TAX POLITICS

ments. Perversely these can exclude genuine small property owners who want to keep their land unspoiled, while favoring large corporate and conglomerate landholders who have the land mainly for speculation and could probably afford the taxes anyway. In some states the local government can decide whether or not to include particular parcels of land (California). California compensates local governments for part of the property tax revenues lost through the assessment cuts, but in most states local taxpayers have to bear this cost themselves.

Another form of assessment break for farmers is the *classified property tax* system discussed in Chapter 7. Under this system property is assessed at different percentages of full value, according to type, and farmland is always at the bottom of the scale. Under classified property taxes the assessment break goes to all farmland, regardless of where it is and who owns it. And of course there is no penalty if the owner sells it or changes its use.

do assessment breaks work?

Even as the use-value assessment programs have spread from state to state, the verdict on them has been clear: they do not work. They have, to be sure, granted temporary property tax relief to some small farmers and rural landowners, perhaps keeping them on the farm a bit longer than they would stay otherwise. But in fulfilling the promises made to voters that they would preserve farmland and open space, they have been failures. New Jersey was losing a larger proportion of its farms each year after its farmland assessment program was enacted in 1965 than before. Even the executive secretary of the New Jersey Farm Bureau, a big booster of the law, had to admit, "whether (it) has been really effective in slowing conversion of farmland to other uses is debatable." In Connecti-

FIGURE 45. STATES WITH DIFFERENTIAL FARMLAND ASSESSMENT PROVISIONS, JANUARY 1, 1973

State	Preferential Assessment	Deferred Taxation	Contracts and Agreements
Alaska		X	
Arkansas	X		
California			X
Colorado	X		
Connecticut		X	
Delaware	X		
Florida	X		
Hawaii			X
Illinois		X	
Indiana	X		
Iowa	X		
Kentucky		X	
Maine		X	
Maryland		X	
Massachusetts			
Minnesota		X	
Nebraska			
New Hampshire		X	
New Jersey		X	
New Mexico	X		
New York		X	
Oregon		X	
Pennsylvania			X
Rhode Island		X	
South Dakota	X		
Texas		X	
Utah		X	
Vermont			X
Virginia		X	
Washington			X
Total	8	15	5

SOURCE: U.S. Department of Agriculture, Rural Development Service.

cut, land near urban areas has been dropping out of the state's farmland assessment program. After a visit to Maryland to witness the results of that state's farmland assessment program, noted conservationist William Whyte wrote in his book *The Last Landscape*:

as far as the eyes could see... preferential assessment was not saving open space. Maryland counties were being developed at about the same rate and the same fashion as suburban counties elsewhere; subdivisions were going up in the usual scattered pattern and to judge from the "for sale" signs that were to be seen on farms, the scattered pattern was certainly going to continue.

A candid state official in Rhode Island replied to a U.S. Senate survey by saying that the farmland assessment law there "is largely ineffective in preserving open space, but does provide a tax shelter for land speculators."

It would be bad enough if the farmland assessment programs simply had failed to preserve open space. In fact, they have often intensified development pressures. By encouraging speculators to hold close-in land off the market temporarily, developers have been encouraged to go deeper into the countryside in search of land they can afford. The area of development expands and once the roads and utilities have been extended out to these hinterlands, the closer-in land is doomed. In California, by removing the lower grade farmlands from potential development, the assessment breaks have actually focused development pressures on the state's best and most vulnerable lands.

The assessment breaks have made farm real estate a choice investment for developers and all kinds of corporations with extra cash. These bid ever more eagerly for the available land, causing assessments and thus property taxes to increase. The high prices in turn entice more genuine farmers into selling. And as more land is enrolled into the farmland assessment programs, local governments try to attract business and industry to make up for the lost revenues—causing the tax breaks to encourage the very thing they are supposed to prevent.

Finally the farmland assessment laws act as a narcotic, lulling people into thinking that the countryside is safe and that all is well. They heard the grand promises that attended passage of the programs. They see pretty farms, unaware that developers have simply leased them to farmers in order to qualify for the assessment break, while they are waiting for the land value to peak. By the time the bulldozers move in, it is too late to do anything to stop them.

As to the rollback penalties, a Maryland assessor computed that speculators actually would come out better with the rollback tax penalty, since this tax replaced the former transfer tax. A Connecticut assessor reckoned that a speculator who held a parcel more than five years would come out ahead after paying that state's special penalty tax. A land speculator described New Jersey's two-year deferred tax penalty by saying that "It ain't nothing."

Not even the binding ten-year contracts required by the Williamson Act in California have kept open lands green. The landowners who expect to sell their land soon simply do not enroll in the program. Speculators—especially large land-development conglomerates—whose development plans encompass ten to thirty years or more, can sign up, get the tax benefits, and then develop the land on schedule after the contract has expired.

Al Parsell, nurseryman and self-styled "swamp Yankee" in Westport, Connecticut, says he doesn't intend to sell any of his land unless he has to at retirement. It has been in his family for 115 years, and he has lived on it with his wife for 51. "I'll tell you that if it weren't for [the farmland assessment law] all this land would go on the market," Parsell says. The proponents of the farmland assessment laws delight in parading honest agrarians like Parsell before the public. But, much as one would like to think otherwise, such yeomen are a tiny minority. "I'm going to farm as long as I can, then sell out at a good profit and retire" is the way an associate planner in Contra Costa County, California, described the attitude of the typical prime-land farmer.

A look at the assessment rolls shows how heavily speculators and corporate sodbusters—as opposed to Farmer Browns—are benefiting from the use-value

162 TAX POLITICS

assessment laws. A moment's reflection suggests why. Before values start escalating, the laws aren't needed. By the time they are, the developers are already in on the action. In New Jersey, a study by the Princeton-based Center for the Analysis of Public Issues showed that International Utilities Corporation (IUC) and Levitt and Sons are getting big tax cuts on thousands of acres under the state's farmland assessment law. In one township, a subsidiary of the Atlantic City Electric Co. has been getting an assessment break of 90 percent per year on a 182-acre tract for which it has had approval to build a planned unit development since 1969. According to Senate testimony, the huge Humble Oil Refinery in Linden, New Jersey, has put 303 acres under the special assessment program.

Of all the corporate land-subsidy programs disguised as property tax breaks for farmers, California's is probably the largest. In 1971 it encompassed over 9.5 million acres, an area larger than New Jersey, Rhode Island, and Connecticut put together, comprising one-quarter of the agricultural land in the state. In 1970 over one-fifth of the land affected by the Williamson Act was held by only ten companies, including Tejon Ranch (Los Angeles Times), Southern Pacific, Kern County Land (Tenneco), Standard Oil of California, the Irvine Co., and Getty Oil. (The second ten on the list are more of the same.) These ten top needy farmers received almost $5 million that year in property tax reductions.

use-value assessments—what are the costs?

Paying the largely corporate landowners while they wait to develop their land is costing state and local taxpayers millions of dollars directly. The indirect costs probably run into the billions.

These are costs the local taxpayers must bear. As millions of suburbanites have learned from sad experience, they could almost tell without looking out the window how rapidly the remaining local farmland is being ranch-housed. They need only look at their property tax bill. Ventura County, California, once estimated that by 1980 local farmers would be paying $15.7 million in property taxes while receiving only $0.4 million in services. (The study apparently omitted, however, the biggest service of all that farmers receive: the increased value of their land, accruing from public expenditures, which they did not realize immediately.) By contrast, the county found that residential areas would cost $96.9 million in services while bringing in only $39.7 million in taxes.

Newcomers moving to these sprawling suburbs have to share the costs, right along with the older residents. They have to pay more for their homes, since the use-value assessment laws enable landowners to hold out until they can get a higher price. Even when such landowners have to pay a "rollback" penalty, in today's tight housing market the levy just gets passed along to the housing consumer. New home-buyers also have the costs—in time as well as money—of long commutes and of general dependence on the automobile. At this writing these costs are not becoming less.

what do we need to do to save farmland and open space?

The basic problem with the use-value assessment laws is that they deal only with the symptoms of development pressures. We bribe the owners of open land not to develop it. Then we sit back, cross our fingers, and hope they won't. But the bribe works only as long as no one comes along offering a better deal. Any effective plan to save farmland and open space must somehow counterbalance the forces that drive up land values.

getting at the source

Three *federal programs* —highways, housing-subsidies, and income tax loopholes—are fueling much of the rush for land that is driving up values and property taxes. The federal highway program has devoured about 100,000 acres per year. Where highways go, housing developments, shopping centers, industrial parks, gas stations, and Burger Kings are soon to follow.

Federal housing policies—and FHA-insured loans in particular—have been heavily biased toward new single-family homes in the suburbs. The overall effect of government housing programs since 1934 has been to construct thirteen homes in the suburbs for every public housing unit built in the center cities.

The federal income tax laws encourage speculators to buy up land, let highways and other publicly financed projects pump up its value, and then sell it and be taxed only at the 50 percent "capital gains" rate. Capital gains often can be combined neatly with the special tax breaks for farmers and tax loss farming. Property taxes and mortgage interest deductions help create the market for houses.

★

Farmers are using more *machinery* to farm efficiently, a trend encouraged by the U.S. Department of Agriculture. To justify the cost, farmers have to expand their operations. High farmland values put the purchase of land often beyond their reach and the farmers opt to rent land from a corporation. Thus the use of more machinery helps create a demand for leased land that encourages corporate land buying.

★

Roads, water, and sewer programs in large measure determine which property is developed and which landowners become rich. They can drive up the land value so that the farmer can no longer afford the property taxes. *Front footage assessments* drive the nail into the coffin. They are a fee the local government levies on landowners for sewers, water mains or sidewalks that run past or across their property, supposedly because these *improvements* enhance the property's value. A charge per foot of a sewer running alongside acres of farmland can run into thousands of dollars.

★

Developers and speculators also can drive farmers off the land by using their influence to change property tax assessments. Pressuring the local government to perform a *revaluation* is one way this is done. Another is to buy a small parcel of rural land at far more than it is worth. The assessor, looking at that sale, assumes that all the land in that area is actually worth that much. He hikes the farmers' assessments, and the "For Sale" signs go up soon thereafter.

★

State and local governments often harass farmers with or without the encouragement of developers. They cut through their land with highways, sewers, gas mains, and power lines, disrupting farm operations so much that the farmer just throws in the towel. Painful experiences with the government's right of *eminent domain* have conditioned many farmers to bristle at the suggestion of "planning" or interference of any kind with their land.

★

In short, increased property taxes are just a symptom of the bundle of policies and pressures that are causing the demise of farmland and open space. Nevertheless, they are critical not only for individual farmers, they are a definite inconvenience to speculators. They impose a cost on holding the land until the profit potential peaks, which cuts into ultimate profits and possibly even forces an owner to sell before he wants to. Thus it comes as no surprise that in some states the big-farm and real estate lobbies have financed expensive campaigns to win voter approval of tax-break referendums. The New Jersey campaign, which went under the slogan "Save Open Space in New Jersey," was staffed by top professionals on leave from two agribusiness concerns. In California some of the largest property owners in the state contributed heavily to the 1966 campaign to pass "Proposition 3," a constitutional amendment allowing the state legislature to enact special low assessments for farmland. A California property tax break for exclusive private golf courses, approved by the voters, was similarly decoyed by the slogan "Keep California Green."

federal, state, and local inheritance taxes

These are based on the fair market-value of the property. People who inherit farmland get caught in the dilemma of either having to sell the land to pay taxes, or else having to go deeply into debt. Congress is considering legislation under which federal estate taxes would be based on the value of the land for farm use. But unless they provide for a recapture with interest of the estate tax forgiven if the land is put to non-farm use, such a law would only encourage wealthy individuals to avoid estate taxes by buying up farmland that could be developed later.

alternative measures

taxes and fees

Paying landowners not to develop their land has not worked. We need to try the opposite approach and impose costs on those who do. This is hardly confiscatory or unjust. Land grows in value largely because of roads, sewers, subways, and other projects the public pays for. In addition, new developments thrust greater burdens upon local taxpayers.

One way to tax development is to charge a stiff fee when owners want to develop open space or have it rezoned for more intense use. Another is to require developers to provide streets, sewers, and other "infrastructure," as well as land for parks and schools, so that the burden of paying for these does not fall on the local taxpayers. A third approach is to subject developers to business license fees, based on the number of units they construct and the land area they consume.

Still another approach is a tax on real estate transactions. Vermont levies a "land gains tax" on sales of all property except single-family homes (including a farm homestead and the acreage around it). The tax is graduated so that the shorter the period the seller owned the property and the larger the profit, the greater the rate of tax.

Similar measures were introduced in 1974–75 in the California, Montana, Hawaii, Washington and Illinois legislatures. The District of Columbia is at this writing considering a tax to deter speculation in inner-city neighborhoods. Howard Samuels of New York estimated during his 1974 gubernatorial campaign that the state would take in an extra $1.2 billion per year if it taxed at 25 percent the land-value increases due to rezoning. The Vermont tax raised $1.2 million in 1974, the first year it was in effect. The legislature had earmarked this revenue for property tax relief. More important, "it has indeed slowed down heretofore unbridled and rampant quick turnovers of land," according to Vermont Governor Thomas P. Salmon. And the state has had no major problems enforcing the tax. Key, says Vermont Tax Commissioner Robert Lathrop, is that the tax be collected at the point of sale, like a sales tax.

development controls

In the past these have not been effective. The main land-use control has been zoning, which has melted like butter under special-interest influence and pressure. Even more effective land-use controls can only go so far. At some point they collide with the last clause of the Fifth Amendment to the U.S. Constitution: "nor shall private property be taken for public use without just compensation." The courts have loosened up somewhat as they realize that the health, safety, and welfare of a community depend on how land is used. Still, in some cases the public must either compensate the owner or back off. Given the prices of land and the lack of public funds, it usually means the latter.

For this reason a plan based on the concept of *development rights* holds special promise. It provides compensation to owners who give up the right to develop their property. Yet it works completely within the private-market system and costs the taxpayers hardly a penny. Instead of zoning controls which try to regulate the development of each parcel of property, a total amount of development is allotted to an entire area. This total pie of development rights is sliced up among the different owners according to the amount of property owned. The owner who wanted to develop intensely would have to buy up development rights from his neighbors. Their land, in turn, would remain in open space, and they would be compensated for their loss. Since their land could not now be developed, the property tax assessment would be in effect a use-value assessment, even if there were no official program by that name.

It is possible to carry the idea a step further. The public could establish agricultural preserves, or otherwise decide where development could and could not take place. Owners in the restricted areas would receive development rights which they could not use but could sell to owners in less restricted areas. These latter owners could then develop their own land more fully. The end result is the same: open space is preserved, the landowners are compensated, and its done without dipping into the taxpayers' pockets.

The development rights approach derives from the way royalties were parceled out among the various property owners when oil was discovered beneath city blocks in midwestern and southwestern cities. It has been proposed as a bill to the Maryland State Senate by State Senator William J. Goodman.

A similar way to compensate owners when land-use restrictions reduce the monetary value of their property was developed by Professor Donald G. Hagman of the UCLA Law School. Called "windfalls and wipeouts," it is based on the simple fact that some property owners benefit—get windfalls—from public actions, while other owners get wiped out. The owner of land next to a new subway stop, highway interchange, or urban renewal area reaps an enormous gain without lifting a finger. The farmer who finds his land zoned strictly for agricultural use, on the other hand, loses the value a developer might have paid.

In the past, public action has been remiss on both counts. It did nothing to recapture the windfall it created. And it has tried to get land-use control on the cheap, without compensating the owners. Windfalls and wipeouts are a natural way out of this dilemma. Tax the windfalls and use the revenues to compensate property owners who have suffered wipeouts.

One of the most potent levers for land-use control is one the public often forgets: the placement of roads, sewers, and utilities. Developers and speculators are well aware of these and get into the act on the ground floor—often by becoming the officials who do the planning.

An even more potent control is an absolute freeze on farmland development. The Canadian province of British Columbia was losing farmland so rapidly that in 1973 it took this firm step, setting up a five-member land commission with the power to restrict land to agricultural use alone.

Another alternative is for the public to *purchase* farm- and open-space lands. This is expensive and is becoming more so. New methods are reducing the costs, however. One such approach is the purchase of development rights, often called *scenic* or *open space easements*. If the goal is simply to preserve open space, and not acquiring recreation areas, the public has no need to purchase all the rights to a property—what lawyers call the *fee*. The current owner can stay on the land, use it as before, or sell it. All he loses is the right to develop, and for this he is fully compensated.

A few states have begun to purchase scenic easements. A Wisconsin study showed that the cost of the program in that state averaged $20 per acre. Suffolk County, on Long Island, New York, has committed itself to spend $15 million over each of the next four years to purchase scenic easements.

The natural resources director of Bucks County, Pennsylvania, has been mulling over a way to turn the easements idea on its head, so as not only to preserve open space, but to generate funds for the program through the program itself. Suppose the county were putting together a conservation district by purchasing easements, and some owners refused to sell. The county might buy their entire fee interest, gaining complete ownership of the property and then sell it in one or more parcels, minus the development rights. This official speculated that enough people would like to live and/or farm in a conservation district, absolutely protected against development, that the county might well be able to sell the land, without the development rights, for more than it cost in the first place.

Land banking is a second and closely related way to reduce the costs to the public of purchasing land. The public sets up a fund and purchases undeveloped land before speculation drives the price beyond reach. As the acreage in the land bank grows larger, the public has several options. It can set part or all of the land aside for a public use—such as a courthouse, schools, or parks. Or it can lease or sell the land, achieving in the process two important goals. One is the generating of revenue, possibly for further land purchases. The second is the guiding of development into the desired areas, which it achieves both through *selecting* the land that is released and the uses that are permitted on that land. In 1974 Fairfax County, Virginia, put $2 million into its land banking fund, $200,000 of which was for its Redevelopment Housing Authority. The county is hoping to purchase as much land as possible before the new Metro

166 TAX POLITICS

rapid transit system, now under construction, sends land values climbing out of sight.

Another method simply applies the circuit breaker idea, to owners of farm and open-space land. Whenever the property tax bill overloads the taxpayer, taking more than a given percent of his income, the state picks up the difference. At this writing, only Michigan has enacted a special farm circuit breaker. To qualify, the landowner must contract not to develop the land for ten years. If the owner lets the contract expire without renewing, he must pay seven years' worth of the back taxes he missed, without interest. The circuit-breaker approach has several advantages. It gives relief only to genuine farmers of modest means, and so bypasses some of the problems posed when absentee speculators exploit use-value assessment programs. It gives relief only according to actual need. The state, and not the local taxpayers, bears the burden. And unlike the use-value assessment programs, it imposes no extra burdens on already overworked assessors.

Another approach involves *agricultural districts*. Under a recent New York law, farmers in an area can establish such a district voluntarily. Once they do, they receive benefits such as protection from roads, power lines, sewers, and from public service district taxes. Since such incursions often are to blame for increasing land values and property taxes, their absence alone should keep property taxes in the districts low. Extra assessment relief is available nevertheless to farmers who want it.

paying for schools

Local property taxes are the basis of public school financing in most of the states, providing close to half of school revenues. To these, the state governments have added two main types of aid, *flat grants* per pupil and *equalizing grants* which supposedly help the neediest school districts the most. These equalizing state grants total over 40 percent of school revenues today. The federal government comes in with another 7 percent.

While some 57 percent of all local collections go to schools, according to 1969-70 data, some state governments play a much larger role than others in paying for education. For example:

	% of state-local property taxes paying for education 1969-70
Arkansas	72.2%
California	51.7%
District of Columbia	34.3%
Massachusetts	51.0%
Oklahoma	77.7%
Tennessee	38.5%

There is also a large difference in the portion of property taxes going to education between urban and rural areas. In the latter, including some suburbs, normally a very high percentage of property taxes goes to schools, because the local governments do not perform many other functions.

The result of basing school funding programs on local property taxes is that the resources available to pay for a child's education depend on an accident—the amount of taxable property in the locality in which the child lives. The taxes which a locality must levy to provide this education depend upon the same accident. Wealthy suburban school districts with large amounts of taxable property, relatively few children, and few service demands competing with education for the property tax dollar can tax themselves lightly and still raise more funds per schoolchild than can districts that are less well-off, even if the latter tax themselves much more heavily. (At the same time, the system gives these suburban districts an incentive to keep out low-income families and their children so as not to dilute their advantage.)

The cities find themselves in a special bind, known by the technical name of *municipal overburden*. They must spend unusual amounts on children who lack advantages at home. The costs of running schools are higher in the cities, as are living costs generally, from teacher salaries to vandalism to insurance to costs of land for new schools. While buffeted on the one side by high school costs, the cities must spread each property tax dollar out over many more nonschool services than the suburbs have to provide. The issue is not one of center cities versus suburbs, however. In fact, many center cities are better off than are poorer suburbs and rural areas. The cities have more commercial and industrial property to tax, and many have won from their state legislatures the power to tax sales and/or income and to tap other sources of revenue.

What of the state equalizing grants? The details of these programs, and the formulas for dispensing them, vary considerably. But most of them are so full of "ceilings," "floors," and compromises to the better-off districts that they close the revenue gaps between wealthy and the poor districts to a very limited degree, if at all. In fact, they can have just the opposite effect. The major part of the Texas "Minimum Foundation Program," for example, subsidizes the salaries of more highly qualified teachers regardless of where they are teaching. As school finance authority Joel D. Berke points out in Answers to Inequality, "(T)he wealthier school districts have the capacity to hire the better teachers and receive more state aid for doing so."

Thus, federal aid programs have been too small and too mixed in their impact to make up for the disparities in the state systems. One can see the overall effect in Bexar County (San Antonio), Texas, where the county's wealthiest school district, Alamo Heights, actually received more state aid per pupil than did the poorest — Edgewood. Alamo Heights, moreover, could raise $333 per pupil from its local property tax, while Edgewood raised only $26, reflecting the

FIGURE 46. CITY-STATE COMPARISON OF PROPORTION OF EXPENDITURES USED FOR EDUCATION, 1969–1970

Percent of Total Local Expenditures Spent for Education

	City-area	All local government in state
NORTHEAST		
Baltimore, Md.	34%	49%
Boston, Mass.	26	45
Newark, N.J.	28	44
Paterson-Clifton-Passaic, N.J.	34	44
Buffalo, N.Y.	34	33
New York, N.Y.	20	33
Rochester, N.Y.	31	33
Philadelphia, Pa.	35	54
Pittsburgh, Pa.	34	54
Providence, R.I.	35	51
MIDWEST		
Chicago, Ill.	30	47
Indianapolis, Ind.	41	54
Detroit, Mich.	37	50
St. Paul-Minneapolis, Minn.	29	48
Kansas City, Mo.	33	52
St. Louis, Mo.	30	52
Cincinnati, Ohio	23	45
Cleveland, Ohio	39	45
Columbus, Ohio	33	45
Dayton, Ohio	38	45
Milwaukee, Wisc.	29	40
SOUTH		
Miami, Fla.	37	48
Tampa-St. Petersburg, Fla.	42	48
Atlanta, Ga.	39	48
Louisville, Ky.	23	56
New Orleans, La.	36	51
Dallas, Texas	39	52
Houston, Texas	45	52
San Antonio, Texas	43	52
WEST		
Los Angeles-Long Beach, Cal.	28	35
San Bernardino-Riverside-Ontario, Cal.	37	35
San Diego, Cal.	33	35
San Francisco-Oakland, Cal.	23	35
Denver, Colo.	34	47
Portland, Ore.	39	53
Seattle-Everett, Wash.	29	52
Average	**33%**	**46%**

SOURCE: National Urban Coalition

fact that the former had $49,478 worth of property to tax per pupil, while Edgewood had only $5,960. It should be added that only 14 percent of the students in Alamo Heights were from minority groups, and the median family income in 1960 was $8,164. The figures for Edgewood were 75 percent minority students and $3,405 median family income.

We can expect major shifts in the portion of local property taxes going to education. Recent court decisions, and public opinion regarding the inequities they have exposed, are compelling the states to pick up a much larger share. Still, small taxpayers will not necessarily gain from these funding shifts. The funding systems the states adopt to replace local property taxes for schools might just hit the small taxpayer from a different direction: especially if they are based on sales taxes, or on payroll taxes disguised as income taxes.

the lawsuits

A wave of lawsuits has been challenging the way states use the local property tax to finance public education.

Despite widespread publicity, the issues have been widely misunderstood and misrepresented. Thus economist and *Newsweek* columnist Milton Friedman informed his readers, one week in February 1972, that these school-finance lawsuits were ruling that "it is wrong for different communities in a state to spend different amounts per child on public schooling." The lawsuits were, he went on with ideological petulance, "seeking the complete equalization of conditions of life—a homogenized society."

Of course the decisions asserted no such thing, as Mr. Friedman could have learned by simply reading them. In the Texas case called *Rodriguez* v. *San Antonio*, the federal district court had gone out of its way to say so:

> In the instant case plaintiffs have not advocated that educational expenditures be equal for each child.

Similarly, a United States district court in Minnesota had said in *Van Dusartz* v. *Hatfield*:

> Neither this case nor Serano (a California case) requires absolute uniformity of school expenditures.

Nor were the court decisions calling for the abolition of property taxes, as others had claimed amidst dire warnings of the end of "local control" and impending takeover by "big brother."

More discussion of these school financing rulings is available in the Bibliographical Note. Here we are concerned with the possible paths for reform.

school finance reform: the options

The court decisions have not been directly about property taxes. They have condemned any state-devised system that makes the resources available to pay for a child's education depend on the wealth of the child's locality.

The decisions do not in any way spell the demise of property taxes though they may encourage changes in the share of local property taxes going to public education.

There appear to be three main directions for school finance reform:

full state funding

The states could take over the entire cost of public education — as Hawaii has done — leaving

FIGURE 47. THE RELATIONSHIP BETWEEN DISTRICT WEALTH AND SCHOOL REVENUES IN BEXAR COUNTY, TEXAS

Selected school districts ranked from high to low by assessed market valuation per pupil	Local	State	Local and state	Federal	Total: local, state, and federal
Alamo Heights	$333	$225	$558	$36	$594
North East	182	233	415	58	468
San Antonio	134	219	353	69	422
North Side	114	248	362	81	443
Harlandale	73	250	323	71	394
Edgewood	26	222	248	108	356

Revenues per Pupil

SOURCE: Joel S. Berke, *Answers to Inequity* (Berkeley, Calif: McCutchan, 1974).

control of the schools with the local school districts. Revenues might come from a statewide property tax replacing local school property taxes, income taxes, sales taxes, and/or other revenue sources. One proposal is to impose a statewide property tax on commercial and industrial property only.

more adequate state compensation for inequities in local resources and funding

An idea that is much discussed under this category is called *power equalizing*. The state would guarantee that a given amount of local tax *effort* yields a given amount of *revenue* per pupil. This would reduce or end the luxurious position of wealthy districts being able to tax themselves lightly and still raise abundant amounts of revenue compared to poorer districts which tax themselves more heavily.

redrawing school district lines so that the resources available to each are fairly uniform

Given the turmoil that arises from efforts to change school district lines, this alternative does not seem likely, even if its object is to equalize tax revenues rather than to achieve racial balance.

Several states at this writing have revised their school finance programs — among them Florida, Kansas, Utah, Minnesota, and Maine. The details of these plans are complex, but in general they have chosen the second path, greater state equalizing of local revenues, combined with ceilings on local property taxes for schools. In some cases, as in Minnesota, the local taxes have been reduced.

What will reforms along these lines mean? It appears that *rural* taxpayers and schoolchildren will come out ahead, getting more school resources while paying fewer taxes. The poorer suburbs will probably find themselves with similar benefits, while the wealthier suburbs will almost certainly find some of their special advantages diminished.

The school-finance reform movement presents a rare opportunity for property tax reform. It will be a long time before the tax again receives such attention, and before legislators are under the gun to produce change. The opportunity appears to be passing by unclaimed, however. The full dimensions of property tax reform and its revenue potentials have gone unnoticed.

As we saw earlier, a modest tax on intangible property alone could raise one-third of the revenues taxes on other property now provide. Since such a tax would be best administered on the state level, it would be an ideal source to tap for increased state funding for education. Assessment reform, progressive property tax rates, curtailed exemptions, service charges on exempt property, and *in lieu* payments on exempt property of the state and federal governments, are equally promising sources.

A statewide property tax on commercial and industrial property holds potential that may not be apparent on the surface. Not only would the statewide tax eliminate the great disparities between localities that are differently endowed with the property, it would also reduce the intense competition between communities to attract such property and end the self-defeating tax breaks that are offered in the process.

Chapter 7
How Property Taxes Work

who levies the property tax

There are over 65,000 units of government which levy their own property tax. They overlap with close to 15,000 assessing districts. There are fewer assessing districts because one assessor often serves several tax units. The assessor puts a value on property and then a school district, a city, a county, a sanitation district, park district, and perhaps others as well, each use this same assessment as the basis of their tax. The pattern varies considerably from state to state. Hawaii has a single assessment head serving just four taxing authorities, while in North Dakota over 1500 assessing units serve more than 2500 local taxing bodies.

★ ★ ★ ★ ★ ★

Today, the property tax is mainly a local tax. It has not always been so. Until the early years of this century, the states gained most of their revenues from property taxes too. Since then, the states have switched to income, sales, and other taxes, leaving the property tax for the localities. Because the state legislatures create local governments, they decide what taxes localities can use. One argument that is made for keeping property taxes local is that property itself is local, and its value is due to *where* it is as much as *what* it is. In addition, local services such as garbage collection, police protection, and road repair, which are paid for by local taxes, provide special benefits to local property owners.

Though state lawmakers are increasingly giving localities the power to levy income, sales, and other taxes beside property taxes — rural-dominated state legislatures often confine such taxes to the large cities — property taxes remain the major source of local revenues.

what is the property tax

The property tax is a tax on the *value* of property — an *ad valorem* tax. More precisely, it is a tax on the assessed valuation of that property.

The property *tax base* — all the property in a given jurisdiction that is subject to property taxes — consists of two kinds of property. The first is *real estate*, which derives its name from the "Royal Estate" — the crown's property. Real estate was originally something that was basically public and common. That was why the crown, or king, could levy a tax on it. Today we consider as real estate land, buildings, and the equipment and machinery that are essential to the functioning of the buildings. Taxes on real estate are taxes on the property itself, not on the person who owns it. (They are *in rem* — on the thing.) When the tax is due, the taxing body has a *lien* on the property. It can take the property if the tax is not paid, to satisfy the debt. But it cannot go after other assets of the person who owns the property.

The other kind of property in the property tax base is *personal property*. There are two types — tangible and intangible. Tangible personal property includes business machinery and equipment, inventories and household possessions. Intangible property consists of paper assets—stocks, bonds—and invisible business property such as goodwill and monopoly position. Many states, as we have seen, have exempted all or part of personal property. Unlike taxes on real property, personal property taxes are usually *in personam*—on the person who owns the property. If the owner tries to avoid the tax by moving the property away, the locality can seize any of his other property for payment, if necessary.

the property tax calendar

Property taxation is a process which repeats itself every year. Specific events happen on specific dates, and you must know these to protect or assert your rights. Tax calendars vary from jurisdiction to jurisdiction. Here,

How Property Taxes Work 171

for example, are the calendars for Los Angeles and for New York City:

★ FIGURE 48. TAX CALENDARS ★

LOS ANGELES COUNTY TAXPAYER'S GUIDE, 1971-1972

March 1: Taxes become a lien on property at 12:01 A.M. (property is assessed as of its condition on this day).

Assessor starts assessment work for ensuing tax year.

Property owners should file statement with assessor between this date and the last Monday in May, the legal deadline for filing statements.

Unsecured (movable) property tax due and payable to tax collector.

July 1 - June 30: Fiscal (budget) year period covered by tax levies.

First Monday in July: Assessor completes assessment roll.

Third Monday in July: Application period for equalization of assessments (appeals) commences.

August 31: Unsecured property taxes become delinquent, if not paid.

September 1: On or before this date local government fixes tax rate for ensuing tax year.

Fourth Monday in September: Equalization hearings (assessment appeals) commence.

November 1: First installment of taxes due (one-half of realty and all of secured personal).

December 10: First installment of taxes delinquent at 5:00 P.M. (if unpaid).

February 1: Second installment of taxes due (second half of real property).

April 10: Second installment of taxes delinquent at 5:00 P.M. (if not paid).

June 8: On or about this date delinquent tax list published.

June 30: On or about this date delinquent property sold to the state for nonpayment of taxes.

First Monday in February: On or before this date municipalities must file copy of ordinance with the county auditor/controller signifying intention of having county assess and collect taxes for city (if municipality chooses to have county government perform these functions for it). This applies to first year only.

Third Monday in August: On or before this date county auditor/controller must notify municipality of the assessed value of the city for ensuing year, where municipal taxes are collected by the county.

Before September 1: City adopts tax rates and immediately furnishes county auditor/controller with a statement or certified copy of ordinance fixing said rates.

NEW YORK CITY PROPERTY TAX CALENDAR

August 1-January 25: Assessors are in the "field" actually making assessments.

January 25: "Taxable status date" (lien date)—the property is taxed as of its condition on this date.

February 1-March 15: Tentative assessments open for public to inspect.

February 1-May 25: Hearings for taxpayer complaints.

May 25: Final assessments open for public to inspect.

June 20: Assessment rolls delivered to City Council.

June 25: City Council sets tax rate.

June 30: Assessment rolls delivered to City Treasurer.

October 24: Last date for filing Petition to Review (a second, formal appeal).

October 1 and April 1: Tax bills due.

The basic patterns are similar even if details are different. In Los Angeles, the lien date is March 1. In New York, it is January 25. Angelenos pay their property taxes on November 1 and on February 1, while New Yorkers pay on October 1 and April 1.

The tax calendar shows you when you should receive your assessment, the deadline for filing an appeal, and other such matters. If public officials haven't prepared one for your community, they should be asked or pressured to do so. Or a group of taxpayers could study the law and prepare a calendar themselves.

The tax calendar is not an invention of your local officials. The State laws and constitutions say what property is taxed, how and when it should be assessed, even how the assessment rolls should be kept. The tax calendar arises almost totally from these state laws. Localities follow the instructions and set their own tax rate so as to raise the revenue they need.

the property tax calendar and the budget process

The property tax calendar is actually a tributary which flows into the local budget process. The primary reason why assessments, appeals, tax bills and the rest must be completed by set dates, is so that local governments can get their tax revenues in hand and pay their bills. Like the property tax process, the local budget process follows a set calendar, often established in part or totally by the state legislature. In states with strong home rule traditions, localities can set down their own procedures to a greater extent than elsewhere.

In general, the local budget process works as follows. The local legislature has final authority for setting the budget. Several months before it does so, the

172 TAX POLITICS

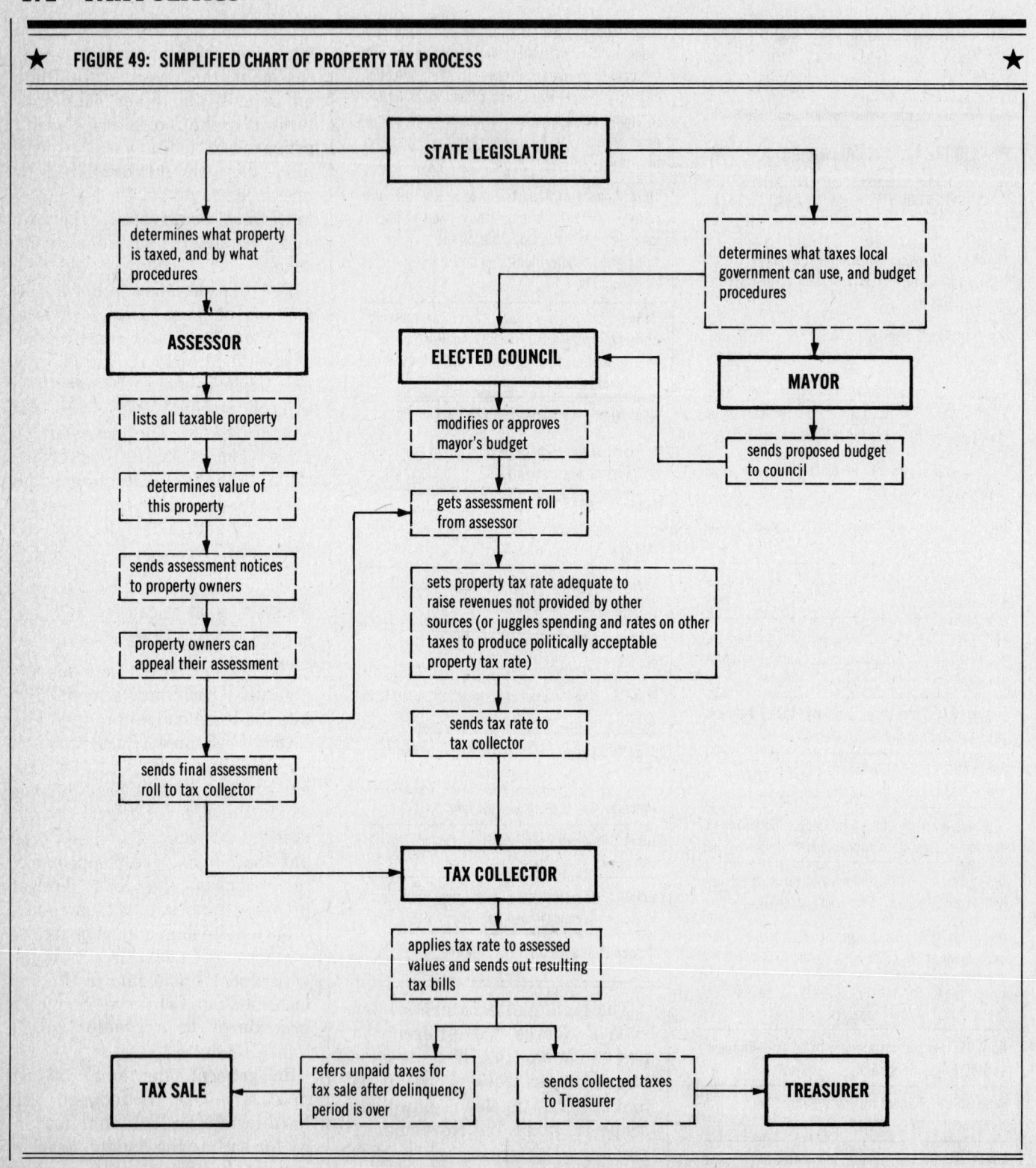

★ **FIGURE 49: SIMPLIFIED CHART OF PROPERTY TAX PROCESS** ★

```
                           STATE LEGISLATURE
                          /                  \
                         /                    \
      determines what property          determines what taxes local
      is taxed, and by what             government can use, and budget
      procedures                        procedures
              |                                   |
              v                                   v
          ASSESSOR          ELECTED COUNCIL <── MAYOR
              |                   |                |
              v                   v                v
      lists all taxable    modifies or approves  sends proposed budget
      property             mayor's budget        to council
              |                   |
              v                   v
      determines value of   gets assessment roll
      this property         from assessor
              |                   |
              v                   v
      sends assessment      sets property tax rate adequate to
      notices to property   raise revenues not provided by other
      owners                sources (or juggles spending and rates on other
              |             taxes to produce politically acceptable
              v             property tax rate)
      property owners can         |
      appeal their assessment     v
              |             sends tax rate to
              |             tax collector
              v                   |
      sends final assessment      |
      roll to tax collector       |
                  \              /
                   v            v
                    TAX COLLECTOR
                         |
                         v
                  applies tax rate to assessed
                  values and sends out resulting
                  tax bills
                       /        \
                      v          v
      TAX SALE <── refers unpaid  sends collected taxes ──> TREASURER
                   taxes for      to Treasurer
                   tax sale after
                   delinquency
                   period is over
```

mayor or executive asks the various departments to submit budgets for the coming year. The mayor's staff then goes over these carefully to hone them down and to make sure they reflect the mayor's priorities. (The Office of Management and Budget—OMB—serves this role at the federal level.)

If the mayor is smart, he or she consults with the local council before submitting a budget to them to avoid embarassing confrontations. When the council gets the suggested budget, it holds public hearings and makes any changes it sees fit. The mayor may have veto power over these changes which the council in turn can override. Even though the council has final say on the budget, the mayor usually has the upper hand. The experts in the mayor's departments spend weeks, possibly months, working up their numbers. The council, with little or no staff, has a few weeks, if that, to review the prodigious balance sheets. Usually it must content itself with across-the-board cuts or guerrilla-type sniping.

All this takes place in the manner of a time-honored ritual. The mayor warns his departments on the tightness of funds, no matter how full the coffers may be. The departments know the mayor is playing this game, so they ignore the crisis rhetoric and ask for whatever increases experience has taught them they can get. When the mayor sends his budget to the council, he embroiders it with adjectives such as "bare-bones" and "austere." This is how he tells the council hands off, and warns that any tampering will result in service cuts and lay-offs for which they will be held responsible. The mayor also wants the public to feel fortunate that it is not being taxed more heavily. Of course, the council makes cuts and the taxpayers scream anyway.

When the budget is final, the property tax rate is set at the level that will raise the necessary revenue. The tax collector sends out the tax bills and the government goes about its business until the budget cycle begins all over again. There are complications, such as revenue shortfalls and supplementary appropriations, but these need not be discussed here.

The budget is an obsession with most local officials. Since property taxes are the prime source of local revenues, they see everything in property tax terms. A new library will add X amount to the millage rate; conversely, a blight of shopping centers or high rise buildings is not an eyesore, or a source of congestion, but a bundle of *ratables* to bolster the property tax base. Even where other revenue sources bulk large, the property tax rate weighs heavily on official minds. "I will not increase the property tax rate" is one of the most frequent—and frequently broken—vows in American politics.

"One of the great arts of the tax game is to design revenue sources so that people will not know they are paying taxes," Arnold Meltsner writes in *The Politics of City Revenue*. "Taxes should not be seen nor felt, only paid." Grants from the state and federal governments, including revenue sharing, rate high on this official pain-avoidance scale. They come from taxes local officials do not levy, and take no blame for. Legalized gambling rates high also. Sales taxes are not quite as painless; still, taxpayers bristle less when they pay in nickles and dimes. Property taxes, with a big bill hitting taxpayers all at one time, are the taxes officials are least fond of. It is not a mystery that cries to abolish the property tax are coming as much from local officials as from local taxpayers.

But property taxes are here, so officials tinker with assessment levels to raise the requisite funds in the politically least risky way. The chronic and often self-defeating search for ratables arises from the effort to raise more revenue without levying more taxes.

The budget calendar often is arranged so that the tax rate is set before the assessments are completed. Rarely are appeals completed before the rate is set. This puts the assessor on the spot to "bring in the values." If his assessments aren't high enough, the tax rate won't produce enough revenue. When mayors vow not to increase the tax rate, it has the same effect on the assessor. Nor do local officials who sit on the assessment review boards like to grant reductions. They also are afraid of wiping out revenues. Later, we look at mass reappraisals as an assessment problem. They, too, frequently stem from budget problems. When local officials want to embark on big new capital improvement programs, such as roads or sewers,

174 TAX POLITICS

they often have to increase the total assessed valuation to be able to sell more bonds, since local bonding power is usually limited to a percentage of assessed property values in the locality.

the tax process

The property tax process has four main steps, which are:

1. Finding and listing taxable property.
2. Assessing, or valuing, the property.
3. Setting the tax rate to apply to this assessed property.
4. Collecting the taxes.

Normally, three different officials, or sets of officials, handle one or more of these steps. The *assessor* finds, lists, and assesses property—steps one and two. The *council* or other elected body makes up the local budget, and then sets a tax rate that will raise enough money to meet that budget—step three. The *tax collector* sends out the tax bills and collects the taxes—step four. (In some places the assessor sends out the tax bills.)

In theory, the assessor is just a lister and appraiser. Normally, he keeps abreast through his own efforts of all the real estate in his jurisdiction, while taxpayers must file reports on their personal property much as they report their income to the IRS. It is true, of course, that a good auditing program is necessary to keep taxpayers honest. If assessors don't have such programs—and they often don't—taxpayers catch on and don't report everything they own. Then the *personal* property tax laws do indeed become a farce.

When the assessor has his list or inventory of property, he has to find the value of it. Except in rare cases where state law sets an arbitrary value on certain kinds of property, the assessor is supposed to determine, as best he can, what the property is really worth—the price a buyer would pay for it.

As soon as the assessor has valued all the property in the locality, property owners should try to find out what their assessments are. This is important because the law provides only a limited time in which to appeal assessments. The laws differ on the notice taxpayers must receive. In some states, the assessor sends out a notice of assessment every year. In others, the taxpayer gets a notice only when his assessment has changed. In still other states the taxpayer gets no notice at all. In New York City, for example, the taxpayer hears nothing about his assessment from the city. Instead, he has to go down to the assessor's office and check for himself. New York taxpayers don't even get a tax bill unless they file a special card with the tax collector. Whether they get the tax bill or not, they still have to pay the taxes.

When appeals are finished, the assessor draws up a final list of assessments. Sometimes this list is called the *certified* assessment roll. The assessor turns the assessment roll over to the local officials who set the budget.

What happens then varies from place to place. If procedures are true to the textbook example, officials will decide how much the locality will spend, and then subtract the amount they will get from other sources: state and federal grants, other local taxes, etc. The property tax will provide the rest, i.e., it is the *residual* tax. Practice is often something else. Officials often adjust their spending to what the property tax and other revenue sources bring in.

There are different ways to express the property tax rate. It can be expressed in *mills*. A mill is one-thousandth of a dollar. Thus a tax rate of 5 mills is half a cent per dollar of assessed value. Or it can be stated in dollars per hundred or per thousand dollars of assessed value.

You may hear mention of an *effective* tax rate. The effective tax rate is the rate you pay on the *full* value of your property. It is usually much less than the *nominal* tax rate. When property is assessed at a fraction of full market value, the nominal tax rate must be high to raise from the fractionated tax base the needed amount of revenue.

Reflecting the nineteenth century state constitutions, property taxes in this country are mainly *flat rate*. Everyone in the same locality pays the same rate, no matter how much their property is worth.

Several states have *tax rate limits*. Usually this is a property tax rate which a local government cannot exceed except under certain conditions, such as when the taxpayers approve. (Often the limits do not apply to interest on debt, however.) Local officials have devised ways to get around these tax rate limits. One way is to increase assessments instead of the tax rate. Another is by setting up *special districts*. Tax rate limits often apply to each separate unit of government rather than to all units together with jurisdiction over the taxpayer. Thus, if a county wants to embark on a big new sewer program, instead of squeezing the sewer program into the county budget, they set up a new unit of government called a *sewer district* which takes a whole new crack at local property taxpayers.

In some states the local budget must be checked by an outside body before it goes into effect. In Massachusetts, for example, the State Department of Taxation checks each local budget, making sure all possible revenue sources have been used. Only then can the local property tax rate become official.

In practice, the tax and budget process is a complex battle. Consider these examples:

The Board of Equalization, controlled by the party opposing the mayor, grants generous assessment cuts to major businesses after the tax rate has been set. The mayor is forced to cut the budget.

The state legislature, dominated by rural and suburban areas, cuts funds that the mayor of the state's largest city had been counting on, again after the tax rate had been set. Undaunted, the mayor goes to Washington and makes the rounds at various Congressional offices and agencies, drumming up funds. The state legislature, not to be one-upped, completely abolishes the program.

The mayor, facing election in the fall, deliberately overestimates the coming year's revenues in order to cut the tax rate. When the revenues fall short, he borrows on the short-term market to make up the deficit. The interest on these notes compels a big leap in the property tax rate the next year.

assessing and the assessor

The assessor's job is as important as it is difficult. A good assessor must know how to keep abreast of the real estate market in his community. He must be an expert on construction costs and on the economics of buying, selling, and operating real estate for profit. In many places he must understand the economics of the mining or timber industries as well. An assessor needs to understand corporate accounting and, increasingly, modern computer techniques. He must be a lawyer, amateur if not actual. An assessor must be able to organize and manage a staff of assistants and mountains of records and paperwork. He must be competent in dealing with the public and the press, and he must be able to navigate the stormy political waters through which his work can take him. He is responsible for thousands of separate parcels of property. If he does not get these onto the tax rolls and assess them properly, then local functions and taxpayers will suffer. How does an assessor carry out his responsibilities?

listing

Listing is the process of finding all the property in a jurisdiction and putting it on the tax rolls. The assessor can draw on three main sources of information. One is taxpayer reporting forms, the system the IRS uses. These are common for personal property, less common for real estate; some states—Texas and Kentucky are among them—require taxpayers to file reports on all their property. The second source is the data network which good assessors establish. They check—or even get copies of—deeds, building permits, zoning changes, and other records which show where property is and what is happening to it. The third source is actual field inspections. These are especially important for buildings under construction and inventories.

Once he has these data, the assessor must assemble them in a useful form. Changes in real estate are recorded on *tax maps*. These are carefully drawn maps showing the location, size, and tax map number for each parcel of real estate in the jurisdiction. Tax maps sometimes include buildings on the property as well. Many smaller jurisdictions do not have these tax maps and have no way of being sure that they have all real estate on the tax rolls.

In many jurisdictions, property data for both real and personal property go onto *property record cards* which list all the information about each property that the assessor needs to determine its value. More advanced assessing offices use computers to transfer the raw property data from the various sources to property record cards.

valuing

The assessor's next step is to ascertain the value of the property on his assessment roll. An assessor is a special kind of appraiser. Private, or *fee* appraisers, determine property values for many different purposes—insurance, corporate mergers, condemnation lawsuits. Assessors determine property values for just one purpose: property taxes. Unlike fee appraisers who can take painstaking care with every property, assessors have a whole community full of properties to appraise. They lack the time and the staff to do a full-fledged appraisal on each. Out of necessity, they have developed techniques to handle large numbers of property on a mass, or assembly-line basis.

It is these so-called *mass appraisal* techniques which really set assessors apart from other appraisers. These techniques can be admirably resourceful and accurate. They can also be utterly fallacious short-cuts that extend or conceal favored treatment for particular taxpayers or enable a lazy or incompetent assessor to get by with little work.

The keystone of assessing is the concept of *market value*, which one court defined as "the price it [the property] would bring if offered on an open market under conditions in which neither buyer nor seller could take advantage of the exigencies of the other." This is the value the assessor is charged by law to find. The word "find" is important; the assessor is not supposed to dream up a value, but rather to arrive at one from factual data about the actual real estate market. There are a few instances, such as farmland assessing, in which the law permits assessors to depart from the market value concept. Such cases are the exception, however, and even here the idea of market value is only modified, not cast out.

Implicit in the market value concept is the standard of "highest and best use." This standard is the source of much confusion. It means that assessors are to look to the most intense and profitable use to which buyers are apt to put the property. A farm surrounded on four sides by residential subdivisions would be assessed at its value for subdividing, not farming; a vacant lot in a downtown business district would be assessed at its value for highrise development, or rather, at the price someone might pay to put a building on it.

In this sense the market value concept is biased towards development. "Highest and best" use is really "most fully developed and profitable" use. Whether most profitable always means best is matter for dispute.

Since market value is the key, why don't assessors merely look at what properties are selling for and be done? Sales prices are probably the best evidence of market value, but they cannot do the job alone. For one thing, there are not always enough sales of a particular kind of property to give the assessor reliable evidence as to value. This is especially true of commercial and industrial properties which tend to be unique, so that the sales price for one does not say much about the value of another. More important, sales *price* does not always reflect market *value*. Speculators often take advantage of uninformed sellers, buying inner-city rowhouses and farmland in the path of development for much less than they are worth. Sellers can also take advantage of buyers. A landowner who knows that a developer needs his parcel to complete a subdivision tract is likely to hold out for the very last dollar. In such cases, it can be argued, the sales price does not truly reflect the value of the property.

For these reasons, assessors consider sales prices just one indicator of value. They use two other methods of finding value called the *cost approach* and *income approach*. In using these approaches the assessor puts himself into the shoes of a prospective buyer and asks himself how much he would be willing to pay for the property in question.

the comparable sales or market data approach

The assessor simply looks up what the particular property, or properties like it, called *comparables*, have sold for recently. He ignores sales that were not "arm's length"—those that were between two family members, for example, or in which the buyer or seller was in special distress, such as a sale of a home after a divorce or death of a spouse. Then the assessor makes adjustments for minor differences between the comparables and the property he is assessing. Adjustments might be for location, the land area, or the condition of the property.

The market data or comparable sales approach works best in assessing homes, which are bought and sold often, and which are sufficiently alike to be useful as comparables. Many assessors think it is the best test, because it is objective.

the cost approach

Under this approach, the assessor figures out how much buildings cost. Then he subtracts an amount to cover wear-and-tear or *depreciation*. Also called the *summation approach*, the cost approach is often the first assessors use. It involves a detailed description of the property—its size, shape, how it is constructed, its condition and age—because only such a description makes possible an accurate cost estimate. Once down on paper, these details can be used in the other approaches to value as well.

There are three different kinds of costs which assessors use: *historical cost*—what it actually cost to build the particular building; *reproduction cost*—what it would cost today to build exactly the same building; and *replacement cost*—what it would cost to construct a building that would perform the same functions as the one in question, using today's materials and technology. For example, someone building a downtown office building today would be more likely to use glass and aluminum than granite and marble.

There are also three different kinds of depreciation which assessors take into account: *physical deterioration*, which is simple wear-and-tear; *functional obsolescence*, which describes an old factory with loading docks built to receive horse-drawn wagons instead of trucks; and finally, *economic obsolescence*, which is a decline in value due to events apart from the building itself. For example, if an airport were built next to a drive-in movie theater the value of the theater would probably go down.

There is a fourth kind of depreciation which assessors are not supposed to consider. *Accountant's* depreciation is a special, rapid form of depreciation that is usually used for income tax purposes. It has little or nothing to do with the actual condition or value of the property. But assessors have slipped this form of depreciation into their calculations to give particular building owners an assessment break.

Assessors cannot afford to investigate fully the actual cost of every building they appraise. Instead they use tables which purport to show the cost of different building components per square or cubic foot of building space. For example, the excavation for a typical ranch house might be computed at 65 cents per square foot of total floor area, the exterior walls at $2.49 per square foot, and so on. There is nothing wrong with such shorthand methods so long as they are based on actual cost data and are up to date. This is not always the case, however.

The cost approach can be very convenient to use. The assessor simply takes the cost of building components from a manual (which he may or may not have prepared himself) and plugs these into the property in question. Training assistants to use the cost approach is also easy. These are reasons assessors tend to use the cost approach more than any other.

the income approach

Assessors often use this approach to value office buildings and other properties that produce income for the owners. In this approach, the assessor tries to reckon the value of the property from the income it produces currently and which it can be expected to produce in the future.

The basic premise is that people who invest in real estate are looking to the income it will yield. An investor interested in buying an office building would want to know how much rental income the building was bringing in and its maintenance cost. He would check the condition of the building and of the neighborhood to see how long it would produce this much income. Then he would figure out how much he should pay. Assessors have reduced these questions down to a system:

1. Estimate the gross annual income.

2. Substract rent loss due to vacancies and "bad debts."

3. Subtract operating expenses.

4. Estimate how many more years this "income stream" will last.

5. Choose a "capitalization rate" and a "capitalization technique." These are formulas for figuring out how much an investor would pay now to get the future income of the building.

Assessors, however, do not have the authority in all states to make property owners submit detailed statements of their costs and income. Nor do they always use this authority. And building owners often ignore requests for data while most assessors lack the legal staffs to put teeth in their requests. Assessors can use the table which real estate trade groups and mortgage lenders prepare to make an educated guess on how much income specific kinds of buildings should produce though many, unfortunately, accept without question oral statements from the owners.

assessing land

An assessment should begin with the land. The site, or location, is often the single most important part of the value of the entire property. Few people would want a home, no matter how lavish and well-appointed, next to a steel mill. Moreover, unlike buildings, land does not wear out for most purposes. To the contrary, it usually increases in value. For these reasons the assessor should consider the land first.

The market value standard applies to land as much as to buildings, but the valuation techniques are different. The cost approach is not useful, because land is not constructed out of parts. The basic methods are therefore the comparable sales and the income approaches.

It is common to assess farm and rural land according to its productivity. Farms are valued according to the crops they can produce, timberland according to the wood it can produce; these are basically applications of the income approach. Industrial land is valued according to its aptness for industrial use, in terms of access to water, sewers, utilities, roads, a labor supply, and the like.

Assessors often reduce such data to unit values. They classify the land according to type and quality, and then develop a standard value per unit of property in each class. For farm and rural land, the unit is a typical value per acre. For industrial land, it is a value per acre or square foot. The assessor is supposed to adjust these numbers for the peculiar features of particular properties.

Commercial and residential land is valued according to "front feet." The theory is that such land is valuable to the extent that it borders on the street. More front feet, for example, mean more display windows that can attract the attention of passersby. For this reason, long shallow lots are considered more valuable than narrow, deep ones of equal area.

In the East, assessors consider a lot one hundred feet deep as the standard. In the West the figure is often higher. They treat this portion of the lot as more valuable than any parts that extend back further.

From these basic assumptions, assessors derive what are called *depth tables*. These enable the assessor to convert quickly the front footage and the depth into a value for the entire lot. The depth tables are constructed according to one of three main rules. One is called the "4-3-2-1 rule," and assumes that the first quarter of the lot going back from the street contains 40 percent of the total value, the second quarter contains 30 percent, and so on. Another, the "Hoffman-Neill rule," says that the first fifty feet of a lot 100 feet deep contain two-thirds of the total value. The third major rule, called the Harper-Edge rule, is based on a slightly more complicated mathematical formula.

It is absolutely essential to remember that none of these approaches to value have any validity of their own. Market value alone is the test, and these techniques are valid only to the extent they help the assessor determine market value. The laws usually require only a result, market value, and leave the assessor to reach that goal as he chooses. Similarly, courts have declined to second-guess the assessor's methods, and have scrutinized instead only the fairness of his results. Thus the assessor, left to his own discretion, can use any approach, or combination of approaches, that he feels is suitable in a particular case.

This vast discretion can create problems and abuses. The depth tables mentioned above are an example. Instead of deriving these from careful study of how buyers and sellers actually value different attributes of building sites, many assessors just insert arbitrary numbers and keep using these year after year. Similarly, in a practice called *indexing*, assessors take a flat figure to reflect general inflation and multiply all the assessments by this amount. Indexing in this way ignores that property values in different neighborhoods change at varying rates that may be more, or less, than the average. Then there are assessors who only increase assessments on properties that are sold. This discriminates against new purchasers in favor of people who have owned their property for a longer time.

Deliberate favors for chosen property owners can be hidden behind a cloud of technical terminology. Taxpayers in Chicago caught the assessor applying depreciation rates—which he called "condition factors"—far in excess of actual declines in value due to wear and tear. Taxpayers in Fairfax, Virginia discovered the assessor granting generous "vacancy allowances" to landlords whose buildings were leased solid for years. There are assessors who make no effort to assess land. Instead they just value the building and assign whatever additional value the property seems to have to the land. This practice usually over-allocates value to the building, where it can be depreciated, much to the owner's delight. There are even assessors who insist that the sharp upward trend in property values over the past forty years does not reflect true market value, only speculation and inflation. Such assessors leave assessments pretty much alone.

Beyond the abuses of misapplied assessing techniques is a more basic question. Are these techniques unbiased and fair, or do they, by their very nature, work to favor particular property owners over others? The depth tables assume that the further back land is from the street, the less valuable it is. Put another way, the larger the parcel, and the greater the percentage of it that is far back from the street, the lower the assessment per unit becomes. Such a technique can easily become a favor to large property owners.

The income approach appears to tilt a favorable balance toward the commercial property owner. For one thing, it turns the property tax into an income tax. The property tax is supposed to tax the *value* of property, not what the property currently produces. The difference is significant. County governments in rural Appalachia have lost millions in property taxes because assessors haven't assessed land rich in oil and minerals until the owners decided to tap these. Thus wealthy mineral owners pay little or no tax until their profit prospects peak. Meanwhile, homeowners are assessed much closer to the market value of their homes, whether or not they are going to sell them.

The income approach can also penalize the efficient property owner who manages his property well and shows a profit, while rewarding the inefficient one who makes less. Assessors are *supposed* to avoid this result by taking into account *economic income*, the income the property should have yielded if it had been well managed, but often fail to do so.

Still another weakness of the income approach is that it can favor tax loss investments. Many investors who buy or build office and apartment buildings do not expect or even want to make a cash profit on them. What they want are artificial tax losses they can deduct from their other income. The value of the property to them is its ability to produce these tax losses. But assessors ignore the way bookkeeping losses can produce tax profits for such investors. Thus they will come up with a low assessment for a new office building that is yielding large tax savings for the owner because looked at in isolation, it is not producing much income.

Perhaps the most serious fault of the income approach is the way it favors commercial property owners over homeowners. When an office-building owner puts in new lighting or paneling, it is an expense that he deducts from the building's income, either all at once or over a period of years. When a homeowner makes such improvments he can deduct nothing. To the contrary, his assessment usually increases.

This inequity was demonstrated in Boston. Assessors used a partial income approach on apartment buildings but the market value, or sales approach, for condominiums, since these are considered a form of single-family housing. When a 114-unit apartment building in downtown Boston was converted into a condominium, the assessment increased 50 percent, simply because of the change in assessment technique. (The assessor later compromised, under pressure of a lawsuit.)

assessing natural resources

Natural resources such as coal and oil are part of the land. Unless specially exempted, they are subject to the property tax. They have been traditionally undervalued and even completely ignored. Yet as they are being

180 TAX POLITICS

depleted, they become more precious and a more important revenue source, and we should consider how they are assessed.

There is no basic difference between exploitable resources and other forms of real estate. Like a building, or even an empty city lot, they provide their owner with revenues. As is the case with a building or lot, much if not all of the revenue will be collected in the future, depending on demand for the property and when the owner decides to exploit it. Investors in natural resource property incur risks comparable to the risks incurred by investors in any other business. These parallels are so close that many economists argue that resources should be treated like any other business property.

There are differences, however, between natural resources and other kinds of real estate. U.S. Steel can move its factories to avoid high taxes, but it cannot move its coal mines. Exxon can move its refineries but not its oil deposits. Thus the local taxing body potentially enjoys an edge over resource owners that it does not have with other property owners.

Another difference is depletion. When an office building is demolished, the owner of the land can put up another one. When oil or coal is exhausted, it is gone for good. The land may be useful for another purpose, but most probably it is not.

Third, the income expected from such resources is often less predictable than income from other forms of real estate.

And finally, environmental and conservation questions enter the property tax issue. Heavy property taxes on minerals encourage the owner to tap these quickly to generate revenues to pay the taxes. Timber may be cut prematurely, and wastefully "clearcut." Coal that otherwise might have been extracted more slowly or conserved may be stripmined. On the other hand, an absence of meaningful property taxes can encourage the resource owners to hoard and drive up prices by keeping their resources off the market.

While some states have evolved alternative taxing policies for resources, such as a "severance tax"—a set fee on each unit mined or drilled—property taxes are still common. The method assessors usually use for valuing resource property is the income approach. Under the income approach, to put it simply, the assessor must determine:

The amount and quality of the resource in the ground

How quickly it can be extracted

How much it will cost to extract the resource

How much the mineral will sell for

These data give the assessor the expected *cash flow* or *income stream*. His next step is to determine how much an investor would pay today to gain access to that income stream in the future—i.e. the *discounted cash flow*. The interest rate, or return, that such an investor would expect each year is called the capitalization rate. Once the mineral has been valued, the assessor proceeds to value the land by usual methods, looking at similar land in his jurisdiction.

It is common for mineral lands to be owned by one party while the right to extract the minerals is leased or sold to another. When the minerals are leased, the owner gets a royalty of a set amount per unit extracted, or a percentage of its value. When the mineral rights are sold, the landowner gets the sales price only. In the former case, the assessor must allocate the total value between the two parties in interest, the royalist and the operator. The royalist's share is normally easier to compute because he has no costs and virtually no risks. A complication arises in some states where a royalty interest is not considered real estate, so that its property tax status might be different.

excuses for low assessments

There are numerous other complications in assessing minerals, and these are often used as excuses for low assessments. We can but mention a few of the more important ones here.

1. Undeveloped vs. Developed Resources

Assessing undeveloped resources is more difficult than assessing resources that are being mined or drilled. Because price, costs, quality, and quantity must be estimated for undevel-

How Property Taxes Work   181

oped resources, many assessors ignore undeveloped resources entirely, so that the owners pay no property taxes on them at all. Such tax breaks are unwarranted. "Generally speaking, any mineral deposit that can be exploited at a profit today, or that will become exploitable within the next few decades, has economic value," write Donald Colby and David Brooks of the U.S. Bureau of Mines in their booklet "Mineral Resource Valuation for Public Policy."

2. Economic vs. Unecomomic Reserves

Assessors usually only assess reserves which are "economic," i.e., reserves which can be extracted profitably using today's technology. In deeming certain reserves "uneconomic" and of no value, assessors downplay two key points. First, rising prices will make reserves that are uneconomic today very economic in the future. And secondly, improvements in mining technology can be expected to further raise reserves from the uneconomic to the economic category.

3. Risk

Assessors often give too much heed to the mineral industry's incessant claims of the "riskiness" of their ventures. The discount or capitalization rate is frequently padded with a generous risk factor that results in a very low assessment. Robert H. Paschall, the widely respected senior petroleum and mining engineer with the California State Board of Equalization, cautions against blowing up the risk factor out of proportion. "The risks in the oil industry," Mr. Paschall says, "are not any greater than they are in other industries and businesses. . . . There may be risks that prevail only in regard to the oil properties, just as there are risks that apply only to laundromats."

4. Depletion

Since minerals will be exhausted, assessors commonly allow mineral owners a return *of* capital as well as a return *on* capital. They assume that owners establish a "sinking fund" to replace the minerals being mined. They allow revenues put into this imaginary fund as an expense for tax purposes. Critics have noted, however, that this allowance results in low assessments for the mineral owners. They point out that many resource owners do not establish a fund, which suggests that the allowance is unwarranted. In any case, the sinking fund allowance appears to apply, at best, to small operators, not to large corporations with ongoing exploration programs which are financed from general company revenues.

Timber is somewhat different from oil, coal, and other minerals. It is basically a crop, which can grow back. Thus the timber industry involves resource management—forest management—to a degree not true of other resources. Since it is widely believed that property taxes can encourage wasteful management, alternative tax policies have been sought.

One alternative has been the forest equivalent of the farmland assessment laws, discussed in Chapter 6. Another has been to refrain from taxing the timber until it is harvested, either through a yield tax on the proceeds of the cut timber, or through a severance tax. Such delayed taxes are said to free the owner from tax pressures to cut excessively or prematurely. Valuation becomes much easier—i.e., the same as other land—since there is no longer a question of how much timber is cut or how much it sells for. (When an owner sells the timber to a related or affiliated company, however, the sales prices may be rigged to avoid taxes.)

One drawback of the delayed taxation of timber is that local governments lose the regular flow of yearly property taxes; instead, revenues come in only when the timber owners decide to cut. If delayed taxes succeed in lengthening the period in which the owner holds the timber before cutting it, then revenues associated with the cutting process—income taxes on the foresters, sales taxes on the harvesting supplies—may dip also. In addition, when taxes are delayed until cutting, the owners may keep their timber off the market (and perhaps create a shortage) while they wait for prices to rise and avoid taxes at the same time. Further, the owner is under less pressure to restock his land quickly. The result can be more "down time," and in the view of many, the waste of a precious asset—timber producing land.

Severance taxes, we should note, are sometimes imposed in

addition to, not instead of, property taxes. In such cases the above problems do not arise.

assessing and computers

Substantial changes in assessing practices are likely to come in the next decade through computers. Since mass appraisal involves the gathering, organizing, and applying of large amounts of data, it is ripe for computer assistance.

Assessors can use computers in two main ways. The first is as mechanical clerks—sending out assessment notices, keeping property descriptions, assembling data used in appraisals. Computerizing such tasks certainly makes the assessor more efficient; it does not signal an automatic improvement in the manner and quality of his work.

A more fundamental application of the computer is its use for making actual appraisals. The basic technique is not difficult. The assessor would list anywhere from ten to one hundred traits for each property—how old it is, how many bathrooms it has, how many spaces in the garage, how large the back yard is. Then he would pick out the properties that had been sold and run them through the computer, along with their sales price. The computer would then correlate sales prices with traits, ranking the latter in order of importance. (It is from this ranking of features from the most important to the least that the technique gets its name *regression analysis*.) The computer would also group the properties into neighborhoods in which the same traits had the same importance. For example, a garage might command a much higher premium in a crowded inner-city neighborhood than in a suburban one, with plenty of on-street parking.

CBM Inc., a Cleveland-based computer consulting firm, has completed such analyses for residential property in Cleveland and in the state of Arizona. In Arizona, the company found that floor space was the single most important factor in determining a home's value. In Cleveland it was the number of plumbing fixtures. The number of spaces in the garage was very important in both cases.

Overall, CBM has found that the eight most important traits for houses in a particular area will account for 90 percent of all sales price variations. The twenty-five most important traits will account for 99 percent of all variations.

With these data under his belt the assessor can turn the process around and use the computer to predict the sales prices of houses based on their traits. The computer would be programmed to identify and "kick out" the properties which did not fit the pattern and needed special attention. Such computerized appraisals can be impressively accurate. A test in Orange County, California, produced residential assessments more than twice as accurate as the nation's best assessors have been producing.

Another advantage of computers is efficiency. They can update the assessment on every residential parcel, each year, at a cost of between 10 and 60 cents per parcel once the system is installed. Several California counties, including Orange and Los Angeles, have been leaders, supported by the highly competent California State Board of Equalization. Under court orders to update assessments each year, Arizona and Maryland are installing computerized systems statewide, and the New York State Board of Equalization has installed a model program in the town of Ramapo. The private appraisers are getting into the act as well. The Society of Real Estate Appraisers has embarked on a program to provide computerized valuations to mortgage lenders and fee appraisers all over the nation. Leaders in the assessing profession have been convinced that computers are the way to go but change has been slow. Out of about 83 million taxable properties nationwide, about 2 million are assessed by regression systems, according to a recent estimate.

A major obstacle to computerized assessing has been the assessors themselves. They and other local officials often fear that computerized systems will severely limit their ability to use assessments for political ends. Staff appraisers fear being reduced to key-punchers, though computer-advocates argue that by getting the routine properties out of the way, computers actually will enable these staff appraisers to focus their energies on the more challenging special cases for which their talents are most needed.

The basic obstacle is once again geography. Of the thousands of local assessing jurisdictions most are too small to move to computers. They resist state assistance which they automatically chastize as "interference," and joining with neighboring units is usually out of the question.

While recognizing their advantages, we need to be cautious of computers nevertheless. They have worked well so far mainly on residential properties in fairly homogenous subdivisions. The more diverse an area, and the more important location factors are to value, the less successful computers have been. It appears possible to develop programs to handle such diversity, but it will take time. Some areas, including Los Angeles County, California, are at work now on ways to use computers to assess commercial and industrial property.

Computers can only be as accurate as the data fed into them. This is the old GIGO principle—Garbage In, Garbage Out. Accurate data have always been essential in assessing, but computers make them even more so. A good many assessors will have to improve their data-gathering significantly if computerization is to work.

Another danger is that computers will further shield the assessor and make it harder than ever for property owners to complain. You can sit down and argue with an appraiser, but who can fight with a third-generation IBM? People who have joined battle with computerized billing foul-ups will not relish what might await them at the assessor's office. Furthermore, once the computerized systems are set up, the assessors who pioneered them will slowly leave the scene. Their places may be taken by others who will accept the systems as given and apply them mechanically, just as today's assessors mechanically apply the valuation tables and formulas devised years ago. There is nothing new about encrusted orthodoxies, but when they take the form of multi-million-dollar capital investments they become especially imposing.

what is a "fair" assessment

There are two legal standards that assessments are supposed to meet: (1) They are supposed to be the full market value or a specific percentage of the full market value of the property, and (2) they are supposed to be uniform.

Originally, the law in just about every state mandated that property be assessed at full market value. For a host of reasons less than half the states today still adhere to that standard. And of those that do, few honor it in practice.

When property tax burdens were low, few taxpayers cared. However, increasing tax rates brought demands for fairness, and *fractional assessments* (assessments at a fraction of the full market value) were challenged. State courts have reacted in two ways. Some, as in Kentucky and Massachusetts, have ruled that the law means what it says, and that assessments must be at full market value. Courts in other states declared (in some cases in contravention of the state constitutions) that fractional assessment was fine as long as everyone was assessed at the same fraction of fair market value, i.e., as long as assessments were *uniform*.

The state legislatures have implemented these court decisions in different ways, and today, the states fall into three basic categories regarding the legal level of property tax assessments.

100 percent full value

Some states adhere to the 100 percent full market value standard out of tradition, others as a result of court rulings. In some cases, though the courts have upheld the standard, their rulings have not been strictly enforced.

fractional assessment

In some states, where the courts have permitted fractional assessment as long as it was uniform, the legislators have stipulated some definite fraction of full market value. In still other states, fractional assessment is the rule although the issue has not come to a head in the courts.

classified assessment levels

In still other states the legislatures established different fractional assessment levels for different kinds of property. These systems are called "classified" because property is divided into classes. Homes would be assessed at one percentage of full market value; businesses, utilities, farms each at yet another, depending on the number of classes the legislature established.

FIGURE 50. ACTUAL LOCAL RESIDENTIAL PROPERTY ASSESSMENT LEVELS COMPARED TO STATE LEGAL STANDARDS, 1971

This table lists the states according to their legal assessment standard. The actual statewide average assessment level is included where that figure is available. The actual assessment level is the key point, for with the exception of a few states, assessments are still far from the level at which the law says they should be.

State	Ratio of Assessed Value to Sales Price [2] (%)	Legal Assessment Standard [1] Level (%)	Valuation Concept	Ratio of Actual Level to Legal Standard (%)
(Full-Value Standard States)				
Oregon	87.1	100	True cash value	87.1
Kentucky	83.8	100	Fair cash value	83.8
Alaska	75.1	100	Full and true value in money	75.1
New Hampshire	65.1	100	Full and true value in money	65.1
Florida	63.2	100	Full cash value	63.2
Maine	52.9	100	At just value in compliance with the laws of the state	52.9
Massachusetts	49.3	100	Fair cash valuation	49.3
Maryland	47.8	100	Full cash value less an allowance for inflation	47.8
District of Columbia	47.5	100	Full and true value in lawful money	47.5
Wisconsin	46.7	100	Full value at private sale	46.7
Delaware	36.5	100	True value in money	36.5
West Virginia	36.2	100	True and actual value	36.2
Virginia	34.8	100	Fair market value	34.8
New Mexico	27.5	100	Assessed in proportion to its value	27.5
Pennsylvania	26.6	100 [3]	Actual value (the price for which the property would sell)	26.6
New York	25.8	100	Full value	25.8
Missouri	23.1	100	True value in money	23.1
Texas	18.0	100	Full and true value in money	18.0
Mississippi	14.7	100	Assessed in proportion to its value	14.7
South Carolina	4.0	100	True value in money	4.0
(Fractional-Value Standard States)				
Tennessee	32.6	35	Actual cash value	93.1
Georgia	35.7	40	Fair market value	89.2
Iowa	23.3	27	Actual value	86.3
Michigan	41.5	50	Full cash value	83.0
California	20.0	25	Full cash value	80.0
Nebraska	27.5	35	Required to be valued at its actual value and assessed at 35%	78.6
Nevada	27.1	35	Full cash value	80.0
Hawaii	54.0	70	Fair market value or a percentage thereof	77.1
Illinois	37.8	50 [4]	Fair cash value	75.6
Ohio	36.9	up to 50 [5]	True value	73.8
Washington	36.1	50	True and fair value	72.2
Kansas	21.3	30	Fair market value	71.0
Indiana	23.5	33 1/3	True cash value	70.6
Colorado	20.7	30	Actual value	69.0

184 TAX POLITICS

How Property Taxes Work

Continued

State	Ratio of Assessed Value to Sales Price [2] (%)	Legal Assessment Standard [1] Level (%)	Valuation Concept	Ratio of Actual Level to Legal Standard (%)
(Fractional-Value Standard States)				
Alabama	19.7	30	Fair and reasonable market value	65.7
Arkansas	12.5	20	True market value in money	62.5
South Dakota	36.5	60	True and full value in money	60.8
Arizona	10.7	18 [6]	Full cash value	59.4
Idaho	10.6	20	Market value	53.0
Oklahoma	18.2	35	Fair cash value	52.0
Utah	14.9	30	Reasonable fair cash value	49.7
North Dakota	15.1	50	Full and true value in money	30.1
Minnesota	8.5	30 [7]	Market value	28.3
Montana	7.7	30 [8]	True and full value	25.7
(Varying valuation — Determined Locally)				
Connecticut	47.8	Up to 100	Uniform % of market value within local district	n.c.
Louisiana	13.1	Not below 25	Actual cash value (land at not less than $1 per acre)	n.c.
New Jersey	58.3	20-100 [9]	Uniform percentage at true value	n.c.
North Carolina	44.6	10	True value in money	n.c.
Rhode Island	50.5	10	Full and fair cash value	n.c.
Vermont	33.3	Up to 100 [10]	Fair market value	n.c.
(Value Determined By State Tax Commission)				
Wyoming	16.6	[11]	Fair value	n.c.

n.c.—Not computed

[1] The "legal standard" rates shown are applicable generally. There are numerous exceptions in several states.

[2] Aggregate assessment — sales price ratio. Residential single-family property.

[3] In fourth to eighth class counties, real property must be assessed at a predetermined ratio not to exceed 75 percent.

[4] "Fair cash value" is defined as 50 percent of the actual value of real and personal property, except in counties of more than 200,000 where real property is classified for tax purposes.

[5] State board of tax appeals authorized to set a fraction for statewide application. In 1972, this fraction was set at 35 percent.

[6] Legal standard varies from 18 to 60 percent depending on class of property.

[7] Estimated. Legal standard varies by class of property. Residential homesteads are assessed at 25 percent on first $12,000 of market value, 40 percent on excess.

[8] Legal standard varies from 1-100 percent depending on class of property.

[9] In a multiple of 10 established by each county board of taxation. If a county fails to establish a uniform percentage, 50 percent level is employed until action is taken.

[10] Uniform percentage, determined locally.

[11] At a fair value in conformity with values and procedures prescribed by the state tax commission.

SOURCE: Advisory Commission on Intergovernmental Relations staff compilation based on data from Commerce Clearing House, State Tax Reporter and U.S. Bureau of the Census, Governments Division.

fractional assessing is not a tax break

What's so bad about assessors who assess us at less than the legal level? Aren't they giving us a break, protecting us from a heavier tax burden? The answer is that fractional assessment is not a break for the taxpayers. By and large, it does not cut taxes. Instead it results in inequitable assessments and taxes, and tends to deny taxpayers the right to an effective appeal. This is why fractional assessment serves not the taxpayer but the assessor himself. As John Shannon, assistant chief of the ACIR, commented, "The lower the assessment level, the larger the administrative graveyard in which the assessor can bury his mistakes."

The secret logic behind fractional assessments is to trick taxpayers out of their right to appeal. Suppose the law says that assessments are to be at 100 percent full market value. You receive an assessment of $20,000 on a home you recently purchased for $30,000. "Gee," you think, "the assessor has been nice to me." But then you find out that your next-door neighbor, whose home is just like yours, was assessed at $5,000 less. You consider complaining. Then you think, "If I complain, the assessor might increase my assessment up to full value. So I had better keep quiet."

Even if a taxpayer sees through this ruse and decides to appeal, in order to show that he is assessed at more than the common level of assessments—or that someone else is assessed at less—he must first know, and then be able to prove, what the common level is. It is no help to know the assessment ratio the assessor claims he uses. What matters is the ratio that actually prevails in the locality, which is probably a good deal lower. (See "How To Make an Assessment-Sales Ratio Study" in Chapter 8.)

Studies have shown that the lower the general level of assessments in a locality, the more inequity there is likely to be between assessments on individual taxpayers. Here is what the U.S. Census Bureau found in a 1966 study of homes in selected areas:

Assessment Level (As a Percent of Full Value)	Percent by Which the Typical Assessment Erred from the Common Level
Under 20%	26.1%
20 to 29.9%	20.7%
30 to 39.9%	18.7%
40% or more	15.8%

SOURCE: James A. Maxwell, *Financing State and Local Government* (Washington, D.C.: The Brookings Institution, 1969), Table 6-10.

In other words, where the average assessment was 40 percent or more of full value, individual assessments were off the mark by an average of 15.8 percent each. But in communities where the assessor was assessing at 20 percent of full value or less, the average taxpayer ended up with an assessment either 26 percent too high or too low. One of two taxpayers living in identical houses could have paid twice as much tax as the other.

Why does inequity increase as the assessment ratio gets lower? One important reason is that the lower the ratio, the more confused taxpayers become, and the less likely they are to complain. Without the check of an inquiring and complaining public, assessors can do much as they please. As tax scholar L.L. Ecker-Racz put it, "Once the assessor departs from true value assessment, the rules of the game go by the board because the taxpayer no longer knows whether he is being treated fairly."

Still, fractional assessing does mean lower assessments. But lower assessments usually do not result in lower taxes. In most cases the local government will simply increase the tax rate to make up for the low assessments and raise the revenue it needs.

Assessors argue that the taxpayers will not accept full value assessments, and that the assessor who tries it will soon be out on his ear. Abrupt assessment increases, for which taxpayers are not prepared, can indeed produce a panic. But states and localities—Richmond, Virginia, and the entire state of Oregon are two—which have made a genuine effort to change gracefully to full value assessments have been able to. Taxpayer fears of this change are greatly exaggerated.

uniformity

In practice, uniformity is the issue that taxpayers have to worry about. Assessments are uniform when they are at the same percentage or ratio of the full value of the property.

Imagine a community with three homes. The first is worth $10,000, the second, $20,000, and the third, $30,000. If assessments are at 100 percent full value, then the total assessed value is $60,000. The first homeowner has one-sixth of this total, the second has one-third, and the third has one-half. These are the shares of the local tax burden each will bear. If assessments are at 50 percent of full value, the first home is assessed at $5,000, the second at $10,000, and the third at $15,000. Though the figures are lower, each still bears the same share of the total assessments—one-sixth, one-third, and one-half. Thus their respective shares of the total tax burden remain the same. It is easy to see from this why courts have favored uniformity over assessment level as the legal standard that must be enforced. In states that prescribe different assessment ratios for different classes of property, there should be uniformity *within* each class.

As we have just shown however, this is true only in theory. In fact uniformity decreases the more assessments dip below the level required by law.

how to tell whether assessments are uniform

To tell whether assessments in your locality are uniform, you need to know two things. The first is the average, or common ratio of assessments to full market values, as reflected by sales prices. The second is the percent by which each individual assessment, on the average, departs from this common level. The common level of assessments is found through an *assessment-sales price ratio study*. The typical error from this common level is shown by the *coefficient of dispersion*. How to compute these is explained in Chapter 8.

how uniform are property tax assessments today?

The U.S. Census Bureau Census of Governments, conducted every five years, shows a striking lack of uniformity (figure 51).

In 1971, only four states had a typical assessment error 15 percent or less. And in only eighteen states—just over one-third—was the assessment error under 20 percent. What this means in dollars and cents is that two identical $30,000 homes in a community, where the common assessment level is 33⅓ percent of market value, should each be assessed at $10,000. However, if the coefficient of dispersion is 20 percent, each of the assessments can be 20 percent off the mark. Thus one home could be assessed at $12,000 and the other at $8,000—a 50 percent difference in tax bills (figure 52).

The local *tax rate* has much to do with the dollar impact of assessment inequities on individual taxpayers. Thus in Manchester, N.H., the 9.7 percent typical assessment error resulted in tax bills off the mark by $91, due to the city's high tax rate, while in New Orleans, Louisiana, the typical over- or underpayment was only $61, even though assessing in that city was less than half as accurate. The reason for the low tax rate in New Orleans is that localities in Louisiana do not rely heavily upon property taxes, a feature common to most of the southern states. Whether tax rates are low or high, taxpayers are still entitled to accurate assessments.

Unequal tax bills are a very unjust result of non-uniform assessment, but the full inequity of this practice becomes apparent only when we see the specific patterns that arise from it.

some neighborhoods are more heavily assessed than others

This practice may express the assessor's and/or the local administration's view that people in some neighborhoods are more or less prone to complain. It may reflect a reward for political support. Or it may be simply the result of the assessor's not keeping assessments in line with changing market values. Since values change more rapidly in some neighborhoods than in others, the assessor's neglect typically results in older and poorer neighborhoods paying more than their share.

The Citizens Action Program (CAP), a broad-based coalition of community groups in Chicago, decided to test in two Chicago neighborhoods the official claim that homes in Chicago were assessed at between 20 percent and 22 percent of their sales or market value. CAP found that homes in South Shore were

188 TAX POLITICS

assessed at 28.4 percent of their sales value, 35.2 percent more than the claimed citywide average. Homes in Beverly were assessed at 26.6 percent of market value, almost one-third more than what the assessor claimed to be the level citywide. The assessor had lowered assessments in South Shore somewhat by 1972, but even then, the typical owner of a $20,000 home there was paying $150 too much in taxes due to the overassessment. And the same homeowner in Beverly was paying $167 too much. Within these neighborhoods, some assessments were as high as 50 percent of market value, some as low as 15 percent.

"There is no rhyme or reason for any particular assessment," CAP said. When taxpayers in the neighborhoods demanded that their assessments be reduced, the assessor refused, saying the time for appeals had passed. The taxpayers would have to wait until next year. But CAP threatened to go to court and finally, the assessor decided to invent a completely new procedure to let the South Shore and Beverly homeowners get the relief they deserved.

In Buffalo, New York, the Erie County Public Interest Research Group made a similar probe in four Buffalo areas: the core area of the city; a fringe area; a lower middle income suburb; and a middle income suburb. Assessments in the first averaged 68 percent of the sales price; in the second 80 percent, in the third 52 percent; and in the fourth 57 percent, even though New York law requires that each homeowner be assessed at the same percentage of the sales value of his property.

The Cayuga County (New York) Citizens Lobby made a study in Auburn, New York, of all the property transfers that occurred between January 1, 1972, and March 31, 1973. As reported in the Auburn Citizen Register, they discovered that the more expensive the home, the lower was the assessment in relation to the home's value.

★ FIGURE 51. ASSESSMENTS ON SINGLE-FAMILY NONFARM HOUSES ★

This table shows in column one the percentage that a typical residential assessment was of the full value of the property in each of the fifty states in 1971. Column 2 shows the degree of assessment uniformity, called the coefficient of dispersion, of the assessments on these homes. The coefficient of dispersion shows the percentage by which the typical assessment is off the mark. Therefore, the higher the coefficient, the more inequity there is between assessments on individual homeowners.

A coefficient of dispersion of ten or under is considered excellent. A coefficient of dispersion of up to 15 percent, and even 20 percent, is considered acceptable.

State	Assessment level Percentage of assessed value to sales price (Ratio)	Assessment uniformity (Percent)
Alabama	19.7	28.1
Alaska	75.1	21.5
Arizona	10.7	24.7
Arkansas	12.5	30.2
California	20.0	15.7
Colorado	20.7	16.9
Connecticut	47.8	16.0
Delaware	36.5	30.0
District of Columbia	47.5	not applicable
Florida	63.2	18.1
Georgia	35.7	23.6
Hawaii	54.0	17.2
Idaho	10.6	31.6
Illinois	37.8	23.0
Indiana	23.5	23.1
Iowa	23.3	22.9
Kansas	21.3	22.5
Kentucky	83.8	12.5
Louisiana	13.1	25.1
Maine	52.9	18.5
Maryland	47.8	19.6
Massachusetts	49.3	18.2
Michigan	41.5	14.6
Minnesota	8.5	22.2
Mississippi	14.7	25.6
Missouri	23.1	26.5
Montana	7.7	23.3
Nebraska	27.5	18.9
Nevada	27.1	13.4
New Hampshire	65.1	15.0
New Jersey	58.3	16.9
New Mexico	27.5	22.8
New York	25.8	26.8
North Carolina	44.6	22.5
North Dakota	15.1	15.7

continued

How Property Taxes Work

FIGURE 51. ASSESSMENTS ON SINGLE-FAMILY NONFARM HOUSES (Continued)

Ohio	36.9	19.5
Oklahoma	18.2	26.1
Oregon	87.1	16.5
Pennsylvania	26.6	30.0
Rhode Island	50.5	24.1
South Carolina	4.0	27.9
South Dakota	36.5	22.3
Tennessee	32.6	21.4
Texas	18.0	25.7
Utah	14.9	24.1
Vermont	33.3	21.2
Virginia	34.8	17.0
Washington	36.1	23.9
West Virginia	36.2	25.7
Wisconsin	46.7	not computed
Wyoming	16.6	25.8

SOURCE: Advisory Commission on Intergovernmental Relations staff compilation based on U.S. Bureau of the Census, 1972 Census of Governments, Vol. I, *Taxable Property Values and Assessment Sales Price Ratios.*

When owners of expensive property are not assessed as they should be, the less-well-off have to pay more to make up the slack. As we have just seen, the failure of assessors to keep assessments up to date is a prime cause of regressive assessment. The technical name for this is *assessment lag.* Since property values normally increase much more rapidly in high-income neighborhoods than in low, assessment lag acts as a taxpayer-financed subsidy for the rich.

The combination of assessment discrimination both against particular neighborhoods and against lower valued properties can result in severe tax burdens on blacks and other low-income groups. This was confirmed in a study which Arthur D. Little, Inc., completed in the early 1970s for the U.S. Department of Housing and Urban Development. It found that properties in blighted, mostly black neighborhoods are carrying *ten times* the tax load of so-called "upward transitional," mainly white neighborhoods. In Providence, Rhode Island, the black South Providence area is carrying five times the load of white College Hill/Fox Point. The sole reason, the report said, was that assessors were bearing down on these neighborhoods much more heavily than they were on their white counterparts.

These findings should not come as a surprise to anyone who has kept even vaguely in touch with the subject. Study after study has reached the same conclusion.

In 1965, Professors Oliver Oldman and Henry Aaron of Harvard University compared property tax assessments in Boston, Massachusetts. They found that single-family homes in West Roxbury, a well-to-do white section, were assessed at 31 percent of their sales value; while in Roxbury, a decaying black ghetto, they were assessed at 54 percent. The gap for apartments in white and black neighborhoods was even greater.

In 1972, the John C. Lincoln Institute of the University of Hartford found two districts in the city of Hartford, Connecticut, where assessments on single-family homes were less than 50 percent of sales prices. These were upper and upper middle income neighborhoods. Three districts where assessments on homes were more than 60 percent of the sales price were mainly black. The gap between assessment levels on two-, three-, and four-family homes was even greater. In a white neighborhood these were assessed at 36 percent of sales prices; in a black neighborhood they were assessed at over 65 percent.

In early 1973, the Connecticut Citizens Research Group in New Haven, Connecticut, released a report by a research team of Yale students which showed a similar pattern in New Haven. Black ward #4, the "Hill," was assessed at 63.4 percent of market value, while white ward #12 was assessed at 37.2 percent.

It is probably the rare assessor who sets out consciously to "get the blacks." The blatant discrimination is much more likely the result of policies and practices that we have already touched upon: assessors failing to keep assessments up-to-date; property values in poor neighborhoods rising very slowly, even falling while jumping quickly in wealthier neighborhoods; assessors taking the path of least resistance—wearing kid gloves when dealing with individuals or groups who are likely to complain and who have clout; renters not seeing their assessments directly and not giving the assessor a hard time since the tax they pay is buried in their rent.

190 TAX POLITICS

★ FIGURE 52. COMPARISON OF ASSESSMENTS AND TAXES ★

This table shows the amount by which the owner of a $30,000 home in sixty-seven major United States cities was over- or undercharged for property taxes in 1971 due to faulty assessing.

The table also shows the wide range of assessment quality and tax burdens for these cities. At one extreme is Manchester, N.H., where the typical assessment on a single-family home was only 9.7 percent off the mark. At the other extreme was Trenton, N.J., where the typical assessment was 54 percent in error.

City	(1) Median Assessment-Sales Price Ratio	(2) Median Assessment on $30,000 Home	(3) Coefficient of Dispersion (Average Error)	(4) Average Error in Assessment on $30,000 Home	(5) Local Tax Rate	(6) Average Local Tax	(7) Average Under- or Over-payment of Tax on $30,000 Home	(8) Difference in Taxes on Over & Under Assessed $30,000 Homes
Birmingham, Ala.	24.7%	$ 7,410	20.9%	$ 1,549	3.6%	$ 267	56	$ 112
Phoenix, Ariz.	11.2	3,360	18.6	625	13.9	467	87	174
Little Rock, Ark.	15.5	4,650	29.1	1,353	7.4	344	100	200
Los Angeles, Cal.	20.3	6,090	15.4	938	13.2	804	124	248
Oakland, Cal.	21.7	6,510	11.0	716	13.5	879	97	194
Sacramento, Cal.	20.4	6,120	12.7	777	14.3	875	111	222
San Diego, Cal.	20.4	6,120	14.4	881	10.2	624	90	180
San Francisco, Cal.	18.9	5,670	27.6	1,565	12.7	720	199	398
Denver, Colo.	22.5	6,750	14.3	965	8.4	567	81	162
Hartford, Conn.	50.2	15,060	16.4	2,545	7.8	1,174	199	398
Wilmington, Del.	58.7	17,610	32.4	5,705	3.8	669	217	434
Washington, D.C.	47.1	14,130	22.5	3,179	3.2	452	102	204
Miami, Fla.	60.8	18,240	14.9	2,718	3.5	638	95	190
Atlanta, Ga.	24.2	7,260	21.1	1,532	4.8	348	74	148
Honolulu, Hawaii	56.1	16,830	17.0	2,861	1.9	320	54	108
Boise, Ida.	12.3	3,690	22.5	830	15.3	565	127	254
Chicago, Ill.	32.3	9,690	28.3	2,742	7.9	766	216	432
Indianapolis, Ind.	26.5	7,950	36.0	2,862	12.3	978	352	704
Des Moines, Iowa	23.0	6,900	19.9	1,373	15.6	1,076	214	428
Wichita, Kan.	24.4	7,320	20.3	1,486	10.6	776	158	316
Louisville, Ky.	83.3	24,990	9.9	2,474	1.0	250	42	84
New Orleans, La.	20.6	6,180	21.6	1,335	4.6	284	61	122
Portland, Me.	53.5	16,050	17.7	2,841	5.3	851	150	300
Baltimore, Md.	57.7	17,310	36.3	6,284	5.8	1,004	364	728
Boston, Mass.	24.8	7,440	27.2	2,024	17.5	1,302	354	708
Detroit, Mich.	42.4	12,720	14.4	1,832	5.8	738	106	212
Minneapolis, Minn.	8.4	2,520	26.5	668	25.4	640	170	340
St. Paul, Minn.	7.9	2,370	26.1	619	23.2	550	144	288
Jackson, Miss.	16.8	5,040	19.3	973	2.7	136	26	52
Kansas City, Mo.		Insufficient Data						
St. Louis, Mo.	31.9	9,570	42.4	4,058	5.6	536	227	454
Billings, Mont.	8.2	2,460	18.6	458	25.2	620	115	230
Omaha, Neb.	27.5	8,250	16.9	1,394	9.6	792	134	268
Las Vegas, Nev.	27.2	8,160	12.5	1,020	5.0	408	51	102
Manchester, N.H.	78.4	23,520	9.7	2,281	4.0	940	91	182

FIGURE 52. COMPARISON OF ASSESSMENTS AND TAXES (Continued)

City	(1) Median Assessment-Sales Price Ratio	(2) Median Assessment on $30,000 Home	(3) Coefficient of Dispersion (Average Error)	(4) Average Error in Assessment on $30,000 Home	(5) Local Tax Rate	(6) Average Local Tax	(7) Average Under- or Over-payment of Tax on $30,000 Home	(8) Difference in Taxes on Over & Under Assessed $30,000 Homes
Newark, N.J.	67.4	20,220	40.0	8,088	8.6	1,739	696	1,392
Trenton, N.J.	37.1	11,130	54.0	6,010	17.5	145	1,052	2,104
Albuquerque, N.M.	26.7	8,010	15.7	1,258	6.2	497	78	156
Buffalo, N.Y.	25.2	7,560	25.6	1,935	16.1	1,217	311	622
New York, N.Y.	28.7	8,610	34.9	3,005	6.0	517	180	360
Rochester, N.Y.	22.3	6,690	22.2	1,485	12.8	856	190	380
Syracuse, N.Y.	26.2	7,860	29.0	2,279	14.6	1,148	332	664
Charlotte, N.C.	48.1	14,430	11.5	1,659	3.6	519	60	120
Fargo, N.D.	16.5	4,950	14.8	748	25.3	1,252	190	380
Akron, Ohio	30.9	9,270	19.5	1,808	5.0	464	90	180
Cincinnati, Ohio	33.8	10,140	34.1	3,458	4.9	497	175	350
Cleveland, Ohio	31.3	9,390	23.5	2,207	6.2	582	137	274
Columbus, Ohio	30.2	9,060	25.1	2,274	4.6	417	104	208
Dayton, Ohio	31.7	9,510	18.4	1,750	5.7	542	100	200
Toledo, Ohio	29.0	8,700	24.1	2,097	5.0	435	105	210
Oklahoma City, Okla.	20.7	6,210	35.7	2,217	9.4	584	208	416
Portland, Ore.	83.7	25,110	13.8	3,465	2.9	728	100	200
Philadelphia, Pa.	44.2	13,260	43.8	5,808	4.5	597	261	522
Pittsburgh, Pa.	36.7	11,010	42.4	4,668	7.1	782	332	664
Providence, R.I.	54.3	16,290	32.7	5,327	5.0	815	267	534
Charlotte, S.C.	4.6	1,380	36.9	509	29.2	403	149	298
Sioux Falls, S.D.	32.6	9,780	18.5	1,809	7.6	743	137	274
Knoxville, Tenn.	31.6	9,480	29.8	2,825	7.3	692	206	412
Memphis, Tenn.	38.1	11,430	18.8	2,149	4.8	549	103	206
Nashville, Tenn.	23.1	6,930	23.2	1,608	6.0	512	96	192
Dallas, Tex.	17.1	5,130	23.7	1,216	9.7	498	118	236
Ft. Worth, Tex.	19.5	5,850	31.5	1,843	10.5	614	193	386
Houston, Tex.	17.5	5,250	24.1	1,265	8.8	462	111	222
Salt Lake City, Utah	15.0	4,500	24.6	1,107	10.6	477	117	234
Richmond, Va.	81.8	24,540	26.0	6,380	2.0	127	128	255
Seattle, Wash.	27.9	8,370	33.0	2,762	4.8	402	133	266
Charleston, W.Va.	28.3	11,490	16.5	1,869	1.8	207	34	68
Milwaukee, Wis.	38.7	11,610	15.5	1,803	10.6	1,230	191	382

Explanation of Table

Column 1: The median assessment sales-ratio for homes in the city. This is the actual common level of assessments, as compared to sales values, calculated by the U.S. Census Bureau. Taxpayers should note that assessors usually claim that the actual common level is much higher than it is in truth. This leads taxpayers to think they are getting a "break" and makes them less likely to appeal.

Column 2: The typical assessment on a $30,000 home in the city. This is computed by multiplying the assessment-sales price ratio in column 1 times $30,000. (To compute the typical assessment for homes worth something other than $30,000, simply multiply that value times the ratio in column 1.) Technically, both the assessment-sales price ratio and the coefficient of dispersion (column 3) might be somewhat different for homes at different levels of value. The Census of Governments does not break its data down to that degree, however, so here the average figures for homes at all price levels are used.

continued

192 TAX POLITICS

> ★ **FIGURE 52. COMPARISON OF ASSESSMENTS AND TAXES (Continued)** ★
>
> **Column 3:** The coefficient of dispersion, or average percentage error of each assessment, as calculated by the U.S. Census Bureau. The higher this percentage, the less uniform the assessor's work, and the greater the inequities to which he is subjecting taxpayers in his jurisdiction.
>
> **Column 4:** The typical error in each assessment of a $30,000 home, plus or minus. This is computed by multiplying the coefficient of dispersion, or average percentage error, in column 3 times the typical assessment for a $30,000 home in column 2. Note that this figure does not show the amount of tax over- or underpayment. It shows the typical variation in the assessments to which the tax rate is then applied.
>
> **Column 5:** The nominal 1971 tax rate for the city, as reported by the U.S. Census Bureau. The nominal tax rate will appear high when the assessment level is low and vice versa. For this reason it cannot be used to compare tax rates between cities that assess at different levels. The nominal tax rate is the taxpayer's total annual tax bill divided by the assessed value of property. This is different from the **effective** rate which tells the taxpayer the rate of tax he is actually paying on the full value of his property. When comparing tax rates in different jurisdictions, it is best to use the effective tax rate.
>
> **Column 6:** The property tax bill of the typical owner of a $30,000 home, computed simply by multiplying the typical assessment for such a home, in column 2, by the nominal tax rate in column 5. Column 6 shows how much tax each owner of a $30,000 home would have paid had assessments been uniform and on the mark.
>
> **Column 7:** The amount by which the typical owner of a $30,000 house paid too much or too little in property taxes because of under- or overassessment. This figure was reached by multiplying the city's tax rate in column 5 times the average assessment error in column 4.
>
> **Column 8:** The difference in taxes paid between two typical under- and overassessed owners of a $30,000 house. For every homeowner who was overassessed by the amount in column 4 there was another who was underassessed by that amount. Thus the spread between the taxes they paid is double the amount in column 7, since column 7 just shows how their tax payments differed from the average. Column 8 shows the actual difference in taxes which a typical underassessed and overassessed owner of a $30,000 house paid. Remember, these two homeowners should have been paying exactly the same amount.
>
> SOURCE: Advisory Committee on Intergovernmental Relations.

"welcome home-buyer"

Many communities give newcomers a grand welcome—a new assessment to match what they paid for their home. Their next-door neighbors may have identical houses but their assessments are not increased. Newcomers are easy targets. They are not familiar with the assessment picture generally, and may not wish to be branded in their new community as complainers and troublemakers. There is another reason for this practice. The normal method for checking assessments is to compare assessed values with the sales prices for properties that have sold. Assessors who up the assessments on these properties only are like students who get a copy of an examination ahead of time. They anticipate the sample on which they will be judged. If those checking the assessor are not careful to compare the assessed values before and after the property was sold, they will fall for the assessor's ruse. In Arkansas, assessors who initially failed to meet the state's standards for accuracy were permitted to see which properties the state had used in its survey. They were able to return to their office, increase assessments on those properties, and pass the follow-up examination with flying colors.

special favors

Perhaps the most primitive form of assessment inequity is special favors for well-connected local eminences—political and business—and their friends. The practice is so blatant that most assessors probably shy away from it. But in smaller jurisdictions it is not uncommon, especially where assessments generally are so erratic that favors of any sort are difficult to detect.

lack of uniformity between homes and commercial and industrial property

We have just discussed the lack of uniformity in assessments on homes. The inequities between assessments on homes, as a class, and assessments on other kinds of property—office buildings, factories, vacant lots, utilities—can be just as great, even greater.

Since there are far fewer sales of these properties than of homes, assessment-sales ratio studies are of uncertain reliability. In New York only about 5 percent of the properties sold in 1971 were commercial and industrial. In California and Texas the figure was 2.3 percent; in Michigan 1 percent. The most valuable commercial and industrial properties are rarely sold—when did you hear last of someone buying a U.S. Steel works or a General Motors assembly plant? The most extensive ratio studies, those of the U.S. Census Bureau, exclude all properties selling for $500,000 or more (prior to 1972 the cutoff was $250,000).

In effect, then, the Census studies give us assessment levels for small- and medium-sized businesses only.

Thus, it becomes necessary to look at specific cases to see what is happening.

Homeowners in Alexandria, Virginia, were hit with bit assessment increases in 1970 and decided to make a detailed study. They found that homes were assessed 14 percent closer to full market value than were commercial properties and apartments. Furthermore, they found that since 1965 the assessor had upped home assessments by an average of 34 percent, while boosting apartment assessments by only 2 percent. The storm of taxpayer protest led to the hiring of a new assessor. After reviewing the assessments for more than a year, the new assessor said, "In general, the allegations made by citizens of underassessment of these classes of property have been borne out." When assessments on mainly high-rise apartments and vacant land were brought up to where they should have been, Alexandria gained so much new property value on its tax roles that it was able to cut the tax rate by 5 cents per $100 assessed valuation.

In the summer of 1970, a University of Texas law student compared assessments on Houston commercial properties with those on homes. She went through back issues of the Houston *Post,* which lists sales of major commercial properties including the sales prices, and looked up a sample of these properties in the assessor's office. It turned out that the assessments were, on the average, only 7.18 percent of the sales price. Yet a recent study of assessments on homes had found that these were almost 18 percent of the sales price. That meant that homes were being assessed over 50 percent higher than were large commercial properties.

Miami Herald reporters John Camp and Ron Sympson concluded in early 1975 that single-family homes in both Dade and Broward counties in southern Florida were assessed more heavily than any other category of property while hotels and commercial buildings were assessed the lightest.

selective underassessment

More important is the selective underassessment of specific large properties. This is the type of underassessment that is least likely to show up in statewide averages, yet it can represent the baldest use of political and economic leverage.

The Citizens Action Program in Chicago was able to show that U.S. Steel's South Works plant was underassessed by almost $150 million.

The Connecticut Citizen Action Group demonstrated that the Uniroyal plant in Middlebury, Connecticut, assessed at a value of $17 million, was actually worth close to $42 million.

How Property Taxes Work 193

The Tax Equity for America (TEA) Party in Philadelphia, was able to show that the new 5 Penn Central Plaza high-rise in that city was underassessed by about $5 million, saving it over $300,000 in property taxes a year.

The full scope of such underassessment probably will never be told, buried as the story is in the assessment records of thousands of jurisdictions. However, it is widespread and costly. Taxpayers should be alert for it in their own communities.

underassessment of land

The underassessment that is most common is that of land, including vacant plots in the inner cities and suburbs, farmland held for speculation, and in many states the vast mineral and resource-bearing lands of the nation's major metal, timber, and energy producers. It also includes the land portion of commercial and industrial real estate generally. Nationwide, homes are assessed, on the average, at 34.1 percent of full value. But vacant lots are assessed at only 27.6 percent, while acreage and farms are assessed at only 22.2 percent—underassessments of 19 percent and 35 percent, respectively.

A check of every property sale in Alameda County, California, in 1966-67 showed that homes were assessed at 19 percent of value; vacant land, at 7.6 percent.

When Bucks County, Pennsylvania, assembled a 3,745-acre flood-control project, it had to pay over $10 million for land that had been on the assessment rolls at about $1 million.

194 TAX POLITICS

The Cherry Hill League found that land under a major Humble Oil Refinery in Linden, N.J., was assessed at between 30 cents and 35 cents per square foot. Residential land in Cherry Hill was assessed at 45 cents to 60 cents per square foot, while the entire Cherry Hill Industrial Park was assessed at 24 cents per square foot. One local land speculator held 84 acres assessed at $42,500, which the township appraised at $1 million to purchase for a landfill.

In 1972 the Anaconda Corporation sold Montana timberland, including a lumber mill, to U.S. Plywood—Champion Papers for $117 million. The property had been assessed at only $9.7 million. Anaconda had been paying property taxes on assessed land values of only $6.43 per acre, even though the land (excluding the mill) sold for over $150 per acre.

Economics students at Indiana University, Bloomington, Indiana, found that four major industrial tracts, belonging to such firms as General Electric, Westinghouse, and RCA, were assessed at between $300 per acre and $1,700 per acre, while adjoining residential land was assessed at a minimum of $5,000 per acre.

The "rollover" is how big Chicago banks welcome the city's April 1 assessment day. Bank accounts in Chicago are subject to a very modest property tax. As April 1 approaches, the banks nevertheless transfer massive amounts either to out-of-state banks or into tax-free government securities. After the dread day is past they sell the securities and take back their accounts. In 1970 five major Chicago banks alone moved over $570 million out of the county in this way. Chicago's taxpayers lost $3 million in revenues as a result.

California companies adopt a similar ploy, the *Wall Street Journal's* William Carley reported. California's property tax applies to business inventories. So companies that ship goods there will keep them in warehouses in Nevada; obligingly, Nevada has a "freeport" law which exempts such goods from its property tax because they are "goods in transit."

Louisiana oil refinery workers report their employers shipping petroleum inventories out-of-state, or hiding them in tanks under abandoned gasoline stations.

The assessment laws in many states invite such practices. They set a particular date as the *lien date*, and only the property that is *in* the jurisdiction on that date is subject to the tax. One way out of the bind would be to apply the tax to the *average amount* of property that the taxpayer had over the course of the year. There would still be enforcement problems, but probably of a lesser order.

Assessors often have a part in tax avoidance. Many just aren't very thorough. They don't keep up-to-date tax maps showing each parcel of property in their locality. They don't check local records, such as building permits and subdivision applications, to make sure they have all new real estate on their rolls. And they never audit businesses to ascertain whether they are reporting all the taxable property, such as machinery and inventories, that they have.

Not long ago a county in New Mexico made a complete reappraisal of all its property. It found 10,000 parcels of real estate that had not been on the tax rolls.

Chicago taxpayers got a surprise several years ago when they learned that the assessor had completely overlooked the O'Hare Motel, built on a former public parking lot at Chicago's famous airport.

The Jacobs Co. of Chicago, a private appraisal consulting firm, made an interesting test. It compared new construction of taxable property reported to the Boston Building Department with the amounts the assessor had added to the assessment rolls. The new construction totaled around $440 million for the two years 1967 and 1968, while the assessor added only about $60 million to the assessment rolls.

In the mountains of Appalachia, it is common for assessors to pretend that coal and mineral deposits do not exist.

Private arrangements between local officials and large industries to keep new plants off the tax rolls for a set number of years have not been unknown.

Developers "arrange" with local officials that new homes will not be assessed until after the developer has sold them.

Sometimes the assessor just looks the other way, even though evidence is literally put before him. This happened in rural Tennessee, where local taxpayers were enraged that assessors were ignoring expensive strip-mining equipment along with the coal the strip-miners were shoveling out. J.W. Bradley, president of Save Our Cumberland Mountains, crawled under the trucks and bulldozers, and copied the registration numbers. He took the data to the assessor, but that stalwart official initially refused to put the equipment onto the tax rolls until finally forced to do so by community pressure.

Careless assessors even omit homes, as reporter Keith George of the

How Property Taxes Work 195

Binghamton (New York) *Press* learned when he drove through Chenango, N.Y., with a book listing town assessments.

A report entitled "Better Assessments for Better Cities," published by the National League of Cities Conference of Mayors, even cites an entire subdivision in Illinois that had been left off the assessment rolls.

revaluations

As we have seen, two of the assessor's main jobs are to keep assessments, or valuations, in line with current market values and to place all taxable property on the assessment rolls.

For a variety of reasons, most assessors do the second job—listing—incompletely, and the first hardly at all. The ensuing assessment chaos and erosion become self-reinforcing. The further assessments lag behind market values, the more local officials dread changing them. In the Deep South and in scattered communities elsewhere, this can go on for thirty to forty years. But usually a lawsuit, state legislation, public pressure, or the sheer need for revenues will force a local government to act. The result is a revaluation or *mass reappraisal*, an experience that more and more jurisdictions are beginning to have regularly every few years. The system seems almost designed to produce taxpayer trauma. Assessment increases that should have occurred gradually, a little bit annually over a period of years, hit the taxpayer all at once.

In many states, the legislature has put the seal of law on assessment lag, requiring localities to conduct mass reappraisals only every six years, ten years, or some other period. These laws practically insure that assessments will not be kept up to date during the intervals, despite state constitutions and statutes that require that assessments be at fair market value, not that they be so only every six or ten years. These laws have promoted even more assessment lag than they appear to do on their face. For example, in Pennsylvania, counties of a certain size are required to reassess once every ten years. County X will conduct a reappraisal in 1975 for the ten-year period 1975-85. Then it will not make another reappraisal until 1995 for the ten-year period 1985-95. Thus, a law that calls for reassessments every ten years serves a practice of making them only every twenty.

Nor are the forces pressing for the reassessment always on the side of the angels. In more than one urban-fringe community, development interests have lobbied for reappraisals so that property taxes on farmers and rural landholders would rise and force them to sell.

Though it would be logical and practical to capitalize on the opportunity of a reappraisal to upgrade the assessor's office, train or hire competent staffs, and install new equipment and procedures that would enable the assessor to keep the property tax rolls up to date, local governments rarely do. Instead they hire a private company, called a *mass appraisal firm*, to come in and do the job lock, stock, and barrel. The assessor's office for the most part sits by and watches.

the reappraisal program

The mass appraisal firm and the locality sign a contract which sets out the rights and obligations of each. A good contract will oblige the mass appraisal firm to perform such tasks as:

1. Make an entirely new list of all the property in the locality.

2. Prepare a new set of tax maps (a separate company may perform this task).

3. Inspect and measure each property inside and out and draw up a description.

4. Make tables showing the costs of different kinds of construction in the locality.

5. Study current sales values in the locality.

6. Work under the supervision of the local assessor or other official.

7. Train the assessor's staff in using the new forms and techniques.

8. Use only trained and qualified personnel.

9. Turn over its data and submit progress reports at regular intervals, and inform the public about the program and supply speakers for taxpayer and civic groups, when requested.

10. Send out notices of new values to property owners, providing adequate procedures and time for review.

11. Defend its work against appeals in court.

The project will take at least nine months to one year, and closer to two to three years in larger jurisdictions. A project director should be on the scene full-time. Employees called *listers* supposedly inspect and measure each property while trained appraisers convert the listers' data into market values, and check the properties themselves. Specialists are supposed to appraise unusual properties such as large commercial buildings and industrial plants on the basis of local cost and sales data gathered by the firm.

The taxpayers may be totally unaware that a reappraisal is taking place. Sometimes, however, an intense public relations campaign is mounted to tell the public how good a job the firm and local officials are doing and how fair the new assessments will be.

When the firm has reached tentative values for all the properties, it sends out a notice to each taxpayer and schedules reviews. Typically, a high school gymnasium or similar facility is converted into a complaint center, and mass appraisal firm employees, sitting behind long tables, speak with anxious taxpayers waiting in long lines.

The mass appraisal firm will be quick to remind one and all that it is not making assessments. In theory, this is correct. It is merely a consulting firm, determining appraisals which the assessor then uses to set assessments. In practice, however, many assessors do not check the appraisal firm's work. If they had this capability, they probably would not have hired the firm to begin with.

When the complaint period is over and the mass appraisal firm has received its final payment, it turns over the new appraisals and records. Usually this does not include the computer programs or other information that would enable the local assessor to update the appraisals himself in later years. In some states, a state department must inspect and approve the project before the locality can accept it.

The assessor then sends out assessment notices to all property owners, informing them not only of their new assessments but also, one hopes, of when and how they can challenge the assessment. Many taxpayers are not aware that the earlier review meeting with the mass appraisal firm, though it can produce a revised appraisal, was only an informal proceeding, and that the formal appeals process begins only when the assessor has determined the assessment. They think that because they have complained once to the mass appraisal firm, they have used up all their rights.

Sometimes localities sign a maintenance contract with the firm. Under a maintenance contract the firm updates its values each year, in effect taking over the local assessor's function. Otherwise the typical pattern is for the assessor to allow the figures to become obsolete until, some years later, the locality has to hire a mass appraisal firm to revise them again.

the mass appraisal industry

The mass appraisal industry had modest beginnings in the 1920s and 1930s but really took off in the early 1950s. The postwar inflation and building boom, along with rising tax rates, caused values to move rapidly, and assessors were not able to keep up with them. As a result, localities increasingly engaged the services of mass appraisal firms.

The industry has been dominated by the aggressive giant, Cole-Layer-Trumble (CLT), whose network of field agents has placed it way ahead of other companies in getting contracts. A second tier of small-to-medium-sized companies tends to focus on particular states and regions and a number of small appraisal companies, often headed by former employees of the larger firms, pick up any local business the other companies somehow missed.

What can go wrong with a mass reappraisal?

When they are dealing with local officials who are inexperienced in mass appraisals and contracts, mass appraisal firms often can write their contracts with localities just the way they want them. CLT told its shareholders confidently in a 1974 report on file at the Securities and Exchange Commission:

During fiscal 1974 the format of CLT's written contracts with its clients was reviewed and revised. The revisions as incorporated in new contractual dealings provide clearly defined limits to the company's responsibility to develop and support for a limited amount of time the information previously supplied to the client.

In short, CLT was rewriting its contracts to give its clients less. And it did not appear to anticipate resistance from them.

Mass appraisal firms approach their work much in the way a highway contractor builds a road. They redo the assessments and get out, leaving the locality to its own devices thereafter. This assures the company of a future need for its services, but it subjects local taxpayers to an endless succession of expensive and painful reappraisals.

On top of this basic weakness have been instances of poor performance. In a 1973 survey by the International Association of Assessing Officers, 31 percent of the assessors rated the work of mass appraisal firms "relatively poor" and another 6 percent rated it "very poor." The industry giant, CLT, has attracted volleys of criticism documented in a full day of hearings before the Senate Subcommittee on Intergovernmental Relations in May 1973. It would be unfair to paint the entire industry with a tar brush. There are many companies, and they are different. Nevertheless, shoddy work has been common enough.

"Listers"—the people who go from property to property recording data about each—are commonly hastily trained temporary workers. They are also often pressured to complete many more properties in a day than they can actually inspect. "Only every third or fourth house" was actually entered for inspection, one lister admitted, even though the company was supposed to enter all the houses. Millions of dollars in tax revenues are at stake when such carelessness occurs in appraising large commercial and industrial properties. Yet in one instance a mass appraisal firm appraised a Chrysler plant by getting figures over the telephone.

Inaccurate records are another problem that has plagued mass appraisals. The assessment chief of New Castle County (Wilmington), Delaware, said he found over one million errors in the initial computer print-out of a mass appraisal there. Knox County, Tennessee, had to spend thousands of dollars to store old assessment records after a reappraisal because the property descriptions produced by the mass appraisal firm were not accurate. In some cases mass appraisal firms have simply copied information from the locality's old records instead of gathering new data.

Mass appraisal is a shorthand. It tries to use data and formulas to put values on a great many properties all at once. Mass appraisal firms have traditionally based their values on costs. They gather local labor and construction costs, insert these into standard formulas and derive a value per square foot for different kinds of buildings. A brick house will be valued at so much per square foot, a wood frame house at a different amount, and so on. Then the firm sends out listers for descriptions of the different properties, plugs in the appropriate values, and makes some adjustments. The result is the appraisal, and it gives rise to two problems. First, in at least one state, Pennsylvania, the use of cost data to make assessments is contrary to state law. A 1975 report of the Pennsylvania Department of Justice cast grave doubt on the legality of the traditional mass appraisal approach in that state. More important is basic accuracy. When property values change rapidly, as they have during the 1960s and 1970s, building costs are an uncertain guide to market value. While mass appraisal firms claim to inject market data into their values, the Pennsylvania attorney general's office was not impressed. At the very best, it said, the standard mass appraisal firm approach could equalize assessments for a year or so. It could not maintain equality over time. "No traditional system," the attorney general's report concluded, "is capable of updating the entire assessment, whether annually, triennially, or at any chosen interval."

The mass appraisal process can tilt toward favoring the largest, most valuable properties. A mass appraisal firm contracts to defend its appraisals in court. Since large property owners are the ones most likely to appeal, the firms are sometimes tempted to placate them in advance by reaching a low appraisal, thus saving themselves the expense of going to court. It is true that local

198 TAX POLITICS

assessors play the same game. But the mass appraisal firms trade on their alleged objectivity and freedom from local pressures. Why should local taxpayers pay a private firm a handsome sum to do what their own assessor was already doing? In 1973, Wilmington, Delaware, officials suspected that the mass appraisal firm hired there had undervalued large commercial, industrial, and estate properties. They employed a private appraiser to recheck the firm's work, who added $9 million to the assessment roll, mainly from those kinds of properties.

When another company merges with or buys a mass appraisal firm, divided loyalties can pose serious questions. Consider CLT, which was purchased in 1970 by the American Appraisal Company of Milwaukee, Wisconsin. (A holding company, American Appraisal Associates, was formed to be the umbrella for both.) American Appraisal was a leading private appraisal firm, doing appraisal work for many of the largest U.S. corporations. As a result of the purchase, CLT was likely to be setting the property tax assessments on corporations which its sister firm had retained as private clients. Clifford Allen, former Nashville assessor and president of the IAAO, and now a U.S. congressman, called this a "secret double agent" arrangement. A divided loyalty could arise in several ways. The mass appraisal firm might be tempted to go light on a particular corporation's assessment so as not to endanger its sister firm's ability to gain that corporation as a client. Or the corporation might suggest to the mass appraisal firm: "Why should we hire you, when your sister firm saddles us with stiff property tax assessments?" In the case of CLT and American Appraisal, their closeness made such dual loyalty a danger. That they were closely connected is advertised in a memo CLT sent to its clients soon after American Appraisal had bought it out, which said in part, "We feel that the alliance of the two companies will enable us to better serve our clients *through the exchange of technical knowledge* and will enable us to offer you total valuation services" (emphasis supplied). Further, many of the officers and directors of CLT served in the same capacity with American Appraisal Associates. Even employees were shifted back and forth between the two companies. Recently American Appraisal sold CLT, and the firm has joined with another mass appraisal firm, the H.L. Yoh Company of Philadelphia, a division of Day and Zimmerman Inc. Cole-Layer-Trumble is not the only mass appraisal firm to have prompted such questions. There have even been companies which themselves have worked both for the local government and for the companies subject to local property taxes. But more information has surfaced about CLT than about any other. And we believe that CLT's corporate maneuvers represent a trend which ought to be discouraged.

Some states have attempted to upgrade the quality of work of mass appraisal firms and to hold them to account. Several maintain lists of "qualified" firms. Georgia and New Jersey, among others, have regulations to which localities must adhere in mass appraisal dealings. (In Georgia, counties must follow the regulations in order to receive state aid in financing the project.) In West Virginia and Tennessee, the state tax departments have played a major part in statewide reappraisal programs.

These efforts have not been great successes. By and large, the lists of qualified firms are based mainly on financial stability, with little or no attention to the firm's past record or competence. And state regulation simply can put the seal of approval on questionable practices, as appears to have been the case in Tennessee, where a local judge criticized the state for its lax supervision of the work of CLT for which it, not the locality—Nashville—had contracted. Local resistance to state "interference" also does not bode well for further efforts along this line.

alternatives

Tax officials are becoming aware of the weaknesses in the current methods, and are looking for alternatives.

statewide assessment

The state of Maryland is now adopting a computer-based statewide system that will be able to update assessments each year. Arizona has already employed such a system for residential property.

joint state-local undertakings

Oregon decided back in 1951 that both a statewide reappraisal of property and an upgrading of property tax administration were necessary. Instead of relying on mass appraisal firms the state decided to make the project a joint state-local undertaking. The state tax commission expanded its own technical staff and entered into agreements with county governments, splitting the costs of the projects 50-50. Here is how Oregon officials explained this decision:

Regardless of the competence of the appraisal firms that most of the counties would have to employ (if the state had simply ordered them to reappraise), there would be less uniformity of performance and less opportunity for the commission to gain insight that would be useful for future supervision. The commission realized, also, that a reappraisal would be financially wasteful unless it could be made the basis for a permanently higher quality of assessment administration. (Emphasis supplied.)

Oregon has achieved this "permanently higher quality of assessment administration." Today, as a result of the decision it made over twenty years ago, its property tax assessing system is one of the best in the country.

New York State has made important progress in state-local assessment cooperation, despite the state's 1,500 local jurisdictions (compared to Oregon's 36) and strong home rule tradition. The state board of equalization has been monitoring carefully the work of mass appraisal firms. More important, it is training local assessors in the use of computers and is providing two computer systems at the state capital in Albany, and two "satellite" systems at strategic centers elsewhere. The board also has contractors working on model systems for all phases of the assessment process.

Nebraska recently enacted an optional state-county reappraisal program. West Virginia replaced CLT with a staff of state appraisers to keep assessments on large commercial and industrial properties statewide up to date and installed a central state system for residential assessments, designed by CBM.

upgrading county assessors' offices

With the backing of a strong and competent state board of equalization, California's larger counties are developing the capacity to update property tax assessments each year, using computers. The California attorney general has ruled the use of mass appraisal firms a violation of state law, no doubt bolstering the state's efforts to strengthen its assessing system.

regional alliances of local governments

Localities which individually would lack the capacity to carry out a reappraisal can pool their resources. This is the approach of the Centralina Council of Governments, a regional council of eight counties and twenty-three cities in North Carolina. The council has developed a revaluation and appraisal program for its members, and it has a computer expert to help them design their own appraisal systems. Members of the council can acquire these services at cost.

local initiatives

Localities of reasonable size — 25,000 to 50,000 population or more—can develop computer-based appraisal systems of their own. In the eary 1970s the assessor of Englewood, New Jersey (population 25,000), decided that the system a conventional mass appraisal firm had installed in 1965 made it impossible to keep assessments abreast of market values. He asked the Research and Technical Services Department of the International Association of Assessing Officers for help. The IAAO concluded that a computer system was feasible for Englewood and recommended ways to implement it. Erie County (Buffalo), New York, and Cuyahoga County (Cleveland), Ohio, have developed their computer-based assessing systems through CBM Inc.

Such options make the unreliability, waste, and taxpayer agony connected with old-style mass reappraisals unnecessary. We need to emphasize again, however, that gathering accurate data to feed the computers will take on new significance as computerized systems become more common. Data collection is one of the major costs in property tax administration and it is an area ripe for improvement.

In the meantime, many communities will not be able to wait until the state reforms the assessment system. They will need to make a reappraisal right away.

200 TAX POLITICS

what local governments and taxpayers can do

If your locality *must* hire a private firm, the local assessor himself should do as much of the job as possible, and make sure that the firm trains his staff to use any new techniques they introduce. The local government might also hire a special outside consultant with mass appraisal experience to oversee and advise on all phases of the project. This consultant should have no business connections within the locality nor with any mass appraisal firms.

If you are in a taxpayer or civic group, or can form one, set up a special committee to monitor the reappraisal. Request that a spokesperson for each mass appraisal firm that wants the job meet with your committee. Find out whether the firm will allow your group to monitor its work in progress. Ascertain exactly how much information the firm will let the taxpaying public see. Will it, for example, open the entire assessment roll *before* the complaint period, so that people can make meaningful comparisons of their appraisals?

choosing the firm

At least fifteen major mass appraisal firms advertise in the *Newsletter of the International Association of Assessing Officers*. A bevy of smaller firms works in various parts of the country. How can a local government avoid making a poor choice? The answer is simple—*search the record*. Yet public officials rarely do. Often they sit spellbound while the larger mass appraisal firms impress them with fancy charts and brochures and promises of modern computer techniques.

Ask each firm that is interested in the job to submit a list of all the projects it has done lately in your region. Contact people in those places—officials, newpapers, taxpayer and civic groups. Try to get all sides. Stay away from firms that have left behind a trail of lawsuits, shoddy work, and ill-will. Remember too that local officials who spend hundreds of thousands of taxpayer dollars on a reappraisal are likely to be defensive about the project.

the mass appraisal contract

Mass appraisals are a "professional service." In some states they are not subject to the requirements of competitive bidding. Where they are, the locality will draw up a list of *specifications for bidders*. This sets out what the locality will expect the firm to do. If the assessor is competent, or if local officials have the prudence to hire a special consultant, the specifications will be quite detailed and demanding. Sometimes state tax departments provide model specifications. Otherwise the "specs" may be little more than an invitation to bid, saying, in effect, "We want a reappraisal. Why don't you make an offer?" The larger firms, with their sales forces and "inside tracks," often know how much the locality expects to spend and gear their bid accordingly.

Local officials should not give the contract automatically to the firm that submits the lowest bid. Some firms bid low and then do slipshod work. Or they may use the initial low bid as a foot in the door for negotiating for additional money later on, and/or for getting a long-term service contract.

Normally the firm puts forth its own contract which its lawyers have drawn up carefully to give the firm the edge on every issue. If no one in the local government has had experience with a reappraisal—as is often the case— this mass appraisal firm proposal becomes the basis for the final agreement. The mass appraisal contract is crucial. No matter what the mass appraisal firm promises, it means nothing if it isn't in writing. Officials can get suggestions from attorneys and officials in communities that have been through a mass appraisal recently. They can also write to the International Association of Assessing Officials for its bibliography on revaluation contracts which includes sample state regulations, bid specifications, and actual contracts. These may not all be good models, but they are something to start with (figure 54).

monitor the project

The worst mass appraisal abuses occur because taxpayers and public officials go to sleep when the private firm takes over. A community should watch over a mass appraisal as carefully as a homeowner would watch over the workmen remodeling his home.

Monitor the project at each step. Make sure the firm produces all the construction cost and property sales data it promised. Check out whether the firm's appraisers make field inspections. See that the company

How Property Taxes Work

★ **FIGURE 53. HOW TO GET FACTS ON A MASS APPRAISAL FIRM** ★

Getting information about mass appraisal firms generally is not easy. And finding out about a particular mass appraisal firm is even harder. Many are "closely held"—their stock is not traded on stock exchanges—so there is little published information about them. And the subject has received scant attention except in journals for assessors. And, even there, most articles have taken great pains not to offend.

Nevertheless, a good place to start is the *Bibliography on Revaluation Projects,* published by the Research and Technical Services Department, International Association of Assessing Officers, 1313 East 60th St., Chicago, Ill., 60637. This bibliography lists standard contracts and specifications for revaluation projects, actual contracts, and articles and reports. Don't take all the contracts as perfect models. And you will note that some of the articles were authored by mass appraisal firm officials and personnel. Nevertheless, the information is useful.

State tax and revenue departments are becoming aware of the mass appraisal firm problem. The IAAO Bibliography lists some that are. A few, like Arkansas, Georgia, Massachusetts, Wisconsin, and New Jersey, have lists of authorized firms. (But be sure to find out the standards firms must meet to get on the lists. Sometimes a firm need only be paying its bills.) Others have regulations governing the firms. The New Jersey State Treasury Department, Division of Taxation, Trenton, N.J., is preparing a report on all mass appraisal work in the state. The state revenue departments in Nebraska, Massachusetts, and Wisconsin—among others—are pressing for legislation that would bring mass appraisal firms more to account.

Newspapers in localities where a particular firm has worked are often a good source. The firm's advertising brochures often list these places. Write to the paper for clippings about the firm. Or have a friend there visit the paper's clipping file. One caution: local papers are sometimes chamber-of-commerce boosters and view a mass appraisal through rose-colored glasses.

Newspapers in the mass appraisal firm's home base are another good source. Town and small-city press are especially prone to write articles about local firms. These may proudly display information about the firm's officers, employees, clients, history, and like matters.

Don't neglect the firm's own promotional literature. The glossy pictures may not help much. But there may be useful leads on clients, officers and directors, branch offices, and companies with which the firm is connected.

Public records are another source. If the firm is "publicly held"—that is, if its stock, or the stock of its parent, is traded on a stock exchange—then the firm must file annual and special reports with the Securities and Exchange Commission in Washington, D.C. On the state and local levels, records to check include:

1. State departments of corporations and taxation; state securities commissions; and departments of state: corporations incorporated, based or doing business in a particular state may have to provide information to these.
2. Reports of campaign contributions (if these are required)—both state and local.
3. Court records—testimony in cases involving the firm is especially valuable.

Publications for investors will have information on "publicly held" firms. *Standard and Poor's* and *Moody's* are corporate directories you can see at most public libraries. Stockbrokers and investment advisors usually have special sources of data on such firms. Check also newspapers and magazines for investors, such as the *Wall Street Journal, Forbes, Barron's* and *Business Week.* The various *Who's Whos* may have information on a firm's officers and directors.

Consult also the *city directory* in the city where the firm is based, or in which it has a branch office.

---

makes new records instead of just copying old ones. Read the company's progress reports. Try to have a member of your committee write a column for the local newspaper telling the public what is going on.

appealing assessments

the appeals system

The appeals system consists of a sequence of panels or boards. The taxpayer who thinks one has not dealt him justice can pursue his case to the next higher level. In general, the procedures become more *formal*, more expensive, and generally more troublesome as one moves up the appeals ladder. On the other hand, the boards themselves generally becomes more professional and objective. There are exceptions to this, however. The authority of the boards varies greatly. Sometimes the boards have progressively broader authority to help the taxpayer as one moves up the ladder; sometimes they have less.

It should be noted that while this discussion concerns complaints about *assessments*, it is also possible to challenge a tax bill. Perhaps the local government did not follow the required procedures in setting the budget. Or perhaps it intends to spend the tax proceeds on illegal purposes. It is possible to challenge a tax payment on such grounds. But the challenge would be through the regular courts of law, not through their special property appeals system.

FIGURE 54. SUGGESTED CONTRACT TERMS FOR A MASS APPRAISAL CONTRACT

(1) Personnel
 (a) The mass appraisal firm (maf) should submit a list of all the personnel it will use on the project, together with their qualifications and training and the function they will perform. It will keep this list up to date. The assessor must approve each employee before he works on the project.
 (b) All personnel shall be hired from the local area whenever possible.
 (c) A minimum number (depending on size of job) of qualified appraisers should be on the job at *all times*.
 (d) All "listers" and "building enumerators" (who are not trained appraisers) should have a minimum amount of training. They should be subject to a definite plan of supervision.

(2) Progress and Control
 (a) The assessor must approve a definite and detailed plan for the project before it begins.
 (b) There shall be a probation period, during which the firm shall complete a sample section of the project. The jurisdiction shall have the right to end the contract if the maf's work on that sample section is not satisfactory.
 (c) The assessor will be appraiser-in-chief, and will make all final decisions on procedures, forms, and assessments.
 (d) The company will submit to the assessor detailed progress reports at regular intervals. These progress reports shall be public information.
 (e) The assessor shall have the authority to inspect the books and records of the appraisal firm relating to the project.
 (f) The maf shall not assign or transfer the contract or any part without written approval of the assessor.

(3) Methods
 (a) The maf shall visit and inspect all properties. It shall attach a snapshot of each property to the property record card.
 (b) The maf shall adhere fully to the provisions of the state law in setting values on property.
 (c) The values for land and buildings shall be listed separately on all property tax records.
 (d) The maf shall prepare data on *local* construction costs and it should use this data to develop a cost manual for all types of property. These manuals shall be completed and approved by the assessor, *before* the valuation work begins. These manuals should be *public information*.
 (e) All allowances for depreciation shall be clearly marked and explained on each property record card.
 (f) All exempt property should be appraised just as all other property and kept on a separate list.
 (g) Qualified appraisers should make a final field inspection and review for each property, and should initial each property card after doing so.
 (h) Any properties that were not on the assessment roll at the beginning of the mass appraisal project should be included on a separate list.

(4) Public Information
 (a) All general information the maf transmits to taxpayers should be approved by the assessor.
 (b) All records, maps, and other data of any kind used in the reappraisal should become public information.
 (c) At least thirty days before the informal review (protest) period, the maf should open to the public a complete list of all assessments, so that taxpayers can compare their own assessments with those of others.
 (d) The maf shall keep a record of each communication with a taxpayer or taxpayer representative regarding the amount of their appraisal. These records shall be public information.

(5) Appeals
 (a) Every taxpayer should have a chance to discuss his own assessment with a qualified appraiser who worked on the project. This person should state briefly in writing his reason for accepting or rejecting the taxpayer's complaint.
 (b) Any group of ten or more taxpayers shall be entitled to an explanation of *any* assessment.

(6) Payments
 (a) The maf should receive regular payments only so long as it performs its work on schedule, and in a satisfactory manner.
 (b) At least fifteen percent of the contract price shall *not* be paid until the project is completed, approved, and accepted, and until *all* appeals are complete.

complaints to the assessor

The first step in appealing an assessment normally is to meet with the assessor. In many states, such a meeting is not part of the formal appeals process. In some states, such as Oregon, taxpayers are required to use this approach before they can pursue their appeal further.

Assessors are not very likely to change an assessment during such a session, unless the taxpayer can point out a glaring error. Nevertheless, the session can be very helpful. The taxpayer can find out how the assessor made the assessment and how he is likely to justify it later.

the local review board

The next step in the appeal process—and for most taxpayers, the last—is a local appeals or review board. Some boards are comprised of local officials—including the assessor himself—or their representatives. Others consist of appointed prominent local citizens who often have substantial interests in real estate—realtors, mortgage lenders, insurance salesmen, builders, and big property owners.

These boards usually have a built-in bias. Assessors do not like to admit that they were wrong. Local officials do not like to grant assessment cuts that will either cost them revenue or else force them to raise the tax rate. People with financial involvements in real estate, direct or indirect, have an obvious interest in the way that real estate is assessed. And appointed officials do not like to offend their political mentors.

second-level review boards

In some states the taxpayer goes before members of the state tax department or of a special commission. In other states there is a special county board of equalization and/or appeals. In still other states the taxpayer goes before a special tax court, or appeals directly to the state court system.

Typically, the second-level review is more formal than the first. Also it might be held at a place distant from the taxpayers. These factors add to the time and expense involved and tend to discourage appeals. Politics weigh into the actions of second-level boards as well. By the time an appeal gets to the second board, the local budget process may be well along. The board may be reluctant to incur the ire of local officials by cutting assessments at that stage. On the other hand, the second-level board may be a bastion of the party opposing that of the local administration. In such cases it might use its power to reduce assessments to undercut and embarrass the locals.

The second-level panels often serve as boards of equalization as well as appeals boards for individual taxpayers. As boards of equalization they adjust assessment levels of entire localities for purposes of state school aid or for taxes that encompass more than one assessing district. This function can divert attention from, and even conflict with, that of adjusting assessments on individual property owners, especially when the board is untrained and understaffed, as is often the case.

Politics, conflicts between state or county officials of one party and local officials of another, and business boosterism can of course enter as readily into the equalization process as into appeals.

the courts

The third level of a property tax assessment review is typically the courts. It may be the regular state court system, or a special tax court created to become expert in tax complexities that ordinary judges often do not understand. Court procedures tend to be complicated and expensive and the vast majority of small taxpayers cannot take their cases this far.

A few states have set up special, more convenient court procedures for small taxpayers—Oregon, Massachusetts, Idaho, and the District of Columbia are examples. An Oregon taxpayer who is not satisfied with the decision of the local board of equalization—the first level of appeal after the required meeting with the assessor—can appeal to a special small claims division of the state tax court. He pays a $1.50 fee, and cases are limited to lands and buildings assessed below $25,000 each.

The courts of different states vary in the extent to which they will question local assessments. Professor Jerome Hellerstein of New York University has classified the state courts into three types.

1. Those that will overrule an assessment only if the taxpayer shows fraud or a clear mistake of law.

2. Those that also overrule an assessment if the assessor lacks substantial evidence to support it.

204 TAX POLITICS

3. Those that start from scratch and reach their own estimate of value.

The appeals procedures of many states are full of both unique technical pitfalls and unusual requirements. In Florida, a taxpayer can put his property up for auction, and if no one bids more than a value he has asserted, that value becomes his assessment. In New Hampshire, a taxpayer must make a special request to the town selectmen or assessor just to find out his assessment. In Rhode Island and West Virginia, a taxpayer appeals directly to the courts. In Vermont, a three-member "board of civil authority" examines properties on which an appeal is filed.

Normally restrained scholars and commissions have used strong language on the subject of local reviews. "Most local review procedure is farcical," conclude economists W. J. Shultz and C. L. Harriss in their textbook, *American Public Finance*. "The protection given the taxpayer by these agencies," adds the Advisory Commission on Intergovernmental Relations, "is limited at best and negligible more often than not."

And local appeals practices, particularly, are likely to bear little resemblance to what is set out in state law. But considering that small taxpayers rarely take an appeal beyond the local board, what taxpayers most need are suggestions for getting satisfaction there.

how to appeal your assessment

find out the property tax schedule

Find it out well in advance. There are definite deadlines for each step of the appeal process. If you miss these deadlines, you are out of luck.

get all the proper forms to appeal

Find out exactly how to fill them out, and any additional steps you need to take. Do not make silly technical errors that can be used to nullify your appeal.

Try not to make statements on the appeals form that will harm your appeal. For example, the form may ask that you state what you think your assessment should be, and why.

Often the law does not require taxpayers to answer all questions. Try to get the assessor to tell you which questions you actually have to answer. Ask him to put it in writing.

talk to someone who can tell you about your rights

See Chapter 8 for details.

know what the board can and cannot do

This will help you in two ways. First, you won't waste time trying to get the board to do something it lacks the power to do. For example, the board may have the power only to lower particular assessments. It may not have the power to change a whole group of assessments at once. And it may not have the power to act on a property—like a large factory—which homeowners think is assessed too low. Taxpayers may have to go to court to get these done.

On the other hand, it may be a good idea to try the local appeals board—if there is time—even if you do not think it can or will act. This can prevent a court from saying later that you did not use all remedies available to you. Further, what the law says the appeals board can do, and what it might do, are two different things. It never hurts to try.

Secondly, if you know what the board can do, it won't be able to bluff you. It won't be able to turn you away with excuses like "Sorry, we can only 'equalize' assessments. We can't help you."

The law isn't always clear on how much authority the board has. But it helps to know just what power it clearly has, and what is fuzzy. Perhaps you can make the fuzzy areas work in your favor.

be clear on the exact grounds

There will be variations from state to state, but in general you can appeal on one of three grounds:

1. *Overassessment*: Technically overassessment occurs when the assessment exceeds the full market value of the property. This rarely happens, because assessors are careful to make sure that everyone's assessment is at least a little below the full market value. Assessors try to make taxpayers believe that overassessment, in this sense, is the only wrong they can appeal. But in practice it is the least important. (As some jurisdictions move to full-value assessing, however,

overassessment will become more important as a grounds for appeal.)

2. *Unequal Assessment:* Ninety-nine times out of a hundred, the small taxpayer's problem, technically, is unequal assessment.

This means simply that his assessment is a higher percentage of his property than are the assessments of others.

To which "others" do you compare your assessment? What if the percentages of assessment level vary so widely that there is no apparent "common level"? These are complex legal questions. But most local boards won't get so technical that you would land in a wrangle over the apparent common level of assessment. If you can show clearly that you have been treated unfairly compared to properties like your own, you will be doing probably all you need to do. In fact, if you tried to do more, the local board might not understand what you were talking about.

3. *Illegal Assessment:* Being too high is not the only reason an assessment might be illegal. The assessor might have assessed property that is supposed to be exempt. Or he may have used a method the law does not allow. Or he may have failed to inspect your house, when the law required him to do so.

Illegal assessment can be the easiest to prove, because it does not involve demonstrating the assessment level for the whole community. It involves merely a point of law—even a technicality, though it probably means having to go to court. Courts, in fact, often welcome such grounds, since they provide a clear-cut and easy basis for deciding a case.

prepare your case thoroughly

It is important to know whether the board consists of laymen or full-time professionals. If the former, you should build your case toward a broad sense of simple equity. If you are dealing with someone who knows the assessment law, you will have to gear your case more to the legal technicalities. Do not worry about splitting legal hairs. This rarely happens at the local appeals level. The more law you can absorb, however, the more the board will see that you mean business.

Never walk cold into a meeting with an assessor or a local appeals board. Have your arguments firmly in mind, and the facts to back them up in hand.

Prepare a clear, solid presentation for the board. Use pictures and copies of documents, wherever possible.

1. Make sure to see your property record card to determine that the information on it is correct and complete. If there are mistakes, or it omits important information, try to make a Xerox copy of the card and bring it with you to the appeal.

If you can, bring *proof* that the record card is wrong. For example, if the card says your house has brick walls, when in fact the walls are wood, bring a picture of your wooden siding.

2. Make a list of the items that you think subtract from the value of your property, and that the assessor didn't take into account. Your list might include items like these:

- unpaved driveway
- basement leaks
- nearby airport (expressway) gives off noise and fumes
- needs new roof (plumbing, wiring, heating, paint job, etc.)
- no hook-up to municipal utilities
- soil is eroding
- restrictions in the deed limit how the property can be used
- high-rises or shopping center going up nearby
- developer promised there would be parks nearby, and then didn't deliver, causing you to pay more for your house than it is worth.

The more problems you can list, the stronger your case will be. And again try to document these points.

3. Find out whether the assessor has included in your assessment items which should not be there. Realtor sales commissions, settlement fees and closing costs are examples. The assessor also might be including personal property such as washers, dryers, stoves, and refrigerators which were purchased with the house but which may be legally exempt.

4. You cannot tell whether or not your own assessment is fair unless you compare it to assessments of others. If you can, find properties that are very much like your own, but are assessed lower. Take a picture of each one. Write beside it the address,

206 TAX POLITICS

the square footage of the lot, the land assessment, the building assessment (if these are listed separately), and any details that show the property is worth at least as much as yours, if not more. Then do the same for properties that are assessed about as much as yours but are clearly worth more. Of course, have a picture of your own house, with the same information, for comparison. It might be a good idea to attach these sheets to your appeal form. But keep a copy of your own to use at the hearing.

5. Find out whether any assessment-sales ratio studies have been done for your jurisdiction. Check the assessor's office, the county board of equalization (if there is one), the state board of equalization, the state tax department, division of property taxes (or its equivalent), and the U.S. Census Bureau's Census of Governments. Check also private civic groups. Citing a ratio study will add weight to your argument and show that you have done your homework.

6. Check out the technicalities. Did the assessor provide you yourself and other taxpayers with notice of your assessment in the manner and in the time required by law? Did he allow you access to assessment records so that you could prepare your appeal? The local review board technically might lack the authority to do anything about these, but if you know about them, and raise them, it may help convince the board that you have been treated unjustly. Or, the board might see that you have a genuine legal complaint, and might give you some relief to head off trouble.

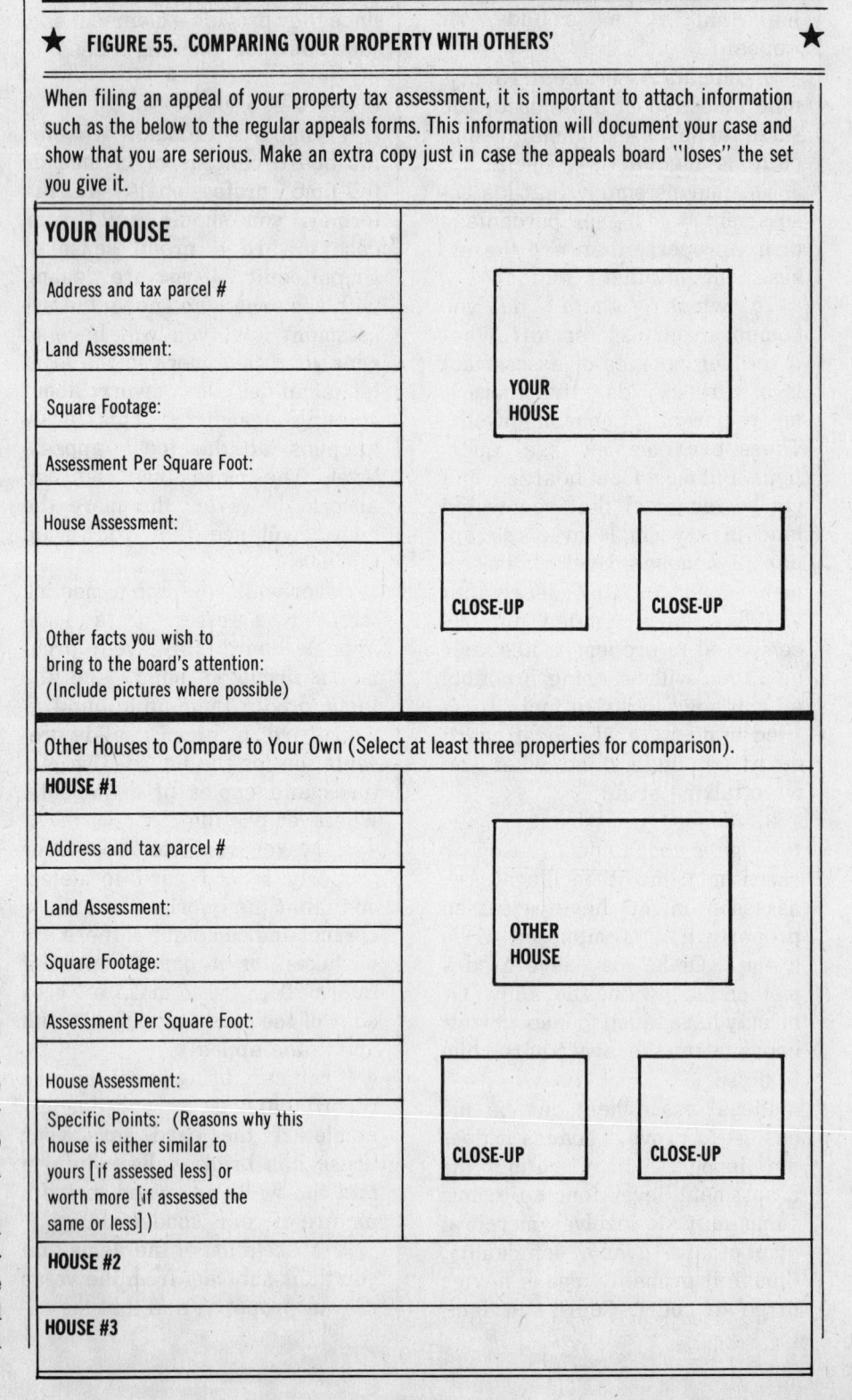

★ **FIGURE 55. COMPARING YOUR PROPERTY WITH OTHERS'** ★

When filing an appeal of your property tax assessment, it is important to attach information such as the below to the regular appeals forms. This information will document your case and show that you are serious. Make an extra copy just in case the appeals board "loses" the set you give it.

YOUR HOUSE

Address and tax parcel #

Land Assessment:

Square Footage:

Assessment Per Square Foot:

House Assessment:

Other facts you wish to bring to the board's attention: (Include pictures where possible)

[YOUR HOUSE]

[CLOSE-UP] [CLOSE-UP]

Other Houses to Compare to Your Own (Select at least three properties for comparison).

HOUSE #1

Address and tax parcel #

Land Assessment:

Square Footage:

Assessment Per Square Foot:

House Assessment:

Specific Points: (Reasons why this house is either similar to yours [if assessed less] or worth more [if assessed the same or less])

[OTHER HOUSE]

[CLOSE-UP] [CLOSE-UP]

HOUSE #2

HOUSE #3

don't raise irrelevant points

The property tax is a tax on the *value* of property. When you appeal a property tax assessment you should focus on that point. Don't complain that your husband or wife is ill or out of work, or that the price of food is going up, or that the local government is spending too much on the courthouse lawn. These things may be true, but appeals boards can't do anything about them and you may irritate them by wasting their time.

Some assessors and appeals boards do respond to hard luck stories. If you are sure yours does, and want to play that game, that's up to you.

an appeals system for the wealthy: the need for reform

Taxpayers who have looked into local appeals practices have found the over-all results that one would expect. The well-to-do use the system most and get most of the benefits.

Homeowners in Alexandria, Virginia studied over 400 decisions of their local review board in 1970 and found that the board had favored, in this order, land speculators, business property owners, slum landlords, and finally, homeowners. The goodwill toward land speculators was not surprising, since the review board consisted largely of realtors.

In a study of appeals in 1970-73, the St. Louis Tax Reform Group found that 87 percent of the appeals in one ward studied were made by real estate companies and that these gained 95 percent of the dollar benefits. The larger property owners tended to do better, even among homeowners.

Official studies similarly have shown that the well-to-do tend to use the appeals process the most. A 1973 study by the Arthur D. Little Co. for the U.S. Department of Housing and Urban Development found that in ten major U.S. cities, only 4.4 percent of the homeowners appealed their assessments, while 10 percent of "small investors" (forty or fewer units) and 24.9 percent of "large investors" did so.

A good appeals system would help to put tax justice within reach of small taxpayers and could be a powerful spur to assessment reform. The following would be useful steps in the right direction:

reliable ratio studies

Each state should compute the assessment ratio for each major type of property in each assessing jurisdiction. It is important that the state make these studies. Local officials have too much at stake in the outcome to be entrusted to do them. Taxpayers should be able to use these ratio studies in their appeals.

adequate notice

Each taxpayer should be entitled to receive a notice of his assessment each year, well before the official appeals and complaint period. The notice should explain in easy-to-understand language what taxpayers must do to appeal. Taxpayers should have access to the entire assessment roll soon enough to help them prepare.

separate and independent appeals system

The property tax appeals system should be as independent as possible from the officials who administer the tax or rely on the tax for revenue. One way to make the appeals system independent is to include it in a special tax court division of the state court system.

simple small claims procedure

Small taxpayers should be able to appeal their assessment in a simple setting like a small claims court. It should not be necessary to have a lawyer.

Taxpayers with a similar complaint should be able to combine their cases so that they do not have to go though the ordeal of appealing one at a time.

If taxpayers win a reduction, local officials should not be able to tie them up in higher and more complicated appeals.

small taxpayer advocate

There might be a special local official to help taxpayers prepare their appeals. This official might have broader powers to act as a tax ombudsman, keeping an eye on all aspects of the property tax system. Montgomery County, Maryland, recently established just such an office.

standards of proof

The standards of proof taxpayers must meet in their appeals should be simple and clear. State lawmakers should remove any old laws or court decisions which impose unfair burdens in this respect.

written records

There should be written records of all property tax appeals, including how the case was handled and why. These records, along with the hearings themselves should be open to the public.

208   TAX POLITICS

challenge assessments of others

Taxpayers should be able to challenge the assessments of property owners other than themselves.

end withholding

Large taxpayers should not be allowed to withhold their entire tax payment while an appeal is pending, since this forces the locality to settle just to get the revenue. Taxpayers should be able to hold back only the disputed amount, if anything.

collecting property taxes

When the local budget-makers have set the tax rate, the tax collector applies this tax rate to the assessed value of each property, and comes up with the amount each property owner must pay. Often, several overlapping units of government send their separate tax rates to a central tax collector who combines them in order to send each taxpayer a single tax bill. Alternately, each separate unit—school districts, water districts, etc—send their own tax bills, so that each property taxpayer receives several. Most local units collect property taxes only once, or at most twice, per year. A few collect four times a year.

Many homeowners do not get their own tax bills. Most people take out a mortgage to buy a home and the bill goes to the bank that holds the taxpayer's mortgage.

escrow accounts

Most mortgage agreements stipulate that the borrower has to pay in monthly installments not just the interest and principal on the mortgage, but the property taxes and insurance fees as well. When local governments collect the property taxes only once (at year's end) or twice a year, the lender gets to invest the "escrowed" money until then.

Escrow accounts are one of the ghosts of the 1930s depression that are still with us. In 1933, over a quarter of the property taxes went unpaid in the nation's 200 largest cities. "More people lost homes because they couldn't pay the tax bill," says a Washington savings and loan official, "than for any other reason." So when the federal government got into the business of insuring mortgages in 1934, to make sure that taxes were paid, it ruled that for any mortgage it insured, the home-buyer would have to pay property taxes (and insurance fees) monthly, with the mortgage payment.

The rule did not prevent the banks from paying interest on the required escrow accounts. And the escrow rule didn't apply at all to "conventional mortgages"—mortgages the federal government did not insure. In fact, on conventional loans many lenders actually did give the borrowers their due, through capitalization: When the homeowner made a monthly tax and insurance payment, the lender cut by that amount the borrower's remaining mortgage debt. Since the debt went down, the interest on the debt went down too. Thus as the property tax and interest payments built up over the year, the homeowner had to pay less interest on his mortgage.

But in the late fifties money became "tight." Loans were hard to get, and interest rates went up. Savings and loans stopped capitalizing the property tax payments. A 1973 survey by the U.S. Savings and Loan League of mainly the larger S&Ls showed that about 16 percent continued to capitalize their borrowers' monthly tax and insurance.

Some pay interest on the escrow accounts. Such institutions are a distinct minority, however. A full 84 percent in the S&L League survey used the escrow system, with few paying interest. Similarly, an informal survey by the *Kiplinger* magazine turned up one commercial bank in eighty that paid interest.

The amounts at stake are not small. In 1971 more than 20 million homeowners—over 60 percent of the total—had mortgaged homes. Their total debt was $227 billion, more than the entire federal budget in 1970. The staff of the House Banking and Currency Committee found in 1972 that the nation's savings and loans held at any one time an average of $1.5 billion in escrows. If the savings and loans invested this billion-and-a-half at just 6 percent, they would gain at least $90 million. S&Ls hold under half the mortgages for single-family homes. Insurance companies and commercial banks are other holders of the homeowner debt.

If the homeowner is tying up money in escrow accounts without any return on it, his loss as a taxpayer is even greater. While property taxes are sitting in bank escrow accounts, local governments have "cash flow" problems. To pay salaries and bills, they borrow "in anticipation of taxes." From whom do they borrow? Local banks.

The Citizens Action Program found that Chicago banks in 1970 were holding at least $200 million in property taxes in their escrow accounts, while the city had to pay over $37.5 million in interest to borrow short-term funds to keep its schools open and other services running.

New York City's June 1974 sale of $800 million in tax anticipation notes at over 7 percent interest would cost the city around $6.6 million, City Controller Harrison J. Goldin said, and come "in large part from the taxes of families who are already struggling to make ends meet."

Not all local governments have the cash-flow problems of Chicago or New York. But the problem turns up in most of the places taxpayers have looked.

Over five years Houston, Texas, has had to borrow $127 million from the Texas Commerce Bank to tide it over until the taxes come in. By the summer of 1973 Houston expected to borrow $35 million more. In 1972, Arlington, Virginia, had to borrow $10 million when it ran out of cash shortly before collection day.

Massachusetts State Senator Jack Backman complained in 1971 that "75 percent to 90 percent of the taxes in our commonwealth are held by banks and other mortgage holders, totaling approximately $1.3 billion per year.... There is no reason why the banks should have in escrow an average of more than half a billion dollars of tax monies, while cities and towns have to borrow from these very same banks while they are waiting for the taxes." Uncle Sam provides the icing on the cake. The banks and other lenders pay no federal income taxes on the interest they get from the local governments.

State lawmakers are offering two solutions. One would have the local governments collect property taxes more often, so they wouldn't run out of cash. State Senator Jack Backman, in fact, wants the local governments to collect their taxes in twelve installments. Backman estimated that Massachusetts cities and towns would get a $200 million windfall the first year, and that they would save a total of $20 million in interest payments thereafter.

The second solution is to require the banks to pay interest on the escrow accounts. Four states—Connecticut, Maryland, Massachusetts, and New York—have taken this step at this writing, and numerous others appear inclined to follow. In addition, Washington, D.C., Attorney Benny Kass has successfully sued the savings and loans there, prompting the payment of interest on the escrows. In theory, one approach does not preclude the other, but in practice frequent collections will considerably reduce the amount of interest an escrow account could earn and would raise the cost of collection. On balance, the better idea seems to be to collect property taxes more often. Local governments then would get their money when they need it—and that, after all, is the purpose of the tax. They would have less need for short-term borrowing at taxpayer expense. And the taxpayer would still have the benefit of paying several smaller bills rather than one big one.

How Property Taxes Work 209

property tax delinquencies

Property taxes which are not paid on time are called *delinquent*. Most states provide a grace period of from two to five years before the taxing unit can take action against the delinquent taxpayer.

In general, the property tax laws enable the local government to foreclose after a set period of time, but they do not *require* the locality to do so. The Ohio Public Interest Action Group (OPIAG) discovered that Franklin County (Columbus) had only *one* attorney to handle all phases of the property tax, of which collections are just one. No wonder delinquencies were backed up for twenty years.

But there is another side to delinquency. Property tax delinquents—people and corporations who don't pay on time—are costing the rest of us large amounts of money.

A main reason why big corporations don't pay property taxes on time is that the penalties, even when localities enforce them strictly, are in effect a low-rate loan from the local government. In April 1969, New York City had $121 million in unpaid property taxes on its books. The *Wall Street Journal* reported:

The city claims that many real estate operators, including some of New York's largest property owners, find it cheaper to withhold their taxes and absorb the penalty, rather than borrow at today's peak rates.

"They hold out for four years and then kick in just before a lien is smacked on their property," a city official says.

Delinquencies in New York City continued to climb, reaching $158 million by 1974.

Businesses also go delinquent in order to bargain down their taxes to a tiny fraction of the original levy. *Chicago Today* disclosed recently that Windy City businesses regularly held back their personal property tax payments, not even bothering to contest them before the regular appeals board. Instead they just sat back and waited to be contacted by the county states attorneys who settled for only 1.7—2.5 cents on the dollar. *Chicago Today* computed the revenue loss for 1972 at $160 million.

Taxpayers lose at least three ways when individuals and corporations don't pay their taxes. First, the local government loses revenue. As a result, it must cut back programs, lay off workers, or borrow at expensive short-term rates. Second, it has to take the time and spend the money to go after the delinquents—when it does. And third, it actually must raise the tax rate to create a special fund to cover future delinquencies.

Renters lose too. Their rents are raised to provide for increasing property taxes. But when the landlord doesn't pay the taxes, the local government may be able to foreclose on the property, board it up, and evict the tenants. This is why tenant groups are calling for laws requiring landlords to set aside property taxes in escrow accounts to be sure they are paid on time.

tax sales

After the grace period, the taxing unit forecloses on the property. The laws of most states make foreclosure a *summary* proceeding which means it can happen very quickly through special, brief court procedures. In some places the local government does not even have to go to court. The last known property owner is supposed to be notified before a foreclosure begins. Often the only notice given and required is a small-print ad in the classified section of the local newspaper.

The foreclosure simply means the local government has asserted its claim to the property. After that, the local government sells the property to recover the taxes due. To sell the property it holds a *tax sale*, a public auction to which everyone, even the delinquent taxpayer himself, can go and bid.

In general, the high bidder at the tax sale gets a certificate of title. In exchange, he pays the taxes due, plus interest, and continues to pay the taxes for two or three years. During those years the former owner can still redeem the property. To do this, the former owner repays the winning bidder the back taxes the latter had picked up, plus interest. The amount of interest, often very high, depends on the way the tax sale was run. When there was *bidding on interest*, the interest is set during the bidding. When there was *bidding on the property*, the interest rate is set by law.

Earlier we mentioned the difference between real estate taxes and personal property taxes. Real estate taxes are called *secured* because the local government feels it has good security on these. The property isn't going anyplace. Personal property taxes normally are called *unsecured* because the owner can move the property away. Usually the delinquency date falls much sooner for unsecured than for secured taxes. And often the local government can seize other property of the delinquent taxpayer, not just the property taxed, in order to collect.

The rules differ from state to state, and even between localities within a state. In Michigan, when the property owner doesn't pay his taxes for three years in a row, the county auctions off the property at a public tax sale. In effect, the "buyer" gets the privilege of paying off the back taxes, and of paying future taxes for eighteen months. If the original owner does not redeem the property by then, by paying back the buyer plus interest, the tax buyer gets the property. If the original owner redeems the property within a year, he must pay the tax buyer what the latter bid at the auction, plus 1 percent interest per month. If the original owner redeems after the first year, the tax buyer can get 50 percent interest.

Tax sales are supposed to be public. In practice, they are often obscure, little-understood procedures that become a private real estate market for a small group of city-hall insiders. The *Detroit Free Press* reported, for example, in 1970 that in Wayne County just three "professionals" bought 85 percent of the property.

Tax buyers have been especially active in urban renewal areas. They make big gains by getting properties at tax sales, then turn around and take part or all of the award when the local government buys them.

Chapter 8
Investigating Property Taxes

We have discussed the various inequities and failings in property taxation. This chapter suggests how to investigate and document these in your own community.

★ ★ ★ ★ ★ ★ ★

how to uncover underassessment

The laws of most states say that "market" value is the standard for property tax assessments, even if they allow the assessor to use just a fraction of that value. It follows that sales price—what someone actually pays for the property when he buys it or a property very much like it — is the acid test for determining whether a property is properly assessed or underassessed.

finding sales prices

The easiest source is one that not many people know about. In many areas there is a special publication or service bureau for realtors and mortgage lenders which lists every property that is sold, along with the sales price and other information. In Philadelphia it is called *The Philadelphia Realty Directory and Service*, published by the Philadelphia Real Estate Directory Inc. In Washington, D.C. it is called *Lusk's Directory*.

You should be able to find such publications at the main public library, or at the municipal reference library, if there is one. If anyone in the assessor's office is friendly, they may have one you can use, or they may suggest where you can get one. Realtors and mortgage lenders (such as savings and loans) and officials for housing and renewal programs are other possible sources. In the Boston area there are services called the Real Estate Guide's Inc. and the Metropolitan Mortgage Bureau. The former charges a fee for each property on which they give information. The second is for members only.

If there is no such publication, then your task is a little harder. Find out first whether there is any government office, state or local, that keeps records of all properties that are bought and sold. In Illinois, for example, every time a property changes hands a so-called "green sheet" must be filed with the Illinois Department of Local Government Affairs.

The recorder of deeds is another possibility. In many states, whenever real estate changes hands, the seller must pay a tax; and tax stamps, showing the sales price, are attached to the deed. The recorder may even keep a separate list of all the properties that are sold each year. The tax stamps are not 100 percent reliable, however. If the buyer "assumed paper" — i.e., if he took over what remained to be paid on the seller's mortgage instead of taking out a new mortgage, this may not appear. Also, there is nothing to stop the buyer from buying more tax stamps than he has to. Some speculators do, to make the property appear to be worth more than it is. Ask some real estate people how reliable the tax stamps are in your area.

If the assessor is doing his job, then he is getting a list of all properties sold from whoever in the local government keeps those records. (In California, however, no one does. The assessor himself has to send a questionnaire to everyone who buys a property.) Perhaps the assessor will let you see this list. If he doesn't, find out whether you have a right to see the list under your state's access-to-information laws.

Another source is the real estate or business page of the local newspaper. These often list, daily or weekly, selected property sales, to give investors an idea of the larger commercial and industrial properties. At least that's a

211

212 TAX POLITICS

start! You should try to weed out all the sales that do not show what the property is actually worth. Sales between family members are an example.

For certain kinds of property you may not be able to find sales prices. You may have to figure out how much a building is worth by finding out how much it cost to build. If the building is new, the construction cost should show the value fairly closely. If you make allowance for wear-and-tear or *depreciation*, you can use this method on older properties too. Companies often brag in press releases and publicity about how much they are putting into a new building or plant. Articles in business publications have this information as well.

If the company doesn't tell the press what a new building is worth, and if there is no other public record, you can "price it out" with the help of construction cost manuals used by assessors, private appraisers and mortgage lenders, or the manuals prepared by state assessment agencies and the larger local assessor's offices.

Forms and reports that businesses have to file with agencies of local, state and federal governments can be an invaluable source. The Uniroyal Corporation in Middlebury, Connecticut had consistently refused to reveal the value of its sprawling Oxford Management and Research Center, either to the town or to the appraisal company the town had hired to redo the assessments. Protests from taxpayers and from a member of the town's board of tax review were to no avail. Then in the spring of 1973, the Connecticut Citizen Action Group, discovered that the plant actually belonged to the Metropolitan Life Insurance Company which had to file an extensive report with the Connecticut Insurance Department each year. In its latest report, Metropolitan had claimed a book value for the center of close to $42 million. United Appraisal of East Hartford had appraised the plant at only about $17 million. The difference came to almost half a million dollars in property taxes which Middlebury was losing each year.

Competitors of the business in question or private appraisers may be willing to give you a rough estimate of what a particular plant is worth. Or, if the plant is new, perhaps the consulting architect, or someone else involved in building it, might do so.

Experts who give such advice may not wish their names made public. In such cases, perhaps they can suggest ways that you can verify what they say from other sources.

If you cannot find out the property's value by any of these direct methods, you may have to piece together information about the property from various sources; information such as the output of factories, the number of people employed, the rents that an office or an apartment building is charging. Then you use this information to estimate what the property must be worth. These indirect methods are not airtight. They are rough, but they will do if they show clearly that an assessment is not anywhere near the actual value.

Thus, if you can find out how many workers there are at a plant, you can often figure out the approximate property value by using industrywide rules of thumb. These are figures, worked up by trade associations, labor unions and government agencies that show the average ratio of workers to property (or *capital*) in a particular industry. Be aware that the proportion of workers to property in an industry may vary with the size of the firm. The bigger firms usually have more property per worker, the smaller firms usually have less. If the rule of thumb you find is a single average for a whole industry, you'll want to take this fact into account.

A recent episode in the tax battle between Gary, Indiana, and its major taxpayer, U. S. Steel, shows how to apply the property-per-worker approach to a single company. The U. S. Steel Company in Gary in effect presents its own assessment to the Gary assessor. It won't let him see its books and even refuses to take out city building permits so as not to give city officials an idea how much its additions and improvements are worth.

To put it mildly, Gary is a city that has problems. Thus Gary Mayor Richard Hatcher has a special interest in seeing that U. S. Steel pays its legal share of taxes. The mayor's finance advisor, Arnold Reingold, used figures from the company's annual reports and other sources and calculated that about 14 percent of U. S. Steel's employees were in Gary. If the ratio of workers to property there was just average, he reasoned, then about 14 per-

Investigating Property Taxes

cent of the company's taxable assets would be in Gary too. Taking these figures, he reached a value of $650 million for Steel's Gary works. This value suggested that the company's assessment was at least $110 million too low.

The value of a factory can also be estimated from its output. The U. S. Iron and Steel Institute, for example, publishes a *Directory of Iron and Steel Works of the United States and Canada* which lists the output of every steel-producing plant.

The Citizens Action Program in Chicago took this approach for the U. S. Steel Company's South Works. CAP discovered that the same two men in the Chicago assessor's office had been assessing U. S. Steel for years, and that these two men had accepted the figures the company provided them without questioning or checking.

Here, step by step, is how CAP pierced U. S. Steel's wall of silence:

1. First, CAP learned that the South Works produced about 3.6 million ingot-tons of raw steel. This was 11.5 percent of all the raw steel the company produced.

2. From the company's annual report, CAP learned that about 80 percent of U.S. Steel's revenues came from producing and fabricating steel.

3. Assuming that about 80 percent of all U.S. Steel's property was involved in steel production (a conservative assumption) and that about 11.5 percent of that amount would be at the South Works, CAP came up with a value, before depreciation, of $789.5 million.

4. To see whether they were on the right track, CAP checked this figure against industrywide estimates. An article in *Fortune* (March 1971) had said that steel mills were costing as much as $350 per ingot-ton of production. CAP's figure came to about $219 per raw ingot-ton. So they were clearly in the ball park.

5. In Illinois, movable equipment in plants is taxed separately, as personal property. So CAP got the assessor's figure for this and subtracted it. That left $757.4 million for the South Works real estate.

6. Next CAP subtracted pollution-control equipment, tax-free under state law. The company wouldn't disclose the figure for South Works. So CAP took the company's total pollution-control expenditure from its annual report and assumed a proportional share went to each of the company's plants. That meant about 11.5 percent of the total was in South Works. So CAP subtracted that amount also; $723.2 million in taxable property was left.

7. Then, from the assessor's records, CAP gleaned the depreciation rate which the Chicago assessor himself applied to U.S. Steel's plant, to take account of wear-and-tear. This rate, which assessor Cullerton called a "condition factor," was 60 percent. That left $433.94 million as CAP's best evaluation of the market value of the plant.

8. The assessor said he took 45 to 55 percent of the market value of industrial property in making an assessment. To be conservative, CAP took 45 percent. Thus by CAP's reckoning, the assessment should have been at least $195.3 million. Instead, U.S. Steel was assessed at only 45.7 million.

9. Then CAP applied the Chicago tax rate to the assessment and found that the underassessment had cost Chicago at least $11.9 million in 1969 and $16.4 million in 1970.

10. Finally, CAP found out the share of local property taxes that went to each of the city taxing authorities. Then it figured out how much each one lost because U.S. Steel was not paying its share. Here is what Chicago taxpayers were losing:

★ **FIGURE 56. TAXES LOST BY CHICAGO PUBLIC AGENCIES DUE TO U.S. STEEL UNDERASSESSMENT** ★

Agency	Taxes Lost 1970	1969
School board	$ 6,445,100	$ 4,572,000
City	$ 6,312,550	$ 4,740,000
County	$ 1,216,700	$ 770,000
Park district	$ 1,167,350	$ 840,000
Sanitary district	$ 559,000	$ 570,000
Chicago City College	$ 509,700	$ 330,000
Forest preserve	$ 180,850	$ 109,000
Mosquito abatement	$ 49,300	$ 40,000
	$16,440,550	$11,971,000

Chicago was losing these amounts from the underassessment of U. S. Steel *alone*. Both the Reingold-Gary and CAP-Chicago techniques gave a low estimate of the underassessment, moreover. Mr. Reingold pointed out that U.S. Steel's book values, in its annual report, listed its Gary land at the land's cost in 1900. An assessor would—or at least should—use the current value of the land. Similarly, Reingold said, the company lists plant and machinery on the balance sheet at their depreciated value. Company accountants use artificial depreciation rates, chopping off a certain amount of value each year, regardless of whether the property actually went down in value by that much. The assessor, by contrast, is supposed to assess according to the actual current value of property. Both Reingold and CAP based their estimates on these conservative balance-sheet figures. CAP's estimate was probably conservative for other reasons as well. CAP assumed, for example, that since 80 percent of U. S. Steel's revenue came from steel production, 80 percent of its property would be devoted to making steel. Yet making steel is more capital-intensive than other U. S. Steel ventures, so the 80 percent figure was probably low. In addition, CAP applied the depreciation rate the assessor himself used. This rate was probably overly generous to the steel companies.

The income approach is difficult for taxpayers to apply, but they can ferret out a number of key points without going through the entire process. You can compare the capitalization rate the assessor is using with the one that investors and mortgage lenders say they use. If there is a difference, ask the assessor why. Similarly, you can check the depreciation factor. Is the assessor allowing overly generous amounts, ignoring what the property is really worth? Does he let the company use the same depreciation for property taxes as for income taxes? You can check for fictional allowances. Some assessors hide tax breaks to new buildings under a "starting-up allowance." This is supposed to compensate for "bugs" plus starting-up costs, but some assessors will grant it even when the building is running just fine right from the start. The number of such ploys is limited only by the assessors' imagination and integrity.

investigating unequal assessments

The basic tool for discovering whether assessments are fair is an *assessment-sales ratio study*. It involves simply comparing property tax assessments with sales prices for the same properties. You can pick out certain properties that sold for the *same amount*, and see if they are assessed the same. Or you can pick out properties that are assessed the same and compare their sales prices.

If you are only trying to find out if the assessment on your own home is fair, you can select just a few properties that are comparable to yours and sold recently. But you may want to compare different kinds of properties: residential and business properties, expensive and average homes, small and large businesses, gas stations and office buildings, developed and vacant land. It all depends on what kind of favoritism you are looking for.

how to make an assessment–sales ratio study

Let's suppose we want to compare the assessment-sales price ratio (another name for the assessment level) of homes with that of business properties in your community. Here is how we might do it.

Step 1. Set up two worksheets, one for homes, the other for business properties (figure 57).

Step 2. Find the properties of each type that have sold during the past year. "Finding Sales Prices" (p. 211) explains how to go about finding this information. Enter the list of properties, the date of sale, and the sales price on your worksheets.

Step 3. Go to the assessor's office to look up the assessment for each property and put it in column 3.

Step 4. Divide the sales price, column 5, into the assessment, column 3. This will give you the assessment-sales ratio. A slide rule or a calculating machine will make this job much easier. The result goes into column 6.

Step 5. Find the common assessment-sales ratio. There are two ways. One is to find the *average*. You just add up the individual ratios in column 6 and divide by the number of items. A better way is to find the *median* instead of the average. To find the median, you list all the ratios in column 7, from the highest to the lowest. Then go halfway down the list. That is, if there are twenty-one items, you take the eleventh from the top. If there are an even number, you take the halfway point between the two middle numbers. The median is better than the average because one or two ratios that are far afield do not throw it all out of kilter.

Put the average or the median, whichever you use, in box 6A at the bottom of column 6.

If the ratios in box 6A for the types of properties you are comparing are close, then these properties are receiving fairly equal treatment. If the ratios are more than five apart, then the assessor is most likely favoring one kind of property over the other. It is important to note that the lower the common assessment-sales ratio, the more important any difference becomes. A gap of say, five, between the common assessment ratio for homes and that for commercial properties means much more if assessments are low, say 20 percent of market value, than if they are higher, say 50 percent. For example, if homes are assessed at 20 percent of full value, and businesses are assessed at 15 percent, then homes are assessed 25 percent too high. But if the figures are 50 percent and 45 percent, then homes are overassessed by only 10 percent.

You can now also answer the question of how close the average ratios are to what the law requires the assessment level to be, and to what the assessor says they are. On looking at the assessment ratios for one category of properties, e.g., individual homes, are they pretty much the same, or are they all over the place? If the latter, you should look for a pattern. Group them according to neighborhoods, and according to the sales price of the home. Is the assessor favoring some of these over others?

Investigating Property Taxes 215

★ **FIGURE 57. SAMPLE WORKSHEET TO FIND ASSESSMENT-SALES RATIO AND COEFFICIENT OF DISPERSION** ★

Title: _____
(Indicate category of property to be listed: homes, industries, etc.)

1 Number each property	2 List information	3 Assessment (Land / Improvement / Total)	4 Date of sale	5 Sales price	6 Assessment-sales ratio (assessment ÷ sales price)	7 Difference between assessment-sales ratio for each property (6) and common ratio (6A)	8 Additional comments
1							
2							
3							
4							
5							

6A Average or Median Assessment-Sales Ratio or Common Assessment level

7A Average assessment error

7B Coefficient of dispersion (7A ÷ 6A)

Column 1 is merely to give a number to every property that you use.

In column 2 you list as much information about the property as you can: the address, the owner, the "tax parcel number," the bank that holds the mortgage (if there is one). You may want to make separate columns for some or all of these items. They are not all necessary right away, but they may be helpful later. If you are pressed for time, just get the address, owner, and tax parcel number.

In column 3 you put the assessment. If it is broken down between land assessment and building assessment on the assessment roll, you should copy both these figures. Be certain to use the assessment that was in effect <u>before</u> the property was sold.

Column 4 is for the date of sale.

Column 5 is for the sales price.

Column 6 is for the assessment-sales ratio, which is just the assessment (column 3) divided by the sales price (column 5).

Column 7 is for the assessment error.

Column 8 is for any comments or remarks about the particular property or sale.

216 TAX POLITICS

finding the coefficient of dispersion

The assessment-sales price study enables us to find the common assessment level for different kinds of property, and to compare these to see if the assessor favors one kind over another. To find out whether the owners of the same kinds of property are treated uniformly, we take the ratio study one step further. No new data are needed. The figure we are going to find, the "coefficient of dispersion," represents the typical assessment error, or injustice, expressed as a percent of the common assessment level. It shows how wide off the common assessment level any one assessment is, on the average.

Step 1. Calculate for each property the difference between its assessment ratio (column 6) and the common assessment level (box 6A) and put it in column 7.

Step 2. Find the average of these differences. Add up all the figures in column 7, and divide the sum by the number of figures in the column. Put the result in box 7A. Now you have the average amount by which the assessor is off the common level on each assessment.

Step 3. To express the average error as a percent of the common assessment level, divide the common ratio in box 6A into the average error in box 7A and put the answer into box 7B.

Now we have the *coefficient of dispersion*. The lower it is, the more uniform assessments are generally. How low should it be? If it is ten or less, the assessor is doing a respectable job. If it is more than 15 percent, he is doing poorly. Experts consider a typical assessment error of between 10

★ **FIGURE 58. FINDING THE TYPICAL ASSESSMENT ERROR: AN ILLUSTRATION** ★

Suppose we have four houses, each of which sold for $30,000. The assessment rolls show the homes assessed at $10,000, $16,000, $22,000, and $28,000. (Remember, they should have been assessed the same.) The assessment-sales price ratios for the three would be:

1) $\dfrac{\$10,000}{\$30,000} = 33\%$ 2) $\dfrac{\$16,000}{\$30,000} = 53\%$

3) $\dfrac{\$22,000}{\$30,000} = 73\%$ 4) $\dfrac{\$28,000}{\$30,000} = 93\%$

To find the median, we rank the four in order, from highest to lowest:

93
73
53
33

Since there are an even number of ratios, we take the middle two and find the halfway point between them:

$$\begin{array}{r} 73 \\ + \ 53 \\ \hline 126 \end{array} \qquad 126 \div 2 = 63$$

Thus the median assessment-sales price ratio, or common assessment level, is 63 percent.

Now we want to find the average deviation from this common level — that is, how much, on the average, each individual assessment was off the mark.

First we find the difference between the common level — the average assessment-sales price ratio — and the ratio for each individual assessment.

$$\begin{array}{cccc} 63 & 63 & 63 & 63 \\ -\ 33 & -\ 53 & -\ 73 & -\ 93 \\ \hline 30 & 10 & -10 & -30 \end{array}$$

(We can disregard plus or minus signs.)

Next we find the average of these differences.

30
10
10
30
——
80               $80 \div 4 = 20$

Thus the average assessment error is 20 percent.

Finally we express this average difference as a percent of the common level:

$$20 \div 63 = .32$$

Thus the coefficient is 32 percent.

In other words, the typical assessment was 32 percent higher or lower than it should have been. This means there could be a 64 percent gap between the assessments of two homeowners who should have been assessed exactly the same.

percent and 15 percent, plus or minus, to be acceptable. Some go as high as 20 percent, mainly in compromise to what they perceive as the situation today. If it is over 20 percent, the sooner you get a new assessor, the better. A coefficient of dispersion of over twenty means that every taxpayer, on the average, is assessed 20 percent too high or too low, and that there are taxpayers who are paying twice as much tax as others even though they should be paying exactly the same.

Assessors who get their typical error down to 5 percent to 10 percent deserve applause. Since market values change constantly, there are genuine problems in cutting the error much below that.

The state department or agency concerned with assessing, the state board of equalization, or even the local assessor, may have done ratio and dispersion studies; or they may have data on hand that will help. These agencies often keep such data close to their chest, so if they tell you "no," check further. The Governments Division of Bureau of the Census, Washington, D.C., every five years conducts a study of "taxable property values" as part of its Census of Governments. The study covers each state, along with selected local areas, and includes assessment ratios and coefficients of dispersion. Get a copy of Volume 2 of the Census of Governments, Parts 1 and 2, from the U.S. Government Printing Office, Washington, D.C., or at a good local library. These agencies often have much more data than they publish.

what to find out about delinquencies

You should find out who the delinquents are and how much they owe. You'll want to know whether they are large corporations or other large taxpayers or small taxpayer hardship cases. The local tax collector or auditor, or the assessor, should have the list. The state tax department also may have at least the total amount of delinquencies for each property tax jurisdiction.

You should know who the officials responsible for delinquents are. Do they have enough staff and budget to do the job? If they can't go after all the delinquencies, how do they choose the ones they do?

What is the penalty for delinquent taxes? Is it high enough to deter the practice?

What percent of the delinquencies are cleared up each year? Has the local government ever had to borrow money, or cut back programs, because taxes aren't being paid on time?

If the assessor or tax collector will not divulge this information, you can try to enlist the help of a public official or a group that needs the revenues that are not being collected. School boards may be especially receptive. Public employees' unions, such as the local chapters of the American Federation of Teachers (AFT) or the American Federation of State, County, and Municipal Employees (AFSCME), have no official authority to get this information but their influence could be important. At a minimum, local governments should be required to publish the list of delinquents and the amount they owe in the newspaper each year.

how to check for nonlisting

Nonlisting is one of the more difficult assessment loopholes to detect since, by definition, it means finding something that isn't on a list. You have no idea, therefore, what or where it might be. On the other hand, the assessor can dispute you when you question his assessments, but there is not much he can say if you turn up property that he doesn't have on the assessment roll.

One way to check up is to make a list of ten or so fairly new factories and office buildings in your community and see if they are on the assessment roll. Find out when they were completed from the occupancy permit and make sure they have been on the rolls since then.

You can also make a list of properties—factories, office buildings, high-rise apartments—that the owners have changed or improved. Go to the local building department and find out from the building permit how much this work cost. (Be aware that the amounts on the building permits usually are at least 20 to 30 percent less than the actual cost of the repairs.) Then look at the assessment records to see if and by how much the assessor changed the assessment. (Remember, the assessment should go up by the percentage of market value that is used in your locality.)

218 TAX POLITICS

If bank accounts in your state are subject to a property tax, compare the average daily deposits in major local banks for the two weeks before and the two weeks after assessment day. You should be able to find this data in Federal Reserve Bank, bankers' trade and chamber of commerce publications. If accounts drop suddenly as assessment day comes near and then shoot up when it is past, they are probably converting their accounts into tax-exempt government securities for a few days to avoid the taxes.

Compare bank statements of total assets, reported to the state banking commission and in reports to shareholders, with property tax assessment for intangible property. You can do the same for other financial institutions, such as insurance companies. Be certain you are clear on the law regarding this property, however—what is taxable, what isn't.

If you live in an area with coal and mineral deposits, are these on the tax rolls? Publications such as *United States Mineral Resources* (Prof. Paper #820), published by the U.S. Geological Survey, will tell you approximately how much of the various types of minerals there are in your state. Compare these figures with statewide totals assessed for property taxes, if your state has this figure.

If construction machinery is taxable in your state, check large construction sites, including strip mines, before, after and on assessment day. Make lists of the property there. Take photographs. Is this property on the assessment rolls. Does the company drive its equipment away before assessment day to avoid the assessment?

Find out if the local building department has a figure for the total amount of new construction in your locality over the past year. Subtract a percent equal to the percent of local real estate that is tax-exempt (unless this tax-exempt property is largely parkland or forests, where much construction is not likely). Then use the actual local assessment-sales price ratio to determine how much of that new property value should be on the assessment rolls. (Remember, you will come up with a very conservative figure because building permits understate the actual cost of new construction.) You will have to take account of old property that increased in value. Find out, if you can, the average percentage increase in local property values during the period you are looking at. The difference between this total and the amount on the new assessment roll is what the assessor allotted to new construction.

Check the records of local or state boards and regulatory agencies to find changes in property value of businesses they regulate. The Citizen Action Program (CAP) in Chicago won a major victory using this approach. From the records of the Illinois Racing Commission, CAP learned that five Cook County racetracks had made major improvements that were not reflected on the assessment rolls. Similarly, CAP learned from records at the Illinois Commerce Commission that the Illinois Central Railroad was no longer using a valuable part of its property for railroad purposes. The Illinois Central is exempt from property taxes, but only for property it uses in railroading. Yet the Chicago assessor had not added to the tax rolls the property the IC was now using commercially. CAP exposed the assessor's omissions, and kept up the pressure on him to act. When the new assessment rolls came out, the racetrack assessments had been raised by almost $3.5 million—an increase of 25 percent—and the Illinois Central's assessment by over $4.5 million.

Make a list of new home developments and check when they went onto the assessment rolls. Did the assessor give the developer a free ride until the properties were sold? If the homes were still not 100 percent completed on assessment day, did the assessor include the work that had been done so far? (Check whether your state laws require the assessing of work in progress.)

One clue to whether property is being left off the tax rolls is the state of the tax maps. Does the assessor keep a complete up-to-date set? If not, how far behind are these maps? Another question is whether the assessor has a good system for keeping track of changes. Does he check exempt property each year to make sure it still qualifies for the exemption? Does he see all building permits and relevant reports of other departments and agencies, does he conduct regular audits?

exempt property

There are two main areas of interest with exemptions. You want to know how diligently your assessor watches tax-exempt property to make sure that such property truly qualifies for the exemption. And you may want to figure out the revenue loss to your community that exemptions produce. In either case you would start out by asking your assessor for the list and total value of exempt properties. [He may not be required by law to have either.]

To check out exempted property, you'll have to know what property is legally exempt in your state.

Assessors often are lax in checking exemptions. Once a property gets onto the exemption list it just stays there, even if the owner puts it to a nonexempt use or sells it to someone else who does. First find out if the assessor makes each owner of exempt property submit a signed application every year. If he doesn't, you can be sure that people who should be paying taxes are receiving a free ride.

Then take a sample of properties from the exemptions list and visit them. You may find properties that have changed use completely—a church torn down to be replaced by an apartment house, for example. Or you may find otherwise exempt property put to a nonexempt use: a church parking lot operated commercially during the week, or doctors running private medical practices out of exempt, supposedly charitable hospitals. (The state laws vary on the uses to which exempt property can be put. Be certain to check on yours.)

Occasionally an assessor comes along who takes the initiative himself. Like Ken Johnson, who was elected assessor of Pierce County (Tacoma), Washington in 1970. Johnson, who openly avows, "I'm a politician and I'm proud of it," set up a special exemption division to investigate and review the seven-thousand-odd exempt properties in Pierce County, worth then about $300 million. Johnson's new "exemption division" did not have to look long or hard. It found, for example, that the American Legion was getting an exemption for a meeting hall that was actually a rental office building. The Legion had not held a meeting in it during the ten-plus years it had owned the building. Churches were claiming exemptions for parsonages that they rented out to others. Churches, hospitals, and other exempt groups were buying up real estate, claiming exemptions on the grounds they intended to build on the land in the future. A nine-acre cemetery on the exemption list turned out to be a parking lot. Another cemetary sported a profit-making mortuary as well as the owner's home.

The exemption division put the dormitories of local universities onto the tax rolls—where the law said they should be. It took away exemptions for hospitals which wouldn't file financial reports. And in what must be a high-water mark in assessing history, it revoked all the exemptions of the Mormon Church when the latter wouldn't produce figures to show that its property was supported through donations and not through profit-making ventures.

All told, in the six months after he took office in January 1971, Johnson had put $31 million worth of property back on the tax rolls. Not all of Johnson's actions stuck. Some failed on appeal. Others were wiped out by the state legislature. But the new assessor was making his point. "Johnson is unpopular with churchmen, legislators, bureaucrats, regents, boards of directors, and even his fellow assessors," wrote the *Snohomish County Tribune*. "The only guy he's getting through to is the taxpayer."

To determine how much revenue the locality is losing each year, you have to apply the tax rate to the total value of exempt property—or as much of it as you can discover and as best as you can figure out its value. What figure you use as your total will, of course, depend on whether you are trying to find only the loss due to illegal exemptions, or whether you are interested in the larger picture of what exemptions cost your community. If you are trying to find the cost of all exemptions, don't forget to include partial exemptions such as those for veterans and the elderly, special low assessments for farms, country clubs, and the like, and items such as business personal property and intangibles. How do you find the value will depend on the kind of property it is. The methods are discussed throughout this chapter and the chapter on assessments.

220 TAX POLITICS

An additional cost factor of exempt properties is the services they enjoy at taxpayers' expense. Various local departments and agencies, or the local executive's office, may have studies showing the cost of providing services to different kinds of property. Local universities may have done such work. Or you might find studies in journals for local officials. Consult the Public Affairs Information Service index, available in larger public libraries. Write the library at the National League of Cities/Conference of Mayors, 1620 I St. N.W., Washington, D.C. 20036. Also the Secretary, Department of Housing and Urban Development, 451 7th St., S.W, Washington, D.C. You can check your local municipal reference library as well.

If you want do your own study, a good model is provided in Chapter 2 of the *Ultimate Highrise*, published by the San Francisco *Bay Guardian*, 1070 Bryant Street, San Francisco, California 94103.

One way to estimate the cost of publicly-provided services is to ask people who provide these same services as a private business. If the city picks up the trash at an exempt luxury "retirement" home, for example, you could call a private refuse hauler and find out what he would charge. You can make a list of all local services and determine the ones for which you want to figure out the costs. Some exempt property does pay for some or all of its own services, so look before you leap.

information on property taxes and how to find it

Do not expect property tax information to leap out at you with a big red sign. The assessment rolls and other records at the assessor's office are just the start. Information about property—where it is, how much it is worth, who owns it—is wherever you find it. How far you dig depends on your purpose.

The most important thing is to get the spirit of the hunt. If you are looking for property values unknown, property owners unknown, and unknown associations and interests of prominent people and corporations, ask yourself, "Where are the footprints on the public record that can tell me what I need to know about this property, or property owner?" The word "public" is essential. Go by the rules. At the same time, citizens should insist on seeing what it is their right to see, and when turned down, they should work through legal channels—the courts, the legislatures, and the press—to end illegal secrecy.

Persistence is the key. At first the information may seem hopelessly scattered, diverse and incomplete. Hoisting heavy deed books off shelves, pouring through page after page of handwritten entries, trying not to breathe the dust, can make you feel like an abused employee in a Dickens-era counting house. But stick with it. You will learn how to use these records.

Another problem can arise: too much data. As page after page of assessments, lot sizes, and sales prices accumulate in your notebook, you might feel swamped. Don't panic. Get the figures. You'll be able to make sense of them later.

A smart citizen investigator does not plunge hastily into a subject he or she knows little about. The first step is to get the lay of the land; and the best way is to talk to as many people as possible who might be in the know. Insiders are especially valuable in providing tips and leads.

Of course many insiders will not want to help. Their stake is in the current system. Do not let them discourage you or turn you off the track.

Here are some people who might help you get started:

Family and Friends. Realtors, business people, or officials may share their knowledge with you even if it is not in their interest.

Mavericks. There are people in almost every line of work, who don't march with the crowd and who would be happy to help people expose problems that may well have bothered them for years.

Adversaries. For almost every power center, political or economic, there is someone who has been battling it, and learning a lot about it in the process. For businesses there are labor unions that keep tabs on company property and profits to bargain over wages. There are attorneys who represent workers, customers, and stockholders in lawsuits against companies. For big corporations, like oil and steel companies, there are often smaller ones—independent refiners and fabricators—that have had to fight them for survival. For almost every successful politician there is one or more others whom that person has defeated. They may well be delighted to tell you where the bodies are buried.

Journalists and Academics. Journalists often know more about local officials and businesses than their editors have allowed them to print. And they know where to go for facts. Teachers and professors, particularly at business schools, often follow certain businesses and industries very closely.

the public record

Everyone has routine encounters *with the law*. People and businesses get permits and licenses, incur health or building inspections, file data with regulatory agencies. Then there are extraordinary encounters, such as breaking the law, being sued by a shareholder or customer, fires and robberies. Encounters with the law usually leave records.

the local government

Deeds are the basic local property record. A deed simply shows when one person or corporation transfers a property right to another. Legally, property is an almost limitless bundle of rights to a thing. This is why there can be several deeds to the same property, granting different rights to different people. The owner may have granted a *mortgage* to a bank; an *easement* (or right of use) to a neighbor; another easement to a power company to run a power line across. The owner still owns the property. He or she has merely granted certain rights to the property to others. Each time this happens, the record goes into the deed books.

The local *recorder of deeds* inserts these deeds into the deed books, in the order in which they are filed. There are usually two indexes for the deed books. One, the *grantee index*, lists each deed according to the person or corporation to whom the right was granted. The *grantor index* lists the deeds according to the person or corporation who gave up, or granted, the right.

When an owner builds a new building or modifies an old one, he has to take out a *building permit*. These are supposed to state the value of the improvement. But owners usually report very low figures, both to ward off a high assessment and to keep the permit fees low, which are often based on the value of the improvement. When the new building is completed, the owner must get an *occupancy permit*.

When a landowner breaks up a large property into smaller parcels, he needs a *subdivision permit*. When the owner wants a change in zoning, he must file an *application* and appear at a hearing. When a business wants to conduct certain activities, it must get *licenses* such as liquor licenses and merchants' licenses. In localities that have *rent control*, building owners must file detailed statements concerning their property and the income it produces, with the rent control board.

In addition, there is information that local governments take upon themselves to get about property. There are *fire inspections, building inspections, and health inspections*. The reports the inspectors make often are public records.

Then there are times when local governments themselves get involved in property transactions. When they need property for schools or roads, they assert *eminent domain* and start a *condemnation* proceeding. In these proceedings the locality and the owner often argue over how much the property is worth. The evidence brought forth can shed light on how much the subject property and property close to it are worth. These condemnation proceedings may well be public records. Local *renewal* and *industrial development* agencies often buy up property, clear it, and then sell or lease it to a private industry or developer. They sometimes even build the factory for the industry. Much information on property values comes out during these proceedings. It may be available to the public. Even if they can withhold information legally, the agencies like to brag about their achievements, and thereby reveal information that can be very useful.

the state government

State departments and agencies deal with many kinds of industries and businesses. State public utilities commissions may be a prime source. They are supposed to regulate (though accommodate is closer to fact) power companies, telephone companies, railroads, etc. The companies have to file detailed financial statements to justify the rates they seek to impose. You may need help to make sense of these statements. But it should be worth the effort. You may well catch the utilities in a double bookkeeping. Normally they are allowed a certain return on capital, which means that the more property they have the higher the rates they can charge. For rate purposes therefore, they try to pad their property value as much as possible, even spending millions on property they don't really need. Do they report these same figures or a lower figure to the local assessor? Catching tax avoiders in self-contradictions that are reflected in public records is a technique citizen investigators often use.

Other state agencies have records on a wide assortment of businesses and properties. These include state tax departments, commerce departments, departments of minerals and natural resources, community and industrial development departments, state land and leasing departments, departments of environmental control and superintendents of state buildings. The secretary of state has information on all corporations doing business in the state. State securities commissions have information on most of the corporations whose stock can be sold there.

How can you find out about this bewildering assortment of departments, agencies, and commissions? Most states publish guidebooks which explain their government to lawmakers and officials. Chambers of commerce, citizen leagues, and other groups often publish similar volumes. They are available from the particular groups and at most public libraries.

Your best bet may be the guidebooks which chambers of commerce, industrial development agencies, and private publishers put out for businesses, explaining exactly which agencies they will have to deal with, and what documents they will have to file should they locate in the state. Normally these are available at law and business libraries, at the chamber of commerce, and from public officials.

Above all, don't forget your "insiders." In the end, they are the best source.

the federal government

The federal government is a great untapped reservoir of information for citizen property tax investigators. True, most of this information can be obtained only in Washington, D.C. But federal agencies often have field offices; sometimes information is available by mail; and your representatives in Congress sometimes can get the information you seek by making a special request for you. In addition, there is a federal Freedom of Information Act to help you get information from federal agencies.

The federal regulatory agencies, like the state utility commissions, require financial reports from the industries under their jurisdiction which are usually public records. The Federal Communications Commission (FCC) goes one step further. It requires every local radio and TV station to keep its files containing this and other information open to the public.

Here is a list of the more important federal agencies and the industries with which they deal.

Atomic Energy Commission (AEC)—Nuclear power plants.

Civil Aeronautics Board (CAB)—Airlines.

Federal Communications Commission (FCC)—Radio and TV stations and networks; telephone and other interstate communications systems.

Federal Reserve Board, Federal Deposit Insurance Corporation, Federal Home Loan Bank Board—Banks and savings and loans.

Federal Maritime Commission (FMC)—Merchant marine.

Federal Power Commission—Power companies which operate interstate; natural gas pipelines.

Federal Trade Commission (FTC)—Many businesses: economic, antitrust and fair-practices data.

General Services Administration (GSA)—Sells and purchases property for the United States government; leases space from private property owners.

Interstate Commerce Commission (ICC)—Railroads, trucking companies, interstate bus companies, barges, "freight forwarders," interstate oil pipelines.

Securities and Exchange Commission (SEC)—Has extensive financial statements and reports of most companies that sell their securities interstate.

Small Business Administration (SBA)—Detailed information on small businesses to which it gives assistance.

Investigating Property Taxes 223

Tennessee Valley Authority (TVA)—Has information (often published in press releases and reports) on plants and industries within the TVA region. Also owns its own power-generating facilities.

The hearings and reports of congressional committees contain a wealth of information about industries and even about particular companies and properties. There are two main reference tools for getting at this information. One is the *Congressional Quarterly Weekly*, which is indexed quarterly and issued as a bound *Congressional Quarterly Almanac* at the end of the year. The other is the Congressional Information Service (CIS), a two-volume compilation of congressional activities. Part 1 is *Abstracts of Congressional Publications and Legislative Histories*; Part 2 is *Index of Congressional Publications* and *Public Laws*. CIS publishes this information periodically along with these year-end wrap-up volumes. Both *CQ* and *CIS* should be available at the largest local library.

Senators and representatives often insert articles, studies, and reports into the *Congressional Record*, which records each day's proceedings on the House and Senate floors. The *Congressional Record* is published daily. Bound, indexed volumes are available at libraries.

Despite these guides and indexes, rich mines of information lie buried in hearings which appear to be on unrelated subjects. The best way to cut through to these is to locate the key staff aides who specialize in the area in which you are interested.

Letters to your representative and senators could begin the search. You can also write to the Congressional Research Service of the Library of Congress. This is Congress's research arm, and if it has happened on Capitol Hill, somebody at CRS probably knows about it.

Another information-gathering arm of Congress is the General Accounting Office (GAO). The GAO is the congressional auditor: at the request of members of Congress it audits programs Congress has enacted and studies the feasibility of new ones. The GAO has studied home-mortgage subsidy programs of the Federal Housing Administration (FHA). And it did a study of the feasibility of savings and loans paying interest on property tax escrow accounts. You can write the Information Officer, GAO, 441 G St., N.W., Washington, D.C. 20001, for a list of the agency's studies and publications.

There is also the executive branch, the president, and the departments and agencies that work under him. In general, the *administrative* agencies, which are offshoots of Congress, grant licenses, regulate rates and practices, and publish statistics related to these. The executive departments, on the other hand, administer federal grant programs, gather data, and enforce the federal laws. In practice though, these functions tend to overlap. The executive departments are subject to the federal Freedom of Information Act, as are the administrative agencies.

These executive departments gather vast amounts of data regarding property and who owns it. They buy property, sell it, manage it, and lease it to and from others. They collect information about property in connection with loan, grant, and statistics-gathering programs. It is hardly possible even to begin to list every such program at every executive branch department. But here are some of the major departments and their more important programs.

Treasury Department—The IRS, part of the Treasury, has a team of over 250 appraisers who appraise for tax purposes all kinds of property, from steel mills to coin collections.

Department of Defense—The DOD has vast amounts of property. It builds plants and leases them to private businesses. It lets out contracts the applications for which might show property values. The Navy has extensive petroleum holdings.

Department of the Interior—Interior has charge of the hundreds of millions of acres in the public domain. On these it leases mineral, timber, grazing, and other rights of access and use to private owners. In some states these leasehold or possessary interests are subject to the property tax. The Bureau of Mines in the Department of Interior has data on most coal mines in the country.

Department of Agriculture—Runs the farm subsidy programs for cotton, tobacco, and other crops. Gathers extensive data on farm real estate values, property taxes, and the like. The Agriculture Department's National Forest Service puts out extensive information on how states tax timber property.

Department of Commerce—Administers a multitude of little-known but important programs in behalf of businesses. Puts out

224 TAX POLITICS

extensive business statistics. The department's Census Bureau is probably the nation's biggest information-gatherer. Every five years the Census Bureau issues a Census of Governments. This includes detailed studies of property tax assessments in urban and selected rural areas throughout the country. These studies contain regrettable omissions but they are probably the most valuable single resource of their type.

Department of Labor—Has information on the output of different industries per worker and per unit of investment. Such information can help in estimating a factory's value from a known quantity, such as its output or the number of people it employs.

Department of Housing and Urban Development—HUD and its agencies like the Federal Housing Administration (FHA) make loans and grants for renovation, renewal, and new home purchases. A property appraisal is involved in each such loan and grant. It does extensive studies of construction and real estate activity.

Department of Transportation—Oversees the national highway program and has extensive statistics on the property this system consumes and affects.

You can write to these federal departments and agencies for lists of the data and publications they can provide, and for general information on what they do. The Federal Power Commission, for example, publishes a *Guide to Public Information* and *An Informal Explanation of the Organization and Work of the Federal Power Commission*. You can get such materials by writing the particular agency's Director of Public Information, Washington, D.C. They can help you greatly in planning your investigation.

The *Congressional Directory*, published by the U.S. Government Printing Office, (and sold by them for $5.75 in paperback) lists every single federal agency, department, and bureau, including major officials, addresses, and phone numbers. You can find a copy at the public library; perhaps your representative could send you a used one from the previous year. Perhaps even more useful is the *United States Government Manual*, published each year by the office of the Federal Register, Archives and Record Service, U.S. Government Printing Office ($5.75 in paper). A useful guide to the major regulatory agencies is *Working on the System*, by James Michael and Ruth Fort, published by Basic Books, 1974. Setting out the major business-oriented programs of the federal government is *The Businessman's Guide to Washington*, by William Ruder and Raymond Nathan (Macmillan Publishers, 1975).

lawsuits

Property owners, individual and corporate, get into lawsuits for a number of reasons. Shareholders sue management for misleading them or for misusing corporate funds. Customers and workers sue companies for injuries they incur from the company's products or on its premises. State and local governments sue to enforce their laws and to condemn property for public use. Heirs of individual property owners have court battles over wills. Corporations often take their disputes with assessors to court.

These actions often bring out information on property values. Corporate assessment appeals can be especially valuable. The records of the lawsuits, including documents and testimony introduced into evidence, are available at the clerk of court's office in the locality where they took place. Usually someone at the clerk's office will show you how to find and use them.

How do you find out about these data-revealing lawsuits? How do you know which court's records to check? In theory, a property owner, and especially a large interstate business, could sue or be sued in any court in the country. There is no way you can check them all. So start with the state and federal courts in your own area. Scan the indexes at the clerk's offices for the name of the property owner in question.

Or, try to find out about particular lawsuits. If the local newspaper keeps a clipping file, and you can get to use it, look under the name of the property owner. You may find news reports of lawsuits. The *New York Times* and the *Wall Street Journal* are likely to report lawsuits involving major corporations. You can find complete indexes to these papers at most good libraries. An even better source on national corporations is the *prospectus* they must send to investors who might purchase their stock. Federal law requires corporations to list in these documents any lawsuits that might affect the value of their stock. You can get a company's latest prospectus from a stockbroker, from the company itself, or at the SEC. Check also the company's 10-K report at the public record

Investigating Property Taxes 225

room of the SEC for events that occurred after the prospectus was published. Moody's guides to corporations list the plant locations of large companies. These locations can be checked out to determine whether the company has been involved in lawsuits.

advertising and unusual events

Corporate boosting and boasting often reveals the value of a new plant or of improvements to old ones. Or it cites the number of employees and what they produce, both clues to property values.

You will find corporate bragging reported, often verbatim, in the local press. For larger companies it appears in national hard-business-news publications like *Forbes, Barron's, Business Week,* the *Wall Street Journal, Nation's Business,* and others aimed at business people and investors. Also check the company's annual report, available from the company or from a stockbroker.

Individuals like to brag as much as corporations do. Few notables and would-be notables can resist the temptation to list their honors and achievements in one of the many *Who's Who's.* There is a large *Who's Who in America,* along with regional volumes (*Who's Who in the Midwest,*), ethnic and religious volumes (*Who's Who in World Jewry, Italian-American Who's Who,*) and business volumes (*Who's Who in Commerce,*). The minibiographies in these contain backgrounds, club and business affiliations, and the like. There may be clues here as to who owns what in your community.

Fires, strikes, oil spills, and accidents of all kinds thrust property owners before the public when they do not wish to be there.

Though often suppressed, some of these events are reported in the local and sometimes in the national press. Digging out old articles from the local newspaper can be easy or hard. It is easy if the paper keeps a clipping file or morgue, and lets the public use it. If the paper has a morgue but doesn't let the public in, perhaps a friendly reporter or a student or professor at a local journalism school could check the files for you. If the local library keeps back copies of the paper on microfilm, that will help. If there is no index, however, you will have to flip through all the back issues. It is much easier to do so with microfilm than with the actual newspapers. People in the community may remember when a particular company or person was in the news. That will help narrow the search. Some groups might even have private indexes or clipping files: the chamber of commerce and municipal reference libraries are examples. Peace, environmental, and labor groups might have clipping files on particular companies.

Doing research in the national press is much easier. The major dailies like the *New York Times* and the *Wall Street Journal* publish indexes that are available at larger libraries. Articles in popular magazines are indexed in the *Reader's Guide to Periodical Literature.* Articles in more specialized journals are indexed in the *Social Sciences and Humanities Index,* the *Business Periodicals Index,* the *Public Affairs Information Service,* and the *Guide to Legal Periodicals.* These too are available at larger libraries.

business information

There is a sprawling network of business information, geared especially to potential investors, consisting of magazines, newsletters, insider reports, bulletins, you name it. The price corporations pay to attract buyers of their stocks and bonds is that they must divulge information about themselves.

The three stalwarts are *Standard and Poor's, Moody's,* and *Dun and Bradstreet.* These multivolume sets overlap to a large degree, providing data on corporate histories, finances, subsidiaries, major lines of business, plant locations, sources of raw materials, markets, anything that might help someone decide whether the company was a wise investment.

Standard and Poor's has a six-volume set with detailed information on over 6,300 of the largest corporations, plus shorter coverage of 6,000 smaller ones. Daily news bulletins on corporate events go into a loose-leaf binder. *S&P* also publishes volumes on all stocks sold on the three major exchanges. Of special interest are its Industrial Surveys, which analyze the economy industry-by-industry; and its Register of Corporations, Directors, and Executives.

Moody's puts out both a manual and a loose-leaf news report service on five important areas: Industries, Banking and Finance, Transportation, Public Utilities, and Municipalities and Government. The

226 TAX POLITICS

latter is especially useful since it shows debt and budget information for all units of government that sell bonds.

Dun and Bradstreet issues a *Million Dollar Directory,* a *Middle Market Directory,* and a *Reference Book of Manufacturers and Corporate Managements.*

You should find these and a host of related publications in the business or reference section of any large library. Bankers, stockbrokers, and investment advisors may also have copies.

The major investor services are very expensive. A few helpful manuals within the budgets of more people are *Fortune's Directory of 1,000 Largest Corporations* and *Fortune's Plant and Product Directory of the 1,000 Largest Industrial Corporations,* both published by Time Inc. in New York City, and the *Forbes Annual Report on American Industry.*

Bond consultants—people who advise investors on bonds to buy—are intensely interested in local property tax matters, since taxes provide the revenues used to pay off many local bonds and are the ultimate security behind them. These bond counselors thus have detailed information on particular local property tax jurisdictions, including the largest taxpayers and the major industries. The *Daily and Weekly Bond Buyer,* 77 Water Street, New York, N.Y. 10005, publishes extensive information along this line. It should be available from local bankers, investment houses and counselors, bond attorneys, and, in larger jurisdictions, from the controller or other official who handles the local government's funds.

Don't forget the people who use these publications daily—the stockbrokers and investment counselors.

Industry directories are gold mines of information. One example is the *Directory of Iron and Steel Works of the United States and Canada,* published by the American Iron and Steel Institute. This directory lists virtually every iron and steel plant in the two countries, including equipment, capacity, and financial information about the companies that own them. Other such directories are *Polk's Bank Directory,* the *Petroleum Registry,* the *Rubber Redbook,* the *Television Factbook* and the *Radio Yearbook.*

Labor unions make studies of central bargaining issues such as how much workers are producing and how much the company can afford to pay them. These studies may reflect on the value of the company's property.

A number of private non-business groups assemble data on major corporations, often from a social reform perspective. Two of these are the Corporate Information Center, Room 846, 475 Riverside Drive. New York, N.Y., and the Council on Economic Priorities, 84 Fifth Avenue, New York, N.Y. 10011, and 250 Columbus Ave., San Francisco, Ca. 94133. These people are experienced in corporate research. If they cannot help you they might well know someone who can.

construction and real estate industry sources

Absolutely basic information services that local realtors use usually list every property that is sold in the area, along with the sales price and the holder of the mortgage. They might even show attachments or liens to the property. There is a different such service for each local area or state. In Boston, Massachusetts, there is the *Real Estate Guide* and the Metropolitan Mortgage Bureau. In Chicago there is *Olcutt's Blue Book of Land Values,* and in Washington, D.C., *Lusk's Directory.* Any realtor, or person interested in real estate, can tell you the name of the publication for your area. You might also check *Klein's Guide to American Directories*, mentioned below.

Then there are guides that tell builders, mortgage lenders, and investors how much it costs to build and maintain certain kinds of buildings. The American Appraisal Co. of Milwaukee, Wisconsin, publishes the *Boeckh Building Valuation Manual,* the F.W. Dodge Corp. of New York, the *Building Cost Calculator and Valuation Guide;* and Marshall and Swift Co. of Los Angeles publishes the *Marshall Valuation Service.*

The Urban Land Institute in Washington, D.C., publishes detailed balance sheets for different kinds of development projects, even including actual case studies. See, for example, its series *The Dollars and Cents of Shopping Centers.* Another

Investigating Property Taxes   227

Institute publication is *Income and Cost of Rental Housing.* The Institute of Real Estate Management in Chicago, gathers data from its members on the costs of managing their properties, and publishes the results according to type of property, region, and the year of construction. An example is its annual *Income Expense Analysis—Apartments, Condominiums and Cooperatives.* Since assessors say they use the income approach to place a value on commercial and rental property, these cost-and-income figures can help you check their work. The Institute also publishes a bimonthly *Journal of Property Management.*

The National Bureau of Research, Burlington, Iowa, publishes a *Shopping Center Directory* which gives "vital facts" on the income and costs of over 15,000 shopping centers throughout the country. The Society of Real Estate Appraisers, in Chicago, puts out a series of guides for appraising different kinds of property.

There are catalogues and price guides for different kinds of equipment and machinery (similar to the "Blue Books" which show the values of used cars). The Equipment Guide Book Company of Palo Alto, California, publishes a line of cost books on building and construction equipment. It is just one of many publishers that serves the building and construction trades. A call to someone involved in this business should yield the names of others. Of course, if you already know what kind of equipment is in a particular plant, you can go right to the manufacturer to find out what it cost.

The property tax divisions of state tax departments often develop construction cost guides for local assessors. The larger assessing offices sometimes develop their own. And private mass appraisal companies often promise in the contract to produce construction-cost information for the locality during a reappraisal.

Investment counselors, bankers and insurance salesmen have developed rules of thumb, which are rough-and-ready formulas for estimating quickly how much property (capital investment) it takes to produce a given level of output in a given industry. These rules of thumb may pop up in articles in business magazines, in the cost manuals, and in conversations with people who use them.

There are also regular reports on construction activity. Two important ones are: the *Construction Bulletin*, published by the Roy Wenzlick Co., St. Louis, Missouri, and the *Dodge Reports*, by the F. W. Dodge Corporation, New York, N.Y. The federal government, especially the Census Bureau and the Department of Housing and Urban Development (HUD), puts out extensive information on construction. For $1.75 a year you can subscribe to the *Bureau of the Census Catalog* which lists such available sources as the bureau's *Monthly Construction Report* and its *Value of New Construction Put in Place.* The Federal Housing Administration (FHA) of the Department of Housing and Urban Development (HUD) has similar statistics related to its mortgage insurance programs. The annual *Savings and Loan Fact Book*, published by the U.S. Savings and Loan League, Chicago, Illinois, contains detailed information on residential construction and financing. The Real Estate Research Corp., also of Chicago, is another source for such information. There are countless bulletins for insiders; like the *Housing Letter*, published by the Housing Institute, in New York City.

Then there are guidebooks to guidebooks, that help you find your way in the confusing maze of business information. Examples are:

Kline's Guide to American Directories,
Bernard Klein, ed. (7th ed., 1968, B. Klein & Co., New York, N.Y.).

Sources of Business Information, Edwin T. Coman, Jr. (University of California, 1970).

Guide to Listings of Manufacturers,
U.S. Chamber of Commerce.

tracing ownership

We've been looking for information that would provide clues to the value of property. There are other questions taxpayers may be asking, such as who *owns* a particular property, what *other* property does that person own, and what are the business interests of public officials, their colleagues and supporters?

To answer these questions you

228 TAX POLITICS

can use the same basic technique shown above. However, there is a common hurdle in trying to find out who owns a particular property. Property owners often do not want anyone to know who they are. Possibly they are trying to assemble a big chunk of property for a new development by buying up smaller ones and don't want the current property owners to catch on and hold out for higher prices. Thus they record the property in the name of a relative or fictional person—a "straw party"—or they establish a "blind trust." Some property owners set up a "dummy" or paper corporation for each property they buy. This way they insulate each one from the legal and financial problems that might befall another. And they can keep their identity a secret too.

Here are some suggestions for cracking these corporate shells.

See who signs the building permits, applications for rezoning, and the like.

Check the mailing address for the dummy corporations and straw parties. Either look them up in the city directory, if there is one, or else go there. You may find a law, real estate, or other office, which will help tell you who the real owner is. On the other hand you may find just a mail drop with a tight-lipped secretary.

If the owner is a corporation, you can check with whoever keeps the records on corporations chartered or doing business in the state. It may be the secretary of state or the state department of corporations. Records for partnerships and trusts may be in a different office. In addition, the local government may have a business license on file. These business and corporate records probably will list the officers and directors.

But even this information will not necessarily help. Real estate manipulators often name their attorneys, obscure relatives, even their secretaries, as the officers and directors of their dummy corporations. This throws people like yourself off the track, not to mention creditors and local enforcement officials. You may have to check any or all of the following trying to identify these fronts:

- telephone directory
- city directory (if there is one)
- birth/marriage/death records
- assessment records (owner index)
- property deeds (grantor and grantee index)
- court records
- *Martindale-Hubbell* lawyer directory

Going through these records can take time. It also may not lead anywhere. You may have to try other ways:

If the building is rented to tenants, you can talk to some of them. Find out where they pay the rent and with whom they deal. These may provide clues.

Talk to the building manager and service employees, such as a janitor. Try to find out who does repairs on the building—plumbing, electrical work, and the like. See what you can learn from them.

Ask the mailman if he has a forwarding address for the owner.

Neighbors often know much about the property around them—especially helpful are those who spend hours on the front porch or stoop, watching the world go by.

From the deed find out from whom the current owner bought the property. That person might tell you who the current owner really is. Also find out from the deed the mortgagees—the persons who loaned money to the current owner. These are sometimes private persons rather than a bank. "Second mortgagees," parties who bought the mortgage from the original lender, are especially likely to be individuals. These mortgage lenders may provide the information you need.

The author once tried to find the address of a New York slum landlord to serve him with the complaint in a tenants' lawsuit. I could find only a mail drop and answering service on East 42nd Street, where a gruff secretary claimed total ignorance. Then I contacted one of the second mortgagees, whose name appeared on the deed. This party turned out to be an elderly gentleman in an old apartment building in the Bronx, who was angry that the current owner had turned the property into a slum. After a long chat the gentleman revealed the owner's actual address.

Consult insiders. Sometimes one or two older residents have all the "dope" on a block or neighborhood. City employees, such as assessors, recorders of deeds, and building inspectors, see many things in the course of their work. It pays to be friendly.

If any prominent persons are subjects of your investigation, do not overlook sources like the various *Who's Who's Blue Books, Social Registers,* and other already mentioned guides to leading lights. Also the *Dun and Bradstreet* and *Standard and Poor* directories of corporate officers and directors; and the *Martindale-Hubbell* law directories and membership lists of local trade and professional groups.

national property tax information

Questions on particular properties, their values and owners, are not the only ones that arise. You may also need comparative data on tax rates, localities and states, or studies showing who pays and who doesn't. You may need to put local findings into a broader context, or perhaps back up your reform proposals.

Nationally, there are two major sources of property tax statistics. The first is the Advisory Commission on Intergovernmental Relations, one of the lesser known but more productive federal agencies. A full-time professional staff issues regular reports on federal-state-local relations that are a gold mine of information. Three invaluable volumes are *The Role of the States in Strengthening the Property Tax*, vols. 1 & 2 (1963), and the 1974 update *The Property Tax in a Changing Environment*; *Federal-State-Local Finances* (annual); and *Financing Schools and Property Tax Relief*. Write for a complete list. Less valuable than the staff reports are the recommendations of the commission. Consisting as it does of politicians of diverse viewpoints, its policy recommendations tend to be compromises.

The second major national source is the U.S. Census Bureau, which every five years issues a comprehensive *Census of Governments*. The census data is the basis of much of the ACIR staff work, and the two work together closely. Volume 2, *Taxable Property Values and Assessment-Sales Price Ratios* is another necessary item on the tax reformer's bookshelf, but all eight volumes are useful. Volume 8 is a guide to the entire set.

Another good source of property tax information is the Senate Subcommittee on Intergovernmental Relations, which has published two volumes of hearings and has issued several reports. Reports and studies are also issued by state tax departments, departments of economic development, local departments of finance, committees and special commissions of state legislatures, and privately funded research bureaus.

how to find the law

We often forget that the law does not belong to lawyers. As complicated as legal matters can be, there is no reason why citizens cannot learn to look up for themselves the property and tax laws and other basic legal information.

Public libraries often have books on law, especially in their reference divisions, but you may have to go to a law library, or to people with special collections on property tax law such as:

Lawyers and law firms, especially those that handle property tax cases.

Public officials: Such as the assessor, controller, or treasurer—anyone whose job is connected with revenues. If officials in your own locality are not helpful, perhaps someone elsewhere will be. State tax and revenue officials are especially likely to have good collections of books and statutes, and even entire reference libraries. Such a library is a gold mine because it is focused on the subjects you need.

Local civic and lobby groups like the League of Women Voters, chamber of commerce, and business-financed civic associations. Especially the business groups often have good collections on local government, law and finances. If the local chapter doesn't have what you need, try the state office.

Municipal reference library. Many local government, law and finances. If the local affairs library in the city hall or courthouse. Some of these try to keep the public out, even though their taxes pay for the library and they have a right to be there. One often can avoid problems at such places by going about one's business with confidence.

Law school libraries can be the best source. The larger the law school, the better the library usually is. On the other hand, the big prestige law schools tend to have a national focus; smaller local law schools may have more material on state and local affairs. Law librarians can be the most helpful people around. If you catch one on a quiet day, you may get red-carpet service.

Consider that what we call "the law" is not in one book or document. It is the combination of:

- The Constitution and laws of the federal government.

- Regulations of federal agencies carrying out federal laws.

- Past decisions of federal courts interpreting the U.S. Constitution and laws.

- The constitutions of the states.

- The laws the state legislatures have passed under these constitutions.

230 TAX POLITICS

- Rules and regulations of state agencies carrying out these laws.
- State court decisions interpreting the state constitutions and laws.
- Opinions of the federal and state attorneys general interpreting their respective constitutions and laws.
- Local ordinances.
- Custom.

In practice, you will be concerned mostly with the state constitution, laws, and court cases. Still, it is important to see the whole picture, beginning with the federal constitution, so as not to leap to conclusions when you find a law or a court decision that seems to say one thing. There may be others that say something else.

federal constitution and laws

The states write the property tax laws. And the state and/or local governments carry them out. But property taxpayers are protected to some extent by the federal constitution and by the laws the U.S. Congress has enacted under it. People who use services that property taxes pay for have this protection too. Most important for property taxpayers is the Fourteenth Amendment to the United States Constitution and the laws enacted under it. The Fourteenth Amendment guarantees all citizens of the United States "equal protection of the laws" and "due process of law."

You can look up the Constitution and laws in two main sources. The *Code of the United States of America* (USC) organizes under appropriate topics the laws Congress has passed at different times. The *United States Code Annotated* (USCA) goes one step further. It prints the code along with notes on important court cases interpreting each section. The USCA has the text of and notes on the Constitution as well.

federal court decisions (including the supreme court) interpreting the federal constitution and laws

Three publishers print the decisions of the U.S. Supreme Court. The West Publishing Co. series is the most complete. West publishes a *Supreme Court Reporter*, as well as a *Federal Reporter* and a *Federal Supplement*; the latter two are opinions of the lower federal courts. In front of each case are "headnotes" which summarize each important point the case decides.

The Lawyers Co-operative Publishing Co. publishes the *United States Supreme Court Reports, Lawyers' Edition*. This series includes each Supreme Court opinion, with notes explaining and commenting on them.

The third series is called *American Law Reports Annotated* (ALR). This series prints important cases, state as well as federal, along with extensive notes. The ALR series is a prime source for comparing the law in different jurisdictions.

How do you find the court cases that deal with your problem? The cases cited in the annotated code make a good starting point.

They will lead you to others, which in turn will refer you to still others. That is how legal research works. You can also go to two legal encyclopedias—*Corpus Juris Secundum* and *American Jurisprudence*. (These are more valuable for the cases they cite than for their statements about the law.) There are also legal treatises, law school casebooks, and law review articles which you can find at a law library.

Each of the three series of published cases has one or more indexes. The West series has a system of digests, with quick summaries of important cases listed under 420 broad topics. West also has a forty-five-volume index called *Words and Phrases*, which enables you to find cases according to important words and phrases they discuss. Instructions for using these and other indexes are in the front. The law librarian or another person in the library should give you a few minutes of their time. See also the guides to legal research at the end of this chapter.

state constitutions and laws

You will find these in the state code for each state. Usually these are kept in a special section of the law library in alphabetical order by state. The state codes are much like the United States Code. Often the first volumes contain the state constitution with annotations. Then come the state laws, also with notes. Finally come several volumes comprising an index. When you use the index, be sure to check under several headings. For example, if you want to find

Investigating Property Taxes 231

the law on assessments, you would check the index under *taxes, property taxes, assessments, counties, local finances,* and the like. Try not to miss important provisions buried in out-of-the-way places.

The back of each volume of the state code contains a "pocket part." This pocket part is like an annual supplement. It brings the code up to date so that a new one doesn't have to be printed each year. Always check the pocket part whenever you use the state code to see if a provision has been amended or repealed. Also, ask the librarian if there are any "slip sheets"—laws passed during the current session of the legislature, which haven't even been printed in a pocket part yet.

regulations of state agencies

State lawmakers can't foresee every single detail when they write a law. They leave to the departments and agencies the job of writing rules and regulations, which apply the law to specific problems, and are supposed to make certain that officials treat everyone the same. The state tax department, for example, may have regulations for local assessors and review boards. Some of these departments issue manuals which the assessor may or may not be required to use. Don't assume a state agency's rules and regulations are the last word. Often they go beyond the law and stand only because nobody has noticed and challenged them.

state court decisions

The more important state court decisions are published by some states. Others rely on the West Publishing Co. reports instead. The bigger states—like California and New York—get a whole volume of West reports to themselves. The other states are lumped together into seven different sets, called the *Atlantic Reporter, Northeastern Reporter, Northwestern Reporter, Pacific Reporter, Southeastern Reporter, Southern Reporter,* and the *Southwestern Reporter.* Don't be surprised to find some states in a different set than you would expect. For example, Massachusetts appears with Ohio and Indiana in the *Northeastern Reporter.* Yet Pennsylvania is with Maine, New Hampshire, and Vermont in the *Atlantic Reporter.*

You find the state court cases that deal with your problem in much the same way as federal cases: in notes to the state code, indexes to the West Co. reporters, treatises, and law review articles. Some states have their own legal encyclopedias which are valuable sources of court cases (see below).

How do you find out if a court ruling in one case has been overruled by a later one, or if a higher court has changed the decision on the same case? You turn to *Shepard's Citations.* This set of big red volumes takes practically every single reported state and federal decision and lists every later decision that upheld it, overruled it, mentioned it, or referred to it in any way. You can find instructions for using *Shepard's* in the front of each volume. By using *Shepard's* you can make sure that the ruling in a particular case is still valid. Always check the most recent volume, along with the older volumes.

opinions of the attorney general

The state attorney general is the state government's lawyer. The governor, heads of his department, and sometimes other officials can turn to him for legal advice. When the attorney gives this advise formally, it is called an *Opinion of the Attorney General.*

These "AG" opinions are not binding and final. Only the state's highest court is the final authority on state law. But the AG opinions carry a great deal of weight. People are very reluctant to do something that they know the attorney general will oppose. Sometimes the AG's opinions appear in the back of each volume of the state court decisions. If you don't find them there, ask the law librarian.

Many people just write to the state attorney general and ask whether he has ever issued an opinion on a particular problem. Usually the AG is glad to send citizens a copy.

local ordinances

These are laws enacted by the local council or other governing body. The state legislature decides how much power the local units have for making their own ordinances. Normally on property taxes the scope of local decision-making is very limited. That is not always the case however. The Cook County (Chicago) Illinois Council, for example, can decide how heavily each type of property

232 TAX POLITICS

will be assessed, and it sets the assessment ratio for each.

A copy of local ordinances should be available at one or more of the following: public library, municipal reference library, city hall, local courthouse, public official's office, local solicitor's office, local law firm. Call the local solicitor clerk of courts, or local council member, if you have trouble locating a copy.

custom

The way officials have "always done it" affects how courts in some states interpret the law. When state lawmakers have been aware of an official practice that was contrary to law and have done nothing about it, the courts give the custom more weight. For example, California law once said that all assessments had to be at 100 percent of fair market value. Assessors had been ignoring this law for "time out of mind." A taxpayer sued to make his local assessor obey the law. The California court said that since the state legislature had known what the assessors were doing and had taken no action, the legislators had put an informal stamp of approval on the assessors' practices. Courts in other states, such as Kentucky, have held that officials who ignore the law do not thereby make the law invalid.

secondary sources

Going to the original laws and court decisions can take time. You can often get a *general* idea of your rights by going to secondary sources.

Perhaps the best secondary source is the *State Tax Law Reporter*, published by Prentice-Hall of Englewood Cliffs, New Jersey. This set pulls together all the tax laws for each state, together with summaries, explanations, indexes, and important legal decisions. There is a looseleaf volume for each state, which is kept up to date with regular bulletins and supplements. There is also a one-volume digest summarizing the tax laws of all the states. The Prentice-Hall series is unfortunately not easy to find. Often only larger law libraries and law firms have it.

The Commerce Clearing House of Chicago publishes a *State Tax Handbook* ($7.50 in paperback) that gives a quick synopsis of the tax provisions for each state. Its weekly *State Tax Review* covers new and proposed legislation, court decisions, and major studies. At $3 a year, it is the tax reformer's buy of the year. Both Prentice-Hall and Commerce Clearing House publish series that may be useful. Write for their lists of publications.

Many states have law *encyclopedias*. These discuss the law topic by topic, citing court cases and statutes. There is usually a pocket part for each volume, bringing it up to date. Law encyclopedias are a handy reference. They provide a quick overview and help you find laws and court cases on specific problems. Their interpretations should always be taken with a grain of salt, however. It just isn't possible to explain the law in nice neat packages the way the encyclopedias try to do.

There are treatises and textbooks which discuss property and property-tax laws for one or many states. Special ones have been written for California and New York, for example. You can find these through the card catalogue at a law library under *taxes, property taxes,* or *property.* Ask the law librarian if you have problems.

Law school casebooks may also be helpful. These are books which reprint court decisions, statutes, articles, and other materials for law school courses. An example is Jerome R. Hellerstein's *State and Local Taxation,* published by the West Publishing Company of St. Paul, Minnesota. The most recent and useful casebook on the subject is *State and Local Taxes and Finance,* by law professors Oliver Oldman and Ferdinand O. Schoettle and published by the Foundation Press of Mineola, New York. This is really a *resource book* as much as a law school casebook and is highly recommended to all trying to understand and take an active role in state or local affairs. It is available at law school bookstores and from the publisher.

Law review articles are one of the very best sources. Law reviews are edited and largely written by law students. Articles in them take specific points of law and explore them in depth. You can find law review articles through the *Reader's Guide to Legal Periodicals.* The guide lists all law review articles according to both author and subject; you use it just as you use the *Reader's Guide to Periodical Literature.* Again, check under several different topic headings to be sure you don't miss an article you should see.

The International Associaton of Assessing Officials (IAAO) in Chicago puts out a monthly *Assessment and Valuation Legal Reporter* which discusses important court decisions in some depth.

Finding the law is a knack you learn from experience. This brief chapter can merely point to the sources available and get you started. A handy yet complete guide to legal research is called *Legal Research in a Nutshell* by Morris L. Cohen, published by the West Publishing Co. It is a pocket-sized paperback and should be available at law school bookstores. Do not overlook footnotes and sources mentioned in law reviews, law school casebooks, and other publications. This information can be their main value.

your right to see public records

The law gives you rights to see public records. These rights are deeply rooted in our legal heritage. Back in 1928 the Michigan Supreme Court said, in upholding a newspaper's right to see certain state records:

If there be any rule of the English common law that denies the public the right of access to public records, it is repugnant to the spirit of our democratic institutions. Ours is a government of the people. Every citizen rules. In Michigan the people elect by popular vote an auditor general . . . He is their servant. His official books and records are theirs. (*Novack* v. *Fuller,* 243 Mich. 200, 219 NW 749)

"It is to the failure of the citizen to assert these rights," the New Jersey Supreme court added in another case "that we must look for those evils that are incident to our government, rather than to a superabundance of zeal in this respect." (*Fagan* v. *State Board of Assessors,* 80 NJ 516, 77At. 1023 1910.) The court upheld the right of a taxpayer, one Mark M. Fagan, to see the assessment records and returns of various railroads and other companies in the state.

Sometimes these rights are expressed in *freedom-of-information* laws. There is evidence that the freedom-of-information laws do not broaden, but rather restrict, the rights which citizens already enjoyed under the "common law"—the legal tradition which was brought over from England and continued here.

The typical state has a very broad freedom-of-information law, providing that, with some exceptions, all official records shall be open to the public unless otherwise provided by specific statutes. It is these "otherwise provided's" that can cause problems.

You will find them in the sections dealing with particular topics and departments. Provisions on property tax records may appear where the state code deals with "Property Taxes," "Assessments," "Cities and Counties," "Local Government," or in some related section. Keep looking until you find them.

Under the usual pattern, the final list of assessments, called the "assessment roll" or "grand list," is open to the public. Also public are the "tax maps."

On the other hand, the laws usually say that financial information about a property owner's business is not open to the public. This makes it hard to check commercial and industrial assessments, which are based largely on such information. The assessment figure itself does not mean much without the supporting data.

Between these two extremes is a large "gray" area. The law varies from state to state, and in many cases the law itself is not clear. When records fall into this gray area, assessors are prone to withhold the information.

Three frequent "gray area" records are:

personal property

Property other than real estate.

property record cards

In some states they are completely closed to the public. In others, taxpayers can see the card for their own property but not for the property of others. And in still other states, taxpayers can see all the record cards.

manuals and handbooks

If taxpayers cannot see these rules, they cannot verify whether the assessor or his assistants follow them.

You can't assume that all the rules in these manuals actually accord with the law. Sometimes whoever writes the rules slips in favors to special interests. This is another reason why all such materials should be completely open to the public.

Sometimes there is a conflict between the state's broad free-

234 TAX POLITICS

dom of information laws, and the specific provisions relating to property taxes. Probably the laws were enacted at different times, and little or no effort was made to coordinate them. Such conflicts leave open the possibility for citizen victories in the courts.

There is a side to citizen access to information that people including legal scholars sometimes forget. No matter how bold the freedom-of-information laws seem on paper, officials can devise ploys to ignore them. For example, assessors have made records available only at inconvenient times. They have refused to provide a place where taxpayers could study and copy them. They have required employees to watch over the taxpayers' shoulders and even hold the records and turn the pages. These ploys can deny citizens their right to know, just as much as locking the records in a file cabinet.

To find out your rights to see property tax records either look up the law yourself or write to your state attorney general. Many attorneys general will send either copies of the law or exact references on where to find them. Other sources of help are your elected state representatives, the American Civil Liberties Union, Sigma Delta Phi (a fraternity of news reporters), the League of Women Voters, and public interest groups. Public Citizen's Freedom of Information Clearinghouse, P.O. Box 19367, Washington, D.C. 20036, has detailed information on freedom-of-information laws generally and your rights under them.

If an official tries to withhold records to which you have a right, you should contact one or more of these groups for legal help. Freedom-of-information cases affect every person in the state. Thus civil rights and public-interest groups might even want to join such a lawsuit.

getting information about business

Some business information is public by law, such as the annual reports of corporations that sell their stock to the public. But by and large freedom-of-information laws do not apply to businesses, and they do not have to allow you on their property.

tips for citizen investigators

When looking into property taxes, there are several points to bear in mind. *Use several methods* whenever you can. Trying more than one approach to a problem is a good check for errors.

Be conservative. Don't build your case on frail reeds. Resolve at least as many close questions against yourself as in your favor.

Ask people who know something about property taxes at each stage of your project. Try to talk to both academics and people with first-hand working experience.

Learn the law. You don't need to learn chapter and verse, but you should get a rough layman's grasp of the law that applies to your investigation. This will help keep you from getting tripped up; for example, from claiming an industry isn't assessed on a piece of equipment when that equipment is exempt by law. Also, it will help you spot where the assessor himself is not following the law.

Do not assume that public officials are your enemies. There are many assessors who genuinely want to serve the public and welcome public pressure that will enable them to do what they have always wanted to do.

Sometimes taxpayers meet a wall of suspicion at the assessor's office. Make sure this wall is not of your own doing. Do not descend on the office with a battalion of cohorts waving notebooks and copying equipment. One or two people can ask for the information you want. The idea is to learn enough so that after the first visit you can find the information you want yourself. You may be the first person they've seen in ages who isn't a tax lawyer or real estate dealer. If you go about your business and show you aren't going to turn the place upside down, they'll get used to you. Remember that the assessor, his office, and staff can be your best source of information. Try to keep this channel open as long as possible, but watch out for assessors who try to act chummy and try to steer you into dead ends.

If the assessor himself won't help you, other officials might. Controller Leonel Castillo in Houston, Texas, has used his office as a base for student investigations of property taxes. County Commissioner Dorothy Shope in Westmoreland County,

Pennsylvania, has given her support to taxpayers' reform efforts. California State Senator Mervyn Dymally, from Los Angeles, has organized a student-staffed "Project Loophole" which lays bare the loopholes in the state's tax system.

Your *attitude* is probably your main obstacle and your greatest potential resource. Many taxpayers feel guilty when they check into local tax and property records, as though they were nosy intruders. That's exactly how tax avoiders and secretive officials hope you will feel. The fact remains that public records are *your* records.

Be persistent. Leave no stone unturned. When the suggestions in this book do not suffice, devise your own.

Try always to find out what *insiders* know or think and try to find out what sources of information they use.

Try to make *copies* of any important information or documents. At the very least, keep precise notes on each item and where you found it. Nothing causes more grief than important nuggets of information for which no one can quite remember the source. Take notes or tape record your interviews if you have permission. If you have to wait and write up the interview afterward, do it immediately. Do not delay. And capture the person's words as exactly as possible. Get *exact references* to specific magazine articles, legal briefs, reports, and the like on the spot.

Keep a *log* of your investigations. Even if it is just a few lines each day, it will help you evaluate your work and sharpen your focus. It also will enable you to pinpoint the dates of specific incidents. For example, if you are denied information you have a right to see, and want to raise the issue later, you will want to know the exact date the denial occurred.

Be alert to *all information* that you come across even if it is beyond your immediate interest. It may be extremely useful later on.

Know your rights as to which information you are entitled to see. If you are denied access, get it in writing. Go home and make a written request. Send it registered mail. Include, if you can, a letter from an attorney stating that the information is public.

Never lie about who you are. On the other hand, you don't have to advertise your purposes. There is no point in making people feel threatened if you can avoid doing so truthfully.

Chapter 9
Property Taxes and Related Battles

Concerned citizens may find themselves fighting a new expressway, high-rise development, pollution, or some other activity they feel threatens the community health and safety. Too often in these cases those involved come off looking like unrealistic "do-gooders." Their concerns for the well-being of the community tend to wilt before the "hard-headed realism" of business people and officials who hammer back with the need for jobs, tax revenues, and growth.

A new highway, it is argued, is necessary to bring more customers and businesses to downtown. High-rises will bolster the property tax base. Cracking down on polluters might drive away industry with its jobs and property tax revenues. Moneyed interests often can parlay these arguments and public anxiety over jobs and taxes into support for their positions.

Citizens who challenge these positions will be whistling in the wind until they learn to meet the dollar arguments head on. And they can. Many of the projects and programs that are destructive to human well-being also have dollars-and-cents consequences which their boosters fail to point out. Property taxes are a major example.

highways

Who hasn't heard the local chamber of commerce and boards of realtors and trade applaud a proposed new highway as a vital shot in the arm for the commercial life-blood of a city? They fail to add that the expressway will drain local revenues as well.

For one, expressways take acres of valuable or potentially valuable property off the tax rolls. That means everyone pays more to make up the difference. By 1968, state and federal governments had bought almost $6.5 billion worth of urban property—a quarter of a billion acres—to turn into expressways. Much of that came out of the property tax bases of the hard-pressed cities. The impact in specific cases can be severe.

Between 1955 and 1969 the Wisconsin County Expressway Commission removed about $10.4 million worth of property from the city of Milwaukee's tax rolls. By 1969 over 22 percent of the city's land area was devoted to streets, alleys, highways, and expressways.

In Chicago, the Citizens Action Program has shown that Mayor Richard Daley's cherished proposal for a Crosstown Expressway would remove from the tax rolls property that now yields approximately $9 million in property taxes each year.

These figures do not include, moreover, the vast urban areas given over to auto-related uses—parking lots, garages, and auto junk yards. These rank among the lowest value uses, and provide less revenue than other uses might.

The problem is especially acute in central business districts where land values are highest and where incursions of streets, expressways, and parking lots are most destructive to the property tax base.

By 1960 a full 35 percent of the land in the Los Angeles central business district had been taken over by streets, and another 21 percent by parking. In Washington, D.C., an even larger portion, 62 percent, was under the internal combustion regime.

In other words, taxpayers in such cities are paying up to a 50 percent surcharge for the servicing of motor vehicles, many of which belong to commuters and

Property Taxes and Related Battles 237

out-of-town truckers, and whose net impact, moreover, may well be to make their own property worth less and their neighborhoods less livable. Sometimes streets do add to adjoining land values but the added costs of repairs, traffic control, and policing the theft and damage attendant to heavy auto use offset these gains.

When stores and factories fall before the bulldozer, not only are their property taxes lost, but sales, income, license, and other taxes are lost as well. Prolonged construction alone, with its noise, soot, and street-clogging equipment, forces many a business near new expressway routes to close. The property that expressways consume is thus just the beginning. Noise and pollution erode the value of nearby property, especially in the cities and suburbs. The *Community Builder's Handbook*, published by the Urban Land Institute in Washington, D.C., thus warns developers:

> Freedom of neighborhoods from the adverse effects of through traffic is highly important. Heavy traffic-volume streets, even freeways if they cut through neighborhoods, exert just as adverse an influence as shoddy developments or unsightly strip commercial and noxious industrial uses. Whenever possible, neighborhoods split by existing or potential major thoroughfares should be avoided. Noise and fumes from cars, trucks, and busses are objectionable.

This was written for hard-headed, dollar-conscious developers, not for idealistic no-growthers.

Readers of suburban newspapers are familiar with articles like the one in the Somerville, Massachusetts, *Times* in March 1970: " 'It's impossible to either sleep or live in peace' was the way Alderman John Holmes described the effect of I-93 traffic on residents of Baily Road." The disgruntled property owners were demanding lower assessments—and they were getting them. Recognizing this value erosion, the Federal Housing Administration (FHA) will no longer insure mortgages on property that is exposed to excessive noise from freeways or from other sources.

It is true that highways and freeways enhance the value of certain kinds of property, mainly in rural areas and near interchanges. Even in these cases, however, it can be shown that the development spurred by the rising property values imposes costs on the local government which translate into higher property taxes.

pollution

So too for pollution. The President's Council on Environmental Quality calculated that by 1968 air pollution had caused over $16 billion of damage a year, $5.2 billion alone to residential property. This figure will rise to $8 billion by 1977, the council estimated, if pollution remains unchecked. Research at Carnegie-Mellon and Pitt universities in Pittsburgh found that dirty air cost each Allegheny County resident $300 annually in damage to health and property (figure 60).

This decay of property values wrought by air pollution and noise shows up in the assessment rolls. As a city or area becomes unpleasant to live in, mobile middle and upper income taxpayers move out. The exodus not only causes property values to decline, the city loses income and sales tax revenues too. The job of keeping or attracting new business and industry becomes more difficult; browsing through the ads that state and local industrial development agencies take out in business magazines shows that environmental amenity is becoming an increasingly important consideration.

★ **FIGURE 59. PAVED ACREAGE IN CITY CENTER** ★

City	Acres in Central Business District		Highways		Parking		Highways & Parking	
Washington	1,152	(100%)	553	(48%)	157	(14%)	710	(62%)
Los Angeles	400	(100%)	140	(35%)	84	(21%)	224	(56%)
Boston	500	(100%)	215	(44%)	15	(3%)	230	(47%)
New York	5,555	(100%)	2,260	(41%)	240	(4%)	2,500	(45%)
Philadelphia	1,395	(100%)	487	(35%)	93	(7%)	580	(42%)

SOURCE: American Municipal Association, "The Collapse of Commuter Service," p. 12 (1960), Department of City Planning, City of Los Angeles.

All in all, pollution can mean that local officials get less revenues, or that they have to apply the tax screws even tighter to raise what they need. Elected officials enjoy doing neither, which is why if you argue against pollution on these grounds, and have facts behind you, you might make some headway.

high-rises

Whether it is the striking contours of San Francisco, or the mixed living neighborhoods near downtown Washington, D.C., or elsewhere, the city councils and boards of trade wax ecstatic over their destruction so that glass-and-steel high-rises can take their place. "Increase the tax base," "revitalize the area," they recite in unison. Like the highway boosters, they do not give an accounting of how much it will *cost* the taxpayers to provide services to the high-rise buildings and their occupants.

A study by the Price Waterhouse consulting firm for the borough of York, in Toronto, Canada, concluded that even a high-rise apartment building housing few schoolchildren would at best impose no large new tax burdens on borough residents. No great revenue gains were seen that would offset the nonrevenue impacts of a high-rise on the community.

Some studies have reached conclusions even less sanguine. To test San Francisco Mayor Joseph Alioto's predictable boosterism: "We need tall buildings because they give us jobs and taxes," the San Francisco *Bay Guardian* set a team of investigators to work. Their study showed that San Francisco's downtown high-rise district actually cost the city $5 million more in services than it contributed in revenues (figure 61).

The reasons why costs have the edge over income are not hard to see. High-rises pack many people into a small area and as former New York City Mayor John Lindsay noted, "Density is responsible for inevitably higher costs for every conceivable service." The New York City police report twice as much crime in high-rise apartments over thirteen stories as in apartment buildings of only three stories. Fire and traffic control, transportation, sanitation, and other costs go up as well. Just consider the fire-fighting equipment a city needs to put out a blaze on the sixtieth floor!

airports

Battles over airports have much in common with those over highways. Promoters of new airports or extensions for old ones point to the new commerce and revenues they will attract. Opponents warn of noise and pollution and argue that extravagant expenditures on airports will pinch funds for other needed forms of transportation.

Airports have serious property tax consequences too. One is the vast amounts of land they consume. Dallas and Fort Worth, Texas, for example, have together bought 17,400 acres—more than Manhattan Island—to build a new airport. The amounts of land devoured are especially striking when they are compared to other forms of transportation. Thus Kennedy, La Guardia, and Newark airports in the New York City metropolitan area occupy 7,800 tax-exempt acres to handle 37 million passengers in 1970, while Pennsylvania and Grand Central Railroad stations were handling 107 million passengers on only 124 acres.

★ **FIGURE 60. ESTIMATED NATIONAL AIR POLLUTION DAMAGE COSTS WITH NO POLLUTION CONTROL, 1968 AND 1977** ★

(In Billions of Dollars)

Damage Class	1968*	1977†
Health	$ 6.1	$ 9.3
Residential property	5.2	8.0
Materials and vegetation	4.9	7.6
Total	$16.2	$24.9

*In 1968 dollars.
†In 1970 dollars.

SOURCE: Larry Barrett and Thomas Waddell, *The Cost of Air Pollution Damages: A Status Report* (Research Triangle Park, N.C.: Environmental Protection Agency, 1973); Environmental Protection Agency, *The Economics of Clean Air*, Senate Document No. 92-67 (Washington: Government Printing Office, 1972).

When the airports are publicly owned, this property is excluded from the local tax base. And not just the land. Some airports, such as those run by the New York Port Authority, lease building space to private concerns—hotels, banks, even industries. Such leased government property can be tax-exempt as well.

Like highways, airports affect the values of property around them. The noise of the huge jets sends neighbors up in arms and causes their property values to plummet. By 1972 lawsuits by enraged neighbors against Los Angeles County's International Airport totaled $4 billion. One study showed that homes in the $25,000-80,000 price range would "definitely" decline in value by up to 80 percent with an airport nuisance nearby. The FHA balks at insuring homes exposed to airport noise. This results in a still greater erosion of the local property tax base, as well as costs to taxpayers when public authorities defend and settle the lawsuits.

shoddy home-construction

In 1972, 718,000 Americans purchased newly built single-family homes, paying an average sales price of $28,000 to do so. If they took out a thirty-year mortgage (typical) at 9 percent effective interest, the real price came to over $81,000. And when closing costs, annual upkeep, and maintenance in the amount of $270 in property taxes, insurance, and other expenses are included, the transaction amounts easily to the single largest expenditure in most people's lives.

It may also be the worst. As builders try to mass-produce houses, shoddy home-construction becomes one of the nation's most expensive consumer rip-offs.

An individual or family stuck with a split-level lemon is really in a bind. A court battle over the purchase price of a shoddy home can be long and expensive. And often not very satisfactory. Moreover, many home-buyers fear that if they raise a stink the word will get around and reduce what they will get for the house when they try to sell it.

Many home-buyers don't realize that their local government has the power—indeed the duty—to stop shoddy home building. The laws vary from state to state and locality to locality. But often a *builder* is required to get an occupancy permit from the local building inspector before the buyer can move in. The builder may have to pass fire and other inspections as well.

The problem is that local officials do not always enforce these laws. They let the builders turn the homes over to the buyers without proper inspections. By the time the buyers learn of the defects, it is too late. Here again, the property tax assessment angle can give the victims a wedge. If a new home has defects, it isn't worth what the buyer paid for it. Since assessors usually peg new home assessments to the sales price, the new homeowner is entitled to a reduction. When homeowners start converging on the assessor's office demanding such reductions, public officials may begin to take notice.

Here is how Patricia Hess, of Columbia, Maryland, put it in a letter to an associate of Ralph Nader after a two-year court battle (and a $5,000 settlement) with the builder of her home, which she and her husband claimed was defect-ridden:

> One approach I would like to mention again is that of having your real estate taxes lowered. ...You simply present your own case to the tax people on the basis that you did not get what you paid for. Since almost all real estate taxes are based on the probable market value of a property, it stands to reason that if you have deficiencies that both you and the assessor were not aware of when you bought the property it is now worth less. If you have documentary evidence, they are obliged to lower your taxes. If this was done in a community on a broad basis and the local government could see their tax base shrinking, they would be eager to properly police the local builders.

strip-mining

Strip-mining is another issue on which opponents are often made to look like unrealistic idealists. When they warn that strip-mining devastates land and pollutes water, the mining companies, utilities, and industrial interests generally paint them as a bunch of impractical featherheads who would rather have all the lights go out than cut a daisy.

The industrialists conjure up what they call the "hard-dollar" benefits of strip-mining—"jobs," "industry," "growth," "a boost to the economy." (One company official even reasoned that devastated strip-mined land would be a

240 TAX POLITICS

FIGURE 61. WHY HIGH-RISES IN SAN FRANCISCO COST TAXPAYERS MORE THAN THEY PROVIDE IN REVENUE

What the Downtown Costs: $67.7 million
(A summary of expenditure apportionments for
San Francisco's Central Business District)

Apportionment by expenditure source[6]	total city '69-'70	apportionable to CBD	CBD's %
A. SERVICES TO PROPERTY[1]			
1. Police protection	$31.5m	$9.5m	30%
2. Fire protection	23.7	5.4	23%
3. Engineering and administration	1.9	.6	31%
4. Streets, sanitation	3.6	.47	13%
5. Sewers, sewage treatment	3.9	.98	25%
6. Municipal railway deficit	19.0	12.45	65%
7. Retirement[2]	28.6	8.6	30%
8. Unaccounted (storm drains & street lights)	9.8	3.2	31%
TOTAL	122.0	41.3	31%
B. COMMUNITY WIDE SERVICES[3]			
1. General[4]	37.81	9.19	25%
2. Welfare	45.24	7.33	16%
3. Debt services	15.73	3.81	25%
TOTAL	98.78	20.33	21%
C. GENERAL ACTIVITIES[5]			
TOTAL	21.66	6.04	28%
TOTAL	242.44	67.68	27.9%

How We Found That High-Rises Cost the City More Tha▶

The *Guardian* research team followed a methodology laid out in "A Cost Revenue Study of the Central Business District," a published dissertation by Raymond J. Green of the Urban Land Institute, on file at the Institute of Government Studies, Berkeley.

Revenues

In fiscal 1970, the latest year for which complete figures were available, total city and county revenue exclusive of school districts was $406.3 million. Federal and state grants accounted for $94.6 million of this, charges for current services and user fees another $61.6 million. The remainder, $250.1 million, came from seventeen local sources. We investigated each of these to determine the amount which came from the Central High-Rise District. Examples:

● Gross receipts tax and sales-and-use tax: we established the percentage of the city's retail sales which occur in the CHD (31.3 percent) by consulting Department of Commerce distribution charts.

● Parking meter and lot revenue: we compiled revenue totals from Police Department account books on the 7,300 CHD meters (51 percent of the city total) and nine CHD off-street garages (100 percent of the total).

Expenditures

Green's study proved an invaluable guide for hacking through the dense jungle of city expenditures. Following Green's method, we divided city expenditures into three

Property Taxes and Related Battles 241

They Pay

categories and computed them as follows:

• Services to property (police, fire, sewage, etc.): we determined these by painstaking examination of the accounts of all city departments engaged in such services and extensive personal interviews with thirty key city officials.

• Community-wide services (health, elections, etc.): we apportioned these according to the only available financial measure of district's worth — the assessed valuation of land and improvements in that district.

• General activities (mayor's office, city attorney, etc.): we apportioned these by multiplying each by the sum of services to property and communitywide services accorded to the CHD, expressed as a percentage of the city total.

Important footnote: Since education provides a service which spreads its value over the entire community, each sector of the city, under Green's methodology, receives educational services in proportion to the assessed value of that sector. San Francisco levies taxes to pay for education by this same method (property taxes), and therefore education revenues and costs for each sector of the city are equal by definition. Since, in addition, the Unified School District is a governmental entity separate from the City and County of San Francisco, we did not further consider it in our report.

What the Downtown Brings in: $62.9 million
(A summary of revenue apportionments from San Francisco's Central Business District)

Apportionment by revenue source[6]	total city '69-'70	apportionable to CBD	CBD's %
1. Property taxes	$161.8m	$39.3m	24%
2. Sales and use taxes	23.8	7.6	32%
3. Hotel occupancy tax	3.9	3.1	80%
4. Business gross receipts tax	9.0	2.9	32%
5. Parking meter and lot revenue	1.3	1.2	93%
6. Construction permits	1.1	.9	80%
7. Real property transfer tax	.4	.1	24%
8. Rents and concessions	.6	.5	83%
9. Franchises	.6	.4	67%
10. Vehicle code and other fines	5.5	1.4	25%
11. State liquor license fee	1.0	.3	30%
12. State property tax relief	4.3	.2	5%
13. State inventory tax relief	1.3	.3	23%
14. State cigarette tax	3.8	.8	20%
15. State motor vehicle tax	9.1	.5	5%
16. State gasoline tax	9.2	.5	5%
17. Earnings from interest	12.1	3.0	25%
TOTAL	249.0	62.9	25.2%

1. Services which can be apportioned to areas of the city where the actual work is performed.
2. Computed on the basis of contributions to retirement on behalf of city employees who service the downtown area.
3. Services whose benefit is felt by the community as a whole and only indirectly by any particular area of the city.
4. These include Corrections, Sheriff's Office, Parks and Recreation, Courts, Library, Community Promotion, Health, Elections, Law Library, and Miscellaneous.
5. These include Board of Supervisors, Mayor's Office, Chief Administrative Officer, County Clerk, Controller, Treasurer, and City Attorney.
6. Figures from fiscal 1970 State Controller's Report.

SOURCE: *The Ultimate Highrise*, published by the San Francisco Bay *Guardian*.

tourist attraction and would thus help the local economy.) Many of these arguments don't stand up. For example, strip-mining employs far fewer people than does deep mining. And it entails no permanent commitment by the company to the community.

Property tax losses are a way that strip-mining causes a hard-dollar loss to local governments and taxpayers. Corporate property tax vandalism is a sober and accurate description. Strip-mining destroys the property on which it occurs. "While mountain land is now assessed for tax purposes at very low values," wrote veteran coal-company battler Harry Caudill, "strip-mining often eliminates it from taxation entirely." If there are buildings, the mining company often levels them as soon as it buys the property, even if it does not intend to begin mining for years to come. Stripping renders soil unfit for use. The blasting, landslides, and acid run-off destroy surrounding property. People move away. All this is in addition to the basic point that the coal companies literally cart away the area's property wealth. "When one ton of coal is mined from Kentucky," wrote the *Kentucky Labor News*, "Kentucky is poorer—forever—by one ton of coal."

Furthermore, stripping imposes enormous costs on the local government—costs the local taxpayers have to bear. Landslides from strip mines block the roads. Overweight coal trucks chew them up. Loaded with silt run-off from strip mines, streams overflow, wrecking bridges, roads, and property. Coal miners laid off as companies switch from deep to strip-mining burden the local welfare rolls.

The property tax destruction has been documented.

Students working under Dr. Theodore J. Voneida at Case Western Reserve University in Cleveland studied the tax records in heavily strip-mined Belmont County in southeastern Ohio. They also used records of the Ohio Division of Mines and Division of Forestry and Reclamation. These showed that the assessed value of buildings per acre in one township decreased from $20 to $9.75 between 1957 and 1970. In Wheeling Township, the average land assessment dropped from $30 an acre in 1957 to $20 an acre in 1963 after heavy stripping. In a neighboring township where there was no stripping, values remained constant.

If there is or may be strip-mining in your area, you can conduct such studies. Public officials and other taxpayers may listen to your arguments against strip-mining more carefully when you show how it erodes the local tax base.

new industry

It is the conventional wisdom among some local officials and chambers of commerce that new factories are the Lord's bounty most ardently to be wished. And the affliction from the other place most to be feared, in this view, is an industry that picks up and goes elsewhere.

Yet it is by no means certain that new industry always benefits local taxpayers, even financially. Studies show that the costs these operations impose on a locality are often greater than the new property taxes and other revenues they provide. In 1970 the United States Department of Agriculture published a study called "The Impact of New Industry on Local Government Finances in Five Small Towns in Kentucky."

In most of the cases studied, the new industry cost the taxpayers more than it provided in new revenue. The harm to local taxpayers was greatest where: (1) the local government offered tax breaks or other inducements, and/or (2) the new plant brought in families with schoolchildren.

It is doubtful as well that local tax breaks are really a major factor in where businesses decide to locate.

"It's not really true that people (i.e. corporations) flee to lower tax jurisdictions," a vice-president for taxes at the Olin Corp. told the *Wall Street Journal*. The official said that access to raw materials, labor, and markets is usually much more important. The chief of business assessments in the Los Angeles County assessor's office provides another example. He points out that aircraft equipment was taxable in California, while it was not in the neighboring states of Arizona and Nevada. Yet California remained a hub of air traffic, while the other two states had very little.

A 1967 study by the U.S. Advisory Commission on Intergovernmental Relations, "State and Local Taxation and Industrial Location," backs up these views. The study concludes: "Between distant states, tax differentials appear to exercise little plant location influence . . . as between neighboring states, there appears to be no clear relationship between industrial growth trends and tax differentials." The study notes the ultimate futility in state efforts to attract new industry through tax breaks. States tend to keep their tax structures in line with those of their neighbors. When one state offers a bonus for industry, its neighbors usually follow suit. Thus they all end up right where they started from, except that their small taxpayers are deeper in the hole for the benefit of business and industry.

Even the effect of property taxes on industrial location within a local area has been seriously questioned. Professor Helene A. Cameron of Ohio State University studied the impact on business of property taxes in Franklin County (Columbus), Ohio, where local tax rates ranged from $27 per $1,000 assessed valuation to $51 per $1,000. As reported by the *Wall Street Journal*, Professor Cameron found that even this difference in tax rates would amount to only 1 percent of a business's operating costs or even less—hardly enough to make property taxes the decisive factor in where the plant would locate.

In some cases, tax differences *can* be the "swing factor" when an industry is choosing localities within a state or metropolitan region. The seven counties in the "Twin Cities" region surrounding Minneapolis and St. Paul, Minnesota, have adopted a simple and logical way to protect themselves and counter this threat. They agreed to share the taxes of any new industry that moved into the region. No longer would they be subject to "tax blackmail" whereby industries play off one locality against another to get the best tax deal.

An even better plan would be to take this idea one step further. The property tax on industry should be statewide. That way, no matter where industries moved within a state, their tax burden would be the same. And since residential property taxes would still be local, taxpayers would keep local control over the taxes they themselves pay. A statewide property tax on business and industry would also help deal with school financing inequities discussed earlier.

The destructive competition between states to attract business and industry would remain. This problem must be solved at the federal level. The federal government should take the same approach it used years ago to stop the erosion of state taxes on gifts and estates. It could establish a generous surtax on business and industry, with a full credit for any state and local takes paid. Under this system, a business or industry would pay at least the set amount no matter where it located, and the efforts of the states to exact a fair share from these taxpayers would be protected.

nuclear power and property taxes

The issues come to a head in conflicts over nuclear power plants. The nuclear power industry is using property taxes the way the early colonists used whiskey and beads—to buy off the natives. Few local officials can resist the tax-revenue bounty that nuclear power plants promise to bring. Local taxpayers usually follow suit.

To be sure, the promises are not empty. In tiny Vernon, Vermont (pop. 1,200), a nuclear plant provided enough new tax revenue to permit a cut in the tax rate from $4.90 per $100 assessed value in 1967 to only $1.83 per $100, even after the town had built new town offices, a new library, a recreation center with an indoor swimming pool, a new garage for highway equipment, and a new school. Since construction of the Pilgrim 1 nuclear plant in Plymouth, Massachusetts, the tax base there has tripled and the plant itself provides half the community's taxes.

These revenue bonanzas have tended to shut people's eyes to the health and safety hazards the plants pose. Within twenty months after opening, the Vermont Yankee plant in Vernon had closed down seventeen times, usually as a result of "accidents" and defects. Yet Mrs. Erma Puffer, a powerful local official, could easily push the problem aside. "Did you ever buy a car that operated 100 percent efficiently when you got it?" Mrs. Puffer asked a reporter for the *Christian Science Monitor*. "The plant is kind of like that car." What does Mrs. Puffer think about the yet-unsolved problem of disposing of nuclear wastes which many feel to be the hidden time-bomb lurking under the nuclear power boom? "If the good Lord is smart enough to let them build a nuclear plant, He's smart enough to give them a way to get rid of the waste," she told the *Monitor*.

The hazards are very real, however. It often falls to the residents of neighboring towns to raise them at hearings over proposed nuclear power sites. These neighbors are exposed directly to the threats, but they do not get to share in the revenues.

Nor is safety the only issue. The growth the plants occasion can show itself a false god. In the five years after Pilgrim 1 was built, Plymouth's population grew so fast that it had to build three schools in one year, among other projects, and the end is not in sight. People who bought homes in jerry-built subdivisions are clamoring for sidewalks and street repairs. By 1974, the *Monitor* reports, the tax rate had already turned up again, and Plymouth was looking to a second and even a third plant to bail it out from the costs of growth.

Here again, the answer is to make the property tax on power plants statewide. This would at least give taxpayers in other localities, who must share the safety hazards, a fair share of the new revenues. And it would enable residents near proposed sites to take a more sober and objective view of whether a nuclear power plant was really compatible with the long-term health, safety, and overall well-being of their communities.

★

Citizens must start to question, with hard facts, the line that commercial and residential development means benefits galore for all. Local bankers, realtors and businesses may gain. But citizens should demand a careful accounting for the total costs and benefits, of which property taxes are a major part.

Chapter 10
Taking Action on Tax Reform

a word about power

Power is the ability to make decisions affecting your life and the lives of others. Remember last April 15 when you filed your income tax return? You had just been required to spend hours filling out complicated forms, listing all your income, and then handing over considerably more than you could afford. How did you feel? Angry? Resentful? Frustrated? Remember picking up the newspaper and seeing those articles that show up every year about all the rich people and corporations skipping their fair share of taxes? You probably had a good glimpse of power at that point—you knew that the powerful could make decisions about you that put money into their pockets.

It is much the same way when you receive your property tax assessment. It seems too high. Or you suspect that there are other people in town who are getting off easy. But when you think about the time and trouble and expense of fighting the assessment, you just sigh and pay up.

★ ★ ★ ★ ★

a study in contrast

GLORIA: How could you cheat on your taxes?

ARCHIE: I'm just, whaddya call it... exercisin' my loopholes, that's all. Like the big guys.

Archie Bunker, however, had second thoughts and ended up quivering in an IRS office trying to explain how he "forgot to put down $680 extra income." By contrast consider the following statement:

"Anybody has a right to evade taxes if he can get away with it. No citizen has a moral obligation to assist in maintaining the government. If Congress insists on making stupid mistakes and passing foolish tax laws, millionaires should not be condemned if they take advantage of them."

The speaker was investment banking baron J. Pierpont Morgan. Rather than ending up in trouble with the IRS, Morgan acquired (and passed on to his family) what is now a multibillion-dollar enterprise. According to a House Banking Committee Report, "Morgan holds 5 percent or more of the common stock in no less than seventy-two major corporations, ... in addition, it has interlocking directorships with 103 major corporations."

The difference between Archie "exercisin' his loopholes" and Mr. Morgan "taking advantage of foolish tax laws" is obvious. Archie exercising his loopholes was like trying to eat the hole of the doughnut—there was nothing for him to take advantage of. On the other hand, the tax laws provide much for Morgan and other special interests to take advantage of. For example, 1972 saw thirteen million-dollar earners who paid no income tax at all.

The difference between Archie and the Morgans *is the difference in political and economic power—how it's acquired, how it works, and how it's kept!* Power allows wealthy special interests to escape paying their taxes and forces you to help make up the difference. Money that stays in their pockets is extracted from yours.

Saul Alinsky has said there are only two types of power: money power and people power. A Federal Reserve Board study found that the wealthiest 20 percent of Americans own 77 percent of the total private wealth of America. That means that a relatively small number of people wield money power. The special interests use money power to protect and expand

245

246 TAX POLITICS

their interests. They use three basic tactics:

Money: To make large campaign contributions and provide other favors to elected officials;

Secrecy: To shield these favors—and the special tax favors provided in return—from public view; and

Propaganda: To lull taxpayers into apathy by confusing the issues with deceptive and misleading arguments.

Against these tactics, average taxpayers need effective countermeasures to shift the balance of power so the tax laws will be written to benefit the majority of Americans instead of the minority of powerful special interests. Since there is a concentration of money power, average taxpayers are left with the other kind of power Alinsky describes: people power.

People power comes from people getting together to work on their common problems, people acquiring the ability to make decisions affecting their own lives, the 80 percent of Americans who share only 23 percent of the wealth.

getting together

People power! Citizen action. The phrases glow with virtue and promise. As we get closer, however, difficulties appear. Our schedules are busy. If we make time, nobody else seems willing to. Even if they do, our high hopes run amok in an endless succession of meetings at which nothing seems to get done. There are difficulties, there always will be. But there are ways to work through them and the effort is worth it.

allies

Many powerful groups have a direct interest in tax reform. So many, in fact, that few have picked up the issue and really pushed it as their own. Groups tend to focus on issues which are theirs alone. Everybody's issues are nobody's issues. For the most part, tax reform coalitions must be deliberately pulled together. First, however, consult the list of tax-reform groups in the Appendix. These groups will be helpful in organizing tax-reform citizen action. But they are not alone in the fight for fair taxes.

Possible allies for a property tax reform drive include:

> People whose paychecks depend on property tax revenues—teachers, police, sanitation workers, all public employees. Teachers' unions and the American Federation of State, County, and Municipal Employees (AFSCME) have shown special interest in local tax issues.

> People who benefit from specific expenditures—users of libraries, parks, zoos, neighborhood groups concerned about trash collections, police protection, rat control, and the like.

> Good government groups, such as the League of Women Voters.

> Labor unions, all of whose members pay property taxes, on their house or in their rents.

> Retired people's groups, the members of which often suffer extra heavy burdens because they live in houses they bought when their incomes were much higher.

One could compile a similar list for income tax issues. Such groups have been testy about alliances. The leaders and staff worry about the compromises an alliance might entail. They don't want to dilute their own influence. A major hurdle is the tendency to think in black-and-white absolutes. "We disagree with them on X and Y, so we better not get mixed up with them on Z." Good politicians know better. Agree where you can. Fix common ends. If you must part ways later, then do so—later.

A systematic approach is important in developing these contacts. You might start with a list of professional fraternal, and social organizations in your town or city. The local chamber of commerce publishes such a list. Consult the Yellow Pages for a list of local unions. (You can supplement this by a look at the *Listing of Reporting Labor Unions*, published by the U.S. Labor Department and available at your library or from the U.S. Government Printing Office.) For a list of religious organizations, again consult the Yellow Pages.

Many of these groups will be interested in working for tax reform. The national headquarters of labor unions are often more informed on such issues than are the locals, so it might pay to contact the national office first. Try to get copies of the AFL-CIO's and UAW's executive board resolutions as well as testimony or other position papers on an individual union's tax-reform position. Most unions have taken very good positions on tax reform. Religious groups such as the Unitarian Church, Religious Society of Friends (Quakers), and the Church of Christ

Taking Action on Tax Reform 247

have "social action" committees which may be especially helpful. And use your imagination to find other groups, such as the local League of Women Voters, Association of University Women, and various consumer groups. (Again, a look at the Yellow Pages, under "Associations," might help.)

It is useful to type information about each organization on a separate 3 by 5 index card. Include the name, address, and phone number of the organization and of the person who coordinates the group. Also list meeting times and other relevant information. Each time you contact the group, make a notation on the card. Note how the organization responded, which members sounded enthusiastic, group actions on tax reform, and the date of your contact. In a month or two, the index file can grow into an invaluable organizing tool.

You might also add index cards for each local periodical you found in *Ayers' Directory of Periodicals*.

building your tax-reform organization

Now you can begin contacting the names you've collected. You don't need to contact large masses of people. In fact, large numbers in the beginning can lead to problems. What you need is a "working committee." You probably have listed at least fifty organizations if you live in a middle-sized city. Each of these organizations has a constituency. Let's say that, of the fifty, you find responsive people in twenty of them. If you get two people from each group to volunteer time, that's forty people. You're well on your way to citizen action for tax justice.

Your working committee is now ready to inform the community on tax issues. You can send speakers to many of the organizations on your list. When speaking on taxes before a group, it's important to give the audience something to do. Perhaps you could pass around a petition (see below). Always get names, addresses, and phone numbers of people interested in the issue. Then follow up. For example, you might ask some to write letters to the editors of local newspapers informing other groups of the opportunity to invite a tax-reform speaker. Others could write on tax action in their organization newsletter, or join in a community petition drive, or in a telephone tree, or volunteer time for investigative work.

Your working committee can set up a formal speakers' bureau once the idea takes hold. It could invite speakers from national tax-reform groups to address community meetings. This is an excellent way to raise money. Ask the speaker if you can sell admissions (at a reasonably low price, of course), while paying only the speaker's expenses without an honorarium. If the speaker agrees, you suddenly have a few dollars for leaflets or newspaper ads.

The St. Louis Tax Reform Group has taken the speaker idea another step. They've made a colorful slide show about tax justice, along with a printed script. They've shown the slides to many groups throughout the Midwest, and then answered questions from the audience. Tax activist Bob Loitz has several copies of the slide show he's lending to groups across the country. You can contact him at P.O. Box 3518, Akron, Ohio 44310.

One or more of the working committee members may want to appear on a local radio talk show to discuss the group's activities and issues of tax justice. Especially around assessment and tax time, your speakers may be in great demand on radio, and even TV talk shows. Also, if you invite outside speakers, try to get them interviewed by your local press before they speak. They might even be taped by a local TV meet-the-press show. Be sure to have the speech covered in local newspapers, too. If you can get a story in the media before the speech, that will bolster your audience.

services

Some tax-reform groups have tried to attract members by offering services. The California Tax Reform Association, for example, made free tax-return advice to all comers, to acquaint more people with tax-reform issues. Other groups, such as the Texas Tea Party, have provided such services to dues-paying members.

Most organizers say it is hard to be an action group and provide services at the same time. One role tends to dominate the other. The California Tax Reform

248 TAX POLITICS

Association found that people would come for the free assistance and then not become involved in the tax-reform campaign.

Property taxes are different on this score, however. Assessment appeals are not just a help to individual property owners. Enough of them together can be a challenge to the whole local assessing system.

getting change

While financial power relies on money, secrecy, and propaganda, people power has its own weapons: investigation, exposure, and political action. Investigation, exposure, and political action can make a difference. In Fort Wayne, Indiana, during the 1970 election, the powerful incumbent Congressman E. Ross Adair (R-Ind.) sent a Chicano to woo Mexican-American voters. However, citizen investigation raised questions about the congressman's true attitudes toward the community. An investigator found, for example, that H. L. Hunt, a right-wing financier who owned six local migrant camps, was a substantial contributor to the campaign. This information was printed in a leaflet and distributed where the congressman's representative spoke. As a result, the congressman lost the Chicano vote, which, in turn, helped lose him the election.

Here, *investigation* uncovered special-interest connections between the congressman and enemies of the Mexican-Americans whose vote the congressman sought. *Exposure* in the form of leaflets alerted the community and suggested questions to be raised with the congressman or his representative; organized *political action*, in the form of the Mexican-American vote, helped the congressman lose the election. The best part is that it took only one person to uncover the information, and two people to print the leaflets and distribute them.

reports

A report is often the best way to release your information to the public and launch a reform drive. It can become the rallying point for further action. CAP's reports on underassessed steel mills, racetracks, office buildings, and other large properties in Chicago led directly to vigorous action campaigns which pressured the assessor into adding millions of dollars to the assessment rolls.

Reports should be short and simple, and focused on a single issue. Boil your data down to three to five pages. Include a chart or graph if helpful. It's fine to put out a lengthy report with all the details. Just realize that only a handful of people will read it. For general distribution you need something shorter. Another advantage of short reports is that making copies is not expensive.

A report is not an action campaign. It is merely the opening shot. Thus it must include, or be accompanied by, demands on specific individuals to take specific steps to correct the problem. Even then, if the report is not followed up with persistent public pressure, it will fall flat.

the media

The media are the eyes and ears of the public. It is possible to reach a few people directly, but to reach many, it is necessary to work through the media. Most editors and reporters think taxes are complicated and deadly dull. It is your job to give the issue life with short, hard-hitting reports, direct challenges to prominent people and interesting actions and events.

It helps to develop a working relationship with one or more local reporters. Find ones who share your interests, help them with information and leads, and **don't always expect credit.** Some tax-reform groups have brought reporters in on their investigations. They supply advance background information which the reporters often develop into complementary stories and follow-up interviews. Such advance work is also a way to "test the waters," to see how much interest a particular story is likely to arouse.

While building allies in the media, it is essential to maintain a healthy arm's length relationship and to respect a journalist's independence.

A press conference is a good way to release a disclosure or report. It lets you reach a group of reporters all at once and allows for questions and answers. Local TV and radio stations often air actual segments of **the conference. To hold a press** conference, you need only a room (or a symbolic location), plenty of copies of your release and report, and advance notice to the media. The location should be *convenient* for the reporters. If a room, it should not be so big that the turnout seems small. Find out the deadlines for morning and evening newspapers, radio and TV shows, and time the conference accordingly.

Access to the media may not be as difficult as you think. "I was amazed," says Akron, Ohio, tax activist Bob Loitz, "at how easy it is for an active citizen to get his story printed in the local paper. I just went in, asked to see the managing editor, and explained why I felt the story was important." Remember the editorial page, and radio and TV editorials as well. A strong editorial can carry weight with public officials, since media support is important to them. Obtain written transcripts of radio and TV editorials to distribute later. In fact, it is very wise to keep a file of all media coverage of your group. Such clippings can be especially useful in fund-raising, because they show you can deliver on your promises.

Sometimes the local media is closely tied to the power interests. What then? You can try meeting with the editor. Once the editor sees you in the flesh, sees that you are not villains but real people with valid concerns, he might be inclined to treat you fairly. Perhaps the paper would give your work unbiased coverage in news columns, even though opposing it in editorials.

Don't forget smaller community papers and shoppers' guides. These often reach a surprisingly large number of people, and the editors crave local news that the major dailies have not touched. *Ayers Directory of Publications*, available at local libraries, lists community papers, and union, trade, religious, and association publications as well.

If the local media is shut tight, try going outside (a good way to exert leverage on local officials anyway). Are there any angles to your story that statewide or even national media might pick up? Perhaps a prominent person or company is involved. Perhaps you could frame your study as a demand on the state legislature for hearings, and then travel to the state capital to release it there. Perhaps a well-known state representative or other person would offer public support. Or a labor union or prominent civic group. It's a scramble. And *you* will have to develop these angles. Busy reporters will not do it for you.

Remember too that newspapers, radio, and TV stations are businesses themselves, with lots of expensive property. In addition, they depend on access to public officials and official records—not to mention emoluments such as free use of the city hall or court house press rooms. Assessors and other officials often use these angles to buy off media criticism. You may choose to expose such goings-on. Before you do, consider whether access to the local media is a bridge you are really ready to burn behind you.

press releases

Give a busy reporter the gist of a story at a glance. The release should contain the key facts, be double- or triple-spaced, not more than one to one-and-a-half pages long, and contain at least one hard-hitting quote from someone in your group. Many reporters will just rewrite a press release and do no more, so be sure you get the meat in. On the other hand, a few experienced reporters regard releases as an effort to spoon-feed them. Get to know your local reporters.

A release can be distributed with a report, handed out at a press conference, or used to announce a demonstration. Be sure to put a release date and time at the top. This is called an embargo: you can distribute the release on a Friday, for example, and if it says on the top, "For release Monday A.M.," the media will not run it until then. It is important also to have at the *top* of the release the names and telephone numbers to be contacted for further information.

Figure 62 is a taxpayer-group press release which received good coverage in Rochester, New York. It concerns high-ranking House Ways and Means Representative Barber Conable (R-N.Y.) and how he serves special interests.

timing

Timing is crucial to an action campaign. A cutting expose or mass demonstration does little good if it is crowded off the front pages by other events, or if it comes at a time of year when nobody is interested. Raise issues when they are hot. A study of property tax assessments will have great impact just after the assessment notices or tax bills are sent out, or when the school

★ FIGURE 62.

METRO-ACT OF ROCHESTER, INC.

277 North Goodman Street
Rochester, New York 14607
(716) 244-7221

FOR IMMEDIATE RELEASE, July 13, 1973

Conable Protects Special Interests

Congressman Barber Conable has introduced a series of bills in this session of Congress which are an affront against local taxpayers, according to a statement released today by Metro-Act of Rochester.

Fred Schaeffer, Metro-Act President, charged that Conable has business and big money interests in mind and not the working man when he sponsors legislation which, for example:

1) would create a $100,000 tax loophole for the Morrison Division of the CIC Corporation of Buffalo, New York;
2) would allow tax write-offs for certain insurance companies, retroactive twenty years;
3) would benefit Page Airways with a $25,000 exemption from import duties.

The largest and most specific case involves the Buffalo-based CIC Corporation, an equipment, motor vehicle, and railroad car leasing outfit, with a Rochester office at 891 Monroe Avenue.

Art North, a Metro-Act Council member and principal researcher of this matter, pointed out that CIC hired a tax specialist named Don Lubick who also is said to advise Congressman Conable, according to the Tax Analysts and Advocates of Washington, D.C. Lubick supposedly suggested to Conable that a bill could solve CIC's problems.

"This is a classic example," said Schaeffer, "of people and institutions in positions of power using that power to influence legislators for their own benefit and not that of the average family and taxpayer."

"It gives us one more concrete example," concluded Schaeffer, "that our present tax system, from the property tax to the income tax, has to be changed quite drastically so the rich don't keep getting richer at the expense of the working people."

Taking Action on Tax Reform 251

board announces a deficit. A study of a congressperson's campaign contributions will mean the most at election time.

It can also help to hitch your release to an event that is likely to gain public attention. This increases the prospects of being covered. For example, if the president of a large corporation is going to receive a good citizenship award at a chamber of commerce banquet, that would be a good time to release a report showing his company is a prime tax avoider.

Even the day of the week is important to consider. Some days are good "news days"; not much is happening and reporters are looking for stories. Other days there is more news than the papers can print. Find out which are the best news days in your area. And don't forget deadlines. Morning and afternoon papers have different ones. Time a press conference or release so that the newspaper friendliest to you gets to print it first.

bringing it back home

It is not hard to connect local tax issues to people's concerns. But how can you hold elected state and federal representatives to account?

voting records on tax issues

The national tax-reform groups listed in the Appendix can help. Try to get behind tricks and ploys. Senate members, for example, sometimes vote for tax reforms only after being assured that the reforms will be dropped in a House-Senate conference on the bill.

campaign contributions

It is one thing simply to report that your representative voted for a special interest. It is much more significant to show that the vote came after the same special interest contributed to the representative's campaign. Does he receive substantial funds from individuals and interests which do not even reside in the district?

absenteeism

How many votes or committee meetings has your representative missed? Missing votes is one way to duck a controversial decision. For example, when a campaign contributor is pressing the representative to vote *for* a bill, and constituents are pressing for a vote *against* the bill, the representative can duck both pressures by claiming an important engagement elsewhere at the time. A report documenting absenteeism is bound to get community attention.

accessibility

How accessible is your representative? Who gets to talk to him on trips home? Does the representative spend most time with local politicians and special-interest groups, or with average taxpayers? You could do a report on the audiences the representative has addressed and the fees or "honorariums" received (these must be reported). You could also report on the difficulties typical taxpayers encounter in getting to see the representative.

financial interests and conflicts of interest

Some representatives have direct interests in industries helped by tax loopholes they support. Former Ways and Means Committee member Joel Broyhill (D-Va.) pushed real estate tax loopholes at the same time he and his family were making millions in that business. Exposure of this conflict helped get Broyhill voted out of office.

do it yourself

You will probably want to tell your story yourself, whether or not you have difficulty breaking into the local media. A typewriter, a mimeo machine, some money for paper and postage, and willing hands are really all you need. An electrostencil machine would save the bother of typing stencils. You can probably borrow the equipment at a church, union, or club. If you can afford it, you can have your material reproduced by an offset printer.

Don't bite off more than you can chew. It is best, for example, not to promise a weekly or monthly newsletter until you have put out a few occasional issues and know what is involved.

Your publications can take many forms. A regular bulletin is essential to building cohesion in a group. Broad-based action groups like the Chicago Citizens Action Program (CAP) and the Arkansas Community Organizations for Reform Now (ACORN) publish regular offset newspapers. Massachusetts Fair Share puts out a

252 TAX POLITICS

monthly magazine. Smaller groups publish mimeo or offset newsletters. A special pamphlet is an excellent way to focus on a major issue. The Philadelphia TEA party put out such pamphlets in its fight for a progressive state income tax.

If you know an artist willing to do drawings and cartoons, all the better. If not, you can get graphics for community newspapers and bulletins from Community Press Features, Urban Planning Aid, 639 Massachusetts Avenue, Cambridge, Massachusetts 02139.

Make it a rule: always have written material to give to people whose support you want.

tactics

Tactics are simply how we use our resources to achieve our ends. The difference between smart and dumb is the difference between good tactics and bad. Tax reformers and their opponents have different resources. Entrenched interests have money and position, and the clout which these entail. Tax reformers have the banner of justice and—potentially at least—the support of large numbers of people. Public outrage and righteous indignation are forces that the powerful and wealthy have great difficulty meeting in kind.

About all they can do is condemn our efforts as demogogic and uncouth. Yet, try to think of a single major social reform—the American Revolution, the freeing of the slaves, the ending of the Vietnam War—that was not ushered in by mass mobilizing of public opinion and pressure. Of which of these achievements do your critics disapprove?

The late Saul Alinsky of Chicago was a master organizer. Even conservative critic William F. Buckley said of him, "Alinsky takes the iconoclast's pleasure in kicking the biggest behinds in town, and the sport is not untempting." In his book, *Rules for Radicals*, he had laid down his

---

★ **FIGURE 63. CITIZENS ACTION PROGRAM NEWSLETTER** ★

CITIZENS ACTION PROGRAM

Vol. 1　　　　October 1971　　　　No. 4
formerly Campaign Against Pollution

LET THE BIG GUYS PAY THEIR SHARE

If Cook County Assessor P. J. Cullerton ran his office legally, our kids wouldn't have to ask for a handout. The schools wouldn't have to close and our taxes wouldn't have to go up.

CAP's goal is fair taxation. If the big industries paid their share of real estate taxes, our children would get the education they deserve without an increase in the homeowners taxes.

On September 9, CAP members voted to change their name to the Citizens Action Program to reflect all of their interests. Pollution, taxes and schools are all affected by the citizens' exclusion from the decision-making. Daley, P. J. and their rich campaign contributors have fleeced the small taxpayers long enough.

-- Continued page two --

Reprinted by permission of Hyde Park Herald & Richard Kimmel.

Passing the hat

tactical principles. We can do no better than to get them from the horse's mouth.

- Power is not only what you have but what the enemy thinks you have.
- Never go outside the experience of your people.
- Wherever possible go outside of the experience of the enemy.
- Make the enemy live up to their own book of rules.
- Ridicule is man's most potent weapon.
- A good tactic is one that your people enjoy.
- A tactic that drags on too long becomes a drag.
- Keep the pressure on.
- The threat is usually more terrifying than the thing itself.
- Pick the target, freeze it, personalize it, and polarize it.
- The price of a successful attack is a constructive alternative.

The kernel of a successful citizen action campaign is right here. Let us expand on several of these pointers.

enjoying your tactics

The Puritan view of civics as a grim churchly enterprise is out. Tactics that are fun are practical. The laziest of us will get moving if a good time is in prospect. This is especially so with taxes. Tax-reform battles can wear on for months. If new and interesting things aren't happening, the troops (not to mention the press and other media) lose interest. City hall has won many battles simply by waiting it out.

Good tactics *are* fun. Picketing a city council meeting, holding a citizens' hearing to air your views, delivering a letter personally to the mayor as a delegation, swamping the assessor's office with telephone calls, or your representative's office with telegrams—these tactics give people a chance to actually work for something with their neighbors. It is exhilarating to find out that we *can* stand up, talk back, and make a difference.

There is no limit to the ways tax reformers can make their point.

Members of the St. Louis Tax Reform Group came to Washington to testify on tax reform, and afterwards delivered a brightly painted cardboard "mailbox" full of letters to Ways and Means Committee Chairman Wilbur Mills, demanding that he act on tax reform.

ACORN took its members on a bus tour (complete with a factual brochure) of the underassessed businesses in Little Rock, Arkansas.

The Citizens Action Program sent a delegation to Chicago Mayor Richard Daley's office just before Christmas, preventing the mayor, who didn't want to face them, from dedicating the nativity scene in the city hall lobby.

Bill Callahan and Ed Schwartz of the Philadelphia TEA Party hiked 105 miles from Philadelphia to the Pennsylvania state capitol in Harrisburg to deliver a tax reform petition to the state legislature. They picked up signatures and support along the way from people who came out to see what these strange "tax walkers" were up to.

Bucks County, Pennsylvania, taxpayers hired a soundtruck to help get people out to their meetings.

Taxpayers in Manassas Park, Virginia—75 strong—took their grievance right to the mayor's front door, and within an hour the town council rescinded a tax increase it recently had voted.

Taxpayers in Westmoreland County, Pennsylvania, attended a county commissioner's meeting to protest a property tax reappraisal, and then marched to the assessor's office to demand to see records which the assessor had been withholding.

While the task at hand is important, the spirit at such outings is almost festive. In Chicago, CAP members visiting over coffee after meetings tell stories not about their kids and lawnmowers, but of "actions" in which they took part that week. "Why don't we do things like this more often," people think. The good tax reformer will give them opportunities to do so.

personalizing the target

The target has to be a person. Constructive conflict does not arise from vague attacks on an unfair tax system. Specific demands must be made of specific people who can act on them. Novelists know that conflict captures interest and leads to growth. Tax reformers can learn it too.

linking up with national groups

By linking up with national organizations, your tax-reform effort can keep current with your representative's legislative activities. At decisive moments, your group can apply pressure to force the representative away from a special-interest decision. By establishing contact with citizen groups, your group can make tax reform a major community issue.

A good example came from citizens of Little Rock, Arkansas,

in response to an effort by Ways and Means Chairman Wilbur Mills to pass a series of special-interest "members bills" in 1972. The action involved a number of bills hammered out in secret committee session that would give generous tax breaks to banks, wealthy foundations, lumber companies, and other special interests. Members of ACORN (Arkansas Community Organizations for Reform Now) got wind of Mills's secret tax loophole plan. Much to Mills's surprise a delegation of citizens appeared at his district office with a message for their congressman. Their message was written on a two-foot-by-three-foot postcard addressed to him. It asked Mills on behalf of the taxpayers of his district to close, rather than open, loopholes for special interests. Two state newspapers, two local TV stations, and even the *Wall Street Journal* covered the story. The message was clear: citizens were keeping an eye on their congressman's activities!

With pressure from his constituents, along with support from tax reformers in the House, Mills was finally forced to withdraw the "members bills" from consideration.

Using teamwork, tax reformers in Congress and Little Rock together saved hundreds of millions of dollars from being lost to the federal Treasury.

specific demands

It sometimes works just to dump a problem in the lap of a high official and demand that he do something. But it is even better to make a specific demand that you know is within his or her powers. The first question, therefore, is "who can do what?" This will take some homework. You will have to find out about the jurisdiction of legislative committees, the tactics available to members of the legislature, the legal authority of state and local officials, and the like. Officials and former officials, reporters and attorneys might help.

Once you've located the person in the best position to do something, then you know where to approach. Or if you want to approach a specific official, you know what demand to make. If the official agrees to meet the demand, request a firm public commitment, preferably in writing.

A good example is the Tax Justice Act of 1975. (See Appendix.) Tax reformers became tired of representatives avoiding firm stands on federal tax reform. So they drafted their own comprehensive reform bill and sought members of Congress to co-sponsor it. Representatives couldn't avoid the issue. They couldn't just mouth a lot of glowing generalities on tax justice. They had to put their name on the line, Yes or No.

vigilance

Sometimes citizen action is reaction, trying to regain lost ground or at least reduce losses. A reappraisal is completed, the assessments go out. By the time taxpayers react the cement is almost dry. When citizens hear of their representative's pro-loophole vote in Congress, the president is ready to sign the bill. Taxpayer groups should take the initiative: attacking the previous year's assessments, demanding more equity before the new values are announced. They can raise questions about a reappraisal before it is completed. They can demand a tax-reform commitment from their representative before the congressional session starts. By moving first, taxpayers can lay a hand on the reins.

Trouble often has its roots at meetings of councils, committees, and boards, which make *decisions that are difficult to reverse later.* The public normally receives little if any advance notice of these meetings and their agendas. Once a tax-reform group gets going, it should have an "alert" committee to call city hall regularly to find out dates and agendas of any meetings that might affect taxes. The groups listed in the Appendix can help you keep an eye on the U.S. Congress.

some specific actions
petitions

Petitions are an excellent way to begin a tax action campaign, for at least four reasons.

First, they create contact with strangers. It is much easier to approach someone for a specific purpose than for just a general discussion. If you have never sought signatures for a petition, try to talk to someone who has experience. There are pointers that can help you.

Second, petitions are probably the most ready way of getting people involved. You accomplish little if you spend five minutes merely talking to someone about tax reform. But a person who signs a petition has become involved. Their action—though small—can provide a foundation to build on. The first step is usually the hardest.

Third, petitions are a sure-fire way to start a mailing list. The problem will be too many names—and not everyone who signs will wish to be contacted again. You can solve this problem by putting a small check on the petition beside the signatures of people who seem particularly responsive. Plan to follow up with that person.

Finally, the main advantage of petitions is the political threat they pose. Bob Loitz of Akron, Ohio, was able to mount a petition drive involving over 200,000 people. The signatures on Bob Loitz's tax petitions are not the source of influence. The influence comes from the recipients not knowing what the signers will do next, while knowing full well what they *could* do. Be sure to remind the recipient of this when you deliver the petitions.

letter-writing campaigns

In March 1972, the United Farm Workers began an unusually effective letter-writing campaign. The story goes like this.

On March 8, Peter Nash, general counsel for the National Labor Relations Board, issued a complaint against the United Farm Workers, claiming the union was conducting an illegal secondary boycott of wines made from grapes grown in the Napa Valley of California. Until Nash's appointment by the Nixon admin-

Taking Action on Tax Reform 255

★ FIGURE 64. THE T.E.A. PARTY PETITION ★

THE T.E.A. PARTY
Tax Equity for America

A petition to the Governor & Legislature

We, the undersigned, believe that it is immoral that governments at all levels are cutting programs that benefit millions of working Americans at a time when large corporations and the rich pay no taxes on much of their income.

We support a change in the Pennsylvania State Constitution to permit the Commonwealth and its political subdivisions to enact graduated taxes on income and wealth levied in accordance with people's ability to pay.

We oppose the efforts of big business and special interests to lower State corporate taxes.

We urge the Legislature to replace regressive sales, property, and wage taxes with progressive taxes on corporate and personal wealth and income so that Pennsylvania can meet its pressing social needs without imposing unfair taxes on ordinary citizens.

SIGNATURE (Written in Ink or Indelible Pencil)	PLACE OF RESIDENCE		DATE OF SIGNING		
	STREET AND NUMBER	CITY - STATE	MO.	DA.	YEAR
1					
2					
3					
4					
5					
6					
7					
8					
9					
10					
11					
12					
13					
14					
15					
16					
17					
18					
19					
20					

Name and address of person circulating this petition.

_____ Zip _____

Please return to
1307 Sansom St., Phila. 19107
(215) KI 5-3031

256 TAX POLITICS

istration, the NLRB had taken the position that the United Farm Workers' boycott was not under their jurisdiction. Clearly a political decision had been made to prevent the farm workers from boycotting.

Since it was a Nixon appointee who brought the situation about, the union decided to focus their efforts on Senator Robert Dole, then chairman of the National Republican Committee. Word went out to boycott offices around the country to begin taking the issue to their communities—urging people to write letters and send telegrams to Senator Dole. In the one-month period prior to a hearing on the complaint, a flood of letters deluged Senator Dole and his office.

Before the date for the hearing, Peter Nash and the NLRB had withdrawn the complaint, and Nash personally made a statement that the United Farm Workers were in fact not under the jurisdiction of the National Labor Relations Board. When the letter campaign was finished, the union had not only won the right to continue boycotting, but had used the NLRB fight to launch their boycott campaign of lettuce.

The secret of success in this case was to find the right target for the letter campaign rather than waste energy on scattered objectives. You don't have to generate a flood of letters to influence your representatives. A significant increase in the mail on tax reform will cause them to take notice. For a congressional office receiving ten letters a month on tax reform, another ten letters a month is a significant increase. Don't discount the importance of letter writing.

using a telephone tree

Akron tax activist Bob Loitz is building a telephone tree to help put citizen pressure on representatives through letters and telegrams just before the key tax votes. "I can think of a number of votes that I have changed before I cast them because of the content of my mail," reports Ways and Means Congressman Sam Gibbons (D-Fla.).

Five people each calling five others who call five more who finally call another five means almost 800 calls can go into a representative within a single day! Contact Bob for further details. Bob also has important suggestions for keeping the calls of high quality, so that the telephone tree does not turn into the old rumor game. Many citizen action groups use telephone trees very effectively, at the local, state, and federal level. When your group is ready, this tool may prove invaluable.

newspaper ads

An advertisement in the local newspaper can supplement a petition drive, if the paper will accept citizen action advertisements. In one sort of ad, a number of people sign an open letter, perhaps to an official, requesting that the official take certain steps. Or the ad itself can be a petition. There can be a coupon at the bottom for the person to sign and send to your group. You can forward all the coupons together to the official in question. Meanwhile, the names and addresses of the signers can help you build your organization. A large ad is not necessary. A small one can work just as well. Request a few thousand extra printed copies (if the price is reasonable) for use later.

tax-day publicity

Taxes are a hot issue in the weeks before April 15, which makes tax day a good time for public displays and other tax action campaigns. In 1973, Fred Harris's New Populist Action (no longer operating) helped groups in thirty-one different cities carry out tax-day activities. Rallies of several hundred people made news in cities from Milwaukee, Wisconsin, to Albuquerque, New Mexico. Frequently, local and state officials were invited to speak on closing tax loopholes. Texas taxpayers distributed over 100,000 leaflets demanding "Take the Rich Off Welfare." After studying the low taxes paid by many corporations, taxpayers in San Francisco, Little Rock, Tallahassee, Minneapolis, Portland, and Philadelphia presented "tax avoider" awards to local corporations including ITT, Alcoa, Honeywell, Georgia-Pacific, Uniroyal, and others. They focused not just on federal income taxes, but on state and local taxes as well.

Tax time is a good opportunity to invite your representative to speak at a tax-reform rally or other meeting. In Philadelphia, Denver, and Cleveland, Representatives Bill Green, Pat Schroeder, and Charles Vanik accepted invitations to preside at 1973 tax day hearings on tax reform. The representatives heard testimony from labor and civic groups and from individual taxpayers angry about their unfair tax burdens. Participation in such rallies tends to strengthen an official's self-image as a reformer and forces him to make his commitment public.

tax clinics

The Movement for Economic Justice has another idea for the weeks before tax day. They can advise your group how to organize tax clinics for people who can't afford to pay to have their tax returns done. Your tax clinic can operate at a high professional level with donated help. You can also inform taxpayers how they can reduce future tax-time woes by getting officials elected who support tax reform.

For further information on establishing a tax clinic, write:

Movement for Economic Justice
1611 Connecticut Ave., N.W.
Washington, D.C. 20009

Another group to contact on establishing tax clinics is:

Community Tax Aid, Inc.
Box 1040, Cathedral Station
New York, New York 10025.

conferences

Conferences and conventions can give a big boost to tax-reform drives. They can draw together people and ideas from across the state and even beyond. They can add the weight of well-known speakers to your cause. They generate enthusiasm and publicity. If you can arrange to publish the proceedings, academic types might even do original research that advances your work. Some organizers feel that a big convention is the way to begin a citizen reform effort. Others feel the convention should be built on strength rather than created from scratch. It takes work to make a meeting or convention succeed, and no detail can be left to chance. The tax-reform meetings we have attended have left these points especially on our minds.

The meeting and workshops must be carefully structured with a definite agenda. It is enraging to drive 300 miles just to sit through a haphazard bull session or to endure a harangue from some pushy individual who has seized the floor. Preliminary memos and advance discussions with participants can help narrow the issues and frame proposals (if there are any) that can be passed. Leave time for informal meetings and open-ended discussions, but do not make these the meat of the conference.

How to prevent the opposite extreme—a railroaded convention at which participants have no real say? The attitude and style of the leaders are key elements. The more groundwork laid beforehand, the less these problems arise.

The meetings should be fast-moving, and start and end *on time.* It is a slap in the face to invite someone to lead a one-hour workshop and then cut it to fifteen minutes because other meetings have run over.

A well-known keynote speaker will help attract people and press. But keep the center of gravity on what your group is here to do. It is not just a celebrity show. Send the speaker a background memo on your

Taking Action on Tax Reform 257

activities beforehand, brief him on the day of the talk, try to enlist his cooperation to focus on the goals of your group.

Provide written materials for people to take back with them—copies of talks and workshop notes, suggestions for local action, names and addresses of participants.

Gain commitments to some form of definite action, perhaps a telephone or letter-writing network to support reform proposals when they arise.

Conferences take more work and time than you think. To get a rough idea, estimate what you will need, and then triple it. It is inviting disaster to try to squeeze the planning of a conference into an already crowded schedule. Make time.

hearings

Public hearings can be an excellent forum. They provide a public platform for your information and views, a chance to confront your opponents and have them subjected to tough questioning, and a chance to show your own group's strength. The information brought forth in good hearings can be invaluable for reform efforts.

Demands for a public hearing can accompany the launching of an issue or the release of a report. The hearings could be before the local council or a federal, state, or local agency (such as the U.S. Treasury, or the state board of equalization, the state legislature, or a committee of the U.S. Congress). Many bodies have a direct or indirect interest in taxes. The education committees of the state and federal legislatures, for example, certainly are concerned with how funds for education are raised.

Hearings are events that should be developed fully. When the Citizens Action Program (CAP) went to the Illinois State Capitol at Springfield to testify on property tax relief for the elderly, it took busloads of elderly people who demanded to meet with their representatives and gained commitments of support. In 1973 members of the St. Louis Tax-Reform Group surprised the House Ways and Means Committee by showing up as a delegation at tax-reform hearings. The committee is not accustomed to hearing from ordinary taxpayers.

If members of the committee or other body holding the hearings are receptive, meet with them or their staffs beforehand. Give them background material and suggest questions to ask other witnesses. They will probably be grateful for the free staff work and the chance to take intelligent positions on the issue.

The hearings themselves will help gain press and media attention. They can be the occasion for a press conference. It will help if your testimony is typed in advance and copies are delivered to the press with a short one-page release. Releasing a study at the hearings will help also, as will an "action," such as packing the hearing room or holding a demonstration outside afterwards.

Official hearings are just one kind. Unofficial "people's hearings" are also a good way to focus attention on an issue. Supporters of the Tax Justice Act of 1975 have held such unofficial hearings in several cities and in the U.S. Capitol. Members of Congress have accepted invitations to take part.

acting on officials

A public official will often be the immediate target of a tax-reform campaign. It is important to know your adversary.

Some officials, especially elected local ones, are media-conscious and are accustomed to battling it out publicly. Their media contacts may enable them to hit back hard. Others, especially appointed bureaucrats and political machine hacks, have loafed in quiet obscurity for years and may be fish out of water if drawn into a public controversy. Still others may be frustrated, beaten idealists who have put up with inequities for years because they found themselves politically powerless to change them. They may privately welcome your activities as giving them a mandate to do what they wanted to do ten years earlier.

Find out the official's soft spot. Elected politicians must guard their public image, especially around election time. Appointees sometimes can be dumped by the one who appoints them. Administrators are subject to a legislative body that sets their budget, and sometimes to outside agencies with powers to audit.

officials acting

Taxes are fertile ground for public officials who want to do something worthwhile and make a name for themselves. Tax systems that can withstand close scrutiny are the exception. Leonel Castillo, the young city controller of Houston, Texas, has shown this by exposing the underassessment of factories, exclusive country clubs, and expensive homes such as those of U.S. Senator Lloyd Bentsen and former Treasury Secretary John B. Connally. Enlisting law students to do research, Castillo launched a "Tax Avoider of the Week" campaign. Representative Charles Vanik (D-Ohio) and his staff have combed corporate reports for each of the past few years to find out how much tax the nation's major corporations are paying. Evan Doss, first black assessor in Mississippi history, has launched a frontal assault on an assessment system blatantly biased toward large white property owners in that state's Claiborne County.

Such officials have learned a lesson that officeholders and potential officeholders might heed. To get where the action is, go where the money is. Controller Castillo was planning to run for the Houston City Council. On reading the city charter, however, he learned that the controller, who handles the city funds, has potential power that most council members would never come close to having. In Washington, D.C., only one department is right next to the White House—the Treasury. The power is where the money is.

elections and taxes

Politicians can become suddenly sensitive to voters around election time. Just before an election is the perfect time for your group to get commitments (specific and public) from candidates. You can demand support of tax reform, public disclosure of special-interest links, pledges to speak frequently before groups of average citizens, and other legitimate demands.

Be sure your group remains nonpartisan. Beyond that, feel free to publicize which candidates support your demands and which candidates oppose them. Elections are also a good time to expose special-interest links to each of the candidates. Your report is sure to get good media coverage. Special-interest links are a hot issue just before elections.

Your action campaign will have many beneficial effects: you will influence the issues in the election and force public discussion of the tax system and the impact of special interests on it. And you may well have many candidates, including the winner, pledged to specific tax reforms.

lawyers and lawsuits

These have a bewitching appeal—the promise of fast action and clear-cut victories. Indeed, lawsuits have scored signal victories for aggrieved taxpayers. A recent lawsuit made the IRS divulge the names of people it was investigating for political reasons. A lawsuit forced the Treasury Department to make public the hitherto secret private rulings it rendered for well-heeled taxpayers. Lawsuits have overturned the assessment systems in a number of states. But lawsuits can also pose problems for broad-based community groups. Lengthy court battles have drained the treasury of more than one such group, while boring the members into inactivity. Lawsuits can play a part, in the context of a larger agenda that keeps members active and involved. The mere threat of a lawsuit can accomplish much. Also, skillfully framed legal action can jar loose information that would not be available otherwise.

Not every lawyer is right for a community or citizen reform group. Lawyers tend to focus solely on winning the case, giving short shrift to how the lawsuit *process* can build the group itself and strengthen it for battles to come. The lawyer needs a sense of the group's broader aims, a feel for politics, and an ability to deal with and use the media. It is essential to agree on the role the group will play in major tactical decisions in the lawsuit *before* the lawyer is retained.

doing it alone

Not all of us can start or want to join a tax-reform group, but we still want to do something. Here are some sugestions.

1. _The Telephone and the Mails_. People do underestimate the power of these tools. All but the most incorrigible elected officials have a pollster in their psyches. Since few have developed effective channels by which voters can get through to them, they tend to grasp at any signs of public opinion available. That is where the phone calls and letters come in.

Letters should be short, to the point, and in your own words. Write out or type the subject of the letter at the top, and underline it. It often helps to show the person to whom you write that others are watching. Suppose you write the assessor. You could make carbon or Xerox copies and send them to the mayor, a state legislator, local news reporters. In the lower left-hand corner write "cc" followed by the names of the people to whom you send copies. If the letter contains new information not publicly known, you could attach a press release to copies and deliver them to the press.

2. _Making Knowledge a Hobby_: Some people make a hobby of sniffing around city hall. On lunch hours and days off they check assessment records, deeds of sale, zoning applications, just to see what's happening. At home they keep clipping files on topics that interest them, and at social gatherings they are alert for information that can help fill in the pieces. You never know when such information will be useful—in an article, a letter to the editor, or to give ammunition to a tax-reform group or advocate. Another way to use information is to make the acquaintance of reporters, elected local and state officials, and their staffs. These people often are too busy to do their own research, and welcome any help they can get. It is also possible to share your findings with reform groups, to help support their demands. But be sure you focus your efforts. Without being organized to demonstrate a particular point, information is confusing rather than useful.

3. *Writing a Column:* You can offer to write feature articles, and/or a regular column for your local newspaper. In the wake of a controversial reappraisal in Wallingford, Connecticut, Elea-

★ FIGURE 65. "TIP TOE THRU THE TAXES," NEWSPAPER COLUMN BY ELEANOR CORAZZINI ★

The Shock Of Reassessment or—

TIP TOE THRU THE TAXES

by Eleanor Corazzini

Wallingford Taxpayers: Have you checked the number of square feet in your home? Do you know what it would cost you for each square foot to replace your home? Do you know how much your home has depreciated since you purchased it?

Your Town Assessor knows the answers to these questions. He knows how much per square foot the land you own should cost. He also knows how much your taxes will be increased based upon the estimated new tax rate of 45 mills. All of this information is in his possession because our town hired experts to determine these facts and whatever United Appraisal Co. concluded, according to our assessor, is right.

My friends, I am not satisfied with the accuracy of United Appraisal Co.'s work. I attempted to discuss my dissatisfaction with our Board of Tax Review. Our Board of Tax Review could not find the time to discuss my dissatisfaction with me nor could they find the time to view my premises. I am still dissatisfied. I couldn't help but notice that our Board of Tax Review found the time to review the accuracy of United Appraisal Co.'s work for International Silver Co.'s Eyelet Specialty Division. They found that United Appraisal Co. was inaccurate and reduced the assessment by $272,000.

It is possible United Appraisal Co. is inaccurate with regard to other properties. Because of these possibilities I have written the following letter to our assessor:

Dear Mr. Kemp,

I request you to make available copies of the following documents prepared by United Appraisal Co. as authorized in Public Bid No. 68-24.

1. Appraisal Schedule
— to include United Appraisal Co.'s detailed investigation of residential, commercial and industrial construction costs in the town, the names of local building material dealers and builders contacted to obtain the costs on material and the prevailing building labor rates and degrees of efficiency in the building trade. Also the results of tests for accuracy of such appraisal schedule and specific location of structures of known value against which Wallingford properties have been tested.

2. Unit Land Value Data and results of test for accuracy
3. Land Value Map
4. Depth Tables
5. Corner Influence Tables
6. Excess Acreage Tables

Please make the requested documents available for inspection on Friday, May 28, 1971 and for as many days thereafter as may be necessary to complete inspection.

Very truly yours,
Mrs. Eleanor Corazzini
148 Fair St.
Wallingford, Conn.

Prior to re-evaluation the assessed value on my property on Fair St. was $10,440. The mill rate for the tax year 1969 was 61. My taxes were $636.84 per year. If the estimates we have seen are correct as to the new mill rate, it will be .045. Multiplying my new valuation by the projected mill rate my taxes will be $969.75. My taxes will increase by $332.91.

Assuming the mill rate for our town were to remain the same until the next general re-evaluation, which will not take place until 1980, I will pay $3,329.10 more in taxes over the next ten years. It is probable that the mill rate will increase each year during the next ten years and therefore I will pay more than $3,329.10 in increased taxes over the next ten years.

Have you multiplied your new valuation by the estimated mill rate for this year? Have you thought about what it will cost you if there is no increase in the mill rate over the estimate for this year, over the next ten years? Have you checked the assessments of people you know and whose properties you know in the same manner?

Revaluation will cost all of us substantial sums over the next ten years. Yet, I am not sure that United Appraisal Co. has been accurate in all its work. I am, therefore, requesting an opportunity to check their work and have requested our assessor to make available to me all of the basis data used in arriving at my re-evaluation.

Taxpayers, check for yourself.
E. Corazzini

May 23, 1971

Taking Action on Tax Reform

nor Corazzini, a housewife, began writing a column called "Tip Toe Thru the Taxes" for the weekly *Wallingford Post*. Before approaching a newspaper, prepare some samples that you can show.

4. *Lawsuits:* Many successful and far-reaching lawsuits can be credited to a single determined taxpayer. The hard work of Martha Hornbeak of Mobile, Alabama, was largely responsible for the 1971 federal court case, *Lee* v. *Boswell*, which compelled the state of Alabama to reform its assessing system, and which set a major precedent in property tax law. Phil and Sue Long, of Bellevue, Washington, have almost singlehandedly opened up the IRS through freedom-of-information lawsuits. It certainly helps if you are a lawyer with time to spare, or know one who will take the case—or at least advise you—as a public service.

lend your weight

Most of us don't like to just go along for the ride. We are reluctant to join groups whose leaders we don't know well, and in which we don't intend to work actively. These are healthy instincts. But the moral and financial support of nonactive members is essential to most reform groups. Everyone cannot do everything. The question to ask is not "Does this group represent my views perfectly?" but rather "Who will be having their way if this group is not on the scene?"

resources—funding

Short-term battles on specific issues often can scrape by on the time and money of the people involved, but long-term reform efforts need to be considered early on.

All fund-raising systems have one thing in common. They aren't easy. Reform groups must chose their tactics carefully to increase their visibility, gain victories, and not waste precious resources. There are several main methods of gaining funding:

membership dues for services

Such services include help on assessment appeals, discounts at certain local merchants and the like. Arkansas Community Organizations for Reform Now (ACORN) has used this method.

door-to-door soliciting

This has proven surprisingly effective when the effort is well planned and sustained. A group called the Illinois Public Action Fund pioneered door-to-door techniques in Chicago and has since helped other groups apply them in California, Massachusetts, and Washington, D.C. With IPAF help, the Chicago Citizen Action Program set up a soliciting program that is raising between $150,000 and $200,000 a year. For further information, write the Illinois Public Action Fund, 57 East Van Buren Street, Chicago, Illinois 60605.

foundation grants

Several foundations have helped to fund local tax-reform activities. For information on these, consult *The Foundation Directory*, available at local libraries. You can get advice on dealing with foundations in *The Bread Game*, $2.95 plus 50 cents postage from Glide Publications, 330 Ellis Street, San Francisco, California 94102. The Youth Project, at 1000 Wisconsin Avenue, Washington, D.C. 20007, helps secure funding for local action groups which involve young people in the process of social change. The Youth Project's resources are limited, but if you write to them, they may be able to help you.

It is important to remember that foundation money can be used only for research and educational activities, not for political organization and pressure.

learning how

We Americans have the idea that citizenship skills are something we inherit from birth, along with our constitutional rights to use them. The notion is quaint but mistaken. Effective citizenship is a craft, sometimes even an art. Training and apprenticeship are invaluable. You can start as a volunteer and go through a self-imposed apprenticeship during which you watch and learn. Or you can go to school. Three programs we know of are:

Midwest Academy, 600 W. Fullerton, Chicago, Illinois 60614.
ACORN, 523 W. 15th Street, Little Rock, Arkansas 72202.
Organize, Inc., 212 Fair Oaks, San Francisco, California 94110.

These programs vary. The Midwest Academy conducts both short workshops in the field and longer-term training sessions in Chicago, in connection with CAP. ACORN's interns work directly in the group's organizing activities, and must agree to stay in Arkansas for a year.

The people who attend these sessions are diverse as well. They focus on substance, not style; tactics, not ideology. The Midwest Academy has trained members of the Communications Workers of America, Stewardesses for Women's Rights, and the Wisconsin Education Association. "The Academy doesn't just teach people how to protest," says its leader Heather Booth. "It teaches how to win."

pitfalls

It would be impossible to spell out all the mistakes possible in getting folks together around tax issues. Here are some things to watch out for.

the "let's study it" pitfall

Before your group takes any action, you will want to know what you are getting into. Since knowledge is a weapon, you will want to be armed with ample knowledge about loopholes, your representative's voting record, or whatever.

Some folks are great for studying a problem. They think that once you have understood a problem then you have solved it. This just isn't so. You can learn everything there is to learn about a tax situation and you still haven't done one thing to help change it. There comes a point at which studying a problem becomes an excuse for lack of action toward resolving the problem.

the "let's educate the people" pitfall

Those who become experts themselves tend to want other people to become experts too. Obviously there has to be education in citizen action. But you can teach people about "oil depletion," "capital gains," "tax loss farming," "intangibles," and "exemptions," and you can bring in a tax lawyer to explain the system to them, and you *still* haven't done anything about their (and your) taxes. Balance is the key word. Remember to teach action tactics as well as the facts about tax reform.

the "let's not get too specific" pitfall

There is a certain security in generalities. As long as we don't give *specific* information, as long as we don't focus on any *specific* corporation, as long as we don't pressure any *specific* senator or representative, we can steer clear of being charged with political motivations, with inaccurate statements, and—more importantly—we do not have to worry about antagonizing anyone. Unfortunately, this process also brings your chance of success to practically zero. If you hope to achieve success, you must have *specific* information, deal with *specific* examples, and pressure *specific* congressmen and officials.

On the other hand, you want to stay on issues. One of the quickest ways to lose credibility in the eyes of the public is to let your efforts degenerate into a personal "mud-slinging" contest about someone's traits or personal habits. Stay on issues, not personalities.

the "let's work it out behind the scenes" pitfall

There have been many cartoons and jokes about "smoke-filled rooms." Closed-door agreements are successful in only one thing—they remove people from the political process and in so doing they prevent democracy from functioning. This pitfall opens the way for all sorts of problems. Officials can flatter people more successfully behind closed doors than in public. Leaders can lose touch with their group's members and can become slowly entwined with their adversaries.

In the long run, the only kind of citizen action which will work is that which is mass-based. Working behind the scenes breeds distrust, as it should. Combine your efforts with the efforts of others and you will be much stronger.

the "chosen few" pitfall

The "chosen few" pitfall is really an attitude. This attitude says that the leadership are really the only ones qualified to make decisions and to speak for your group. Implied in this attitude is the converse—the people outside the leadership somehow don't have what it takes to say or do the right thing. This attitude also breeds distrust. Try to elect leaders who don't have the "chosen few" attitude.

the expertise pitfall

Americans have succumbed to the cult of the expert. Officials regularly exploit this weakness. They try to debunk taxpayer investigations as the work of a "bunch of amateurs." But the issue is *their performance*, not your qualifications. Officials make such a to-do over "expertise" because it wraps them in a safe aura of mystery and puts them beyond public scrutiny. Nowhere does the Constitution say

Taking Action on Tax Reform 263

people must be experts before exercising their constitutional rights. When anyone makes this demand, it is the system, not our qualifications, that must be examined.

the "sunlight" pitfall

When the headlines scream out our charges, the editorials pick up our cause, we feel that something has happened that is setting things right. It isn't. Publicity does nothing by itself. People must be impressed by the facts and act on them. People in power are expert at letting things blow over. Follow-up is 90 percent of the job.

the "personality" pitfall

Interviews, headlines, TV and radio appearances are intoxicating. "Maybe running for the state legislature, or even Congress, wouldn't be such a bad idea...," we think. "Personalities don't produce; they spend their time having their hair done," Boston author George V. Higgins has said.

the discouragement pitfall

More than one would-be researcher has come back from an official's office dejected. "They wouldn't let me see the property record cards" or "They wouldn't let me see the campaign finance reports," our researcher says. "That finishes our survey." It doesn't. Shift focus, and the denial becomes an invitation to victory. The issue now is *official secrecy*. In many ways, secrecy is an easier issue to handle than assessments or campaign contributions. It is cut-and-dried. It provokes immediate public outrage. Court challenges to secrecy are quicker and less complicated than are other kinds of lawsuits.

Taxpayers in Westmoreland County, Pennsylvania, were denied the right to see the assessor's property record cards. Rather than be discouraged, they went to court and won a victory which opened up the property record cards to taxpayers throughout the state. If your opponents so generously offer to dig their own graves, by all means let them.

the "knights on white horses" pitfall

Don't look for knights on white horses. Even if they appear, you can't trust them. The only strength you can count on is the broad-based citizen organization you build. By all means try to draw powerful allies to your side: the state's attorney general, the revenue committee of the state legislature, consumer and public-interest groups. Just don't expect them to be saviors.

Carefully hone and focus the issue to their interests before approaching them. Try to devise the easiest and least time-consuming role they could play and still help the cause. Don't cart boxes and briefcases full of records, documents, and research materials into people's offices—until they ask for them.

the politicians pitfall

Rose Krause and Karen Kline helped organize a Summit County, Ohio, fight against an unfair piggyback sales tax the county commissioners wanted to impose. They successfully gathered over 40,000 petition signatures to put the issue to the voters on the November ballot. A local politician offered help to the campaign and, as soon as the referendum drive caught fire, claimed all the credit in media stories. The group had to oppose and finally stop him in a personal confrontation. Recalling the lessons of their campaign, they warn: "Beware the politicians who will offer help and then sit back to manipulate you for their own personal political gain; the fight can be won without them."

the "details" pitfall

We are all inclined to get swept up in the "big issues" and to forget the details. But more action campaigns have failed through a lack of transportation to demonstrations and baby-sitting services than through a lack of righteousness and vision. Ignore the details at your peril.

wrapping it up

GLORIA: Listen little girl, what can you do about taxes?

ARCHIE: By golly, us little people's been messed up over by them...whaddya call'm... oh yea...the "loopholes" long enough. I'm gonna talk to the guys down at Kelsey's. Gloria, get on the phone with them pinco student buddies of yours and tell 'em to put their brains where their mouths is. Let's get this here great country of ours movin' again!

Although these words weren't actually spoken on "All in the Family," they might have been. Instead of ending up quivering in an IRS office, Archie could have done something about his problem. So can you. Citizen action certainly isn't a new idea. The 200th anniversary of the Boston Tea Party is past. Let's make it a time people 200 years from now will want to celebrate.

Appendix

the tax justice act: an agenda for reform

A significant step forward in citizen action toward reform of the federal income tax has been the creation, in 1974, of the National Committee for Tax Justice (NCTJ). The NCTJ is a loose coalition of groups from around the country who have been coordinating their activities on behalf of tax reform. In 1974, committee members successfully pushed for the elimination of the oil depletion allowance. In 1975, they drafted a comprehensive tax-reform bill as a focus for the individual groups' reform activities. The result is the Tax Justice Act of 1975—an agenda of tax reforms—which has been introduced in the 94th Congress by more than thirty members of the House of Representatives (bill number H.R. 10086). The committee's long-range goal is to secure the passage of legislation which embodies the reforms contained in the Tax Justice Act. To this end, the NCTJ has begun to work with others to set up local citizen tax-reform organizations in key House Ways and Means and Senate Finance Committee districts to counter the traditionally one-sided special-interest influence over our tax laws. These organizations, by pressuring their representatives to adopt tax-reform positions, and exposing non-tax-reform positions, hope to significantly change the voting behavior of key committee members or have them replaced by more reform-minded individuals. What follows is a summary of the Tax Justice Act adapted from a flyer prepared by one NCTJ member, CP PAX of Massachusetts. More complete information is available from the National Committee for Tax Justice, 1611 Connecticut Ave., N.W., Washington, D.C. 20009.

★ ★ ★ ★ ★ ★ ★

The Tax Justice Act: A Summary

Federal income taxes were originally designed to be progressive—the wealthy paid more of their income in taxes; low and middle income families less. But now the system is riddled with tax loopholes for special interests. It is so inequitable that wealthy individuals often pay little or no taxes and so complex that ordinary wage earners often must pay for professional help to complete their tax returns.

The Tax Justice Act of 1975 meets these inequities head on. Drafted by tax reform and community groups and tax experts, the Tax Justice Act (TJA) is a balanced revenue package. It provides substantial tax savings for low and middle income families by closing the major tax loopholes for large corporate and individual incomes.

The great majority of Americans bear increasingly unfair tax burdens. But to win any real changes in the tax system, we must turn our frustration and anger into an organized demand for tax justice.

Tax justice is up to you!

Tax Savings

Tax credits distribute TJA savings fairly to all taxpayers. Middle and low income taxpayers need tax relief now more than ever. The recent inflation report from the Joint Economic Committee revealed a startling fact—tax payments outstripped all other increases in the consumer's budget in 1974. The average tax bill for a moderate income family was up 25% in 1974!

Figure A shows how the TJA provisions for tax credits would benefit the average family of four. The tax savings are entirely paid for by the loopholes closed in the TJA.

Appendix 265

The tax credit works like this: Under existing tax law you can deduct $750 from your income for each personal exemption you claim. If you are in the 20% tax bracket this means $150 less tax that you have to pay (20% x $750). But for the rich taxpayer in the 70% bracket, the savings for the same exemption is $525 (70% x $750). This is $525 cash in his pocket compared to $150 in yours.

But a tax credit is subtracted from the final tax bill. *The TJA substitutes a $250 credit for the personal deduction.* So every taxpayer gets $250 off the tax bill for each dependent, no matter what the tax bracket.

The TJA also substitutes a 25% tax credit for the present personal deductions (standard deduction or itemized deductions). It works exactly like the tax credit for personal exemptions: every $100 deduction now puts $70 in the pocket of the wealthy in the 70% bracket taxpayer, but returns only $14 to the lowest (14%) bracket wage-earner. *The TJA would take $25 off of everyone's tax for each such $100 expense.*

Business Tax Subsidies and Foreign Earnings

The corporate tax rate of 48% is a myth. Few large corporations pay that rate. Instead they take advantage of various business tax subsidies and special tax treatment of foreign income. Figure B shows taxes paid by several large corporations in 1973. (This figure shows the U.S. tax rate on worldwide income.)

As corporations pay less than their share, the tax burden shifts more and more to low and middle income taxpayers. Corporate income tax payments, as a percentage of federal revenue receipts, declined from 33.6% in 1944 to 14.6% in 1974. During the same time individual income and payroll taxes soared from 49% in 1944 to approximately 74% in 1974.

The TJA will reverse this trend. It will:

Repeal the Investment Tax Credit

The TJA repeals this subsidy which now gives companies 10c back for every $1 they spend on new machinery (10% directly off their tax bill), at a cost of $8 billion to us each year. This is supposed to stimulate production and lower unemployment, but it does little in times like these when most plants are operating at reduced capacity. They don't even use all of their existing machinery, so why do they need new equipment?

Eliminate Accelerated Depreciation Allowances

It is only fair that businesses take reasonable deductions for the aging, exhaustion, and wear of their machinery, buildings, etc. But the tax law provides numerous complex schemes to

---

★ **FIGURE A. TAX LIABILITY UNDER TAX JUSTICE ACT COMPARED TO PRESENT TAX CODE** ★

Married Couple With 2 Dependents

Adjusted Gross Income	Present Tax Law [1]	Tax Justice Act [2]	Income Tax Savings	Present 1975 Social Security Tax [3]
$ 1,000	$ 0 [4]	$ 0 [4]	$ 0	$ 59
3,000	0 [4]	0 [4]	0	176
5,000	0 [4]	0 [4]	0	293
6,000	35 [4]	0 [4]	35	351
8,000	347	0	347	468
10,000	709	345	364	585
12,500	1,165	885	280	731
15,000	1,612	1,410	202	825
17,500	2,036	1,936	99	825
20,000	2,538	2,528	10	825
25,000	3,630	3,958	(328) [5]	825
50,000	11,345	13,935	(2,590)	825

[1] Computed without reference to the tax tables for adjusted gross incomes under $10,000. Figures based on 1975 law and includes the $30 credit per exemption.

[2] Computed using the 25 percent credit in lieu of deductions and a $250 tax credit in lieu of personal exemption.

[3] Assumes payroll tax deductions for one worker in each family. Social security tax is included here to show that taxpayers paying either low federal income taxes or none at all still pay social security taxes.

[4] If the family qualifies for the earned income credit, a refund will be given of: $100 on $1,000 income; $300 on $3,000 income; $300 on $5,000 income; and $165 on $6,000 income.

[5] ( ) indicates additional tax due.

NOTE: All figures were computed using deductions equal to 17 percent of adjusted gross income, or the standard deduction, whichever was applicable.

266 TAX POLITICS

allow deductions much greater than the actual exhaustion of the property—in order to stimulate selected businesses and sectors of the economy. *The TJA eliminates the Asset Depreciation Range (ADR) that arbitrarily speeds up all such depreciation by 20% and requires straight line depreciation on real estate instead of any of the accelerated computations now in use.*

★ FIGURE B. INCOMES AND TAXES ★

Companies that paid no federal income tax in 1973:

	Net Income (in millions)	Tax Paid	Rate (percent)
Freeport Minerals Co.	$ 23.9	None	0
Texas Gulf Inc.	57.4	None	0
United Airlines	28.7	None	0
Trans-World Airlines	58.0	None	0
Gould of New York	208.3	None	0
American Electric Power	194.3	None	0
Western Bancorporation	97.7	None	0
Chemical New York Corp.	74.7	None	0
Bankers Trust Corp.	81.7	None	0
Continental Illinois Corp.	107.8	None	0

Companies that paid less than 10 percent income tax in 1973:

	Net Income (millions)	Tax Paid (thousands)	Rate (percent)
International Harvester	$ 72.3	$ 30	.06
Kennecott Copper Corp.	211.9	100	.4
LTV Corp.	83.2	100	1.2
Anaconda Co.	78.1	1,058	1.4
Occidental Petroleum	80.5	1,423	1.5
Texaco Inc.	1,817.3	20,000	2.3
Chase Manhattan Corp.	170.7	4,100	2.5
Gulf Oil Corp.	744.0	23,000	3.1
McDonnell Douglas Corp.	300.2	8,508	2.2
Standard Oil of Ohio	113.0	3,837	2.5
El Paso Natural Gas	104.1	4,758	4.5
Mobil Oil	573.0	43,500	5.0
Uniroyal, Inc.	58.7	3,818	8.0
International Minerals	73.0	9,242	7.1
Chrysler Corp.	393.7	28,400	7.5
Gulf & Western Industries	71.0	9,400	7.8
National Cash Register	91.8	8,249	9.0
Southern Railway Co.	108.2	9,828	9.1
Union Oil Co. of Calif.	209.3	19,700	9.6
Continental Oil Co.	287.8	28,828	9.9

Limit Farm Loss Deductions

By special accounting procedures, farmers can take deductions for farming expenses long before they have to pay taxes on the profits for their products. The great fluctuations of good and bad years justify these special allowances for the real farmer. But corporations and the wealthy now use these provisions as massive tax shelters to offset their other income. This loophole not only costs us $840 million in lost taxes, but also favors the huge farming conglomerates over the small independent farmer. *The TJA would limit an individual's deductions for farm losses to that person's farm income plus $10,000 of non-farm income.*

Repeal the Oil and Mineral Tax Subsidies

The 1975 Tax Reduction Act repealed the oil depletion allowance for all oil companies except the independent producers who can continue to take the 22% allowance on the first 2,000 barrels per day (bpd). At the average U.S. price of $7.50 per barrel, that adds up to almost $5.5 million in gross income per year (larger gross income than 99.8% of all other U.S. businesses make). In addition, oil and gas companies can still deduct "intangible expenses," which are approximately 80% of the total drilling costs, immediately instead of gradually over the life of the well. *The TJA repeals both subsidies for all foreign and domestic operations.*

End the Special Treatment of Overseas Subsidiaries of Corporations

At present earnings of all overseas subsidiaries are totally untaxed until brought into this country. When and if they are brought in, all taxes and royalties paid to other countries can be deducted on a dollar-for-dollar basis from the U.S. tax liability. While some allowances for these expenses are justifiable, these excessive provisions in effect reward corporations for building factories overseas instead of at home where they would provide jobs for American workers. *The TJA ends the deferral of tax on overseas earnings, requires that credits for foreign taxes be computed strictly on a country-by-country basis, and ensures that royalties will be treated only as ordinary expense deductions, not as foreign tax credits.*

Eliminate the Tax Subsidies for Exportation

Special corporate subsidiaries, called DISCs, which are set up to export American products to foreign countries are taxed at 1/2 the normal rate. A 14% tax cut is also given to corporations doing business outside the U.S. in the Western Hemisphere. These subsidies cut corporate taxes while not stimulating U.S. production and employment. At a time when many products are scarce in the U.S., it makes little sense to subsidize overseas products with $2 billion of our tax dollars annually. *The TJA would eliminate all special provisions for Domestic International Sales Corporations (DISCs), and Western Hemisphere Trade Corporations (WHTCs).*

Estate and Gift Taxes

The present estate tax is paid by only 8 percent of all estates. But even those that do pay the tax pay at low actual rates. Ten-million-dollar estates, for example, pay an average tax of 17%—much less than the 77% they are supposed to pay.

Integrate the Estate and Gift Tax Systems

Now people can get around the progressive estate tax rates by transferring some of their property during their lifetime by gift. Taxes are paid at the lower end of the two gift and estate tax rates. *The Tax Justice Act integrates the estate and gift taxes to eliminate this inequity and to insure that the same progressive rates would apply to the total wealth, whatever the form of the gift.*

Eliminate Generation-Skipping Trusts

These trusts allow wealthy individuals to transfer property to their children and then to later generations and only pay an estate tax once, instead of paying it each time the estate is transferred. *The TJA closes this loophole with a substitute tax.*

Limit the Estate and Gift Charitable Deductions

Under present law, unlimited estate and gift tax deductions can be made for gifts to charities, including the personal family foundation. *The TJA would limit these deductions to 50% of the value of the estate or of lifetime gifts to bring them into line with the current charitable deductions limit (50% of income) in the income tax structure.*

Aid to State and Local Governments

Replace Interest Exemption With Direct Federal Payment of Interest on State and Local Bonds

Interest paid on state and local bonds is now totally exempt from federal income tax. Special treatment of these bonds is justifiable because of the need for these governments to raise funds, but the $1.9 billion savings for states and towns costs the U.S. Treasury $2.5 billion in lost taxes. Wealthy bondholders and commercial banks receive the extra benefits. Under the TJA, the federal government would directly pay localities 40% of the interest on new bonds (except for "industrial development bonds") and eliminate the middlemen.

Wealthy Individuals, Capital Gains

Repeal the $100 Dividend Exclusion

Current tax law allows an individual to exclude from gross income $100 of dividends received on corporate stock, costing the Treasury $340 million in lost taxes. There is no similar exclusion for interest received on savings accounts, which is a much more common form of investment by middle and low income taxpayers. *The TJA eliminates this inequity by abolishing all dividend exclusions.*

Limit Deductions for Mortgage Interest and Property Taxes

These deductions now amount to nearly 1/3 of all personal deduc-

268 TAX POLITICS

tions and benefit most the wealthy individual with large vacation homes and other property. No benefits at all are available to renters. *The TJA limits these deductions to amounts paid on the taxpayer's own residence. The deductions cannot exceed interest paid on the first $50,000 of a mortgage and the property taxes paid on property assessed at $70,000. No deductions will be allowed for rental or investment property in excess of the income from it.*

Repeal the 50% Maximum Tax

Currently, while paying no more than 50% taxes on "earned income," a taxpayer may be paying little or no tax on unearned income such as interest on municipal bonds or revenue from oil investments. Therefore, the rate on such a taxpayer's total income is often very low. This special limitation benefits only wealthy individuals between the 50 and 70% tax bracket. *The TJA abolishes the over-all limitation of a 50% tax on earned income. Higher rates will apply where applicable under current law.*

Eliminate the Special Treatment of Capital Gains and Losses

Currently the income from capital (stocks, real estate, equipment, etc., held more than 6 months) is taxed at 1/2 the rate that wages are taxed. This is the largest single loophole, costing us about $10 billion per year. And 94% of these benefits go to those with incomes over $10,000. *The TJA would eliminate this special treatment entirely. It would also make capital losses fully deductible from ordinary income (instead of only 50% deductible) just as ordinary business expenses.*

Close the Loophole for Capital Gains Transferred at Death

Now, if a rich uncle leaves someone $100,000 worth of property, a minimal estate tax may be paid, but the capital gains on the property while he owned it—even if it had gained thousands of dollars—is never taxed. In addition, if the heir never sells the property tax free capital gains will accumulate from generation to generation. *The TJA would tax this accumulated gain before the property is transferred. The only exceptions would be transfers between husband and wife, and exemption of the first $25,000 from a family home, business, or farm.*

tax reform groups

The following is a list of groups which work on a number of tax-reform issues and are members of the National Committee for Tax Justice.

Americans for Democratic Action [ADA]: This lobbying organization supports liberal candidates and issues such as tax reform, curbing inflation, cutting defense spending, and Democratic party charter reform, and has local chapters in many areas of the country. There is a bi-monthly newsletter called the *ADA Newsletter*, which deals with Capitol Hill legislation, and a monthly publication called *ADA World*, which covers a wider range of activities and individual chapter projects. Contact ADA at 1424 16th St., N.W., Washington, D.C. 20036.

Arkansas Community Organizations for Reform Now [ACORN]: This group was founded in 1970 and has become a statewide organization with forty-five affiliates and nearly 5,000 low- to moderate-income member families. They work on a wide range of community and statewide issues such as education, utilities, community improvements, and general tax reform. The group publishes a monthly newspaper called *ACORN News*; operates a tax clinic; has led a campaign on the state level against tax breaks; lobbies in the state legislature for reform of sales taxes, state income taxes, and numerous other programs which focus on tax matters; and is involved in federal income tax reforms. For more information write to ACORN, 523 15th St., Little Rock, Arkansas 72202.

California Tax Reform Association: This organization began as a free tax clinic for low- and middle-income citizens, and now includes public education on tax reform by helping to organize other groups and tax clinics in California. They have developed a California Tax Justice Act for greater state tax equity, and lobby for state and federal tax reform. They publish a monthly newspaper called *Tax Back Talk*, which deals with local and state tax issues. They can be reached at 909 12th St., Sacramento, California 95814.

Citizens for Participation in Political Action [CP PAX]: This organization of 3,000 members has a wide range of activities, including a tax-reform task force and federal tax-reform lobbying efforts. The task force has spearheaded a campaign against Congressman James Burke because of his anti-tax-reform votes in the Ways and Means Committee. They are involved in other state and local issues including reform of state sales taxes, establishment of rent control and rent control boards throughout the state, a peace action campaign dealing with nuclear disarmament issues, gun control drives, and unifying people behind reform candidates for various political offices. They publish a regular newsletter called *CP PAX*, which tells the people of Massachusetts what they are doing. Contact them at 11 South St., Boston, Massachusetts 02111.

Delaware Citizens Coalition for Tax Reform: This group was founded in 1973 by Ted Keller to educate people of Delaware about tax inequities at all levels of government, and to help to mobilize them into an effective force for tax reform. *Citizens Voice* is their publication, informing the public of the group's activities, such as efforts to block enactment of a state sales tax, and a successful attempt to change the state tax laws to make banks pay their fair share of income tax. For more information contact the group at 1225 Lakewood Dr., Wilmington, Delaware 19803.

Movement or Economic Justice [MEJ]: This group tries to build a broad base of support for significant changes in the American economic system, especially changes which affect the distribution of wealth, income, resources, and services. MEJ has helped to establish free income tax clinics in many localities. Through the tax clinics MEJ advises taxpayers on strategies for tax reform. Through its published handbook on property tax reform and its monthly bulletin, *Just Economics*, MEJ serves as a clearinghouse for hundreds of local community organizations on tax reform, and a wide range of economic issues. Their address is 1611 Connecticut Ave., N.W., Washington, D.C. 20009.

New York Citizens for Tax Reform: This group was formed as part of the Tax Action Campaign in the spring of 1973. Its activities have centered in the New York city area, though its membership comes from all over New York state. It has focused primarily on encouraging members of Congress to support the Tax Justice Act of 1975. Its board of directors is made up of tax experts in the New York area interested in federal tax reform. They publish a periodical called *TEA* (Tax Equity for America) *Leaf*, which deals with the group's activities. They can be reached by writing to Dr. Filer, Professor of Law, University of Hofstra Law School, 1000 Fulton Ave., Hempstead, New York 11553.

Ohio Tax Equity for America [TEA] Party: This group began as a petition campaign calling for comprehensive reform of the federal income tax system and evolved into an organization which assists tax groups getting started in other states. Its activities have included a telephone network in each of Ohio's twenty-three congressional districts so that citizens can be alerted promptly when tax-reform issues arise; studies of property tax assessments; investigations of the tax-reform records of members of Congress; drives to eliminate various tax subsidies like the oil depletion allowance. To contact the group write to Ohio TEA Party, P.O. Box 3518, Akron, Ohio 44310.

Philadelphia Tax Equity for America [TEA] Party: The TEA Party is an organization of over 600 Pennsylvania citizens working for progressive tax reform at all levels of government. They published the *Homeowner's Guide to the Property Tax*, which has information on assessment appeal procedures. They do other work aimed at property tax reform, and have worked for a progressive state income tax as well as for reforms in federal taxes. The group has established free tax assistance clinics throughout the state and provides education workshops on tax reform and citizen action. Contact them at 4839 Germantown Ave., Philadelphia, Pennsylvania 19144.

Public Citizen's Tax Reform Research Group: Founded by Ralph Nader in 1971, our group is made up of tax professionals who lobby directly for tax reform in the U.S. Congress, work for reforms in the administration of the tax laws by the IRS, and provide support for state and local tax reforms. TRRG has developed information for taxpayers regarding federal, state, and local tax-reform issues; operation and reform of the IRS; how taxes work, who benefits from tax loopholes; how our tax laws are written and how citizens can work for reform. All of this

270 TAX POLITICS

work appears in our monthly newspaper, *People & Taxes*. Write to People & Taxes, P.O. Box 14198, Ben Franklin Station, Washington, D.C. 20044.

St. Louis Tax Reform Group: This group was founded in 1972 to work for progressive tax reform at all levels of government. It now has members throughout Missouri, but the majority are concentrated in the St. Louis area. Its activities have included campaigns to end the sales tax on food and medicines, support for legislation to make the state income tax system more progressive, and an education and lobbying effort to end federal tax subsidies for oil companies. They publish a monthly newsletter called *Beyond Just Gripes*, which deals with the St. Louis group's activities, and have also published a property tax assessment study which triggered a mass assessment appeals project by low-income homeowners. To contact the group, write to 4236 McPherson St., St. Louis, Missouri 63108.

Tax Analysts and Advocates: This group was established by Thomas Field, a former Treasury official, in 1970. The group publishes a weekly journal called *Tax Notes*, which examines in detail current tax-reform issues, including an analysis of tax bills introduced in Congress. The Tax Analysts division makes specialized tax information services available to the news media and the Tax Advocates division conducts a public-interest tax law practice. For more information write to Tax Analysts and Advocates, 732 17th St., N.W., Washington, D.C. 20006.

Taxation with Representation: This group is a public-interest taxpayer's lobby that deals with federal tax issues. Its main goal is to represent the public interest with skilled professionals when tax issues are being discussed in Congress. Its expert members testify before congressional committees for the public interest. TWR also prepares detailed "scorecards" of tax-reform votes in the Congress ranking every senator and representative on the basis of recorded votes. Similar scorecards are prepared for the House Ways and Means and Senate Finance Committees. All members receive a quarterly newsletter dealing with these issues. Sample copies of this newsletter and other information can be obtained by writing to TWR at 2369 North Taylor St., Arlington, Virginia 22207.

Texas Tax Equity for America [TEA] Party: This group is working for tax reforms primarily at the state and local level. They also support federal tax reform and the Tax Justice Act of 1975. The group helps to organize smaller groups or chapters throughout Texas to fight for tax reform, and helps to support candidates for state and local office concerned about tax equity in Texas. They can be reached at 3725 Acorn Circuit, Beaumont, Texas 77703.

Some other multi-issue groups which work on tax-reform issues include:

Americans Nonpartisan for Tax Equity [ANTE]: This group is working toward tax reform at all levels of government. The group has been involved in a campaign to change the views of federal and state legislators so that they will vote for tax reform. It has been involved in a number of state tax-reform campaigns including the creation of a new California state tax bracket rate for the higher income people and the reform of property tax assessment procedures for senior citizens. Its monthly publication, *Tax Action*, informs people of California of what ANTE and other statewide tax-reform groups are doing. *Tax Action* contains articles on the politics of taxation and what tax reform means to the average citizen. For more information, contact ANTE at P.O. Box 612, Loma Linda, California 92354.

Citizen Action League: This group was founded in 1973 to fight electric utility rate hikes. Since then, it has branched out to organize mass meetings and membership drives for tax reform at the state and local level, and for other issues. Other chapters of the organization are located in San Mateo and Los Angeles. They publish a monthly newsletter called *Citizen Action News* which describes the group's activities. They can be reached by writing to Citizen Action League, 593 Market St., San Francisco, California 94104.

Citizens Action Program (CAP): This well-established community-based group in the Chicago area is concerned about many issues affecting its members. CAP has been involved in property tax reform, redlining, pollution issues, and others. It has exposed the underassessment of property taxes for businesses, and has successfully fought the underassessment of steel mills and race tracks in the Chicago area. CAP publishes a quarterly newsletter called *Action*, which describes these issues and what it and other groups are doing. CAP can be reached at 2200 N. Lincoln St., Chicago, Illinois 60614.

Citizens League: This Minnesota group, a twenty-year-old organization, conducts policy studies on state and local issues. Its sizable membership includes 3,000 individuals and 550 institutions. It has two publications: *Citizens League Newsletter*, which deals with the activities of the organization, and *Public Life*, published by its small tax-exempt foundation, which describes trends and developments emerging on the public finance horizon. Its activities include property tax reform, the public finance process, and investigations of how the tax dollar is spent. The group can be reached at 84 S. 6th St., Minneapolis, Minnesota 55402.

Massachusetts Fair Share: This is a citizen action organization fighting for basic economic justice for all low- and middle-income families. The group is involved with issues such as high utility rates, local and state level tax reform, property tax reform, unemployment, public transportation, and other issues of vital concern to their members and the citizens of Massachusetts. They publish a monthly news magazine called *The Fair Fighter*, which describes the group's activities and important issues. They can be contacted by writing to them at 364 Boylston St., Boston, Massachusetts 02116.

Metro-Act of Rochester: This community-based group is involved with a variety of local issues and reforms. They achieved significant tax reform in the city of Rochester, and discuss local tax issues in a bi-weekly publication called *Metro-Logue*. Metro-Act also helps to organize community groups for a progressive tax system and against any form of property tax. For more information contact them at 8 Prince St., Rochester, New York 14607.

Public Interest Economics Center and Foundation [PIE-C and PIE-F]: This group was formed to launch a movement within the economics profession analogous to public-interest law and public-interest science. The group recruits and organizes professional economists and students of economics to do *pro bono* or low-fee work for citizen and consumer groups. It provides various forms of citizen education in economics, and publishes a bimonthly newsletter called *PIE-F*. The group is especially interested in tax legislation which distorts economic gains in our system, such as the depletion allowance for oil companies. It has published a book dealing with reform of the banking system. For more information on the group write to them at 1714 Massachusetts Ave., N.W., Washington, D.C. 20036.

The Student Public Interest Research Groups (PIRGs): PIRGs are student-run organizations, modeled after the Ralph Nader organization in Washington, to challenge the unresponsive seats of power in government and business. Since 1971, the PIRGs have demonstrated that students engaged in public-interest research with a full-time professional staff can successfully overcome the intransigent nature of big business and government bureaucracy. PIRGs are presently operating on college campuses in some twenty-two states across the country. Their scope of activities includes tax reform, health and safety projects, human rights projects, environmental protection, government responsiveness, and consumer protection. PIRGs have their own publications, with a central newsletter called *PIRG News*, available from the Public Citizen Action Group (CAG), 133 C St., S.E., Washington, D.C. 20003. A PIRG directory is available from CAG.

Save Our Cumberland Mountains [SOCM]: This group was founded in 1971 to stop strip-mining and gain more adequate taxation of coal lands in six counties in eastern Tennessee. The group has won a court suit compelling the state of Tennessee to assess the coal lands, and it has scored victories against strip-mining and overweight coal trucks. SOCM does local organizing in other coal mining regions of Tennessee and helps to form small community groups or chapters of SOCM in these regions. It publishes the monthly *SOCM Newsletter*. SOCM can be reached at Box 457, Jacksboro, Tennessee 37757.

Bibliographical Note

income taxes

Writings on federal income tax reform and reform of the Internal Revenue Service appear in remarkably small numbers. Most of them are highly technical and, often, exceedingly dull to all but the professional tax expert. Income tax readings also tend to deal with descriptions of the present system and how one can survive in it as taxpayer or tax practitioner. Few focus on reform issues and fewer aim their reform discussions at average citizens.

An important step toward tax reform is informing citizens about the present system and how they can help to change it. We hope that this book helps to accomplish that goal. There are other information resources available as well.

A good overview of who pays tax, who doesn't, and why is Philip M. Stern's well-known and very readable book, *The Rape of the Taxpayer* (New York: Vintage, 1972). The book is a bit outdated in its description of the legislative process but on substance it is still very worthwhile. If this book doesn't make you angry, nothing will.

Americans for Democratic Action publishes a quick and readable summary of tax-reform issues entitled "A Guide to the American Loophole System" (A.D.A., 1424 16th St., N.W., Washington, D.C. 20036, $1.00).

Another simple overview of tax-reform issues is found in a twelve-page summary of the Tax Justice Act of 1975 described in the Appendix. The summary is available from the National Committee for Tax Justice (1611 Connecticut Ave., N.W., Washington, D.C. 20009).

Of course, an invaluable source of easily understandable and comprehensive tax-reform issues is our own *People & Taxes* newspaper, published monthly by Public Citizen's Tax Reform Research Group. *People & Taxes* discusses federal, state, and local tax-reform issues as well as reforms of the Internal Revenue Service. It contains articles on what is happening in Congress, at the IRS, in local agencies, and with citizen tax-reform groups around the country. In the past, *People & Taxes* has discussed who benefits from tax breaks, how our tax laws work, how taxes affect other areas of your life, tax-reform proposals—good and bad—the rights of average taxpayers vs. IRS authority, and political use and abuse of the IRS. Sample copies are available from *People & Taxes* (P.O. Box 14198, Ben Franklin Station, Washington, D.C. 20044). Complete twelve-issue sets of Volumes II (1974) and III (1975) are available, while they last, for $2.00 per set. Individual subscriptions are $7.50 for one year and $13.00 for two years. (Business, professional, and institutional subscriptions are $12.00 and $21.50.)

Tax Notes, a weekly newspaper published by Tax Analysts and Advocates (732 17th St., N.W., Washington, D.C. 20006), is a very useful tool for tax reformers. It has articles on various tax-reform issues, analyzes tax legislation, and covers what is happening concerning taxes in Congress and the administration. Also featured are specific departments covering corporate tax burdens filed with the SEC, IRS Manual Changes, summaries of tax changes published in the *Federal Register*, summaries of *Congressional Record* statements on tax issues, and a review of public correspondence and Treasury reports on specific legislation. *Tax Notes* is primarily geared to providing information on tax reform to the press but it is an excellent resource for tax reformers who can afford it. Yearly subscriptions are $45.00 ($25.00 to the press) and ex-

Bibliographical Note

change subscriptions are available. Write for a free sample.

For the more serious student of tax reform, several other books are recommended. Joseph A. Pechman's *Federal Tax Policy* (Washington, D.C.: The Brookings Institution, 1971) is a comprehensive look at tax policy and tax reform. Pechman, an economist, is well versed in tax-reform issues. His book, while somewhat technical, is meant for the serious non-tax expert. He does a good job of discussing some historical development, the basic equity and tax policy questions surrounding the various federal taxes, and what kind of reforms are needed. The book sometimes gets bogged down in economic detail and the legislative section is a bit simplistic and out of date, but discussions of specific tax issues are generally well laid out and understandable. In short, the book is a fine overview of basic tax policy issues (i.e., how should we tax corporations; should we have a tax on consumption instead of income; what's wrong with the payroll tax, etc.).

Another more technical but important little book is Pechman's latest, *Tax Reform: The Impossible Dream?*, which he wrote with George Break (Washington, D.C.: The Brookings Institution, 1975, $2.50). This is a short, concise, and serious effort to discuss the existing tax structure and how it could be reformed. Many of the ideas have been around for a while, others are new. All are worth reading about.

An interesting book describing major tax loopholes left untouched by the Tax Reform Act of 1969 is *Halfway to Tax Reform* by Joseph Ruskay and Richard Osserman (Bloomington, Ind.: University of Indiana Press, 1971, $8.95). This book does an excellent job of discussing how tax breaks work and who can benefit from them. The book is several years old but, sadly, all the tax loopholes discussed are still on the books.

The concept of tax expenditures discussed in Chapter 2 was developed primarily by Harvard Law Professor Stanley S. Surrey while he was assistant Treasury secretary. His latest book, *Pathways to Tax Reform*, (Cambridge, Mass.: Harvard University Press, 1973, $12.00), is by far the most thoughtful and comprehensive treatment of tax expenditures and their key role in the tax-reform debate. The book sometimes becomes detailed beyond the needs of most tax reformers, but if you want to focus in on tax expenditures, it is invaluable. The price, however, may dictate a trip to the library.

A well-written article on replacing unfair and inefficient tax expenditures with direct expenditures is "Alternatives to Utilization of the Federal Income Tax System to Meet Social Problems" by Paul McDaniel (*Boston College Law Review*, June, 1970). And consult the Congressional Joint Economic Committee study, "Economics of Federal Subsidy Programs" (January 1972), on details of direct subsidies and tax subsidies to various industries.

Under the new budget law tax expenditure budgets such as the one in this book are prepared by the Congress and the administration. They are available in the House and Senate Budget Committee's *Report on the First Concurrent Resolution on the Budget* for each fiscal year, and each year in the president's Special Analyses of the Budget of the United States Government.

Who pays taxes and who benefits from tax breaks is at the core of the tax-reform debate. The charts and tables in this book should be adequate for most readers, but other statistics are available. The most comprehensive compilation of income tax statistics appears in the Treasury Department's *Statistics of Income* series. Individual Statistics of Income are published for each year in a short *Preliminary Statistics of Income* version (the latest is for 1974) and a very complete final *Statistics of Income* (the latest is for 1973). These publications include information on how many taxpayers, in what income brackets, take advantage of exemptions, deductions, and other tax preferences; on sources of income; on state and regional collections of federal tax; on payments of minimum tax on tax preferences, and more. Also available are similar publications on *Estate Tax Returns*, *Business Tax Returns*, *Corporation Tax Returns*, *Foreign Income and Taxes of Corporations*, and *Sales of Capital Assets* (capital gains). Statistics of Income publications are on sale from the Superintendent of Documents (U.S. Government Printing Office, Washington, D.C. 20402). Write for a listing of the latest ones.

The erosion of the corporate income tax base and how specific large corporations use tax preferences to cut their tax bill are now revealed in reports filed with the Securities and Exchange Commission. A compilation of these reports in chart form shows how specific tax write-offs reduce each corporation's taxes. Such charts, grouped by industry, appear semiannually in *Tax Notes*, a weekly publication of Tax Analyists and Advocates (732 17th St., N.W., Washington, D.C. 20006). Write to them for information. Summaries also appear periodically in *People & Taxes*.

A detailed and fairly technical treatment of the erosion of the individual tax base by tax preferences appears in "Individual Income Tax Erosion by Income Classes" by Joseph A. Pechman and Benjamin A. Okner (1972). Reprints are available free of charge from the Brookings Institution (1775 Massachusetts Ave., N.W., Washington, D.C. 20036).

Finally, the burden of our present tax system is detailed in another book by Pechman and Okner entitled *Who Bears the Tax Burden?* (Washington, D.C.: The Brookings Institution, 1974). This book is very difficult for all but economists to understand. Most of its conclusions depend on numerous economic variations and assumptions. We have tried to synthesize some of these and hope that will be sufficient for most of our readers. Students of the property tax might be bothered by Pechman and Okner's rigid income bias, viewing all equity in light of the taxpayer's income. Nevertheless, for answering the question "Who bears the tax burden?" as far as existing data permit, they deserve credit.

A good overview of Congress and how it works is offered by a very readable Ralph Nader Congress Project book, *Who Runs Congress?* by Mark Green (New York: Bantam/Grossman, 1975). More details of the tax legislative process are contained in the lengthy Congress Project study *The Revenue Committees: A Study of the House Ways and Means and Senate Finance Committees and the House and Senate Appropriations Committees* (New York: Grossman, 1975). This volume, along with others on five important congressional committees, should be of interest to anyone who wants to know more about how the Congress functions and who and what influences our nation's lawmakers.

Political scientists tend to write like political scientists. They build models, quantify data, and construct theories and profiles of the legislative process that sometimes bear little relation to the real thing. One political scientist, John F. Manley, has written about the Ways and Means Committee and the result, while more dynamic than one might fear, is still a fairly dry treatise. However, *The Politics of Finance: The House Committee on Ways and Means* (Boston: Little, Brown and Co., 1970) is interesting for what it says, if not for how it says it. The book is fairly dated because of the numerous changes in the House committee in the last six years, but if you like this kind of treatment look for it in your local library.

A more up-to-date description of one battle in the tax legislative process appears in Joe Klein's detailed, yet very amusing article on the 1974 fight over the oil depletion allowance, "The Fanne Fox Memorial Tax Bill" (*Rolling Stone Magazine*, No. 177, January 1975, p. 29).

Also on the same subject is an article by Edward F. Morrison, a former legislative assistant to Representative Charles Vanik, "Energy Tax Legislation: The Failure of the 93rd Congress" (*Harvard Journal on Legislation*, Vol. 12, No. 3, April 1975).

Lobbying is obviously central to the legislative process. One interesting piece for an historical perspective that is still often valid is Stanley Surrey's article "The Congress and the Tax Lobbyist" (*Harvard Law Review*, Vol. 70, 1975, p. 1145).

An interesting look at more up-to-date tax lobbying is "Tax Report/Attorneys perform dual role as lobbyists, policy makers," a short article by Daniel J. Balz in *National Journal* (October 4, 1975, p. 1379). And a new and very comprehensive directory of all lobbyists can be found in most libraries—a useful investigative tool for those sorting out money and influence in Washington—*The Washington Influence Directory* by Ed Zuckerman (Washington, D.C.: Amward Publications, 1975, $25.00)

The best broad guide to literature about the IRS is "A Classified, Selective Bibliography on the Administration and Operations of the Internal Revenue Service" by Robert Sperry, in the *National Tax Journal* (Vol. XXV, No. 1).

While scholarly articles about IRS procedures and policies

Bibliographical Note 275

abound, there is only one fairly current book on the tax agency's organization. It is *The Internal Revenue Service* (New York: Praeger, 1970), by John C. Chommie, a law professor. This book provides a good overview of the way the agency functions, but it is somewhat out of date.

The most thorough and current description of the way IRS practices affect individuals can be found in the unpublished *Report to the Administrative Conference of the United States on Some Administrative Procedures of the Internal Revenue Service*. The report was written for the Administrative Conference, an independent federal agency, by a team of tax experts headed by Charles Davenport, now assistant director for tax policy in the Congressional Budget Office. The report reviews IRS procedures in audits, appeals, collections, and taxpayer services. It also analyzes and makes recommendations concerning the IRS summons power, the use of civil penalties, and tax return confidentiality. The study is nearly 1,000 pages long and contains hundreds of informative footnotes. It is a "must" for serious students. Arrangements to see this report can be made by contacting the Administrative Conference (2120 L St., N.W., Suite 500, Washington, D.C. 20037).

The next best resource for those interested in taxpayer problems is the *Senate Hearings on Internal Revenue Service Taxpayer Assistance and Compliance Programs*, FY 1974, before the Subcommittee on the Department of the Treasury, U.S. Postal Service and General Government Appropriations, 93rd Cong., 2d Sess. (1974). The hearings, contained in one 889-page volume, have testimony and data regarding a broad spectrum of taxpayer problems. They also contain the only report on IRS audit practices ever made public. The report is titled "The Audit Story" (Doc. 5667, Rev. 10-72). Although the IRS had published similar "official use only" studies for the previous ten years, it stopped compiling the report after this one was made public.

The Senate *Hearings on Internal Revenue Service Taxpayer Assistance and Compliance Programs*, FY 1975, contain further valuable data on IRS procedures, including jeopardy assessments and forcible collection.

Up-to-date statistics on IRS taxpayer services, compliance activities, tax fraud investigations, legal actions, planning and research, etc., can be found in IRS Publication 55, *Annual Report, Commissioner of Internal Revenue*. It is for sale by the Superintendent of Documents (U.S. Government Printing Office, Washington, D.C. 20402).

For a look at the accuracy of IRS tax advice, see *Telephone Assistance to Taxpayers Can be Improved*, Report to the Joint Committee on Internal Revenue Taxation by the Comptroller General of the United States, June 10, 1975, GGD-75-69.

Information about the number of taxpayers who seek assistance in tax return preparation and about the quality of return preparation is contained in *Regulation of Income Tax Return Preparers*, Hearing before a Subcommittee of the Committee on Government Operations, House of Representatives, 92nd Cong., 2d Sess. (1972).

Although scholarly articles on audits and appeals seem to be aimed at tax practitioners rather than at the unrepresented taxpayer, they still contain helpful advice. The mysteries of IRS audit procedures are explained by former Commissioner Mortimer Caplin in "How to Handle a Federal Income Tax Audit" (*The Tax Counselor Quarterly*, Spring 1972).

To find out about the IRS's legal authority to examine tax returns, read "IRS Right to Examine: What and Whose Records, When and How Often (*The Journal of Taxation*, September 1961).

There is a graphic description of the difficulties tax practitioners face in IRS administrative appeals proceedings in the last few pages of "Conference and Review Procedures in Field Audit Division" by present Commissioner Donald C. Alexander (*New York University Institute on Federal Taxation*, Vol. 21, 1963). The description of the IRS district conferee's adversarial role makes it clear that unrepresented taxpayers haven't much of a chance for equitable treatment in this proceeding.

The best article we found on the collection process is "What a Taxpayer Can Do When a Case Has Been Turned Over for Collection," by Marvin J. Garbis (*New York Institute on Federal Taxation*, 1971).

property taxes

The late nineteenth and early twentieth centuries were the golden age of writing on state and local finances. Richard T. Ely, in *Taxation in American States and Cities* (New York: Crowell, 1888) and Jens Jensen, in *Property Taxation in the United States* (Chicago: University of Chicago Press, 1931), searched out with tireless curiosity existing tax systems and actual administrative practices in American states and localities, developing concrete data invaluable to legislators, citizen-reformers, and tax administrators. Their observations were informed, moreover, by a sense of equity and social justice.

Today's economists have retreated to a numbers hothouse they call "econometrics." They provide lots of data but often tell little about the way things are. Perhaps the best work of our uninspired contemporaries is L.L. Ecker-Racz's *The Politics and Economics of State and Local Finance* (Englewood Cliffs, N.J.: Prentice Hall, 1970). Ecker-Racz is a man of humane and generous instincts who has himself worked in public finance, federally and locally.

Students will probably find themselves looking at other books, such as James A. Maxwell's *Financing State and Local Governments* (Washington, D.C.: The Brookings Institution, 1965) and *Public Finance* (New York: Ronald Press, 1971), by George Break and Robert Rolph. These are useful, but elevate numbers over experience. The richness of concrete detail found in Ely and Jensen, the harkening to actual practice, is lacking.

A good example of a new genre of studies of finances in specific states and localities from a reform viewpoint is *The Rich Get Richer and the Poor Pay Taxes* (1974) by the Massachusetts Public Finance Project (360 Washington St., Lynn, Mass. 01901) which has produced over thirty studies of state and local finances in Massachusetts. Another example, which focuses on the budget process instead of the tax structure, is *Understanding San Francisco's Budget* (1973) by Richard Hayes of the San Francisco Study Center (Box 5646, San Francisco, Calif. 94101). These would serve as admirable models for studies elsewhere.

Texts on property taxes tend to be all alike mainly because they get their information from one another. Dick Netzer's *The Economics of the Property Tax* (Washington, D.C.: The Brookings Institution, 1966) is the major recent work on the subject. Mr. Netzer is a careful scholar who asks good questions, but he passes too quickly over administrative problems. Because his (and everyone else's) data are based on assessments that everyone knows are inaccurate, they must be viewed critically.

Two series of publications encompass property taxes in broad scope. The Committee on Resources and Economic Development (TRED, c/o University of Wisconsin Press, Box 1379, Madison, Wis. 55701) calls together scholars from all over the country each year to discuss a tax-related policy question. The papers presented have been published annually by the University of Wisconsin Press. TRED leans toward site-value taxation, but in a less dogmatic way than hardcore Georgists. *Property Taxation, Housing, and Urban Growth*, is a symposium of public officials and scholars published by the Urban Institute in Washington, D.C. It has more breadth than depth, but contains the kinds of insights that only informal discussion can provoke.

The published proceedings of the annual conventions of the International Association of Assessing Officers (IAAO, 1313 E. 60th St., Chicago, Ill. 60637) are less useful than other IAAO publications, such as its *Assessor's Journal* and special reports.

Who Bears the Tax Burden? (Washington, D.C.: The Brookings Institution, 1974) by Joseph Pechman and Benjamin Okner, like Netzer's book, is flawed by being based on wildly inaccurate data, i.e., existing assessments. Moreover, Pechman and Okner have a rigid income bias, viewing all equity in light of the taxpayer's income. Nevertheless, for answering the question "Who bears the tax burden?" as far as existing data permit, they deserve credit.

How the property tax process really works is something known only to close followers of any particular city hall. It all begins with the local budget process; *Understanding San Francisco's Budget,* mentioned above, will make you aware of the kinds of political tugs and pulls to look for in your own community. Somewhat more general and academic is *Municipal Budgeting: A Primer for Elected Officials* (Washington, D.C.: Joint Center for Political Studies, 1974) by Jesse Burkhead and Paul Bringewatt.

The closest thing to an assessor's desk manual is John Keith's *Property Tax Assessment Practices* (Monterey Park, Calif.: Highland Publishing Co., 1966). How the assessor's office really works is a strange world of compromises to short funds, political pressures, and human frailty. On tax sales, deed recordation, and such real estate esoterica, almost any real estate text seems to be about as good as the others.

On appraising, Bonbright's classic *The Valuation of Property* (New York: McGraw-Hill, 1937) still reigns. The IAAO publishes materials for both beginners and advanced assessors. Essays on the use of computers in assessing lie scattered through various IAAO publications. Robert Gustafson of the California State Board of Equalization has made some of the best contributions, for example, "Developing a Central EDP System," in *International Property Assessment Administration,* Vol. 2 (Chicago: IAAO, 1970). The CBM corporation of Cleveland, Ohio, has explained advanced computer-assisted assessing techniques in clear language in its project report *Summary of the Research and Validation Phase of the Cuyahoga County, Ohio Computer Assisted Mass Appraisal System* (CBM, Inc. 24100 Chagrin Blvd., Cleveland, Ohio 44122). The inequity of property tax assessing is still among the neglected backwaters in American public administration. An uncommonly readable excursion appeared in a special edition of *Nation's Cities* magazine (May 1970) entitled "Better Assessments for Better Cities." President Johnson's Commission on Urban Problems (the "Douglas Commission") gave significant space to assessment shortcomings in its report, *Building the American City* (House Document No. 91-34, December 1968). Richard Almy of the IAAO's Research Department is at work now on an ambitious nationwide project which will attempt to correlate particular assessment practices with quality of performance.

Countless reports have been prepared on assessment practices in specific states and localities—reports as important as they have been ignored. People who have read the so-called Silverherz Report, published by the New York State Tax Commission in the 1930's (John D. Silverherz, *The Assessment of Real Property in the United States—Special Report of the State Tax Commission,* No. 10, 1936, Albany, N.Y.) say it is perhaps the best. Of the many I have seen, Roland Hatfield's "Report to Governor's Minnesota Property Tax Study Advisory Committee" (Governor's office, St. Paul, Minn.) is exceptionally candid. The reports of blue ribbon panels and commissions comprised of interest-group maharajahs—industry, utilities, bankers, labor unions, government officials—are invariably a gruel of platitudes and compromises, though the staff reports prepared for such panels are often valuable.

Private consulting firms have produced valuable studies of property tax administration. Notable is the 1971 report on Boston's assessing ills, "The Assessing Function in Boston," prepared for the Boston Finance Commission by the Jacobs Co., Inc. (53 W. Jackson Blvd., Chicago, Ill. 60604).

Ordinary taxpayers have begun producing their own reports of local property tax administration. For information on receiving sample copies, write the Public Citizen Tax Reform Research Group, Box 14198, Ben Franklin Station, Washington, D.C. 20044. Some of these have been included in the 1972 and 1973 hearings on property taxes, available from the Senate Subcommittee on Intergovernmental Relations, Washington, D.C. 20510.

A good model of what citizens can uncover about a state or local property tax system is *Mississippi Property Tax: Special Burden for the Poor* (Black Economic Research Center, Jackson, Miss.) by Barbara Phillips and Joseph Huttie, Jr. This report focuses on the gothic difficulties Mississippi's first black assessor, Evan Doss, confronted upon being elected in that state's Claiborne County.

The doings and misdoings of property tax assessors have received only occasional attention from the press. George Crile's

278 TAX POLITICS

piece on the Gary, Indiana, assessor, "A Tax Assessor Has Many Friends," which appeared in the November 1972 *Harper's* shows what a fruitful line of inquiry this is.

Materials on private mass appraisal firms are few and far between. The 1973 property tax hearings, above, contain over 100 pages of information the Public Citizen Tax Reform Research Group assembled on this subject. The IAAO has published some fairly innocuous bibliographies. *Improving Real Property Tax Administration*, a primer for local officials (New York State Board of Equalization and Assessment, Empire State Plaza, Albany, N.Y. 12223) cites the inadequacy of current mass appraisal practices, but without specifics.

Sources on property tax law appear in Chapter 8. The law school casebooks, such as Oldman and Schoettle's *State and Local Taxes and Finance* (Mineola, N.Y.: The Foundation Press, 1974) and Hellerstein's *State and Local Taxation* (St. Paul, Minn.: West Publishing, 1969), the former being the more recent and better, raise the proper questions for lawyers. The state statutes will tell you how the appeals system is supposed to work.

A number of state and local reform groups, such as the Missouri Tax Justice Project ("A Homeowner's Guide to Property Tax Appeals," P.O. Box 8052, St. Louis, Mo. 63156), the New York Public Interest Research Group ("Homeowner's Guide to Property Taxes," 5 Beekman St., New York, N.Y.), and the Connecticut Citizen Action Group (*A Citizen's Handbook for Property Taxpayers*, 57 Farmington Ave., Hartford, Conn. 06105)—to name just three—have published homeowner's guides for assessment appeals. Private attorneys and individuals have done the same: Two examples are James A. Newslow's *A Taxpayer's View Into the Window of the Assessors' Office in Massachusetts* (Needham, Mass., 1970) and New York attorney Irving Lew's *Real Estate Tax Reduction Manual* (Jamaica, N.Y.: Battery Park Book Co., 1961). The latter is geared mainly to commercial properties. Such manuals tend to come and go; it will take a lot of searching to find any for your own area.

Chicanery in the assessment appeals process is a fertile subject the media have touched but lightly, The bellwether was James Phelan's piece in the September 10, 1966, *Saturday Evening Post* on the scandal that rocked the state of California. This article is overflowing with tips and leads still waiting for reporters elsewhere to pursue.

Exposés of property tax delinquencies, tax sales, and tax escrows appear now and then in local newspapers. Textbooks for realtors and bankers set out the mechanics along with the viewpoint of the people who make money by them.

There has been a flowering of books, pamphlets, and articles on preserving farmland and open space, including tax and other aspects. The Center for Rural Studies, 345 Franklin Street, San Francisco, California, has published an extensive bibliography (cost: $1.25), which is probably the place to begin.

William H. Whyte was one of the first to see the futility in the "farmland assessment" laws, which he expresses in his book *The Last Landscape* (New York: Doubleday, 1968). Subsequent studies have laid out the abuse of these tax breaks in more detail. See, for example, *Politics of Land* by Robert Fellmeth (New York: Grossman, 1973) and *Misplaced Hopes, Misspent Millions* (Princeton, N.J.: Center for Analysis of Public Issues, 1972).

Local concern over dwindling open space and irresponsible developers has spawned an assortment of action guides on how to stop them. It is hard to do better than *Guiding Growth: A Handbook for New Hampshire Townspeople* by the Society for the Protection of New Hampshire Forests (5 S. State St., Concord, N.H. 03301). The New York State Department of Agriculture has produced an admirable series of booklets on that state's "Agricultural District" program.

The People's Land (Emmaus, Pa.: Rodale, 1975), edited by Peter Barnes, is a basic text for people who want to find out about our land, who has it, how they got it, what they are doing with it, and how we can get it back. More focused on taxes and preservation techniques, but still elementary, is *The Good Earth of America* (Englewood Cliffs, N.J.: American Assembly, Prentice-Hall, 1974), a collection of mild essays, edited by C. Lowell Harriss.

A literature is budding forth on land gains and speculation taxes. UCLA law professor Donald

Hagman's HUD-sponsored project on windfalls and wipeouts already has yielded some valuable articles, such as "Trading Windfalls for Wipeouts" (*Planning*, September, 1974), and more are coming. In a recent article in the *Washington Law Review*, "Vermont Tax Gains Realized from the Sale or Exchange of Land Held Less than Six Years" (Vol. 49, 1974), Mary Miles Treachout evaluates Vermont's speculation tax. Orville Grimes, Jr., of the staff of the International Bank for Reconstruction and Development, has prepared a report entitled "Urban Land and Public Policy: Social Appropriation of Betterment," on real estate speculation and gains taxes throughout the world.

On speculation generally, see Leonard Downie, Jr.'s *Mortgage on America* (New York: Praeger, 1974).

Cities face preservation problems too, when developers threaten to level landmark buildings and integral neighborhoods to replace them with parking lots and high-rises. Strategies for containing rural despoilation can be applied in cities. A recent effort on these lines is *Space Adrift—Saving Urban Landmarks through the Chicago Plan* (Urbana, Ill.: University of Illinois Press, 1974), available from the National Trust for Historic Preservation. Professor Hagman's law school casebook, *Public Planning and Control of Urban Land Development* (St. Paul, Minn.: West Publishing, 1973) is thorough, and contains so much besides law cases that non-lawyers should find it a valuable resource.

Good for starters on the assessment of oil and minerals are "The Valuation of Oil and Mineral Rights" (International Association of Assessing Officers, 1313 E. 60th St., Chicago, Ill. 60637) and "Mineral Resources Valuation for Public Policy" by Donald Colby and David Brooks of the U.S. Bureau of Mines (Department of Interior, Washington, D.C.). The Forest Service of the U.S. Department of Agriculture provides information on the property taxation of timber. Larger law libraries have volumes setting out in detail the laws relating to oil and mineral assessment.

The writing on timber and mineral taxation has been dominated by people who work for the resource corporations or who sympathize with them. There have been a few bright spots, however. See, for example, Mason Gaffney's "Editor's Conclusion" in *Extractive Resources and Taxation* (Madison, Wisc.: University of Wisconsin Press, 1967), and Mr. Gaffney's more recent paper, "Taxes on Yield, Property, Income, and Site: Effects on Forest Revenues and Management," available from the British Columbia Institute for Economic Policy Analysis (3771 Haro Rd., Victoria, B.C.). Not completely agreeing with Gaffney, but offering another fresh view, is "Evaluating Forest Tax Alternatives for Oregon," a study prepared for the Oregon Legislative Interim Committee on Revenue by W. David Klemperer, a forest economist based in Salem, Oregon.

Exemptions are one side of property taxation that have received much attention recently. Alfred Balk's *The Free List* (New York: Russell Sage Foundation, 1971) showed a popular audience the scope of exempt real estate. *The Churches: Their Riches, Revenues, and Immunities* (New York: Robert B. Luce, 1969) by Martin A. Larson and C. Stanley Lowell, takes special aim on exempt property of religious bodies. A 1973 Report of the National Tax Association, *The Erosion of the Ad Valorem Real Estate Tax Base* (21 E. State St., Columbus, Ohio 43215) goes into somewhat more technical detail. It has a good bibliography.

The General Services Administration issues each year a summary of federal property holdings, entitled *Inventory Report on Real Property Owned by the United States Throughout the World* (General Services Administration, Washington, D.C. 20405).

All the attention on exempt real estate has upstaged other kinds of exemptions that are equally important. Professors Lester Snyder of the University of Connecticut Law School, Donald Hagman of UCLA, and Lester Thurow of MIT have resurrected the intangible property exemptions (stocks, bonds, and the like) for much needed criticism. An article entitled "Taxing the Unlanded Gentry" by Snyder appears in the Fall 1971 *Connecticut Law Review* (Vol. 4, No. 2). Hagman's article, "VIT for VAT: is a Valorem Intangibles Tax A Democratic Alternative for a Value Added Tax?" (#MR-172, 1972) was published by the institute of

280 TAX POLITICS

Government and Public Affairs at UCLA. Thurow's article, "Net Worth Taxes," appeared in the *National Tax Journal* (Vol. 25, 1972).

An important step toward controlling exemptions and other loopholes is a tax expenditure budget. The best versions are available from the budget committees of the U.S. House and Senate. The President's Office of Management and Budget (OMB) includes a tax expenditure budget in its annual budget report which has omitted important favors to wealthy interests. Outside of the federal studies, only the California State Department of Finance is compiling such budgets, and copies are available from the department in Sacramento, California. (An example is "1974-75 Tax Expenditure Report.") Other states should follow their lead.

Private Wealth and Public Education (Cambridge, Mass.: Harvard University Press, 1970) by John Coons, William Clune, and Stephen Sugarman, was the fountainhead of the legal challenges to local school financing systems. A good assessment of the changes that book helped bring is Joel S. Berke's *Answers to Inequity* (Berkeley, Calif.: McCutchan, 1974). All the commotion predictably gave rise to a flurry of commissions and reports—such as the "Fleischman Commission," *Report of the New York State Commission on the Quality, Cost, and Financing of Elementary and Secondary Education* (Manly Fleischman, Chairman, Albany, N.Y., 1972)—which have produced an appearance of action, voluminous reports, and occasionally some useful information. A good number of these, along with other sources, are listed in Berke's ample bibliography.

Coordinating the school finance reform lawsuits has been the Lawyers Committee for Civil Rights Under Law (733 15th St., N.W., Room 520, Washington, D.C. 20005). They are the people to contact for the latest in this fast-developing area.

There are several good, solid guides for doing research on individuals and businesses concerned with property. The top spot on my list goes to *People Before Property* published by Urban Planning Aid (639 Massachusetts Ave., Cambridge, Mass. 02139, 1972). This is one of the few handbooks that really tell you what you need to know. Though based on Massachusetts, it is useful anywhere. It is hoped it will inspire similar efforts in other states and cities.

Focusing on the effective use of research is "Tactical Investigations for People's Struggles" (Public Citizen Action Group, 133 C St., S.E., Washington, D.C. 20003) by Barry Greever. This booklet deserves far more attention than it has received. In a similar vein is a pamphlet called "The Care and Feeding of Power Structures" by Jack Minnis. More systematic is William Domhoff's "Researching the Governing Class of America." Both of these are available from the New England Free Press (60 Union Sq., Somerville, Mass. 02143). Still more extensive is the *NACLA Research Methodology Guide* published by the North American Congress on Latin America (P. O. Box 57, Cathedral Station, New York, N.Y. 10025).

More sources appear throughout Chapter 8 on investigation.

Everybody's talking and writing about "citizen action" but those who are genuinely helpful usually speak from firsthand experience. Saul Alinsky's writings and *Organize—My Life as a Union Man* (Boston: Beacon Press, 1971) by Wyndham Mortimer are examples. Such books can also give a sense of rootedness by linking us to the tradition of social activism and change that is as old as society.

The magnum opus of organizing and social action is probably Gene Sharp's three-volume *The Politics of Nonviolent Action* (Boston: Porter Sargent, 1973). These cover the theory and history and are replete with fascinating illustrations. The bibliography will keep you reading for years.

How People Get Power (New York: McGraw-Hill, 1970) is a thoughtful book by seasoned Appalachian poet-organizer Si Kahn, especially valuable in smaller and rural localities. The Movement for Economic Justice (1609 Connecticut Ave., N.W., Washington, D.C. 20009) has produced a hundred-page "Property Tax Organizing Manual" that anyone considering a property tax action campaign should have.

Books about organizing tend to overlook the views and needs of property owners and of middle income people generally. *Property Power* (New York: Doubleday, 1972) by Mary Anne Guitar does

Bibliographical Note 281

not. Rooted in the experience of a Connecticut exurbanite, it suggests "how to keep the bulldozer, the power line, and the highwayman away from your door."

Some of the best writings on organizing and citizen action are mimeographed sheets passed among social action groups and used in local organizer training programs. The Midwest Academy (600 W. Fullerton Ave., Chicago, Ill. 60614) has assembled a notebook full of these; it would be worth attending one of their two-week sessions just to receive a copy. Such papers often appear in polished-up form in publications not widely known, such as *Working Papers for a New Society*, published quarterly by the Cambridge Policy Studies Institute (123 Mt. Auburn St., Cambridge, Mass. 02138).

Don't overlook books for corporate movers and shakers— titles such as Robert Townsend's *Up the Organization* (New York: Fawcett World Library, 1971) and Peter and Hull's *The Peter Principle* (New York: William Morrow, 1969). They provide good clues on what makes large institutions (public or private— there's not much difference) tick.

There hasn't been much fresh thinking about property taxes for the last thirty years at least. Reformers, such as there were, plugged away for much needed improvement in administration, and for relief from what they considered a regressive levy. A wave of new interest is represented by *Property Tax Reform* (Washington, D.C.: Urban Institute, 1973) edited by George Peterson, which represents some outposts of respected opinion. Professors Donald Hagman, Lester Snyder, and Lester Thurow are the exceptions. They have pretty much gone it alone in advancing the inclusion of paper property in the tax base—an idea whose time is coming.

Assessment reform is pretty well covered by the ACIR, the IAAO, and various state and local consulting reports mentioned throughout this book. The problem is not what to do, but how to get it done.

Then there are still the Georgists, who want to end taxes on buildings and put the whole burden on land. They are persistent iconoclasts with some keen insights and you may want to read Henry George's classic *Progress and Poverty* (New York: Robert Schalkenbach Foundation, 1971). The work of M. Mason Gaffney, an economist with a Georgist bent, deserves serious attention. See, for instance, *Extractive Resources and Taxation* (Madison: University of Wisconsin Press, 1967), which he edited.

On public enterprises as a revenue source, nothing has come along to match Carl Thompson's *Municipal Ownership* (New York: B. W. Huebsch, 1917). Something should.

For keeping up to date on tax developments, see the publications listed above. The only national publication dealing specifically with tax reform is our own *People & Taxes*. Sample copies are available from the Public Citizen Tax Reform Research Group (Box 14198, Ben Franklin Station, Washington, D.C. 20044).

Index

Page numbers in boldface type refer to figures.

Aaron, Henry, 146, 189
ability-to-pay principle, 3–4
  in colonial times, 11
  present undermining of, 13–14, **14**
accelerated deductions, 47
accelerated depreciation, 9, 31, 34, 58–9
  ADR system, 58–9, 91, 95, 112–13, 266
    tax benefits by income class, **42–3**
  for real estate, 59–60
  for rental units, 45
  and the Tax Justice Act of 1975, 265–6
accountant's depreciation, 177
Adair, E. Ross, 248
Adjusted Gross Income (AGI), 39, 109
  and social security payments, 66–7
administrative appeals conferences (IRS), 127
Administrative Procedures Act, 112
Advisory Commission on Intergovernmental Relations (ACIR), 13, 31, 145–6, 147, 229, 242
agricultural districts, and land-use control, 166
Agricultural Department
  farm real estate data, 223
  new industry study, 242
airports, and poverty values, 238–9
Alabama
  assessing system, 261
  federal aid to, 23
  revenue sources, 23, **24**
Albert, Rep. Carl, 92
alcoholic beverage taxes, 5, 7, 21, **25**, 28
Alexander, Donald C., 129, 135, 275

Alexandria, Va., property assessment in, 193
Alinsky, Saul, 245–6, 252–3, 280
Alioto, Mayor Joseph, 238
Allen, Clifford, 198
Almanac of American Politics, 137, 142
Almy, Richard, 277
amendments, to tax legislation, 91, 93–4, 100–3
American Appraisal Associates, 198
American Bar Association, 86, 108, 135
American Council on Education, 53
American Law Reports Annotated (ALR), 230
American Medical Association, 80–1, 88
American Mining Congress, 95, 112
American Petroleum Institute, 90, 95, 104
Americans for Democratic Action (Washington, D.C.), 268, 272
Americans Nonpartisan for Tax Equity (ANTE), 270
amusements taxes, **25**, 28
Anaconda Corporation, 194
Andrews, Rep. Ike F., 139, 140
Appalachia, property assessments in, 152, 153, 156, 179
appeals
  income taxes, 127–30
    appeal procedure, 128
    appellate conferences, 127, 129
    district conferences, 127, 129
    90-day letters, 127, 129
    tax courts, 126, 129–30
    30-day letters, 127, 129
  property taxes, 174, 186, 201, 203–8

  comparison of property, 205–6 **206**
  reforms, 207–8
  review boards, 203
  See also audits
appellate conferences, 127, 129
Archer, Rep. Bill, 78, 90
Arkansas Community Organizations for Reform Now (ACORN), 251, 253, 254, 261, 268
armed forces personnel, tax preferences for, **42**
arrest records, of elected officials, 142
Articles of Confederation, 7
assessing for property taxes, 153, 170, 175–208
  appeals, 174, 186, 201, 203–8
  assessments and taxes compared, **190–2**
  assessor's role, 174–5
  black neighborhoods, 189
  classified assessment levels, 183, **185**
  commercial property, 192–3
  comparable sales (market value) approach, 176–7
  computers, use of, 182–3, 199
  cost (summation), 177
  and economic income, 179
  fractional assessment, 183, **184–5**, 186
  income approach, 177–8, 179
  land assessment, 178–9, 193–5
  legal standards, 183, **184–5**
  listing of property, 174
  and local tax rates, 187, **190–1**
  mass appraisal techniques, 173–4, 176, 195–201
  natural resources, 179–82
  nonlisting, 217–18

284 TAX POLITICS

(assessing for property taxes, *cont.*)
　overassessment, 204–6, 207
　reappraisals, 195–6, 199–201
　residential property, **184–5**, **188–9**, **190–2**
　state-local undertakings, 199
　underassessment, 193–5
　unequal assessments, 214–17
　uniformity, 183, 187–95, 216–17
　valuing, 175–86
Assessment and Valuation Legal Reporter (IAAO), 233
assessment lag, 189, 195
assessment-sales price ratio studies, 186, 187, **190–2**, 214–17
　commercial property, 192–3
　how to make, 214–17
　and property tax appeals, 206
Asset Depreciation Range (ADR) system, 58–9, 91, 95, 112–13, 266
　hearings on, 112–13
Atlanta, Ga., property taxes, 145, **145**
Atlantic City Electric Company, 162
Atomic Energy Commission, 153, 222
Auburn, N.Y., property assessment in, 188
"Audit of Returns . . ." (IRS), 122
"Audit Story, The" (PCTRRG), 122
audits, of income taxes, 119–26.
　　See also appeals
　compliance levels, **121**
　computers, use of, 121
　depletion allowances, 52
　field audits, 122
　freuency of (1971–73), **123**
　and income class, 122
　notification letters, 124
　office audits, 122
　self-help advice, **126**
　taxpayers' rights, 123, 126
automobile industry
　exemption from property taxes, 149
　lobbyists, 90–1
automobiles, efficiency tax on, 90
Ayer's Directory of Periodicals, 247, 249

Backman, Jack, 209
Bafalis, Rep. L. A., 78, 81
Balk, Alfred, 279
Baltimore, enterprise revenues, 29
Balz, Daniel J., 274
banks, taxation of, 19
　escrow account for property taxes, 194, 208–9, 218
　and municipal bonds, 70
Barnes, Peter, 278
Barr, Joseph, 108
Bayh, Sen. Birch, 113
benefits principle, 4, 5
Bennett, Sen. Wallace, 94, 96–7, 102, 111
Bentsen, Sen. Lloyd, 78, 98, 101, 258
Berke, Joel, 167, 280
Bethlehem Steel Corporation, 156
Bexar City, Tex., school finances in, 167–8, **168**
Bibliography on Revaluation Projects (IAAO), **201**
bill-drafting. *See* mark-up sessions
blind persons, tax preferences for, **43**
Boeckh Building Valuation Manual, 226
Boggs, Hale, 80–1
Boggs, Thomas, 80–1
bond consultants, and property tax data, 226
bonds, tax-exempt interests on, 31, 45, 69–71, 85. *See also* intangible property
　and assessed property values, 174
　interest from local government, 147
　and Tax Justice Act, 267
　tax preference by income class, **43**
Booth, Heather, 262
Boston
　paved acreage, **237**
　property taxes, 145, **145**, 152, 158, 179, 189, 194, 226
　real estate information, 211
Bradley, J. W., 194
Brannon, Gerard, 44, 95
Bread Game, The (Glide Publications), 261
Bringewatt, Paul, 277

British Columbia, land-use controls in, 165
broadcasting stations
　ownership, 141
　tax-reform coverage, 248–9
Brock, Sen. William, 78, 95, 97, 98
Brooks, David, 181, 279
Brotzman, Rep. Donald, 50, 83, 92, 105
Broyhill, Rep. Joel, 83, 251
　special-interest ties, 139–40
Buckley, William F., 252
Bucks County, Pa.
　debt service for schools, 147
　property assessment, 193
　scenic easements, 165
Buffalo, N.Y., property assessments, 188
Building the American City (House Document), 277
building permits, 221, 229. *See also* construction industry
Bureau of the Census Catalog, 227
Bureau of Internal Revenue, 113, 116. *See also* Internal Revenue Service
Burke, Rep. James A., 78, 81, 88, 269
Burkhead, Jesse, 277
Burleson, Rep. Omar, 78, 91
business, taxation of
　inventories, 13
　loan interest, 57
　property taxes, 13, 31, 143, 144, **144**, 145–50, 169
　underassessment, 192–5
　tax shelters, 48–9
　See also investment tax credit
Business-Industry Political Action Committee (BIPAC), 137
business machinery, evaluation of, 227
business publications, 225–6
Businessman's Guide to Washington (Ruder and Nathan), 224
Byrd, Sen. Harry F., Jr., 78
Byrnes, Rep. John W., 80, 102

California
　air traffic, 242

Index 285

(California, cont.)
  farmland assessment law, 157
  leasehold interests, 156
  property tax assessment, 182–3, 193, 194, 199
  use-value assessment, 158, 159, 160, **160**, 161–3
California Tax Reform Association, 247–8, 268
Callahan, Bill, 253
Cameron, Helene A., 243
campaign contributions, xvi, 79–80, 88, 104, 105
  disguising of, 138
  information sources, 140–2
  tax preferences, **43**
  and tax reform, 251
capital gains, 63–6
  auditing of, 52
  charitable gifts, 56
  double taxation of, 64, 65
  estate taxes, 65, 66, 268
  exemptions, 14, 16, 17–18, 31
    benefits by income class, **43**
  and income-averaging, 64
  inequities in, 40
  and inflation, 64–5
  and land speculation, 163
  $100 dividend exclusion, 267–8
  and tax deferrals, 64–5, 66
  and Tax Justice Act, 267, 268
  and tax shelters, 48–9
capital-intensive industry subsidies, 58–9
capital investment, and the ADR system, 58–9
capitalization rate
  of natural resources, 180
  and property tax payments, 143, 208–9
  on real estate, 177
Caplin, Mortimer, 123, 275
Carey, Gov. Hugh, 83
Carley, William, 194
carriage tax, 7–8
Castillo, Leonel, 234, 258
Caudill, Harry, 242
CMB, Inc., 277
Center for the Analysis of Public Issues, 162
Center for Rural Studies, 278

Census Bureau, 224, 227, 229
Census of Governments, 217, 224, 229
Chamber of Commerce, 88, 95, 137
Chamberlain, Charles, 80, 83
Chapoton, John, 112
Chapoton, O. Don, 112
charitable deductions, 34, 38, 39–40
  inequities in, 40
  vs. matching grants, 53, 56–7
  tax preferences for, **42**
  and Tax Justice Act, 267
Chicago, property taxes in, **145**, 210, 226, 227
  banks' evasion of, 194
  and freeway construction, 236
  residential property, 187–8
  underassessment of U.S. Steel, 213, **213**, 214
child care expenses, deductability of, **42**
Chommie, John C., 274
Chrysler Building (N.Y.C.), 157
Chrysler Corporation, 89, 91, 99
  property tax exemptions, 149
circuit breakers, on property taxes, 158, 166
cities
  freeway construction and land values, 236–7
  municipal overburdens, 166–7
  property taxes, 145, **145**
  school financing, 166–7, **167**
Citizen Action League (San Francisco), 270
Citizens Action Program (Chicago), 213, 218, 236, 248, 251, 253, 258, 261, 70–1
  newsletter, **252**
Citizens for Participation in Political Action (CPPAX), 268–9
Citizens League (Minn.), 271
citizenship training programs, 261–2
City Directories, 140, 141
Civil Aeronautics Board (CAB), 222
Civil War, taxation during, 8, 25
claims courts, tax appeals in, 127
Clancy, Rep. Donald D., 78
classified property tax, 160
Cleveland, Pres. Grover, 8

Clune, William, 280
coal resources, assessment of. *See* mineral resources
Code of the U.S.A. (USC), 230
coefficient of dispersion, in sales price studies, 216–17
Cohen, Edwin S., 108–9, 112
Cohen, Morris L., 233
Cohen, Sheldon, 112
Colby, Donald, 181, 279
Cole-Layer-Trumble, Inc., 196–8, 199
"Collection Process, The" (IRS), 133
Collier, Rep. Harold, 83
colonial taxation, 7
  state and local taxes, 10–11
Columbus, Ohio, taxation in, 26
Coman, Edwin T., Jr., 227
Commerce Department, 223–4
commercial property assessment, 178, 192–3
  and sales prices, 212–14
Committee on Resources and Economic Development, 276
Committee on Standards of Official Conduct (House of Representatives), 140
Common Cause, 97, 98, 105, 113, 142
Community Builder's Handbook (ULI), 237
Community Press Features, 252
Community Tax Aid, Inc., 257
compromise offers, for delinquent taxes, 133
computer programming
  in income tax audits, 121, 131, **132**
  in property tax assessment, 182–3, 199
Conable, Rep. Barber B., 78, 82, 249, **250**
Conference Committee, 101–3
  and special interest amendments, 102–3
Congress, 75, 106. *See also* House of Representatives; Senate
  conflicts of interest, 251
  expertise of committees, 45–6
  and oil depletion allowance, 61
  as source of tax legislation, 87
  tax expenditure programs, 41
  tax-writing committees, 53, **76–7**, 78–85, 107. *See also* House

286 TAX POLITICS

(Congress, cont.)
    Ways and Means Committee; Senate Finance Committee
    vote recording, 141
Congress Project Study (Nader), 137, 141, 274
Congressional Budget Act (1974), 35
Congressional Directory, 224
Congressional Information Service (CIS), 223
Congressional Profiles, 137, 142
Congressional Quarterly, 137, 142
Congressional Quarterly Weekly, 223
Congressional Record, 140, 223
Congressional Record Index, 139–40, 141
Congressional Research Service, 223
Connally, John B., 41, 44, 258
Connecticut
    capital gains tax, 27
    commercial property assessment, 193
    early taxation, 10, 11
    transfer tax, 159, **160**, 160–1
Connecticut Citizen Action Group, 212, 278
Connery, Vincent, 132–3
Consolidated Edison Corporation, 91
Constitution
    Article I taxing powers, 7–8
    Fourteenth Amendment, 230
    Sixteenth Amendment, 5, 8
Construction Bulletin (Weinzlich Co.), 227
construction industry
    new construction assessment, 218
    and property tax data, 226–7
    shoddy techniques, 239
construction machinery assessment, 218
consumer credit, deduction of interest, 57
Continental Congress, 7
Coons, John, 280
copper industry, depletion allowance for, 111
Corazzini, Eleanor, 259–61
Corman, Rep. James C., 78, 87
Corporate Information Center, 226

corporations
    advertising, public relations campaigns, 104–5
    auditing of, 122
    federal bail-outs for, 88, 99
    foreign subsidiaries, 18–19, 267
    income taxes
        advantages of incorporation, 67–8
        effective tax rate, reduction of, **18**
        exemptions, subsidies, 9, 31, 67–8, 91
        federal taxes, 15, 16–19
        graduated scale, 67–8
        history of, 9
        vs. individual income rates, **17**
        progressivity in, 17–19
        revenues to federal government, xv, **22**
        state taxes, **24, 25,** 26, 27
        Subchapter S corporation, 68
        surtax exemptions, 67–8
        worldwide income, effective tax rate on, 18–19, **19**
    land-subsidy programs, 161–3
    and mass appraisal firms, 197–8
    pension plans, 72–4
    and property ownership, 228
    property tax delinquencies, 209
    prospectuses, 224–5
    and Tax Justice Act, 265–6
cost approach, in assessment, 177
cost depletion allowances, 61
    benefits by income class, **42**
Cotter, Rep. William R., 78
Council on Economic Priorities, 226
court records, and property tax data, 224
courts. *See* lawsuits; tax courts; U.S. Supreme Court
Crane, Rep. Philip M., 78
Cranston, Alan, 101
Crile, George, 277–8
Cumulative Bulletins (IRS), **114**
current-use assessments, of farmland, 159, **160,** 160–1
Curtis, Sen. Carl T., 78
Curtis, Thomas, 93
customs duties, 22

Daily and Weekly Bond Buyer, 226
dairy industry, campaign contributions of, 139
Daley, Mayor Richard, 236, 253
Dallas-Fort Worth airport, 239
Davenport, Charles, 275
David, Martin, 113
Davis, Charles W., 138
death transference tax, capital gains on, 28–9, 268. *See also* estate taxes
debt-ceiling bills, 1974 hearings on, 95, 96
deeds to property, 221, 229
Defense Department, property leases, 153, 223
deferred taxation, on farmland, 159, **160**
Deffett, George H., 60, 88
Delaware
    mass appraisals in, 197, 198
    revenue sources, 23, **24**
    taxation policies, 23, 27
Delaware Citizens Coalition for Tax Reform, 269
delinquent taxes, collecton of, 130–6
    bills and seizure notices, **132**
    collection procedure, 132–3, **134**
    complaints, **132**
    computer errors, 131, 132
    forcible collections, 130–1
    installment plans, 133
    interest charges, 127
    jeopardy assessments, 135
    liens, 135
    offers in compromise, 133
    property taxes, 209–10
    protected property, 135
    seizure by geographical area, **131**
Democratic party
    caucuses and House amendments, 93
    Steering and Policy Committee, 82
    tax policy, 109
Denver, property taxes in, **145**
departments of government. *See* Agriculture Department; Interior Department; *etc.*
depletion allowances, 31, 98, 109. *See also* oil depletion allow-

(depletion allowances, *cont.*)
ance; mineral depletion allowance
me-too-ism, 46
percentage depletion, 60–3
and property taxes, 180, 181–2
and tax regulations, 111–12
depreciation, in property assessment, 177, 179, 213, 214
determination letters (IRS), **114**, 117
Detroit, local taxes in, 27
development rights, and land use, 164–5
depth tables, for land assessment, 178, 179
direct subsidies, 34, 41, 52–3
Directory of Iron and Steel Works, 213, 226
DISC export and tax subsidy, 44–5, 89, 91, 95, 110
and Tax Justice Act, 267
district conferences, for tax appeals, 126, 128
district courts, 126
Dodge, Mrs. Horace, 81
Dodge Corporation, 226, 227
Dodge Reports, 227
Dole, Sen. Robert, 78, 95, 97, 98, 256
Dollars and Cents of Shopping Centers (ULI), 226–7
Domestic International Sales Corporations (DISCs), 267. *See also* Disc export tax subsidy
Domhoff, William, 280
Doss, Evan, 258, 277
Douglas, Sen. Paul, 80
Downie, Leonard, Jr., 279
Drew, Elizabeth, 82
Du Pont, Irenee, 21
Du Pont family, 46, 86
dummy corporations, 228
Dun and Bradstreet publications, 225, 226, 228
Duncan, Rep. John J., 78
Dymally, Mervyn, 235

easements, open and scenic, 165
Ecker-Racz, L. L., 186, 276
economic policy and taxation, 4–5

effective tax rate, vs. nominal rate, 174
Ehrlichman, John D., 116
Eisenstein, Louis, 16
elasticity principle, 5
elected officials, 137–42
information on, 140–42
and tax-reform groups, 251, 258–9
Ely, Richard T., 276
eminent domain, right of, 163, 221
Energy Conservation Bill (1975), 81–2, 84, 90, 93–4, 97–9
amendments to, 93–4
Senate mark-up session, 97–9
Environmental Protection Agency, 86
Equipment Guide Book Company, 227
Ervin, Sen. Sam, 113
escrow accounts, for property taxes, 208–9
estate taxes, 6–7, 267–8
capital gains on, 65, 66
exemptions, 21
farmland, 164
federal taxes, 20–1, 22, 28
state taxes, 28–9, 30
and Tax Justice Act, 267
excess profits tax, 9
Excise Tax Reduction Act (1965), 21
excise taxes, 21–2. *See also* sales taxes
effective rates, **21**
history of, 7–8
Executive Departments, and property tax data, 223–4. *See also* Transportation Department; Treasury Department; *etc.*
export profits, exemption of, 44–5. *See also* DISC export tax subsidy

faculty tax (Great Britain), 11
Fagan, Mark M., 233
Fannin, Sen. Paul J., 78, 96
farms, farmland
assessment programs, 31, 158–66
federal programs, 162–3
estate taxes, 164

machinery and corporate lease programs, 163
and market values, 176
property taxes, 143, **144**, 158–66
reforms, alternatives, 164–6
vs. road, water, and sewer programs, 163, 165
speculation and development, 161–3
tax subsidies, 48–9, 266
Federal Communications Commission (FCC), 222
federal highway program, 162
Federal Housing Administration (FHA), 223, 224, 227, 237, 239
federal housing programs, 162–3
Federal Maritime Commission (FMC), 222
Federal Power Commission (FPC), 222, 224
Federal Reserve Board, 222
Federal Tax Policy (Pechman), 273
federal taxation, 15–22
average vs. upper income burden, **32**
budget receipts by source, **16**
history of, 7–10
revenue sources, **15**, **22**
See also corporations: income taxes; estate taxes; excise taxes; individual income taxes; property taxes; state taxes; *etc.*
Federal Trade Commission (FTC), 222
fee appraisers, 175–6
Fellmeth, Robert, 278
Fialka, John, 118
Field, Thomas F., 112, 270
Filer, Dr., 269
fiilms, assessed as property, 149
Financing Schools and Property Tax Relief (ACIR), 229
Finch, Robert H., 117
Fisher, Rep. Joseph, 78
flat rates, of taxation, 6, 27, 174
Fleischman, Manly, 280
Florida
commercial property assessment, 193

288 TAX POLITICS

(Florida, cont.)
   property tax appeals, 204
   retirement tax havens, 28
Ford, Pres. Gerald R., 35, 85, 109
Ford, Rep. Harold E., 78
Ford Motor Company, 90
foreign tax credit, to oil companies, 109
Fort, Ruth, 224
Fortune's directories, 226
Foundation Directory, 141
foundations
   grants for tax-reform study, 261
   tax exemptions for, 45
Fourteenth Amendment, 230
Fowler, Henry, 111
fractional assessment, 183, **184–5**, 186
Franklin, Benjamin, 10
Freedom of Information Act, 222, 223, 233, 234, 261
French and Indian War (1755), 11
Frenzel, Rep. Bill, 78, 81
Friedman, Milton, 168
front footage assessments, 163

Gaffney, Mason, 146, 279, 281
gambling, vs. direct taxes, 173
Garbis, Marvin, J., 130, 275
Gary. Ind., vs. U.S. Steel Corporation, 212–13, **213**, 214
General Accounting Office, 135, 223
General Services Administration, 222
   Inventory Report, 279
   office building leases, 139–40
George, Henry, 281
George, Keith, 194–5
Georgia, mass appraisal regulations, 198
Gibbons, Rep. Sam M., 46, 50, 78, 82, 94, 113, 256
GI bill benefits, exemption of, **43**
gift taxes
   federal, 20–1, 22, 28
   state, 28–9
   and Tax Justice Act, 267
Girard, Stephen, 10
Goodell, Richard, 118
Goodman, Sen. William J., 165

government property, leasing of, 153, 156–7, 158
grants, vs. direct taxes, 173
Gravel, Sen. Mike, 78, 97, 98
Great Britain, colonial tax policies, 7
Green, Mark, 274
Green, Raymond J., **240–1**
Green, Rep. William J., 78, 83, 93, 94, 257
Greenspan, Alan, 86
Greever, Barry, 142, 280
Griffin, Sen. Robert, 95
Griffiths, Rep. Martha, 83
Grimes, Orville, Jr., 279
guidebooks, to state governments, 222
Guitar, Mary Anne, 280–1
Gustafson, Robert, 277

Hagman, Donald, 148, 165, 278–9, 281
Haines, Daniel, 11–12
Halfway to Tax Reform (Ruskay and Osserman), 273
handbooks, to property tax laws, 233–4
Hansen, Sen. Clifford P., 78
Harberger, Arnold C., 61
Harper-Edge rule, for land assessment, 178
Harris, Fred, 256
Harriss, C. L., 204, 278
Hart, Sen. Gary, 101
Hart, Sen. Philip, 101
Hartford, Conn., property tax assessment, 189
Hartke, Sen. Vance, 78, 94
Haskell, Sen. Floyd K., 37, 78, 84, 85, 87, 95, 98, 102
Hatcher, Richard, 212
Hatfield, Sen. Mark, 38
Hatfield, Roland, 277
Hathaway, Sen. William, 78, 84, 85, 95, 102
Hawaii
   property assessments, 170
   restrictive land agreements, 159, **160**
   school financing, 168–9

   state income tax, 26
Hayes, Richard, 276
hearings, on tax legislation, 95–7, 257–8
Hellerstein, Jerome, 203–4, 232, 278
Helstoski, Rep. Henry, 78, 91
Herman, Tom, 119
Hess, Patricia, 239
Hewlett-Packard Corporation, 45
Hickman, Frederic, 85, 91–2, 107
Higgins, George V., 263
high-rise buildings
   cost vs. revenue study, **240–1**
   and property values, 236, 238
highway construction, and property taxes, 236–7
Hodge, Edwin Jr., 138
Hoffman-Neill rule, for land assessment, 178
Hollings, Sen. Ernest F., 84, 100–1
Holmes, John, 237
home insulation, tax credit for, 81
home mortgage interest deductions, 34, 38–9, 40, **43**, 86, 91. *See also* property taxes
   home ownership promotion, 45, 91
   and savings interest deduction, 50–2
   as tax expenditure, 55
   and Tax Justice Act, 267–8
Homeowner's Guide to the Property Tax, 269
homestead exemptions, 148, 149
Hornbeak, Martha, 261
hospitals, property tax exemptions to, 219
House of Representatives
   and campaign contributions, 140
   power relationships, 82–4
   and tax legislation, 87–94
House Rules Committee, 92–3
House Ways and Means Committee, 38, 40, 60, 78–9, 82–90, 107
   chairman's role, 89
   hearings, 50, 87–8
   members' role, 89–90
   membership, 78–9
   power relationships, 82–4
   professional staff, 89–90
   and tax-reform legislation, 83–4
   and tax shelters, 50

(Ways and Means Committee, *cont.*)
  Treasury Department investigation (1951–53), 113
housing developments, and accelerated depreciation, 60
housing subsidies, 38–9
  depreciation deductions, by income class, **43**
Housing and Urban Development, Department of, 220, 224, 227
Houston, Tex., property taxes in, 145, **145**, 193
Humble Oil Corporation, 162
Hunt, Albert, 98, 99
Hunt, H. L., 248
Hunter, Edward O., 126
Huttie, Joseph Jr., 277

Ikard, Frank, 104
Illinois, tax policies in, 27, 195
Illinois Public Action Fund, 261
incentive exemptions, to industry, 149
Income and Cost of Rental Housing (ULI), 227
income taxes
  elasticity of, 5
  history of, 8–10
  progressive rates, 5–6
  See also corporations: income taxes; individual income taxes
income-averaging, and capital gains, 64
income-security transfer payments, 66–7
Independent Gas Producers of America, 90
Independent Natural Gas Association, 104
Independent Petroleum Association of America, 104
Independent Petroleum Producers of America, 90, 95
indexes
  newspapers, periodicals, 225
  property tax laws, 230–1
indexing, of property values, 178
Indiana, tax policies in, 27, 194
individual income taxes
  federal taxes, 15–16

burden by income class, 22, **23**
high-income returns, xv
high vs middle-income families, xv
progressive rates, 6
state taxes, 23, **24**, 25–7
and tax shelters, **48**, **49**
and tax preferences, 16
industrial development bonds, 156
industrial land, assessment of, 178, 212–14
industry, statewide taxation of, 242–3
industry directories, 226
inflation, and capital gains rates, 64–5
information letters (IRS), **114**, 117
Inland Steel Corporation, 137
inspections (fire, building, health), and property data, 221, 239
installment plans, for tax delinquencies, 133
Institute of Real Estate Management (Chicago), 227
institutions, exemption from property taxes, 148, 151, **152**, 157–8, 219
  payments in lieu of taxes, 158
insurance premiums, deductability of, **42**
intangible expenses, deductions for, 62–3
intangible property, taxation of, 12, 13, 31, 170, 218. *See also* bonds; property taxes
  bibliography, 279–80
  exemption of, 148, 149, **150**
  and school financing, 169
Interior Department, leases of rights, 223
Internal Revenue Code, 103, **114**
Internal Revenue Service, 75, 107, 117–36. *See also* appeals; audits
  administrative appeals, conferences, 127, 129
  audits, 119–26
  bibliography on, 274–5
  binding rulings, 117
  Cumulative Bulletins, **114**
  delinquent taxes, collection of,

130–36
"determination letters," **114**, 117
"friends" and "enemies" list, 113
information letters, **114**, 117
interpretative rulings, 116–17
Legislation and Regulation Division, 107, **114**
political influences, 116
political investigations, 259
"private" ("letter") rulings, **114**, 116–17
property tax appraisals, 223
"revenue rulings," **114**
self-assessment system, 118
and tax policies, 107–10
tax returns, assistance in filing, 118–19
  employee advice, 119
  error rate, 118
and tax subsidy administration, 52–3
technical advice, 117
International Association of Assessing Officers (IAAO), 197, 199, 200, 201, 233
  publications, 276, 277, 278, 279
International Utilities Corporation, 162
Interstate Commerce Commission (ICC), 222
investigating manuals, 142
investment tax credit, 34, 41, 44, 46
  benefits by income class, **43**
  and job development, 68–9
  and Tax Justice Act, 265
investor service manuals, 226

Jackson, Justice Robert, 75, 135
Jacobs, Rep. Andy, Jr., 78, 81
Jacobs Company, Inc., 277
Jensen, Jens, 11, 276
jeopardy assessment procedure, 135
job development credit, 68–9
Johnson, Ken, 219
Johnson, Pres. Lyndon B., 9, 85, 108
Joint Committee on Internal Revenue Taxation, 87, 90, 81
Jones, Rep. James R., 78

Kahn, Si, 153, 156, 280

290 TAX POLITICS

Kansas City, Mo., local taxes in, 27
Karth, Rep. Joseph E., 78, 81, 82
Kass, Benny, 209
Keller, Ted, 269
Kellogg foundation, 137–8
Kelly Act (1846), 11
Kennedy, David M., 112
Kennedy, Sen. Edward, 86, 95, 100, 101
Kennedy, Pres. John F., 85, 86
Keogh plans, 71
Ketchum, Rep. William M., 78
Keys, Rep. Martha, 78
Korean War, taxation during, 9
Klein, Joseph, 274
Klein's Guide to American Directories, 226, 227
Klemperer, W. D., 279
Kline, Karen, 263
Krause, Rose, 263

Labor Department, and property tax data, 224
labor unions, 88
    and property tax data, 226
    and tax reform, 246
land, property taxes on, 143–4, 158–66. *See also* farms, farmland; mass appraisal firms
    assessment of, 178–9
    underassessment of, 153, 193–5
land banking, 165–6
land gains tax, 164
land speculation, 31
    vs. assessment laws, 161–3
    biblography on, 278–9
    controls for, 164–6
Landrum, Rep. Phil M., 78
Larson, Dr. Martin A., 150–1, 279
Lathrop, Robert, 164
law encyclopedias, 230, 231, 232
law libraries, and property tax information, 229
law school casebooks, and property tax laws, 232
lawsuits
    and property tax data, 224–5
    and tax-reform groups, 259, 261
Lawyers Committee for Civil Rights Under Law, 280

Lawyers Co-operative Publishing Company, 230
League of Women Voters, 246, 247
leasing, of government property, 153, 156–7, 158
Lederer, Lewis, 131
Lee v. Boswell (Ala.), 261
Legal Research in a Nutshell (Cohen), 233
letter-writing campaigns, for tax reform, 255–6, 259
levies, on wages, 131
Lew, Irving, 278
licenses, for business activities, 221
lien, notices of, 135
lien dates, for property taxes, 194
life insurance savings, deductability of interest, **43**
Lindsay, Mayor John V., 239
Little, Arthur D., Inc., 189, 207
Litton Industries, 100
loans, deductability of interest on, 57
lobbyists, lobbying, xv, 79–84. *See also* special-interest groups
    bibliography, 274
    employment of Congressional retirees, 80
    and hearings on tax legislation, 88
    and mark-up sessions, 88, 90–1
    me-too-ism, 46
    registration of, 140–1
    and tax preferences, 33
    and tax regulations, 110
local ordinances, and property taxes, 231–2
local taxes, 23–32. *See also* property taxes; state taxes
    average vs. upper income burden, **32**
    deductability of, 54
    history of, 10–13
    revenue distribution, **26**
    sales taxes, **26**, 27–8
    and school support, 12, 147, 166–9
    special districts, 175
Lockheed Corporation, 86, 89, 91, 99, 100, 156
Loitz, Bob, 247, 249, 255, 256
Long, Phil and Sue, 119, 261
Long, Sen. Russell B., 78, 84–6, 90,

94–101 *passim*, 111, 112
    and the Senate Finance Committee, 84–5
    on tax credits, 98
loopholes, exemptions, 6–7, 13. *See also* tax expenditures
Los Angeles
    paved acreage, 236, **237**
    property taxes in, **145**, **171**
    taxpayers' guide, **172**
Louisiana
    property taxes, 145
    revenue sources, 23, **24**, 31
Louisville, Ky., local taxes in, 26–7
Lowell, C. Stanley, 150–1, 279
Lubick, Don, **250**
Lundberg, Ferdinand, 53–4
Lusk's Directory, 211
Lynn, Arthur, 11, 12

Magnuson, Sen. Warren, 100, 101
Manchester, N.H., property assessments in, 187
Manley, John F., 274
Manual on Money and Politics (Common Cause), 142
market value, 176, 211
mark-up sessions
    House of Representatives, 88–90
    Senate, 97–9
    and vote recording, 141
Marshall Valuation Service, 226
Martin, Rep. James G., 78
Martindale and Hubbell's Law Directory, 138, 140, 228
Maryland
    early taxation, 10, 11
    farmland assessment, 158, 161
mass appraisals, 173–4, 176, 195–201, 227
    bibliography, 278
    contracts, 200–1, **202**
    investigation of, 200–1, **201**
    specifications for bidders, 200
Massachusetts
    early taxation, 10, 11
    farmland in, 158
    flat rate system, 27
    local budgets, 175
    property tax collection, 209

Massachusetts Fair Share, 251–2, 271
Massachusetts Port Authority, 156
Massachusetts Public Finance Project, 276
Massena, N.Y., tax base of, 143
Maxwell, James A., 276
Mayer, Louis B., 46, 86
McClure, Harold, 104
McDaniel, Paul, 56, 273
McDonnell-Douglas Corporation, 86, 100
medical expenses, deductability of, **42**, 57–8
Mellon, Andrew, 46
Mellon National Bank and Trust, 138
Meltsner, Arnold, 173
Merrill, Charles, 86
Metcalf, Sen. Lee, 101
Metro-Act of Rochester (N.Y.), **250**, 271
Metropolitan Life Insurance Company, 212
Michael, James, 224
Michigan
   flat rate system in, 27
   property taxes in, 149, 210
Midwest Academy (Chicago), 261–2, 281
Mikva, Rep. Abner, 78
military disability pensions, tax preferences for, **42**
Mill, John Stuart, 4
Mills, Rep. Wilbur D., 33, 38, 44, 45, 78, 79, 80, 87–8, 90, 102, 253, 254
   campaign violations (1972), 138–9
   and House Ways and Means Committee, 83, 89
   members' bills (1972), 254
mineral depletion allowances, 46, 60, 61. *See also* oil depletion allowances
   and Tax Justice Act, 264, 266
   and Treasury Department, 111–12
mineral resources
   assessment of, 153, 180–2, 218
   leasing of rights, 153, 156
Minneapolis, Minn., property taxes in, **145**, 243

Minnesota, farmland assessment in, 159, **160**
Minnis, Jack, 280
Mississippi, property taxes in, 258, 277
Missouri Tax Justice Project, 278
Mobil Oil Corporation, 86, 100
Mondale, Sen. Walter F., 78, 84, 85, 94, 97, 98
Monsanto Chemical Company, 116
Montana, property taxes, and revenue sources, 23, **24**
Montoya, Sen. Joseph, 133
Moody's guides, 225–6
Morgan, J. P., 245
Morrison, Edward F., 274
mortgage interest deductions. *See* home mortgage interest deductions
mortgage payments, and property taxes, 208–9
mortgages, and property ownership investigations, 228
Mortimer, Wyndham, 280
motor fuel and vehicle taxes, 12, **25**, 28, 54
   tax preferences by income class, **42**
Mott, Stewart, 16
Movement for Economic Justice, 257, 269, 280
municipal overburdens, 166–7
Muskie, Sen. Edmund, 113

NACLA Research Methodology Guide, 280
Nader, Ralph, 98, 102, 112, 113
   Congress Project, 137, 141, 274
Nash, Peter, 255–6
Nathan, Raymond, 224
National Association of Manufacturers, 88, 90, 95
National Association of Realtors, 95
National Bureau of Research (Iowa), 227
National Committee for Tax Justice (NCTJ), 264, 272
National Journal Reports, 142
National Labor Relations Board, 255–6

National League of Cities, 220
National Republican Congressional Committee, 138
Nation's Cities magazine, 277
natural resources:
   assessment of, 153, 179–82
   bibliography, 279
   exploration and development deductions, **42**
   leasing of, 153, 156, 158
Nebraska
   public enterprises in, 31
   state-county reappraisal program, 199
Nelson, Sen. Gaylord, 45, 78, 84–5, 94, 96, 97
Netzer, Richard, 144, 148, 149, 276
Nevada
   "freeport" law, 194
   as retirement tax haven, 28, 29
New Jersey
   farmland assessment, 158, 159, 160, **160**, 161, 163
   mass appraisal regulations, 198
   property taxes, 11–12, 143, 145
   reappraisals, 194, 199, 201
   rejection of income tax, 14
   revenue sources, 23, **24**
New Hampshire
   dividend taxes, 27
   property taxes, 23
   revenue sources, 23, **24**
New Haven, Conn., Property tax assessment, 189
New Mexico, property taxes in, 194
New Orleans, property taxes in, 187
New Populist Action, 256
New York City
   airports, 238–9
   paved acreage, **237**
   property taxes, 145, **145**, **171**, 209
New York Port Authority, leasing activities, 156
New York Public Interest Research Group, 278
New York State, property values in, 164, 199
Newark, N.J., exempt property in, 152
newsletters, of tax-reform groups, 251–2, 268–71

292 TAX POLITICS

Newslow, James A., 278
newspapers
    press releases, 249, **250**, 251
    and property tax data, 224, 225
    and special-interest legislation, 137, 139, 140
    tax-reform coverage, 249, 259–61
Nixon, Pres. Richard M., 44, 85, 104, 108, 112, 113
    and oil industry, 109
Nolan, John, 113
nonlisting, of property, 217–18
North, Arthur, **250**
North Carolina, property taxes, 199
North Dakota, property assessment, 170
nuclear power, and property taxes, 243–4

occupancy permits, 221, 239
office building leases, 139–40
Office of International Tax Counsel, 107
Office of Management and Budget, 41, 110, 173, 280
Office of Public Records, 141
Office of Records and Registration, 138
Office of Tax Analysis, 107
Office of the Tax Legislative Counsel, 107
offset procedure, in collecting delinquent taxes, 130
Ohio
    early taxation, 11
    local taxes, 26
    property taxes, 11, 209, 243
    state income taxes, 26
    strip-mining, 242
Ohio Public Interest Action Group (OPIAG), 209
Ohio TEA Party, 269
oil depletion allowance, 31, 34, 38, 45, 83, 84, 93
    auditing of, 52
    cost vs. percentage depletion, 60–3
    and House Rules Committee, 92
    intangible drilling, 60, 62
    1974 Senate hearings, 95–6
    and resource allocation, 46
    and Tax Justice Act, 100–1, 102–3, 264, 266
    and Treasury Department, 111–12
oil industry
    drilling credit, 84
    excess profits tax, 95–6
    foreign tax credit, 109
    lobbying organizations, 90, 91, 95, 104
    tax avoidance, 19
    windfall profits, 109
Okner, Benjamin, 16, 17, 31, 146, 274, 276
old age, tax preferences, **42**, **43**
Oldman, Oliver, 189, 232, 278
Oregon
    reappraisal programs, 186, 199, 203
    tax courts, 203
Organize, Inc. (San Francisco), 261
Osserman, Richard, 273
overassessment, of property, 204–6, 207
ownership of property, investigation of, 227–8

Packwood, Sen. Robert, 78, 95, 97
Paine, Thomas, 7, 27
Pan American Airlines, 89, 91, 99
panic of 1893, 8
Parsell, Al, 161
partnerships, taxation of, **48**, 68
Paschall, Robert H., 181
Pathways to Tax Reform (Surrey), 273
payroll taxes. *See* social security taxes
Pechman, Joseph, 16, 17, 31, 146, 273, 274, 276
Pennsylvania
    flat rate system in, 27
    mass appraisals, 197
    reassessments of property, 195
Pension Act of 1973, 71–2
pension plans, 71–4
    corporate contribution, 72–3
    high vs. low-income benefits, **42**, **73**
    for the self-employed, **42**, 71–2, 73–4
    tax integrations, 73, **73**
People Before Property (UPA), 280
People and Taxes (PCTRRG), 141, 270, 272, 274, 281
percentage depletion allowances, 60–3
Percy, Sen. Charles, 52
personal exemptions
    and Tax Justice Act, 265
    tax preferences by income class, **42**
Peterson, George, 281
Petroleum Industry Information Committee, 104
Pew Memorial Trust, 137–8
Phelan, James, 278
Philadelphia
    commercial property assessment, 193
    early taxation, 10
    local taxes, 27
    paved acreage, **237**
Philadelphia TEA Party, 252, 253, 269
    petition, **255**
Phillips, Barbara, 277
Pickle, Rep. J. J., 78
Pike, Rep. Otis, G., 78, 81
Plymouth, Mass., nuclear power in, 243–4
Political Awareness Fund, 139
Politics of Finance, The (Manley), 274
pollution control, tax subsidies for, 45, 46, 213
    damage costs, **238**
    and industrial development bonds, 156
    and property values, 236, 237–8
Populist party, 3, 8
Poor Tax (Great Britain), 11
Poor's Registry of Executives, 138, 140, 141
preferential assessments, of farmland, 159, **160**, 160–1
President's Council on Environmental Quality, 237
press releases, of tax-reform groups, 249, **250**, 251
private letter rulings (IRS), **114**, 116–17

Index 293

professional groups, and tax legislation, 86–7
professional incorporation, tax advantages of, 73, **74**
profit-sharing plans, 71
progressive tax rates, 5–7
property, IRS seizure of, 130–1, 134–5
property deeds, 221, 229
property record cards, 175, 233
Property Tax in a Changing Environment, The (ACIR), 229
property tax laws, 229–33
   assessor's role, 234–5
   custom, 232
   indexes, 230–1
   local laws, 231–2
   manuals, 233–4
   public records, 233–4
   secondary sources, 232–3
   state laws, 230–1
property taxes, xv, 143–69, 170–210. *See also* property tax laws
   abolishing of, 147–8
   appeals, 174, 186, 201, 203–8
   assessing, 153, 170, 175–208, 211–14. *See also* assessing for property taxes
   bibliography, 276–81
   capitalization of, 143
   collection, 208–10
   classified, 160
   commercial and industrial, 143, 144, **144**, 149–50, 169
   delinquencies, 209–10
      investigation of, 217
   disparities between states, 145, **145**
   effective rates, **146**
   elasticity of, 5
   escrow accounts, 208–9
   exempt property, 31, 148–58, 219–20
      benefits by income class, **43**
   and family income, 145–6, **146**
   farms, farmland, 143, **144**, 158–66
   government property, 153, 156–7, 158
   history of, 11–13
   interest deductions, 267–8
   investigation of, 220–7, 229

and local budget processes, 171, 172–4
nonassessment, 53
nonlisting, 217–18
ownership, tracing of, 227–8
personal property, 149–50, **150–1**, 170, 210
   assessment of, 174
   tangible and intangible, 170
progressivity of, 6, 146–7
ratables, 173
real estate, 148, 150–2, 226–7
rental housing, 143, 144–5, 157
residential, 143, 144–5, **145**
residential vs. business, xv
and school finances, 12, 147, 166–9
state and local, 23, **24**, 25
tax bases, 13, 170
tax calendars, 171–4
and tax expenditure, 55
tax rates, 174
taxed vs. untaxed property, 149, **150–1**
taxpayer advocates, 207
underassessment, 153, 211–14
proportional taxation, 6
prospectuses, and property tax data, 224
Providence, R. I., property assessment, 189
Proxmire, Sen. William, 51, 99
Public Affairs Information Service, 220
public assistance payments, exemption of, 66
public authorities, property leases, 156–7
Public Citizen Tax Reform Research Group, xvi, 88, 90, 105, 122, 137, 139, 141, 269–70
   publications, 277, 278
Public Citizen's Freedom of Information Clearinghouse, 234
public employees' unions, and propetry tax data, 217
Public Interest Economics Center, 141, 271
Public Interest Research Group (PIRG), 112, 270
public property, exemption from taxation, 148
public records, and property data, 221–5
public relations campaigns, of corporations, 104–5
public utility taxes, **25**, 28, 30, **30**, 31
   and property taxes, 143, 221–2

railroad retirement payments, **42**, 66
railroads, coal-hauling write-offs for, 81
Rangel, Rep. Charles B., 78, 91
Rape of the Taxpayer, The (Stern), 272
ratables, in local budgets, 173
ratio studies, assessment to sales price, 186, 187, **190–2**, 192–3, 206, 207, 214–17
Reagan, Gov. Ronald, 149
real estate
   property taxes, 148, 150–2, 226–7
   straight-line depreciation, 266
   underassessment of, 31
real estate directories, 211
real estate interest groups, 88
   campaign contributions, 139–40
   See also land speculation
reappraisals, for property taxes, 195–6, 199–201
"Recordkeeping Requirements and a Guide to Tax Publications" (IRS), **120**
recycling resources, tax credit for, 46, 61, 82, 86, 91, 94, 98
regression analysis, in property assessment, 182
regressivity, in taxation, 6–7, 14–15
regulatory agencies, and property tax data, 222–4
Reingold, Arnold, 212, 214
religious organizations
   exemption from property taxes, 151, 157, 219
   and tax reform, 246–7
rent control, and property evaluation, 221
rental units
   depreciation of, 45, 59–60
   benefits for, by income class, **43**

(rental units, *cont.*)
   and property taxes, 143, 144–5, 157, 210
Report . . . on Some Administrative Procedures of the IRS (Davenport), 275
Republican party, tax policies, 109
residential property assessment, 178, **184–5**, **188–9**, 192–3
   assessments and taxes compared, **190–2**
   vs. commercial property, 192–3
restrictive agreements, on land, 159–60
retired people's tax-reform groups, 246
retirement income, exemption of, **43**, 66–7. *See also* pension plans
Reuss, Rep. Henry, 87, 109, 113
Revenue Act of 1918, 8–9
Revenue Act of 1963, 9
Revenue Act of 1971, 9, 91, 96, 102
   depreciation law, 113
   and DISC export subsidy, 44–5
revenue rulings, **114**
revenue-sharing programs, 38, 45, 54, 71
Rhode Island, farmland assessment law, **160**, 161
Ribicoff, Sen. Abraham, 78, 84–5, 94, 97
Riddel, James "Dick," 80
Riley, Ed. 16
Rinfret, Pierre, 44, 59
risk-taking, and capital gains, 64, 65
Rochester, N.Y., tax reform in, 249, **250**, 271
Rockefeller, Gov. Nelson, 156
Rodriguez v. San Antonio, 168
Rogers, Walter, 104
Rogovin, Mitchell, 112
Role of the States . . . Property Tax (ACIR), 229
rollback taxes, on farm assessments, 159, 161
Roosevelt, Pres. Theodore, 28
Rostenkowski, Rep. Daniel, 78
Roth, Sen. William V., 78, 95
Rowe, Mass., tax base of, 143
Ruder, William, 224

Rules for Radicals (Alinsky), 252–3
rules of thumb, for evaluating industral property, 212, 227
Ruskay, Joseph, 273

St. Louis Tax Reform Group, 247, 253, 258, 270
sales prices, of property
   location of, 211–12
   vs. market value, 176, 211
   worker-to-property ratios, 212–13
sales taxes
   deductability of, 54
   elasticity of, 5
   general sales taxes, 27–8
   local taxes, **26**, 27–8
   special taxes, 25, 28
   state taxes, 23, **24**, **25**, 27–8
   use taxes, 27
Salmon, Gov. Thomas P., 164
Samuels, Howard, 164
Samuelson, Paul, 44
San Antonio, Tex., school financing, 167–8, **168**
San Francisco, high-rise vs. revenue study, 238, **240–1**
Savannah, Ga., early public enterprises in, 10
Save Our Cumberland Mountains, 271
Savings and Loan Fact Book (USSLL), 227
savings interest exemption, 50–2, 85, 92–3
savings and loan institutions
   capitalization of tax payments, 208–9
   lobbyists, 91
scenic easements, 165
Schaeffer, Fred, **250**
Schneebeli, Rep. Herman T., 78, 137–8
Schoettle, Ferdinand O., 232, 278
scholarships, fellowships, deductability of, **42**
school financing
   federal aid programs, 167–8
   and property taxes, 12, 147, 166–9
   reforms, 168–9
   state grants, 166, 167

Schroeder, Pat, 257
Schultz, George P., 85, 109
Schwartz, Ed, 253
Seattle, Wash.
   leasing of public property, 156
   property taxes, **145**
secrecy, of public officials, 97, 263
secured vs. unsecured taxes, 210
Securities and Exchange Commission, 222, 274
self-employed individuals, pension plans for, **42**, 71–2
Seligman, E. R. A., 12
Senate
   campaign contributions, 140
   power relationships, 84–5
   tax legislation procedures, 95–103
      Conference Committee, 101–3
      floor procedures, 99–101
      hearings, 95–7
      mark-up sessions, 97–9
Senate Finance Committee, 38, 41, 78–9, 84–5, 94–5, 111–12
   and depletion allowances, 111–12
   and Long, Sen. Russell B., 84–5
   membership, 78–9
   Republicans and Democrats on, 94–5
   secrecy, 97
Senate Hearings on IRS Taxpayer Assistance (1974), 275
services, taxation of, 27
severance taxes, 180, 181–2
Shannon, John, 186
Sharp, Gene, 280
Shepard's Citations, 231
Shope, Dorothy, 234–5
Shopping Center Directory (NBR), 227
Shultz, W. J., 204
Silverherz, John D., 277
Simon, John, 17, 18, 85, 95
Simon, William, 62, 109, 110
simpliform tax plan, 38
Sixteenth Amendment, 5, 8
Small Business Administration (SBA), 222
small businesses, taxation of, **49**, 68
small claims courts
   income tax appeals, 127, 129–30
   property tax appeals, 203–4, 207

Index 295

Small Savers Act of 1974, 50
Smathers, George, 80
Smith, Adam, 3–4
Smith, William, 132
Snyder, Lester B., 149, 279, 281
Social Security Act of 1935, 9
social security (payroll) taxes, 6, 7, 14, 19–20, **20**, 66–7
   burden by income class, 22, **23**
   effective rates, **20**
   exemption of, 66–7
      by income class, **42**
   history, 9, **9**
   regressivity of, 19–20
Society of Real Estate Appraisers (Chicago), 227
solar heating, tax credit for, 81, 82
Sources of Business Information (Coman), 227
special districts, and local taxation, 175
special-interest groups, xv, xvi, 75, **76**–7, 79–82, 137–42. *See also* lobbyists; tax-reform campaigns
   amendments to tax bills, 91
   campaign contributions, 79, 88
   influences in Congress, 79–82
   tax legislation for, 86, 88, 90–1, 99–100, 103–5
   and Tax Reform Act (1969), 49–50, 86, 100
Sperry, Robert, 274
Standard and Poor's index, 225, 228
Stark, Rep. Fortney H., 78, 91
state attorneys general, property tax opinions, 231
State and Local Taxation (Hellerstein), 232
State and Local Taxes and Finance (Oldman and Schoettle), 232
State Tax Handbook (CCH), 232
State Tax Law Reporter, 232
state taxes, 23–32
   average vs. upper income burden, **32**
   collections by source, **25**
   corporate income taxes, **24**, **25**, 26, 27
   deductability of, 43, 54

estate taxes, 28–9, 30
flat rate system, 27
gift taxes, 28–9
history, 10–13
   adoption by states, 25–6, **29**
individual income taxes, 5, 23, **24**, 25–7
progressive rates, 27
property taxes, 23, **24**, 25, **144** n.9, 147–8, 221–2
   laws, 230–1
public utilities, **25**, 28, 30, **30**, 31
regressivity in, 13–14
revenue sources, 23, **24**, 25
   separation of, 12
sales taxes, 23, **24**, 25, **25**, 27–8
Statistics of Income (Treasury Department), 49, 273
Stebbins, Mary, 10
steel industry
   campaign contributions, 138
   property taxes, 212–14
Steiger, Rep. William A., 78, 81
Stephens, E. Edward, 130
Sterne, Philip M., 272
stock dividends, taxation of, xv, 18, 31, 64, 65
   tax preferences by income class, **43**
straight-line depreciation, 58–60
strip-mining, and property tax losses, 239, 242
stumpage fees, 156
subdivision permits, 221
subsidies, 34, 41, 52–3. *See also* tax expenditures
suburbs
   and FHA programs, 162–3
   school financing, 166
   use-value assessment laws, 162
Sugarman, Stephen, 280
summation approach, in assessing property, 177
sumptuary taxes, 5
Supreme Court. *See* U.S. Supreme Court
Surrey, Stanley, S., 9, 35, 38, 52, 85, 98, 107, 273, 274
Swope, Mary Hill, 86
Tactical Investigation for Peoples'

Struggles (Greever), 142
Talmadge, Sen. Herman E., 78
Tariff Bill of 1894, 8
tariff bills, and special-interest legislation, 99
Tax Analysts and Advocates, 105, 141, 220, 272
tax avoidance awards, to corporations, 256
tax base, erosion of, 13, 14, **14**, 15, 170
tax calendars, for property taxes, 171–4
tax clinics, 257, 268, 269
tax courts, 126, 129–30, 203–4, 207
   property tax appeals, 203–4, 207
   settlements, 129–30
   small-case division, 127, 129
tax credits, 40, **40**
   refundability, 98
   and Tax Justice Act, 264–5, **265**
tax deferrals, 64–6
tax expenditure budgets, 157
   bibliography, 280
tax expenditures, 5, 33–74
   accelerated deductions, 47
   administrative costs, 52–3
   average saving by income class, **42–3**
   bibliography, 273
   Congressional procedures, 41
   deductions, 54–8
   defined, 34–5
   vs. direct subsidies, 34, 41, 45–6, 52–3
   and federal budget, 35, **36**–7
   federal subsidies, FY 1975, **45**
   inequities in, 38–40
   and market mechanism, 46–8
   pluralism vs. private decision-making, 53
   reforms, 35, 38
   taxpayer support of, 53–4
Tax Foundation, 104–5
tax guides, **120**
tax history, 7–13
   federal taxes, 7–10
   state and local taxes, 10–13
tax integrations, and private pensions, **73**

tax laws, implementation of, **114–15**
tax legislation process, 82–103
  amendments, 91, 93
  flow chart, **76–7**
  hearings, 87–8
  mark-up sessions, 88–90, 97–9
  open rules procedure, 93–4
  Senate procedures, 95–103
  sources of, 85–7
  special-interest legislation, 86, 88, 90–1, 99–100
    vs. public interests, 103–5
  and Treasury Department staff, 91–2
tax maps, 175, 218
Tax Notes (TAA), 141, 270, 272–3, 274
tax rate structures, 5–6
  "effective" tax rates, 6
Tax Reduction (Justice) Act of 1975, 84, 86, 87, 93, 94, 100–3, 254, 258, 264–8
  and Conference Committee, 102–3
  and oil depletion allowance, 100–3
  and Senate Finance Committee, 99
  summary, 264–8
Tax Reform Act of 1969, 9, 85, 108, 110, 112
  and accelerated depreciation, 59–60
  and charitable foundations, 137
  special-interest provisions, 49–50, 86, 100
  taxable bonds, and federal subsidies, 70
tax-reform groups, 87, 137–9, 245–63, 268–71
  bibliography, 280–1
  campaigns, 245–63
    coalitions, 246–7
      letter-writing, 255–6, 259
      working committees, 247
  conferences, 257
  and elected officials, 105–6, 251, 258–9
  fund raising, 261
  investigations, 105–6, 248
  and legislation, 87, 137–8
  media coverage, 248–9
  national groups, alliances with, 253–4
  newsletters, 251–2, 268–71
  pitfalls, 262–3
  and political processes, 75
  public hearings, 257–8
  services, 247–8
  specific targets, demands, 253–4, 262
  tactics, 252–4
  tax-day publicity, 256–7
Tax Reform (Pechman), 273
tax regulations, 107, 110–13, **114–15**
  and depletion allowances, 111–12
  interpretive, 110–12
  legislative, 112–13
tax returns, preparation of, 118–19, **120**, **121**
  commercial firms, 118–19, **121**
  do-it-yourself suggestions, **120**
  IRS assistance, 118–19
tax rulings (IRS), 116–17
tax sales, for delinquent property taxes, 210
tax shelter investments, 47–50
  deferral aspect, 47, 48
  farming, 31
  and land assessments, 179
  leverage aspect, 48
tax stamps, and sales prices of property, 211
taxation, burden of, 3–7
  ability-to-pay principle, 3–4
  average vs. upper income burden, 31, **32**
  benefits principle, 4, 5
  and economic policy, 4–5
  elasticity principle, 5
  flat rates, 6
  by income class, **23**
  individual vs. corporate, **22**
  progressive rates, 5–7
  proportional, 6
  regressivity, 6, 7
  sumptuary taxes, 5
Taxation with Representation, 105, 140, 270
Taxpayer Compliance Measurement Program (TCMP), 119–21
Taxpayer Service Representatives, 119
Taxpayer Service Specialists, 119
telephone campaigns, for tax reform, 256, 259
Tennessee
  commercial property taxes, 194
  dividend taxes, 27
  mass appraisals in, 197, 198
Tennessee Valley Authority (TVA), 223
termination of tax year procedure, 134
Texas
  Minimum Foundation Program, 167–8, **168**
  tax-reform groups, 247, 258
Texas TEA Party, 247, 270
Thompson, Carl D., 31, 281
Thrower, Randolph, 112, 116
Thurow, Lester, 279–80, 281
timber industry
  bibliography, 279
  capital gains preference, **42**
  delayed taxation of, 181
  government leases, 153, 156
tobacco taxes, 5, 21, **25**, 28
Toronto, Ont., high-rise construction in, 238
Townsend, Robert, 281
transfer payments, exemption of, 66–7
transfer taxes, on land, 159, 161
Transportation Department, 224
Treachout, M. M., 279
Treasury Department, 41, 107–36. *See also* Internal Revenue Service
  Individual Statistics of Income, 49, 273
  private rulings, 259
  secretary of the Treasury, 107, 108
  staff, 86, 87, 91–2
  and tax expenditure budgets, 157
  and tax legislation, 85–6, 91–2
  and tax policy, 75, 107–10
  and tax reforms, 108
  tax regulations, 107, 110–13
Treasury Tax Reform Studies (Treasury Department), 108
tuition tax credit, 137

Ullman, Rep. Al, 78, 79, 80, 81, 83–4, 89, 92, 101, 102–3
Ultimate Highrise (San Francisco Bay Guardian), 220
underassessment, of property, 193–5
　investigation of, 211–14
unemployment insurance payments, exemption of, **42**, 66
unemployment rates, and investment incentives, 69
unequal assessments, 205
Union Carbide Corporation, 45
Union Oil Company, 139
Uniroyal Corporation, 86, 100, 193
United Auto Workers, 113
United Farm Workers, 255–6
United States Code Annotated (USCA), 230
United States Government Manual, 224
United States Mineral Resources, 218
universities, tax exemptions for, 157, 158, 219
Urban Land Institute, 226–7, 237
urban renewal agencies, 221
use taxes, 7
use-value assessments, of farmland, 159–63
U.S. Forest Service, 152, 153, 156
U.S. Steel Corporation, 193
　underassessment of, 212–13, **213**, 214
U.S. Supreme Court, 5
　Flint v. Stone Tracy Co., 8
　McCulloch v. Maryland, 148
　Pollack v. Farmers' Loan, 8
　property tax laws, 230
　Springer v. United States, 8
　U.S. v. Hylton, 7, 8
　U.S. v. Kahriger, 135–6

Van Dusartz v. Hatfield (Minn.), 168

Vander Veen, Rep. Richard F., 78, 91
Vanderjagt, Rep. Guy, 78, 81
Vanik, Rep. Charles, 18–19, 50, 78, 103, 257, 258
Ventura City, Calif., property taxes in, 162
Vermont
　early taxation, 11
　land gains tax, 164
　nuclear power, 243
veterans' disability compensation, exemption of, **43**, 66
Vietnam war surcharge, 9, 108
Virginia
　early property taxes, 11
　land banking in, 165–6
Voneida, Theodore J., 242

Waggonner, Rep. Joe O. Jr., 78, 90, 91
Wall Street Journal, 137, 139, 224, 225
Walters, Johnnie, 117
War of 1812, 8
Washington, George, 7
Washington, D.C., paved acreage in, 236, **237**
Washington Influence Directory, 141, 274
Washington Post, 137, 139
Washington State, property tax exemptions, **154–5**, 219
welfare payments, exemption of, **42**, 66
West Publishing Company, law series, 230–1
West Virginia, reappraisel programs, 198, 199
Western Electric, xv
Western Hemisphere Trade Corporations (WHTCs), 267

Westinghouse, **xv**
Whiskey Rebellion (1791), 3, 7–8
White Plains, N.Y., exempt property in, 152
Whitten, Les, 101
Who Bears the Tax Burden? (Pechman and Okner), 274
Who Runs Congress? (Green), 274
Who's Who, 142, 225, 228
Whyte, William H., 161, 278
Williamson Act, 161, 162
Willsey, Burke, 112
Wisconsin
　federal aid to, 23
　highway construction, 236
　income taxes, 25–6
　revenue sources, 23, **24**
Wolfman, Bernard, 113
Woods, Rose Mary, 116
Woodworth, Dr. Lawrence, 87, 90, 91, 97, 98, 99
Work Incentive (WIN), tax credit, 52
worker-to-property ratios, in sales prices, 212–13
Working on the System (Michael and Fort), 224
workmen's compensation benefits, deductability of, **42**
World War I, taxation during, 8–9
World War II, taxation during, 9

"Your Federal Income Tax" (IRS), **120**
Youth Project, The (Washington, D.C.), 261

zoning, and land use control, 164, 221
Zuckerman, Ed, 274

ABOUT THE AUTHORS

The Tax Reform Research Group was established in 1972 as part of Ralph Nader's Public Citizen organization. Located in Washington, D.C., the tax group has been working on behalf of ordinary taxpayers toward reform of federal, state, and local tax laws and the administration of those laws by the IRS and local officials. Its full-time staff of eight testifies and lobbies in Congress on federal tax reforms, works for changes in the IRS, provides information and resources to local tax-reform groups, collaborates with those groups to reform local property and other tax laws, and publishes research and information on various tax-reform issues in its monthly newspaper, *People & Taxes*. This book is based on the knowledge the authors have gained working with the Tax Reform Research Group.

Robert M. Brandon joined the Public Citizen Tax Reform Research Group in February 1973 and is currently its director. He took a Juris Doctor degree from the National Law Center of George Washington University in 1972 and is a member of the District of Columbia bar and its section on taxation. An Associate Professorial Lecturer in Law at George Washington University, he has been teaching tax policy and tax reform since 1974. In 1971-72, he directed the Task Force on Drug Abuse, a private, foundation-sponsored project.

Jonathan Rowe graduated from the University of Pennsylvania Law School in 1971. As a VISTA volunteer he did tenant organizing on Manhattan's Lower East Side and worked with a Neighborhood Youth Corps program. He was with the Public Citizen Tax Reform Research Group from its beginning in 1972 until January 1976 when he joined the staff of District of Columbia Council member Marion Barry to work on revenue and budget matters.

Thomas H. Stanton received his Juris Doctor from Harvard Law School in 1970 and is a member of the bar of the District of Columbia. He was the Public Citizen Tax Reform Research Group's first director in 1972 and 1973 and Professorial Lecturer in Law at George Washington University, where he taught a course on tax reform strategies for several years. He is currently initiating a project on housing for the Center for Study of Responsive Law.